# Decisions on
# The Rules of Golf
# 2006-2007

*Official Rulings on over*
*1200 Golf Situations*

By the United States Golf Association®
and The R&A

© Copyright 2005 by the

United States Golf Association®

All rights reserved


For more information on the USGA®, contact:

United States Golf Association®
Golf House
Far Hills, New Jersey 07931
T 908 234-2300


Printed in the United States of America


*Cover photo of Golf House by Kim Barney © USGA*

# INTRODUCTION TO THE DECISIONS ON THE RULES OF GOLF

Each year, the United States Golf Association and The R&A receive thousands of phone calls and letters regarding clarification of the Rules of Golf. In order to help millions of golfers around the world better understand how these detailed Rules are applied and interpreted, the USGA and R&A developed the comprehensive Decisions on the Rules of Golf. The topics of Etiquette, Definitions, and the Rules of Play are discussed at length. The format is geared towards questions and answers and is designed to be used as a reference at home, or right on the golf course.

Since 1951 the USGA and R&A have been meeting regularly in order to establish a uniform code of Rules. Decisions on the Rules of Golf is the result of these meetings. However, each year brings about a whole new round of questions not specifically addressed in the Rules of Golf. Committees meet from both organizations to discuss these new questions — anything from water hazards, and points of relief, to how to play a ball near a dead elk — and arrive at a decision with which both the USGA and R&A agree. Decisions on the Rules of Golf is amended every two years in order to keep up on the ever evolving game of golf.

The partnership of the USGA and The R&A has worked to further the understanding and enjoyment of the game of golf. With their official expertise, golf enthusiasts can rest assured that even the most unusual situations can be addressed. Whether it's a question of casual water, loose impediments, or line of play, no answer is out of bounds.

# CONTENTS

**Contents of Index** .................................................................. c-1

**Index** .................................................................................... i-1

**SECTION I**   Etiquette ........................................................... 1
**SECTION II**  Definitions ........................................................ 3
**SECTION III** The Rules of Play ............................................ 12

**The Game**
  1. The Game .................................................................... 12
  2. Match Play .................................................................. 29
  3. Stroke Play .................................................................. 47

**Clubs and the Ball**
  4. Clubs ............................................................................ 57
  5. The Ball ....................................................................... 70

**Player's Responsibilities**
  6. The Player ................................................................... 76
  7. Practice ...................................................................... 107
  8. Advice; Indicating Line of Play .................................. 115
  9. Information as to Strokes Taken .............................. 123

**Order of Play**
  10. Order of Play ............................................................ 130

**Teeing Ground**
  11. Teeing Ground ......................................................... 136

**Playing the Ball**
  12. Searching for and Identifying Ball .......................... 142
  13. Ball Played as It Lies ................................................ 146
  14. Striking the Ball ....................................................... 176
  15. Substituted Ball; Wrong Ball .................................. 188

**The Putting Green**
  16. The Putting Green ................................................... 201
  17. The Flagstick ............................................................ 216

**Ball Moved, Deflected or Stopped**
  18. Ball at Rest Moved .................................................. 226
  19. Ball in Motion Deflected or Stopped ..................... 255

**Relief Situation and Procedure**
  20. Lifting, Dropping and Placing; Playing from Wrong Place .................. 266
  21. Cleaning Ball ............................................................ 298
  22. Ball Assisting or Interfering With Play ................... 300
  23. Loose Impediments ................................................. 303
  24. Obstructions ............................................................ 311
  25. Abnormal Ground Conditions, Embedded Ball
      and Wrong Putting Green ....................................... 328
  26. Water Hazards (Including Lateral Water Hazards) ... 354
  27. Ball Lost or Out of Bounds; Provisional Ball ......... 370
  28. Ball Unplayable ........................................................ 390

**Other Forms of Play**
   29. Threesomes and Foursomes ................................................................. 397
   30. Three-Ball, Best-Ball and Four-Ball Match Play ............................ 402
   31. Four-Ball Stroke Play ........................................................................... 415
   32. Bogey, Par and Stableford Competitions ........................................ 420

**Administration**
   33. The Committee ..................................................................................... 425
   34. Disputes and Decisions ...................................................................... 461

**Appendix I: Local Rules; Conditions of the Competition .......................... 474**
   Contents .......................................................................................................... 474
   Part A: Local Rules ...................................................................................... 476
   Part B: Specimen Local Rules ................................................................... 478
   Part C: Conditions of the Competition .................................................. 487

**Appendix II: Design of Clubs ..................................................................... 493**

**Appendix III: The Ball ................................................................................. 501**

**Miscellaneous Decisions ............................................................................ 502**

**Decisions Applicable Only in the United States of America ................... 503**

**Principal Changes Since 2004-2005 .......................................................... 507**

# INTRODUCTION TO INDEX

The Index consists of over 5000 entries each of which refers to a Decision by number. Decisions relating to a given topic are grouped under a heading, which should be thought of as a keyword. There are 250 separate headings, of which there are two kinds — those that have entries (Decisions) and those that simply refer to other more appropriate headings. Decisions entered under headings with a larger number of entries are sometimes grouped under subheadings for further efficiency. The Contents section that precedes the actual Index is a listing of all the headings found in the Index. It is the entry point into the Index and a familiarity with these headings will make using the Index easier. Each of the over 1200 Decisions in the book is listed in the Index. Nearly every Decision appears under several separate headings to increase the chances of finding the proper Decision relating to a given situation.

Efficient and timely use of the Decisions book suggests that one should first become skillful in finding in the Index a Decision that most closely relates to the situation at hand. For example, assume a situation in match play where a player lifts his ball without marking its position under a mistaken belief that his next stroke is conceded. Within the Contents, identify the headings (keywords) that might be examined — Ball Lifted, Concession, Marking Position of Ball or Putting Green. The relevant Decision (2-4/3) is found under each of these headings and is also found under the heading Equity. If the Contents is not consulted first, one might select a keyword that is not listed as a heading, and much effort might be expended without success. For instance, potential keywords such as "ball picked up" or "ball not marked" are not headings in the Index; the proper terms that are found in the Contents are "Ball Lifted" or "Marking Position of Ball." Reference to the Contents will efficiently lead an inquirer to the proper heading and increase the likelihood of finding the appropriate Decision.

# CONTENTS OF INDEX

**Abnormal Ground Conditions** ................................................................ i-1
    *See also* Burrowing Animal, Reptile or Bird; Casual Water, Embedded Ball; Ground Under Repair; Material Piled for Removal; Pitch-Mark; Reasonable Evidence; Status of Object

**Addressing the Ball** ................................................................................. i-1
**Advice** ........................................................................................................ i-2
**Aeration Holes and Plugs** ..................................................................... i-3
**Agreement to Waive Rules** ................................................................... i-3
**Animal** *See* Ants and Ant Hills; Bees; Burrowing Animal, Reptile or Bird; Crab; Crawfish; Dog; Insects; Snake; Worm

**Ants and Ant Hills** ................................................................................. i-3
    *See also* Greenkeeper and Hole Made by Greenkeeper; Insects; Loose Impediments

**Area of Intended Swing** ........................................................................ i-3
    *See also* Improving Area of Intended Stance or Swing, Position or Lie of Ball, or Line of Play or Putt

**Artificial Devices and Unusual Equipment** ...................................... i-4
    *See also* Status of Object

**Artificial Objects** *See* Obstructions
**Artificially-Surfaced** *See* Obstructions
**Assistance** ................................................................................................ i-5
    *See also* Ball Assisting or Interfering with Play; Exerting Influence on Ball; Four-Ball Match Play; Four-Ball Stroke Play

**Ball** ............................................................................................................. i-6
    *See also* Addressing the Ball; Ball Assisting or Interfering With Play; Ball at Rest Moved; Ball Deflected or Stopped; Ball Dropped or Re-Dropped; Ball Lifted; Ball Mark; Ball Overhanging Hole; Ball Placed or Replaced; Ball Touched; Ball Unfit for Play; Cleaning Ball; Embedded Ball; Exchanging Ball; Exerting Influence on Ball; Hole Made by Greenkeeper; Holed or Holing Out; Lie of Ball Altered; Lost Ball; Out of Bounds; Provisional Ball; Searching for and Identifying Ball; Second Ball; Status of Object; Stroke; Substituted Ball; "X-Out" Ball

**Ball Assisting or Interfering with Play** ............................................... i-6
    *See also* Assistance; Exerting Influence on Ball

**Ball at Rest Moved** ................................................................................. i-7
    *See also* Ball Deflected or Stopped; Ball Touched

**Ball Deflected or Stopped** .................................................................. i-10
    *See also* Ball at Rest Moved; Exerting Influence on Ball

**Ball Drop (Dropping Zone)** ................................................................ i-11
**Ball Dropped or Re-Dropped** ............................................................ i-11
    *See also* Ball Lifted; Ball Placed or Replaced; Local Rules

**Ball Identifying** *See* Searching for and Identifying Ball
**Ball Interfering with or Assisting Play** *See* Ball Assisting or Interfering with Play
**Ball Lifted** ............................................................................................... i-15
**Ball Mark** ................................................................................................ i-18
    *See also* Ball-Marker; Pitch-Mark

**Ball-Marker** ............................................................................................ i-18
    *See also* Ball Mark; Marking Position of Ball; Status of Object

**Ball Overhanging Hole** ....................................................................... i-19
**Ball Placed or Replaced** ..................................................................... i-19
**Ball Touched** ......................................................................................... i-21
    *See also* Ball at Rest Moved

**Ball Unfit for Play** ................................................................................ i-21
    *See also* Unplayable Ball

**Ball Unplayable** *See* Unplayable Ball
**Bandage** .................................................................................................. i-21
**Beach** ...................................................................................................... i-21
**Bees** ......................................................................................................... i-21
    *See also* Insects

**Bird** *See* Burrowing Animal, Reptile, or Bird

## Contents of Index

**Bogey Competition** .................................................................................................. i-22
*See also* Stableford Competition
**Boundary Fence, Line, Wall or Stakes** ................................................................... i-22
*See also* Marking or Defining Course; Out of Bounds; Status of Object
**Bridge** ........................................................................................................................ i-23
**Bunker** ....................................................................................................................... i-23
*See also* Sand
**Burrowing Animal, Reptile or Bird** ....................................................................... i-26
*See also* Abnormal Ground Conditions; Casual Water; Ground Under Repair;
Reasonable Evidence; Reptile; Status of Object
**Bush** *See* Leaves; Tree or Bush
**Caddie** ........................................................................................................................ i-28
**Canceling Scores** *See* Course Unplayable or Closed; Discontinuance and Resumption
of Play
**Car** *See* Status of Object
**Cart** *See* Golf Cart; Trolley
**Cart Path** *See* Roads and Paths
**Casual Water** ............................................................................................................. i-29
*See also* Abnormal Ground Conditions; Reasonable Evidence
**Chipper** ...................................................................................................................... i-31
*See also* Club(s)
**Claims and Disputes** ................................................................................................ i-31
*See also* Committee; Penalty Imposed, Modified or Waived by Committee; Referee
**Cleaning Ball** ............................................................................................................. i-33
**Close of Competition** ............................................................................................... i-34
*See also* Committee; Conditions of Competition; Handicap and Handicap Competition;
Penalties Imposed, Modified or Waived by Committee; Scores and Score Cards
**Closely Mown Area** *See* Fairway and Closely Mown Areas
**Clubhouse or Half-Way House** ............................................................................... i-35
**Club(s)** ....................................................................................................................... i-35
*See also* Grip; Grounding Club; Status of Object; Stroke
**Committee** ................................................................................................................ i-37
*See also* Claims and Disputes; Close of Competition; Conditions of Competition;
Course Unplayable or Closed; Discontinuance and Resumption of Play; Doubt
Regarding Facts; Local Rules; Marking or Defining Course; Observer; Penalties
Imposed, Modified or Waived by Committee; Referee
**Concession** ................................................................................................................ i-42
*See also* Default; Four-Ball Match Play; Foursomes; Singles Match; Wrong Information
**Conditions of Competition** ..................................................................................... i-43
*See also* Committee; Local Rules
**Concurrent Four-Ball and Singles Matches** *See* Singles Match
**Concurrent Match and Stroke Play** *See* Singles Match
**Course** *See* Course Unplayable or Closed; Out of Bounds; Marking or Defining Course
**Course Unplayable or Closed** ................................................................................. i-44
*See also* Discontinuance and Resumption of Play
**Course Marking** *See* Marking or Defining Course
**Course Record** .......................................................................................................... i-44
**Crab** ............................................................................................................................ i-44
**Crawfish** .................................................................................................................... i-45
*See also* Burrowing Animal, Reptile or Bird
**Damage** ..................................................................................................................... i-45
*See also* Ball Unfit for Play; Club(s); Ground Under Repair; Repair
**Dangerous Situations** .............................................................................................. i-45
**Default** ...................................................................................................................... i-46
*See also* Concession; Halved Hole
**Defining Course** *See* Marking or Defining Course
**Deflected Ball** *See* Ball Deflected or Stopped
**Delay, Undue** *See* Undue Delay
**Dew** ............................................................................................................................ i-46

## Contents of Index c-3

**Directly Attributable** ............................................................................................. i-46
**Direction Post** ....................................................................................................... i-46
    *See also* Status of Object
**Discontinuance and Resumption of Play** ............................................................. i-46
**Disputes** *See* Claims and Disputes
**Distance, Distance Information and Distance Markers** ...................................... i-47
    *See also* Measuring
**Divot and Divot Hole** ........................................................................................... i-48
**Dog** ...................................................................................................................... i-48
**Doubt as to Procedure** ......................................................................................... i-48
    *See also* Doubt Regarding Facts; Provisional Ball; Second Ball; Serious Breach of Rules
**Doubt Regarding Facts** ........................................................................................ i-49
    *See also* Committee; Doubt as to Procedure
**Drainpipe** ............................................................................................................. i-51
**Dropping Zone** *See* Ball Drop (Dropping Zone)
**Elevated Power Line** *See* Power Line
**Embedded Ball** ..................................................................................................... i-51
    *See also* Pitch-Mark
**Environmentally-Sensitive Area** ........................................................................... i-51
**Equipment** ........................................................................................................... i-52
    *See also* Artificial Devices and Unusual Equipment; Club(s); Golf Cart; Status of Object; Trolley
**Equity** .................................................................................................................. i-52
**Etiquette** ............................................................................................................. i-55
**Exchanging Balls** ................................................................................................. i-55
    *See also* Substituted Ball
**Excluding Operation of Rule** *See* Agreement to Waive Rules
**Exerting Influence on Ball** ................................................................................... i-55
    *See also* Serious Breach of Rules
**Failure to Hole Out** ............................................................................................. i-57
    *See also* Holed or Holing Out
**Fairway and Closely Mown Areas** ....................................................................... i-57
    *See also* Embedded Ball; Through the Green
**Fence** ................................................................................................................... i-58
    *See also* Boundary Fence, Line, Wall or Stake; Wall
**Flagstick** .............................................................................................................. i-59
    *See also* Putting Green
**Flowers** ................................................................................................................ i-60
**Footprint(s)** ......................................................................................................... i-60
    *See also* Abnormal Ground Conditions; Bunker; Damage; Ground Under Repair; Spike Marks
**Footwear** ............................................................................................................. i-61
**Four-Ball Match Play** ........................................................................................... i-61
    *See also* Default; Four-Ball Stableford Competition; Four-Ball Stroke Play; Wrong Information
**Four-Ball Stableford Competition** ....................................................................... i-62
    *See also* Four-Ball Match Play; Four-Ball Stroke Play
**Four-Ball Stroke Play** .......................................................................................... i-62
    *See also* Four-Ball Match Play; Four-Ball Stableford Competition
**Foursomes** ........................................................................................................... i-63
**Frost** .................................................................................................................... i-64
**Fruit** .................................................................................................................... i-64
**Gallery** *See* Spectator
**Gallery-Control Stake, Rope or Line** .................................................................... i-64
    *See also* Obstructions; Status of Object
**Gate** .................................................................................................................... i-64
**Glove** ................................................................................................................... i-64
    *See also* Equipment; Tape
**Golf Cart** ............................................................................................................. i-65
    *See also* Equipment; Status of Object; Trolley

**Grass or Turf** .................................................................................................... i-65
    *See also* Fairway and Closely Mown Areas; Spike Marks; Testing
**Gravel** *See* Stone(s), Rock(s) or Gravel
**Greenkeeper and Hole Made by Greenkeeper** ................................................. i-66
**Grip** .................................................................................................................... i-66
    *See also* Club(s)
**Ground Under Repair** ....................................................................................... i-67
    *See also* Abnormal Ground Conditions; Burrowing Animal, Reptile or Bird; Casual Water; Marking or Defining Course; Reasonable Evidence; Tree or Bush
**Grounding Club** ................................................................................................. i-69
    *See also* Addressing the Ball
**Groups and Grouping** ........................................................................................ i-70
    *See also* Time of Starting
**Half-Way House** *See* Clubhouse or Half-Way House
**Halved Hole** ....................................................................................................... i-70
    *See also* Concession; Default
**Handicap Competition and Handicap Strokes** ................................................ i-71
    *See also* Claims and Disputes; Close of Competition; Scores and Score Cards
**Hazard** *See* Bunker; Water Hazards
**Heather** .............................................................................................................. i-72
**Hole** .................................................................................................................... i-72
    *See also* Ball Overhanging Hole; Claims and Disputes; Concession; Flagstick; Holed or Holing Out; Putting Green
**Hole-Liner** *See* Hole
**Hole Made by Greenkeeper** *See* Greenkeeper and Hole Made by Greenkeeper
**Hole Plug** ........................................................................................................... i-73
**Holed and Holing Out** ....................................................................................... i-73
    *See also* Failure to Hole Out; Stroke
**Honor** ................................................................................................................. i-74
    *See also* Order of Play; Playing Out of Turn
**Ice** *See* Casual Water; Loose Impediments; Obstructions
**Identifying Ball** *See* Lost Ball; Searching for and Identifying Ball
**Imposed Penalty** *See* Penalties Imposed, Modified or Waived by Committee
**Improving Area of Intended Stance or Swing, Position or Lie of Ball, or Line of Play or Putt** ............................................................................................................ i-75
    *See also* Area of Intended Swing; Lie of Ball Altered; Line of Putt; Line of Play; Stance
**Improving Area of Intended Swing** *See* Area of Intended Swing; Improving Area of Intended Stance or Swing, Position or Lie of Ball, or Line of Play or Putt
**Improving Lie of Ball** *See* Improving Area of Intended Stance or Swing, Position or Lie of Ball, or Line of Play or Putt
**Improving Line of Play** *See* Improving Area of Intended Stance or Swing, Position or Lie of Ball, or Line of Play or Putt; Line of Play
**Improving Line of Putt** *See* Improving Area of Intended Stance or Swing, Position or Lie of Ball, or Line of Play or Putt; Line of Putt
**Improving Position of Ball** *See* Improving Area of Intended Stance or Swing, Position or Lie of Ball, or Line of Play or Putt
**Improving Stance** *See* Improving Area of Intended Stance or Swing, Position or Lie of Ball, or Line of Play or Putt; Stance
**Incorrect Information** *See* Incorrect Information on Rules; Wrong Information
**Incorrect Information on Rules** ........................................................................ i-76
    *See also* Information as to Strokes Taken; Wrong Information
**Indicating Line for Putting** ............................................................................... i-77
    *See also* Improving Area of Intended Stance or Swing, Position or Lie of Ball, or Line of Play or Putt; Indicating Line of Play; Line of Play; Line of Putt; Putting Green
**Indicating Line of Play** ..................................................................................... i-77
    *See also* Indicating Line of Putt; Line of Play; Line of Putt
**Information as to Strokes Taken** ..................................................................... i-77
    *See also* Wrong Information
**Injury** *See* Physical Problem

Contents of Index    c-5

**Insects** ..................................................................................................................................... i-78
    *See also* Burrowing Animal, Reptile or Bird; Loose Impediments; Status of Object
**Instruction** *See* Advice
**Integral Part of Course** ......................................................................................................... i-78
    *See also* Fence; Gate; Marking or Defining Course; Obstructions; Wall
**Interference** *See* Ball Assisting or Interfering with Play; Exerting Influence on Ball
**Lateral Water Hazards** *See* Water Hazards
**Leaves** ..................................................................................................................................... i-78
    *See also* Pine Needles; Status of Object; Tree or Bush
**Lie of Ball Altered** ................................................................................................................ i-79
    *See also* Improving Area of Intended Stance or Swing, Position or Lie of Ball, or Line of Play or Putt
**Lightning** ............................................................................................................................... i-79
    *See also* Dangerous Situations; Discontinuance and Resumption of Play; Rain; Weather Conditions; Wind
**Line of Play** .......................................................................................................................... i-79
    *See also* Improving Area of Intended Stance or Swing, Position or Lie of Ball, or Line of Play or Putt; Indicating Line of Play
**Line of Putt** .......................................................................................................................... i-81
    *See also* Hole; Improving Area of Intended Stance or Swing, Position or Lie of Ball, or Line of Play or Putt; Indicating Line for Putting; Putting Green
**Local Rules** .......................................................................................................................... i-82
    *See also* Conditions of Competition
**Loose Impediments** ............................................................................................................ i-85
    *See also* Status of Object
**Lost Ball** ............................................................................................................................... i-86
    *See also* Provisional Ball; Reasonable Evidence; Searching For and Identifying Ball
**Man-Made Reservoir** .......................................................................................................... i-89
**Marker** ................................................................................................................................... i-89
    *See also* Ball-Marker; Scores and Score Cards
**Marking or Defining Course** .............................................................................................. i-89
    *See also* Abnormal Ground Conditions; Boundary Fence, Line, Wall or Stakes; Committee; Fence; Ground Under Repair; Local Rules; Obstructions; Out of Bounds; Teeing Ground and Tee-Markers; Water Hazards
**Marking Position of Ball** .................................................................................................... i-91
    *See also* Ball-Marker
**Match Play** *See* Claims and Disputes; Concession; Halved Hole; Information as to Strokes Taken; Wrong Information
**Material Piled for Removal** ............................................................................................... i-92
    *See also* Greenkeeper and Hole Made by Greenkeeper; Ground Under Repair; Status of Object
**Maximum Available Relief** ................................................................................................ i-92
    *See also* Nearest Point of Relief
**Measuring** ............................................................................................................................ i-92
    *See also* Distance and Distance Markers
**Method of Making Stroke** *See* Stroke
**Modified Penalty** *See* Penalties Imposed, Modified or Waived by Committee
**Molehill** ................................................................................................................................ i-93
    *See also* Status of Object
**Moss** ..................................................................................................................................... i-93
**Moved and Moving Ball** *See* Ball at Rest Moved; Ball Deflected or Stopped
**Multiple Penalty Situations** ............................................................................................... i-93
**Mushroom** ........................................................................................................................... i-94
**"Nassau" System of Scoring** ............................................................................................. i-94
**Natural Objects** *See* Loose Impediments
**Nearest Lie Most Similar** ................................................................................................... i-94
    *See also* Lie of Ball Altered
**Nearest Point of Relief** ...................................................................................................... i-94
    *See also* Maximum Available Relief

**Observer** .................................................................................................................... i-95
*See also* Committee; Referee
**Obstructions** .............................................................................................................. i-95
*See also* Integral Part of Course; Loose Impediments; Reasonable Evidence; Status of Object
**Ocean** ........................................................................................................................ i-99
**Official** *See* Committee; Referee
**Order of Play** ............................................................................................................ i-99
*See also* Order of Play in Foursomes and Threesomes; Playing Out of Turn; Stroke Canceled or Recalled
**Order of Play in Foursomes and Threesomes** ...................................................... i-100
**Out of Bounds** .......................................................................................................... i-100
*See also* Boundary Fence, Line, Wall or Stakes; Marking or Defining Course; Provisional Ball
**Out of Turn** *See* Order of Play
**Outside Agency** ........................................................................................................ i-103
*See also* Ball Deflected or Stopped; Loose Impediments; Status of Object
**Pace of Play** .............................................................................................................. i-104
*See also* Undue Delay
**Par Competition** ...................................................................................................... i-104
*See also* Bogey Competition; Stableford Competition
**Path** *See* Roads and Paths
**Penalties Imposed, Modified or Waived by Committee** ........................................ i-104
*See also* Close of Competition; Committee; Multiple Penalty Situations
**Physical Problem** .................................................................................................... i-105
**Pine Needles** ............................................................................................................ i-105
*See also* Leaves; Tree or Bush
**Pitch-Mark** .............................................................................................................. i-105
*See also* Ball Mark; Embedded Ball
**Plants** *See* Flowers; Heather; Moss; Mushroom; Status of Object; Tree or Bush; Tumbleweed
**Playing from Wrong Place** *See* Wrong Place
**Playing Out of Turn** ................................................................................................ i-105
*See also* Honor; Order of Play; Order of Play in Foursomes and Threesomes
**Play-Off and Ties** .................................................................................................... i-106
**Plumb-Line** .............................................................................................................. i-106
**Power Line** .............................................................................................................. i-106
**Practice** .................................................................................................................... i-106
**Practice Swing** ........................................................................................................ i-107
**Prize** ........................................................................................................................ i-108
**Provisional Ball** ...................................................................................................... i-108
*See also* Lost Ball; Out of Bounds; Second Ball
**Putting Green** .......................................................................................................... i-109
*See also* Ball Overhanging Hole; Flagstick; Hole; Hole Plug; Improving Area of Intended Stance or Swing, Position or Lie of Ball, or Line of Play or Putt; Indicating Line for Putting; Line of Putt; Wrong Putting Green
**Rain** *See* Discontinuance and Resumption of Play; Weather Conditions
**Rake** .......................................................................................................................... i-113
*See also* Bunker; Improving Area of Intended Stance or Swing, Position or Lie of Ball, or Line of Play or Putt; Line of Play; Obstruction; Status of Object
**Reasonable Evidence** .............................................................................................. i-113
*See also* Abnormal Ground Conditions; Burrowing Animal, Reptile or Bird; Casual Water; Ground Under Repair; Lost Ball; Obstructions; Outside Agency; Provisional Ball; Water Hazards
**Recording Scores** *See* Marker; Scores and Score Cards
**Re-Dropping Ball** *See* Ball Dropped or Re-Dropped
**Referee** .................................................................................................................... i-114
*See also* Committee; Observer
**Refusal to Comply with Rule** ................................................................................ i-114

# Contents of Index    c-7

**Relief**.................................................................................................................................. **i-114**
    *See also* Burrowing Animal, Reptile or Bird; Casual Water; Embedded Ball; Ground Under Repair; Maximum Available Relief; Nearest Point of Relief; Obstructions

**Repair**................................................................................................................................ **i-116**
    *See also* Damage; Ground Under Repair

**Replacing Ball** *See* Ball Placed or Replaced

**Reptile** *See* Burrowing Animal, Reptile or Bird

**Resumption of Play** *See* Discontinuance and Resumption of Play

**Roads and Paths**................................................................................................................ **i-116**
    *See also* Status of Object

**Rock** *See* Stone(s), Rock(s) or Gravel

**Roots**................................................................................................................................. **i-117**
    *See also* Tree or Bush

**Rough**............................................................................................................................... **i-117**
    *See also* Through The Green

**Saliva**................................................................................................................................ **i-118**
    *See also* Loose Impediments

**Sand**................................................................................................................................. **i-118**
    *See also* Bunker

**Scores and Score Cards**.................................................................................................... **i-118**
    *See also* Information as to Strokes Taken; Marker

**Searching for and Identifying Ball**..................................................................................... **i-120**
    *See also* Lost Ball

**Second Ball**....................................................................................................................... **i-121**
    *See also* Doubt as to Procedure; Provisional Ball; Serious Breach of Rules

**Serious Breach of Rules**.................................................................................................... **i-122**
    *See also* Agreement to Waive Rules; Etiquette

**Shoes** *See* Footwear

**Shrubs** *See* Leaves; Status of Object; Tree or Bush

**Singles Match**.................................................................................................................. **i-123**

**Slow Play** *See* Undue Delay

**Snake**............................................................................................................................... **i-124**
    *See also* Burrowing Animal, Reptile or Bird; Status of Object

**Spectator**......................................................................................................................... **i-124**
    *See also* Outside Agency

**Spike Mark(s)**.................................................................................................................. **i-125**
    *See also* Damage; Improving Area of Intended Stance or Swing, Position or Lie of Ball, or Line of Play or Putt; Line of Putt; Putting Green

**Sportsmanship Code**....................................................................................................... **i-125**
    *See also* Etiquette

**Stableford Competition**.................................................................................................. **i-125**
    *See also* Bogey Competition; Four-Ball Stableford Competition

**Stakes**............................................................................................................................. **i-125**
    *See also* Boundary Fence, Line, Wall or Stakes; Status of Object

**Stance**............................................................................................................................ **i-126**
    *See also* Addressing the Ball; Improving Area of Intended Stance or Swing, Position or Lie of Ball, or Line of Play or Putt

**Starting, Starting Time** *See* Groups and Grouping; Time of Starting

**Status of Object**............................................................................................................. **i-127**

**Steps**.............................................................................................................................. **i-129**
    *See also* Obstructions

**Stipulated Round**.......................................................................................................... **i-129**
    *See also* Artificial Devices and Unusual Equipment

**Stone(s), Rock(s) or Gravel**........................................................................................... **i-130**
    *See also* Loose Impediments; Status of Object; Wall

**Stopped Ball** *See* Ball Deflected or Stopped

**Striking the Ball** *See* Stroke

**Stroke**........................................................................................................................... **i-131**
    *See also* Artificial Devices and Unusual Equipment; Concession; Handicap Competition and Handicap Strokes; Practice; Practice Swing; Stroke-and-Distance; Stroke Cancelled or Recalled; Wrong Ball

**Stroke-and-Distance** .................................................................................. i-132
**Stroke Canceled or Recalled** ................................................................... i-134
    *See also* Ball Deflected or Stopped; Order of Play; Order of Play in Foursomes and Threesomes; Stroke-and-Distance; Teeing Ground
**Stroke Play** *See* Doubt as to Procedure; Failure to Hole Out; Scores and Score Cards; Second Ball
**Substituted Ball** ......................................................................................... i-135
    *See also* Exchanging Balls
**Sudden-Death Play-Off** *See* Play-Off; Ties
**Suspension of Play** *See* Discontinuance and Resumption of Play
**Tape** ............................................................................................................. i-136
**Team Competition** ..................................................................................... i-136
**Tee** ................................................................................................................ i-136
    *See also* Status of Object; Teeing Ground and Tee-Markers
**Teeing Ground and Tee-Markers** ............................................................ i-136
    *See also* Marking or Defining Course; Status of Object; Stroke-and-Distance; Tee
**Temporary Obstructions** *See* Local Rules
**Terminology** ............................................................................................... i-138
**Test or Testing** ........................................................................................... i-139
**Three-Ball Match Play** ............................................................................. i-139
**Through the Green** ................................................................................... i-139
*See also* Fairway and Closely Mown Areas; Rough
**Ties** *See* Play-Off and Ties
**Time of Starting** ........................................................................................ i-140
    *See also* Course Unplayable or Closed; Groups and Grouping
**Touching Ball** *See* Ball Touched
**Towel** ........................................................................................................... i-141
**Trademark** .................................................................................................. i-141
**Tree or Bush** ............................................................................................... i-141
    *See also* Leaves; Pine Needles; Status of Object
**Trolley** ......................................................................................................... i-142
    *See also* Equipment; Golf Cart
**Tumbleweed** ............................................................................................... i-143
**Turf** *See* Grass and Turf
**Umbrella** ..................................................................................................... i-143
**Undue Delay** .............................................................................................. i-143
    *See also* Pace of Play
**Unplayable Ball** ......................................................................................... i-143
    *See also* Ball Unfit for Play
**Waived Penalty** *See* Penalties Imposed, Modified or Waived by Committee
**Wall** .............................................................................................................. i-145
    *See also* Boundary Fence, Line, Wall or Stakes; Fence; Integral Part of Course; Obstructions; Status of Object
**Water Hazards** ........................................................................................... i-145
    *See also* Marking or Defining Course; Provisional Ball; Reasonable Evidence
**Weather Conditions** .................................................................................. i-149
    *See also* Course Unplayable or Closed; Discontinuance and Resumption of Play
**Wind** *See* Weather Conditions
**Worm** ........................................................................................................... i-149
**Wrong Ball** ................................................................................................. i-149
**Wrong Information** .................................................................................. i-151
    *See also* Claims and Disputes; Incorrect Information on the Rules; Information as to the Strokes Taken
**Wrong Place** ............................................................................................... i-153
    *See also* Serious Breach of Rules
**Wrong Putting Green** ............................................................................... i-155
**Wrong Teeing Ground** ............................................................................. i-155
    *See also* Teeing Ground and Tee-Markers
**"X-out" Ball** ............................................................................................... i-155

# INDEX

## Abnormal Ground Conditions

*See Also* Burrowing Animal, Reptile or Bird; Casual Water, Embedded Ball; Ground Under Repair; Material Piled for Removal; Pitch-Mark; Reasonable Evidence; Status of Object

| | |
|---|---|
| aeration holes | 25/15 |
| clarification of point where ball "last entered" abnormal ground condition when ball lost in condition | 25-1c/1.5 |
| cracks in earth | 25/12 |
| crawfish mound | 25-1b/18 |
| edging grooves around putting green; Local Rule allowing relief | 33-8/24 |
| improving line of play when taking relief from abnormal ground conditions | 25-1b/3 |
| molehills | 25/23 |

nearest point of relief
- determining club, address position, direction of play and swing used to identify nearest point of relief ... 24-2b/1
- diagrams illustrating nearest point of relief ... 25-1b/2
- diagram illustrating player unable to determine nearest point of relief ... 24-2b/3.7
- player determines nearest point of relief but physically unable to play intended stroke ... 24-2b/3
- player does not follow recommended procedure in determining nearest point of relief ... 24-2b/2

reasonable evidence
- ball lost in abnormal ground condition; drop made under Rule 25-1c; original ball then found within five minutes ... 25-1c/2.5
- meaning of "reasonable evidence" ball lost in abnormal ground condition ... 25-1c/1

| | |
|---|---|
| rut made by tractor | 25/16 |
| soft, mushy earth | 25/1 |
| sunken hole plug | 25/17 |

## Addressing the Ball

ball dropped in improper manner moves when addressed; player then lifts ball and drops it in proper manner ... 20-2a/4

ball moves after being addressed
- after stance taken in hazard without club ... 18-2b/2
- and comes to rest out of bounds ... 18-2b/9
- and falls into hole ... 18-2b/10
- and then stopped by player's club ... 18-2b/12
- ball moves downward in rough; will not remain at rest when replaced ... 20-3d/3
- ball perched on heather moves after stance taken when club rested on heather ... 18-2b/6
- competitor invokes Rule 3-3; second ball played first from spot where original ball lay ... 3-3/14
- in water in water hazard; played while still moving ... 14-6/1
- on putting green when player attempts to brush insect from it ... 23-1/12
- player steps away from ball after addressing it; ball then moves ... 18-2b/7
- player steps away from ball after addressing it, lifts ball and replaces it; ball then moves ... 18-2b/8
- provisional ball moves after being addressed; whether penalty canceled if provisional ball never becomes ball in play ... 15/7
- stance taken and clubhead grounded in front of ball ... 18-2b/5.5
- when some other agency strikes it ... 18-2b/11

ball moves before being addressed
- after club grounded but before stance completed ... 18-2b/4
- after stance taken but before club grounded ... 18-2b/1
- ball replaced at rest; thereafter ball moved by wind before being addressed ... 18-1/12
- while player in process of taking stance in bunker ... 18-2b/3

| | |
|---|---|
| ball oscillates during address | 18/2 |
| casual water in bunker touched with club; whether club grounded | 13-4/7 |

## Addressing the Ball (continued)

grounding club
- in front of ball and taking stance then ball moves; whether ball addressed .... 18-2b/5.5
- in tall grass; when club considered grounded ............................................. 18-2b/5
- outside water hazard prior to stroke at ball in hazard ............................... 13-4/29
- presses down sand behind ball through the green ...................................... 13-2/12

order of play in foursome play if player accidentally moves ball after address ............. 29-1/5

original ball out of bounds; ball re-teed under stroke-and-distance touched at
      address and falls off tee ......................................................................... 11-3/3

stance in bunker taken
- then player smoothes footprints after deciding to play different type of stroke ...... 13-4/27
- without club; whether ball addressed .............................................................. 13-4/24

stroke misses ball; ball then accidentally knocked off tee .................................... 11-3/1

when ball addressed
- by player who putts "side-saddle" .............................................................. 18-2b/5.7
- in bunker .................................................................................................. 13-4/23

## Advice

absent partner gives advice before joining match ........................................... 30-3a/2

asking
- accuracy of distance marker .................................................................... 8-1/3
- advice between rounds in 36-hole match .................................................. 8-1/19
- advice when play suspended .................................................................... 8-1/20
- distance between objects ......................................................................... 8-1/2
- length of hole ........................................................................................... 8-1/1
- whereabouts of another player's ball ...................................................... 8-1/5

club selection
- after playing to green, player asks what club opponent or fellow-competitor
      used for similar stroke ..................................................................... 8-1/7
- comment about club selection made after stroke ................................... 8-1/8
- double caddie informs one employer about club used by other .............. 8-1/12
- looking into another player's bag to determine club used ...................... 8-1/10
- misleading statement about club selection purposely made ................... 8-1/9
- player asks opponent or fellow-competitor about club used at previous hole ......... 8-1/6
- towel removed covering another player's clubs to determine club used ........ 8-1/11

concurrent four-ball and singles matches; whether partners may exchange
      advice on singles match after result of hole or match in four-ball decided ........ 30-3/1

electronic device used to seek or give advice during stipulated round .......... 14-3/16

given on request; penalties in various forms of play ..................................... 8-1/25

instruction
- caddie swings club to show player how to play shot ............................... 8-1/15
- competitor, after finishing hole, demonstrates to fellow-competitor how
      to play shot .................................................................................. 8-1/14
- player gives opponent or fellow-competitor instruction during round ...... 8-1/13

play of wrong ball not rectified on advice of Committee member ................... 33-7/5

player putting for half given advice by opponent ............................................ 2-2/1

player who has not yet played seeks advice from player who has finished round ........ 8-1/18

request for advice made in error to opponent's caddie; withdrawn before
      advice given ...................................................................................... 8-1/17

suggesting fellow-competitor deem ball unplayable ....................................... 8-1/16

team competition
- advice given by team captain or by team coach not authorized to give advice ...... 8-1/24
- advice given by team captain while playing ............................................. 8/2
- advice given by team mate in another group in stroke play .................... 8-1/21
- condition of team competition stipulates who may give advice, such as
      team captain or amateur ............................................................... 8/1
- team mate in gallery hits ball to green to show player whether green will hold ........ 8-1/23
- team mates playing as fellow-competitors exchange advice ................... 8-1/22
- whether team captain authorized to give advice may be required to keep
      off putting greens ......................................................................... 8-2b/4

## Aeration Holes and Plugs

| | |
|---|---|
| holes | 25/15 |
| plugs | 23/12 |

## Agreement to Waive Rules

agreement
- not to tee off in prescribed order in match play to save time .................. 1-3/1
- that side losing after 18 holes of 36-hole match will concede match ............ 1-3/7
- to concede short putts ........................................................ 1-3/2
- to consider hole halved during play of hole ................................... 2-1/1.5
- to consider hole halved made when players not able to resolve Rules problem ...... 2-1/1
- to play out of turn made between competitors but not for purpose of giving one of them an advantage ................................................... 10-2c/2
- to repair spike marks on one another's line of putt made by player and opponent or fellow-competitor ................................................ 1-3/3

ball assisting fellow-competitor on putting green; procedure for Committee member if competitor does not lift ball ........................................ 22/7

breach of Rule by opponent
- discussed between player and opponent; penalty not applied ................... 1-3/4
- disregarded by player ......................................................... 2-5/1
- neither player nor opponent aware; penalty not applied ....................... 1-3/5
- procedure for valid claim .................................................... 2-5/2

competitor requests ball in position to assist him not be lifted .................. 22/6
handicap stroke given at wrong hole in error ..................................... 6-2a/2
incorrect procedure agreed to in error by player and opponent; whether valid claim can be made after procedure followed .................................... 2-5/8.5

marker attests wrong score
- knowingly ..................................................................... 1-3/6
- knowingly; competitor unaware score wrong .................................... 6-6a/5

player reaching third-round of match play disqualified for agreeing to waive Rules in first-round match .................................................... 34-1a/1
players unaware penalty incurred ................................................. 1-3/5
replaying match when play discontinued instead of resuming from where play stopped ........................................................................ 2-1/6
two holes purposely omitted in match ............................................ 2-1/4

wrong form of play used
- in match discovered after play of 9th hole ................................... 6-1/1
- in match; players agree losing side will default to winners .................. 33-1/4
- to decide which side will concede match ...................................... 2-4/21

## Ants and Ant Hills

*See also* Greenkeeper and Hole Made by Greenkeeper; Insects; Loose Impediments

danger from fire-ants ............................................................. 33-8/22

dangerous situation
- meaning of "dangerous situation" ............................................. 1-4/11
- relief procedure .............................................................. 1-4/10

Local Rule deeming hard conical ant hills as ground under repair ................. 33-8/22
status of ant hill ............................................................... 23/5

## Area of Intended Swing

*See also* Improving Area of Intended Stance or Swing, Position or Lie of Ball, or Line of Play or Putt

breaking branch
- interfering with backswing on teeing ground ................................ 13-2/14
- on backswing and swing discontinued ........................................ 13-2/14.5
- with practice swing; area of intended swing finally used not affected by branch .... 13-2/24

diagram illustrating player unable to determine nearest point of relief .......... 24-2b/3.7

"fairly taking his stance"
- explanation of "fairly taking his stance" ................................... 13-2/1
- player allowed to play in any direction in "fairly taking his stance" ........ 13-2/1.5

## Area of Intended Swing (continued)

- player attempts to take stance fairly but improves line of play by moving interfering growing object .......... 13-2/1.1
- player under tree changes intended direction of play and fairly takes stance second time .......... 13-2/1.7

improved by
- bending boundary fence .......... 13-2/18
- bending branch with hand; also club grounded and loose impediments moved in hazard; whether multiple penalties apply .......... 13-4/28
- bending grass in removal of loose impediments .......... 13-2/13
- moving growing or fixed object situated out of bounds .......... 13-2/19
- pushing off-course fence leaning across boundary to upright position .......... 13-2/20
- removing boundary stake interfering with swing .......... 13-2/17
- removing immovable obstructions .......... 13-2/15
- repairing pitch-mark made by ball on previous stroke .......... 13-2/21
- replacing or removing undetached divot .......... 13-2/5
- shaking water from tree branch interfering with backswing .......... 13-2/23
- taking stance fairly then changing direction of play .......... 13-2/1.7

knocking down leaves with practice swing; whether area of intended swing improved .......... 13-2/22
movable part of drainage hose interferes with player's swing .......... 24-2b/15.3
natural object interfering with swing moved to determine if loose; whether breach of Rule 13-2 .......... 13-2/26
obstruction in ground under repair interferes with player's swing .......... 24-2b/10
player breaches two Rules with different penalties; more severe penalty applied .......... 1-4/15
player determines nearest point of relief but physically unable to play intended stroke .......... 24-2b/3
position of ball worsened when obstruction removed; player replaces obstruction; whether area of intended swing improved .......... 13-2/15.5
probing near ball for tree roots or rocks; whether permitted .......... 13-2/27
removing dew or frost; whether permitted .......... 13-2/35
stake supporting tree broken in attempt to remove it .......... 13-2/16
tree in area of ground under repair interferes with swing at ball outside area .......... 25-1a/1

## Artificial Devices and Unusual Equipment

*See Also* Status of Object

adhesive tape .......... 14-3/8
artificial limbs .......... 14-3/15
binoculars .......... 14-3/3
booklet providing distances between various points .......... 14-3/5
bottled drink used as level .......... 14-3/12.5
compass used during round .......... 14-3/4
distance measuring device .......... 14-3/0.5
distance meter attached to golf cart .......... 14-3/1
elastic bandage worn .......... 14-3/7
electronic device or instrument
- containing distances between various points .......... 14-3/5.5
- transmitter contained in ball .......... 14-3/14
- use of electronic devices .......... 14-3/16
- used to find ball .......... 14-3/14

golf ball artificially warmed .......... 14-3/13.5
golf ball warmer or hand warmer used .......... 14-3/13
gradient measuring device .......... 14-3/0.5
hand warmer .......... 14-3/13.5
holding ball in hand against grip when putting .......... 14-3/6
Local Rule permitting use of distance measuring device .......... 14-3/0.5
pencil used to gauge distance .......... 14-3/2
player putts with one hand and steadies himself with club in other hand .......... 14-3/9
player with injured right wrist inserts left thumb under elastic bandage on right wrist and hand .......... 14-3/7

Index **I-5**

plumb-line
- club used as .................................................................................................. 14-3/12
- used during round ........................................................................................ 14-3/11

reflectors (non-circular) on flagsticks aid in use of distance-measuring
  devices; whether permitted ....................................................................... 17/3.5
score card used to gauge distance ................................................................... 14-3/2
standard spectacles and field glasses .............................................................. 14-3/3
stretching device ............................................................................................ 14-3/10.5
training or swing aid, such as weighted head cover or "doughnut" on club,
  used to make stroke or practice swing ..................................................... 14-3/10
wind gauge ..................................................................................................... 14-3/0.5

## Assistance

*See also* Ball Assisting or Interfering with Play; Exerting Influence on Ball; Four-Ball Match Play; Four-Ball Stroke Play

ball mark in position to assist player; whether player may prevent repair by
  opponent .................................................................................................... 16-1c/2
ball-marker of player in position to assist opponent or fellow-competitor;
  whether player may move it if opponent or fellow-competitor objects ..... 20-1/11
caddie
- hires boy to carry most of player's clubs but does not assist player in any
  other way; whether player has two caddies ............................................. 6-4/4
- inadvertently positioned on extension of line of play or putt behind ball ... 14-2/4
- shields player from sun during stroke ......................................................... 14-2/3
- takes player's glove to him at tee while another caddie or friend assists him
  by carrying player's clubs forward; whether player has two caddies ...... 6-4/4.5
player
- aligns partner's club before stroke .............................................................. 14-2/1
- directs caddie not to search for ball until others can assist ........................ 27/1
- holds ball in hand against grip to assist in putting ..................................... 14-3/6
- holds umbrella over own head during stroke ............................................. 14-2/2
- late for starting time provided medical assistance at scene of accident;
  whether circumstances warrant waiving penalty of disqualification
  under Rule 6-3a ...................................................................................... 6-3a/1.5
- places club on ground to assist in aligning feet for stroke ......................... 8-2a/1
- repairs spike marks in vicinity of hole that might assist him in subsequent
  play of hole ............................................................................................. 16-1c/4
- seeks assistance of others in removing large loose impediment ................ 23-1/3
- smoothes irregularities in bunker after playing out of turn in match;
  opponent recalls stroke; whether smoothing assists player in
  subsequent play of hole .......................................................................... 13-4/39
- smoothes irregularities in bunker after stroke but before ball extricated;
  opponent or fellow-competitor claims smoothing assisted player in
  subsequent play of hole .......................................................................... 13-4/36
- with artificial arm uses club with attachment to grip or shaft to assist
  him to hold club; whether permitted ...................................................... 14-3/15
player's breach of Rule assists partner
- absent player joins match during play of hole; stroke played by him
  assists partner ......................................................................................... 30-3a/1
- loose impediment in bunker lifted when player's and partner's balls
  lie in bunker; infringement assists partner's play (match play) ............. 30-3f/1
- loose impediment in bunker lifted when player's and partner's balls
  lie in bunker; infringement assists partner's play (stroke play) ............. 31-8/1
- player putts partner's ball by mistake; opponents claim partner also
  disqualified for hole because action assisted him .................................. 30-3d/1
- playing away from hole to assist partner ................................................... 30-3f/6
- practice stroke played from near partner's ball after player picks up ....... 30-3f/7
- putting out after concession of stroke; act assists partner ......................... 2-4/6
- stroke made by player disqualified for hole assists partner ....................... 30-3f/8

## Ball

*See also* Addressing the Ball; Ball Assisting or Interfering With Play; Ball at Rest Moved; Ball Deflected or Stopped; Ball Dropped or Re-Dropped; Ball Lifted; Ball Mark; Ball Overhanging Hole; Ball Placed or Replaced; Ball Touched; Ball Unfit for Play; Cleaning Ball; Embedded Ball; Exchanging Ball; Exerting Influence on Ball; Hole Made by Greenkeeper; Holed or Holing Out; Lie of Ball Altered; Lost Ball; Out of Bounds; Provisional Ball; Searching for and Identifying Ball; Second Ball; Status of Object; Stroke; Substituted Ball; "X-Out" Ball

- artificially warmed .................................................................................................... 14-3/13.5
- borrowing balls from another player; whether permitted ............................................ 5-1/5
- effect of state of match penalty for breach of "One Ball" condition in four-ball play ........ 30-3/2
- explanation of "any ball he has played" ....................................................................... 18/7
- holding ball in hand against grip when putting ........................................................ 14-3/6

List of Conforming Golf Balls
- ball to be removed from List used ................................................................... US/5-1/102
- condition in effect; ball not on list played as provisional ball ................................. 5-1/3
- penalty for breach of condition requiring use of ball on List of Conforming Golf Balls changed by Committee ............................................... 5-1/2
- status of ball not on List ...................................................................................... US/5-1/101

non-conforming ball
- one stroke played with non-conforming ball; whether Committee may waive disqualification penalty ............................................................... 5-1/1
- used for stroke with provisional ball that never becomes ball in play .................. 5-1/3

optional conditions of competition
- "One Ball" condition; prohibiting changing brands or types of golf balls during stipulated round .............................................................................. App I-C-1c
- requiring use of ball named on current List of Conforming Golf Balls ............ App I-C-1b

status of
- abandoned ball ......................................................................................................... 24-1/2
- ball not on List of Conforming Golf Balls ....................................................... US/5-1/101
- ball to be removed from List of Conforming Golf Balls ................................... US/5-1/102
- broken piece of ball swung at and struck by player mistaking it for his ball lying in heavy grass ............................................................................... 15/3
- "X-out" ball .............................................................................................................. 5-1/4

- trademark aimed along line of putt when ball replaced .................................................. 20-3a/2
- use of ball containing electronic transmitter ................................................................ 14-3/14

## Ball Assisting or Interfering with Play

*See also* Assistance; Exerting Influence on Ball

ball assisting play
- competitor not given opportunity to lift ball assisting fellow-competitor ................ 3-4/1
- competitor requests ball in position to assist him not be lifted; whether request proper .................................................................................... 22/6
- lifted by opponent then replaced at player's request; player's putt strikes opponent's ball; opponent lodges claim ............................................ 22/5
- on putting green in position to assist fellow-competitor; procedure for Committee member if competitor does not lift ball ................................... 22/7
- player requests ball of another player be lifted in absence of reasonable possibility it might assist play ......................................................... 22/3
- request to lift ball that might assist partner not honored ....................................... 30-3f/11

ball interfering with play
- abandoned ball lies against player's ball; procedure for player ................................ 24-1/2
- ball replaced on putting green while another ball in motion after stroke; player re-lifts ball in belief moving ball might strike it ........................... 16-1b/2
- kicked accidentally by player asked to lift it due to interference ............................ 20-1/13
- lie of ball lifted from bunker altered by another player's stroke ............................ 20-3b/1
- mental interference by another ball; whether player may have ball lifted under Rule 22-2 ........................................................................................ 22/1
- mud adheres to ball when lifted under Rule not permitting cleaning; whether ball may be replaced with mud facing different direction ...................... 21/5

Index  I-7

- player claims ball lying 30 yards away interferes with his play;
  whether request reasonable .................................................................................... 22/2
- player plays out of turn instead of complying with opponent's
  request to lift ball due to interference ................................................................ 10-1c/2
- player requests ball of another player be lifted in absence of reasonable
  possibility it might interfere with play ................................................................ 22/3
- two balls lie together in hazard and neither identifiable; procedure for players .......... 1-4/6

**Ball at Rest Moved**
*See also* Ball Deflected or Stopped; Ball Touched
after address
- and comes to rest out of bounds ............................................................................ 18-2b/9
- and then stopped by player's club ......................................................................... 18-2b/12
- ball dropped in improper manner moves when addressed; player
  then lifts ball and drops it in proper manner .......................................... 20-2a/4
- ball falls into hole ..................................................................................................... 18-2b/10
- ball in rough moves downward when addressed; ball will not
  remain at rest when replaced ................................................................................ 20-3d/3
- ball moves in water hazard after address; played while still moving ............... 14-6/1
- ball oscillates during address .................................................................................... 18/2
- by ball played from elsewhere .............................................................................. 18-2b/11
- competitor invokes Rule 3-3; second ball played first from spot
  where original ball lay ............................................................................................ 3-3/14
- foursome partner accidentally moves ball after address; effect on
  order of play ............................................................................................................... 29-1/5
- on putting green when player removes loose impediment ........................... 23-1/12
- player addresses ball, steps away; ball then moves .......................................... 18-2b/7
- player addresses ball, steps away, lifts ball and replaces it; ball then moves ........ 18-2b/8
- provisional or second ball moves after address; whether penalty
  cancelled if it never becomes ball in play ............................................................ 15/7
after club grounded
- ball perched on heather moves when club rested on heather ........................ 18-2b/6
- but before stance completed ................................................................................. 18-2b/4
after loose impediment touched or moved
- ball in hazard moves after loose impediment outside hazard moved ........... 18-2a/5
- ball in hazard moves when loose impediment in hazard removed .............. 13-4/15
- ball through the green moves after removal of nearby loose impediment ...... 18-2a/30.5
- ball touched with fir cone or stick to prevent movement when
  loose impediments removed .............................................................................. 18-2a/32
after stance taken
- but before address ................................................................................................... 18-2b/1
- in hazard without club ........................................................................................... 18-2b/2
ball falls into bunker when person walks nearby ..................................................... 18/10
ball in tree moved
- circumstances in which player not penalized .................................................... 18-2a/27
- circumstances in which player penalized ........................................................... 18-2a/28
- ball in fork of tree moves in relation to ground ................................................. 18/3
- knocked down by outside agency ........................................................................ 18-1/9
- replacement of ball not possible ............................................................................ 18-2a/29
- player climbs tree to play stroke; ball falls to ground ..................................... 18-2a/26
- striking at tree branch to move ball lodged beyond reach in branch ........... 14/7
ball moved
- by backward movement of club after stroke misses; ball comes to
  rest out of bounds .................................................................................................... 18-2a/22
- by fellow-competitor; competitor's ball thought to be wrong ball
  picked up at competitor's request ........................................................................ 18-2a/16
- by foot during removal of loose impediment on putting green ................... 23-1/11
- by golf cart shared by two players ........................................................................ 18/8
- by opponent in playing his own ball .................................................................... 18-3b/1

## Ball at Rest Moved *(continued)*

- by player accidentally during suspension of play ............................................. 18-2a/25
- by player, original lie altered; player places ball in wrong place and plays ............ 18-2a/21.3
- by player in playing wrong ball in bunker ........................................................... 18-2a/21
- by player in kicking ball accidentally when asked to lift it due to
  interference ............................................................................................... 20-1/13
- by practice swing prior to tee shot ..................................................................... 18-2a/19
- by practice swing when ball in play .................................................................... 18-2a/20
- by putter dropped by player approaching ball to lift it ........................................ 20-1/14
- by removal of player's foot after ball stopped by same foot ................................. 19-2/1
- by stone dislodged by partner's or opponent's stroke .......................................... 18-1/8
- by towel of player dropped on ground and blown onto ball ................................. 18-2a/17
- in measuring to determine if re-drop required ................................................... 18-6/1
- in removing ball-marker after replacing ball ....................................................... 20-3a/1
- prior to address then accidentally stopped by player's club; player
  removes club and ball rolls away ................................................................. 19-2/1.5
- vertically downward ............................................................................................ 18/1
- while player in process of taking stance in bunker ............................................. 18-2b/3

ball played from within ground under repair retrieved by player and
relief taken under ground under repair Rule .............................................. 18-2a/8

by another ball
- accidentally dropped by opponent or fellow-competitor ...................................... 18/7.5
- after player addresses ball .................................................................................. 18-2b/11
- balls inadvertently exchanged by players after one ball strikes and
  moves other ................................................................................................ 15-1/2.5
- competitor and fellow-competitor unaware ball moved by
  fellow-competitor's ball until after completion of hole .............................. 18-5/3
- competitor's ball played from putting green strikes ball on green
  belonging to competitor playing in another group ..................................... 19-5/2
- opponent's ball knocked away by player after concession moves
  player's ball ................................................................................................. 18-2a/18
- original ball strikes and moves provisional ball .................................................. 19-5/5
- original ball strikes second ball or vice versa ..................................................... 3-3/7
- provisional ball strikes original ball ................................................................... 18-5/2
- wrong ball played by opponent moves player's ball ............................................ 18-5/1

by another player making stroke
- competitor's ball in bunker played by fellow-competitor; ball
  remains in bunker; competitor plays ball from new location .................... 18-4/1
- competitor's ball knocked out of bunker by fellow-competitor's
  stroke at own ball ....................................................................................... 18-4/2
- opponent's stroke disturbs bushes causing player's ball to move ....................... 18-3b/2
- player plays own ball and accidentally moves partner's ball with
  club during stroke ....................................................................................... 30-3f/9

by caddie
- ball accidentally stepped on by opponent's caddie .............................................. 18-3b/3
- shared by members of opposite sides in four-ball match .................................... 30/1
- shared by opponent's side in four-ball match ..................................................... 30/2

by outside agency
- ball at rest kicked away from hole by spectator attending flagstick ..................... 18-1/10
- ball in tree knocked down by outside agency .................................................... 18-1/9
- ball not found; either moved by outside agency or lost ...................................... 18-1/1
- ball stolen by outside agency from unknown spot .............................................. 18-1/5
- ball visible from tee disappears or moved by outside agency while
  play suspended ............................................................................................ 6-8d/4
- lost ball treated as moved by outside agency in absence of
  reasonable evidence to that effect .............................................................. 27-1/2.5
- player unaware ball moved by outside agency does not replace ball ................... 18-1/3
- spectator says ball moved by outside agency but player not sure;
  procedure for player if Committee decision not possible in
  reasonable time ........................................................................................... 18-1/4

by water
- ball moved into bounds by flow of water in water hazard ........................................... 26-1/8
- ball moved out of bounds by flow of water in water hazard ..................................... 26-1/7
- ball moves in water in water hazard after address; played while still moving.............. 14-6/1
- ball moved by casual water while play suspended .......................................................... 18-1/11
by wind
- ball replaced instead of played from new location ...................................................... 18-2a/7
- ball moved by tumbleweed blown by wind ..................................................................... 18-1/6
- ball in plastic bag moves when bag blown to new position by wind ....................... 18-1/7
- ball moved by wind while play suspended ........................................................................ 18-1/11
concurrent four-ball and singles matches
- player causes partner's ball to move; whether penalty stroke
   applies to player's singles match ................................................................................. 30-3/1
- player causes opponent's ball to move; whether penalty stroke
   applies to player's singles match with other opponent........................................... 30-3/1
club breaks during downswing
- swing completed but misses ball; clubhead falls and moves ball ................................ 14/5
- swing stopped short of ball; clubhead falls and moves ball .......................................... 14/4
dropped ball comes to rest and then rolls out of bounds.................................................... 20-2c/3.5
during backswing ball moves; ball struck while still in motion .......................................... 14-5/1
flagstick
- ball overhanging hole rolls away or falls in hole when flagstick removed ............ 16-2/4
- ball overhanging hole moves and strikes flagstick being removed........................... 16-2/5
- ball resting against flagstick moves away from hole when flagstick
   removed by opponent or fellow-competitor......................................................... 17-4/3
- ball resting against flagstick moves away from hole when flagstick
   removed by player; ball not placed on lip of hole ................................................ 17-4/4
- when used for measuring or when accidentally dropped on ball ....................... 18-2a/24
meaning of "directly attributable" in Rules 20-1 and 20-3a................................................ 20-1/15
meaning of when moved ball to be replaced deemed not "immediately
  recoverable" ..................................................................................................................... 18/11
player breaches two Rules with different penalties; more severe penalty applied ............. 1-4/15
player takes several practice swings near ball and touches grass behind
  ball; ball moves .................................................................................................................. 18-2a/30
position of ball marked before obstruction removed; ball moves when
  ball-marker removed........................................................................................................ 24-1/5
putting green
- after ball addressed on putting green ball moved in removal
   of loose impediment.................................................................................................... 23-1/12
- ball blown into hole by competitor not replaced and holed out ................................ 3-2/2
- ball falls into hole after being addressed ........................................................................ 18-2b/10
- ball knocked from lip of hole in disgust ........................................................................ 18-2a/23
- ball oscillating in wind pressed into surface of putting green ................................ 18-2a/6
- ball replaced at rest thereafter moved by wind ............................................................. 18-1/12
- ball replaced on putting green but ball-marker not removed;
   ball then moves ............................................................................................................ 20-4/1
- competitor's ball played from putting green strikes ball on
   green belonging to competitor playing in another group ................................. 19-5/2
- fellow-competitor's ball knocked from lip of hole by competitor
   not replaced ................................................................................................................. 3-2/1
- fellow-competitor marks and lifts player's ball without authority............................ 20-1/4
- opponent's ball knocked away by player after concession moves
   player's ball ................................................................................................................... 18-2a/18
- opponent marks and lifts player's ball without authority ......................................... 20-1/2
- player addresses ball, steps away, lifts ball and replaces it; ball then moves........ 18-2b/8
- player jumps close to hole to cause ball to drop; ball does not move ..................... 1-2/3.8
- player jumps close to hole to cause ball to drop; ball falls into hole ...................... 1-2/4
- player throws putter at ball after leaving putt short .................................................... 1-2/4.5
searching for ball
- ball covered by sand in bunker moved from buried lie during search .................... 12-1/2
- player kicks ball while probing for it in water in water hazard ................................ 12-1/5

## Ball at Rest Moved (continued)

spot where moved ball originally lay not determinable; player places
    ball instead of dropping it .................................................................... 18-2a/21.5

teeing ground
- ball swung at within teeing ground falls off tee when stroke just
  touches it; player lifts, re-tees and plays ball............................................ 18-2a/2
- player misses tee shot; tees ball lower before playing next stroke .............. 18-2a/1
- stroke misses ball; then accidentally knocked off tee .................................. 11-3/1

## Ball Deflected or Stopped

*See also* Ball at Rest Moved; Exerting Influence on Ball

by ball at rest
- ball replaced on putting green while another ball in motion; replaced
  ball subsequently deflects moving ball ................................................... 16-1b/3
- competitor not given opportunity to lift his ball that assists
  fellow-competitor .................................................................................. 3-4/1
- competitor's ball played from putting green deflected by balls
  of two fellow-competitors ...................................................................... 19-5/3
- competitor's ball played from putting green strikes ball on green
  belonging to competitor playing in another group .................................. 19-5/2
- competitor's ball played from putting green touches but does not
  move ball of fellow-competitor lying on green ........................................ 19-5/4
- opponent's or fellow-competitor's ball played from putting green
  strikes player's ball that was lifted and set aside on green ....................... 19-5/1
- original ball strikes provisional ball ........................................................... 19-5/5
- original ball strikes second ball or vice versa .............................................. 3-3/7
- provisional ball strikes original ball ........................................................... 18-5/2

by equipment of player or partner
- club when ball moves after address ......................................................... 18-2b/12
- club when ball moves prior to address; player removes club and
  ball rolls away ....................................................................................... 19-2/1.5
- clubs belonging to different side but carried in same bag .......................... 19-2/5
- competitor's golf bag and then his caddie ................................................ 19-2/7
- face of club after striking pipeline ............................................................ 14-4/2
- face of club after stroke when ball falls and sticks to mud thereon............. 14-4/1
- golf cart being pulled by opponent or fellow-competitor ........................... 19-2/6
- opponent's or fellow-competitor's bag left ahead by shared caddie ........... 19-2/8
- trolley after first being deflected by trolley of opponent or fellow-competitor ........... 19-3/3

by flagstick, flag or hole-liner
- flag when flagstick attended .................................................................... 17-3/5
- flagstick attended by opponent or fellow-competitor not removed from hole .......... 17-3/2
- flagstick attended by partner without authority of player ......................... 17-3/4
- flagstick being removed when ball moves while overhanging hole ........... 16-2/5
- flagstick lying on ground ......................................................................... 17-3/3
- hole-liner and thereafter bounces out of hole ........................................... 16/5
- hole-liner pulled out with flagstick........................................................... 17/8

by golf cart shared by two players ..................................................................... 19/1

by opponent, caddie or equipment in match play
- opponent or caddie deflects ball dropped under Rule by player................. 19-3/2
- opponent standing out of bounds and ball comes to rest out of bounds .... 19-3/1
- opponent's trolley then strikes player's trolley.......................................... 19-3/3
- player attending flagstick for opponent .................................................... 30-3f/5
- tee marking position of ball .................................................................... 20-1/17

by outside agency
- ball dropped on moving ball by opponent or fellow-competitor ................ 19-5/1.7
- ball played at another hole ...................................................................... 19-1/10
- direction post ......................................................................................... 19-1/1
- dog on putting green when stroke played from off putting green .............. 19-1/6
- dog on putting green when stroke played from on putting green .............. 19-1/7
- golf cart shared by two players ................................................................ 19/1

Index  I-11

- fellow-competitor, deliberately .................................................................... 19-1/5
- fellow-competitor's or opponent's trolley then strikes player's trolley ..... 19-3/3
- knob falls from top of flagstick as attendant removes flagstick and
   deflects ball ............................................................................................... 17/9
- other than worm or insect and stroke from putting green not replayed ............... 19-1/3
- maintenance vehicle deflects ball out of bounds; substituted ball
   played from spot where original ball deflected ............................................. 20-7/1
- pipeline then deflected by face of club ................................................... 14-4/2
- spectator when stroke played from putting green ................................. 19-1/4
- spectator when stroke played from through the green.......................... 19-1/4.1
- stroke of player in another group ............................................................ 19-1/2
- tree branch before striking ground when dropped ................................. 20-2c/1.3
by player or partner
- after ball popped up then swung at in disgust ....................................... 14/6
- ball stopped by player's foot; ball moves when foot removed................ 19-2/1
- player knocks partner's putted ball back to him while still in motion
   after having passed hole ................................................................................ 1-2/7
- player catches ball in hole with one hand after putting with other hand ............... 1-2/5
- when flagstick attended by partner without authority of player ................ 17-3/4
- where next stroke must be played from when ball purposely stopped
   or deflected by player or partner ............................................................ 1-2/5.5
by player's own caddie
- dropped ball rolls toward or into position where re-drop would be
   required; caddie stops ball before it comes to rest ................................. 20-2c/4
- standing in bounds; ball comes to rest out of bounds ........................... 19-2/2
- standing out of bounds; ball comes to rest on course ........................... 19-2/3
- standing out of bounds; ball comes to rest out of bounds .................... 19-2/4
Local Rule for ball deflected by
- power line, tower or pole requiring cancelation and replay of stroke
   without penalty ......................................................................................... 33-8/13
- sprinkler head; allowing replay of stroke without penalty; whether
   authorized ................................................................................................. 33-8/12
- temporary power lines and cables ........................................................... App I-B-6b
- unattended flagstick; waiving penalty for ball striking unattended
   flagstick; whether authorized .................................................................. 33-8/11

### Ball Drop (Dropping Zone)
lateral water hazard
- defined as water hazard ........................................................................... 26/3.5
- part of lateral water hazard where impossible to drop not nearer hole ............... 33-2a/9
- permissible dropping area under lateral water hazard Rule so
   narrow player has difficulty dropping within it ..................................... 26-1/19
Local Rule
- allowing drop on green side of water hazard when ball fails to clear
   hazard; whether authorized .................................................................... 33-8/2
- allowing line-of sight relief without penalty from protective fence
   near line of play ........................................................................................ 33-8/18
- providing relief from paved path in all cases to ball drop (dropping
   zone) when nearest point of relief effectively gives no relief;
   whether authorized .................................................................................. 33-8/19
marking island green ....................................................................................... 33-2a/10
procedure for dropping and re-dropping on ball drop (dropping zone)
   established by Local Rule ........................................................................ 33-8/34
tree falls onto fairway during stipulated round ............................................. 25/9.5

### Ball Dropped or Re-Dropped
*See also* Ball Lifted; Ball Placed or Replaced; Local Rules
ball accidentally dropped by opponent or fellow-competitor on player's ball
- at rest .......................................................................................................... 18/7.5
- in motion after stroke from putting green .............................................. 19-5/1.7

## Ball Dropped or Re-Dropped *(continued)*

ball deemed unplayable
- and dropped then deemed unplayable second time; player wishes to proceed under stroke-and-distance .................................................................................... 28/6.5
- at base of cliff and player wishes to drop within two club-lengths of point above ball ........................................................................................................ 28/12
- dropped in ground under repair from which play prohibited; ball then dropped under ground under repair Rule ........................................... 25-1b/14.5
- dropped outside bunker under option requiring drop in bunker ..................... 28/10
- in tree and player opts to drop within two club-lengths ................................... 28/11
- in water hazard; dropped in hazard and played .................................................. 20-7/2
- in water hazard; substituted ball dropped in hazard without lifting original; error discovered before stroke played ................................................ 20-7/2.5
- player deems provisional ball unplayable and drops ball; original ball then found .................................................................................................... 27-2b/6.5
- player who deems ball unplayable under Rule 28a must drop only at place from which last stroke played ............................................................... 28/5
- through the green dropped in hazard ................................................................... 28/4
- through the green dropped in water hazard; player elects not to play ball and wishes to proceed under water hazard Rule .................................. 28/4.5

ball embeds when dropped
- in fairway .................................................................................................................... 25-2/2
- procedure if ball again embeds when re-dropped ............................................. 25-2/2.5

ball lifted without authority
- and dropped away from boundary stake under obstruction Rule .................. 18-2a/3
- and dropped away from movable obstruction ................................................... 18-2a/4
- ball played from ground under repair abandoned and relief taken under ground under repair Rule .......................................................................... 18-2a/8.5

bunker
- ball believed lost in bunker; competitor drops and plays substituted ball in bunker; then original ball found outside bunker .................................. 20-7c/3
- ball deemed unplayable through the green dropped in hazard ....................... 28/4
- ball dropped outside bunker under option requiring drop in bunker ............ 28/10
- ball to be dropped in bunker, dropped outside bunker so it will roll into bunker to avoid ball embedding in bunker ................................................ 25-1b/7
- smoothing footprints created in bunker on line of play when required to enter bunker to retrieve ball ......................................................................... 13-2/29.3

by whom and how to drop
- ball dropped in other than prescribed manner moves after address and before re-drop .................................................................................................. 20-2a/4
- ball dropped in improper manner and wrong place ......................................... 20-2a/3
- ball spun by player when dropping ...................................................................... 20-2a/2
- ball substituted mistakenly when dropped ......................................................... 20-6/3
- caddie holds back tree branch to prevent branch from deflecting dropped ball .......................................................................................................... 20-2a/5
- penalty when ball dropped in other than prescribed manner ........................ 20-2a/1
- who drops ball in foursome play .......................................................................... 29/4

changing relief option
- dropped ball first strikes course outside where applicable Rule requires; whether player may change relief option when re-dropping ............. 20-6/2
- dropped ball first strikes course outside where applicable Rule requires; whether player may replace ball in original location ......................... 20-6/5
- dropped ball rolls to position requiring re-drop; whether player may change relief option when re-dropping ...................................................... 20-2c/5
- dropped ball strikes player; whether player may change relief option when re-dropping ........................................................................................ 20-2a/6
- player drops ball in bunker under first option of Rule 25-1b(ii); player then wishes to proceed under second option to drop outside bunker ..................................................................................................... 25-1b/9

- player lifts ball from bunker intending to drop under first option
of Rule 24-2b(ii); player then wishes to proceed under second
option to drop outside bunker .................................................................................. 24-2b/5
- point where ball last crossed margin of lateral water hazard
determined and ball dropped; point then proves to be wrong
point; whether player may change relief option when re-dropping .................. 26-1/16

dropped ball rolls toward or into position where re-drop would be
required; caddie stops ball before it comes to rest .................................................. 20-2c/4

dropping instead of placing or placing instead of dropping
- ball dropped instead of being replaced after being lifted
without authority ......................................................................................................... 18-2a/9
- ball dropped third time when placement required after second drop .................. 20-2c/2
- ball moved accidentally; spot where ball originally lay not
determinable; player places ball instead of dropping it ..................................... 18-2a/21.5
- ball placed when required to be dropped or dropped when
required to be placed .................................................................................................. 20-6/1
- ball placed instead of dropped on bank of water hazard to
prevent ball rolling into water ................................................................................. 26-1/10
- ball placed instead of dropped when obvious dropped ball
will roll into position where re-drop will be required .......................................... 20-2c/3

improving area in which ball to be dropped
- ball played from bunker goes out of bounds or lost; player
smoothes footprints or tests condition of bunker before dropping
another ball in bunker ............................................................................................... 13-4/37
- divots replaced in area in which ball to be dropped ................................................. 13-2/4.5
- loose impediments removed from area in which ball to be dropped ....................... 23-1/6
- pitch-mark in dropping area repaired before ball dropped ...................................... 13-2/10
- player smoothes irregularities in bunker after playing out of turn
in match play; opponent then recalls stroke and player must drop
ball in smoothed area ................................................................................................ 13-4/39
- sand or loose soil removed from dropping area .......................................................... 13-2/11

Local Rule
- allowing drop opposite to spot where ball comes to rest in lateral
water hazard; whether authorized ........................................................................... 26-1/20
- ball drop (dropping zone) established by Local Rule; clarification of
procedure for dropping and re-dropping ................................................................ 33-8/34
- permitting re-dropping or placing when dropped ball embeds in
bunker; whether authorized ..................................................................................... 33-8/28
- wrong putting green; deemed to include apron to prohibit dropping
on and play from .......................................................................................................... 33-8/33

lost ball
- ball believed lost in bunker; competitor drops and plays substituted
ball in bunker; then original ball found outside bunker ...................................... 20-7c/3
- ball dropped and played under ground under repair Rule in absence
of reasonable evidence original ball lost in ground under repair ...................... 25-1c/2
- ball dropped where original ball lost; ball then played ............................................. 27-1/3
- explanation of how to determine "estimated spot" for dropping when
specific spot cannot be determined exactly ........................................................... 20-2c/1.5
- original ball found within five-minute search period after substituted
ball dropped at spot of previous stroke .................................................................. 27-1/2
- original ball found within five-minute search period after substituted
ball dropped at spot of previous stroke; original ball played ............................. 27-1/2.3

measuring for dropping and re-dropping
- ball moved in measuring to determine if re-drop required ....................................... 18-6/1
- club to be used in measuring ........................................................................................... 20/1
- directly through fence, tree or wall or across ditch .................................................. 20-2b/2
- player must continue measuring with club originally used for
subsequent measuring ................................................................................................. 20/1

player drops ball after play suspended for dangerous situation .................................... 6-8b/8

## Ball Dropped or Re-Dropped *(continued)*

player invokes Rule 3-3 (doubt as to procedure)
- ball dropped in wrong place and played; second ball dropped in right place; both balls played out .................................................. 3-3/3
- ball dropped in wrong place but not played; second ball dropped in right place; both balls played out ............................................... 3-3/4
- competitor announces intention to play two balls; plays original ball before dropping second ball then elects not to play second ball ............ 3-3/7.5
- competitor drops one ball in accordance with two different Rules instead of playing second ball .......................................................... 3-3/11
- competitor drops one ball in accordance with two different Rules instead of playing second ball; dropped ball rolls back into condition from which relief taken ................................................... 3-3/12
- competitor lifts and drops original ball then places second ball where original ball lay and plays it ........................................................ 3-3/13
- whether score with second ball counts if dropped in wrong place and played ................................................................................. 3-3/5

player mis-hits ball when distracted by accidentally dropped ball ....................... 1-4/1

player picks up without completing hole; drops ball where partner's ball lies and plays practice stroke ........................................................... 30-3f/7

reasonable evidence
- original ball lost in abnormal ground condition or obstruction; substituted ball dropped under applicable Rule; whether re-drop required if finding original demonstrates drop made in wrong place .......... 25-1c/2.5
- original ball in water hazard; substituted ball dropped under water hazard Rule; whether re-drop required if finding original demonstrates drop made in wrong place ............................................... 26-1/3.5

water hazard
- ball deemed unplayable in water hazard, dropped in hazard and played .............. 20-7/2
- ball deemed unplayable through the green dropped in hazard ..................... 28/4
- ball deemed unplayable through the green dropped in water hazard; player elects not to play ball and wishes to proceed under water hazard Rule ........................................................... 28/4.5
- ball dropped twice then placed where second drop struck course and played; first drop should have been played as it lay ....................... 18-2a/10
- ball placed instead of dropped on bank of water hazard to prevent ball from rolling into water .......................................................... 26-1/10
- ball dropped and played under water hazard Rule; original ball found outside hazard .................................................................. 26-1/3
- impossible to drop not nearer hole than point where ball last crossed margin of lateral water hazard ............................................. 26-1/18
- Local Rule allowing drop opposite to spot where ball comes to rest in lateral water hazard; whether authorized ................................... 26-1/20
- meaning of "behind" in Rule 26-1 ....................................................... 26-1/1.5
- part of lateral water hazard where impossible to drop not nearer hole ............... 33-2a/9
- permissible dropping area under lateral water hazard Rule so narrow player has difficulty dropping within it ....................................... 26-1/19
- player proceeding under water hazard Rule drops ball in another hazard ............ 26-1/2
- point where ball last crossed margin of lateral water hazard determined; ball dropped but not played; point then proves to be wrong point .................................................................................. 26-1/16
- point where ball last crossed margin of lateral water hazard determined; ball dropped and played; point then proves to be wrong point .......... 26-1/17

whether glove used to mark dropping area is equipment .............................. 20-2a/7
whether player may drop ball into area from which play prohibited ................. 20-7/3
whether player may substitute ball when re-dropping under Rule allowing substitution ............................................................... 20-6/4
whether re-drop required
- after relief from obstruction taken for stroke toward green, same obstruction interferes with stance for necessary sideways stroke ........ 24-2b/9.5

Index **I-15**

- ball accidentally deflected by opponent or his caddie when dropped ..................... 19-3/2
- ball dropped from casual water in bunker at point of maximum
  relief rolls elsewhere ................................................................................................ 25-1b/6
- ball dropped from ground under repair area rolls to position
  where area interferes with stance ........................................................................... 20-2c/0.5
- ball never strikes ground when dropped ................................................................... 20-2b/1
- ball strikes tree branch then ground when dropped ................................................. 20-2c/1.3
- ball dropped under Rule 20-5 strikes course through the green
  within inches of and not nearer hole than spot in bunker where
  previous stroke played .............................................................................................. 20-5/2
- ball dropped under Rule 24-2b rolls nearer hole than nearest point
  of relief but not nearer than where it originally lay ............................................... 20-2c/1.7
- ball dropped under unplayable ball Rule comes to rest in original
  position or another unplayable position ................................................................ 28/3
- ball rolls towards hole when dropped at spot from which previous
  stroke played ............................................................................................................. 20-2c/1.5
- dropped ball comes to rest and then rolls out of bounds ........................................ 20-2c/3.5
- dropped ball rolls out of prescribed dropping area ................................................. 20-2c/1
- pine needles piled for removal interfere with lie; after drop taken
  pine needles interfere with line of play .................................................................. 25-1b/17
- player takes relief from area of casual water; ball comes to rest in
  position where another area of casual water interferes ........................................ 20-2c/7
- player takes relief from area of ground under repair and condition
  interferes for stroke with club not used to determine nearest point
  of relief ...................................................................................................................... 20-2c/0.8
- player takes relief from immovable obstruction; dropped ball rolls
  nearer obstruction than nearest point of relief; player changes clubs
  and obstruction no longer interferes ...................................................................... 20-2c/0.7

wrong ball
- dropped and played under stroke-and-distance procedure; original ball
  then found ................................................................................................................. 28/14
- dropped under unplayable ball Rule but not played ................................................. 15/13
- dropped under unplayable ball Rule within two club-lengths and played
  before error discovered ............................................................................................ 28/15
- in bunker deemed unplayable, dropped in bunker and played; ball then
  discovered to be wrong ball ..................................................................................... 15/14
- original ball found within five-minute search period after substituted
  ball dropped; original ball played ........................................................................... 27-1/2.3

## Ball Lifted

assisting or interfering with play
- assisting ball lifted by opponent replaced on request; player's ball then
  strikes opponent's ball and opponent lodges claim .............................................. 22/5
- ball assisting fellow-competitor on putting green; procedure for Committee
  member if competitor does not lift ball ................................................................. 22/7
- competitor not given opportunity to lift ball assisting fellow-competitor ............. 3-4/1
- competitor requests ball in position to assist him not be lifted; whether
  request proper ........................................................................................................... 22/6
- player requested to lift ball due to interference plays out of turn instead ............ 10-1c/2
- request to lift ball that might assist partner not honored ....................................... 30-3f/11
- mental interference by another ball ........................................................................... 22/1
- player claims that another ball lying 30 yards away interferes with his play ....... 22/2
- player requests another player to lift his ball in absence of reasonable
  possibility ball might interfere or assist ................................................................. 22/3

ball at rest moved
- accidentally kicked by player asked to lift it due to interference ........................... 20-1/13
- ball dropped in improper manner moves when addressed; player
  then lifts ball and drops it in proper manner ........................................................ 20-2a/4
- ball moved by putter dropped by player approaching ball to lift it ....................... 20-1/14
- player addresses ball, steps away, lifts ball and replaces it; ball then moves ....... 18-2b/8

## Ball Lifted (continued)

ball-marker moved accidentally by player who marked position of ball
    and lifted it ................................................................................................. 20-1/6
ball with mud adhering lifted under Rule not permitting cleaning,
    rotated when replaced .................................................................................. 21/5
by caddie without authority
    - competitor's ball lifted without authority by fellow-competitor's caddie
      who subsequently substitutes another ball which competitor plays ............. 20-1/5
    - considering it unplayable .......................................................................... 18-2a/15
    - for identification ........................................................................................ 18-2a/14
    - in water hazard ............................................................................................ 26-1/9
    - opponent's caddie lifts player's ball after player claims another ball ........... 18-3b/4
    - opponent's caddie lifts player's ball which may or may not have been
      out of bounds ............................................................................................ 18-3b/5
by opponent or fellow-competitor without authority
    - by fellow-competitor .................................................................................... 20-1/4
    - by opponent ................................................................................................ 20-1/2
    - by opponent after marking it; player lifts ball-marker and claims
      hole; opponent disputes claim ................................................................. 20-1/3
    - by opponent because player reported wrong score in match play ................ 9-2/6
    - by opponent in four-ball match ................................................................. 30-3f/10
    - competitor's ball thought to be wrong ball picked up by fellow-competitor
      at competitor's request ........................................................................... 18-2a/16
    - fellow-competitor lifts competitor's ball and sets it aside; competitor
      plays ball from where set aside................................................................. 15-3b/3
by player (or partner) without authority
    - and cleaned ............................................................................................... 18-2a/13
    - and dropped away from boundary stake under obstruction Rule .............. 18-2a/3
    - and dropped away from movable obstruction .......................................... 18-2a/4
    - and re-dropped when it should have been played as it lay; ball then
      lifted again and placed ........................................................................... 18-2a/10
    - and thrown into pond in anger ................................................................ 18-2a/13
    - ball in play under stroke-and-distance procedure lifted when original
      ball found and played ................................................................................ 15/5
    - ball played from teeing ground of hole to be played later in round
      lifted; ball replaced at spot from which lifted and played out when
      that hole subsequently reached ................................................................ 11-5/5
    - ball played from teeing ground wrongly thought out of bounds lifted;
      competitor plays another ball from tee .................................................. 18-2a/11
    - ball played from within ground under repair retrieved by player and
      relief taken under ground under repair Rule ........................................... 18-2a/8
    - ball swung at within teeing ground falls off tee when stroke just
      touches it; player lifts, re-tees and plays ball........................................... 18-2a/2
    - before being holed out; opponent then picks up his ball claiming
      player loses hole........................................................................................ 2-5/3
    - competitor picks up second ball, completes hole with original ball
      and plays from next tee ............................................................................. 3-3/8
    - dropped instead of being replaced ............................................................. 18-2a/9
    - due to misunderstanding Committee member's instructions ................... 34-3/3.5
    - player makes several strokes on wrong putting green after lifting
      and replacing ball..................................................................................... 25-3/2
    - provisional ball lifted in erroneous belief original ball in bounds ........... 27-2b/8
    - provisional ball lifted subsequently becomes ball in play......................... 27-2b/9
    - provisional ball lifted; subsequently becomes ball in play;
      ball not replaced but played from wrong place...................................... 27-2b/10
changing relief option
    - dropped ball first strikes course outside where applicable Rule
      requires; whether player may change relief option when re-dropping................ 20-6/2
    - dropped ball first strikes course outside where applicable Rule
      requires; whether player may replace ball in original location ........................... 20-6/5

- dropped ball rolls to position requiring re-drop; whether player
  may change relief option when re-dropping ............................................. 20-2c/5
- dropped ball strikes player; whether player may change relief option
  when re-dropping ........................................................................................... 20-2a/6
- player drops ball in bunker under first option of Rule 25-1b(ii); player
  then wishes to proceed under second option to drop outside bunker ............. 25-1b/9
- player lifts ball from bunker intending to drop under first option of
  Rule 24-2b(ii); player then wishes to proceed under second option to
  drop outside bunker ..................................................................................... 24-2b/5
- point where ball last crossed margin of lateral water hazard
  determined and ball dropped; point then proves to be wrong
  point; whether player may change relief option when re-dropping ................. 26-1/16
competitor invokes Rule 3-3; lifts and drops original ball ....................................... 3-3/13
competitor who lifts his and fellow-competitor's balls inadvertently
  exchanges them when replaced ...................................................................... 15-2/4
concessions
- fellow-competitor lifts competitor's ball conceding next stroke
  in stroke play ................................................................................................ 18-4/3
- player concedes match due to misconception as to opponent's score
  at last hole and lifts opponent's ball ............................................................. 2-4/14
- player concedes opponent's next stroke and plays before opponent has
  opportunity to lift ball ................................................................................... 2-4/8
- player lifts ball in mistaken belief that next stroke conceded ........................ 2-4/3
- whether lifting opponent's ball-marker considered concession of
  next stroke ..................................................................................................... 2-4/5
- whether picking up opponent's ball considered concession of next stroke .... 2-4/4
- player shakes opponent's hand and picks up opponent's ball in
  erroneous belief match over .......................................................................... 2-4/17
lie of lifted ball in bunker altered by another player's stroke ............................. 20-3b/1
loose impediments
- affecting lie moved when ball lifted through the green ................................ 23-1/7
- affecting lie removed while ball lifted through the green ............................. 23-1/8
- removed after player lifts ball deemed unplayable in bunker ...................... 13-4/35.7
meaning of
- "directly attributable" in Rules 20-1 and 20-3a ............................................ 20-1/15
- "good reason to lift" when play suspended .................................................. 6-8c/1
player entitled to relief without penalty lifts ball then chooses not to take free relief
- replaces ball and plays it from original position ........................................... 18-2a/12
- wishes to proceed under unplayable ball Rule ............................................. 18-2a/12.5
position of ball not marked when lifted for identification, intention to lift
  not announced and ball cleaned beyond extent necessary to identify it ............. 21/4
provisional ball lifted
- in erroneous belief original ball in bounds .................................................. 27-2b/8
- subsequently becomes ball in play .............................................................. 27-2b/9
- subsequently becomes ball in play; provisional ball not replaced
  but played from wrong place ........................................................................ 27-2b/10
putting green
- ball knocked aside after marking position instead of lifted ......................... 20-1/22
- ball lifted and thrown into lake; player then announces ball was
  unfit for play ................................................................................................ 5-3/3.5
- ball lifted because player feared ball might move ........................................ 16-1b/1
- ball lifted by fellow-competitor who sets it aside; competitor plays
  ball from where set aside ............................................................................. 15-3b/3
- ball lifted by player who sets it aside; opponent's or fellow-competitor's
  ball subsequently strikes player's ball .......................................................... 19-5/1
- ball lifted by player who sets it aside; played from where set aside ............. 15/4
- ball lifted and replaced by player who then makes several strokes
  on wrong putting green ................................................................................ 25-3/2
- ball lifted without its position being marked in mistaken belief it is
  wrong ball .................................................................................................... 20-1/1

## Ball Lifted (continued)
- ball moved by putter dropped by player approaching ball to lift it ...................... 20-1/14
- ball overhanging hole lifted, cleaned and replaced; ball then falls into hole ............ 16-2/0.5
- ball placed ahead of ball-marker and then rolled or slid back to
 original position ..................................................................................... 16-1a/17
- ball putted from wrong place lifted and putted from right place ........................... 20-7c/2
- ball replaced while another ball in motion; player re-lifts ball thinking
 moving ball might strike it ....................................................................... 16-1b/2
- ball replaced while another ball in motion; replaced ball deflects
 moving ball ............................................................................................. 16-1b/3
- ball resting against flagstick lifted before being holed .......................................... 17-4/1
- ball resting against flagstick lifted before being holed; others in
 match pick up mistakenly believing player won hole .................................. 30-3f/3
- ball returned to spot from which it was lifted by rolling it with putter ............... 16-1d/3

teeing ground
- ball played from teeing ground of hole to be played later in round
 lifted; ball replaced at spot from which lifted and played out when
 that hole subsequently reached ............................................................... 11-5/5
- ball played within teeing ground barely moved by first stroke; player
 lifts and re-tees ball................................................................................. 18-2a/2

to determine whether it is
- embedded in its own pitch-mark ................................................................... 25-2/7
- in burrowing animal hole .............................................................................. 25/21

unfit for play
- ball lifted and thrown into lake; player then announces ball was unfit
 for play ................................................................................................... 5-3/3.5
- Committee involvement when opponent, marker or fellow-competitor
 not readily available ................................................................................ 5-3/7
- lifted under another Rule and cleaned; ball then determined unfit for play ......... 5-3/6

unplayable ball
- after declaring ball unplayable and lifting it, player discovers ball was
 in ground under repair ............................................................................ 28/13
- caddie lifts ball considering it unplayable ..................................................... 18-2a/15
- player deems ball unplayable in bunker; lifts ball and then removes
 loose impediment from bunker................................................................ 13-4/35.7
- player entitled to relief without penalty lifts ball then decides not to
 take relief and wishes to proceed under unplayable ball Rule ...................... 18-2a/12.5

when player entitled to replace lifted ball in original position ........................................... 20-6/5
whether player himself must lift ball.................................................................................. 20-1/0.5

## Ball Mark

*See also* Ball-Marker; Pitch-Mark

ball embedded in side of hole
- all of ball below lip of hole............................................................................. 16/2
- all of ball not below lip of hole...................................................................... 16/3

removal of dew or frost from line of putt
- incidental to repair of ball marks on putting green..................................... 13-2/35
- other than incidental to repair of ball marks ............................................... 16-1a/3

repair of ball mark
- in position to assist opponent ...................................................................... 16-1c/2
- on putting green by caddie without player's authority; whether permitted ............... 6-4/10
- partially on and partially off putting green ................................................. 16-1c/1.5
- second time ................................................................................................... 16-1c/1
- spike mark on line of putt repaired during repair of ball mark .................... 16-1a/16
- that damaged hole......................................................................................... 16-1a/6

## Ball-Marker

*See also* Ball Mark; Marking Position of Ball; Status of Object

ball lifted from putting green by player; caddie places ball behind
 ball-marker; whether ball in play.......................................................................... 20-4/2

Index **I-19**

ball lifted on putting green placed ahead of ball-marker and then
    rolled or slid back to original position.................................................................. 16-1a/17
ball moved in removing ball-marker after replacing ball ..................................................... 20-3a/1
ball replaced on putting green but ball-marker not removed; ball then moves................ 20-4/1
ball-marker moved by wind or casual water during stipulated round.......................... 20-1/10.5
incorrect information causes opponent to lift ball-marker; whether
    lifting of marker equivalent of next stroke................................................................ 9-2/5
lie altered by act of marking position of ball ................................................................ 20-1/15.5
lifted
    - ball marked and lifted by opponent without player's authority;
        player lifts ball-marker and claims hole; opponent disputes claim ..................... 20-1/3
    - by outside agency.................................................................................................... 20-1/9
    - by player mistakenly believing he won hole ......................................................... 20-1/8
meaning of "directly attributable" in Rules 20-1 and 20-3a.......................................... 20-1/15
method used to mark position of ball.............................................................................. 20-1/16
moved accidentally
    - by player after having moved loose impediments ............................................. 20-1/12
    - by opponent's caddie ............................................................................................... 20-1/7
    - by player ................................................................................................................. 20-1/5.5
    - by player after having moved loose impediments ............................................. 20-1/12
    - by player in process of marking position of ball ................................................. 20-1/6
moved off green by wind or casual water while play suspended ................................ 20-1/10
placing object marking position of ball other than behind ball .................................. 20-1/19
player measures clubhead-length to side of ball and places ball-marker ............... US/20-1/100
player places ball-marker approximately two inches behind ball .................................. 20-1/20
position of ball
    - marked before obstruction removed; ball moves when ball-marker
        removed .................................................................................................................. 24-1/5
    - marked with tee ....................................................................................................... 20-1/17
in position to assist another player.................................................................................. 20-1/11
tee marking position of player's ball deflects opponent's ball .......................................... 20-1/17
whether lifting opponent's ball-marker considered concession of next stroke ............... 2-4/5

### Ball Overhanging Hole

casting shadow on ball overhanging hole....................................................................... 16-2/3
falls into hole after
    - addressed by player................................................................................................ 18-2b/10
    - concession of next stroke........................................................................................ 2-4/2
    - player waits 40 seconds .......................................................................................... 16-2/1
fellow-competitor's ball knocked from lip of hole by competitor not replaced ................ 3-2/1
flagstick
    - ball overhanging hole rolls away or falls in hole when flagstick removed ............ 16-2/4
    - ball overhanging hole moves and strikes flagstick being removed....................... 16-2/5
knocked away by opponent before player determines status ............................................ 16-2/2
lifted cleaned and replaced; ball then falls into hole....................................................... 16-2/0.5
player jumps close to hole to cause overhanging ball to drop
    - ball does not move ................................................................................................. 1-2/3.8
    - ball falls into hole .................................................................................................... 1-2/4

### Ball Placed or Replaced

after relief taken from obstruction for stroke towards green, obstruction
    interferes with stance for necessary sideways stroke; whether ball
    should be re-dropped or placed where it first struck course............................ 24-2b/9.5
ball dropped instead of placed or replaced
    - ball dropped third time when placement required after second drop ................. 20-2c/2
    - ball lifted without authority dropped instead of replaced ..................................... 18-2a/9
    - ball dropped when required to be placed; correction of error.................................. 20-6/1
ball placed instead of dropped or re-dropped
    - ball moved accidentally; spot where ball originally lay not
        determinable; player places ball instead of dropping it................................... 18-2a/21.5

## Ball Placed or Replaced (continued)

- ball placed on bank of water hazard instead of dropped to prevent
  ball rolling into water ............................................................................... 26-1/10
- ball placed when required to be dropped; correction of error .................... 20-6/1
- when obvious dropped ball will roll into position where re-drop
  will be required ............................................................................................ 20-2c/3

ball with mud adhering lifted under Rule not permitting cleaning
  rotated when replaced ........................................................................................ 21/5

ball-marker
- ball moved in removing ball-marker after replacing ball ......................... 20-3a/1
- ball replaced on putting green but ball-marker not removed; ball
  then moves ................................................................................................... 20-4/1
- lifted by outside agency ................................................................................ 20-1/9
- lifted by player mistakenly believing he won hole ...................................... 20-1/8
- moved accidentally by player .................................................................... 20-1/5.5
- moved accidentally by player in process of marking position of ball ......... 20-1/6
- moved off green by wind or casual water while play suspended ............. 20-1/10

competitor invokes Rule 3-3; second ball played first from spot where
  original ball lay ................................................................................................. 3-3/14

competitor lifts and drops original ball then places second ball where
  original ball lay and plays it ............................................................................ 3-3/13

in wrong place
- ball resting against flagstick moves away from hole when flagstick
  removed by player; ball not placed on lip of hole ..................................... 17-4/4
- competitor repeatedly replaces ball nearer hole on green .......................... 33-7/6
- on putting green and holed ......................................................................... 20-7c/1

lie of ball to be replaced altered
- and spot where ball originally lay not determinable; procedure
  player must use .......................................................................................... 20-3b/5
- by act of marking position of ball ............................................................ 20-1/15.5
- in bunker by another player's stroke ......................................................... 20-3b/1
- in hazard; lifted to determine whether unfit for play .................................. 5-3/5
- when stepped on accidentally by player; ball placed in wrong
  place and played .................................................................................... 18-2a/21.3

Local Rule permitting re-dropping or placing when dropped ball
  embeds in bunker; whether authorized ........................................................ 33-8/28

meaning of
- "directly attributable" in Rules 20-1 and 20-3a ......................................... 20-1/15
- "estimated spot" for placing when specific spot cannot be
  determined exactly ................................................................................... 20-2c/1.5

method used to mark position of ball ................................................................... 20-1/16
moved by wind after being replaced .................................................................... 18-1/12
player addresses ball, steps away, lifts ball and replaces it; ball then moves ........ 18-2b/8

putting green
- ball lifted by player from putting green and placed by caddie
  behind ball-marker ....................................................................................... 20-4/2
- ball oscillating in wind pressed into surface of putting green ..................... 18-2a/6
- ball overhanging hole lifted, cleaned and replaced; ball then falls
  into hole ..................................................................................................... 16-2/0.5
- ball replaced at wrong place on putting green and holed ........................... 20-7c/1
- ball replaced on putting green but ball-marker not removed; ball
  then moves ................................................................................................... 20-4/1
- ball replaced on putting green while another ball in motion; player
  re-lifts ball thinking moving ball might strike it ......................................... 16-1b/2
- ball replaced on putting green while another ball in motion; replaced
  ball deflects moving ball ............................................................................. 16-1b/3
- ball resting against flagstick moves away from hole when flagstick
  removed by player; ball not placed on lip of hole ..................................... 17-4/4
- competitor repeatedly replaces ball nearer hole on green .......................... 33-7/6
- player addresses ball, steps away, lifts ball and replaces it; ball then moves ....... 18-2b/8
- player returns ball to spot from which it was lifted by rolling it with putter ........ 16-1d/3

Index **i-21**

   - replaced ball rolls into hole .................................................................................. 20-3d/1
   - trademark aimed along line of putt when ball replaced.................................... 20-3a/2
removal of loose impediments from spot on which ball to be placed ................ 23-1/6.5
replacement of ball not possible
   - ball dislodged from tree by outside agency ........................................................ 18-1/9
   - ball dislodged from tree by player ................................................................... 18-2a/29
   - ball in bunker moves when obstruction removed; whether player
      may press ball into sand or take relief outside bunker if not possible
      to replace or place in bunker not nearer hole ................................................ 20-3d/2
   - ball in rough moves downward when addressed; ball will not remain
      at rest when replaced ....................................................................................... 20-3d/3
when player entitled to replace ball in original position after lifting with
     intention of taking relief under Rule ................................................................... 20-6/5
whether player himself must place or replace ball ............................................. 20-3a/0.5

### Ball Touched

*See also* Ball at Rest Moved
accidentally
   - in removing loose impediments ...................................................................... 18-2a/31
   - original ball out of bounds; ball re-teed under stroke-and-distance
      touched at address and falls off tee ................................................................. 11-3/3
   - with club in bunker or water hazard; ball does not move .............................. 13-4/12
purposely
   - ball on putting green rotated without marking position ................................ 18-2a/33
   - half-buried ball rotated for identification purposes in hazard ...................... 12-2/3
   - half-buried ball rotated for identification purposes through the green ........ 12-2/2
   - holding ball in place while removing obstruction ........................................... 24-1/4
   - stick or fir cone placed against ball to prevent movement when
      loose impediments removed .......................................................................... 18-2a/32

### Ball Unfit for Play

*See also* Unplayable Ball
ball breaks into pieces as result of striking paved cart path .................................... 5-3/4
ball deemed unfit during hole earlier in round put back into play later in round ........ 5-3/2
ball fit for play deemed unfit during play of hole; player substitutes and
     plays another ball................................................................................................. 5-3/3
ball thought unfit for play
   - Committee involvement when opponent, marker or fellow-competitor
      not readily available ......................................................................................... 5-3/7
   - lifted under another Rule and cleaned; ball then determined unfit for play............... 5-3/6
   - in bunker or water hazard lifted to determine if unfit; whether permitted ....... 5-3/5
claim that player's ball unfit for play disputed by opponent or fellow-competitor............ 5-3/8
loose impediment affecting lie
   - moves when ball lifted to determine if unfit .................................................... 23-1/7
   - removed while ball lifted to determine if unfit for play .................................. 23-1/8
player claims ball with no visible external damage unfit because of
     internal damage................................................................................................... 5-3/1
player lifts ball from putting green and throws it into lake; announces
     ball was unfit for play........................................................................................ 5-3/3.5

### Bandage

player with injured wrist wears elastic bandage.................................................... 14-3/7
used as aid in gripping .............................................................................................. 14-3/7

### Beach

treating ocean and beach as through the green.................................................... 33-2a/8

### Bees

*See also* Insects
discontinuing play due to bee sting........................................................................ 6-8a/3
interfering with play ................................................................................................ 1-4/10
meaning of dangerous situation ............................................................................. 1-4/11

## Bogey Competition

*See also* Stableford Competition

| | |
|---|---|
| competing simultaneously in Bogey or Stableford and stroke-play competitions | 32-1/1 |
| omitting holes in Bogey or Stableford competition | 32-1/2 |
| recording of lower gross score does not affect result of hole | 32-2a/5 |
| when practice between holes permitted | 7-2/1 |

## Boundary Fence, Line, Wall or Stakes

*See also* Marking or Defining Course; Out of Bounds; Status of Object

| | |
|---|---|
| ball enters burrowing animal hole | |
|   - in bounds and comes to rest out of bounds | 25-1b/24 |
|   - out of bounds and comes to rest in bounds | 25-1b/23 |
| ball in drainpipe under course; entrance to drainpipe out of bounds | 24-2b/12 |
| ball in unmarked ditch in bounds; opposite margin out of bounds; relief options for player | 26/3 |
| ball lifted and dropped away from boundary stake under obstruction Rule | 18-2a/3 |
| ball lost in underground drainpipe; entrance to drainpipe out of bounds | 24-3b/1 |
| boundary altered by unauthorized removal of boundary stake | 33-2a/19 |
| dropped ball comes to rest and then rolls out of bounds | 20-2c/3.5 |
| establishing boundary line inside fence on property line | 33-2a/15 |
| exposed water pipe adjacent and parallel to boundary fence causes problems; suggested procedure | 33-2a/1 |
| flow of water moves ball | |
|   - into bounds in lateral water hazard | 26-1/8 |
|   - out of bounds in water hazard | 26-1/7 |
| improving position of ball by bending boundary fence | 13-2/18 |
| internal boundary between holes; whether permitted | 33-2a/12 |
| Local Rule | |
|   - deeming ball in bounds until beyond boundary wall | 33-2a/16 |
|   - deeming interior boundary fence immovable obstruction; whether authorized | 33-8/14 |
|   - to prevent cutting across "dog-leg;" deeming ball out of bounds that crosses boundary even if it recrosses boundary and comes to rest on same part of course; whether authorized | 33-8/38 |
| marking environmentally-sensitive areas; recommendations for Committee | 33-8/41 |
| moving ball lying against fence by striking other side of fence | 14-1/5 |
| obstruction interferes with abnormal stroke; because of proximity to boundary fence abnormal stroke reasonable in circumstances | 24-2b/17 |
| part of boundary fence within boundary line | 24/4 |
| part of fence off course leans across boundary and interferes with swing | 13-2/20 |
| provisional ball played from point nearer hole than visible original ball; player erroneously thought original ball out of bounds | 27-2c/3 |
| public road defined as out of bounds divides course; status of ball crossing road | 27/20 |
| regression under unplayable ball Rule; ball near boundary fence | 28/5 |
| relief from immovable obstruction incidentally results in relief from boundary fence | 24-2b/6 |
| relief from immovable obstruction parallel to boundary fence in most cases would result in relief from boundary fence; recommendation for Committee | 33-2a/1 |
| removal of boundary post or stake | |
|   - on line of play; replaced before playing | 13-2/25 |
|   - interfering with swing | 13-2/17 |
| river or other body of water adjacent to hole but off club property | 33-2a/11 |
| status of | |
|   - angled supports or guy wires supporting boundary fence | 24/2 |
|   - boundary stakes having no significance in play of hole being played | 24/5 |
|   - concrete bases of boundary fence posts | 24/3 |

# Index

- displaced boundary stake .................................................................. 33-2a/20
- gate in boundary fence ............................................................................ 27/18
- stile attached to boundary fence ............................................................. 24/1

striking ball interfered with by boundary fence with half inch backswing ........... 14-1/4
when ball inside boundary fence considered out of bounds ............................... 27/19

## Bridge

ball lying on elevated bridge over deep hollow; how nearest point
    of relief determined ........................................................................... 24-2b/11
grounding club on bridge in water hazard; whether permitted ....................... 13-4/30

## Bunker

*See also* Sand

ball at rest moved
- accidentally by player in playing wrong ball in bunker ............................ 18-2a/21
- after loose impediment outside hazard moved ........................................ 18-2a/5
- after stance taken in hazard without club .............................................. 18-2b/2
- ball falls into bunker when person walks nearby .................................... 18/10
- competitor's ball knocked out of bunker by fellow-competitor's
  stroke at own ball ................................................................................ 18-4/2
- competitor's ball played by fellow-competitor in bunker not replaced ......... 18-4/1
- while player in process of taking stance in bunker ................................. 18-2b/3
- when loose impediment removed .......................................................... 13-4/15
- wrong ball played from bunker by opponent moves player's ball .............. 18-5/1

ball believed lost in bunker; competitor drops and plays substituted
    ball in bunker; then original ball found outside bunker ............................ 20-7c/3

ball deemed unplayable
- ball lying on grass-covered ground within bunker deemed unplayable ........ 28/9
- dropped in bunker and played; ball then discovered to be wrong ball ........ 15/14
- dropped outside bunker under option of unplayable ball Rule
  requiring drop in bunker ..................................................................... 28/10
- in bunker; player lifts ball and then removes loose impediment
  from bunker ...................................................................................... 13-4/35.7
- through the green dropped in hazard ................................................... 28/4

ball enters burrowing animal hole in bunker and comes to rest
    underneath putting green ....................................................................... 25-1b/25

ball hit out of bounds from bunker; player's drop under Rule 20-5
    strikes course through the green within inches of and not
    nearer hole than spot in bunker where previous stroke played ..................... 20-5/2

ball in motion after stroke on putting green deflected into bunker by
    ball played at another hole ........................................................................ 19-1/10

ball overhangs edge of bunker; whether considered in bunker ............................ 13/3
ball played back into water hazard from putting green side of hazard ................ 26-1/6
bunker totally under repair; Committee options ................................................. 25/13

casual water
- ball dropped from casual water in bunker at point of maximum
  relief rolls elsewhere ............................................................................ 25-1b/6
- ball dropped in bunker under first option of Rule 25-1b(ii); player
  then wishes to proceed under second option to drop outside bunker ......... 25-1b/9
- ball lifted from bunker by player intending to drop under first
  option of Rule 25-1b(ii); player then wishes to proceed under
  second option to drop outside bunker .................................................... 24-2b/5
- ball required to be dropped in bunker, dropped outside bunker
  so it will roll into bunker to avoid embedding in bunker ......................... 25-1b/7
- explanation of "maximum available relief" from casual water in bunker ..... 25-1b/5
- Local Rule providing relief from flooded bunker without penalty
  outside bunker; whether authorized ...................................................... 33-8/27
- player's options when bunker completely covered by casual water ............ 25-1b/8
- touching casual water in bunker with club ............................................ 13-4/7

club accidentally touches ball in bunker; ball does not move ............................ 13-4/12

## Bunker *(continued)*

embedded ball
- in bunker lifted to determine whether unfit for play ..................................................... 5-3/5
- in grass bank or face of bunker ......................................................................................... 25-2/5
- in lip of bunker ...................................................................................................................... 13/4
- Local Rule permitting re-dropping or placing when dropped ball
  embeds in bunker; whether authorized ..................................................................... 33-8/28

grounding club
- bare earth wall of bunker touched on backswing ........................................................ 13-4/34
- cane or club used to enter or leave bunker when ball lies in bunker ..................... 13-4/3.5
- clubhead used to search for ball covered by sand in bunker ..................................... 12-1/1
- ground in bunker or water hazard touched with club while
  probing for ball believed covered by loose impediments ........................................ 12-1/4
- leaning on club in bunker while waiting to play ........................................................... 13-4/2
- loose impediments moved and area of intended swing improved
  in hazard; whether multiple penalties apply .............................................................. 13-4/28
- mound made by burrowing animal touched with backswing in bunker ................... 13-4/5
- sand in bunker touched during backswing ................................................................... 13-4/31
- sand in bunker touched when ball lies outside bunker .............................................. 13-4/1
- several practice swings touch ground in bunker ........................................................... 13-4/3
- several practice swings touch ground in bunker; player advised
  of breach then makes several more practice swings ................................................. 1-4/13
- several practice swings touch ground in bunker then player makes
  stroke and ball remains in bunker; player makes several similar
  practice swings before next stroke ............................................................................... 1-4/14
- solidly embedded stone in hazard touched with club during backswing ................ 13-4/6

hitting sand in bunker after failing to extricate ball
- in foursome match ................................................................................................................ 29/5
- in four-ball match; partner's ball also in same bunker ................................................ 30-3f/2
- in individual play .................................................................................................................. 13-4/35
- player hits ball from bunker into grass bank then hits sand in
  bunker with club; thereafter ball rolls back into bunker ...................................... 13-4/35.5

identifying ball
- half-buried ball in bunker touched or rotated for identification purposes ............... 12-2/3
- two balls lie together in bunker; neither identifiable .................................................... 1-4/6

lie in bunker altered
- by another player taking stance ...................................................................................... 20-3b/2
- by another player's stroke .................................................................................................. 20-3b/1
- greenkeeper rakes bunker when player's ball lies therein improving
  lie of ball or line of play ................................................................................................... 13-2/4
- prior to resumption of play ................................................................................................ 6-8d/2

Local Rule
- allowing free drop outside bunker or smoothing of sand in bunker
  damaged by play of children; whether authorized .................................................... 33-8/9
- deeming material similar to sand to have same status as sand ............................... 33-8/40
- deeming stacked turf bunker faces (whether grass covered or
  earthen) as not closely mown ......................................................................................... 33-8/39
- permitting re-dropping or placing when dropped ball embeds
  in bunker; whether authorized ....................................................................................... 33-8/28
- providing relief without penalty from flooded bunker ................................................ 33-8/27

loose impediment
- accidentally moved in bunker .......................................................................................... 13-4/13
- ball outside bunker; stone in bunker on line of play pressed
  down or removed ................................................................................................................ 13-2/31
- bunker covered by leaves; player touches leaves during backswing ...................... 13-4/33
- club touches partially embedded pine needle on backswing in bunker ................. 13-4/32
- competitor lifts loose impediment in bunker when his ball and
  partner's ball in bunker .................................................................................................... 31-8/1
- ground in bunker or water hazard touched with club while
  probing for ball believed covered by loose impediments ........................................ 12-1/4

Index    **I-25**

**B**

- partner's, opponent's or fellow-competitor's divot comes to rest
 near player's ball in bunker ................................................................. 13-4/18
- pine cone falls from tree and comes to rest behind ball lying in bunker ................ 13-4/18.5
- player accidentally kicks pine cone into bunker and picks it up ........................ 13-4/14
- player lifts loose impediment in bunker when his ball and partner's
 ball in bunker ................................................................................ 30-3f/1
- player moves loose impediments when approaching ball in hazard ................ 13-4/13.5
- player removes loose impediment affecting opponent's lie in bunker ................ 1-2/6
- removal of obstruction in bunker would move loose impediment .................... 1-4/5
- top of ball in bunker covered by leaves but part of ball visible from
 another angle .................................................................................. 12-1/3

obstruction
- ball dropped in bunker under first option of Rule 24-2b(ii); player
 then wishes to proceed under second option to drop outside
 bunker ....................................................................................... 25-1b/9
- ball lifted from bunker by player intending to drop under first
 option of Rule 24-2b(ii); player then wishes to proceed under
 second option to drop outside bunker ....................................................... 24-2b/5
- ball lying on obstruction in bunker ................................................................. 13/5
- loose impediment in bunker will move when obstruction lying
 against ball removed ................................................................................ 1-4/5
- rake removal causes ball in bunker to move; whether player
 may press ball into sand or take relief outside bunker if not
 possible to replace or place in bunker not nearer hole ........................................ 20-3d/2

placing ball instead of dropping when obvious dropped ball will roll
 into bunker requiring re-drop .......................................................... 20-2c/3
player proceeding under water hazard Rule drops ball in bunker or
 another water hazard .................................................................... 26-1/2
player's lie through the green affected by sand from partner's, opponent's,
 or fellow-competitor's stroke from bunker ............................................. 13-2/8.5

rake
- ball in bunker moves when rake removed; whether player may press
 ball into sand or take relief outside bunker if not possible to replace
 or place in bunker not nearer hole .................................................... 20-3d/2
- handle stuck in bunker before stroke ................................................. 13-4/22
- placed in bunker before stroke ............................................................ 13-4/20
- thrown into bunker before stroke ....................................................... 13-4/21
- whether rakes should be placed in or outside bunkers ............................ Misc./2

searching for ball
- ball removed from buried lie in bunker during search ............................ 12-1/2
- clubhead used to search for ball covered by sand in bunker ................... 12-1/1

smoothing irregularities in bunker; whether permitted
- after announcing intention to proceed under Rule 28a outside
 bunker and lifting ball ...................................................................... 13-4/35.8
- after ball played out of bunker before dropping another ball in bunker ............. 13-4/37
- after ball played out of bunker; ball later returns to smoothed area ................... 13-4/38
- after footprints made in bunker on line of play ................................... 13-2/29
- after footprints made in bunker on line of play when required to
 enter bunker to retrieve ball ............................................................ 13-2/29.3
- after footprints made in search for ball in bunker ............................... 13-4/11
- after making stroke but before ball extricated .................................... 13-4/36
- after playing out backwards; smoothed area on line of play .................. 13-4/37.5
- after playing out of turn; opponent recalls stroke ............................... 13-4/39
- after stance taken in bunker; player decides to play different shot ........ 13-4/27
- by greenkeeping staff member when player's ball lies therein ............. 13-2/4
- footprints made in bunker by opponent or fellow-competitor on
 extension of player's line of play ..................................................... 13-2/29.5
- player preparing to play from bunker requests another player
 that just played from bunker to smooth his footprints ....................... 13-4/19
- situated between ball and hole ........................................................... 13-2/28

## Bunker *(continued)*

stance
- ball moves after stance taken in bunker without club ............................................. 18-2b/2
- ball moves while player in process of taking stance in bunker ............................. 18-2b/3
- knocking down side of bunker to level stance ..................................................... 13-3/3
- lie in bunker altered by another player taking stance ........................................ 20-3b/2
- taken some distance from where ball lies in bunker to simulate
  next stroke .............................................................................................................. 13-4/25
- taken in bunker then player changes clubs and takes second stance ................. 13-4/26
- taken in bunker without club .................................................................................. 13-4/24
- when stance taken in bunker .................................................................................. 13-4/23

status of
- ball on edge of bunker overhanging sand ............................................................... 13/3
- dead land crab in bunker .......................................................................................... 23/6
- half-eaten pear in bunker ......................................................................................... 23/3
- insect on ball in bunker ......................................................................................... 23-1/5.5
- sand spilling over margin of bunker ........................................................................ 13/1
- stone serving as part of drain in bunker ................................................................ 24/7
- tree in bunker ............................................................................................................ 13/2

testing condition of bunker
- ball outside bunker; stone in bunker on line of play pressed down
  or removed ............................................................................................................. 13-2/31
- ball played from bunker goes out of bounds or lost; player tests
  condition of bunker or smoothes footprints before dropping
  another ball in bunker ......................................................................................... 13-4/37
- before deciding whether to play stroke from outside bunker through it .............. 13-2/30
- player in bunker takes firm stance and then smoothes footprints
  after deciding to play different type of shot ..................................................... 13-4/27
- player uses cane or club to enter or leave bunker when ball lies therein ........... 13-4/3.5
- rake handle stuck in bunker before stroke ............................................................ 13-4/22
- rake thrown into bunker before stroke .................................................................. 13-4/21
- smoothing sand in bunker after stroke but before ball extricated ...................... 13-4/36
- stance in bunker taken without club ...................................................................... 13-4/24
- taking firm stance in bunker some distance from ball in bunker to
  simulate next stroke ............................................................................................ 13-4/25
- taking stance in bunker and then changing clubs ................................................ 13-4/26
- umbrella or rake placed in bunker before stroke ................................................. 13-4/20

when ball addressed in bunker .................................................................................. 13-4/23

whether player in match play may play next stroke from bunker after
result of hole decided ............................................................................................ 7-2/1.5

wrong ball
- ball deemed unplayable in bunker dropped in bunker and played;
  ball then discovered to be wrong ball ................................................................. 15/14
- in playing wrong ball in bunker player accidentally moves own ball ................ 18-2a/21
- played from bunker by opponent moves player's ball ........................................... 18-5/1
- player concedes hole; then opponent's previous stroke discovered
  played with wrong ball from bunker ................................................................. 2-4/9.5

## Burrowing Animal, Reptile or Bird

*See also* Abnormal Ground Conditions; Casual Water; Ground Under Repair; Reasonable
Evidence; Reptile; Status of Object

after five-minute search, ball found in hole made by burrowing animal,
reptile or bird ............................................................................................................ 27/7

ball enters burrowing animal, reptile or bird hole
- in bounds and comes to rest out of bounds ........................................................ 25-1b/24
- in bunker and comes to rest underneath putting green .................................... 25-1b/25
- out of bounds and comes to rest in bounds ....................................................... 25-1b/23

ball interfered with by hole next to tree or bush made by burrowing
animal, reptile or bird
- for reasonable sideways stroke ............................................................................. 25-1b/22

Index I-27

- stroke toward green not reasonable because of position of tree ............................ 25-1b/21
- unreasonable to play stroke due to bush ........................................................ 25-1b/19
- unreasonable to play stroke because of tree ................................................... 25-1b/20

bird nest interferes with stroke ................................................................................. 1-4/9

bunker or water hazard
- ball enters burrowing animal, reptile or bird hole in bunker; comes to rest underneath putting green ........................................................... 25-1b/25
- relief taken from hole made by burrowing animal, reptile or bird by player unaware ball in water hazard; error discovered before ball played ................................................................................................ 25-1b/26
- touching mound made by burrowing animal, reptile or bird with backswing ................................................................................................... 13-4/5

crawfish mound interferes with stance or swing ...................................................... 25-1b/18

diagram illustrating player unable to determine nearest point of relief ................... 24-2b/3.7

footprint of burrowing animal, reptile or bird; whether relief available ...................... 25/19.5

lifting ball
- to determine whether it lies in hole made by burrowing animal, reptile or bird ........................................................................................ 25/21
- to determine whether it lies in hole made by burrowing animal, reptile or bird; Committee involvement when opponent, marker or fellow-competitor not readily available ................... 5-3/7
- with mud adhering to it to determine whether in hole made by burrowing animal, reptile or bird; ball rotated when replaced ................................ 21/5

line of play improved when relief taken from burrowing animal, reptile or bird hole ............................................................................................... 25-1b/3

Local Rule
- declaring severe damage by non-burrowing animals as ground under repair .................................................................................................... 33-8/32.5
- deeming hard conical ant hills as ground under repair ........................................... 33-8/22

nearest point of relief
- determining club, address position, direction of play and swing used to identify nearest point of relief .............................................. 24-2b/1
- diagrams illustrating nearest point of relief ........................................................ 25-1b/2
- from cart path in burrowing animal hole; nearest point of relief from burrowing animal hole back on cart path .......................................... 1-4/8
- player determines nearest point of relief but physically unable to play intended stroke ................................................................................... 24-2b/3
- player does not follow recommended procedure in determining nearest point of relief .................................................................................. 24-2b/2
- player entitled to relief without penalty from burrowing animal hole lifts ball; chooses not to take relief and wishes to proceed under unplayable ball Rule ......................................................... 18-2a/12.5

reasonable evidence ball lost in burrowing animal, reptile or bird hole; drop made under Rule 25-1c; original ball then found within five minutes .................................................................................................. 25-1c/2.5

relief taken from hole made by burrowing animal, reptile or bird
- ball comes to rest in position where another such hole interferes ....................... 20-2c/7
- line of play improved .............................................................................................. 25-1b/3
- player unaware ball in water hazard; error discovered before ball played ............ 25-1b/26

snake
- dangerous snake interferes with play ..................................................................... 1-4/10
- when outside agency; when loose impediment ...................................................... 23/6.5

status of
- molehills ................................................................................................................ 25/23
- footprint of burrowing animal, reptile or bird ...................................................... 25/19.5
- snake ...................................................................................................................... 23/6.5

touching mound made by burrowing animal, reptile or bird with back swing in bunker ............................................................................................. 13-4/5

## Caddie

acts which caddie may perform ................................................................................ 6-4/10
advice
- caddie swings club to show player how to play shot ....................................... 8-1/15
- request for advice made in error to opponent's caddie withdrawn
  before advice given ........................................................................................ 8-1/17
application of penalty when player has multiple caddies ................................... 6-4/5.5
ball deflected or stopped by caddie
- ball strikes opponent's or fellow-competitor's bag left ahead by
  shared caddie ................................................................................................. 19-2/8
- ball strikes player's caddie and comes to rest out of bounds ........................ 19-2/2
- ball strikes player's caddie standing out of bounds and comes to
  rest on course ................................................................................................. 19-2/3
- ball strikes player's caddie standing out of bounds and comes to
  rest out of bounds .......................................................................................... 19-2/4
- competitor's ball strikes golf bag and then his caddie .................................... 19-2/7
- dropped ball accidentally deflected by opponent's caddie ............................. 19-3/2
- dropped ball rolls toward or into position where re-drop would
  be required; caddie stops ball before it comes to rest............................... 20-2c/4
ball lifted by caddie
- considering it unplayable without authority of player ............................. 18-2a/15
- fellow-competitor's caddie lifts competitor's ball without
  authority; caddie subsequently substitutes another ball when
  replaced which competitor plays ................................................................. 20-1/5
- for identification without authority of player ........................................... 18-2a/14
- in water hazard without player's authority................................................... 26-1/9
- opponent's caddie lifts player's ball after player claims another ball ........... 18-3b/4
- opponent's caddie lifts player's ball which may or may not have
  been out of bounds ..................................................................................... 18-3b/5
ball moved by caddie
- of opponent when accidentally stepped on .................................................. 18-3b/3
- shared by members of opposite sides in four-ball match ................................. 30/1
- shared by opponent's side in four-ball match moves player's ball ................... 30/2
ball thrown into bounds by outside agency and played
- caddie aware of action of outside agency ......................................................... 15/9
- neither player nor his caddie aware of action of outside agency .................... 15/10
casual water mopped up on line of play by caddie ............................................. 13-2/34
competitor withdraws during round and carries fellow-competitor's
  clubs for remainder of round............................................................................ 6-4/9
conditions and restrictions
- acts which caddie may perform .................................................................... 6-4/10
- prohibiting use of caddies; restricting who may caddie ............................ App I-C-3
during round caddie gets putter from clubhouse and gives it to
  player; whether player may tell caddie to take it back
  and get different club....................................................................................... 4-4a/1
effect of state of match penalty when one partner has more
  than one caddie in four-ball play..................................................................... 30-3/2
inadvertently positioned on extension of line of play or putt behind ball ............ 14-2/4
incorrect information given by caddie................................................................... 9-2/1
meaning of "specific directions" in definition of caddie......................................... 6-4/1
player directs caddie not to search for ball until others can assist .......................... 27/1
player in competition caddies for another player in same event ........................... 6-4/8
putting green
- ball thrown to caddie for cleaning comes to rest in lake................................ 15-2/1
- ball-marker moved by opponent's caddie accidentally.................................... 20-1/7
- caddie inadvertently positioned on extension of line of putt behind ball...... 14-2/4
- caddie practices on or tests putting green surfaces of course
  before stroke-play round ............................................................................. 7-1b/5

- line of putt damaged accidentally by caddie of opponent or
      fellow-competitor .................................................................................. 16-1a/13
  - shadow cast on putting green by caddie to indicate line of putt ............... 8-2b/1
  - surface roughened by caddie but player does not benefit........................ 16-1d/6
  - touched by caddie or partner to indicate line of play before player
      chips from off green................................................................................ 8-2b/3
  - while attending flagstick caddie suggests player aim at foot;
      whether breach of any Rule .................................................................. 8-2b/2
shared or double caddie
  - ball moved by caddie shared by members of opposite sides in
      four-ball match ......................................................................................... 30/1
  - ball moved by caddie shared by opponent's side in four-ball match ........... 30/2
  - ball strikes opponent's or fellow-competitor's bag left ahead by
      shared caddie .......................................................................................... 19-2/8
  - ball strikes opponent's or fellow-competitor's cart being pulled
      by double caddie ..................................................................................... 6-4/6
  - double caddie informs one employer about club used by other ............... 8-1/12
shields player from sun during stroke ...................................................................... 14-2/3
smoothing footprints made in search for ball in bunker before stroke.......... 13-4/11
status of
  - ball placed behind ball-marker on putting green by caddie so
      player can assess line of putt ................................................................ 20-4/2
  - carts pulled by double caddie.................................................................... 6-4/6
  - individual who transports player's clubs on motorized golf cart or trolley ............... 6-4/2.5
transportation condition breached by caddie ..................................................... 33-1/9.5
tree branch held back by caddie to prevent branch from deflecting
   dropped ball ..................................................................................................... 20-2a/5
whether ball cleaned by act of caddie throwing it to player .................................... 21/3
whether player has more than one caddie
  - additional person(s) carry items, other than clubs, for player ............. 6-4/5.3
  - another caddie or friend carries clubs while player's caddie returns
      to tee with player's glove ....................................................................... 6-4/4.5
  - changing caddies during round ................................................................. 6-4/7
  - competitor withdraws during round and carries fellow-competitor's
      clubs for remainder of round................................................................. 6-4/9
  - player hires boy to carry all of player's clubs except putter .................... 6-4/4
  - player with clubs transported on motorized golf cart hires individual
      to perform all other functions of caddie ............................................... 6-4/3
  - umbrella carrier employed in addition to caddie ...................................... 6-4/5

## Casual Water

*See also* Abnormal Ground Conditions; Reasonable Evidence
ball in casual water
  - difficult to retrieve ........................................................................................ 25-1/1
  - within ground under repair......................................................................... 25-1b/11
  - within ground under repair; whether player entitled to
      take relief from both conditions in single procedure ......................... 25-1b/11.5
ball lost in either water hazard or casual water overflowing hazard ................... 1-4/7
ball moved by wind or casual water while play suspended ............................... 18-1/11
ball-marker moved
  - off green by wind or casual water while play suspended ......................... 20-1/10
  - by wind or casual water during stipulated round ...................................... 20-1/10.5
ball played from area of casual water, lost in same area ...................................... 25-1c/3
brushing aside or mopping up casual water on line of putt............................... 16-1a/1
bunker completely covered by casual water
  - Local Rule providing relief from flooded bunker without penalty
      outside bunker; whether authorized ................................................... 33-8/27
  - player's options ............................................................................................. 25-1b/8

## Casual Water (continued)

changing relief option
- dropped ball first strikes course outside where applicable Rule requires; whether player may change relief option when re-dropping ............ 20-6/2
- dropped ball first strikes course outside where applicable Rule requires; whether player may replace ball in original location ............ 20-6/5
- dropped ball rolls to position requiring re-drop; whether player may change relief option when re-dropping ............ 20-2c/5
- dropped ball strikes player; whether player may change relief option when re-dropping ............ 20-2a/6
- player drops ball in bunker under first option of Rule 25-1b(ii); player then wishes to proceed under second option to drop outside bunker ............ 25-1b/9
- player lifts ball from bunker intending to drop under first option of Rule 25-1b(ii); player then wishes to proceed under second option to drop outside bunker ............ 24-2b/5

clarification of point where ball "last entered" casual water when ball lost in condition ............ 25-1c/1.5
covering teeing ground ............ 25-1b/4
diagram illustrating player unable to determine nearest point of relief ............ 24-2b/3.7
explanation of "maximum available relief" from casual water in bunker ............ 25-1b/5
hole surrounded by casual water ............ 33-2d/2
improving line of play when taking relief from casual water ............ 25-1b/3

Local Rule
- permitting re-dropping or placing when dropped ball embeds in bunker; whether authorized ............ 33-8/28
- providing relief from flooded bunker without penalty outside bunker; whether authorized ............ 33-8/27

meaning of "reasonable evidence" in Rule 25-1c ............ 25-1c/1

mistaken for water hazard
- original ball played under water hazard Rule ............ 25-1b/12
- substituted ball played under water hazard Rule ............ 25-1b/13

mopping up casual water on line of play ............ 13-2/34

nearest point of relief
- determining club, address position, direction of play and swing used to identify nearest point of relief ............ 24-2b/1
- diagrams illustrating nearest point of relief ............ 25-1b/2
- from cart path in casual water; nearest point of relief from casual water back on cart path ............ 1-4/8
- player determines nearest point of relief but physically unable to play intended stroke ............ 24-2b/3
- player does not follow recommended procedure in determining nearest point of relief ............ 24-2b/2

on putting green casual water
- intervenes between ball off green and hole ............ 25-1a/2
- nearest point of relief off green ............ 25-1b/10
- visible when player walks beside line of putt but not visible elsewhere ............ 25/5
- whether player entitled to relief for intervention; ball on green, nearest point of relief off green ............ 25-1b/10.5

overflow from water hazard ............ 25/2
pitch-mark filled with casual water ............ 25/3
player entitled to relief without penalty from casual water lifts ball; chooses not to take relief and wishes to proceed under unplayable ball Rule ............ 18-2a/12.5
player takes relief from area of casual water and ball comes to rest in position where another area of casual water interferes; whether re-drop required ............ 20-2c/7
player unable physically to determine nearest point of relief ............ 24-2b/3.5
reasonable evidence ball lost in casual water; drop made under Rule 25-1c; original ball then found within five minutes ............ 25-1c/2.5

Index **I-31**

removal of casual water or loose impediments on putting green
    by Committee ................................................................................................. 33/1
removing casual water from hole ................................................................... 16-1a/4
soft, mushy earth .................................................................................................. 25/1
stroke at ball not reasonable due to interference by immovable
    obstruction and casual water ................................................................. 24-2b/19
touching casual water in bunker with club ..................................................... 13-4/7
water visible as result of undue effort with feet ............................................... 25/4

## Chipper

*See also* Club(s)
status of ............................................................................................................... 4-1/3

## Claims and Disputes

*See also* Committee; Penalty Imposed, Modified or Waived by Committee; Referee
after competition closed in stroke play
    - competitor correctly advised he incurred penalty by
        fellow-competitor; competitor disagrees and fails to
        include penalty in returned score card; Committee
        advised of incident after close of competition ..................................... 34-1b/1.5
    - failure to sign score card discovered ............................................... 34-1b/2
    - omission of penalty stroke in competitor's score discovered ................... 34-1b/1
    - play of wrong ball not rectified in stroke play discovered ....................... 34-1b/3
    - change to weight of club during round discovered after close
        of competition ........................................................................................ 34-1b/4
    - wrong score in qualifying round discovered during match play ............ 34-1b/7
after match played to conclusion
    - breach of 14-club Rule discovered after match concluded but
        before result officially announced ........................................................ 2-5/5.5
    - hole inadvertently omitted in match; error discovered after
        match concluded ...................................................................................... 2-1/3
    - incorrect information on penalty applicable to player given by
        opponent; error discovered after match result announced;
        player then makes claim ........................................................................ 2-5/10
    - player concedes match after winning it when opponent
        lodges invalid claim regarding strokes taken ...................................... 2-4/15
    - player omits penalty stroke when advising opponent as to score
        for hole; error discovered after match conceded by opponent ............. 9-2/10
    - valid timely claim made after concession of match ............................... 2-4/16
    - wrong handicap used in match by mistake; error discovered
        after result officially announced .......................................................... 6-2a/5
    - wrong information given after play of last hole; claim made
        after result announced ............................................................................ 2-5/11
assisting ball lifted by opponent replaced on request; player's ball
    then strikes opponent's ball and opponent lodges claim ............................. 22/5
breach of Rule by opponent
    - discussed between player and opponent; penalty not applied ................. 1-3/4
    - disregarded by player; whether permitted ................................................ 2-5/1
    - neither player nor opponent aware; penalty not applied ......................... 1-3/5
    - procedure for valid claim .......................................................................... 2-5/2
Committee error
    - disqualification penalty wrongly applied to winner of event; error
        discovered after two other competitors play off for first place ............ 34-1b/5
    - pace of play condition breached; Committee does not penalize
        player believing he had already lost hole ............................................. 34-3/2
    - player plays based on incorrect ruling; procedure for player
        when error discovered ............................................................................ 34-3/3
    - winner's score not posted due to Committee error ................................. 34-1b/6
    - wrong ball penalty not included in competitor's score due to
        incorrect Committee ruling; during subsequent round error
        discovered and penalty applied retroactively; competitor objects ....... 34-3/1

**Claims and Disputes** *(continued)*

determination of honor at next tee following disputed hole ............................................ 10-1a/2
disagreement with referee's decision ................................................................................ 34-2/4
failure to include penalty in score
- competitor correctly advised he incurred penalty by fellow-competitor; competitor disagrees and fails to include penalty in returned score card; Committee advised of incident after close of competition ........................................................................... 34-1b/1.5
- penalty stroke omitted when score card returned ............................................... 34-1b/1
- player advancing to fourth-round in match play disqualified for wrong score in qualifying round; options for Committee ..................... 34-1b/8
- players in match unaware penalty incurred ................................................................. 1-3/5
handicap
- extra handicap stroke taken by mistake in handicap match; status of late claim ................................................................................................ 2-5/13
- failure to determine handicaps prior to start of match ............................................... 6-2a/1
- handicap stroke claimed after hole conceded ............................................................ 6-2a/4
- handicap stroke wrongly claimed at hole; error discovered before hole completed ....................................................................................... 6-2a/3
- wrong handicap knowingly used in stroke play; error discovered after competition closed ............................................................................................... 6-2b/2
- wrong handicap recorded on score card by Committee error; discovered before competition closed ....................................................... 6-2b/3.5
- wrong handicap used in match by mistake; error discovered after result officially announced .......................................................................... 6-2a/5
- wrong handicap used in stroke play by mistake; error discovered after competition closed ....................................................................................... 6-2b/1
late claim
- after playing wrong ball, player wins hole with original ball; opponent does not lodge claim during hole; claim lodged next day ...................... 2-5/4
- breach of 14-club Rule discovered after match concluded; claim made before result officially announced .............................................. 2-5/5.5
- extra stroke taken by mistake in handicap match; status of late claim .................. 2-5/13
- foursome side drives for three holes in wrong order; opponents make claim during third hole ......................................................................... 29-2/2
- hole won with wrong ball and partner picks up; error discovered at next hole .............................................................................................................. 30-3d/2
- hole won with wrong ball; error discovered at next hole; opponent claims previous hole .................................................................................. 9-2/8
- incorrect procedure agreed to in error by player and opponent; whether valid claim can be made after procedure followed ......................... 2-5/8.5
- player agreeing with opponent that hole halved realizes after match he won hole and should have won match; player then makes claim .............................................................................................................. 2-5/9
invalid claim
- not disputed ................................................................................................................. 2-5/5
- player concedes hole on basis of invalid claim ......................................................... 2-4/12
- player concedes match after winning it when opponent lodges invalid claim regarding strokes taken ........................................................ 2-4/15
match discontinued by agreement due to rain; player subsequently wishes to resume
- opponent refuses although course playable ............................................................. 6-8a/5
- opponent refuses on ground course unplayable ...................................................... 6-8a/6
player plays partner's ball; error discovered after opponents have played next strokes ...................................................................................... 30-3d/3.5
player reaching third-round of match play disqualified for agreeing to waive Rules in first-round match .............................................................. 34-1a/1
players in singles match accompanied by third party; one player objects .......................... 2/1
player's claim ball unfit for play disputed by opponent ..................................................... 5-3/8

Index **I-33**

result of hole in dispute
- ball marked and lifted by opponent without player's authority; player lifts ball-marker and claims hole; opponent disputes claim .................................................................. 20-1/3
- determination of honor at next tee following disputed hole .................... 10-1a/2
- hole won with wrong ball; error discovered at next hole; opponent claims previous hole ................................................................. 9-2/8
- player and opponent agree hole halved; after match result posted player realizes he won hole and should have won match; player then makes claim ................................................................ 2-5/9
- player lifts ball before holing out; opponent then picks up his ball claiming player loses hole ................................................................ 2-5/3
- players on opposite sides exchange balls during play of hole and their partners pick up; error discovered at next hole ............................ 30-3d/3
- player with lost ball concedes hole; ball then found in hole ...................... 2-4/11

score card
- competitor correctly advised he incurred penalty by fellow-competitor; competitor disagrees and fails to include penalty in returned score card; Committee advised of incident after close of competition ................................................................ 34-1b/1.5
- failure to sign score card discovered after competition closed ................ 34-1b/2
- marker refuses to sign competitor's score card after dispute resolved in favor of competitor ................................................................ 6-6a/4
- penalty stroke omitted on score card returned by player ........................... 34-1b/1
- wrong handicap recorded on score card by Committee error; discovered before competition closed ................................................... 6-2b/3.5

second ball played in match play; whether permitted .............................. 3-3/9
spectator says ball moved by outside agency; player not sure; procedure for player if Committee decision not possible in reasonable time .................................................................................. 18-1/4

state of match misunderstood
- players mistakenly believe match all square after 18 holes and play extra hole without making claim ................................................... 2-5/6
- players leave last green under impression match over later realize it was all square; whether late claim valid .................................. 2-3/1
- rightful winner of match makes no claim and agrees to play extra holes .................... 2-5/7
- true state of match not determinable ........................................................ 34-3/5

when match result "officially announced" ................................................ 2-5/14
whether competitor played from outside teeing ground disputed at end of round .................................................................................. 34-3/4
wrong ruling accepted by players from person not on Committee; match played to conclusion based on ruling; whether Committee should consider late claim ....................................................... 2-5/8

## Cleaning Ball

acts which caddie may perform; cleaning ball ........................................ 6-4/10
ball
- dropped away from obstruction immediately after resumption of play; whether player may lift, clean and place ball under Rule 6-8d(ii) ........ 6-8d/3
- lifted from putting green thrown to caddie for cleaning comes to rest in lake; player substitutes another ball ........................................ 15-2/1
- lifted from wrong putting green, cleaned and replaced; player holes out in two strokes; error then discovered; penalties and procedure for player ................................................................................ 25-3/2
- lifted without authority and cleaned ....................................................... 18-2a/13
- overhanging hole lifted, cleaned and replaced; ball then falls into hole .................... 16-2/0.5
- rubbed on putting green for cleaning purposes; whether putting green tested .................................................................................. 16-1d/5
- thought unfit for play lifted under another Rule and cleaned; ball then determined unfit for play ............................................................ 5-3/6

I-34   Index

## Cleaning Ball *(continued)*

ball lifted under Rule not permitting cleaning
- determining whether ball embedded .................................................................... 25-2/7
- determining whether ball lies in burrowing animal hole ........................................ 25/21
- half-buried ball in rough rotated instead of lifted for
  identification purposes ...................................................................................... 12-2/2
- mud adheres to ball when lifted; whether ball may be
  replaced with mud facing different direction ...................................................... 21/5
- position of ball lifted for identification not marked, intention
  to lift not announced, and ball cleaned beyond extent
  necessary to identify it ....................................................................................... 21/4

caddie places ball lifted for cleaning immediately behind player's
  ball-marker on putting green so player can assess line of putt;
  whether ball in play ................................................................................................ 20-4/2
lime from gallery-control line adheres to ball; whether player may remove lime ........... 21/1
sand from another player's stroke from bunker affects player's lie
  through the green; equity procedure entitling player to clean
  ball and remove sand deposited by stroke ............................................................... 13-2/8.5
two balls lie together in hazard; neither identifiable; equity procedure
  allowing ball farther from hole to be lifted and cleaned to extent
  necessary for identification ..................................................................................... 1-4/6
whether action constitutes cleaning of ball
- caddie throws ball to player ...................................................................................... 21/3
- grass adhering to ball removed .................................................................................. 21/2
- half-buried ball in rough rotated instead of lifted for identification purposes ............ 12-2/2
- insect on ball removed .............................................................................................. 23-1/5
- rubbing ball on putting green for cleaning purposes; whether
  putting green tested ............................................................................................... 16-1d/5

## Close of Competition

*See also* Committee; Conditions of Competition; Handicap and Handicap Competition;
Penalties Imposed, Modified or Waived by Committee; Scores and Score Cards

Committee procedures when player in match play disqualified for
  wrong score in qualifying round ............................................................................... 34-1b/8
Committee errors and mistakes
- disqualification penalty wrongly imposed by Committee on
  event winner; error discovered after completion of play-off
  between two other competitors ............................................................................. 34-1b/5
- handicap incorrectly calculated and posted by Committee;
  wrong competitor named event winner ................................................................... 6-2b/3
- handicap misapplied by Committee to qualifying score;
  incorrect match-play draw posted ........................................................................... 33-5/3
- miscalculation of correct net score or application of wrong
  handicap results in wrong competitor receiving prize ............................................. 33-5/2
- players wrongly advised as to condition regarding handicaps ................................ 33-1/12
- winner's score not posted ......................................................................................... 34-1b/6
- wrong handicap applied results in another competitor receiving prize ................... 33-5/2
- wrong handicap mistakenly recorded on score card ................................................. 6-2b/3.5
player errors and mistakes discovered after close of competition
- competitor correctly advised he incurred penalty by
  fellow-competitor; competitor disagrees and fails to
  include penalty in returned score card ................................................................... 34-1b/1.5
- competitor failed to sign score card ......................................................................... 34-1b/2
- marker not appointed by Committee signed score cards ......................................... 6-6b/5
- penalty stroke omitted when score card returned ..................................................... 34-1b/1
- play of wrong ball in stroke play not rectified ........................................................... 34-1b/3
- player disqualified for wrong score in qualifying round
  discovered during match play ................................................................................ 34-1b/7
- weight of club changed during round ..................................................................... 34-1b/4
- wrong handicap in match play mistakenly used by player ........................................ 6-2a/5

Index **I-35**

- wrong handicap in stroke play knowingly used .................................... 6-2b/2
- wrong handicap in stroke play recorded by partner in
  foursome competition .................................................................. 6-2b/2.5
- wrong handicap in stroke play used by mistake ............................... 6-2b/1

## Clubhouse or Half-Way House

due to inoperable motorized cart players discontinue play and
  return to clubhouse; whether reason for discontinuance satisfactory ..... 6-8a/4
entering clubhouse or half-way house for refreshment during round ......... 6-8a/2.7
watching television for 45 minutes after nine holes ................................. 6-8a/1
window of clubhouse opened and ball played through window ................. 24-2b/14

## Club(s)

*See also* Grips; Grounding Club; Status of Object; Stroke
another caddie or friend carries clubs while player's caddie
  returns to tee with players glove ................................................. 6-4/4.5
attachment to grip of club of player with artificial arm ............................. 14-3/15
ball deflected or stopped by clubs belonging to different side
  but carried in same bag ............................................................... 19-2/5
ball moved by putter dropped by player approaching ball to lift it ............ 20-1/14
borrowing
- another player's putter during round to make practice stroke ......... 4-4a/13
- fellow-competitor's putter ............................................................. 4-4a/12
- partner's putter ............................................................................. 4-4b/1
breach of 14-club Rule
- borrowing fellow-competitor's putter .......................................... 4-4a/12
- borrowing partner's putter ........................................................... 4-4b/1
- clarification of match-play penalty .............................................. 4-4a/9
- clarification of stroke-play penalty .............................................. 4-4a/10
- discovered after match concluded but before result officially announced .... 2-5/5.5
- excess club declared out of play before round and placed
  on floor of golf cart ..................................................................... 4-4c/1
- excess club discovered before player plays from 2nd tee but
  after opponent or fellow-competitor plays ................................. 4-4a/11
- excess club put in player's golf bag after player has counted
  his clubs at 1st tee; error discovered after player starts round ........... 4-4a/6
- fellow-competitor's club put in competitor's bag by mistake
  during round used unintentionally by competitor ........................ 4-4a/5
- player discovers he has 15 clubs at 2nd hole; opponent
  refuses to apply penalty ............................................................. 1-3/4
breaking during swing
- club breaks during backswing; swing completed ......................... 14/2
- club breaks during downswing; swing completed but misses
  ball; clubhead falls and moves ball ............................................ 14/5
- club breaks during downswing; swing stopped short of ball;
  clubhead falls and moves ball .................................................... 14/4
- clubhead separates from shaft on downswing ............................ 14/3
caddie hires boy to carry all of player's clubs except putter .................... 6-4/4
club used as flagstick to mark position of hole ....................................... 17-3/6
club placed beside or behind ball to indicate line of play ....................... 8-2a/2
clubhead cleaned in water of water hazard when ball lies therein .......... 13-4/40
competitor withdraws during round
- carries fellow-competitor's clubs for remainder of round ............ 6-4/9
- puts his clubs in fellow-competitor's bag ................................... 4-4a/3
concurrent four-ball and singles matches
- player starts round with 15 clubs; whether four-ball partner
  incurs penalty in singles match ................................................. 30-3/1
- player starts round with non-conforming club; whether player's
  partner disqualified in his singles match .................................. 30-3/1
condition of competition requiring use of driving club listed on current List of
  Conforming Driver Heads ........................................................... App I-C-1a

**Club(s)** *(continued)*
damaged club; whether replacement permitted
- club broken due to habit of hitting head of club on ground ................................. 4-3/9
- club broken on practice ground while play suspended ................................. 4-3/11
- club broken while used as cane ................................................................ 4-3/7
- club damaged in normal course of play breaks into pieces when repaired ................. 4-3/3
- club rendered unfit for play by outside agency or opponent's side ....................... 4-3/9.5
- material in head of metal wood club broken away from shell ............................. 4-1/2
- player starting with 13 clubs breaks club in anger and replaces it ....................... 4-3/8

diagram illustrating player unable to determine nearest point of relief ................ 24-2b/3.7
excess club
- club broken into pieces prior to round discovered in player's bag
  during round ................................................................................... 4-4a/14
- club of player put in another player's bag by mistake during
  suspension of play ........................................................................... 4-4a/5.5
- declared out of play before round and placed on floor of golf cart ....................... 4-4c/1
- declared out of play during round; whether it may replace club
  damaged later in round ...................................................................... 4-4c/2
- discovered before player plays from 2nd tee but after opponent or
  fellow-competitor plays ..................................................................... 4-4a/11
- lost club of another player carried in player's bag ....................................... 4-4a/8
- put in player's golf bag after player has counted his clubs at 1st tee;
  error discovered after player starts round ............................................... 4-4a/6

face of club
- applying chalk; whether permitted ......................................................... 4-2/3
- applying saliva; whether permitted ......................................................... 4-2/4
- ball adheres to face of club after stroke ................................................... 1-4/2
- ball falls on club face after stroke and sticks to mud thereon ........................... 14-4/1
- ball strikes pipeline and on rebound deflects off face of club ........................... 14-4/2
- groove space to width ratio less than 3 to 1 as required by Rules ..................... US/4-1/100

grip
- attachment to grip of club of player with artificial arm ................................. 14-3/15
- changing clubs because of wet grips ....................................................... 4-3/5
- holding ball in hand against grip when putting ........................................... 14-3/6

leaning on club in hazard while waiting to play ............................................... 13-4/2
indicating alignment or distance
- player aligns partner's club before stroke ................................................. 14-2/1
- placing club on ground to align feet ....................................................... 8-2a/1
- placing club on ground to indicate distance for pitch-shot ............................. 8-2a/3

marking position of hole with club instead of flagstick ................................... 17-3/6
meaning of
- damage sustained in "normal course of play" ............................................. 4-3/1
- "repair" .......................................................................................... 4-3/2

measuring
- borrowed club used for measuring purposes ............................................. 20/2
- club to be used in measuring ................................................................ 20/1
- club-lengths directly through fence, tree or wall, or across ditch ................... 20-2b/2

nearest point of relief
- determining club, address position, direction of play and
  swing used to identify nearest point of relief ............................................ 24-2b/1
- dropped ball rolls nearer condition than nearest point of
  relief; whether re-drop necessary if player changes clubs
  and condition no longer interferes ........................................................ 20-2c/0.7
- club used to determine nearest point not used for next stroke ...................... 24-2b/4
- diagrams illustrating nearest point of relief ............................................. 25-1b/2
- player determines nearest point of relief but physically unable
  to play intended stroke ....................................................................... 24-2b/3
- player does not follow recommended procedure in determining
  nearest point of relief ......................................................................... 24-2b/2

Index **I-37**

- player takes relief from condition; whether re-drop required if condition interferes for stroke with club not used to determine nearest point of relief .................................................................. 20-2c/0.8
non-conforming club
 - carried but not used ................................................................................. 4-1/1
 - Committee member rules non-conforming club conforms with Rules; player uses club ................................................................. 34-3/1.5
partners' clubs carried in one bag ............................................................... 4-4a/4
player holds grip of club with one hand and strikes shaft with other hand to move ball; whether ball fairly struck at ........................... 14-1/6
player steadies himself with club in one hand and putts with other hand ..................... 14-3/9
player throws putter at ball after leaving putt short .................................... 1-2/4.5
player uses club or cane to enter or leave hazard when ball lies in hazard ................. 13-4/3.5
playing characteristics of club changed
 - lead tape applied to clubhead or shaft before start of round ....................... 4-1/4
 - lead tape applied to clubhead or shaft during round ................................. 4-2/0.5
 - material applied to clubhead to reduce glare ............................................. 4-2/1
 - other than in normal course of play; modifying penalty for holing short putt with such club ..................................................... 4-3/4
 - weight of club changed during round; breach discovered after competition closed ......................................................................... 34-1b/4
 - while play suspended; error discovered before play resumed ..................... 4-2/2
playing stroke with back of clubhead ......................................................... 14-1/1
putting with wrong end of putter ................................................................. 14-1/3
replacement of club; whether permitted
 - because of wet grip ................................................................................. 4-3/5
 - between rounds in 36-hole match ......................................................... 4-4a/2
 - broken on practice ground while play suspended ................................. 4-3/11
 - for stroke-play play-off ........................................................................... 4-3/12
 - lost during round .................................................................................... 4-3/10
returning to tee to retrieve forgotten club; whether play unduly delayed .......... 6-7/1
status of
 - chipper ................................................................................................... 4-1/3
 - individual who transports player's clubs on motorized golf cart or trolley ........ 6-4/2.5
stopped on downswing by agency other than player ....................................... 14/1
striking ball with billiard-type motion .......................................................... 14-1/2
tape used to bind fingers together to aid in gripping club ........................... 14-3/8
touching casual water in bunker with club ................................................... 13-4/7
training club or swing aid
 - carrying weighted training club .............................................................. 4-4a/7
 - stretching device used to make practice swing ................................. 14-3/10.5
 - weighted headcover or "doughnut" on club used to make stroke or practice swing ............................................................................... 14-3/10
used as plumb line ......................................................................................... 14-3/12
using more than one club to make stroke at ball ......................................... 14-1/7
when club considered added ......................................................................... 4-4a/1

## Committee

*See also* Claims and Disputes; Close of Competition; Conditions of Competition; Course Unplayable or Closed; Discontinuance and Resumption of Play; Doubt Regarding Facts; Local Rules; Marking or Defining Course; Observer; Penalties Imposed, Modified or Waived by Committee; Referee

attachment to grip of club of player with artificial arm; Committee deems attachment gives player undue advantage .................................. 14-3/15
ball moved out of bounds by flow of water in water hazard; suggested preventative measure ................................................................................ 26-1/7
canceling round in stroke play
 - guidelines on whether to cancel round ................................................... 33-2d/1
 - incorrect information on Rules given by Committee to competitor(s) significantly affects competition result ................................................. 34-3/1.5

## Committee (continued)

Committee decision required when doubt exists as to questions of fact
- ball cleaned through act of caddie throwing it to player ............................................. 21/3
- ball deliberately deflected or stopped through the green by spectator ................ 19-1/4.1
- ball falls into bunker when person walks nearby .................................................... 18/10
- ball knocked away along line of putt after player concedes
    opponent's stroke ............................................................................................. 16-1d/2
- ball lifted by opponent's caddie when ball may have been out of bounds ............. 18-3b/5
- ball moved after player takes practice swings touching grass behind ball ............ 18-2a/30
- ball moved in water in water hazard after address ................................................ 14-6/1
- ball not found; either moved by outside agency or lost ......................................... 18-1/1
- ball played from putting green touches but does not move other
    ball on green .................................................................................................... 19-5/4
- ball played in water hazard and lost not unidentified ............................................. 26/5
- ball played out of bunker, player grounds club, ball rolls back into
    bunker ............................................................................................................. 13-4/35.5
- ball strikes hole-liner pulled out with flagstick ...................................................... 17/8
- ball visible from tee disappears or moved by outside agency while
    play suspended ................................................................................................ 6-8d/4
- balls inadvertently exchanged by competitors at unknown place ........................... 15-1/2
- cleaning clubhead in water hazard when ball lies in hazard .................................. 13-4/40
- dispute as to whether competitor played outside teeing ground ............................ 34-3/4
- hole at which wrong ball played unknown ............................................................. 15-1/3
- meaning of "reasonable evidence" in Rule 26-1 .................................................. 26-1/1
- player alters path of clubhead to avoid striking ball; whether
    player intended to make stroke ........................................................................ 14/1.5
- player proceeds on Committee ruling based on available facts;
    subsequent facts prove ruling incorrect ............................................................ 34-3/7
- player proceeds on Committee ruling based on player's version
    of facts; player's version later found incorrect .................................................. 34-3/8
- player uses half-inch backswing; whether ball pushed or fairly struck at .............. 14-1/4
- provisional ball not distinguishable from original ball ........................................... 27/11
- score card alleged incorrect by spectators ............................................................ 6-6d/5
- true state of match not determinable ................................................................... 34-3/5
- when stance in bunker taken ............................................................................... 13-4/23

Committee error
- competitor wins competition with incorrect handicap due to
    Committee error; error discovered several days later ........................................ 6-2b/3
- incorrect ruling; correction of ............................................................................. 34-3/1
- incorrect ruling; whether player should be exempt from penalty
    and for what duration ...................................................................................... 34-3/1.5
- incorrect ruling puts player at serious disadvantage ............................................. 34-3/3.3
- misapplication of handicap by Committee affects match-play draw;
    error discovered during first-round matches ..................................................... 33-5/3
- pace of play condition breached; Committee does not penalize
    player believing he had already lost hole ......................................................... 34-3/2
- play of wrong ball not rectified in stroke play; Committee did not
    ask if error rectified; error discovered after competition closed ........................ 34-1b/3
- play of wrong ball not rectified on advice of Committee member ......................... 33-7/5
- player plays based on incorrect ruling; procedure for player when
    error discovered ............................................................................................... 34-3/3
- referee authorizes player to infringe Rule ............................................................. 34-2/2
- referee reverses ruling made at last hole of match after players
    leave putting green .......................................................................................... 34-2/5
- referee reverses ruling made on previous hole after play of next hole begun ........ 34-2/6
- winner wrongly disqualified; error discovered after two other
    competitors play off for first place ................................................................... 34-1b/5
- winner's score not posted due to Committee error ............................................... 34-1b/6
- wrong form of play (four-ball instead of foursome) used in match as
    result of Committee error ................................................................................. 6-1/1

- wrong handicap applied by Committee results in player not receiving prize ...... 33-5/2
- wrong handicap recorded on score card by Committee; error discovered
    before competition closed .................................................................................... 6-2b/3.5
- wrong handicap used due to Committee misinformation ........................................ 33-1/2
Committee intervention
- ball assisting fellow-competitor on putting green; procedure for
    Committee member if competitor does not lift ball ................................................ 22/7
- ball thought unfit for play; Committee involvement when
    opponent, marker or fellow-competitor not readily available ............................... 5-3/7
- competitor correctly advised he incurred penalty by fellow-competitor;
    competitor disagrees and fails to include penalty in returned score
    card; Committee advised of incident after close of competition ..................... 34-1b/1.5
- hole damaged; Committee involvement required if Committee
    member readily available ...................................................................................... 16-1a/6
- in match play in absence of referee .............................................................. US/34-3/100
- in match play when search exceeds five minutes ........................................ US/34-3/101
- member of Committee finds player's original ball; player prefers to
    continue with provisional ball ................................................................................ 27-2/2
- referee warns player to infringe Rule ...................................................................... 34-2/3
- retroactive appointment of marker by Committee ................................................. 33-1/5
Committee options
- bunker totally under repair ....................................................................................... 25/13
- casual water covering entire teeing ground .......................................................... 25-1b/4
- casual water surrounding hole .............................................................................. 33-2d/2
- holes relocated and/or tee-markers moved during stroke-play round .................. 33-2b/1
- relocating hole when damaged after ball already positioned nearby
    on putting green ................................................................................................. 33-2b/2
- tree falls onto fairway during stipulated round ...................................................... 25/9.5
competitor plays second ball without announcing intention to invoke
    Rule 3-3 and fails to report facts to Committee ..................................................... 3-3/6.5
concurrently playing four-ball and singles matches ................................................... 30-3/1
concurrently playing match and stroke play
- one player in match competes concurrently in stroke-play competition ................ 33-1/6
- competitor in stroke-play event without marker joins two players
    engaged in match; whether breach of combining match and stroke play ............ 33-1/5
conditions of competition
- altering conditions after competition starts ............................................................ 33-1/1
- condition regarding footwear ................................................................................ 33-1/14
- golf cart used in competition; whether permitted .................................................. 33-1/8
- making competitors responsible for adding scores ............................................... 33-1/7
- number of holes of stroke-play competition reduced during competition ............. 33-1/2
- prohibiting players from having person(s) in addition to caddie
    carry items, other than clubs, for them .............................................................. 6-4/5.3
- restriction on which partner in foursome competition may play
    from 1st tee ....................................................................................................... 33-1/3.5
- transportation condition breached by caddie ........................................................ 33-1/9.5
defaulting player plays informal match with opponent and wins ................................ 2-4/18
defining bounds, margins and marking course
- attachment to flagstick to indicate position of hole on green ..................................... 17/1
- boundary altered by unauthorized removal of boundary stake ........................... 33-2a/19
- declaring area as ground under repair during round ............................................ 33-2a/2
- declaring damage due to heavy rain and traffic ground under repair
    during round ..................................................................................................... 33-2a/3
- deeming area of adjoining hole out of bounds for play of particular
    hole but not for play of other holes ................................................................. 33-2a/14
- deeming area of adjoining hole out of bounds for stroke played from
    teeing ground only; whether authorized ......................................................... 33-2a/14
- deeming body of water as both water hazard and lateral water hazard ............... 33-2a/7
- deeming water hazard as lateral water hazard in play from forward
    tee by Local Rule ............................................................................................... 33-2a/6

**Committee** *(continued)*
- - different colored flags used to indicate position of hole on green ............... 17/2
- - displaced boundary stake ............... 33-2a/20
- - distance markers ............... 33/5
- - exposed water pipe adjacent and parallel to boundary fence causes problems; suggested procedure ............... 33-2a/1
- - half of double green serving hole not being played ............... 25-3/1
- - map of putting green indicating hole position displayed at tee ............... 33/6
- - marking island green ............... 33-2a/10
- - part of lateral water hazard where impossible to drop not nearer hole ............... 33-2a/9
- - river or other body of water adjacent to hole but off club property ............... 33-2a/11
- - treating ocean and beach as through the green ............... 33-2a/8
- - where to place lines or stakes defining margin of water hazard ............... 33-2a/4

discontinuance and resumption of play
- - competitor refuses to start or picks up because of weather conditions; round subsequently canceled ............... 33-2d/3
- - competitors playing hole when play suspended discontinue play immediately but then complete hole before Committee orders resumption of play ............... 6-8b/1
- - drop from obstruction made immediately after resumption of play; whether player may lift and clean or substitute then place ball under Rule 6-8d(ii) ............... 6-8d/3
- - explanation of "good reason to lift" when play suspended ............... 6-8c/1
- - guidelines on whether to cancel round ............... 33-2d/1
- - play suspended by Committee; competitor does not resume play at time ordered by Committee ............... 6-8b/6
- - player claiming danger from lightning, refuses to resume play when resumption ordered by Committee ............... 6-8b/5
- - player discontinues play due to physical problem ............... 6-8a/3
- - player drops ball after play suspended for dangerous situation ............... 6-8b/8
- - player plays out of turn in match play after play suspended by Committee and after opponent discontinues play ............... 6-8b/3.5
- - players discontinue play due to inoperable motorized cart ............... 6-8a/4
- - players discontinue play for refreshments ............... 6-8a/2.5
- - when players must be present for resumption of play ............... 6-8b/9

dispute as to whether competitor played from outside teeing ground ............... 34-3/4
flagstick; whether tapered or varying diameters permitted ............... 17/3
handicap
- - alteration of handicap stroke table for matches beginning other than at first hole ............... 33-4/1
- - competitor disqualified from handicap event claims gross prize ............... 33-1/13
- - misapplication of handicap affects match-play draw ............... 33-5/3
- - wrong handicap allowance used in match ............... 6-2a/6
- - wrong handicap applied by Committee results in player not receiving prize ............... 33-5/2
- - wrong handicap used due to Committee misinformation ............... 33-1/12

hole at which wrong ball played unknown ............... 15-1/3
incorrect procedure agreed to in error by player and opponent; whether valid claim can be made after procedure followed ............... 2-5/8.5
line of play improved or worsened by fellow-competitor while discussing with Committee member whether competitor entitled to free relief ............... 1-2/1.5
match begun in ignorance that course closed ............... 33-2d/4
match-play finalists both disqualified ............... 33/3
meaning of "serious breach of etiquette" ............... 33-7/8
mushroom growing on line of putt ............... 16-1a/15
opponent disputes player's claim that ball unfit for play ............... 5-3/8
player lifts ball without authority due to misunderstanding Committee member's instructions ............... 34-3/3.5
player proceeds under inapplicable Rule; guidelines for Committee in determining Rule to apply ............... 34-3/6

# Index  I-41

player reaching fourth-round of match play disqualified for wrong
    score in qualifying round; options for Committee ................................................. 34-1b/8
player reaching third-round of match play disqualified for agreeing
    to waive Rules in first-round match........................................................................ 34-1a/1
play-offs and ties
- determining winner and positions in stroke-play play-off when
    player disqualified or concedes............................................................................. 33-6/3
- groupings for stroke-play play-off............................................................................... 33-3/4
- players decide method of settling tie when Committee fails to do so ...................... 33-6/4
- score cards in sudden-death play-off......................................................................... 33-5/1
postponement of final match due to injury of player........................................................ 6-3a/1
relocating hole when damaged after ball already positioned nearby
    on putting green........................................................................................................ 33-2b/2
removal of casual water or loose impediments on putting green by Committee .............. 33/1
score cards
- competitor's failure to countersign score card blamed on lack
    of time provided by Committee ........................................................................... 33-7/3
- competitor's returned score card has wrong or no name on it................................. 6-6d/4
- in sudden-death play-off............................................................................................. 33-5/1
- marker disappears with competitor's score card....................................................... 6-6b/6
- marker not appointed by Committee signs score cards............................................ 6-6b/5
- not returned promptly due to Committee failure to advise
    competitors where to return cards ...................................................................... 6-6b/4
- requirement that score be entered into computer ................................................... 6-6b/8
- total score recorded by competitor incorrect ........................................................... 6-6d/2
- when score card considered returned ...................................................................... 6-6c/1
second ball played despite adverse ruling by Committee member................................... 3-3/2
spectators allege competitor's score incorrect................................................................... 6-6d/5
status of
- half of double green serving hole not being played ................................................. 25-3/1
- team captain or coach................................................................................................. 33-1/11.5
- starting time fixed by players ..................................................................................... 33-3/1
- tree basins .................................................................................................................... 33-2a/10.5
- two holes on each green of nine-hole course ........................................................... 16/7
- wrong ruling accepted by players from person not on Committee .......................... 2-5/8
teeing ground
- competitors determine spot from which to play from tee when
    both tee-markers missing ..................................................................................... 11-4b/3
- competitors estimate area of teeing ground when one tee-marker missing............. 11-4b/2
- play from wrong teeing ground attributed to Committee failure to
    indicate hole numbers on teeing ground............................................................. 11-5/2
true state of match not determinable................................................................................... 34-3/5
time of starting
- all competitors must be present ................................................................................. 6-3a/2
- circumstances which warrant waiving disqualification penalty for lateness ............ 6-3a/1.5
- competitors determining own groupings and starting times ................................... 33-3/3
- meaning of "time of starting"...................................................................................... 6-3a/2.5
- player not present at time of starting; course closed at that time ............................ 33-3/2
- starting players from 1st and 10th tees...................................................................... 33-1/3
- status of starting time fixed by players ...................................................................... 33-3/1
- when players must be present for resumption of play ............................................. 6-8b/9
waiving, modifying or imposing disqualification penalty
- application of disqualification penalty in team competition in which
    not all team members' scores count for each round ......................................... 33/8
- authority to waive or modify disqualification penalty................................................ 33-7/1
- circumstances which warrant waiving disqualification penalty for lateness ............ 6-3a/1.5
- competitor repeatedly replaces ball nearer hole on green ....................................... 33-7/6
- competitor seeks help from fellow-competitor to avoid penalty .............................. 33-7/7
- competitor unaware of penalty returns wrong score; whether
    waiving or modifying disqualification penalty justified ...................................... 33-7/4.5

## Committee (continued)
- modifying penalty for not holing out in stroke play ..................... 33-7/2
- modifying penalty for returning wrong score ............................ 33-7/4
- player intentionally gives incorrect information on Rules ............... 9/1
- wrong form of play used in match; players agree losing side will default to winners ............................................... 33-1/4

when match result "officially announced" ................................. 2-5/14
whether player disqualified in match-play event entitled to prize won prior to disqualification ................................. 33/7
wrong form of play used in match play ................................... 6-1/1
wrong handicap
- recorded on score card by Committee; error discovered before competition closed .................................... 6-2b/3.5
- used in stroke play by mistake; error discovered after competition closed ............. 6-2b/1

## Concession

*See also* Default; Four-Ball Match Play; Foursomes; Singles Match; Wrong Information

agreement that side losing after 18 holes of 36-hole match will concede match ..... 1-3/7
agreement to concede short putts .......................................... 1-3/2
agreement to consider hole halved during play of hole ..................... 2-1/1.5
ball falls into hole after concession of next stroke ...................... 2-4/2
ball resting against flagstick; putt conceded and ball removed before player can remove flagstick ................................. 17-4/2
competitor concedes fellow-competitor's short putt and knocks ball away ..... 3-2/1
concurrent four-ball and singles matches; whether concessions made under various circumstances apply to only four-ball or singles match or both ........................................... 30-3/1
conscious failure to correct opponent's misunderstanding of state of match; what constitutes wrong information ..................... 9-2/12
defaulting player plays informal match with opponent and wins ............. 2-4/18
determining winner and positions in stroke-play play-off when player disqualified or concedes ...................................... 33-6/3
fellow-competitor lifts competitor's ball conceding next stroke in stroke play ..... 18-4/3
foursome match conceded by play of singles match ......................... 2-4/21
implied concession of hole withdrawn ..................................... 2-4/13
incorrect information given by player corrected before opponent plays next stroke but after opponent concedes player's putt ............. 9-2/7
opponent's ball knocked away by player after concession moves player's ball ..... 18-2a/18
opponent's misreading of number on player's ball results in agreement that player lost hole for playing wrong ball ......................... 9-2/11
player concedes hole
- after which opponent discovered to have played wrong ball .............. 2-4/9
- after which discovered opponent's previous stroke played with wrong ball from hazard ............................................. 2-4/9.5
- after which opponent plays wrong ball .................................. 2-4/10
- handicap stroke claimed after hole conceded ........................... 6-2a/4
- on basis of invalid claim ............................................. 2-4/12

player concedes match
- after winning it when opponent lodges invalid claim regarding strokes taken .................................................. 2-4/15
- due to misconception as to opponent's score at last hole .............. 2-4/14

player concedes opponent's next stroke
- and knocks or rolls ball to opponent .................................. 16-1d/1
- and knocks opponent's ball away along own line of putt ................ 16-1d/2
- and knocks opponent's ball into hole .................................. 2-4/1
- then plays before opponent has opportunity to lift ball ............... 2-4/8

player lifts ball or ball-marker
- in mistaken belief that next stroke conceded .......................... 2-4/3
- mistakenly believing he won hole ...................................... 20-1/8

Index    I-43

- of opponent and shakes opponent's hand in erroneous belief match over ............... 2-4/17
- whether lifting opponent's ball-marker considered concession of next stroke ............ 2-4/5
- whether picking up opponent's ball considered concession of next stroke ................. 2-4/4

player omits penalty stroke when advising opponent as to score for hole;
    error discovered after match conceded by opponent ............................................... 9-2/10
player unable to meet match-play schedule defaults; schedule then
    changed and player requests reinstatement .......................................................... 2-4/20
player with lost ball concedes hole; ball then found in hole ........................................... 2-4/11
putting out after concession of stroke ................................................................................ 2-4/6
result of match when player dormie and opponent concedes ............................................. 2-3/2
stroke concession refused by player and withdrawn by opponent; player
    then putts and misses ............................................................................................... 2-4/7
three holes played out of sequence in match ..................................................................... 2-1/5
valid timely claim made after concession of match ........................................................... 2-4/16
winner of match wishes to default to beaten opponent ..................................................... 2-4/19

## Conditions of Competition

*See also* Committee; Local Rules

agreement that side losing after 18 holes of 36-hole match will concede match ................. 1-3/7
altering conditions after competition starts; whether permitted ....................................... 33-1/1
borrowing balls from another player when "One Ball" condition in effect ......................... 5-1/5
both players in match late for time of starting ................................................................... 6-3a/3
caddies; prohibiting use of caddies or restricting who may caddie .............................. App I-C-3
changing partner in foursome play after player drives from first tee ................................. 29/1
competitors play two holes not included in stipulated round ............................................. 3/2
condition
- making competitors responsible for addition of hole scores on
    score cards; whether permitted ............................................................................ 33-1/7
- of team competition stipulating person authorized to give advice
    must be team captain and/or amateur ........................................................................ 8/1
- prohibiting players from having person(s) in addition to caddie
    carry items, other than clubs, for them ............................................................... 6-4/5.3
- regarding footwear .................................................................................................... 33-1/14
- requiring alterations on score card be initialed; whether permitted ...................... 6-6a/6
- requiring immediate discontinuance of play; guidelines for
    waiving or modifying disqualification penalty for failure to
    discontinue play immediately ............................................................................... 6-8b/7
- requiring scores be entered into computer by players; whether permitted .......... 6-6b/8
- restricting which partner in foursome competition may play from 1st tee ........ 33-1/3.5
discontinuance of play
- for refreshment ........................................................................................................ 6-8a/2.5
- guidelines for waiving or modifying disqualification penalty
    for failure to discontinue play immediately when immediate
    discontinuance condition in effect ......................................................................... 6-8b/7
driving clubs; requiring use of driving club listed on List of Conforming
    Driver Heads ............................................................................................................ App I-C-1a
golf cart used in competition; whether permitted ............................................................. 33-1/8
group plays from wrong teeing ground; whether Committee should
    waive penalties because Committee failed to indicate hole
    numbers on teeing ground ...................................................................................... 11-5/2
incorrect information on conditions
- given by player ............................................................................................................. 9/1
- given by Committee member; whether player should be exempt
    from penalty and for what duration .................................................................... 34-3/1.5
match decided by wrong form of play by agreement of players ...................................... 33-1/4
number of holes of stroke-play competition reduced during
    competition; options available to Committee ....................................................... 33-1/2
pace of play condition breached; Committee does not penalize player
    believing he had already lost hole ........................................................................... 34-3/2

**Conditions of Competition** *(continued)*

restrictions on balls used
- "One Ball" condition; prohibiting changing brands or types of golf balls during stipulated round; specimen optional condition ......... App I-C-1c
- effect of state of match penalty for breach of "One Ball" condition in four-ball play ................................................................. 30-3/2
- requiring use of ball named on current List of Conforming Golf Balls; specimen optional condition ........................................ App I-C-1b
- requiring use of ball on List of Conforming Golf Balls; penalty for breach ...................... 5-1/2
- requiring use of ball on List of Conforming Golf Balls; provisional ball played not on list .................................................................. 5-1/3

score cards and scores
- making competitors responsible for addition of hole scores on score cards; whether permitted ...................................................... 33-1/7
- requiring alterations on score card be initialed; whether permitted ....................... 6-6a/6
- requiring scores be entered into computer by players; whether permitted .................. 6-6b/8

starting players from 1st and 10th tees .................................................................... 33-1/3

status of
- starting time fixed by players ........................................................................... 33-3/1
- team captain or coach ...................................................................................... 33-1/11.5

team competition
- condition stipulates person authorized to give advice must be team captain and/or amateur .................................................... 8/1
- no action taken to stop team captain giving advice without authority ................... 8-1/24
- team captain gives advice while playing ........................................................... 8/2
- whether team captain authorized to give advice may be required to keep off putting greens ................................................................. 8-2b/4

time of starting, all competitors must be present ...................................................... 6-3a/2
transportation condition breached by caddie ............................................................ 33-1/9.5
umbrella carrier employed in addition to caddie ....................................................... 6-4/5

wrong form of play used
- in match play by mistake; error discovered after nine holes ................................ 6-1/1
- players agree losing side will default to winners ................................................. 33-1/4
- to decide which side will concede match .......................................................... 2-4/21

wrong handicap
- allowance used in match .................................................................................. 6-2a/6
- knowingly used in stroke play; error discovered after competition closed ............ 6-2b/2
- used due to Committee misinformation ........................................................... 33-1/12

**Course Unplayable or Closed**

*See also* Discontinuance and Resumption of Play

canceling or suspending play
- casual water completely covers teeing ground .................................................. 25-1b/4
- guidelines on whether to cancel round ........................................................... 33-2d/1
- hole surrounded by casual water ................................................................... 33-2d/2

competitor refuses to start or picks up because of weather conditions; round subsequently canceled ................................................................ 33-2d/3
match begun in ignorance that course closed ........................................................... 33-2d/4
match discontinued by agreement; one player subsequently wishes to resume
- opponent refuses although course playable ................................................. 6-8a/5
- opponent refuses on basis course unplayable .............................................. 6-8a/6

player not present at time of starting; course closed at that time ............................ 33-3/2
player unable to meet match-play schedule defaults; course unplayable on scheduled day of match; player requests reinstatement ................ 2-4/20

**Course Record**

guidelines and recommendations ........................................................................... Misc./1

**Crab**

status of dead land crab ........................................................................................ 23/6

Index  I-45

## Crawfish

*See also* Burrowing Animal, Reptile or Bird
mound made by crawfish interferes with stance or swing ................................. 25-1b/18

## Damage

*See also* Ball Unfit for Play; Club(s); Ground Under Repair; Repair
ball
 - damaged internally .................................................................................................. 5-3/1
 - deemed unfit for play played at later hole ....................................................... 5-3/2
 - not unfit for play deemed unfit ............................................................................. 5-3/3
club
 - broken due to habit of hitting head of club on ground ............................... 4-3/9
 - broken into pieces prior to round discovered in player's bag during round ............. 4-4a/14
 - broken while used as cane ...................................................................................... 4-3/7
 - changing clubs because of wet grips .................................................................. 4-3/5
 - damaged in normal course of play breaks into pieces when repaired ...... 4-3/3
 - excess club declared out of play during round; whether it may
    replace a club damaged later in round ........................................................... 4-4c/2
 - lead tape applied to clubhead or shaft during round ................................... 4-2/0.5
 - material in head of metal wood club broken away from shell .................. 4-1/2
 - meaning of damage sustained in "normal course of play" ......................... 4-3/1
 - meaning of "repair" .................................................................................................. 4-3/2
 - player starting with 13 clubs breaks putter in anger and replaces it ....... 4-3/8
 - playing characteristics of club changed while play suspended; error
    discovered before play resumed ...................................................................... 4-2/2
 - rendered unfit for play by outside agency or opponent's side .................. 4-3/9.5
 - short putt holed with club whose playing characteristics changed
    other than in normal course of play; whether Committee should
    waive or modify disqualification penalty ....................................................... 4-3/4
hole
 - damaged; procedure for player ............................................................................. 16-1a/6
 - ball damages side of hole ....................................................................................... 16/3
 - relocating hole when damaged after ball already positioned nearby
    on putting green .................................................................................................... 33-2b/2
 - repaired by player after holing out but before opponent,
    fellow-competitor or partner holes out ........................................................ 1-2/3.5
 - touching inside of hole to repair damage; whether permitted .................. 16-1a/5
line of putt
 - altered purposely by stepping on it by opponent or fellow-competitor ....... 1-2/1
 - damaged accidentally by opponent, fellow-competitor or their caddies ..... 16-1a/13
Local Rule
 - allowing free drop outside bunker or smoothing of sand in bunker
    damaged by play of children; whether authorized ................................... 33-8/9
 - allowing free relief from damage made by insects ........................................ 33-8/21
 - declaring severe damage by non-burrowing animals as ground
    under repair ............................................................................................................. 33-8/32.5
 - permitting relief from extensive damage to course due to heavy
    rain and foot traffic .............................................................................................. 33-2a/3
 - permitting repair of turf plugs on putting green not 4-1/4 inches
    in diameter ............................................................................................................... 33-8/30
 - wrong putting green deemed to include apron to prevent damage thereto ........ 33-8/33
repair of spike mark damage
 - around hole ................................................................................................................... 16-1c/4
 - on competitor's line of putt by fellow-competitor, sanctioned or
    tacitly approved by competitor ........................................................................ 13-2/36

## Dangerous Situations

bees interfere with play ..................................................................................................... 1-4/10
condition requiring immediate discontinuance of play; guidelines for
    waiving or modifying disqualification penalty for failure to
    discontinue play immediately ............................................................................ 6-8b/7

## Dangerous Situations (continued)
| | |
|---|---|
| danger from fire-ants | 33-8/22 |
| definition | 1-4/11 |
| rattlesnake interferes with play | 1-4/10 |

## Default

*See also* Concession; Halved Hole

after defaulting to opponent
| | |
|---|---|
| - player wins informal match with opponent; who Committee should decide advances | 2-4/18 |
| - because player unable to play match as scheduled, matches postponed due to unplayable course conditions; player requests reinstatement | 2-4/20 |

after winning
| | |
|---|---|
| - match, player wishes to default to losing opponent; whether permitted | 2-4/19 |
| - several matches, player disqualified from competition for wrong score in stroke-play qualifying; Committee options regarding defeated opponents and remaining matches | 34-1b/8 |
| sides agree to play match using wrong form of play with losers defaulting to winners | 33-1/4 |

## Dew

| | |
|---|---|
| removing dew or frost | |
| - from line of putt | 16-1a/3 |
| - near ball or from line of play | 13-2/35 |
| testing surface of putting green behind ball for presence of dew | 16-1d/4 |

## Directly Attributable

| | |
|---|---|
| "directly attributable;" meaning of in Rules 20-1 and 20-3a | 20-1/15 |
| ball moved accidentally | |
| - by flagstick when measuring | 18-2a/24 |
| - by foot of player asked to lift due to interference | 20-1/13 |
| - by foot of player during removal of loose impediment on putting green | 23-1/11 |
| - during removal of movable obstruction | 24-1/4 |
| - when flagstick removed as ball overhangs hole | 16-2/4 |
| - when kicked while lying in long grass inside water hazard while player probes for it in water | 12-1/5 |
| ball-marker moved accidentally | |
| - by player after moving loose impediments on putting green | 20-1/12 |
| - by player in process of marking position of ball | 20-1/6 |
| - by putter dropped by player approaching ball to lift it | 20-1/14 |
| holding ball in place while removing movable obstruction; whether permissible | 24-1/4 |

## Direction Post

*See also* Status of Object
| | |
|---|---|
| ball deflected by direction post | 19-1/1 |

## Discontinuance and Resumption of Play

| | |
|---|---|
| asking advice when play suspended | 8-1/20 |
| casual water covering teeing ground; whether Committee should discontinue play | 25-1b/4 |
| Committee guidelines on whether to cancel round | 33-2d/1 |
| competitor refuses to start or picks up because of weather conditions; round subsequently canceled | 33-2d/3 |
| due to inoperable motorized cart | 6-8a/4 |
| due to physical problem | 6-8a/3 |
| during suspension of play | |
| - ball moved accidentally by player | 18-2a/25 |
| - ball moved by wind or casual water | 18-1/11 |
| - ball visible from tee prior to suspension disappears or moved by outside agency before play resumed | 6-8d/4 |
| - ball-marker moved off green by wind or casual water | 20-1/10 |
| - club put in another player's bag by mistake | 4-4a/5.5 |

Index    I-47

entering clubhouse or half-way house for refreshment during round .................. 6-8a/2.7
for refreshment.................................................................................................. 6-8a/2.5
guidelines for waiving or modifying disqualification penalty for
      failure to discontinue play immediately ................................................. 6-8b/7
hole surrounded by casual water....................................................................... 33-2d/2
hole-liner not sunk deep enough; whether discontinuance of play permitted............... 16/4
lie altered
  - by natural causes during discontinuance of play ........................................... 6-8d/1
  - in bunker prior to resumption of play ............................................................ 6-8d/2
Local Rule permitting competitors to discontinue play by agreement
      in bad weather; whether authorized..................................................... 33-8/5
match discontinued by agreement
  - cannot be resumed until three days later; one player wishes to
    play on competition course prior to resumption ....................................... 7-2/10
  - due to rain one player subsequently wishes to resume; opponent
    refuses although course playable ............................................................. 6-8a/5
  - due to rain one player subsequently wishes to resume; opponent
    refuses on ground course unplayable ...................................................... 6-8a/6
  - players may play first 12 holes following day if match
    discontinued on 13th tee previous day .................................................... 7-2/11
  - replaying match when play discontinued instead of resuming
    from where play stopped ........................................................................... 2-1/6
meaning of "good reason to lift" when play suspended ......................................... 6-8c/1
old hole plug on line of putt not repairable; whether players may
      discontinue play to request help from Committee................................. 16-1c/3
play suspended by Committee
  - competitor does not resume play at time ordered by Committee.............................. 6-8b/6
  - competitor wishes to complete hole; fellow-competitor does not;
    whether competitor may play alone and complete hole ........................ 6-8b/3
  - competitors discontinue play of hole immediately then resume
    play and complete hole before Committee orders resumption of play ............... 6-8b/1
  - options for players if one competitor in group has played from tee ........................ 6-8b/2
  - player drops ball after play suspended for dangerous situation .............................. 6-8b/8
  - player plays out of turn in match after play suspended by
    Committee and after opponent discontinues play................................ 6-8b/3.5
  - player wishes to practice after scheduled resumption but
    before group plays.................................................................................... 7-2/12
player claiming danger from lightning, refuses to resume play when
      resumption ordered by Committee........................................................ 6-8b/5
player unable to resume suspended match at scheduled time........................... 6-8b/4
playing characteristics of club changed while play suspended; error
      discovered before play resumed ................................................................. 4-2/2
replacement of club broken on practice ground while play suspended;
      whether permitted ................................................................................. 4-3/11
resumption of play
  - ball dropped away from obstruction immediately after
    resumption of play; whether player may lift and clean or
    substitute then place ball under Rule 6-8d(ii)......................................... 6-8d/3
  - when players must be present .................................................................... 6-8b/9
returning to tee to retrieve forgotten club........................................................... 6-7/1
taking shelter while waiting to play..................................................................... 6-8a/2
time permitted for search for lost ball if play suspended during search........................ 27/1.5
tree falls onto fairway during stipulated round ................................................. 25/9.5
watching television for 45 minutes after nine holes ........................................... 6-8a/1

**Distance, Distance Information and Distance Markers**

*See also* Measuring
asking
  - accuracy of distance marker; whether advice ............................................... 8-1/3
  - distance between objects; whether advice ................................................... 8-1/2
  - length of hole information; whether advice ................................................. 8-1/1

### Distance, Distance Information and Distance Markers (continued)

devices used in measuring or determining distance
- distance meter attached to golf cart .................................................. 14-3/1
- electronic device containing distance measurements between
    various points ............................................................................. 14-3/5.5
- pencil or score card used to gauge distance ..................................... 14-3/2
- reflectors (non-circular) on flagsticks aid in use of distance
    measuring devices; whether permitted ...................................... 17/3.5

distance markers indicating distance to putting green
- asking if distance marker accurate; whether advice ....................... 8-1/3
- whether permitted ............................................................................. 33/5

illustrations of holes with distance measurements between various points
- booklet containing ............................................................................. 14-3/5
- electronic device containing ............................................................. 14-3/5.5

Local Rule permitting use of distance measuring device ..................... 14-3/0.5
mark placed by player to indicate distance for pitch shot ................... 8-2a/3
vertical distance
- ball moves vertically downward; whether ball has moved by definition ............. 18/1
- ball moves vertically downward when addressed; will not remain
    at rest when replaced ................................................................. 20-3d/3
- nearest point of relief; ball lying in burrowing animal hole under
    ground on course ......................................................................... 25-1b/23
- nearest point of relief; ball lying in drainpipe under ground on course ............. 24-2b/12
- nearest point of relief; ball lying on elevated obstruction ........................ 24-2b/11
- unplayable ball in tree; player opts to drop within two club-lengths ......... 28/11
- unplayable ball at base of cliff; player wished to drop within two
    club-lengths of point above ball at top of cliff ........................... 28/12

### Divot and Divot Hole

another player's divot comes to rest near player's ball already in bunker ........ 13-4/18
ball rolls towards hole when dropped behind divot hole at spot
    where previous stroke played ................................................... 20-2c/1.5
folded over, partially attached divot near player's ball; whether
    removal or replacement permitted ........................................... 13-2/5
on line of play; whether replacement permitted ................................ 13-2/6
original lie altered and spot where ball originally lay not determinable;
    which procedure takes precedence ........................................... 20-3b/5
player makes divot hole affecting area of intended stance of partner,
    opponent or fellow-competitor ................................................. 13-2/8.7
replaced in area where ball to be dropped ........................................ 13-2/4.5
when divot considered replaced .......................................................... 13-2/7

### Dog

ball deflected or stopped by dog on putting green
- after stroke from off green ................................................................ 19-1/6
- after stroke from green ..................................................................... 19-1/7

### Doubt as to Procedure

*See also* Doubt Regarding Facts; Provisional Ball; Second Ball; Serious Breach of Rules
determining which ball counts when two balls played under Rule 3-3
- guidelines for determining which ball counts when player
    proceeds under Rule 3-3 ............................................................. 3-3/0.5
- whether score with second ball counts if dropped in wrong place and played ............. 3-3/5
explanation of "any ball he has played" ............................................. 18/7
player invokes Rule 3-3 (doubt as to procedure)
- after playing original ball .................................................................. 3-3/6
- ball dropped in wrong place and played; second ball dropped in
    right place; both balls played out ............................................... 3-3/3
- ball dropped in wrong place but not played; second ball dropped
    in right place; both balls played out .......................................... 3-3/4

Index  I-49

- ball played under water hazard Rule; original ball then found in
 hazard and holed out as second ball .................................................................. 26-1/5
- ball selected by player to count lifted and not holed out; player
 holes out with other ball; plays from next teeing ground .......................... 3-3/8
- guidelines for determining which ball counts when player
 proceeds under Rule 3-3 .................................................................................. 3-3/0.5
- in match play; whether permitted .................................................................... 3-3/9
- intention to play two balls announced; competitor plays original
 ball before dropping second ball; elects not to play second ball ............ 3-3/7.5
- original ball lifted and dropped then competitor places second
 ball where original ball lay and plays it ........................................................ 3-3/13
- plays second ball first then plays original ball; whether order
 of play permitted .............................................................................................. 3-3/14
- provisional ball used as second ball when not determinable
 whether original ball out of bounds ............................................................... 3-3/1
- second ball played despite adverse ruling by Committee member .............. 3-3/2
- second ball played without announcing intention to invoke
 Rule 3-3 and competitor fails to report facts to Committee .................... 3-3/6.5
- single ball dropped in accordance with two different Rules
 instead of playing second ball ........................................................................ 3-3/11
- single ball dropped in accordance with two different Rules
 instead of playing second ball; dropped ball rolls back into
 condition from which relief taken ................................................................. 3-3/12
- three balls played by competitor doubtful of rights; whether permitted ..... 3-3/10
match play
- Local Rule allowing play of second ball in match play;
 whether authorized ............................................................................................ 33-8/3
- player invokes Rule 3-3 in match play; whether permitted............................ 3-3/9
- procedure for valid claim .................................................................................... 2-5/2
original ball strikes second ball or vice versa............................................................. 3-3/7
spectator says ball moved by outside agency but player not sure;
 procedure for player if Committee decision not possible
 in reasonable time................................................................................................ 18-1/4
wrong ball played in belief it is provisional or second ball ..................................... 15/7

## Doubt Regarding Facts

*See also* Committee; Doubt as to Procedure
ball at rest
- falls into bunker when person walks nearby ....................................................... 18/10
- moves after player takes practice swings touching grass behind ball ................ 18-2a/30
- moves after removal of nearby loose impediment ............................................... 18-2a/30.5
ball not found
- either in water hazard or casual water overflowing hazard............................. 1-4/7
- either lodged in water hazard or lost outside water hazard........................... 26-1/1
- either lost in casual water or in high rough or hollow not
 visible from tee..................................................................................................... 25-1c/1
- either moved by outside agency or lost ............................................................ 18-1/1
- treated as moved by outside agency in absence of reasonable
 evidence to that effect ......................................................................................... 27-1/2.5
- visible from tee; disappears or moved during suspension of play ............... 6-8d/4
ball(s) not identifiable
- ball believed his by player lost in deep water after stroke from
 within water hazard ............................................................................................. 26/5
- player unable to distinguish his ball from another ball ............................................. 27/10
- provisional ball not distinguishable from original ball ................................................ 27/11
- wrong ball played by competitor and lost; may have been
 ball of fellow-competitor...................................................................................... 15-3b/1
ball overhanging hole moves when flagstick removed; whether
 directly attributable to removal not determinable................................................. 16-2/4

## Doubt Regarding Facts (continued)

clubhead cleaned with water in water hazard after stroke from
    hazard fails to extricate ball; stroke from ball's new location
    clearly unreasonable .................................................................................... 13-4/40
during downswing player purposely tries to stop club; swing carries
    clubhead beyond ball; whether stroke made........................................... 14/1.5
hole-liner pulled out with flagstick deflects ball; not known whether
    hole-liner moving or stationary ................................................................. 17/8
location unknown
  - ball of player lifted by opponent's caddie claiming it was out of
    bounds; whether original position of ball in or out of bounds
    not determinable .................................................................................... 18-3b/5
  - ball overshooting green deliberately stopped or deflected by
    spectator; ball would have come to rest just short of or in
    water hazard ........................................................................................... 19-1/4.1
  - ball stolen by outside agency from unknown spot.................................. 18-1/5
  - balls inadvertently exchanged by competitors either during play
    of previous hole or between play of two holes ................................... 15-1/2
  - fellow-competitor asserts, at completion of stipulated round,
    competitor played from outside teeing ground on 15th hole;
    competitor asserts he played within teeing ground ........................... 34-3/4
player proceeds on Committee ruling
  - based on available facts; subsequent facts prove ruling incorrect ........... 34-3/7
  - based on player's version of facts; player's version later found incorrect ...... 34-3/8
player uses half inch backswing; whether ball pushed or fairly struck at ......... 14/1/4
players unable to resolve Rules problem agree to consider hole halved ............ 2-1/1
spectators claim score for hole higher than score returned on score
    card by player........................................................................................... 6-6d/5
state of match at end of stipulated round disputed; Committee cannot
    determine true state of match................................................................ 34-3/5
timing of events unknown
  - ball played from bunker to grass bank rolls back into bunker;
    player in frustration hits sand with club; not determinable
    whether ball returned to bunker before sand struck ......................... 13-4/35.5
  - hole at which wrong ball played unknown ............................................. 15-1/3
  - player may have failed to discontinue play immediately as
    required by Appendix I-C-5 Condition ................................................. 6-8b/7
when stance taken in bunker ................................................................................. 13-4/23
whether action causes breach of Rule
  - ball moves in water in water hazard after address; whether action
    of player or water current caused movement not known ....................... 14-6/1
  - competitor's ball played from putting green comes to rest
    touching ball of fellow-competitor on green; whether competitor's
    ball stopped or deflected or fellow-competitor's moved not known .................... 19-5/4
  - flagstick removed without authority by opponent or
    fellow-competitor while player's ball in motion after stroke;
    players unsure whether ball might have reached hole
    when flagstick removed.......................................................................... 17-2/2
  - player attempts to take stance fairly and moves growing
    or fixed object (i.e. branch or boundary stake); player
    abandons stance and object probably returns to original
    position; player then takes stance without moving object ................. 13-2/1.1
  - player concedes opponent's next stroke and knocks ball away
    along own line of putt............................................................................ 16-1d/2
  - player unsure whether partially embedded stone considered
    loose impediment or fixed..................................................................... 23/2
  - throwing ball to caddie may have cleaned it; ball lifted under
    Rule prohibiting cleaning ...................................................................... 21/3

whether ball not on current List of Conforming Balls conforms to Rules ............... US/5-1/101
wrong ball
    - balls inadvertently exchanged by competitors either during play
       of previous hole or between play of two holes ............................................................ 15-1/2
    - competitor plays wrong ball and loses it; may have been ball of
       fellow-competitor ........................................................................................................... 15-3b/1
    - hole at which wrong ball played unknown ........................................................................ 15-1/3
    - player unable to distinguish his ball from another ball ............................................. 27/10
    - provisional ball not distinguishable from original ball ............................................... 27/11

### Drainpipe

ball in drainpipe under course; entrance to drainpipe out of bounds ........................ 24-2b/12
ball lost in underground drainpipe .......................................................................................... 24-3b/1
status of movable part of drainage hose .............................................................................. 24-2b/15.3

### Embedded Ball

*See also* Pitch-Mark

ascertaining whether ball embedded
    - lifting ball to determine whether embedded in own pitch-mark .............................. 25-2/7
    - lifting ball to determine whether embedded in own pitch-mark;
       Committee involvement when opponent, marker or
       fellow-competitor not readily available .................................................................. 5-3/7
    - when ball considered embedded in ground .................................................................. 25-2/0.5
ball bounces out of its pitch-mark and spins back into it ..................................................... 25-2/1
ball embedded
    - in fruit .................................................................................................................................. 23/10
    - in grass bank or face of bunker ........................................................................................ 25-2/5
    - in ground under repair in closely mown area ............................................................... 25-2/4
    - in hazard; lifted to determine whether unfit for play ................................................... 5-3/5
    - in lip of bunker .................................................................................................................... 13/4
    - inside circumference of hole; all of ball below lip of hole .......................................... 16/2
    - inside circumference of hole; all of ball not below lip of hole ................................... 16/3
    - within teeing ground ......................................................................................................... 25-2/8
ball on steep bank driven straight into ground ..................................................................... 25-2/6
ball returns to pitch-mark from prior stroke .......................................................................... 25-2/3
dropped ball
    - embeds ................................................................................................................................ 25-2/2
    - embeds; procedure if ball again embeds when re-dropped ...................................... 25-2/2.5
Local Rule
    - allowing relief through the green for ball embedded in
       own pitch-mark ............................................................................................................ App I-B-3a
    - permitting re-dropping or placing when dropped ball embeds in
       bunker; whether authorized ..................................................................................... 33-8/28
pitch-mark of previous stroke (ball embedded) in dropping area repaired
       before ball dropped .............................................................................................................. 13-2/10
pitch-mark of previous stroke (ball not embedded) in area of intended
       swing repaired before ball played ...................................................................................... 13-2/21

### Environmentally-Sensitive Area

marking environmentally-sensitive areas; recommendations for Committee ............. 33-8/41
player enters environmentally-sensitive area to retrieve ball ........................................... 33-8/42
stroke made from
    - environmentally-sensitive area ........................................................................................ 33-8/43
    - environmentally-sensitive area; significant advantage gained ................................. 33-8/44
strokes made from place where play not permitted, including
       environmentally-sensitive areas .......................................................................................... 25-3/2

## Equipment

*See also* Artificial Devices and Unusual Equipment; Club(s); Golf Cart; Status of Object; Trolley

ball deflected, stopped or moved by
- another ball accidentally dropped by opponent or fellow-competitor ...................... 18/7.5
- bag of competitor and then his caddie ................................................................. 19-2/7
- bag of opponent or fellow-competitor left ahead by shared caddie ......................... 19-2/8
- cart or trolley of opponent or fellow-competitor; thereafter strikes
    cart or trolley of player or partner ................................................................... 19-3/3
- cart pulled by opponent or fellow-competitor ....................................................... 19-2/6
- cart shared by two players; ball at rest moved ....................................................... 18/8
- cart shared by two players; ball in motion deflected ............................................... 19/1
- clubs belonging to different side carried in same bag ............................................. 19-2/5
- tee marking position of player's ball ..................................................................... 20-1/17
- towel dropped by player and blown by wind ......................................................... 18-2a/17

borrowing equipment from another player (i.e. balls, towels, gloves,
    tees, etc); whether permitted ............................................................................ 5-1/5
cap used to remove loose impediment from line of putt ............................................. 16-1a/8
club put in another player's bag by mistake during suspension of play ........................ 4-4a/5.5
condition prohibiting players from having person(s) in addition to caddie
    carry items, other than clubs, for them ............................................................. 6-4/5.3
explanation of "any ball he has played" ..................................................................... 18/7
Local Rule clarifying status of motorized golf carts and persons driving them ............. 33-8/4
non-conforming club ruled conforming by Committee member; player
    uses club ............................................................................................................ 34-3/1.5
person(s) other than caddie
- carry items, other than clubs, for player during round ........................................... 6-4/5.3
- hired to carry umbrella for player ........................................................................ 6-4/5
status of
- glove used as indicating mark ............................................................................... 20-2a/7
- golf carts pulled by double caddie ........................................................................ 6-4/6
- person in shared golf cart ..................................................................................... 19/2
towel
- borrowed from another player; whether permitted ............................................... 5-1/5
- covering another player's clubs removed by player to find out club used ................ 8-1/11
- dropped by player; blows onto and moves ball ..................................................... 18-2a/17
- placed under knees to play stroke ........................................................................ 13-3/2
- used by Committee member to remove casual water or loose
    impediments on putting green .......................................................................... 33/1
- used by player to brush aside loose impediments on line of putt ............................ 16-1a/8
- used to mop up casual water ................................................................................ 16-1a/1
- waved to encourage insect in bunker to move ....................................................... 23-1/5.5

## Equity

advice in team competition
- no action taken to stop team captain without authority from giving advice ............. 8-1/24
- player's team mate in gallery hits ball to green to show player whether
    green will hold .................................................................................................. 8-1/23
ball or ball-marker deflected, lifted or moved
- ball deliberately deflected or stopped by fellow-competitor on putting green ........... 19-1/5
- ball deliberately deflected or stopped by spectator; stroke played from
    putting green .................................................................................................... 19-1/4
- ball in bunker moves when obstruction removed; whether player
    may press ball into sand or take relief outside bunker if not
    possible to replace or place in bunker not nearer hole ........................................ 20-3d/2
- ball in tree dislodged by outside agency ................................................................. 18-1/9
- ball in tree dislodged by player; replacement of ball not possible ............................ 18-2a/29
- ball lifted and dropped away from movable obstruction ......................................... 18-2a/4
- ball moved accidentally by player in playing wrong ball in bunker .......................... 18-2a/21

- ball moved by fellow-competitor's ball; competitor and
  fellow-competitor unaware until after completion of hole ...................... 18-5/3
- ball moved in measuring to determine if re-drop required ......................... 18-6/1
- ball stolen by outside agency from unknown spot ................................ 18-1/5
- ball thrown into bounds by outside agency and played; neither
  player nor caddie aware of action of outside agency ................................... 15/10
- ball-marker moved by opponent's caddie accidentally ............................... 20-1/7
- caddie shared by opponents' side in four-ball match moves player's ball ................. 30/2
- lifting ball to determine whether embedded in own pitch-mark ..................... 25-2/7
- lifting ball to determine whether it lies in burrowing animal hole ................... 25/21
- opponent's caddie lifts player's ball after player claims another ball .................... 18-3b/4
- player lifts ball in mistaken belief that next stroke conceded ......................... 2-4/3
- player's golf cart being pulled by opponent or fellow-competitor
  without player's knowledge deflects ball .................................................. 19-2/6
- spectator deflects or stops ball through the green ................................. 19-1/4.1
- whether lifting opponent's ball-marker considered concession
  of next stroke ................................................................................ 2-4/5
bird's nest interferes with stroke ................................................................ 1-4/9
bunker smoothed after player lifts ball and states intention to proceed
  under Rule 28a ............................................................................ 13-4/35.8
club
- ball adheres to club face after stroke ................................................. 1-4/2
- broken into pieces prior to round discovered in player's bag during round ............. 4-4a/14
- Committee member rules non-conforming club conforms with Rules;
  player uses club ....................................................................... 34-3/1.5
- playing characteristics of club changed while play suspended; error
  discovered before play resumed ...................................................... 4-2/2
- rendered unfit for play by outside agency or opponent's side .................... 4-3/9.5
concession
- opponent's ball in position to assist player; player concedes
  opponent's next stroke and plays before opponent has
  opportunity to lift ball ................................................................. 2-4/8
- player lifts ball in mistaken belief that next stroke conceded ......................... 2-4/3
- player putts out after concession of stroke; act assists partner ..................... 2-4/6
- whether lifting opponent's ball-marker considered concession of next stroke ............. 2-4/5
dangerous situation
- danger from fire-ants .................................................................. 33-8/22
- meaning of term ........................................................................ 1-4/11
- rattlesnake or bees interfere with play ............................................... 1-4/10
determination of honor at next tee following disputed hole ............................ 10-1a/2
divot hole just made affects area of intended stance of another player ...................... 13-2/8.7
divots replaced in area in which ball to be dropped ..................................... 13-2/4.5
dropped ball embeds; procedure if ball again embeds when re-dropped ................... 25-2/2.5
flagstick
- ball overhanging hole moves and strikes flagstick being removed ....................... 16-2/5
- player's ball strikes flagstick deliberately left in hole by opponent
  or fellow-competitor attending flagstick ............................................. 17-3/2
- removed flagstick being held by player subsequently moved ........................ 17-1/8
- stuck into green some distance from hole by practical joker .......................... 1-4/3
gate in boundary fence ........................................................................ 27/18
hazard
- ball dropped from casual water in bunker at point of maximum
  relief rolls elsewhere ................................................................... 25-1b/6
- ball in bunker moves when obstruction removed; whether player
  may press ball into sand or take relief outside bunker if not
  possible to replace or place in bunker not nearer hole .......................... 20-3d/2
- ball lost in either water hazard or casual water overflowing hazard ..................... 1-4/7
- insect flying in water hazard swatted away ........................................ 13-4/16.5
- lie in bunker changed by another player taking stance ............................. 20-3b/2

## Index

**Equity** *(continued)*
- partner's, opponent's or fellow-competitor's divot comes to rest near player's ball in bunker .................................................. 13-4/18
- two balls lie together in hazard and neither identifiable; allowable procedure for players .................................................. 1-4/6

incorrect ruling; whether player should be exempt from penalty and for what duration .................................................. 34-3/1.5

loose impediments affecting lie
- moved when ball lifted through the green .................................................. 23-1/7
- removed while ball lifted through the green .................................................. 23-1/8
- removal of obstruction in hazard would move loose impediment .................................................. 1-4/5

match discontinued by agreement
- cannot be resumed until three days later; one player wishes to play on competition course prior to resumption .................................................. 7-2/10
- on 13th tee cannot be resumed until following day; players wish to play first 12 holes prior to resuming match .................................................. 7-2/11

nearest point of relief from cart path in casual water; nearest point of relief from casual water back on cart path .................................................. 1-4/8

player breaches Rule or Rules either more than once or with different penalties
- advised of breach of Rule; player breaches same Rule prior to stroke .................................................. 1-4/13
- breaches Rules more than once prior to stroke; whether multiple penalties applied .................................................. 1-4/12
- breaches same Rule before and after stroke .................................................. 1-4/14
- breaches two Rules with different penalties; more severe penalty applied .................................................. 1-4/15

player distracted by ball dropped accidentally by another player mis-hits ball .................................................. 1-4/1

player entitled to lie, line of play and stance when ball comes to rest after stroke
- divot hole just made by another player affects player's area of intended stance .................................................. 13-2/8.7
- footprints made in bunker on extension of player's line of play by opponent or fellow-competitor .................................................. 13-2/29.5
- lie or line of play affected by pitch-mark made by another player's ball after player's ball came to rest .................................................. 13-2/8
- lie changed by removal of gallery-control stake .................................................. 20-3b/3
- lie of ball lifted from heel print in bunker altered by another player's stroke .................................................. 20-3b/1
- lie in bunker changed by another player taking stance .................................................. 20-3b/2
- line of putt altered purposely by opponent or fellow-competitor by stepping on it .................................................. 1-2/1
- line of putt damaged accidentally by opponent, fellow-competitor or their caddies .................................................. 16-1a/13
- partner's, opponent's or fellow-competitor's divot comes to rest near player's ball in bunker .................................................. 13-4/18
- player's lie affected by sand from partner's, opponent's, or fellow-competitor's stroke from bunker .................................................. 13-2/8.5
- position of ball worsened when obstruction removed; player replaces obstruction .................................................. 13-2/15.5

player in anger strikes ball played by player in following group .................................................. 1-4/4
player places mark to indicate distance for pitch shot .................................................. 8-2a/3

player advancing in match play disqualified for
- agreeing to waive Rules in earlier match; options for Committee .................................................. 34-1a/1
- wrong score in qualifying round .................................................. 34-1b/8

provisional ball
- not distinguishable from original ball .................................................. 27/11
- player wishing to render original ball lost plays next stroke with provisional ball out of turn .................................................. 27-2b/1
- struck by original ball .................................................. 19-5/5
- when provisional ball holed becomes ball in play .................................................. 27-2b/2

putting green
- ball deliberately deflected or stopped on putting green by fellow-competitor .................................................. 19-1/5
- ball-marker moved by opponent's caddie accidentally .................................................. 20-1/7

Index **I-55**

- ball played from putting green deliberately deflected or stopped
  by spectator .................................................................................................. 19-1/4
- opponent's ball in position to assist player; player concedes
  opponent's next stroke and plays before opponent has
  opportunity to lift ball ................................................................................. 2-4/8
- player lifts and replaces ball then makes several strokes on wrong
  putting green .............................................................................................. 25-3/2
- player lifts ball in mistaken belief next stroke conceded ................................. 2-4/3
- player lifts opponent's ball-marker in mistaken belief he won hole ................. 2-4/5
- player plays away from hole to assist partner .............................................. 30-3f/6
- player putts out after concession of stroke; act assists partner ...................... 2-4/6
- relocating hole when damaged after ball already positioned
  nearby on putting green ............................................................................ 33-2b/2

teeing ground
- ball embeds in own pitch-mark in teeing ground ......................................... 25-2/8
- ball lies in or on movable obstruction within teeing ground .......................... 25-2/8
- competitors estimate area of teeing ground when one tee-marker missing ..... 11-4b/2
- competitors determine spot from which to play when both
  tee-markers missing ................................................................................. 11-4b/3
- determination of honor at next tee following disputed hole .......................... 10-1a/2
time of starting; both players in match late .................................................... 6-3a/3
tree falls onto fairway during stipulated round .............................................. 25/9.5
wrong ball played but hole unknown ............................................................ 15-1/3

## Etiquette

action contrary to spirit of game
- competitor seeks help from fellow-competitor to avoid penalty .................... 33-7/7
- conscious failure to correct opponent's misunderstanding of state of match .. 9-2/12
club thrown, slammed or struck on ground or tree .......................................... 4-3/1
in gesture of sportsmanship, opponent removes loose impediment
  affecting lie of player in hazard ................................................................... 1-2/6
Local Rule for breach of sportsmanship code; whether permitted ............... US/33-8/101
meaning of "serious breach of etiquette" ....................................................... 33-7/8
player refuses to tell opponent number of strokes taken ............................... 9-2/3.5
practice putt made by player before opponent holes out .................................. 30/6
request to attend flagstick declined by opponent or fellow-competitor .......... 17-1/2

## Exchanging Balls

*See also* Substituted Ball
balls inadvertently exchanged
- by competitors at unknown place ............................................................... 15-1/2
- by partners in four-ball Stableford competition ......................................... 32-2b/1
- by players after one ball strikes and moves other ..................................... 15-1/2.5
- by players between holes ........................................................................... 15-1/1
- by players on opposite sides during play of hole and their partners
  pick up; error discovered at next hole ..................................................... 30-3d/3
- competitor lifts his and fellow-competitor's ball; balls exchanged
  when replaced .............................................................................................. 15-2/4
- when recovered from water hazard ........................................................... 15-1/4
competitor plays wrong ball and loses it; wrong ball may have been
  fellow-competitor's ball .............................................................................. 15-3b/1

## Exerting Influence on Ball

*See also* Serious Breach of Rules
ball popped up then swung at in disgust ......................................................... 14/6
ball purposely deflected or stopped
- by fellow-competitor .................................................................................. 19-1/5
- by player; where next stroke played from ................................................. 1-2/5.5
- caddie stops ball before it comes to rest after player drops and it rolls
  toward or into position where re-drop required ...................................... 20-2c/4

**Exerting Influence on Ball** (continued)
- catching ball in hole with one hand after putting with other hand ......................... 1-2/5
- on putting green by spectator .................................................. 19-1/4
- through the green by spectator ................................................ 19-1/4.1

flagstick
- adjusted to more favorable position ........................................... 17/4
- attended without player's authority or knowledge before stroke; attendance ceases upon instruction of player after stroke ..................... 17-2/1
- opponent or fellow-competitor attends flagstick for player; deliberately fails to remove it.......................................................... 17-3/2
- opponent or fellow-competitor removes flagstick without authority while player's ball in motion .......................................... 17-2/2
- opponent or fellow-competitor removes flagstick without authority while player's ball overhangs hole causing it to move ........... 16-2/4
- opponent or fellow-competitor removes obstruction affecting player's play ................................................................. 24/16

flagstick not in hole moved
- attended flagstick removed from hole after stroke; attendant places flagstick on ground then lifts it while ball still in motion .......... 17-1/6
- flagstick held away from hole prior to stroke by opponent or fellow-competitor; moved to prevent ball from striking it ...................... 17-1/8
- flagstick lying on ground prior to stroke; lifted by opponent or fellow-competitor to prevent ball from striking it ............................. 1-2/3
- flagstick lying on ground prior to stroke within reach of opponent or fellow-competitor lifted to prevent ball from striking it ................. 17-1/7

loose impediments
- affecting opponent's lie in hazard removed by player .......................... 1-2/6
- assisting player's play not removed by player or removed by opponent or fellow-competitor ................................................. 23-1/10
- assisting player's play removed by opponent or fellow-competitor then replaced by player ................................................. 23-1/10
- brushed along line of putt rather than to side .............................. 16-1a/10

putting green
- ball mark in position to assist opponent repaired by player.................. 16-1c/2
- ball-marker placed in front of ball .......................................... 20-1/19
- ball overhanging hole knocked away by opponent before player determines status ............................................................... 16-2/2
- ball placed ahead of ball-marker and rolled or slid back to original position .......... 16-1a/17
- ball putted with one hand; caught in hole with other hand ..................... 1-2/5
- ball replaced on putting green while another ball in motion; player re-lifts ball thinking moving ball might strike it ................................. 16-1b/2
- ball replaced on putting green while another ball in motion; replaced ball deflects moving ball ................................................. 16-1b/3
- casting shadow on ball overhanging hole ..................................... 16-2/3
- hole repaired by player after holing out but before opponent, fellow-competitor or partner holes out ..................................... 1-2/3.5
- jumping close to hole when ball overhangs it; ball does not move............ 1-2/3.8
- jumping close to hole when ball overhangs it; ball falls into hole ............ 1-2/4
- line of putt altered purposely by opponent or fellow-competitor by stepping on it ................................................................. 1-2/1
- line of putt damaged accidentally by opponent, fellow-competitor or their caddies ................................................................ 16-1a/13
- line of putt shielded from wind by laying golf bag nearby ...................... 1-2/2
- player knocks partner's putted ball back to him while still in motion after having passed hole ...................................................... 1-2/7
- putter thrown at ball by player after leaving putt short....................... 1-2/4.5
- spike mark damage repaired on player's line of putt by fellow-competitor; player sanctions or tacitly approves repairs ........... 13-2/36

Index  I-57

serious breach of exerting influence
- application of Rule 1-2 disqualification penalty in team competition
   in which not all team members' scores count for each round .................. 33/8
- ball deliberately deflected or stopped on putting green by fellow-competitor............. 19-1/5
- opponent or fellow-competitor attending flagstick for player
   deliberately fails to remove it; ball strikes flagstick ................................... 17-3/2
spinning ball when dropping................................................................................ 20-2a/2
tree branch
- held back by caddie to prevent branch from deflecting dropped ball.................. 20-2a/5
- moved by competitor improving or worsening fellow-competitor's
   line of play while discussing with Committee member whether
   free relief available................................................................................ 1-2/1.5

## Failure to Hole Out

*See also* Holed or Holing Out
ball blown into hole by competitor not replaced and holed out........................... 3-2/2
ball resting against flagstick
- lifted before being holed .................................................................................. 17-4/1
- next stroke conceded and ball removed by opponent before player
   can remove flagstick ................................................................................... 17-4/2
competitor in error does not hole out; error corrected before playing
   from next tee ............................................................................................... 3-2/3
fellow-competitor knocks competitor's ball away from hole "conceding"
   next stroke; ball not holed by competitor .................................................... 3-2/1
intention to play two balls (under Rule 3-3) announced by competitor
- after playing original ball, competitor elects not to play second ball ............. 3-3/7.5
- second ball not holed out ............................................................................... 3-3/8
Local Rule for temporary putting green waives requirement to hole out;
   whether authorized.................................................................................... 33-8/1
modifying disqualification penalty for not holing out in stroke play;
   whether permitted..................................................................................... 33-7/2
player fails to hole out; marker knowingly attests wrong score........................... 1-3/6
putting with one hand and catching ball in hole with other hand...................... 1-2/5
stroke-play play-off
- competitors do not complete play-off hole or holes because one
   competitor disqualified or withdraws......................................................... 33-6/3
- next stroke of competitor "conceded" and ball lifted by fellow-competitor ........... 18-4/3
two balls in play simultaneously at different holes ............................................. 1-1/1

## Fairway and Closely Mown Areas

*See also* Embedded Ball; Through the Green
ball embedded
- in grass bank or face of bunker ....................................................................... 25-2/5
- in ground under repair in closely mown area ................................................. 25-2/4
ball on steep bank driven straight into ground .................................................. 25-2/6
ball stolen by outside agency from unknown spot .............................................. 18-1/5
balls of opponents on opposite sides of fairway; procedure for referee
   in determining ball farther from hole........................................................ 10-1b/1
dropped ball embeds
- in fairway on impact ....................................................................................... 25-2/2
- in fairway on impact; procedure if ball embeds again when re-dropped .......... 25-2/2.5
dropping from rough to fairway in obtaining relief from immovable
   obstruction or abnormal ground condition; whether permitted................ 24-2b/8
internal boundary between holes; whether permitted ....................................... 33-2a/12
lifting ball to determine whether embedded in its own pitch-mark.................. 25-2/7
Local Rule
- allowing free relief for ball in water hazard within limits of
   fairway; whether authorized..................................................................... 33-8/36
- allowing line-of-sight relief from irrigation-control boxes near
   fairways; whether authorized ................................................................... 33-8/17

## Fairway and Closely Mown Areas *(continued)*
- deeming stacked turf bunker faces (whether grass covered or earthen) as not closely mown .................................................. 33-8/39
- establishing procedure for "preferred lies" or "winter rules" ............... App I-B-3b
- granting relief from ground under repair in fairway of 1st hole only during play of that hole; whether authorized ...................... 33-8/23
- permitting relief from intervention by immovable obstructions in closely mown areas near putting greens ............................... App I-B-5
- providing relief from unsurfaced road crossing fairway for tee shot only; whether authorized ................................................... 33-8/20
- providing relief in all cases on fairway side of paved path, or ball drop (dropping zone), when nearest point of relief effectively gives no relief; whether authorized .............................................. 33-8/19
- wrong putting green; deemed to include apron to prohibit dropping on and play from .......................................................................... 33-8/33

pitch-mark in fairway dropping area repaired before ball dropped ............... 13-2/10
player finds ball and hits it to player who lost it .............................................. 7-2/5.5
player's ball deflected by stroke of player in another group .............................. 19-1/2
putting on fairway while waiting to play to green ............................................... 7-2/2
relief taken from obstruction for stroke towards green; same obstruction then interferes with stance for necessary sideways stroke to fairway ............ 24-2b/9.5
status of
- aeration holes and plugs ............................................................................ 23/12
- fallen tree attached to stump .................................................................... 25/9
tree falls onto fairway ....................................................................................... 25/9.5

## Fence
*See also* Boundary Fence, Line, Wall or Stake; Wall
boundary fence
- ball enters burrowing animal hole in bounds near boundary fence and come to rest underground out of bounds; status of ball and procedure for player .................................................................. 25-1b/24
- bowed inside boundary line interferes with lie of ball; whether player entitled to relief ................................................................ 24/4
- club strikes other side of boundary fence to move ball lying against it ................. 14-1/5
- exposed water pipe parallel to boundary effectively gives free relief from boundary fence; suggested solution for Committee ................. 33-2a/1
- gate in boundary fence; whether movable or deemed fixed .................. 27/18
- Local Rule deeming interior boundary fence immovable obstruction; whether permitted ......................................................... 33-8/14
- near player's ball necessitates abnormal stroke; obstruction interferes with abnormal stroke; whether player entitled to relief ................... 24-2b/17
- relief from immovable obstruction incidentally results in relief from boundary fence .......................................................................... 24-2b/6
- swing using half inch backswing used to strike ball lying close to boundary fence ............................................................................ 14-1/4
- whether ball lying inside boundary fence considered out of bounds .......... 27/19
- whether boundary fence leaning away from course must be straightened ........... 33-2a/20
- whether boundary fence leaning toward or onto course may be straightened improving position of ball ......................................... 13-2/18
- whether boundary line may be established inside fence on property line .......... 33-2a/15
Local Rule
- allowing line-of sight relief without penalty from protective fence near line of play ................................................................ 33-8/18
- deeming interior boundary fence immovable obstruction; whether authorized .................................................................................. 33-8/14
measuring club-length(s) through fence; whether permitted ............................ 20-2b/2

Index  I-59

nearest point of relief
- from fence determined for stroke with 4-iron; when dropped,
  ball rolls to position where stroke with 4-iron still has interference
  but stroke with other club player wishes to use does not; whether
  ball must be re-dropped .................................................................................. 20-2c/0.7
- not possible to determine by simulating required address position
  because fence physically prevents player from taking stance;
  recommended procedure to follow ................................................................ 24-2b/3.5
part of fence off course leans across boundary and interferes with player's
  swing; whether player entitled to relief .............................................................. 13-2/20
recommendations for Committee; how to prevent access to
  environmentally-sensitive areas with fencing and warning signs ...................... 33-8/41
removing part of fence improves line of play; whether permitted ............................ 13-2/32.5
status of
- stile attached to boundary fence ...................................................................... 24/1
- angled supports or guy wires supporting boundary fence ............................... 24/2
- concrete bases of boundary fence posts ........................................................... 24/3

## Flagstick

*See also* Putting Green

adjustment of; player's rights ...................................................................................... 17/4
attendant removes flagstick
- holds it upright behind hole with bottom of flagstick touching
  putting green; whether breach of Rule 8-2b ................................................... 17-1/4.5
- knob then falls from top of flagstick and deflects ball ....................................... 17/9
attendant stands behind hole ..................................................................................... 17-1/4
attended or removed by
- opponent or fellow-competitor without authority before stroke;
  attendance ceases on instruction of player after stroke ................................... 17-2/1
- opponent or fellow-competitor without authority while player's
  ball in motion ................................................................................................... 17-2/2
- partner without express authority; ball strikes flagstick or partner ................... 17-3/4
- referee, observer or marker at player's request .................................................. 17-1/3
ball
- at rest kicked away from hole by spectator attending flagstick ........................ 18-1/10
- lodged in flag attached to flagstick ................................................................... 17/6
- moved by flagstick when used for measuring or when accidentally
  dropped on ball ................................................................................................ 18-2a/24
- overhanging hole moves when flagstick removed ............................................ 16-2/4
ball resting against flagstick but not holed
- lifted by opponent after opponent concedes next stroke ................................. 17-4/2
- lifted by player ................................................................................................... 17-4/1
- lifted by player; opponent lifts his ball claiming player loses hole .................. 2-5/3
- lifted by player; others pick up mistakenly believing player won hole ........... 30-3f/3
- moved when flagstick removed by opponent or fellow-competitor ................. 17-4/3
- moved when flagstick removed by player; ball not placed on lip of hole ....... 17-4/4
ball strikes flagstick
- flag struck by ball when flagstick attended ...................................................... 17-3/5
- lying on ground ................................................................................................ 17-3/3
- opponent or fellow-competitor attending flagstick for player fails
  to remove it; player's ball strikes flagstick ........................................................ 17-3/2
- or partner when attended by partner without express authority of player .... 17-3/4
- when ball overhanging hole moves during flagstick removal ......................... 16-2/5
- wrong ruling accepted by players from person not on Committee;
  match played to conclusion based on ruling; whether Committee
  should consider late claim ................................................................................ 2-5/8
caddie while attending flagstick suggests player aim at foot; whether
  breach of any Rule ................................................................................................ 8-2b/2
club used as flagstick to mark position of hole ......................................................... 17-3/6

### Flagstick (continued)

dimensions and attachments
- attachment indicates position of hole on green; whether permitted ......................... 17/1
- different colored flags to indicate position of hole on green;
  whether permitted .......................................................................................... 17/2
- non-circular reflectors on flagsticks aid use of distance measuring
  devices; whether permitted ......................................................................... 17/3.5
- tapered or of varying diameters; whether permitted ......................................... 17/3
- USGA recommendations ............................................................................ US/17/100

holding flagstick with one hand and putting with other hand;
  whether permitted ......................................................................................... 17-1/5

hole-liner pulled out of hole with flagstick
- ball falls into unlined hole ................................................................................. 17/7
- ball strikes hole-liner ......................................................................................... 17/8

holing out without ball touching flagstick in hole; whether possible........................... 17-3/1

Local Rule
- prohibiting removal of flagstick; whether authorized .................................... 33-8/10
- waiving penalty for ball striking unattended flagstick; whether authorized .......... 33-8/11

meaning of "stands near the hole"............................................................................. 17-1/1

moved or lifted when not in hole to prevent ball from striking it
- after stroke, attended flagstick removed from hole, placed on ground
  then lifted while ball still in motion ............................................................. 17-1/6
- removed flagstick lying on putting green when stroke made lifted
  while ball in motion ....................................................................................... 1-2/3
- removed flagstick placed on ground prior to stroke; lifted after stroke made............. 17-1/7
- removed flagstick being held by opponent or fellow-competitor moved
  when ball in motion ...................................................................................... 17-1/8

request to attend flagstick declined by opponent or fellow-competitor..................... 17-1/2

player attending flagstick for opponent struck by ball of opponent's
  partner who played out of turn...................................................................... 30-3f/5

stuck into green some distance from hole by practical joker ..................................... 1-4/3

### Flowers

deeming small area of rare plants close to putting green
  environmentally-sensitive area ..................................................................... 33-8/41
establishing boundary line inside fence on property line to protect flower bed............. 33-2a/15
Local Rule requiring relief under penalty from plantation or nursery;
  whether permitted ....................................................................................... 33-8/29

### Footprint(s)

*See also* Abnormal Ground Conditions; Bunker; Damage; Ground Under Repair; Spike Marks

extensive damage from spectator traffic due to heavy rain and wet
  conditions; Committee options .................................................................... 33-2a/3

in bunker or water hazard
- altered by another player's stroke while player's ball lifted from
  heel print because of interference ............................................................. 20-3b/1
- altered during suspension of play by greenkeeping staff ............................. 6-8d/2
- altered during suspension of play by natural causes .................................... 6-8d/1
- created by another player who just played from bunker; player
  preparing to play from same bunker requests footprints be smoothed ............ 13-4/19
- created by children; whether Local Rule providing relief authorized ....................... 33-8/9
- created during search for ball, smoothed before stroke made from bunker ........ 13-4/11
- created and then smoothed by player on line of play before
  stroke made outside bunker ...................................................................... 13-2/29
- created on line of play by player required to retrieve ball under Rule............... 13-2/29.3
- created on extension of line of play by opponent or fellow-competitor ............ 13-2/29.5
- player's foot stops ball; when foot removed, ball rolls into footprint ..................... 19-2/1
- smoothed after original stance taken when player decides to play
  different type of shot .................................................................................. 13-4/27
- smoothed after stroke played from bunker lost or goes out of
  bounds and before substituted ball dropped in bunker ............................... 13-4/37

Index I-61

- smoothed after ball played out of bunker; ball returns to smoothed area on subsequent stroke .................................................................... 13-4/38
- smoothed by player after playing out of turn in match play; opponent recalls stroke and player must drop ball in smoothed area ............. 13-4/39
- smoothed on line of play before stroke played from outside bunker .................... 13-2/28
- smoothed on line of play before stroke played from outside bunker; whether multiple penalties apply ............................................................... 1-4/12

Local Rule providing relief from damage, including footprints, in bunkers caused by children; whether authorized ............................................... 33-8/9

status of footprint of burrowing animal, reptile or bird ...................................... 25/19.5

## Footwear

condition prohibiting use of metal or traditionally designed spikes ..................... 33-1/14

## Four-Ball Match Play

*See also* Default; Four-Ball Stableford Competition; Four-Ball Stroke Play; Wrong Information

absent partner
- gives advice before joining match ........................................................... 30-3a/2
- joins match during play of hole ............................................................. 30-3a/1
- joins partner in stroke play after fellow-competitor plays from teeing ground but before partner plays ................................................ 31-2/1

advice
- given by absent partner before joining match ........................................... 30-3a/2
- given on request; penalties in various forms of play .................................. 8-1/25

ball of player moved or lifted without authority
- by caddie shared by player and opponent in four-ball match ...................... 30/1
- by caddie of opponents in four-ball match ............................................... 30/2
- by player's partner playing his ball .......................................................... 30-3f/9
- by opponent in four-ball match ............................................................... 30-3f/10

borrowing putter from partner ................................................................. 4-4b/1

breach of Rule by opponent
- discussed between player and opponent; penalty not applied ................... 1-3/4
- disregarded by player; whether permitted ............................................... 2-5/1
- neither players nor opponents aware; penalty not applied ....................... 1-3/5
- procedure for valid claim ...................................................................... 2-5/2

breach of Rule in four-ball match; whether partner assisted
- absent partner joins match during play of hole ........................................ 30-3a/1
- after picking up at hole, player drops ball near partner's ball and plays practice stroke ........................................................................... 30-3f/7
- hitting sand in bunker with club after failing to extricate ball; partner's ball in same bunker ............................................................... 30-3f/2
- loose impediment in bunker lifted by player when his and partner's balls in bunker .................................................................................. 30-3f/1
- player disqualified for next hole plays that hole ....................................... 30-3f/8
- playing away from hole to assist partner ................................................. 30-3f/6
- request to lift ball that might assist partner not honored .......................... 30-3f/11

concurrent four-ball and singles matches
- whether concessions made under various circumstances apply to only four-ball or singles match or both .............................................. 30-3/1
- whether partners may exchange advice on singles match after result of hole or match in four-ball decided .................................................. 30-3/1

determination of honor in four-ball match in which points awarded for both better-ball and aggregate scores ................................................ 30/3

effect of state of match penalties in four-ball match ..................................... 30-3/2

flagstick
- ball resting against flagstick lifted by player and not holed; others in match pick up mistakenly believing player won hole; error then discovered ...................................................................................... 30-3f/3
- partner attends flagstick without express authority of player; ball strikes flagstick or partner ................................................................ 17-3/4
- player attending flagstick for opponent struck with ball played by opponent's partner played out of turn from deep bunker ..................... 30-3f/5

**Four-Ball Match Play** *(continued)*

handicap allowances in four-ball match if player with lowest handicap
   unable to compete .................................................................................................. 30-3a/3
hitting sand in bunker with club after failing to extricate ball;
   partner's ball in same bunker ............................................................................. 30-3f/2
incorrect ruling by Committee places player at serious disadvantage;
   when ruling can be reversed ............................................................................. 34-3/3.3
loose impediment in bunker lifted by player when his and partner's
   balls in bunker .................................................................................................... 30-3f/1
practice
   - after picking up at hole, player drops ball near partner's ball and
     plays practice stroke ....................................................................................... 30-3f/7
   - player practice putts after he and partner have holed out but before
     opponents hole out ............................................................................................ 30/6
   - player practice putts on previous green after partner drives from next tee ............ 30-3f/12
   - when practice between holes permitted .............................................................. 7-2/1
provisional ball; order of play when played other than from teeing ground ................... 10/4
putting green
   - player entitled to putt stands on another player's line of putt ................................ 30-3c/1
   - player knocks partner's putted ball back to him while still in
     motion after having passed hole ....................................................................... 1-2/7
   - player walks off green under mistaken impression partner halved
     hole; player then returns to putt for half ............................................................ 30/4
   - player with putt for half picks up in error at suggestion of opponent
     based on misunderstanding ............................................................................... 30/5
   - putting out after concession of stroke; partner yet to complete hole ...................... 2-4/6
   - ragged edge of hole repaired by player after holing out but before
     opponent(s) or partner holes out ...................................................................... 1-2/3.5
   - touching putting green to point out partner's line for putting;
     player incidentally touches own line of putt ..................................................... 30/2.5
   - waiving turn to putt in four-ball match .............................................................. 30-3c/2
side plays out of turn from tee; opponents require one member of side
   to replay but not other ........................................................................................ 30-1/1
wrong ball
   - player plays partner's ball ................................................................................ 30-3d/1
   - player plays partner's ball; error discovered after opponents
     have played next strokes .................................................................................. 30-3d/3.5
   - player "wins" hole with wrong ball; partner picks up; error
     discovered at next hole ..................................................................................... 30-3d/2
   - players on opposite sides unknowingly exchange balls during
     hole; both their partners pick up; error discovered at next hole ......................... 30-3d/3
wrong information given by player out of contention in four-ball match play ............ 30-3f/4

**Four-Ball Stableford Competition**

*See also* Four-Ball Match Play; Four-Ball Stroke Play
breach of Rule by both partners at same hole .................................................................. 32-2b/1
practice between holes; when permitted .......................................................................... 7-2/1
score card
   - different score card returned when original lost or damaged ............................. 6-6a/7
   - scores of partners transposed at hole but not to side's advantage ....................... 32-2a/1
   - scores of partners transposed at hole to side's advantage ................................... 32-2a/2

**Four-Ball Stroke Play**

*See also* Four-Ball Match Play; Four-Ball Stableford Competition
absent player joins partner after fellow-competitor(s) play from teeing
   ground but before partner plays ......................................................................... 31-2/1
breach of 14-club Rule by partner in stroke play discovered at 8th hole;
   where penalty strokes applied .............................................................................. 4-4a/10
effect of state of match penalties in four-ball stroke play ............................................... 30-3/2

flagstick attended by partner without express authority of player; ball
    strikes flagstick or partner .................................................................................. 17-3/4
loose impediment in bunker lifted by competitor when his and partner's
    balls in bunker ........................................................................................................ 31-8/1
minus or zero net score; whether permitted .............................................................. 2-1/2
order of pay between partners
    - extent to which side may play in order it considers best .............................. 31-5/2
    - partner waives turn to play; circumstances under which he may
        complete hole ................................................................................................. 31-5/1
partner with opportunity for better score leaves green without holing out;
    error corrected before playing from next tee ...................................................... 3-2/3
playing away from hole to assist partner ................................................................. 30-3f/6
ragged edge of hole repaired by player after holing out but before
    fellow-competitor(s) or partner holes out ........................................................ 1-2/3.5
practice
    - after picking up at hole, competitor drops ball near partner's
        ball and plays practice stroke .................................................................... 30-3f/7
    - competitor practices on previous green after partner plays from next tee ............... 30-3f/12
    - when practice between holes permitted ............................................................ 7-2/1
score card
    - different score card returned when original lost or damaged ..................... 6-6a/7
    - gross score of partner with better net score omitted from score card ....... 31-4/1
    - lower gross score attributed to wrong partner on score card .................... 31-7a/2
    - partners' scores transposed at hole but not to side's advantage in
        handicap competition .................................................................................. 32-2a/1
    - score recorded for competitor for hole not completed; partner's
        lower score also recorded ............................................................................ 31-7a/1
wrong handicap used due to Committee misinformation .................................. 33-1/12

## Foursomes

both player and partner drive at same tee in foursome play ............................... 29-1/9
breach of Rule by opponent
    - discussed between player and opponent; penalty not applied ..................... 1-3/4
    - disregarded by player; whether permitted ........................................................ 2-5/1
    - neither players nor opponents aware; penalty not applied ........................... 1-3/5
    - procedure for valid claim ...................................................................................... 2-5/2
changing partners after driving from first tee; whether permitted ....................... 29/1
concession of foursome match decided by play of singles match ...................... 2-4/21
condition of competition designates which foursome partner must play
    from 1st tee; whether permitted ........................................................................ 33-1/3.5
disputes and claims in foursome match
    - procedure for valid claim ...................................................................................... 2-5/2
    - side drives for three holes in wrong order; opponents make claim
        during third hole ........................................................................................... 29-2/2
dropping ball under Rule; which partner must drop ............................................. 29/4
foursome match
    - begun as four-ball match; error discovered at 9th hole ................................. 6-1/1
    - played as four-ball match by agreement of players ...................................... 33-1/4
hitting sand in bunker with club after failing to extricate ball; whether
    side incurs penalty ................................................................................................ 29/5
mixed foursome in which different tees used by men and women; tee
    shot out of bounds ................................................................................................ 29/2
order of play between foursome partners
    - if player accidentally moves ball after address ............................................... 29-1/5
    - if provisional ball played ...................................................................................... 29-1/3
    - if stroke accidentally misses ball ........................................................................ 29-1/6
    - if swing misses ball on purpose ......................................................................... 29-1/7
    - if tee shot out of bounds ..................................................................................... 29/2
    - if tee shot played outside teeing ground in match recalled by opponents ............. 29-1/1

## Foursomes (continued)
- - if tee shot played outside teeing ground in stroke play ............................................. 29-1/2
- - if wrong ball played .................................................................................................. 29-1/8
- - side drives for three holes in wrong order; opponents make claim during third hole ................................................................................................................. 29-2/2

partners' clubs carried in one bag; whether permitted ...................................... 4-4a/4
penalty in "Pinehurst" foursome not related to ball holed out ................................. US/29-1/100
player practice putts on previous green after partner drives from next tee ...................... 29/3
player misses ball
- - accidentally, when making stroke ............................................................................ 29-1/6
- - purposely, so partner would play stroke over water ................................................ 29-1/7

provisional ball in foursome competition
- - order of play when played other than from teeing ground ........................................... 10/4
- - which partner must play provisional ball ................................................................. 29-1/3
- - wrong partner plays provisional ball ........................................................................ 29-1/4

score card
- - different score card returned when original lost or damaged ..................................... 6-6a/7
- - incorrect handicap for partner in foursome stroke-play competition discovered after competition closed .......................................................... 6-2b/2.5
- - individual handicaps of partners not recorded on score card ................................... 6-2b/4

stroke play
- - competitor plays from outside teeing ground in foursome stroke play; partner replays stroke ......................................................................................... 29-1/2
- - order of play in foursome stroke play when wrong ball played ................................ 29-1/8
- - signing of score card in foursome stroke play ............................................................. 29/6

wrong partners drive for both sides in foursome match ........................................... 29-2/1

## Frost
removal of frost or dew
- - from line of putt .................................................................................................... 16-1a/3
- - near ball or on line of play .................................................................................... 13-2/35

## Fruit
ball embedded in fruit; whether free relief available ............................................... 23/10
status of
- - fruit skins ................................................................................................................ 23/4
- - half-eaten pear ...................................................................................................... 23/3

## Gallery-Control Stake, Rope or Line
*See also* Obstructions; Status of Object

interference by line used for gallery-control purposes ......................................... 24-2b/20
lime used to mark lines for gallery-control purposes adheres to ball .................... 21/1
Local Rule deeming lines used for gallery-control purposes ground under repair .................................................................................................. 24-2b/20
removal of
- - gallery-control rope by player worsens position of ball; player replaces rope ....................................................................................... 13-2/15.5
- - gallery-control stake by marshal worsens lie of player's ball ................................ 20-3b/3

## Gate
gate in boundary fence; whether movable or deemed fixed ..................................... 27/18

## Glove
*See also* Equipment; Tape

another caddie or friend carries clubs while player's caddie returns to tee with player's glove .................................................................................. 6-4/4.5
applying adhesive tape to glove; when permitted ................................................... 14-3/8
used as indicating mark struck by ball when dropped under Rule; whether glove equipment ....................................................................... 20-2a/7

Index  I-65

### Golf Cart

*See also* Equipment; Status of Object; Trolley
ball deflected or stopped by
- golf cart shared by two players .................................................................................. 19/1
- player's golf cart being pulled by opponent or fellow-competitor ........................... 19-2/6

ball moved by golf cart shared by two players ............................................................... 18/8

caddie
- breaches transportation condition ............................................................................ 33-1/9.5
- Local Rule clarifying status of person(s) hired by player(s) to drive
    motorized golf cart .................................................................................................... 33-8/4
- player with clubs transported on motorized golf cart hires individual
    to perform all other functions of caddie ................................................................. 6-4/3

club rendered unfit for play when struck by golf cart of opponent,
    fellow-competitor or other outside agency ............................................................. 4-3/9.5

distance meter attached to golf cart; whether artificial device .................................... 14-3/1

excess club declared out of play before round and placed on floor of golf cart ........ 4-4c/1

inoperable motorized cart causes players to discontinue play;
    whether discontinuance permitted .......................................................................... 6-8a/4

Local Rule clarifying status of motorized golf carts and persons driving them ......... 33-8/4

player builds stance by positioning golf cart beneath tree but corrects
    error before playing stroke ....................................................................................... 13-3/5

status of
- carts pulled by double caddie .................................................................................... 6-4/6
- individual who transports player's clubs on motorized golf cart or trolley ............ 6-4/2.5
- person in shared golf cart .......................................................................................... 19/2

used in competition; whether permitted ....................................................................... 33-1/8

### Grass or Turf

*See also* Fairway and Closely Mown Areas; Spike Marks; Testing
ball lies outside ground under repair area; long grass within area
    interferes with swing ................................................................................................. 25-1a/1

ball lying on grass-covered ground within bunker deemed unplayable;
    explanation of relief options .................................................................................... 28/9

ball-marker when placed presses down grass
- changing lie of ball .................................................................................................... 20-1/15.5
- in front of ball on putting green .............................................................................. 20-1/19

ball moves
- after player touches grass behind ball and takes several practice
    swings near ball ......................................................................................................... 18-2a/30
- vertically downward in long grass ............................................................................ 18/1
- when club rested on same grass or heather as ball perched on ............................ 18-2b/6

ball played out of bunker onto grass bank; player hits sand with club; ball
    then rolls back into bunker ...................................................................................... 13-4/35.5

bunker face or bank
- ball embedded in grass bank or face of bunker; whether area
    considered closely mown ......................................................................................... 25-2/5
- Local Rule deeming stacked turf bunker faces (whether grass covered
    or earthen) as not closely mown .............................................................................. 33-8/39

"embedded;" when ball considered embedded in ground ............................................. 25-2/0.5

gallery-control stake removed by marshal without sanction of player;
    turf in front of ball raised ........................................................................................ 20-3b/3

"grounded;" when club considered grounded in grass .................................................... 18-2b/5

line of putt altered purposely by opponent or fellow-competitor by
    pressing down or stepping on raised tuft of grass ................................................. 1-2/1

Local Rule
- deeming grass-covered cable trenches as ground under repair ............................. App I-B-6a
- deeming stacked turf bunker faces (whether grass covered or
    earthen) as not closely mown .................................................................................. 33-8/39

removal of grass adhering to ball; whether permitted .................................................. 21/2

**Grass or Turf** *(continued)*

shadow cast around ball next to hole by player believing grass will
    wilt causing ball to fall into hole ................................................................. 16-2/3
status of
    - grass-covered areas in bunkers ........................................................................ 13/2
    - grass cuttings ................................................................................................... 25/11
    - non-growing plants, including grasses, within area of ground under repair ........... 25/10.9
    - turf raised by underground pipe ....................................................................... 24/14
stone near ball presses down grass when rolled away by player; whether
    breach of any Rule ............................................................................................ 13-2/13
teeing ground
    - breaking off grass behind ball on teeing ground ................................................ 13-2/3
    - player misses tee shot; presses down turf behind ball before next stroke ............ 13-2/2
testing grass to determine whether attached or loose impediment
    - long blade of grass through the green moved to determine if
        attached or loose; whether permitted ......................................................... 13-2/26
    - raised tuft of grass on line of putt brushed to determine if attached
        or loose; whether permitted ......................................................................... 16-1a/11
touching grass with club during practice swing in hazard ........................................ 13-4/4
underground pipe raises turf above it; whether raised turf considered
    part of obstruction ............................................................................................ 24/14

**Greenkeeper and Hole Made by Greenkeeper**

aeration holes; status of ....................................................................................... 25/15
bunker raked by greenkeeper when player's ball lies therein; lie of ball
    or line of play improved ................................................................................... 13-2/4
club rendered unfit for play after struck by greenkeeper's vehicle ........................... 4-3/9.5
fallen tree in process of being removed by greenkeeper; whether
    ground under repair .......................................................................................... 25/7
hole made by greenkeeper
    - aeration holes ................................................................................................. 25/15
    - explanation of "hole made by greenkeeper" in definition of
        ground under repair .................................................................................... 25/14
    - hole of removed stake defining water hazard .................................................... 25/18
    - sunken hole plug .............................................................................................. 25/17
    - two holes on each green of nine-hole course; status of hole not in use .............. 16/7
maintenance vehicle deflects ball out of bounds; substituted ball played
    from spot where original ball deflected ............................................................ 20-7/1
player's lie in bunker altered prior to resumption of play by
    - greenkeeping preparations .............................................................................. 6-8d/2
    - natural causes ................................................................................................. 6-8d/1
rut made by tractor
    - status of ......................................................................................................... 25/16
    - believing Committee might declare rut ground under repair,
        competitor announces intention to play two balls;
        plays original ball before dropping second ball; elects
        not to play second ball ................................................................................ 3-3/7.5
sunken hole plug; status of ................................................................................... 25/17
two holes on each green of nine-hole course; whether permitted;
    status of hole not in use .................................................................................. 16/7

**Grip**

*See also* Club(s)
attachment to grip of club of player with artificial arm ........................................... 14-3/15
binding fingers together with tape to aid in gripping .............................................. 14-3/8
changing clubs because of wet grips ..................................................................... 4-3/5
holding ball in hand against grip when putting ...................................................... 14-3/6

## Ground Under Repair

*See also* Abnormal Ground Conditions; Burrowing Animal, Reptile or Bird; Casual Water; Marking or Defining Course; Reasonable Evidence; Tree or Bush

ball lost
- ball played from area of ground under repair, lost in same area ............................ 25-1c/3
- ball played under Rule for ball lost in ground under repair after
   another ball played under stroke-and-distance procedure ........................................ 15/8
- clarification of point where ball "last entered" ground under
   repair when ball lost in condition ................................................................................ 25-1c/1.5
- in tree in ground under repair ........................................................................................ 25/10
- Local Rule declaring accumulations of leaves (at specified
   holes) through the green as ground under repair ...................................................... 33-8/31
- meaning of "reasonable evidence" ball lost in ground under repair ...................... 25-1c/1
- player proceeds as if ball lost in ground under repair without
   reasonable evidence ........................................................................................................ 25-1c/2
- whether provisional ball becomes ball in play if original ball
   lost in ground under repair ............................................................................................ 27-2c/1.5

ball played from ground under repair then relief taken under
       ground under repair Rule
- original ball abandoned ..................................................................................................... 18-2a/8.5
- original ball retrieved by player ....................................................................................... 18-2a/8

ball thought unfit for play; lifted under relief from ground under
       repair procedure and cleaned; ball then determined unfit for play ....................... 5-3/6

Committee options
- declaring area as ground under repair during competition round ......................... 33-2a/2
- extensive damage due to heavy rain and traffic declared ground
   under repair ........................................................................................................................ 33-2a/3
- referee's authority to declare ground under repair ...................................................... 34-2/1

competitor invokes Rule 3-3 (doubt as to procedure)
- competitor drops one ball in accordance with two different Rules
   instead of playing second ball ......................................................................................... 3-3/11
- competitor drops one ball in accordance with two different Rules
   instead of playing second ball; dropped ball rolls back into
   condition from which relief taken .................................................................................. 3-3/12
- competitor lifts and drops original ball then places second ball
   where original ball lay and plays it ................................................................................. 3-3/13

explanation of "hole made by greenkeeper" in definition of ground under repair............ 25/14

fallen tree
- attached to stump .............................................................................................................. 25/9
- in fairway after play begun ............................................................................................... 25/9.5
- in process of being removed ........................................................................................... 25/7

improving line of play when taking relief from ground under repair ......................... 25-1b/3

interference by ground under repair and some other condition
- ball embedded in ground under repair in closely mown area .................................. 25-2/4
- ball in casual water within ground under repair .......................................................... 25-1b/11
- ball in casual water within ground under repair; whether player
   entitled to take relief from both conditions in single procedure .............................. 25-1b/11.5
- Local Rule deeming ground under repair adjacent to
   artificially-surfaced cart path to have same status as path ....................................... 33-8/25
- obstruction in ground under repair interferes with player's swing ...................... 24-2b/10

Local Rule
- altering ground under repair relief procedure to require player to
   drop behind condition; whether authorized ................................................................ 33-8/26
- declaring accumulations of leaves (at specified holes) through the
   green as ground under repair ......................................................................................... 33-8/31
- declaring severe damage by non-burrowing animals as ground
   under repair ........................................................................................................................ 33-8/32.5
- deeming ground under repair adjacent to artificially-surfaced
   cart path to have same status as path .......................................................................... 33-8/25

**Ground Under Repair** *(continued)*
- deeming hard conical ant hills as ground under repair ................................. 33-8/22
- granting relief from ground under repair in fairway of 1st hole
  only during play of that hole; whether authorized ................................. 33-8/23
- permitting relief from extensive damage to course due to heavy
  rain and traffic ......................................................................................... 33-2a/3
- procedure for dropping and re-dropping on ball drop (dropping
  zone) established by Local Rule ............................................................. 33-8/34
- providing relief from unsurfaced road for tee shot only; whether
  authorized ................................................................................................ 33-8/20

marking environmentally-sensitive area as ground under repair ..................... 33-8/41

material piled for removal
- fallen tree in process of being removed ........................................................ 25/7
- grass cuttings ............................................................................................... 25/11
- pine needles piled for removal interfere with line of play after
  ball dropped away .................................................................................... 25-1b/17

nearest point of relief
- ball dropped from immovable obstruction rolls nearer obstruction
  than nearest point of relief; whether re-drop required if player
  changes clubs and obstruction no longer interferes (also applies
  to similar interference from ground under repair) ................................ 20-2c/0.7
- club used to determine nearest point of relief not used for next stroke ........ 24-2b/4
- determining club, address position direction of play and swing
  used to identify nearest point of relief .................................................... 24-2b/1
- diagram illustrating player unable to determine nearest point of relief ........ 24-2b/3.7
- diagrams illustrating nearest point of relief ................................................ 25-1b/2
- dropped ball rolls nearer obstruction than nearest point of relief;
  whether re-drop necessary if player changes clubs and obstruction
  no longer interferes ................................................................................. 20-2c/0.7
- from cart path in casual water; nearest point of relief from casual
  water back on cart path ........................................................................... 1-4/8
- measuring across ground under repair in obtaining relief ........................... 25-1b/15
- player determines nearest point of relief but physically unable to
  play intended stroke ................................................................................ 24-2b/3
- player does not follow recommended procedure in determining
  nearest point of relief .............................................................................. 24-2b/2
- player takes relief from area of ground under repair; condition
  interferes for stroke with club not used to determine nearest
  point of relief ........................................................................................... 20-2c/0.8
- player unable physically to determine nearest point of relief ....................... 24-2b/3.5
- two equidistant nearest points of relief meet requirements of
  ground under repair Rule ........................................................................ 25-1b/16

order of play when two balls lie in ground under repair and both
  players take relief ........................................................................................... 10/1

play prohibited from area of ground under repair
- ball dropped in ground under repair from which play prohibited
  after being deemed unplayable; ball then dropped under ground
  under repair Rule .................................................................................... 25-1b/14.5
- ball lifted and replaced then player makes several strokes
  from place where not permitted ............................................................. 25-3/2
- stroke played from environmentally-sensitive area marked as
  ground under repair ................................................................................ 33-8/43
- whether player may drop ball into ground under repair from
  which play prohibited .............................................................................. 20-7/3

player enters environmentally-sensitive area marked as ground under
  repair to retrieve ball ..................................................................................... 33-8/42

player entitled to relief from ground under repair lifts ball
- player then replaces ball and plays from original position ........................... 18-2a/12
- chooses not to take relief and wishes to proceed under unplayable
  ball Rule .................................................................................................... 18-2a/12.5

# Index I-69

reasonable evidence ball lost in ground under repair; drop made
    under Rule 25-1c; original ball then found within five minutes ...................... 25-1c/2.5
status of
- aeration holes .................................................................................................. 25/15
- aeration plugs .................................................................................................. 23/12
- ball lost in tree in ground under repair ........................................................... 25/10
- bunker totally under repair ............................................................................. 25/13
- cracks in earth ................................................................................................. 25/12
- fallen tree ........................................................................................................ 23/7
- fallen tree attached to stump ......................................................................... 25/9
- fallen tree in process of being removed ......................................................... 25/7
- grass cuttings .................................................................................................. 25/11
- hole not in use when two holes on each green of nine hole course .............. 16/7
- hole of removed stake defining water hazard ............................................... 25/18
- non-growing plants within area of ground under repair ............................. 25/10.9
- old hole plug sunk or raised on line of putt .................................................. 16-1c/3
- rut made by tractor ......................................................................................... 25/16
- severe damage by non-burrowing animals .................................................. 33-8/32.5
- sunken hole plug ............................................................................................. 25/17
- tree roots outside ground under repair growing from tree inside
    ground under repair ...................................................................................... 25/10.7
- tree stump ....................................................................................................... 25/8
whether player entitled to relief under ground under repair Rule
- ball deemed unplayable and lifted; player then discovers ball
    was in ground under repair .......................................................................... 28/13
- ball in tree in ground under repair ................................................................. 25/10.5
- ball outside ground under repair area but tree within area
    interferes with swing .................................................................................... 25-1a/1
- line of putt damaged accidentally by opponent, fellow-competitor
    or their caddies ............................................................................................. 16-1a/13
- sideways stroke behind tree ........................................................................... 25-1b/22
- tree prevents stroke towards green ............................................................... 25-1b/21
- unreasonable to play stroke due to bush ....................................................... 25-1b/19
- unreasonable to play stroke because of tree ................................................. 25-1b/20
whether re-drop required if ball dropped from ground under repair
    area rolls to position where condition interferes with stance ........................ 20-2c/0.5

## Grounding Club

*See also* Addressing the Ball
"grounded;" when club considered grounded in grass ....................................... 18-2b/5
addressing ball
    - stance taken and clubhead grounded in front of ball; whether
        ball addressed ............................................................................................. 18-2b/5.5
    - when ball addressed by player putting "side-saddle" ................................. 18-2b/5.7
ball moves after
- player addresses it and then steps away ....................................................... 18-2b/7
- player grounds club but before stance completed ....................................... 18-2b/4
- player takes several practice swings near ball and touches grass
    behind ball .................................................................................................... 18-2a/30
- stance taken but before ball addressed ........................................................ 18-2b/1
ball perched on heather moves when club rested on heather ............................ 18-2b/6
ball played from bunker onto grass bank; player hits sand with club;
    ball then rolls back into bunker .................................................................... 13-4/35.5
club grounded outside water hazard while addressing ball in hazard ............... 13-4/29
club touches
- ball in bunker or water hazard accidentally; ball does not move ................ 13-4/12
- bare earth wall of bunker during backswing ............................................... 13-4/34
- bridge in water hazard in addressing ball .................................................... 13-4/30
- casual water in bunker .................................................................................. 13-4/7
- grass in hazard during practice swing ......................................................... 13-4/4

**Grounding Club** *(continued)*
- ground in hazard while probing for ball believed covered by loose impediments .................................................................................................. 12-1/4
- ground in hazard with practice swing causing loose impediments to move; player also improves area of intended swing by bending branch ............................................................................................................. 13-4/28
- ground in hazard with practice swing; stroke played fails to extricate ball; before next stroke club touches ground in hazard with another practice stroke ................................................................ 1-4/14
- ground in hazard with several practice swings ...................................................... 13-4/3
- ground in hazard with several practice swings; player advised of breach then makes several more such swings ........................................ 1-4/13
- leaves in hazard during backswing ........................................................................ 13-4/33
- mound made by burrowing animal in bunker during backswing ..................... 13-4/5
- partially embedded pine needle in bunker during backswing ......................... 13-4/32
- sand in bunker during backswing ......................................................................... 13-4/31
- sand in bunker when ball lies outside bunker ...................................................... 13-4/1
- sand through the green behind ball during backswing .................................... 13-2/9
- sand through the green when ball addressed, pressing it down ..................... 13-2/12
- solidly embedded stone in hazard during backswing ....................................... 13-4/6

hitting sand in bunker with club after failing to extricate ball
- in four-ball match; partner's ball in same bunker ............................................. 30-3f/2
- in foursome match; partner to play next stroke; position of ball not improved ................................................................................................................ 29/5
- in singles play ......................................................................................................... 13-4/35

leaning on club in hazard while waiting to play ................................................. 13-4/2

**Groups and Grouping**

*See also* Time of Starting

competitors determine own groupings; whether permitted ............................... 33-3/3
groupings for stroke-play play-off; guidelines for Committee ............................ 33-3/4
in anger, player strikes ball played by player in following group .................... 1-4/4

play suspended by Committee
- competitor wishes to complete hole; fellow-competitor does not; whether competitor may play alone and complete hole ............................ 6-8b/3
- one competitor in group has played from tee; options for players in group .......... 6-8b/2
- player wishes to practice after scheduled resumption but before group plays ........... 7-2/12

team mates playing as fellow-competitors exchange advice; whether permitted ................. 8-1/22

time of starting
- player late but group unable to play due to delay .......................................... 6-3a/4
- player late but in time to play in correct order ............................................... 6-3a/2

**Halved Hole**

*See also* Concession; Default

advice given by player to opponent putting for half ......................................... 2-2/1

agreement between player and opponent that hole halved
- after match result posted player realizes he won hole thus should have won match; player then makes claim ......................................... 2-5/9
- after second strokes on par 5 hole ...................................................................... 2-1/1.5
- when Rules problem cannot be resolved .......................................................... 2-1/1

ball overhanging hole after stroke for half knocked away by opponent before player determines status ................................................. 16-2/2

believing he won hole, player picks up opponent's ball-marker; opponent's putt was for half; whether picking up ball-marker considered concession .............................................................................................. 2-4/5

determination of honor at next tee following disputed hole .......................... 10-1a/2

incorrect information
- causes opponent mistakenly to think he has putt for half; opponent holes putt and then error discovered ......................................... 9-2/14
- reported by player causes opponent with stroke for half to pick up ball ........... 9-2/6

player walks off green under mistaken impression partner halved
  hole returns and putts for half; whether permitted .................................................. 30/4
four-ball competition
 - player waives turn to putt; later wishes to putt for half ............................................ 30-3c/2
 - player with putt for half picks up based on misunderstanding
  of partner's score following statement by opponent ............................................ 30/5
 - players on opposite sides exchange balls during play of hole and
  their partners pick up; error discovered at next hole ........................................... 30-3d/3
result of match when player dormie and opponent concedes ............................................. 2-3/2
time of starting; both players in match late .................................................................. 6-3a/3

## Handicap Competition and Handicap Strokes
*See also* Claims and Disputes; Close of Competition; Scores and Score Cards
competitor disqualified from handicap event for playing off
  higher handicap; whether eligible for gross prize in same event ...................... 33-1/13
Committee error
 - competitor wins competition with wrong handicap due to
  Committee error; error discovered after close of competition ............................. 6-2b/3
 - misapplication of handicap affects match-play draw; error
  discovered during first round matches; Committee options ................................... 33-5/3
 - player in four-ball match uses wrong handicap due to Committee
  misinformation .................................................................................................. 33-1/12
 - wrong handicap applied by Committee results in player not
  receiving prize; error discovered after close of competition ................................. 33-5/2
 - wrong handicap printed on score card issued by Committee not
  corrected by competitor; error discovered before competition closed ............... 6-2b/3.5
determining honor
 - in handicap match ................................................................................................. 10-1a/1
 - in handicap stroke-play competition ..................................................................... 10-2a/1
 - in handicap Stableford competition ...................................................................... 32-1/3
failure of players to determine handicaps prior to start of match
  results in one player not receiving handicap stroke at hole ................................. 6-2a/1
four-ball handicap competition
 - competitor holes out; partner forgets about handicap stroke, does
  not hole out and does not lift ball-marker; before playing from
  next teeing ground partner remembers handicap stroke, returns
  to green, and holes out ....................................................................................... 3-2/3
 - gross score of partner with better net score not recorded by marker;
  error discovered after score card returned to Committee ..................................... 31-4/1
 - player in match uses wrong handicap due to Committee misinformation ................ 33-1/12
 - player in match with lowest handicap unable to participate;
  handicap allowances to be used ........................................................................ 30-3a/3
foursome handicap competition
 - competitors fail to record individual handicaps on score card
  returned to Committee ......................................................................................... 6-2b/4
 - wrong handicap recorded by competitor for partner;
  error discovered after competition closed .......................................................... 6-2b/2.5
handicap stroke
 - claimed after hole conceded ................................................................................. 6-2a/4
 - competitor holes out; partner forgets about handicap stroke,
  does not hole out and does not lift ball-marker; before playing
  from next teeing ground partner remembers handicap stroke,
  returns to green, and holes out .......................................................................... 3-2/3
 - given at incorrect hole in error ............................................................................. 6-2a/2
 - taken by player at hole by mistake; status of late claim ....................................... 2-5/13
 - wrongly claimed at hole; error discovered before hole completed .................... 6-2a/3
handicap stroke allocation table altered by Committee for matches
  beginning other than at first hole; whether permitted ....................................... 33-4/1
minus or zero net score; whether permitted ................................................................ 2-1/2

Index

**Handicap Competition and Handicap Strokes** *(continued)*
player wins handicap match using posted handicap; Committee
 determines player's handicap too high due to failure to observe
 Equitable Stroke Control; whether Committee should disqualify
 player .................................................................................................... US/6-2a/100
Stableford, Par or Bogey handicap competition
 - determination of honor (Stableford only) ............................................... 32-1/3
 - lower gross score on score card affects result of hole (Stableford only) ................ 32-2a/3
 - lower gross score on score card does not affect result of hole
  (Stableford only) ................................................................................. 32-2a/4
 - lower gross score on score card does not affect result of hole (Par and Bogey) .......... 32-2a/5
 - partner's scores transposed at hole but not to side's advantage ................... 32-2a/1
 - partners' scores transposed at hole to side's advantage ............................... 32-2a/2
wrong handicap
 - applied by Committee results in player not receiving prize;
  error discovered after close of competition ........................................... 33-5/2
 - competitor disqualified for returning score card with higher
  handicap in first round of competition in which best two of
  four scores determines winner; whether competitor disqualified
  for entire competition ......................................................................... 6-2b/5
 - knowingly used by competitor in stroke play; error discovered
  after competition closed ...................................................................... 6-2b/2
 - players use full handicap difference in match because unaware of
  condition providing 3/4 of difference be used; error discovered
  after match result decided ................................................................... 6-2a/6
 - recorded by competitor for partner in foursome stroke play
  competition; error discovered after competition closed .................... 6-2b/2.5
 - printed on score card issued by Committee not corrected by
  competitor; error discovered before competition closed ................... 6-2b/3.5
 - used by player in four-ball match due to Committee misinformation ............. 33-1/12
 - used by player in match by mistake; error discovered after result
  officially announced ............................................................................ 6-2a/5
 - used by player in stroke-play competition by mistake; error
  discovered after competition closed ................................................... 6-2b/1

**Heather**
ball perched on heather moves when club rested on heather .......................... 18-2b/6

**Hole**
*See also* Ball Overhanging Hole; Claims and Disputes; Concession; Flagstick; Holed or Holing Out; Putting Green
ball at rest kicked away from hole by spectator attending flagstick .................. 18-1/10
ball blown into hole by competitor not replaced and holed out ........................ 3-2/2
ball embedded in side of hole
 - all of ball below lip of hole ........................................................................ 16/2
 - all of ball not below lip of hole ................................................................... 16/3
ball knocked away from lip of hole in disgust ................................................... 18-2a/23
ball overhanging hole
 - casting shadow on ball overhanging hole ................................................. 16-2/3
 - falls into hole after being addressed ....................................................... 18-2b/10
 - falls into hole after concession of next stroke ........................................ 2-4/2
 - falls into hole after player waits 40 seconds .......................................... 16-2/1
 - fellow-competitor's ball knocked from lip of hole by competitor
  not replaced ......................................................................................... 3-2/1
 - knocked away by opponent before player determines status .................. 16-2/2
 - lifted, cleaned and replaced; ball then falls into hole ............................ 16-2/0.5
 - player jumps close to hole to cause ball to drop; ball does not move .......... 1-2/3.8
 - player jumps close to hole to cause ball to drop; ball falls into hole ........... 1-2/4
ball resting against flagstick moves away from hole when flagstick
 removed by player; ball not placed on lip of hole ................................. 17-4/4

Index **I-73**

ball rolls into hole after being replaced on putting green...................................................20-3d/1
booklet providing distances to holes from various points......................................................14-3/5
concession
   - ball falls into hole after concession of next stroke .........................................................2-4/2
   - player concedes opponent's next stroke and then knocks opponent's
      ball into hole...................................................................................................................2-4/1
   - player with lost ball concedes hole; ball then found in hole .......................................2-4/11
damaged hole
   - ragged edge repaired by player after holing out but before
      opponent, fellow-competitor or partner holes out...................................................1-2/3.5
   - when repair permitted and procedure for player .......................................................16-1a/6
flagstick attendant stands behind hole...................................................................................17-1/4
hole-liner
   - ball strikes edge of hole-liner and bounces out of hole ..................................................16/5
   - not sunk deep enough; relief available to player.............................................................16/4
   - pulled out with flagstick; ball falls into unlined hole ......................................................17/7
   - pulled out with flagstick; hole-liner deflects ball .............................................................17/8
holes relocated and/or tee-markers moved during stroke-play round .................................33-2b/1
hole surrounded by casual water ...........................................................................................33-2d/2
marking position of hole with club instead of flagstick.........................................................17-3/6
meaning of "stands near the hole"..........................................................................................17-1/1
old hole plug sunk or raised on line of putt..........................................................................16-1c/3
original ball discovered in hole after player searches five minutes
      then continues play with provisional ball ........................................................................1-1/3
player holes short putt; another player alleges ball removed from hole
      before at rest ....................................................................................................................16/5.5
player plays away from hole to assist partner ......................................................................30-3f/6
player putts with one hand and catches ball in hole with other hand..................................1-2/5
position of hole on green indicated by
   - attachment to flagstick ........................................................................................................17/1
   - different colored flags .........................................................................................................17/2
   - flagstick with tapered or varying diameters.....................................................................17/3
   - map of putting green indicating hole location displayed at tee......................................33/6
procedure for Referee in determining ball farther from hole ..............................................10-1b/1
relocating hole when damaged after ball already positioned nearby
      on putting green ..........................................................................................................33-2b/2
removing casual water from hole..........................................................................................16-1a/4
spike mark damage around hole repaired; whether permitted ...........................................16-1c/4
touching inside of hole..........................................................................................................16-1a/5
two holes on each green of nine-hole course ..........................................................................16/7

## Hole Plug

Local Rule permitting repair of turf plugs on putting green not
   4-1/4 inches in diameter......................................................................................................33-8/30
old hole plug sunk or raised on line of putt; relief available to player .........................16-1c/3
spike mark on line of putt pressed down when player repairs old hole
      plug; whether permitted .............................................................................................16-1a/16.5
status of sunken hole plug ........................................................................................................25/17

## Holed and Holing Out

*See also* Failure to Hole Out; Stroke
advice given by player after holing out to opponent with putt for half ..............................2-2/1
ball embedded in side of hole
   - all of ball below lip of hole................................................................................................16/2
   - all of ball not below lip of hole.........................................................................................16/3
ball overhanging hole falls into hole
   - after being addressed ....................................................................................................18-2b/10
   - as flagstick removed from hole .......................................................................................16-2/4
   - striking flagstick while being removed from hole..........................................................16-2/5
ball played under water hazard Rule; original ball then found in hazard
      and holed out as second ball.............................................................................................26-1/5

### Holed and Holing Out (continued)

ball replaced, putted from wrong place and
- holed .................................................................................................................... 20-7c/1
- lifted then putted from right place ......................................................... 20-7c/2

ball still moving in bottom of hole as player removes it; whether ball holed ....... 16/5.5
competitor in error does not hole out; error corrected before playing from next tee .......... 3-2/3
competitor practices putting on 18th green immediately after holing out
    in first round of stroke-play competition played over consecutive
    days; whether practice between rounds ....................................................... 7-2/8
damaged hole repaired after player holes out but before opponent,
    fellow-competitor or partner holes out............................................................ 1-2/3.5
flagstick
- ball holed while flagstick in hole after stroke from putting
    green; player claims ball did not touch flagstick............................ 17-3/1
- ball resting against flagstick lifted before being holed ........................ 17-4/1
- ball resting against flagstick; putt conceded and ball removed
    by opponent before player can remove flagstick ............................. 17-4/2
- player putts with one hand and holes ball while holding
    flagstick with other hand ................................................................... 17-1/5
four-ball match play; player with putt for half picks up in error at
    suggestion of opponent based on misunderstanding............................ 30/5
Local Rule for temporary putting green waives requirement to hole
    out; whether authorized................................................................................. 33-8/1
modifying penalty for not holing out in stroke play............................................. 33-7/2
original ball discovered in hole after
- five-minute search and continuation of play with provisional ball ........................... 1-1/3
- player concedes hole thinking ball lost............................................................. 2-4/11
- player puts another ball into play .................................................................... 1-1/2
- wrong ball played.............................................................................................. 1-1/4
player lifts ball before holing out; opponent then picks up his ball
    claiming player loses hole............................................................................... 2-5/3
player putts with one hand and catches ball in hole with other hand............... 1-2/5
practice putt made by player after he and partner have holed out
    but before opponents hole out ..................................................................... 30/6
stance astride or touching extension of line of putt behind ball used
    inadvertently or to avoid other player's line while holing short putt .............. 16-1e/2
when provisional ball holed becomes ball in play............................................... 27-2b/2
whether ball considered holed
- ball blown into hole by competitor not replaced and holed out .................... 3-2/2
- ball removed from hole while still bouncing in bottom of hole-liner ............. 16/5.5
- hole-liner pulled out with flagstick; ball falls into unlined hole .................... 17/7
- lifted ball replaced on putting green; ball then rolls into hole ..................... 20-3d/1

### Honor

*See also* Order of Play; Playing Out of Turn
determination of honor
- at next tee following disputed hole ............................................................... 10-1a/2
- in four-ball match in which points awarded for both better-ball
    and aggregate scores .................................................................................. 30/3
- in handicap match ........................................................................................... 10-1a/1
- in handicap Stableford competition ............................................................... 32-1/3
- in handicap stroke play .................................................................................. 10-2a/1
- when opponent requires player with honor to cancel stroke
    played from outside teeing ground ........................................................ 11-4a/1

Index    I-75

## Improving Area of Intended Stance or Swing, Position or Lie of Ball, or Line of Play or Putt

*See also* Area of Intended Swing; Lie of Ball Altered; Line of Putt; Line of Play; Stance

area in which ball to be dropped or placed; whether improved by
- removing sand or loose soil ................................................................................ 13-2/11
- repairing pitch-mark ............................................................................................ 13-2/10
- replacing divots .................................................................................................... 13-2/4.5

area of intended swing; whether improved by
- act that also causes ball to move and whether multiple penalties apply ........... 1-4/15
- bending boundary fence ..................................................................................... 13-2/18
- bending shrub with hand .................................................................................... 13-4/28
- breaking branch interfering with backswing on teeing ground ......................... 13-2/14
- breaking branch on backswing; swing discontinued ......................................... 13-2/14.5
- breaking branch; player then chooses different direction of play; new area of intended swing not affected by broken branch ............................ 13-2/24
- knocking down leaves with practice swing ........................................................ 13-2/22
- moving growing or fixed object situated out of bounds ..................................... 13-2/19
- moving loose impediment in hazard accidentally .............................................. 13-4/13
- moving loose impediments by walking to ball and taking stance in hazard ..... 13-4/13.5
- moving natural object to determine whether attached or loose impediment ... 13-2/26
- pushing off-course fence leaning across boundary to upright position ............ 13-2/20
- removing boundary stake ................................................................................... 13-2/17
- removing immovable obstruction ...................................................................... 13-2/15
- removing moss or creepers in tree ..................................................................... 13-2/37
- repairing pitch-mark made by ball on previous stroke ...................................... 13-2/21
- replacing or removing undetached divot interfering with backswing ............... 13-2/5
- shaking water from tree branch interfering with backswing ............................ 13-2/23
- taking stance fairly ............................................................................................. 13-2/1
- taking stance fairly then changing direction of play .......................................... 13-2/1.7

line of play; whether improved by
- creating and then smoothing footprints in bunker on line of play .................... 13-2/29
- mopping up casual water ................................................................................... 13-2/34
- moving interfering growing object in attempting to take stance fairly ............. 13-2/1.1
- moving tree branch affecting fellow-competitor's line of play while discussing with Committee member whether fellow-competitor entitled to free relief ............................................... 1-2/1.5
- pressing down stone in bunker when ball lies through the green .................... 13-2/31
- removing casual water from hole ...................................................................... 16-1a/4
- removing dew or frost ........................................................................................ 13-2/35
- removing part of fence ....................................................................................... 13-2/32.5
- removing stone from wall .................................................................................. 13-2/32
- replacing divot in divot hole .............................................................................. 13-2/6
- replacing divot; when divot replaced ................................................................ 13-2/7
- sanctioning repair of spike mark by fellow-competitor .................................... 13-2/36
- smoothing irregularities in bunker after player lifts ball and states intention to proceed under Rule 28a ....................................................... 13-4/35.8
- smoothing irregularities in bunker when ball lies through the green .............. 13-2/28
- taking relief from abnormal ground condition .................................................. 25-1b/3
- taking stance fairly then changing direction of play ......................................... 13-2/1.7
- testing condition of bunker before deciding whether to play through it ......... 13-2/30

line of putt; whether improved by
- removing casual water from hole ...................................................................... 16-1a/4
- removing dew or frost ........................................................................................ 13-2/35
- sanctioning repair of spike mark by fellow-competitor .................................... 13-2/36
- stepping on; when done purposely by opponent or fellow-competitor ........... 1-2/1
- walking on; when done accidentally or intentionally ....................................... 16-1a/12

lie or position of ball; whether improved by
- alteration through natural causes during suspension of play .......................... 6-8d/1
- alterations made by greenkeeping staff during suspension of play ................. 6-8d/2
- bending boundary fence .................................................................................... 13-2/18

### Improving Area of Intended Stance or Swing, Position or Lie of Ball, or Line of Play or Putt (continued)

- bending grass in removal of loose impediments ............................................................. 13-2/13
- breaking off grass behind ball on teeing ground ................................................................ 13-2/3
- greenkeeping staff member raking bunker when player's ball in bunker ................... 13-2/4
- marking position of ball................................................................................................. 20-1/15.5
- moving loose impediment affecting lie when ball through the green lifted under Rule requiring replacement ........................................................................ 23-1/7
- moving loose impediment in hazard accidentally ......................................................... 13-4/13
- moving loose impediments when approaching ball in hazard ................................. 13-4/13.5
- placing umbrella or rake in hazard ................................................................................... 13-4/20
- pressing down irregularities on teeing ground after missed tee shot prior to next stroke .......................................................................................................... 13-2/2
- pressing down sand behind ball through the green during address ........................ 13-2/12
- probing near ball for tree roots or rocks through the green ....................................... 13-2/27
- removing dew or frost ........................................................................................................ 13-2/35
- removing loose impediment affecting after lifting ball under Rule requiring replacement ....................................................................................................... 23-1/8
- removing loose impediment affecting opponent's lie in hazard ................................... 1-2/6
- removing sand behind ball with backswing ..................................................................... 13-2/9
- replacing obstruction which worsened player's lie when removed ........................ 13-2/15.5
- replacing or removing undetached divot interfering with backswing ......................... 13-2/5
- smoothing irregularities in bunker after stroke but before ball extricated .............. 13-4/36
- taking stance fairly .............................................................................................................. 13-2/1
- taking stance fairly then changing direction of play ................................................... 13-2/1.7
- throwing rake into bunker ................................................................................................ 13-4/21
- touching grass with club during practice swing in hazard ............................................ 13-4/4
- using cane or club to enter or leave bunker when ball lies in bunker .................... 13-4/3.5

stance or area of intended stance; whether improved by
- moving interfering growing object in attempting to take stance fairly ................. 13-2/1.1
- moving loose impediment in hazard accidentally ......................................................... 13-4/13
- moving loose impediments when approaching ball in hazard ................................. 13-4/13.5
- replacing divot just taken by another player ................................................................ 13-2/8.7
- taking stance fairly .............................................................................................................. 13-2/1
- taking stance fairly in any direction player chooses ................................................... 13-2/1.5
- taking stance fairly then changing direction of play ................................................... 13-2/1.7

### Incorrect Information on Rules

*See also* Information as to Strokes Taken; Wrong Information
given by Committee
- correction of incorrect ruling made during subsequent round of competition; whether permitted ........................................................................................ 34-3/1
- non-conforming club ruled conforming; player uses club .......................................... 34-3/1.5
- places player at serious disadvantage ............................................................................ 34-3/3.3
- player proceeds based on incorrect Committee ruling; guidelines for Committee when error discovered ........................................................................ 34-3/3
- player proceeds on Committee ruling based on available facts; subsequent facts prove ruling incorrect ................................................................... 34-3/7
- player proceeds on Committee ruling based on player's version of facts; player's version later found incorrect .......................................................... 34-3/8
- whether player should be exempt from penalty and for what duration ................. 34-3/1.5

given by player; guidelines for Committee when incorrect information given in ignorance and knowingly .................................................................................... 9/1

match play
- incorrect information on penalty applicable to player given by opponent; error discovered after match result announced; player then makes claim ............................................................................................................. 2-5/10
- incorrect procedure agreed to in error by player and opponent; whether valid claim can be made after procedure followed ................................. 2-5/8.5

- ruling made at final hole reversed by referee after players have
    left putting green but before result officially announced ....................... 34-2/5
- ruling made on previous hole reversed by referee after play of
    next hole begun.................................................................................... 34-2/6
- wrong ruling accepted by players from person not on Committee;
    match played to conclusion based on ruling; whether Committee
    should consider late claim ................................................................... 2-5/8

## Indicating Line for Putting

*See also* Improving Area of Intended Stance or Swing, Position or Lie of Ball, or Line of Play or Putt; Indicating Line of Play; Line of Play; Line of Putt; Putting Green
ball-marker in position to assist player in lining up putt ................................. 20-1/11
caddie while attending flagstick suggests player aim at foot; whether
    breach of any Rule ............................................................................... 8-2b/2
condition authorizes team captains to point out line for putting but
    requires they keep off putting greens.................................................. 8-2b/4
line scratched on putting green to mark position of ball .................................. 20-1/16
putting green touched by player in pointing out partner's line for
    putting; player incidentally touches own line of putt; whether
    multiple penalties apply ........................................................................ 30/2.5
shadow cast by caddie to indicate line for putting ............................................ 8-2b/1
trademark aimed along line of putt when ball replaced; whether permitted ............. 20-3a/2

## Indicating Line of Play

*See also* Indicating Line of Putt; Line of Play; Line of Putt
club placed on ground to align feet................................................................. 8-2a/1
object or mark placed
- beside or behind ball to indicate line of play ................................................ 8-2a/2
- indicating distance for pitch shot................................................................. 8-2a/3
putting green touched to indicate line of play before player chips from
    off putting green ................................................................................... 8-2b/3
trademark aimed along line of play when ball replaced under Rule;
    whether permitted ................................................................................ 20-3a/2

## Information as to Strokes Taken

*See also* Wrong Information
"as soon as practicable" in Rule 9-2; meaning of ........................................... 9-2/1
conscious failure to correct opponent's misunderstanding of state of
    match; what constitutes wrong information ..................................... 9-2/12
four-ball match; player with putt for half picks up in error at suggestion
    of opponent based on misunderstanding ........................................... 30/5
incorrect information given
- by competitor in sudden-death play-off....................................................... 9-3/1
- by player's partner or caddie to opponent .................................................. 9-2/2
- voluntarily by player to opponent................................................................ 9-2/3
player concedes match after winning it when opponent lodges invalid
    claim regarding strokes taken ............................................................. 2-4/15
player tells opponent he will proceed under water hazard Rule; changes
    mind after opponent plays .................................................................. 9-2/13
withholding information as to strokes taken
- player refuses to tell opponent number of strokes taken ............................ 9-2/3.5
- until opponent's turn to play ....................................................................... 9-2/4
wrong score for player reported to opponent
- after play of hole; error not corrected; when penalty applicable ............ 9-2/15
- error discovered several holes later ........................................................... 9-2/9
- opponent mistakenly thinks he has putt for half; opponent holes
    putt then error discovered ................................................................... 9-2/14
- opponent with chance for half picks up ..................................................... 9-2/6
- penalty stroke omitted when opponent advised of score for hole;
    error discovered after match conceded by opponent ....................... 9-2/10

## Insects

*See also* Burrowing Animal, Reptile or Bird; Loose Impediments; Status of Object.
after ball addressed on putting green, ball moved during attempt to
    brush insect from it .................................................................................................... 23-1/12
dangerous situation
  - bees interfering with play ............................................................................................. 1-4/10
  - fire-ants interfering with play ..................................................................................... 33-8/22
  - meaning of "dangerous situation" ............................................................................. 1-4/11
discontinuing play due to bee sting .................................................................................. 6-8a/3
Local Rule
  - allowing free relief from damage made by insects ..................................................... 33-8/21
  - deeming hard conical ant hills as ground under repair ............................................. 33-8/22
removal of insect from ball; whether permitted .............................................................. 23-1/5
status of
  - ant hill .............................................................................................................................. 23/5
  - insect flying in water hazard ...................................................................................... 13-4/16.5
  - insect on ball in bunker or water hazard ................................................................... 23-1/5.5
  - spiders (insect-like creatures) and spider webs ........................................................ 23/5.5

## Integral Part of Course

*See also* Fence; Gate; Marking or Defining Course; Obstructions; Wall
Committee
  - exposed water pipe adjacent and parallel to boundary fence; in
    most cases player would be entitled to drop away from fence by
    taking free relief from water pipe; suggested procedure for Committee .......... 33-2a/1
  - immovable obstruction relief incidentally results in relief from
    boundary fence ...................................................................................................... 24-2b/6
  - may declare artificial surfaces and sides of roads and paths integral
    parts of course ...................................................................................................... App I-A-5c
  - responsibility for clarifying status of objects that may be obstructions ............... App I-A-5a
grounding club on construction deemed integral part of course in bunker
    or water hazard .......................................................................................................... 13-4/30
improving line of play by removing stone from wall ........................................................ 13-2/32
incorrect procedure agreed to in error by player and opponent thinking
    road obstruction; whether valid claim can be made after procedure
    followed and opponent discovers road deemed integral part of course .............. 2-5/8.5
status of
  - stile attached to boundary fence ................................................................................ 24/1
  - tree basins ................................................................................................................... 33-2a/10.5
unsure whether road obstruction or integral part of course
  - competitor invokes Rule 3-3; whether score with second ball counts
    if played from wrong place ................................................................................... 3-3/5
  - competitor plays second ball; fails to announce intention to invoke
    Rule 3-3; fails to report facts to Committee ...................................................... 3-3/6.5
window of clubhouse opened and ball played through it .............................................. 24-2b/14

## Leaves

*See also* Pine Needles; Status of Object; Tree or Bush
Local Rule
  - declaring accumulations of leaves (at specified holes) through
    the green as ground under repair ........................................................................ 33-8/31
  - providing relief from accumulations of leaves in bunkers ..................................... 13-4/33
practice swing knocks down leaves ................................................................................... 13-2/22
top of ball covered by leaves in hazard but part of ball visible from
    another angle ............................................................................................................. 12-1/3
touching
  - ground in bunker or water hazard with club while probing for
    ball believed covered by leaves ............................................................................ 12-1/4
  - leaves during backswing for stroke in bunker or water hazard .......................... 13-4/33

## Lie of Ball Altered

*See also* Improving Area of Intended Stance or Swing, Position or Lie of Ball, or Line of Play or Putt

| | |
|---|---|
| act of marking position of ball alters lie | 20-1/15.5 |
| ball stepped on accidentally by player; original lie altered; player places ball in wrong place and plays | 18-2a/21.3 |
| divot made by stroke of partner, opponent or fellow-competitor comes to rest near player's ball in bunker; whether player entitled to relief | 13-4/18 |
| embedded ball in hazard lifted to determine whether unfit for play; procedure if original lie altered | 5-3/5 |
| gallery-control stake removed without sanction of player; lie of ball worsened; procedure for player | 20-3b/3 |
| in bunker | |
| - by stance taken by another player | 20-3b/2 |
| - by stroke made by another player while ball lifted from bunker | 20-3b/1 |
| - prior to resumption of play by greenkeeper | 6-8d/2 |
| - prior to resumption of play by natural causes | 6-8d/1 |
| lie worsened | |
| - obstruction removed by player worsens lie of ball; player replaces obstruction restoring original lie; whether permitted | 13-2/15.5 |
| - lie of ball to be replaced altered and spot where ball originally lay not determinable; procedure player must use | 20-3b/5 |
| loose impediment affecting lie | |
| - moves when player lifts ball through the green under Rule | 23-1/7 |
| - of player in hazard removed by opponent in gesture of sportsmanship | 1-2/6 |
| obstruction removed by player worsens lie of ball; player replaces obstruction restoring original lie; whether permitted | 13-2/15.5 |
| pine cone falls from tree and comes to rest behind ball lying in bunker; whether player entitled to relief | 13-4/18.5 |
| pitch-mark made by ball of partner, opponent or fellow-competitor affects lie of player's ball | 13-2/8 |
| prior to resumption of play by natural causes | 6-8d/1 |
| sand from bunker stroke by partner, opponent, or fellow-competitor affects player's lie on apron next to putting green | 13-2/8.5 |
| wind causes ball on putting green to oscillate; player presses ball into surface of putting green to stop oscillation | 18-2a/6 |

## Lightning

*See also* Dangerous Situations; Discontinuance and Resumption of Play; Rain; Weather Conditions; Wind

| | |
|---|---|
| claiming danger from lightning, player refuses to play when resumption ordered by Committee | 6-8b/5 |
| failure to discontinue play immediately; guidelines for waiving or modifying disqualification penalty when App I-C-5 condition in effect | 6-8b/7 |

## Line of Play

*See also* Improving Area of Intended Stance or Swing, Position or Lie of Ball, or Line of Play or Putt; Indicating Line of Play

| | |
|---|---|
| ball mark partially on and partially off putting green on player's line of play; whether repair permitted | 16-1c/1.5 |
| ball outside bunker; stone in bunker on line of play pressed down or removed | 13-2/31 |
| barn doors opened by player to play shot through barn | 24-2b/15 |
| bending grass in removal of loose impediments | 13-2/13 |
| boundary post on line of play removed by player then replaced before stroke played | 13-2/25 |
| caddie | |
| - inadvertently positioned on extension of line of play behind ball | 14-2/4 |
| - touches putting green to indicate line of play before player chips from off green | 8-2b/3 |
| casual water on putting green intervenes between ball off green and hole | 25-1a/2 |

Index

**Line of Play** *(continued)*

clubhouse window opened by player and ball played through window ............. 24-2b/14
club placed on ground to align feet................................................................................ 8-2a/1
competitor sanctions repair of spike damage on his line of putt by
      fellow-competitor ............................................................................................. 13-2/36
divot replaced in divot hole on line of play ................................................................ 13-2/6
"fairly taking his stance"
    - explanation of "fairly taking his stance" ............................................................. 13-2/1
    - player allowed to play in any direction in "fairly taking his stance" .......... 13-2/1.5
    - player attempts to take stance fairly but improves line of play
      by moving interfering growing object ........................................................ 13-2/1.1
    - player under tree, changes intended direction of play and fairly
      takes stance second time ............................................................................... 13-2/1.7
footprints
    - created and then smoothed in bunker on line of play by player ................ 13-2/29
    - created and then smoothed in bunker on line of play by player
      required to enter bunker to retrieve ball ................................................... 13-2/29.3
    - made in bunker on extension of player's line of play by opponent
      or fellow-competitor ................................................................................... 13-2/29.5
    - player preparing to play from bunker requests another player that
      just played from bunker to smooth his footprints ....................................... 13-4/19
greenkeeper rakes bunker when player's ball lies therein improving lie
      of ball or line of play ............................................................................................ 13-2/4
immovable obstruction on player's line of play removed by outside agency ......... 13-2/33
Local Rule allowing line-of-sight relief from
    - irrigation-control boxes near fairways; whether authorized ........................ 33-8/17
    - protective fence near line of play without penalty ........................................ 33-8/18
mark placed by player to indicate distance for pitch shot ......................................... 8-2a/3
object placed beside or behind ball to indicate line of play ....................................... 8-2a/2
obstruction interferes with abnormal stroke; abnormal stroke reasonable
      in circumstances ............................................................................................ 24-2b/17
pine needles piled for removal interfere with line of play after ball
      dropped away ................................................................................................. 25-1b/17
pitch-mark made by partner's, opponent's or fellow-competitor's
      ball affects player's line of play ......................................................................... 13-2/8
probing near ball for tree roots or rocks; whether permitted ................................ 13-2/27
relief from obstruction interfering with swing incidentally gives
      relief from intervention on line of play ......................................................... 24-2b/7
removal of casual water or loose impediments
    - mopping up casual water on line of play ...................................................... 13-2/34
    - mopping up casual water on line of putt ...................................................... 16-1a/1
    - on putting green by Committee ............................................................................ 33/1
    - removing casual water from hole ................................................................... 16-1a/4
removal of dew or frost .............................................................................................. 13-2/35
smoothing irregularities in bunker
    - after playing backwards out of bunker player smoothes bunker
      on line of play for next stroke ..................................................................... 13-4/37.5
    - situated between ball and hole; ball lies outside bunker ............................. 13-2/28
status of moss or creepers in tree and on ground ..................................................... 13-2/37
testing condition of bunker before deciding whether to play through it .............. 13-2/30
whether line of play improved by
    - creating and then smoothing footprints in bunker on line of play ............ 13-2/29
    - mopping up casual water .................................................................................. 13-2/34
    - moving interfering growing object in attempting to take stance fairly ...... 13-2/1.1
    - pressing down stone in bunker when ball lies through the green ............ 13-2/31
    - removing casual water from hole ................................................................... 16-1a/4
    - removing dew or frost ..................................................................................... 13-2/35
    - removing part of fence ................................................................................. 13-2/32.5
    - removing stone from wall ............................................................................... 13-2/32

- replacing divot in divot hole .................................................................................. 13-2/6
- replacing divot; when divot replaced................................................................... 13-2/7
- sanctioning repair of spike mark by fellow-competitor ............................................. 13-2/36
- smoothing irregularities in bunker after player lifts ball and
  states intention to proceed under Rule 28a ................................................. 13-4/35.8
- smoothing irregularities in bunker when ball lies through the green................. 13-2/28
- taking relief from abnormal ground condition .............................................. 25-1b/3
- taking stance fairly then changing direction of play........................................... 13-2/1.7
- testing condition of bunker before deciding whether to play through it ............ 13-2/30

# Line of Putt

*See also* Hole; Improving Area of Intended Stance or Swing, Position or Lie of Ball, or Line of Play or Putt; Indicating Line for Putting; Putting Green
"line of putt;" illustration and meaning of in context of "standing astride
  or on line of putt"................................................................................. 16-1e/1
ball placed in front of ball-marker and rolled or slid back to original position ................ 16-1a/17
ball mark repaired second time; whether permitted ................................................. 16-1c/1
ball-marker positioned to side or in front of ball; whether permitted .......................... 20-1/19
caddie
  - casts shadow to indicate line for putting ............................................................. 8-2b/1
  - inadvertently positioned on extension of line of putt behind ball ......................... 14-2/4
casual water
  - mopped up or brushed aside from line of putt by player ......................................... 16-1a/1
  - removed from putting green by Committee .................................................... 33/1
  - removed from hole by player .......................................................................... 16-1a/4
  - visible when player walks beside line of putt but not visible elsewhere .................. 25/5
damaged accidentally by opponent, fellow-competitor or their caddies ........................ 16-1a/13
depression in putting green from removed partially embedded acorn
  repaired by player................................................................................ 16-1a/7
dew or frost removed from line of putt .................................................................. 16-1a/3
extension of line of putt behind ball
  - caddie inadvertently positioned on ..................................................................... 14-2/4
  - meaning of "extension of line of putt behind ball" in context
    of standing astride or on line of putt ................................................................. 16-1e/1
  - stood on or astride of inadvertently or to avoid other player's line
    while holing short putt .................................................................................... 16-1e/2
flagstick attendant stands behind instead of beside hole; whether permitted............... 17-1/4
hole
  - damaged; when repair permitted and procedure for player......................................16-1a/6
  - inside of hole touched; whether line of putt touched ................................................ 16-1a/5
  - ragged edge repaired by player after holing out but before
    opponent, fellow-competitor or partner holes out................................................... 1-2/3.5
loose impediment(s)
  - brushed along line of putt then to side ....................................................... 16-1a/10
  - palm of hand used to brush line of putt about one dozen
    times to remove small leaves ................................................................ 16-1a/9
  - removed from putting green by Committee................................................................. 33/1
  - cap or towel used to remove loose impediments from line of putt.............................. 16-1a/8
mushroom growing on line of putt................................................................................16-1a/15
old hole plug sunken or raised on line of putt........................................................... 16-1c/3
opponent's next stroke conceded; player knocks ball away along
  own line of putt ........................................................................................ 16-1d/2
player entitled to putt stands on another player's line of putt ........................................ 30-3c/1
player touches putting green to point out partner's line for
  putting and incidentally touches own line of putt; whether
  multiple penalties apply ............................................................................. 30/2.5
shielding line of putt from wind; whether permitted ......................................... 1-2/2

## Line of Putt (continued)
spike mark
- competitor sanctions or tacitly approves repair of spike damage on his line of putt by fellow-competitor .................. 13-2/36
- on line of putt pressed down when player repairs old hole plug ............ 16-1a/16.5
- on line of putt repaired during repair of ball mark ................. 16-1a/16
- player and opponent or fellow-competitor agree to repair spike marks on one another's line of putt .......................... 1-3/3
- raised tuft of grass on line of putt brushed or tested to determine whether loose ................................... 16-1a/11

status of worm partially underground ................. 23/8
trademark on ball aimed along line of putt when ball replaced ............. 20-3a/2
walking on line of putt
- accidentally by player ................................ 16-1a/12
- accidentally by opponent, fellow-competitor or their caddies and damaged .................................. 16-1a/13
- intentionally by player ............................. 16-1a/12
- purposely and altered by opponent or fellow-competitor .................. 1-2/1

whether line of putt improved by
- removing casual water from hole ......................... 16-1a/4
- removing dew or frost .................................. 13-2/35
- sanctioning repair of spike mark by fellow-competitor ............ 13-2/36
- stepping on; when done purposely by opponent or fellow-competitor ........... 1-2/1
- walking on; when done accidentally or intentionally .................. 16-1a/12

## Local Rules
*See also* Conditions of Competition
abnormal ground conditions
- allowing free relief from damage made by insects ............ 33-8/21
- allowing relief through the green for ball embedded in own pitch-mark; specimen Local Rule ............ App I-B-3a
- altering ground under repair relief procedure to require player to drop behind condition; whether authorized ............ 33-8/26
- declaring areas of course as ground under repair from which play prohibited and relief must be taken; specimen Local Rule .......... App I-B-1a
- declaring severe damage by non-burrowing animals as ground under repair .................................. 33-8/32.5
- declaring temporary accumulations of leaves (at specified holes) through the green as ground under repair ............ 33-8/31
- declaring temporary accumulations of leaves in bunkers ground under repair .................................. 13-4/33
- declaring unsurfaced road ground under repair for tee shot only; whether authorized ............................. 33-8/20
- deeming fire-ant mounds or hills ground under repair ............ 33-8/22
- deeming ground under repair adjacent to artificially-surfaced cart path to have same status as path ............ 33-8/25
- deeming hard conical ant hills as ground under repair ............ 33-8/22
- deeming lines used for gallery-control purposes ground under repair ............ 24-2b/20
- deeming mushrooms growing on line of putt as ground under repair ............ 16-1a/15
- granting relief from ground under repair in fairway of 1st hole only during play of that hole; whether authorized ............ 33-8/23
- "preferred lies" or "winter rules;" specimen Local Rule ............ App I-B-3b
- providing relief from exposed tree roots without penalty; whether authorized ............................. 33-8/8
- providing relief from flooded bunker without penalty outside bunker; whether authorized ............ 33-8/27
- requiring player to take relief under penalty from tree nursery (or plantation) from which play prohibited; whether authorized ............ 33-8/29
- requiring relief away from young trees to prevent damage; specimen Local Rule ............ App I-B-2

Index  I-83

bad weather; permitting competitors to discontinue play by
   agreement; whether authorized ............................................................... 33-8/5
ball drop (dropping zone)
 - for island putting green ............................................................................... 33-2a/10
 - for part of lateral water hazard where impossible to drop not nearer hole ............... 33-2a/9
 - for relief from area containing young trees ............................................. 33-8/26
 - for relief from lateral water hazard with bunker adjacent ...................... US/33-8/100
 - procedure for dropping and re-dropping when ball drop
   (dropping zone) established by Local Rule............................................... 33-8/34
 - providing relief from paved path in all cases to ball drop
   (dropping zone) when nearest point of relief effectively gives
   no relief; whether authorized ................................................................... 33-8/19
 - when protective fence intervenes on line of play..................................... 33-8/18
bunker
 - damaged by children; allowing drop outside bunker or
   smoothing of sand without penalty; whether authorized ...................... 33-8/9
 - deeming material similar to sand to have same status as sand............... 33-8/40
 - deeming stacked turf bunker faces (whether grass covered or
   earthen) as not closely mown .................................................................. 33-8/39
 - establishing ball drop (dropping zone) through the green for
   relief from lateral water hazard with bunker adjacent........................... US/33-8/100
 - permitting re-dropping or placing when dropped ball embeds
   in bunker; whether authorized ................................................................ 33-8/28
 - totally under repair; options for Committee ............................................ 25/13
cleaning ball in specified areas of course other than putting green;
   specimen Local Rule ................................................................................... App I-B-3a
distance measuring devices; permitting use.................................................. 14-3/0.5
doubt as to rights or procedure in match play, allowing play of
   second ball; whether authorized ............................................................... 33-8/3
environmentally-sensitive areas; specimen Local Rule clarifying
   relief procedures......................................................................................... App I-B-1b
establishing sportsmanship code................................................................... US/33-8/101
flagstick
 - prohibiting removal of flagstick; whether authorized ............................. 33-8/10
 - waiving penalty for ball striking unattended flagstick; whether
   authorized ................................................................................................... 33-8/11
free relief procedure agreed to in error by player and opponent
   thinking road obstruction; whether valid claim can be made
   after procedure followed and opponent discovers road deemed
   integral part of course by Local Rule....................................................... 2-5/8.5
incorrect information about Local Rule given by Committee member;
   whether player should be exempt from penalty and for what duration .......... 34-3/1.5
motorized golf carts and persons appointed to drive them; clarifying status ................ 33-8/4
obstructions
 - allowing free relief from immovable water hazard stake for ball
   lying in water hazard; whether authorized ............................................. 33-8/15
 - allowing line of play relief without penalty from intervention
   by immovable obstruction within two club-lengths of putting
   green; specimen Local Rule ..................................................................... App I-B-5
 - allowing line-of-sight relief from irrigation-control boxes near
   fairways; whether authorized .................................................................. 33-8/17
 - allowing line-of-sight relief without penalty from protective
   fence near line of play ............................................................................. 33-8/18
 - allowing replay of stroke without penalty when sprinkler head
   deflects ball; whether authorized ............................................................ 33-8/12
 - deeming all stakes on course (except boundary stakes) immovable
   obstructions ............................................................................................... 33-8/16
 - deeming boundary stakes having no significance in play of hole
   being played as immovable obstructions ............................................... 24/5
 - deeming ground under repair adjacent to artificially-surfaced cart
   path to have same status as path ............................................................ 33-8/25

## Local Rules (continued)

- deeming interior boundary fence immovable obstruction; whether authorized ............................................................................................................ 33-8/14
- deeming stones in bunkers movable obstructions; specimen Local Rule ................ App I-B-4
- providing relief from temporary immovable obstructions; specimen Local Rule ........................................................................................................... App I-B-6a
- providing relief from temporary power lines and cables; specimen Local Rule ........................................................................................................... App I-B-6b
- providing relief from unsurfaced road for tee shot only; whether authorized ............................................................................................................ 33-8/20
- providing relief in all cases on fairway side of paved path, or ball drop (dropping zone), when nearest point of relief effectively gives no relief; whether authorized ................................................................... 33-8/19

out of bounds
- deeming area of adjoining hole out of bounds for play of particular hole but not for play of other holes .................................................................... 33-2a/14
- deeming area of adjoining hole out of bounds for stroke played from teeing ground only; whether authorized ................................................... 33-2a/14
- deeming area surrounding teeing ground in bounds for tee shot and out of bounds thereafter; whether authorized ........................................... 33-2a/13
- deeming ball in bounds until beyond boundary wall ...................................... 33-2a/16
- deeming ball out of bounds that crosses public road defined as out of bounds even though it may lie on another part of course ...................... 27/20
- deeming boundary stakes having no significance in play of hole being played as immovable obstructions ........................................................... 24/5
- deeming interior boundary fence immovable obstruction; whether authorized ............................................................................................................ 33-8/14
- to prevent cutting across "dog-leg;" deeming ball out of bounds that crosses boundary even if it recrosses boundary and comes to rest on same part of course; whether authorized ...................................................... 33-8/38

power line, tower or pole deflects ball; requiring cancelation and replay of stroke without penalty ..................................................................................... 33-8/13

"preferred lies" or "winter rules;" specimen Local Rule ............................................... App I-B-3b

putting green
- allowing relief from edging grooves around putting green ............................... 33-8/24
- deeming mushrooms growing on line of putt as ground under repair ............ 16-1a/15
- permitting repair of turf plugs on putting green not 4-1/4 inches in diameter ........................................................................................................... 33-8/30
- requiring players to putt continuously on putting green until ball holed; whether authorized ....................................................................... 33-8/7
- waiving requirement to hole out when temporary putting green used; whether authorized ............................................................................ 33-8/1

temporary power lines and cables; specimen Local Rule ............................................ App I-B-6b

water hazards
- allowing drop on green side of water hazard when ball fails to clear hazard; whether authorized ........................................................................... 33-8/2
- allowing drop opposite to spot where ball comes to rest in lateral water hazard; whether authorized .................................................................. 26-1/20
- allowing drop within water hazard behind point where ball lies unplayable in same hazard; whether authorized ........................................ 33-8/37
- allowing free relief for ball in water hazard; whether authorized ................... 33-8/36
- allowing free relief from immovable water hazard stake for ball lying in water hazard; whether authorized ..................................................... 33-8/15
- deeming body of water as both water hazard and lateral water hazard ........... 33-2a/7
- deeming body of water as water hazard from back tee and lateral water hazard from forward tee .................................................................. 33-2a/6
- defining areas not meeting definition of lateral water hazard, such as rough and unplayable areas adjacent to fairways, as lateral water hazard; whether authorized .................................................... 33-8/35
- establishing ball drop (dropping zone) for island putting green ..................... 33-2a/10

- establishing ball drop (dropping zone) for part of lateral water
   hazard where impossible to drop not nearer hole .................................................. 33-2a/9
- establishing ball drop (dropping zone) through the green for
   relief from lateral water hazard with bunker adjacent.............................. US/33-8/100
wrong putting green; deemed to include apron to prohibit dropping
   on and play from........................................................................................................ 33-8/33

## Loose Impediments

*See also* Status of Object
affecting lie
- moved when ball lifted through the green .................................................... 23-1/7
- removed while ball lifted through the green ................................................. 23-1/8
- of opponent in hazard removed by player in gesture of sportsmanship..................... 1-2/6
assistance in removing large loose impediment ..................................................... 23-1/3
ball through the green moves after removal of nearby loose impediment..................... 18-2a/30.5
ball touched
- accidentally in removing loose impediments .............................................. 18-2a/31
- with fir cone or stick to prevent movement when loose
   impediments removed ...................................................................................... 18-2a/32
bending grass in removal of loose impediments ..................................................... 13-2/13
breaking off part of large loose impediment ............................................................ 23-1/4
bunker or water hazard
- accidentally moving loose impediment in hazard........................................ 13-4/13
- ball in hazard moves after loose impediment outside hazard moved .................... 18-2a/5
- ball in hazard moves when loose impediment removed ............................ 13-4/15
- ball outside bunker; stone in bunker on line of play pressed
   down or removed................................................................................................ 13-2/31
- bunker covered by leaves; player touches leaves during backswing........................ 13-4/33
- club touches partially embedded pine needle on backswing in bunker................ 13-4/32
- competitor lifts loose impediment in bunker when his ball and
   partner's ball in bunker ........................................................................................ 31-8/1
- ground in hazard touched with club while probing for ball
   believed covered by loose impediments ........................................................... 12-1/4
- grounding club, moving loose impediments and improving
   area of intended swing in hazard..................................................................... 13-4/28
- insect on ball in bunker ............................................................................... 23-1/5.5
- loose impediment in water hazard partially covering wrong ball removed................ 13-4/16
- loose impediments removed from water hazard; player then
   decides not to play from hazard .......................................................................... 13-4/17
- pine cone falls from tree and comes to rest behind ball lying in bunker................ 13-4/18.5
- player accidentally kicks pine cone into bunker and picks it up ........................... 13-4/14
- player deems ball unplayable in bunker; lifts ball and then
   removes loose impediment from bunker ........................................................ 13-4/35.7
- player lifts loose impediment in bunker when his ball
   and partner's ball in bunker ............................................................................... 30-3f/1
- player moves loose impediments when approaching ball in hazard ................. 13-4/13.5
- player removes loose impediment affecting opponent's lie in hazard..................... 1-2/6
- removal of obstruction in hazard would move loose impediment ............................. 1-4/5
competitor seeks help from fellow-competitor to move loose
   impediment to avoid penalty............................................................................. 33-7/7
intervene between embedded ball and ground (criteria for being embedded).................... 25-2/0.5
meaning of "solidly embedded" in definition of loose impediments .......................... 23/2
means by which loose impediments may be removed ........................................... 23-1/1
natural object interfering with swing moved to determine whether loose ................... 13-2/26
putting green
- after ball addressed on putting green, ball moved in attempting
   to brush insect from it........................................................................................ 23-1/12
- ball moved accidentally by foot during removal of loose
   impediment on putting green............................................................................ 23-1/11
- ball-marker moved accidentally by player after having moved
   loose impediments ............................................................................................. 20-1/12

### Loose Impediments (continued)

- brushing loose impediments along line of putt rather than to side .................. 16-1a/10
- brushing loose impediments off line of putt with palm of hand ........................ 16-1a/9
- player repairs depression on line of putt created when
  partially embedded acorn removed ............................................................ 16-1a/7
- raised tuft of grass on line of putt brushed to determine whether loose ................. 16-1a/11
- removal of casual water or loose impediments on putting
  green by Committee ........................................................................................ 33/1
- removing loose impediment from line of putt with cap or towel ........................... 16-1a/8

removing
- loose impediment lying out of bounds ................................................................ 23-1/9
- loose impediments affecting player's play by opponent or fellow-competitor ........... 23-1/10
- loose impediments from area in which ball to be dropped ..................................... 23-1/6
- loose impediments from spot on which ball to be placed ....................................... 23-1/6.5
- sand or loose soil from dropping area ................................................................. 13-2/11

status of
- aeration plugs ................................................................................................ 23/12
- ant hill ........................................................................................................... 23/5
- ball embedded in fruit ..................................................................................... 23/10
- bird's nest ....................................................................................................... 1-4/9
- clod of earth .................................................................................................... 23/13
- dead land crab ................................................................................................ 23/6
- dew or frost on line of putt .............................................................................. 16-1a/3
- dew or frost other than on line of putt .............................................................. 13-2/35
- divot partially attached and folded over ............................................................ 13-2/5
- embedded acorn ............................................................................................. 23/9
- fallen tree ...................................................................................................... 23/7
- finely crushed shells ...................................................................................... 33-8/40
- fruit skins ...................................................................................................... 23/4
- grass adhering to ball ..................................................................................... 21/2
- grass cuttings ................................................................................................. 25/11
- gravel used to surface road or path .................................................................. 23/14
- half-eaten pear ............................................................................................... 23/3
- insect flying in water hazard .......................................................................... 13-4/16.5
- insect on ball ................................................................................................. 23-1/5
- insect on ball in bunker .................................................................................. 23-1/5.5
- insect-like creatures ....................................................................................... 23/5.5
- large stone removable only with much effort .................................................... 23-1/2
- lava dust ........................................................................................................ 33-8/40
- loose soil remaining when molehill swept flat ................................................. 23/11
- moss or creepers in tree and on ground ........................................................... 13-2/37
- pine needle partially embedded ....................................................................... 13-4/32
- pine needles piled for removal ........................................................................ 25-1b/17
- saliva ............................................................................................................. 25/6
- snake, alive and dead ..................................................................................... 23/6.5
- solidly or partially embedded stone ................................................................. 23/2
- spiders and spider webs ................................................................................. 23/5.5
- worm partially underground ........................................................................... 23/8

when loose impediment transformed into obstruction ............................................. 23/1

### Lost Ball

*See also* Provisional Ball; Reasonable Evidence; Searching For and Identifying Ball

ball dropped and played under ground under repair Rule in absence
  of reasonable evidence original ball lost in ground under repair .................... 25-1c/2
ball dropped where original ball lost; ball then played ......................................... 27-1/3

ball lost
- either water hazard or casual water overflowing hazard ................................. 1-4/7
- in tree in ground under repair ....................................................................... 25/10
- in underground drainpipe .............................................................................. 24-3b/1

ball played from bunker goes out of bounds or lost; player tests condition of bunker or smoothes footprints before dropping another ball in bunker ..................................................................... 13-4/37
ball played from ground under repair abandoned and relief taken under ground under repair Rule ................................................... 18-2a/8.5
ball played in ground under repair area lost in same area ................... 25-1c/3
ball played out of turn from tee abandoned and another ball played in proper order ............................................................................... 10-2c/1
ball played under Rule for ball lost in ground under repair after another ball played under stroke-and-distance procedure ............. 15/8
ball visible from tee disappears or moved by outside agency while play suspended ..................................................................................... 6-8d/4
identifying ball by brand and number only ............................................... 12-2/1
meaning of "reasonable evidence" in Rule 26-1 ....................................... 26-1/1
original ball found
 - after more than five-minute search; ball then played ....................... 27/8
 - and played after another ball put into play ......................................... 15/5
 - ball assumed in water hazard found outside hazard after another ball played under stroke-and-distance procedure .............................. 26/6
 - ball believed lost in bunker; competitor drops and plays substituted ball in bunker; then original ball found outside bunker ................ 20-7c/3
 - ball in tree identified but not retrieved ............................................... 27/14
 - ball played under water hazard Rule; original ball then found outside hazard ......................................................................................... 26-1/3
 - ball thought lost found before another ball put into play ............... 27/16
 - found in burrowing animal hole after five-minute search ............... 27/7
 - identification of ball through testimony of spectator ...................... 27/12
 - member of Committee finds player's original ball; player prefers to continue with provisional ball ............................................................. 27-2/2
 - original ball beyond provisional ball; player searches briefly for original ball, plays provisional ball and then finds original ball ..... 27-2b/3
 - original ball played after provisional ball played from point nearer hole than original ball likely to be ..................................................... 27-2b/5
 - player abandons original ball and walks forward to play provisional ball; original ball then found .................................................................. 27-2b/6
 - player discovers original ball in hole after searching five minutes and then continuing play with provisional ball ............................... 1-1/3
 - player unable to distinguish his ball from another ball .................... 27/10
 - player wishes to ignore original ball and continue play with provisional ball ........... 27-2c/2
 - player with lost ball concedes hole; ball then found in hole ............ 2-4/11
 - provisional ball played from beyond where original ball likely to be but not beyond where original ball found ......................................... 27-2b/4
 - provisional ball played in erroneous belief it is original ball .......... 27-2b/7
 - status of original ball if another ball played under stroke-and-distance procedure ......................................................... 27/17
 - time permitted for search when lost ball found and then lost again .......... 27/3
 - within five-minute search period after substituted ball dropped at spot of previous stroke ................................................................................ 27-1/2
 - within five-minute search period after substituted ball dropped; original ball played ............................................................................... 27-1/2.3
 - within five-minute search period after substituted ball teed but not played ............. 27-1/1
 - within five-minute search period not identified until after period elapses ............... 27/5.5
 - wrong ball deemed unplayable played under stroke-and-distance procedure; original ball then found ................................................... 28/14
player plays wrong ball and loses it; may have been fellow-competitor's ball .............. 15-3b/1
player unable to find his ball because another player has played it ................... 27/6

## Lost Ball *(continued)*

provisional ball
- announcement requirements .................................................................... 27-2a/1
- continuation of play with provisional ball without searching for
  original ball ............................................................................................ 27-2b/1
- member of Committee finds player's original ball; player prefers
  to continue with provisional ball ........................................................... 27-2/2
- not distinguishable from original ball .......................................................... 27/11
- order of play when played other than from teeing ground ......................... 10/4
- original ball beyond provisional ball; player searches briefly for
  original ball, plays provisional ball and then finds original ball .......... 27-2b/3
- original ball played after provisional ball played from point nearer
  hole than original ball likely to be ....................................................... 27-2b/5
- play of provisional ball in absence of reasonable possibility original
  ball lost or out of bounds ..................................................................... 27-2a/3
- played from beyond where original ball likely to be but not beyond
  where original ball found ..................................................................... 27-2b/4
- played in erroneous belief it is original ball ............................................. 27-2b/7
- played solely in belief original ball might be in water hazard ................. 27-2a/2
- player abandons original ball and walks forward to play provisional
  ball; original ball then found ............................................................... 27-2b/6
- player discovers original ball in hole after searching five minutes
  and then continuing play with provisional ball ....................................... 1-1/3
- player plays provisional ball in belief original might be lost outside
  water hazard; then determines no possibility ball lost outside
  water hazard ......................................................................................27-2a/2.5
- player wishes to ignore original ball and continue play with provisional ball ......... 27-2c/2
- possibility that original ball in water hazard may not preclude
  play of provisional ball ......................................................................... 27-2c/1
- possibly lost or out of bounds; third ball played with no announcement ........... 27-2a/4
- time permitted for search for original ball and provisional ball ................... 27/4
- whether provisional ball becomes ball in play if original ball lost
  in ground under repair .......................................................................27-2c/1.5
re-drop required when proceeding under lost ball Rule; whether
  player may substitute when re-dropping ..................................................... 20-6/4
searching
- after putting another ball into play ............................................................... 27/9
- ball covered by sand in bunker removed from buried lie during search ......... 12-1/2
- Committee intervention in match play when search exceeds
  five minutes ...................................................................................... US/34-3/101
- electronic instrument used to search for ball ............................................ 14-3/14
- for ball for ten minutes ................................................................................ 6-7/2
- player directs caddie not to search for ball until others can assist ............... 27/1
- player searching for ball mistakes his ball for opponent's then
  discovers mistake after five-minute search period ................................. 27/5
- smoothing footprints made in search for ball in bunker before
  playing stroke from bunker ................................................................ 13-4/11
- time permitted for search after wrong ball played ....................................... 27/2
- time permitted for search for original ball and provisional ball ................. 27/4
- time permitted for search if play suspended during search .................... 27/1.5
- with clubhead for ball covered by sand in bunker ..................................... 12-1/1
treating lost ball as moved by outside agency
- in absence of reasonable evidence to that effect ..................................27-1/2.5
- rather than lost ........................................................................................... 18-1/1
unidentifiable ball played in water hazard and lost ............................................. 26/5
whether player entitled to ascertain whereabouts of opponent's ball
  that may be lost before playing ............................................................... 9-2/16

# Index    I-89

**Man-Made Reservoir**
whether considered water hazard .................................................................................. 26/4

**Marker**
*See also* Ball-Marker; Scores and Score Cards
appointment of marker
- lone competitor appoints own marker when Committee fails to do so ................. 6-6a/1
- retroactive appointment of marker by Committee ........................................ 33-1/5
competitor plays several holes without marker ............................................... 6-6a/2
competitor withdraws during round; continues as fellow-competitor's marker
    and caddies for him for remainder of round; whether permitted ......................... 6-4/9
flagstick attended by marker at player's request; whether permitted ...................... 17-1/3
hole scores
- entered in wrong boxes; marker corrects error by altering hole numbers
   on score card ........................................................................................ 6-6a/3
- for first nine holes recorded in boxes for second nine and vice versa .................. 6-6d/3
score card
- competitor corrects score after marker signs and leaves scoring area ................ 6-6b/7
- marker disappears with competitor's score card .......................................... 6-6b/6
- marker other than one appointed by Committee signs competitors'
   score cards ........................................................................................... 6-6b/5
- marker refuses to sign competitor's score card after dispute resolved
   in favor of competitor by Committee ...................................................... 6-6a/4
- signatures of marker and competitor in wrong places ................................... 6-6b/1
- when score card considered returned to Committee ..................................... 6-6c/1
wrong score knowingly attested by marker
- competitor aware score wrong ................................................................... 1-3/6
- competitor unaware score wrong .............................................................. 6-6a/5

**Marking or Defining Course**
*See also* Abnormal Ground Conditions; Boundary Fence, Line, Wall or Stakes; Committee;
Fence; Ground Under Repair; Local Rules; Obstructions; Out of Bounds; Teeing Ground and
Tee-Markers; Water Hazards
declaring area as ground under repair during competition round ....................... 33-2a/2
Local Rule
- allowing drop on green side of water hazard when ball fails to clear
   hazard; whether authorized ................................................................... 33-8/2
- allowing drop within water hazard behind point where ball lies
   unplayable in same hazard; whether authorized ....................................... 33-8/37
- allowing free relief for ball in water hazard within limits of
   fairway; whether authorized ................................................................. 33-8/36
- allowing free relief from immovable water hazard stake for ball
   lying in water hazard; whether authorized ............................................. 33-8/15
- declaring accumulations of leaves (at specified holes) through the
   green as ground under repair ................................................................. 33-8/31
- declaring extensive damage due to heavy rain and traffic as
   ground under repair ............................................................................. 33-2a/3
- declaring severe damage by non-burrowing animals as ground
   under repair ...................................................................................... 33-8/32.5
- deeming area of adjoining hole out of bounds for play of
   particular hole but not for play of other holes ......................................... 33-2a/14
- deeming area of adjoining hole out of bounds for stroke played
   from teeing ground only; whether authorized ......................................... 33-2a/14
- deeming area surrounding teeing ground in bounds for tee shot
   and out of bounds thereafter; whether authorized ................................... 33-2a/13
- deeming ball in bounds until beyond boundary wall ................................... 33-2a/16
- deeming ground under repair adjacent to artificially-surfaced
   cart path to have same status as path .................................................... 33-8/25
- deeming hard conical ant hills as ground under repair ............................... 33-8/22
- deeming interior boundary fence immovable obstruction;
   whether authorized ............................................................................. 33-8/14

### Marking or Defining Course (continued)

- defining given part of body of water as water hazard from
  back tees and by Local Rule lateral water hazard from forward tees .................. 33-2a/6
- defining given part of body of water as water hazard in play of
  one hole and by Local Rule lateral water hazard in play of another hole ........ 33-2a/7
- to prevent cutting across "dog-leg;" deeming ball out of bounds
  that crosses boundary even if it recrosses boundary and comes
  to rest on same part of course; whether authorized ............................................. 33-8/38

out of bounds objects and procedures
- angled supports or guy wires supporting ....................................................................... 24/2
- boundary stakes having no significance in play of hole being played ....................... 24/5
- concrete bases of boundary fence posts ......................................................................... 24/3
- displaced boundary stake ............................................................................................ 33-2a/20
- establishing boundary line inside fence on property line ....................................... 33-2a/15
- gate in boundary fence ...................................................................................................... 27/18
- internal boundary between holes .............................................................................. 33-2a/12
- Local Rule deeming area of adjoining hole out of bounds for play
  of particular hole but not for play of other holes ................................................. 33-2a/14
- Local Rule deeming area of adjoining hole out of bounds for stroke
  played from teeing ground only; whether authorized .......................................... 33-2a/14
- Local Rule deeming area surrounding teeing ground in bounds for
  tee shot and out of bounds thereafter; whether authorized ................................ 33-2a/13
- Local Rule deeming ball in bounds until beyond boundary wall ......................... 33-2a/16
- Local Rule deeming interior boundary fence immovable obstruction;
  whether authorized ..................................................................................................... 33-8/14
- Local Rule to prevent cutting across "dog-leg;" deeming ball out of
  bounds that crosses boundary even if it recrosses boundary and
  comes to rest on same part of course; whether authorized ................................. 33-8/38
- part of boundary fence within boundary line ................................................................ 24/4
- preventive measures when flow of water moves ball out of bounds
  in water hazard ............................................................................................................... 26-1/7
- procedure for treating exposed water pipe adjacent and parallel
  to boundary .................................................................................................................. 33-2a/1
- public road defined as out of bounds divides course; status of
  ball crossing road ............................................................................................................ 27/20
- river or other body of water adjacent to hole but off club property ................... 33-2a/11
- stake defining out of bounds removed during competition
  without authority ........................................................................................................ 33-2a/19
- stile attached to boundary fence ...................................................................................... 24/1
- unmarked water hazard with margin out of bounds ....................................................... 26/3
- when ball inside boundary fence considered out of bounds ......................................... 27/19
- whether internal boundary between holes allowed ................................................. 33-2a/12

putting green
- attachment to flagstick to indicate position of hole on green ...................................... 17/1
- different colored flags used to indicate position of hole on green .............................. 17/2
- half of double green serving hole not being played ................................................... 25-3/1
- map of putting green indicating hole position displayed at tee ..................................... 33/6
- marking island green ................................................................................................... 33-2a/10
- two holes on each green of nine-hole course .................................................................. 16/7
- whether flagstick may have tapered or of varying diameters ....................................... 17/3

recommendations for marking or defining
- distance markers .................................................................................................................. 33/5
- tree basins ............................................................................................................... 33-2a/10.5

teeing ground
- Local Rule deeming water hazard as lateral water hazard in
  play from forward tee .................................................................................................. 33-2a/6
- map of putting green indicating hole position displayed at tee ..................................... 33/6
- play from wrong teeing ground attributed to Committee
  failure to indicate hole numbers on teeing ground ................................................... 11-5/2

# Index    I-91

water hazard
- ball within natural margin of water hazard but outside
  stakes defining margin ............................................................................. 26/2
- defining part of body of water as water hazard and remainder
  as lateral water hazard ........................................................................ 33-2a/7
- defining rough and unplayable areas adjacent to fairways
  (areas not meeting definition of lateral water hazard) as lateral
  water hazard ......................................................................................... 33-8/35
- lateral water hazard defined as water hazard ........................................ 26/3.5
- Local Rule allowing drop on green side of water hazard when
  ball fails to clear hazard; whether authorized ................................... 33-8/2
- Local Rule allowing drop within water hazard behind point
  where ball lies unplayable in hazard; whether authorized ............. 33-8/37
- Local Rule allowing free relief for ball in water hazard within
  limits of fairway; whether authorized ................................................. 33-8/36
- Local Rule allowing free relief from immovable water hazard
  stake for ball lying in water hazard; whether authorized ............... 33-8/15
- Local Rule deeming given part of body of water as water hazard
  from back tees and lateral water hazard from forward tees ............ 33-2a/6
- Local Rule deeming given part of body of water as water hazard
  in play of one hole and lateral water hazard in play of another hole ........ 33-2a/7
- marking and defining margins of water hazards; where to
  place lines and/or stakes .................................................................... 33-2a/4
- marking environmentally-sensitive areas; recommendations
  for Committee ..................................................................................... 33-8/41
- marking island green .............................................................................. 33-2a/10
- marking ocean and beach as through the green; whether permitted ........... 33-2a/8
- marking river or other body of water adjacent to hole but
  off club property ................................................................................. 33-2a/11
- marking water hazard with bunker adjacent ................................... US/33-8/100
- part of lateral water hazard where impossible to drop not nearer hole ........... 33-2a/9
- permissible dropping area under lateral water hazard Rule
  so narrow player has difficulty dropping within it ............................. 26-1/19
- preventive measures when flow of water moves ball out of
  bounds in water hazard ....................................................................... 26-1/7
- unmarked water hazard with margin out of bounds .............................. 26/3

## Marking Position of Ball
*See also* Ball-Marker

acceptable and unacceptable methods for marking position of ball ............. 20-1/16
acts which caddie may perform; including marking position of ball ............. 6-4/10
ball lifted by player without marking position
- and match conceded due to player's misconception as to
  opponent's score at hole .................................................................... 2-4/14
- before holing out; opponent then picks up his ball claiming
  player loses hole .................................................................................. 2-5/3
- in mistaken belief next stroke conceded by opponent ............................. 2-4/3
- when given wrong information by fellow-competitor in
  sudden-death play-off ........................................................................ 9-3/1
- when lifted for identification; intention to lift not announced;
  ball cleaned beyond extent necessary to identify it; whether
  multiple penalties apply ...................................................................... 21/4
- when mistaken for wrong ball .................................................................. 20-1/1
- without authority due to misunderstanding Committee
  member's instructions ........................................................................ 34-3/3.5
ball-marker
- lifted after player given incorrect information by opponent ...................... 9-2/5
- moved accidentally by player after having moved loose impediments .......... 20-1/12
- placed approximately two inches behind ball ...................................... 20-1/20
- placed other than behind ball ............................................................... 20-1/19
- player measures clubhead-length to side of ball and places ball-marker ...... US/20-1/100

### Marking Position of Ball *(continued)*
ball moves when
- accidentally kicked by player asked to lift it due to interference ............................ 20-1/13
- ball-marker removed ................................................................................................. 24-1/5
- player drops putter on ball while approaching to lift it ............................................. 20-1/14

claims and disputes
- player lifts ball resting against flagstick without marking
  or holing out; after making stroke and learning of player's
  actions opponent lifts his ball and claims hole .................................................. 2-5/3
- opponent marks and lifts player's ball without authority;
  player lifts ball-marker and claims hole; opponent disputes claim .................... 20-1/3

competitor invokes Rule 3-3; lifts and drops original ball then places
  second ball where the original marked and plays it ........................................... 3-3/13
fearing ball might move on putting green, player lifts ball ............................................ 16-1b/1
knocking ball aside after marking position before lifting ............................................... 20-1/22
lie of ball altered due to act of marking ........................................................................ 20-1/15.5
meaning of "directly attributable to the specific act" in the context of
  marking or replacing in Rules 20-1 and 20-3a ................................................... 20-1/15
player's ball resting against flagstick lifted without being holed;
  others in match pick up mistakenly believing player won hole .......................... 30-3f/3
rotating ball without marking position or lifting
- in bunker for identification purposes ....................................................................... 12-2/3
- in rough for identification purposes ........................................................................ 12-2/2
- on putting green to align trademark ....................................................................... 18-2a/33

substituted ball mistakenly placed on putting green instead of original
  then lifted and original replaced before stroke played ....................................... 15-2/2

### Material Piled for Removal

*See also* **Greenkeeper and Hole Made by Greenkeeper; Ground Under Repair; Status of Object**

pine needles piled for removal interfere with line of play after ball
  dropped away ..................................................................................................... 25-1b/17
status of
- fallen tree .................................................................................................................. 23/7
- fallen tree in process of being removed .................................................................. 25/7
- grass cuttings ............................................................................................................ 25/11
- tree stump ................................................................................................................ 25/8

### Maximum Available Relief

*See also* **Nearest Point of Relief**

ball dropped from casual water in bunker at point of maximum
  available relief rolls elsewhere ........................................................................... 25-1b/6
ball dropped in bunker under first option of Rule 25-1b(ii) at point
  of maximum available relief; player then wishes to invoke
  second option to drop outside bunker ................................................................ 25-1b/9
ball lifted from bunker by player intending to drop under first option
  of Rule 25-1b(ii) at point of maximum available relief; player then
  wishes to proceed under second option to drop outside bunker ....................... 24-2b/5
bunker completely covered by casual water; player's options ...................................... 25-1b/8
bunker totally under repair ............................................................................................ 25/13
explanation of "maximum available relief" from casual water in bunker ................... 25-1b/5

### Measuring

*See also* **Distance and Distance Markers**

across ground under repair in obtaining relief .............................................................. 25-1b/15
ball moved
- by flagstick when used to measure or when dropped on ball ................................. 18-2a/24
- while measuring to determine if re-drop required ................................................. 18-6/1
borrowing club for measuring purposes ....................................................................... 20/2
club-lengths directly through fence, tree or wall or across ditch ................................. 20-2b/2
club to be used in measuring ......................................................................................... 20/1

use of distance meter attached to golf cart; whether permitted .......................... 14-3/1
vertical distance
- nearest point of relief; ball lying in burrowing animal hole under
 ground on course ........................................................................................... 25-1b/23
- nearest point of relief; ball lying in drainpipe under ground on course ............ 24-2b/12
- nearest point of relief; ball lying on elevated obstruction ...................................... 24-2b/11
- unplayable ball in tree; player opts to drop within two club-lengths ...................... 28/11
- unplayable ball at base of cliff; player wished to drop within two
 club-lengths of point above ball at top of cliff ................................................. 28/12

## Molehill

*See also* Status of Object

loose soil remaining when molehill swept flat ........................................................ 23/11
status of molehill ................................................................................................. 25/23

## Moss

status of moss in tree and on ground ................................................................... 13-2/37

## Multiple Penalty Situations

breach of 14-club Rule at two or more holes
- clarification of match-play penalty ...................................................................... 4-4a/9
- clarification of stroke-play penalty ...................................................................... 4-4a/10
breaches of Rule(s) more than once prior to stroke; whether multiple
 penalties apply ..................................................................................................... 1-4/12
ball at rest moves
- after address; ball then stopped by player's club ................................................ 18-2b/12
- before address; accidentally stopped by player's club; player removes
 club and ball rolls away .................................................................................... 19-2/1.5
- in hazard when loose impediment removed ...................................................... 13-4/15
- when stepped on and original lie altered; player places ball in
 wrong place then plays it .............................................................................. 18-2a/21.3
ball deflected or stopped
- by competitor's golf bag and then his caddie ..................................................... 19-2/7
- by player's caddie standing in bounds and comes to rest out of bounds ............ 19-2/2
- by player's caddie standing out of bounds and comes to rest out of bounds ...... 19-2/4
- by player's foot then ball moves when foot removed .......................................... 19-2/1
- competitor's ball played on putting green deflected by balls of
 two fellow-competitors ..................................................................................... 19-5/3
ball dropped in improper manner and in wrong place ........................................... 20-2a/3
ball lifted
- and changed during play of hole to aid identification ......................................... 15/6.5
- and re-dropped when it should have been played as it lay;
 ball then lifted again and placed .................................................................. 18-2a/10
- and thrown into pond in anger ........................................................................ 18-2a/13.5
- by caddie on own initiative for identification ..................................................... 18-2a/14
- for identification not marked, intention to lift not announced
 and ball cleaned beyond extent necessary to identify it ................................... 21/4
ball played
- following procedure for ball lost in ground under repair (Rule 25-1c)
 after another ball played under stroke-and-distance procedure ........................ 15/8
- from ground under repair then original ball abandoned and
 relief taken under ground under repair Rule ................................................ 18-2a/8.5
- two wrong balls played between strokes with ball in play ................................. 15-3b/2
bunker or water hazard
- after taking firm stance in bunker, player smoothes footprints
 and changes club before playing .................................................................. 13-4/27
- ball in hazard moves when loose impediment removed ................................. 13-4/15
- casual water mistaken for water hazard; substituted ball played
 under water hazard Rule ............................................................................... 25-1b/13
- ground in hazard touched with several practice swings ................................ 13-4/3

### Multiple Penalty Situations (continued)
- ground in hazard touched with several practice swings; player advised of breach then makes several more such swings ........................ 1-4/13
- prior to stroke from hazard, practice swing touches ground in hazard and moves loose impediments; also area of intended swing improved by bending branch .................................................. 13-4/28

competitor's ball played by fellow-competitor; competitor substitutes another ball at wrong place, plays it and then abandons it and plays out original ball from right place .......................................... 20-7c/4

foursome stroke play; ball played from outside teeing ground; partner replays stroke .................................................................... 29-1/2

general principles applying to multiple breaches of Rule(s)
- Rule(s) breached more than once prior to stroke; whether multiple penalties apply .................................................................. 1-4/12
- player advised of breach of Rule prior to stroke; player breaches same Rule again prior to stroke ........................................................ 1-4/13
- same Rule breached before and after stroke .......................................... 1-4/14
- two Rules with different penalties breached; more severe penalty applied ........... 1-4/15
- two wrong balls played between strokes with ball in play ............................ 15-3b/2

### Mushroom
growing on line of putt .......................................................................... 16-1a/15

### "Nassau" System of Scoring
player who wins first nine holes withdraws during second nine ........................ US/2-3/100

### Nearest Lie Most Similar
*See also* Lie of Ball Altered

ball accidentally stepped on altering original lie; player places ball in wrong place and plays ........................................................ 18-2a/21.3

lie of ball changed by removal of gallery-control stake ............................... 20-3b/3

lie of embedded ball in hazard altered when lifted to determine whether unfit for play .............................................................. 5-3/5

### Nearest Point of Relief
*See also* Maximum Available Relief

casual water on putting green
- interferes with lie of ball; nearest point of relief off green ................... 25-1b/10
- intervenes on line of putt; nearest point of relief off green ................... 25-1b/10.5

club used to determine nearest point of relief not used for next stroke ............... 24-2b/4

determining nearest point of relief
- recommended procedure ..................................................................... 24-2b/1
- diagrams illustrating recommended procedure ........................................ 25-1b/2
- recommended procedure not followed by player in determining nearest point of relief ......................................................... 24-2b/2
- nearest point of relief located where player not able to play intended stroke ..................................................................... 24-2b/3
- nearest point of relief at physically inaccessible spot; procedure for player ............................................................................ 24-2b/3.5
- diagrams illustrating examples of nearest point of relief at physically inaccessible spots ................................................... 24-2b/3.7
- two equidistant nearest points of relief meet requirements of Rule ............... 25-1b/16
- when relief from two conditions permitted in single procedure .................... 1-4/8
- when bird's nest interferes with stroke ................................................ 1-4/9
- when rattlesnake or bees interfere with play; relief procedure ................... 1-4/10

line of play
- relief from obstruction interfering with swing incidentally gives relief from intervention on line of play ................................... 24-2b/7
- relief taken from other condition improves line of play ............................ 25-1b/3

Local Rule
- allowing relief from edging grooves around putting green ....................... 33-8/24
- providing relief in all cases on fairway side of paved path, or
    ball drop (dropping zone), when nearest point of relief effectively
    gives no relief; whether authorized................................................................. 33-8/19
- wrong putting green deemed to include apron to prohibit dropping
    on and play from.......................................................................................................... 33-8/33
measuring from nearest point of relief across ground under repair
    to determine dropping area; whether permitted ..................................... 25-1b/15
replacing or placing moved ball in bunker not nearer hole not possible;
    whether player may press ball into sand or take relief outside bunker .......... 20-3d/2
whether re-drop required if
- ball dropped from area of ground under repair rolls to position
    where same area interferes with stance .................................................... 20-2c/0.5
- ball dropped from area of ground under repair then same area
    interferes for stroke with club not used to determine nearest
    point of relief ........................................................................................................... 20-2c/0.8
- ball dropped from immovable obstruction rolls nearer hole than
    nearest point of relief but not nearer than where it originally lay.............. 20-2c/1.7
- ball dropped from immovable obstruction rolls nearer obstruction
    than nearest point of relief but player changes clubs and
    obstructions no longer interferes .................................................................. 20-2c/0.7
- dropped ball required to first strike course within bunker instead
    strikes course outside bunker then rolls into it......................................... 25-1b/7
- dropped ball strikes course within prescribed dropping area and
    rolls outside that area ........................................................................................ 20-2c/1
- relief taken from obstruction for stroke toward green; same
    obstruction interferes with stance for necessary sideways stroke.................... 24-2b/9.5
whether relief permitted from two conditions in single procedure
- ball in casual water within ground under repair...................................... 25-1b/11.5
- relief from cart path in casual water; relief from casual water
    back on cart path.................................................................................................. 1-4/8

## Observer
*See also* Committee; Referee
flagstick attended by observer, referee or marker at player's request................. 17-1/3

## Obstructions
*See also* Integral Part of Course; Loose Impediments; Reasonable Evidence; Status of Object
after relief taken from obstruction second obstruction interferes ................... 24-2b/9
area of intended swing
- improved by removing immovable obstruction ............................................. 13-2/15
- interfered with by obstruction in ground under repair ......................... 24-2b/10
artificial object out of bounds
- interference by immovable artificial object situated out of bounds ..................... 24-2b/21
- movable artificial object lying out of bounds ................................................... 24-1/3
artificially-surfaced road or path
- competitor not sure whether road considered obstruction
    or integral part of course, invokes Rule 3-3; whether score
    with second ball counts if played from wrong place ................................ 3-3/5
- competitor not sure whether road considered obstruction or
    integral part of course, plays second ball; fails to announce
    intention to invoke Rule 3-3 and to report facts to Committee .............. 3-3/6.5
- free relief agreed to in error by player and opponent thinking
    road obstruction; whether valid claim can be made after relief
    taken and opponent discovers road deemed integral part of course ................ 2-5/8.5
- gravel used to surface road; whether movable if player chooses
    to play ball as it lies ........................................................................................... 23/14
- Local Rule deeming ground under repair adjacent to
    artificially-surfaced path as part of path ..................................................... 33-8/25

## Obstructions (continued)

- Local Rule providing relief from unsurfaced road for tee shot only; whether authorized .................................................. 33-8/20
- meaning of "artificially-surfaced" ........................................................... 24/9

ball deflected
- by direction post ........................................................................................ 19-1/1
- by sprinkler head; Local Rule allowing replay of stroke without penalty; whether authorized .................................................................. 33-8/12

ball dropped in obtaining relief from obstruction
- from rough to fairway; whether permitted ........................................... 24-2b/8
- immediately after resumption of play; whether player may lift and clean or substitute then place ball under Rule 6-8d(ii) ............. 6-8d/3
- on ball drop (dropping zone) established by Local Rule; procedure for dropping and re-dropping .................................................................. 33-8/34
- strikes course within prescribed dropping area then rolls out of prescribed area; whether ball must be re-dropped ........................ 20-2c/1

ball in plastic bag moves when bag blown to new position by wind ........ 18-1/7
ball lifted and dropped away from movable obstruction ......................... 18-2a/4
ball marked before obstruction removed; ball moves when ball-marker removed .................................................................................... 24-1/5
ball played from obstruction, lost in same obstruction ............................ 25-1c/3
ball substituted by mistake in taking relief from cart path; correction of error procedure ........................................................................................ 20-6/3
barn doors opened to play shot through barn; whether permitted ......... 24-2b/15

boundary fence
- angled supports or guy wires supporting boundary fence .................. 24/2
- concrete bases of boundary fence posts .................................................. 24/3
- exposed water pipe adjacent and parallel to boundary fence causes problems; suggested procedure .................................................. 33-2a/1
- gate in boundary fence ............................................................................... 27/18
- Local Rule deeming interior boundary fence immovable obstruction; whether authorized ............................................................. 33-8/14
- part of boundary fence within boundary line ....................................... 24/4
- part of fence off course (not boundary fence) leans across boundary and interferes with swing ........................................................ 13-2/20
- relief from immovable obstruction incidentally results in relief from boundary fence ................................................................................. 24-2b/6
- relief from immovable obstruction parallel to boundary fence in most cases would result in relief from boundary fence; recommendation for Committee ............................................................... 33-2a/1
- stile attached to boundary fence ............................................................... 24/1

boundary stakes
- ball lifted and dropped away from boundary stake under obstruction Rule .......................................................................................... 18-2a/3
- displaced boundary stake ........................................................................... 33-2a/20
- having no significance in play of hole being played .............................. 24/5
- removal of boundary stake interfering with swing ................................ 13-2/17

bridge
- ball lying on elevated obstruction over deep hollow; where to drop ..... 24-2b/11
- grounding club on bridge in water hazard .............................................. 13-4/30

bunker
- ball dropped in bunker under first option of Rule 24-2b(ii); player then wishes to proceed under second option to drop outside bunker ........................................................................................... 25-1b/9
- ball lifted from bunker by player intending to drop under first option of Rule 24-2b(ii); player then wishes to proceed under second option to drop outside bunker ................................................... 24-2b/5
- ball lying on obstruction in bunker; whether ball considered in bunker ................. 13/5

- rake removal causes ball in bunker to move; whether player may press ball into sand or take relief outside bunker if not possible to replace or place in bunker not nearer hole ......................... 20-3d/2
- rakes; whether they should be placed in or outside bunkers ................... Misc./2
- stone serving as part of drain in bunker; whether obstruction or loose impediment .......................................................................................... 24/7

clubhouse window opened; ball played through it; whether permitted .................. 24-2b/14

drainpipe
- ball in drainpipe under course; entrance to drainpipe out of bounds ................ 24-2b/12
- ball lost in underground drainpipe ............................................................. 24-3b/1

flagstick
- after stroke, attended flagstick removed from hole, placed on ground then lifted while ball still in motion ............................................... 17-1/6
- ball lodged in flag attached to flagstick .................................................................. 17/6
- lying on putting green removed by player to prevent another player's ball from striking it.......................................................................... 1-2/3

holding ball in place while removing movable obstruction................................ 24-1/4

line of play improved
- by removing part of fence ....................................................................... 13-2/32.5
- by removing stone from wall ...................................................................... 13-2/32
- in taking relief from obstruction interfering with swing player incidentally gains relief from intervention on line of play .................. 24-2b/7

Local Rule
- allowing free relief from immovable water hazard stake for ball lying in water hazard; whether authorized ...................................... 33-8/15
- allowing line-of sight relief without penalty from protective fence near line of play............................................................................................ 33-8/18
- allowing line-of-sight relief from irrigation-control boxes near fairways; whether authorized ..................................................................... 33-8/17
- allowing replay of stroke without penalty when sprinkler head deflects ball; whether authorized ................................................................ 33-8/12
- deeming all stakes on course (except boundary stakes) immovable obstructions ................................................................................................ 33-8/16
- deeming ground under repair adjacent to artificially-surfaced cart path to have same status as path........................................................ 33-8/25
- deeming interior boundary fence immovable obstruction; whether authorized .................................................................................... 33-8/14
- procedure for dropping and re-dropping on ball drop (dropping zone) established by Local Rule............................................. 33-8/34
- providing relief from temporary power line and cables ..................... App I-B-6b
- providing relief from unsurfaced road for tee shot only; whether authorized .................................................................................... 33-8/20
- providing relief in all cases on fairway side of paved path, or ball drop (dropping zone), when nearest point of relief effectively gives no relief; whether authorized ...................................... 33-8/19
- requiring cancelation and replay of stroke without penalty when ball deflected by power line, tower or pole ..................................... 33-8/13

meaning of
- "artificially-surfaced"................................................................................... 24/9
- point where ball "last entered" ground under repair when ball lost in condition ............................................................................... 25-1c/1.5
- "reasonable evidence" ball lost in ground under repair ............................................. 25-1c/1

mental interference by obstruction................................................................. 24-2a/1

nearest point of relief
- club used to determine nearest point of relief not used for next stroke .............. 24-2b/4
- determining club, address position, direction of play and swing used to identify nearest point of relief................................................ 24-2b/1
- diagrams illustrating nearest point of relief......................................................... 25-1b/2
- diagrams illustrating player unable to determine nearest point of relief .............................................................................................. 24-2b/3.7

### Obstructions (continued)

- dropped ball rolls nearer hole than nearest point of relief but not nearer than where it originally lay ............ 20-2c/1.7
- dropped ball rolls nearer obstruction than nearest point of relief; whether re-drop necessary if player changes clubs and obstruction no longer interferes .................... 20-2c/0.7
- from cart path in casual water; nearest point of relief from casual water back on cart path .................... 1-4/8
- Local Rule providing relief in all cases on fairway side of paved path, or ball drop (dropping zone), when nearest point of relief effectively gives no relief; whether authorized .................... 33-8/19
- measuring across ground under repair in obtaining relief; whether permitted .................... 25-1b/15
- player determines nearest point of relief; intended stroke from that point physically impossible .................... 24-2b/3
- player does not follow recommended procedure in determining nearest point of relief .................... 24-2b/2
- player takes relief properly from ground under repair; same condition interferes for stroke with club not used to determine nearest point of relief .................... 20-2c/0.8
- player physically unable to take stance to determine or establish location of nearest point of relief .................... 24-2b/3.5
- two equidistant points meet requirements of nearest point of relief from obstruction or ground under repair .................... 25-1b/16

player entitled to relief from immovable obstruction lifts ball then
- chooses not to take relief and wishes to proceed under unplayable ball Rule .................... 18-2a/12.5
- replaces ball and plays it from original position .................... 18-2a/12

position of ball worsened when obstruction removed; player replaces obstruction .................... 13-2/15.5

probing near ball for presence of immovable obstruction .................... 13-2/27

reasonable evidence ball lost in obstruction; drop made under Rule 24-3; original ball then found within five minutes .................... 25-1c/2.5

removal of obstruction
- in hazard would move loose impediment .................... 1-4/5
- on player's line of play by opponent or fellow-competitor .................... 24/16
- on player's line of play by outside agency .................... 13-2/33

stake supporting tree broken in attempt to remove it .................... 13-2/16

stance
- after relief taken from obstruction for stroke towards green, obstruction interferes with stance for necessary sideways stroke .................... 24-2b/9.5
- ball dropped from immovable obstruction rolls to position where it interferes with stance; whether re-drop required .................... 20-2c/0.5
- player physically unable to take stance to determine or establish location of nearest point of relief .................... 24-2b/3.5

status of
- abandoned ball .................... 24-1/2
- angled supports or guy wires supporting boundary fence .................... 24/2
- artificially-surfaced road or path .................... 24/9
- barn doors .................... 24-2b/15
- clubhouse window .................... 24-2b/14
- concrete bases of boundary fence posts .................... 24/3
- flagstick when ball overhangs hole .................... 16-2/4
- gate in boundary fence .................... 27/18
- gravel used to surface road .................... 23/14
- half-eaten pear .................... 23/3
- line or mark on ground for gallery-control purposes consisting of lime or paint .................... 24-2b/20
- movable part of drainage hose .................... 24-2b/15.3
- part of boundary fence within boundary line .................... 24/4

Index   I-99

- part of fence off course leaning across boundary ........................... 13-2/20
- paved area .................................................................................................. 24/10
- parked car .................................................................................................... 24/8
- tee-markers after first stroke ................................................................. 11-2/1
- tree basins ............................................................................................ 33-2a/10.5
- turf raised by underground pipe ............................................................ 24/14
- wooden or earthen steps ......................................................................... 24/12
- wooden planks ........................................................................................... 24/11

stone
- broken away from retaining wall in water hazard ............................... 24/6
- line of play improved by removing stone from wall ..................... 13-2/32
- serving as part of drain in bunker ............................................................ 24/7

teeing ground; ball lies in or on movable obstruction ............................ 25-2/8
when loose impediment transformed into obstruction ............................. 23/1
whether player entitled to relief if
- obstruction interferes but ball unplayable due to some other condition .......... 24-2b/16
- obstruction interferes with abnormal stroke; abnormal stroke
    reasonable in circumstances .......................................................... 24-2b/17
- obstruction interferes with abnormal stroke; abnormal stroke
    not reasonable in circumstances ................................................... 24-2b/18
- obstruction interferes with stroke but stroke at ball not reasonable
    due to interference by casual water ............................................. 24-2b/19

### Ocean

treating ocean and beach as through the green ..................................... 33-2a/8

### Order of Play

*See also* Order of Play in Foursomes and Threesomes; Playing Out of Turn; Stroke Canceled or Recalled

competitor arrives late for scheduled tee time but in time to play in
    correct order; whether late for tee time .......................................... 6-3a/2
competitor objects to fellow-competitor putting out of turn ............ 10-2b/1
competitors in stroke play agree to play out of turn but not for
    purpose of giving one of them advantage ..................................... 10-2c/2
determining ball farther from hole; procedure for referee ............... 10-1b/1
determining honor
- at next tee following disputed hole ..................................................... 10-1a/2
- in four-ball match in which points awarded for both better-ball
    and aggregate scores ................................................................................ 30/3
- in handicap match ................................................................................. 10-1a/1
- in handicap Stableford competition ................................................... 32-1/3
- in handicap stroke play ......................................................................... 10-2a/1
- when opponent requires player with honor to cancel stroke
    played from outside teeing ground .............................................. 11-4a/1
four-ball competition
- determination of honor in four-ball match in which points
    awarded for both better-ball and aggregate scores ........................ 30/3
- extent to which partners may play in order they consider best ............... 31-5/2
- partner waives turn to play; circumstances under which he
    may complete hole ............................................................................ 31-5/1
- player entitled to putt stands on another player's line of putt ............. 30-3c/1
- side plays out of turn from tee; opponents require one member
    of side to replay but not other ....................................................... 30-1/1
- waiving turn to putt in four-ball match play ..................................... 30-3c/2
holes played out of sequence
- competitors play two holes not included in stipulated round ................ 3/2
- starting players from 1st and 10th tees; whether permitted ............. 33-1/3
- three holes played out of sequence in match .......................................... 2-1/5
meaning of "immediately" when stroke to be canceled ........................ 30-1/1

I-100  Index

## Order of Play (continued)

playing from outside teeing ground or from wrong teeing ground in match play
- stroke canceled by opponent; correct order of play .................................................. 11-4a/1
- stroke canceled by opponents in foursome match; which partner
  replays stroke .................................................................................................. 29-1/1
- stroke goes out of bounds; procedure if stroke not recalled by opponent ............. 11-5/3
request for player to replay stroke withdrawn after opponent plays ............................... 10-1c/1
provisional ball; order of play when played other than from teeing ground................... 10/4
stroke(s) played out of turn
- ball played out of turn from tee abandoned and another ball
  played in proper order .................................................................................... 10-2c/1
- player attending flagstick for opponent struck by ball of opponent's
  partner who played out of turn ...................................................................... 30-3f/5
- player plays out of turn from tee in three-ball match; one opponent
  requests replay and other does not ................................................................ 30-2/1
- player requested to lift ball due to interference plays out of turn instead ............ 10-1c/2
- players agree not to tee off in prescribed order to save time .............................. 1-3/1
- side plays out of turn from tee; opponents require one member
  of side to replay but not other ....................................................................... 30-1/1
when both balls
- lie in ground under repair and both players take relief ..................................... 10/1
- lie in lateral water hazard and both players take relief...................................... 10/2
- lost in lateral water hazard ............................................................................... 10/3
withholding information on strokes taken until opponent's turn to play ...................... 9-2/4

## Order of Play in Foursomes and Threesomes

ball played from outside teeing ground
- which partner must replay stroke .................................................................... 29-1/1
- wrong partner replays stroke in stroke play .................................................... 29-1/2
both partners drive at same tee in foursome match............................................................ 29-1/9
foursome partner accidentally moves ball after address ................................................... 29-1/5
foursome partner misses ball
- accidentally, when making stroke ..................................................................... 29-1/6
- purposely, so partner would play ball over water ............................................. 29-1/7
provisional ball
- played by wrong member of side ..................................................................... 29-1/4
- which partner must play provisional ball ......................................................... 29-1/3
side drives for three holes in wrong order; opponents make claim
  during third hole .......................................................................................... 29-2/2
wrong ball played in foursome stroke play........................................................................ 29-1/8
wrong partners drive for both sides in foursome match.................................................... 29-2/1

## Out of Bounds

*See also* **Boundary Fence, Line, Wall or Stakes; Marking or Defining Course; Provisional Ball**
ball comes to rest out of bounds
- ball accidentally strikes opponent standing out of bounds
  and comes to rest out of bounds ..................................................................... 19-3/1
- ball dropped in ball drop (dropping zone) rolls out of bounds;
  whether ball must be re-dropped .................................................................... 33-8/34
- ball dropped, comes to rest and then rolls out of bounds ..................................... 20-2c/3.5
- ball dropped under Rule 20-5 strikes course through the green
  within inches of and not nearer hole than spot in bunker where
  previous stroke played ................................................................................... 20-5/2
- ball enters burrowing animal hole in bounds and comes to
  rest out of bounds............................................................................................ 25-1b/24
- ball lost in underground drainpipe or culvert with entrance
  out of bounds .................................................................................................. 24-3b/1
- ball moved accidentally by backward movement of club after
  stroke misses; ball comes to rest out of bounds ............................................. 18-2a/22
- ball moved out of bounds by flow of water in water hazard ......................... 26-1/7

Index  I-101

- ball moves after address and comes to rest out of bounds ......................................... 18-2b/9
- ball played from bunker out of bounds or lost; player tests
    condition of bunker or smoothes footprints before dropping
    another ball in bunker ................................................................................................... 13-4/37
- ball played from outside teeing ground goes out of bounds ..................................... 11-4b/6
- ball played from water hazard to out of bounds ........................................................ 26-1/10
- ball played out of bounds from wrong teeing ground in match not recalled ........ 11-5/3
- ball thrown into bounds by outside agency and played;
    caddie aware of action of outside agency ..................................................................... 15/9
- ball thrown into bounds by outside agency; neither player nor
    caddie aware of action of outside agency ................................................................... 15/10
- explanation of options under Rule 26-2b if ball played from
    water hazard comes to rest out of bounds ................................................................ 26-2/1
- maintenance vehicle deflects ball out of bounds; substituted
    ball played from spot where original ball deflected ................................................. 20-7/1
- mixed foursome in which different tees used by men and
    women; tee shot out of bounds ...................................................................................... 29/2
- opponent's caddie lifts player's ball which may or may not
    have been out of bounds ............................................................................................... 18-3b/5
- original ball and provisional ball found out of bounds ............................................ 27-2c/4
- original ball out of bounds; ball re-teed under stroke-and-distance
    touched at address and falls off tee ............................................................................ 11-3/3
- player strikes ball out of bounds, picks up, drops ball where
    partner's ball lies and plays practice stroke ............................................................. 30-3f/7
- player's ball strikes own caddie; ball comes to rest out of bounds ........................... 19-2/2
- player's ball strikes own caddie standing out of bounds and
    comes to rest out of bounds ........................................................................................... 19-2/4
- stroke played from environmentally-sensitive area defined as
    out of bounds ................................................................................................................ 33-8/43
- stroke played with ball lying out of bounds .................................................................. 15/6
- teed ball missed then hit out of bounds ......................................................................... 20-5/1
- wrong ball found out of bounds, played under stroke-and-distance
    procedure; original ball then found in bounds ......................................................... 15/12
- wrong ball hit out of bounds; another ball played under Rule 27-1;
    original ball then found nearby .................................................................................... 15/11
ball moved into bounds by flow of water in lateral water hazard ..................................... 26-1/8
ball wrongly thought out of bounds lifted; competitor plays another
    ball from tee .................................................................................................................. 18-2a/11
objects defining out of bounds
    - angled supports or guy wires supporting ..................................................................... 24/2
    - ball lifted and dropped away from boundary stake under obstruction Rule ........ 18-2a/3
    - boundary stakes having no significance in play of hole being played ....................... 24/5
    - concrete bases of boundary fence posts ......................................................................... 24/3
    - deeming ball in bounds until beyond boundary wall .............................................. 33-2a/16
    - establishing boundary line inside fence on property line ...................................... 33-2a/15
    - exposed water pipe adjacent and parallel to boundary fence
        causes problems; suggested procedure .................................................................... 33-2a/1
    - gate in boundary fence .................................................................................................... 27/18
    - identifying stake defining out of bounds removed during
        competition without authority ............................................................................... 33-2a/19
    - improving position of ball by bending boundary fence ............................................ 13-2/18
    - internal boundary between holes ............................................................................. 33-2a/12
    - marking environmentally-sensitive areas; recommendations
        for Committee ........................................................................................................... 33-8/41
    - moving ball lying against fence defining out of bounds by
        striking other side of fence ........................................................................................ 14-1/5
    - part of boundary fence within boundary line .............................................................. 24/4
    - relief from immovable obstruction incidentally results in relief
        from boundary fence ................................................................................................ 24-2b/6

## Out of Bounds *(continued)*

- removal of boundary stake interfering with swing .................................................. 13-2/17
- removal of boundary stake on line of play but replaced before stroke ................. 13-2/25
- river or other body of water adjacent to hole but off club property ..................... 33-2a/11
- stile attached to boundary fence ................................................................................ 24/1
- when ball inside boundary fence considered out of bounds ...................................... 27/19

objects lying out of bounds
- burrowing animal hole out of bounds, ball enters it and comes
  to rest in bounds .......................................................................................................... 25-1b/23
- entrance to drainpipe out of bounds, ball found or lost in
  drainpipe under course ............................................................................................... 24-2b/12
- entrance to drainpipe out of bounds, ball lost in drainpipe out of bounds ........... 24-3b/1
- improving area of intended swing by moving growing or fixed
  object situated out of bounds ................................................................................... 13-2/19
- interference by immovable artificial object situated out of bounds .................... 24-2b/21
- movable artificial object lying out of bounds ........................................................... 24-1/3
- part of fence off course leans across boundary and interferes with swing .......... 13-2/20
- removal of loose impediment lying out of bounds .................................................. 23-1/9
- unmarked water hazard with left-hand margin out of bounds .................................. 26/3

Local Rule
- boundary stakes having no significance in play of hole being played ....................... 24/5
- deeming area of adjoining hole out of bounds for play of
  particular hole but not for play of other holes ...................................................... 33-2a/14
- deeming area of adjoining hole out of bounds for stroke played
  from teeing ground only; whether authorized ....................................................... 33-2a/14
- deeming area surrounding tee in bounds for tee shot and
  out of bounds thereafter; whether authorized ...................................................... 33-2a/13
- deeming ball in bounds until beyond boundary wall ............................................... 33-2a/16
- public road defined as out of bounds divides course; status of
  ball crossing road ........................................................................................................ 27/20
- to prevent cutting across "dog-leg;" deeming ball out of bounds
  that crosses boundary even if it recrosses boundary and comes
  to rest on same part of course; whether authorized ............................................. 33-8/38

player enters environmentally-sensitive area to retrieve ball ............................................ 33-8/42
player's ball strikes own caddie standing out of bounds and comes
  to rest on course ................................................................................................................ 19-2/3
provisional ball
- announcement of .......................................................................................................... 27-2a/1
- determining who plays provisional ball in foursome .................................................. 29-1/3
- lifted in erroneous belief original ball in bounds ....................................................... 27-2b/8
- not distinguishable from original ball ........................................................................... 27/11
- played from point nearer hole than visible original ball;
  player erroneously thought original ball out of bounds ...................................... 27-2c/3
- played in absence of reasonable possibility original ball lost or
  out of bounds ................................................................................................................ 27-2a/3
- played in erroneous belief it is original ball .............................................................. 27-2b/7
- possibly lost or out of bounds; third ball played with no announcement ........... 27-2a/4
- used as second ball when not determinable whether original
  ball out of bounds ........................................................................................................ 3-3/1

re-drop required when proceeding under out of bounds Rule;
  whether player may substitute when re-dropping ........................................................ 20-6/4
relief from immovable obstruction incidentally results in relief
  from boundary fence ........................................................................................................ 24-2b/6
whether player entitled to ascertain whereabouts of opponent's ball
  that may be out of bounds before playing .................................................................... 9-2/16

# Index I-103

**Outside Agency**
*See also* Ball Deflected or Stopped; Loose Impediments; Status of Object
ball at rest
- kicked away from hole by spectator attending flagstick ............................ 18-1/10
- moved by tumbleweed blown by wind................................................................ 18-1/6
ball dislodged in tree knocked down by outside agency ........................................ 18-1/9
ball dropped accidentally by opponent or fellow-competitor on
  player's moving ball on putting green............................................................. 19-5/1.7
ball in plastic bag moves when bag blown to new position by wind .................. 18-1/7
ball not found; either moved by outside agency or lost
- criteria necessary to treat ball as moved by outside agency ........................ 18-1/1
- treated as moved by outside agency in absence of reasonable
  evidence to that effect ................................................................................... 27-1/2.5
ball played from another hole deflects player's ball in motion
  after stroke on putting green......................................................................... 19-1/10
ball stolen by outside agency from unknown spot ................................................ 18-1/5
ball visible from tee disappears or moved by outside agency
  while play suspended..................................................................................... 6-8d/4
ball-marker lifted by outside agency........................................................................ 20-1/9
borrowing balls or towel from another player or outside agency ........................ 5-1/5
club rendered unfit for play by outside agency ...................................................... 4-3/9.5
competitor seeks help from fellow-competitor to avoid penalty.......................... 33-7/7
dog picks up or deflects ball on putting green after stroke
- from off green................................................................................................. 19-1/6
- from green...................................................................................................... 19-1/7
flagstick removed whereupon knob falls from it and deflects ball in motion.......... 17/9
hole-liner pulled out with attended flagstick deflects ball in motion after stroke........... 17/8
immovable obstruction on player's line of play removed by outside agency ........... 13-2/33
maintenance vehicle deflects ball out of bounds; player drops
  substituted ball near spot where vehicle deflected original ball
  and plays it..................................................................................................... 20-7/1
meaning of "good reason to lift" when play suspended, such as
  possibility outside agency may take ball .................................................... 6-8c/1
movable obstruction removed by outside agency; position of ball
  worsened; player replaces obstruction ....................................................... 13-2/15.5
person(s) other than caddie carry items, other than clubs, for player.................. 6-4/5.3
player plays ball moved or lifted by outside agency from new position
- caddie aware ball moved from out of bounds onto course;
  does not inform player ................................................................................ 15/9
- neither player nor caddie aware ball moved from out of bounds onto course........ 15/10
- neither player nor caddie aware ball moved until next hole begun................. 18-1/3
- without competitor's knowledge, fellow-competitor lifts competitor's
  ball and sets it aside; competitor plays ball from where set aside ........... 15-3b/3
player's ball deflected by stroke of player in another group .................................. 19-1/2
snake; when outside agency.................................................................................... 23/6.5
spectator says ball moved by outside agency but player not sure; procedure
  for player if Committee decision not possible in reasonable time............ 18-1/4
sprinkler head deflects ball; Local Rule allowing replay of stroke
  without penalty; whether authorized ............................................................ 33-8/12
steps on ball in tall grass; original lie altered and spot where ball
  originally lay not determinable; procedure player must use..................... 20-3b/5
stone dislodged by partner's or opponent's stroke moves player's ball .............. 18-1/8
stroke not replayed as required by Rule 19-1 after ball played from
  putting green deflected by moving outside agency .................................... 19-1/3
team captain or coach; status of............................................................................ 33-1/11.5
umbrella carrier employed in addition to caddie; whether second
  caddie or outside agency .............................................................................. 6-4/5

## Pace of Play

*See also* Undue Delay
Committee does not penalize player in breach of pace of play condition
    believing player had already lost hole ............................................................... 34-3/2
players agree not to tee off in prescribed order to save time ................................. 1-3/1

## Par Competition

*See also* Bogey Competition; Stableford Competition
recording of lower gross score does not affect result of hole ........................... 32-2a/5
when practice between holes permitted ................................................................. 7-2/1

## Penalties Imposed, Modified or Waived by Committee

*See also* Close of Competition; Committee; Multiple Penalty Situations
authority to waive or modify disqualification penalty ....................................... 33-7/1
Committee error
  - disqualification penalty wrongly applied to winner of event; error
    discovered after play-off for first conducted with two other competitors ........ 34-1b/5
  - incorrect ruling by Committee in first-round affecting competitor's
    score corrected during second round ............................................................... 34-3/1
condition of competition
  - requiring immediate discontinuance of play in dangerous situations;
    guidelines for waiving or modifying disqualification penalty for
    failure to discontinue immediately .................................................................. 6-8b/7
  - use of ball not on List of Conforming Golf Balls imposes penalty
    other than disqualification; whether permitted ............................................... 5-1/2
incorrect information on Rules given to partner, opponent or fellow-competitor ............. 9/1
Local Rule
  - allowing drop on green side of water hazard when ball fails to
    clear hazard; whether authorized .................................................................... 33-8/2
  - providing relief without penalty from flooded bunker ................................... 33-8/27
  - requiring player to take relief under penalty from tree nursery
    (or plantation) from which play prohibited; whether authorized .................... 33-8/29
  - waiving penalty for ball striking unattended flagstick; whether authorized ...... 33-8/11
  - waiving requirement to hole out when temporary putting green used;
    whether authorized ......................................................................................... 33-8/1
meaning of "serious breach of etiquette" ............................................................... 33-7/8
tee-markers moved by player ................................................................................. 11-2/2
time of starting
  - all competitors must be present ..................................................................... 6-3a/2
  - circumstances which warrant waiving disqualification penalty
    for lateness ..................................................................................................... 6-3a/1.5
  - meaning of "time of starting" ......................................................................... 6-3a/2.5
whether Committee may waive or modify penalty
  - competitor resumes play after suspension not at time ordered by
    Committee (early or late) ................................................................................ 6-8b/6
  - failure to countersign score card blamed on lack of time provided
    by Committee ................................................................................................. 33-7/3
  - failure to hole out in stroke play ................................................................... 33-7/2
  - non-conforming club carried but not used .................................................... 4-1/1
  - play of wrong ball not rectified on advice of Committee member ............... 33-7/5
  - practice on course between stroke-play rounds ............................................ 7-1b/2
  - practice on course between stroke-play round and play-off on same day ......... 7-1b/3
  - short putt holed using club with playing characteristics changed
    other than in normal course of play ............................................................... 4-3/4
  - single stroke played with non-conforming ball ............................................ 5-1/1
  - wrong score returned on score card .............................................................. 33-7/4
  - wrong score returned on score card because player unaware of
    penalty incurred ............................................................................................. 33-7/4.5

whether Committee should impose penalty
- application of disqualification penalty in team competition in
   which not all team members' scores count for each round ...................... 33/8
- Committee suspends play; one player in match discontinues
   immediately; other player completes hole playing successive
   strokes out of turn ................................................................................ 6-8b/3.5
- competitor advised during round he incurred penalty by
   fellow-competitor; competitor disagrees and fails to include
   penalty in returned score card; Committee advised of
   incident after close of competition ..................................................... 34-1b/1.5
- consciously failing to correct opponent's misunderstanding
   of state of match ..................................................................................... 9-2/12
- knowingly giving incorrect information on Rules ............................................ 9/1
- playing away from hole to assist partner ..................................................... 30-3f/6
- refusing to identify ball ................................................................................. 27/13
- refusing to resume play (claiming danger from lightning) when
   resumption ordered by Committee .......................................................... 6-8b/5
- repeatedly replacing ball nearer hole on green ............................................ 33-7/6
- seeking help of fellow-competitor moving loose impediment to
   avoid penalty should removal causes ball to move ................................. 33-7/7

## Physical Problem

artificial limbs ............................................................................................... 14-3/15
discontinuing play
- due to physical problem ........................................................................... 6-8a/3
- for refreshment ........................................................................................ 6-8a/2.5
elastic bandage used by player with injured wrist ............................................ 14-3/7
postponement of final match due to injury of player ........................................ 6-3a/1

## Pine Needles

*See also* Leaves; Tree or Bush
club touches partially embedded pine needle on backswing in bunker ....................... 13-4/32
piled for removal interfere with line of play after ball dropped away ........................ 25-1b/17

## Pitch-Mark

*See also* Ball Mark; Embedded Ball
ball
- bounces out of its pitch-mark then spins back into it ................................... 25-2/1
- lifted to determine whether embedded in its own pitch-mark ..................... 25-2/7
- returns to pitch-mark from prior stroke .................................................... 25-2/3
casual water contained in embedded ball's pitch-mark; relief options
   available to player ........................................................................................ 25/3
made by ball of partner, opponent or fellow-competitor affects player's
   lie or line of play; whether player entitled to free relief ........................... 13-2/8
repaired
- eliminating interference with player's backswing; whether permitted ................. 13-2/21
- in area where ball to be dropped through the green; whether permitted ............ 13-2/10
when ball considered "embedded" in its own pitch-mark .............................. 25-2/0.5

## Playing Out of Turn

*See also* Honor; Order of Play; Order of Play in Foursomes and Threesomes
limitations on authority of partners to play in order they consider best ........................ 31-5/2
Local Rule requiring continuous putting on putting greens; whether authorized ...... 33-8/7
match play
- player asked to lift ball plays out of turn instead ................................ 10-1c/2
- player requests opponent to replay stroke played out of turn;
   request withdrawn after player plays and before opponent replays;
   whether opponent may replay stroke ..................................................... 10-1c/1
- player smoothes bunker after playing out of turn; opponent recalls
   stroke; player must drop ball in smoothed area; whether player
   subject to penalty ................................................................................. 13-4/39

### Playing Out of Turn (continued)
- player wishing to render original ball lost plays subsequent stroke with provisional ball out of turn ................................................................ 27-2b/1
- players agree not to tee off in prescribed order to save time .......................... 1-3/1
- in four-ball match, side plays out of turn from tee; opponents require one member of side to replay but not other .............................................. 30-1/1
- in three-ball match, player plays out of turn from tee; one opponent requests replay, other opponent does not ................................................ 30-2/1

stroke play
- ball played out of turn from tee abandoned; competitor plays another ball in proper order ........................................................................ 10-2c/1
- competitor objects to fellow-competitor putting out of turn; various circumstances discussed ............................................................. 10-2b/1
- competitor wishing to render original ball lost plays subsequent stroke with provisional ball out of turn ............................ 27-2b/1
- fellow-competitors agree to play out of turn to save time; whether agreement to waive Rule ............................................................ 10-2c/2

### Play-Off and Ties
match play
- players agree on method of settling tie when Committee fails to do so ................. 33-6/4
- mistakenly believing match all square after 18 holes, players play extra holes and determine winner; error then discovered .......................... 2-5/6
- rightful winner of match makes no claim and agrees to play extra holes ............... 2-5/7

stroke play
- competition over 36 holes on two courses; player completes first round, practices on same course, later in play-off on that course ................ 7-1b/4
- competitor who practices on competition course after qualifying round subsequently in play-off on same day ........................................ 7-1b/3
- determining winner and positions in stroke-play play-off when player disqualified or withdraws .................................................................. 33-6/3
- disqualification penalty incurred by competitor in play-off; whether penalty applies to entire competition ................................................ 3/1
- fellow-competitor lifts competitor's ball conceding next stroke in stroke-play play-off .............................................................................. 18-4/3
- groupings for stroke-play play-off ........................................................... 33-3/4
- replacement before play-off of club broken in anger during round ..................... 4-3/12
- score cards in sudden-death play-off ....................................................... 33-5/1
- wrong information given by competitor in sudden-death play-off results in fellow-competitor lifting ball and incurring penalty ........................ 9-3/1

### Plumb-Line
club used as plumb-line ................................................................................ 14-3/12
plumb-line used during round ....................................................................... 14-3/11

### Power Line
Local Rule requiring cancelation and replay of stroke without penalty when ball deflected by power line, tower or pole ....................... 33-8/13
relief from temporary power lines and cables; specimen Local Rule .............. App I-B-6b

### Practice
before or between rounds
- caddie practices on or tests putting green surfaces of course before stroke-play round ........................................................................ 7-1b/5
- competitor practices putting on 18th green immediately after finishing first round of stroke-play competition played over consecutive days ........................................................................... 7-2/8
- competitor practices putting on 3rd green after finishing hole during first round of 36-hole stroke-play competition .............................. 7-1b/7
- competitor who practices on competition course after qualifying round subsequently in play-off on same day ........................................ 7-1b/3

Index **I-107**

 - match discontinued by agreement on 13th tee cannot be resumed until following day; players may play first twelve holes prior to resuming match ............................................................................................ 7-2/11
 - one practice stroke played on course before stroke-play round ................... 7-1b/1
 - stroke play over 36 holes on two courses; player completes first round and practices on same course; player later in play-off on that course .................................................................................................. 7-1b/4
 - stroke play over 54 holes on consecutive days; second round canceled and competitor practices on course following cancelation ..................... 7-1b/6
during round
 - competitor practices putting on 3rd green of 9-hole course during 18-hole stroke-play competition ............................................................................ 7-2/9
 - completing hole in match play after result of hole decided ...................... 7-2/1.5
 - explanation of "strokes played in completing play of a hole" ................... 7-2/1.7
 - in anger player hits ball played by player in following group; whether stroke considered practice stroke ....................................................... 1-4/4
 - in four-ball, player disqualified for next hole plays that hole; whether strokes played on that hole were practice strokes ................. 30-3f/8
 - hitting plastic ball before playing ball in play ............................................... 7-2/4
 - hitting practice range ball back to range ....................................................... 7-2/5
 - player after picking up drops ball where partner's ball lies and plays practice stroke ............................................................................................ 30-3f/7
 - player finds ball and hits it to player who lost it; whether stroke considered practice stroke ........................................................................... 7-2/5.5
 - player in four-ball match practices on previous green after partner drives from next tee ............................................................................. 30-3f/12
 - player in foursome match practices putts on previous green after partner drives from next tee .................................................................................. 29/3
 - player plays practice putt after he and partner have holed out but before opponents hole out ................................................................................... 30/6
 - player practices putting off green while waiting to putt ............................... 7-2/3
 - player practices with another player's putter ............................................. 4-4a/13
 - putting on fairway while waiting to play to green ........................................ 7-2/2
 - replacement of club broken on practice ground while play suspended; whether permitted ................................................................................... 4-3/11
 - when practice between holes permitted ....................................................... 7-2/1
play discontinued by players in match by agreement on 13th hole cannot be resumed until following day; players may play first twelve holes prior to resuming match ............................................................. 7-2/11
play suspended by Committee; player wishes to practice after scheduled resumption but before group plays ........................................................ 7-2/12
practice swing dislodges concealed ball ................................................................... 7-2/7
waiving penalty for practice on course .................................................................. 7-1b/2

## Practice Swing

area of original intended swing improved when branch broken with practice backswing; area of intended swing finally used not affected by branch ........................................................................................... 13-2/24
ball moved
 - player takes several practice swings near ball in play and touches grass behind ball; thereafter ball moves ................................................. 18-2a/30
 - prior to tee shot accidentally by practice swing ........................................ 18-2a/19
 - when in play accidentally by practice swing ............................................. 18-2a/20
concealed ball dislodged by practice swing .............................................................. 7-2/7
club damaged while making practice swing; whether considered damaged in "normal course of play" .................................................................. 4-3/1
ground in hazard
 - touched with several practice swings ............................................................ 13-4/3
 - touched with several practice swings; player advised of breach then makes several more such swings ......................................................... 1-4/13
 - not touched however grass touched with club during practice swing ................ 13-4/4

### Practice Swing *(continued)*

leaves knocked down with practice swing .................................................. 13-2/22
player breaches Rule(s) either more than once or with different penalties
- ground in hazard touched with several practice swings; player advised
of breach then makes several more such swings ................................... 1-4/13
- ground in hazard touched with practice swing; stroke played fails
to extricate ball; before next stroke club touches ground in
hazard with another practice swing ........................................................... 1-4/14
- breaches two Rules with different penalties; more severe penalty applied ......... 1-4/15
stretching device used to make practice swing ................................................. 14-3/10.5
training or swing aid, such as weighted headcover or "doughnut" on club,
used to make practice swing; whether permitted ......................................... 14-3/10

### Prize

due to Committee error
- incorrectly calculated handicap for competitor posted resulting in
competitor winning event; error discovered several days later ................ 6-2b/3
- winner of event erroneously disqualified; Committee holds play-off
between two other competitors; error discovered after play-off
but before close of competition ............................................................... 34-1b/5
- winner's score not posted; Committee awards prize to another
competitor; error discovered next day ..................................................... 34-1b/6
- wrong handicap deducted from competitor's score resulting in
player not receiving prize; error discovered after close of competition ........ 33-5/2
player disqualified in
- match-play event; whether eligible for prize won prior to disqualification ........ 33/7
- stroke-play handicap event; whether eligible for gross prize ...................... 33-1/13

### Provisional Ball

*See also* Lost Ball; Out of Bounds; Second Ball

announcement requirements before provisional ball played .............................. 27-2a/1
Committee member finds player's original ball; player prefers
to continue with provisional ball ....................................................................... 27-2/2
condition requiring use of ball on List of Conforming Golf Balls;
player uses ball not on list as provisional ................................................. 5-1/3
deemed unplayable; player drops ball; original ball then found ....................... 27-2b/6.5
divots replaced in area in which provisional ball to be dropped ....................... 13-2/4.5
explanation of "any ball he has played" ........................................................ 18/7
foursome competition
- provisional ball played by wrong member of side .................................. 29-1/4
- determining which partner plays provisional ball ................................... 29-1/3
lifted
- in erroneous belief original ball in bounds ............................................. 27-2b/8
- subsequently becomes ball in play; penalty and procedure for player ............ 27-2b/9
- subsequently becomes ball in play; competitor then plays
from wrong place ................................................................................. 27-2b/10
meaning of "goes forward to search" ............................................................ 27-2a/1.5
moves after being addressed; whether penalty canceled if provisional
ball never becomes ball in play ....................................................................... 15/7
order of play when played other than from teeing ground ................................. 10/4
original ball
- and provisional ball found out of bounds ............................................. 27-2c/4
- and provisional ball not distinguishable from each other .......................... 27/11
- and provisional ball; time permitted for search ..................................... 27/4
- found by Committee member; player prefers to continue
with provisional ball .......................................................................... 27-2/2
- found in hole after five-minute search and continuation of play
with provisional ball ........................................................................... 1-1/3
- found; player wishes to ignore it and continue play with provisional ball ........ 27-2c/2
- not searched for; player continues play with provisional ball ..................... 27-2b/1

Index  I-109

- played after provisional ball played from point nearer hole
  than original ball likely to be ................................................................. 27-2b/5
- search abandoned; player walks forward to play provisional ball;
  original ball then found ........................................................................ 27-2b/6
- searched for briefly; player plays stroke with provisional from
  nearer hole than where original likely to be; original ball then found ............ 27-2b/3
- strikes provisional ball .............................................................................. 19-5/5
- struck by provisional ball ......................................................................... 18-5/2

played
- and possibly lost or out of bounds; third ball played with no announcement.... 27-2a/4
- as second ball when player not able to determine whether original
  ball in or out of bounds........................................................................... 3-3/1
- in absence of reasonable possibility original ball lost or out of bounds................ 27-2a/3
- from beyond where original ball likely to be but not beyond
  where original ball found ....................................................................... 27-2b/4
- from point nearer hole than visible original ball; player erroneously
  thought original ball out of bounds ....................................................... 27-2c/3
- from tee; player deems original ball unplayable while still on tee
  and plays third ball; claims third ball lying three ....................................... 28/2
- in belief original ball might be in water hazard or lost outside
  water hazard or out of bounds ................................................................ 27-2c/1
- in belief original ball might only be in water hazard (no possibility
  of being out of bounds or lost outside water hazard) ............................. 27-2a/2
- in belief original might be lost outside water hazard; thereafter player
  determines no possibility ball lost outside water hazard .................. 27-2a/2.5
- in erroneous belief it is original ball....................................................... 27-2b/7
player wishes provisional ball to serve as ball in play if original
  unplayable or in water hazard ..................................................................... 27-2/1
time permitted for search for original ball and provisional ball ........................... 27/4
when holed provisional ball becomes player's ball in play .............................. 27-2b/2
whether provisional ball becomes ball in play if original ball lost in
  ground under repair .................................................................................. 27-2c/1.5
wrong ball played in belief it is provisional ball .................................................. 15/7

## Putting Green

*See also* Ball Overhanging Hole; Flagstick; Hole; Hole Plug; Improving Area of Intended Stance or Swing, Position or Lie of Ball, or Line of Play or Putt; Indicating Line for Putting; Line of Putt; Wrong Putting Green

ball at rest moved
- player addresses ball, steps away, lifts ball and replaces it; ball then moves ........ 18-2b/8
- player knocks opponent's ball away after concession; ball strikes
  and moves player's ball ............................................................................ 18-2a/18
- player's foot accidentally moves ball during removal of loose
  impediment on putting green................................................................. 23-1/11

ball deflected or stopped on putting green
- after stroke from off green ...................................................................... 19-1/6
- after stroke from green ............................................................................ 19-1/7
- ball played at another hole deflects player's ball in motion
  after stroke played from putting green.................................................. 19-1/10
- by ball replaced while other ball in motion ........................................... 16-1b/3
- by moving outside agency; stroke not replayed ..................................... 19-1/3
- deliberately by spectator ......................................................................... 19-1/4
- player knocks partner's putted ball back to him while still in
  motion after having passed hole............................................................ 1-2/7
- stroke played from putting green strikes ball on green belonging
  to competitor playing in another group................................................ 19-5/2
- stroke played from putting green touches but does not move
  ball of fellow-competitor lying on green .............................................. 19-5/4

ball enters burrowing animal hole in bunker and comes to rest
  underneath putting green........................................................................ 25-1b/25
ball knocked from lip of hole in disgust.............................................................. 18-2a/23

## Putting Green *(continued)*

ball lifted
- because player feared ball might move .................................................. 16-1b/1
- cleaned and replaced; ball then falls into hole ........................................ 16-2/0.5
- on putting green placed ahead of ball-marker and then rolled or
    slid back to original position .................................................................. 16-1a/17

ball mark
- in position to assist opponent repaired by player ................................... 16-1c/2
- partially on and partially off putting green on line of play ..................... 16-1c/1.5
- repaired second time .............................................................................. 16-1c/1
- spike mark repaired during repair of ball mark ...................................... 16-1a/16

ball-marker
- ball replaced ahead of ball-marker then player rolls or slides
    ball back to original position ............................................................... 16-1a/17
- ball replaced but ball-marker not removed; ball then moves ................. 20-4/1
- caddie places lifted ball behind ball-marker so player can assess
    line for putting; whether ball in play .................................................. 20-4/2
- moved accidentally by player after having moved loose impediments ... 20-1/12
- placed other than behind ball; whether permitted ................................ 20-1/19
- whether lifting opponent's ball-marker considered concession
    of next stroke ..................................................................................... 2-4/5
- whether player may use object other than ball-marker or coin
    to mark position of ball ....................................................................... 20-1/16

ball oscillating in wind pressed into surface of putting green ....................... 18-2a/6

ball overhanging hole
- casting shadow on ball overhanging hole ............................................... 16-2/3
- falls into hole after being addressed ....................................................... 18-2b/10
- ball falls into hole after concession of next stroke ................................. 2-4/2
- falls into hole after player waits 40 seconds .......................................... 16-2/1
- fellow-competitor's ball knocked from lip of hole by competitor
    not replaced ........................................................................................ 3-2/1
- knocked away by opponent before player determines status ................ 16-2/2
- lifted, cleaned and replaced; ball then falls into hole ............................. 16-2/0.5
- player jumps close to hole to cause ball to drop; ball does not move .... 1-2/3.8
- player jumps close to hole to cause ball to drop; ball falls into hole ...... 1-2/4

ball putted from wrong place lifted and putted from right place ................... 20-7c/2

ball replaced
- at wrong place on putting green and holed ............................................ 20-7c/1
- ball-marker not removed after ball replaced; ball then moves ............... 20-4/1
- by rolling it to correct spot with putter ................................................... 16-1d/3
- trademark aimed along line of putt; whether permitted ......................... 20-3a/2
- while another ball in motion; replaced ball re-lifted because
    moving ball might strike it .................................................................. 16-1b/2
- while another ball in motion; replaced ball subsequently
    deflects moving ball ........................................................................... 16-1b/3

bottled drink used to gauge slope of putting green; whether permitted ....... 14-3/12.5

caddie
- casts shadow to indicate line of putt ....................................................... 8-2b/1
- inadvertently positioned on extension of line of putt behind ball ............ 14-2/4
- places lifted ball behind ball-marker so player can assess line
    for putting; whether ball in play ......................................................... 20-4/2
- practices on or tests putting green surfaces of course
    before stroke-play round .................................................................... 7-1b/5
- roughens surface of putting green but player does not benefit .............. 16-1d/6
- touches putting green to indicate line of play before player chips
    from off green ..................................................................................... 8-2b/3

casual water on putting green
- brushing aside or mopping up casual water on line of putt .................... 16-1a/1
- intervenes between ball off green and hole ............................................ 25-1a/2
- nearest point of relief off putting green .................................................. 25-1b/10

- removal of casual water or loose impediments on
  putting green by Committee..................................................................................33/1
- visible when player walks beside line of putt but not visible elsewhere .................25/5
- whether player entitled to relief for intervention if ball on
  putting green and nearest point of relief off putting green.........................25-1b/10.5
club used as plumb-line..............................................................................................14-3/12
competitor mistakenly substitutes another ball on putting green;
  error discovered after stroke played from next teeing ground................................15-2/3
concession
- agreement to concede short putts .............................................................................1-3/2
- ball falls into hole after concession of next stroke ....................................................2-4/2
- lifting opponent's ball-marker; whether considered concession of next stroke ......2-4/5
- of stroke refused by player and withdrawn by opponent;
  player then putts and misses .....................................................................................2-4/7
- opponent's ball knocked away by player after concession
  moves player's ball.................................................................................................18-2a/18
- picking up opponent's ball; whether considered concession of next stroke ............2-4/4
- player concedes opponent's next stroke and knocks ball
  away along own line of putt ..................................................................................16-1d/2
- player concedes opponent's next stroke and plays before opponent
  has opportunity to lift ball .........................................................................................2-4/8
- player concedes opponent's next stroke and rolls or knocks
  ball to opponent....................................................................................................16-1d/1
- player concedes opponent's next stroke and then knocks
  opponent's ball into hole ...........................................................................................2-4/1
- player lifts ball in mistaken belief that next stroke conceded ...................................2-4/3
- putting out after concession of stroke.......................................................................2-4/6
double green; whether portion serving hole not being played
  considered wrong putting green...............................................................................25-3/1
extension of line of putt behind ball
- caddie inadvertently positioned on .........................................................................14-2/4
- meaning of "extension of line of putt behind ball" in context
  of standing astride or on line of putt....................................................................16-1e/1
- stood on or astride of inadvertently or to avoid other
  player's line while holing short putt......................................................................16-1e/2
flagstick
- attended without authority before stroke; attendance ceases
  upon instruction of player after stroke...................................................................17-2/1
- held upright by attendant behind hole with bottom of flagstick
  touching putting green; whether breach of Rule 8-2b ........................................17-1/4.5
- holding with one hand and putting with other hand; whether permitted ............17-1/5
- removed without authority by opponent or fellow-competitor
  while player's ball in motion ...................................................................................17-2/2
flagstick moved or lifted when not in hole to prevent ball from striking it
- after stroke, attended flagstick removed from hole, placed on
  ground then lifted while ball still in motion .............................................................17-1/6
- removed flagstick on putting green when stroke made;
  lifted while ball still in motion ..................................................................................1-2/3
- removed flagstick placed on ground prior to stroke within
  reach of opponent or fellow-competitor; lifted after stroke made ........................17-1/7
- removed flagstick held by opponent or fellow-competitor;
  moved while ball in motion .....................................................................................17-1/8
four-ball match play
- partner waives turn to putt...................................................................................30-3c/2
- player knocks partner's putted ball back to him while still in
  motion after having passed hole...............................................................................1-2/7
- player with putt for half picks up in error at suggestion of opponent
  based on misunderstanding .......................................................................................30/5

**Putting Green** (continued)
line of putt
- altered purposely by opponent or fellow-competitor by stepping on it ...... 1-2/1
- brushing aside or mopping up casual water on line of putt .................. 16-1a/1
- caddie casts shadow to indicate line of putt ......................................... 8-2b/1
- caddie while attending flagstick suggests player aim at foot;
  whether breach of any Rule ............................................................. 8-2b/2
- casual water visible when player walks beside line of putt but not
  visible elsewhere .............................................................................. 25/5
- damaged accidentally by opponent, fellow-competitor or their caddies ........... 16-1a/13
- meaning of "line of putt" in context of "standing astride or
  on line of putt" ................................................................................ 16-1e/1
- mushroom growing on line of putt ..................................................... 16-1a/15
- old hole plug sunk or raised on line of putt ...................................... 16-1c/3
- player entitled to putt stands on another player's line of putt ........... 30-3c/1
- player touches putting green in pointing out line for putting
  for partner and incidentally touches own line of putt .................. 30/2.5
- player walks on line of putt ................................................................ 16-1a/12
- removal of casual water or loose impediments on putting
  green by Committee ....................................................................... 33/1
- removing dew or frost from line of putt ............................................. 16-1a/3
- shielding from wind .............................................................................. 1-2/2
Local Rule
- allowing relief from edging grooves around putting green .................. 33-8/24
- deeming material similar to sand to have same status as sand ........... 33-8/40
- requiring players to putt continuously on putting green until
  ball holed; whether authorized ...................................................... 33-8/7
- waives requirement to hole out for temporary putting green;
  whether authorized ........................................................................ 33-8/1
- wrong putting green; deemed to include apron to prohibit
  dropping on and play from ........................................................... 33-8/33
map of putting green indicating hole position displayed at tee;
  whether permitted ............................................................................... 33/6
marking island green; recommendations for Committee ........................ 33-2a/10
mud on ball touches putting green but ball itself does not touch green;
  whether ball considered on putting green ........................................... 16/1
player putts with one hand and catches ball in hole with other hand ...... 1-2/5
practice putting
- off green while waiting to putt ........................................................... 7-2/3
- on fairway while waiting to play to green ......................................... 7-2/2
- on previous green player in four-ball match practices after partner
  drives from next tee ...................................................................... 30-3f/12
- with another player's putter during round ....................................... 4-4a/13
rotating ball on putting green without marking position ..................... 18-2a/33
rubbing ball on putting green for cleaning purposes ............................ 16-1d/5
spike mark(s)
- competitor sanctions repair of spike damage on his line of putt
  by fellow-competitor ...................................................................... 13-2/36
- line of putt altered purposely by opponent or fellow-competitor
  by stepping on it ............................................................................. 1-2/1
- line of putt damaged accidentally by opponent, fellow-competitor
  or their caddies .............................................................................. 16-1a/13
- player and opponent or fellow-competitor agree to repair
  spike marks on one another's line of putt ................................... 1-3/3
- pressed down when player repairs old hole plug ............................. 16-1a/16.5
- repair of spike mark damage around hole ....................................... 16-1c/4
- repaired during repair of ball mark .................................................. 16-1a/16

team competition
- player's team mate in gallery hits approach shot to show player
whether putting green will hold ................................................................. 8-1/23
- whether team captain authorized to give advice may be required
to stay off putting greens ........................................................................ 8-2b/4
testing surface of putting green for wetness; whether permitted ................... 16-1d/4
trademark aimed along line of putt when ball replaced; whether permitted ............ 20-3a/2

## Rake

*See also* Bunker; Improving Area of Intended Stance or Swing, Position or Lie of Ball, or Line of Play or Putt; Line of Play; Obstruction; Status of Object
ball in bunker moves when rake removed; whether player may press
ball into sand or take relief outside bunker if not possible to
replace or place in bunker not nearer hole .............................................. 20-3d/2
bunker entered by player to remove rake on line of play; player smoothes
footprints restoring line of play before playing stroke ........................... 13-2/29
rake handle stuck in bunker before stroke................................................................ 13-4/22
rake or umbrella placed in hazard before stroke ..................................................... 13-4/20
rake thrown into bunker before stroke...................................................................... 13-4/21
whether rakes should be placed in or outside bunkers ......................................... Misc./2

## Reasonable Evidence

*See also* Abnormal Ground Conditions; Burrowing Animal, Reptile or Bird; Casual Water; Ground Under Repair; Lost Ball; Obstructions; Outside Agency; Provisional Ball; Water Hazards
ball lost in abnormal ground condition
- ball dropped and played under ground under repair Rule in absence
of reasonable evidence original ball lost in ground under repair .............. 25-1c/2
- ball dropped with reasonable evidence; original ball then found
within five minutes............................................................................. 25-1c/2.5
- ball found in burrowing animal hole after five-minute search ................... 27/7
- ball in casual water difficult to retrieve ................................................................ 25-1/1
- Local Rule declaring accumulations of leaves (at specified holes)
through the green as ground under repair............................................. 33-8/31
- meaning of "reasonable evidence" in Rule 25-1c ........................................ 25-1c/1
- whether provisional ball becomes ball in play if original ball lost
in ground under repair ........................................................................ 27-2c/1.5
ball lost in obstruction
- underground drainpipe.......................................................................................... 24-3b/1
- underground drainpipe with entrance out of bounds............................. 24-2b/12
ball in water hazard
- ball assumed in water hazard found outside hazard after another ball
played under stroke-and-distance procedure ........................................ 26/6
- ball dropped with reasonable evidence; original ball then found
within five minutes............................................................................... 26-1/3.5
- ball played under water hazard Rule; original ball then found
outside hazard ....................................................................................... 26-1/3
- ball played under water hazard Rule without reasonable evidence
original ball in hazard; original ball then found in hazard .................... 26-1/4
- meaning of "reasonable evidence" in Rule 26-1 ........................................... 26-1/1
- player plays provisional ball in belief original might be lost outside
water hazard; player then discovers no possibility ball lost outside
water hazard .......................................................................................... 27-2a/2.5
- unidentifiable ball played in water hazard and lost ..................................... 26/5
ball moved by outside agency
- ball not found; either moved by outside agency or lost ............................... 18-1/1
- competitor plays wrong ball and loses it; wrong ball may have been
fellow-competitor's ball......................................................................... 15-3b/1
- treated as moved by outside agency rather than lost in absence of
reasonable evidence .............................................................................. 27-1/2.5
identifying ball by brand and number only .......................................................... 12-2/1

## Referee

*See also* Committee; Observer

| | |
|---|---|
| authority to declare ground under repair | 34-2/1 |
| authorizes player to infringe Rule | 34-2/2 |
| ball thought unfit for play; referee's involvement when opponent, marker or fellow-competitor not readily available | 5-3/7 |
| Committee intervention in match play in absence of referee | US/34-3/100 |
| flagstick attended by referee at player's request; whether permitted or recommended | 17-1/3 |
| imposes penalty for previous hole after play of next hole begun | 2-5/12 |
| incorrect ruling by referee places player at serious disadvantage; when ruling may be reversed | 34-3/3.3 |
| player disagrees with referee's decision; whether decision may be referred to Committee | 34-2/4 |
| procedure for determining ball farther from hole | 10-1b/1 |
| reverses ruling | |
| - made at last hole of match after players leave putting green | 34-2/5 |
| - made on previous hole after play of next hole begun | 34-2/6 |
| warns player about to infringe Rule | 34-2/3 |
| when match result "officially announced" | 2-5/14 |

## Refusal to Comply with Rule

| | |
|---|---|
| competitor not given opportunity to lift ball assisting fellow-competitor before fellow-competitor plays | 3-4/1 |
| player concedes opponent's next stroke then plays before opponent has opportunity to lift ball | 2-4/8 |
| player claiming danger from lightning, refuses to play when resumption of play ordered by Committee | 6-8b/5 |
| player refuses to tell opponent how many strokes he has taken | 9-2/3.5 |
| player requests opponent's ball be lifted because it might assist opponent's partner; opponent does not lift ball and opponent's partner plays | 30-3f/11 |

## Relief

*See also* Burrowing Animal, Reptile or Bird; Casual Water; Embedded Ball; Ground Under Repair; Maximum Available Relief; Nearest Point of Relief; Obstructions

| | |
|---|---|
| after relief taken from obstruction | |
| - for stroke towards green, obstruction interferes with stance for necessary sideways stroke | 24-2b/9.5 |
| - from rough to fairway in obtaining relief from obstruction | 24-2b/8 |
| - second obstruction interferes | 24-2b/9 |
| ball at base of cliff; player wishes to drop within two club-lengths of point above ball | 28/12 |
| ball dropped from ground under repair area rolls to position where area interferes with stance; whether re-drop required | 20-2c/0.5 |
| ball in casual water, difficult to retrieve | 25-1/1 |
| ball in tree; player opts to drop within two club-lengths | 28/11 |
| ball lies on mound made by burrowing animal; unreasonable to play stroke due to bush | 25-1b/19 |
| ball played on wrong putting green after lifting and replacing | 25-3/2 |
| ball rolls towards hole when dropped at spot from which previous stroke played | 20-2c/1.5 |
| cast of burrowing animal interferes with | |
| - sideways stroke; when relief granted | 25-1b/22 |
| - stroke towards green; tree prevents such stroke | 25-1b/21 |
| changing relief option | |
| - dropped ball first strikes course outside where applicable Rule requires; whether player may change relief option when re-dropping | 20-6/2 |

- dropped ball first strikes course outside where applicable Rule
  requires; whether player may replace ball in original location ............................. 20-6/5
- dropped ball rolls to position requiring re-drop; whether player may
  change relief option when re-dropping ............................................................. 20-2c/5
- dropped ball strikes player; whether player may change relief option
  when re-dropping ............................................................................................ 20-2a/6
- player drops ball in bunker under first option of Rule 25-1b(ii); player
  then wishes to proceed under second option to drop outside bunker .............. 25-1b/9
- player lifts ball from bunker intending to drop under first option
  of Rule 24-2b(ii); player then wishes to proceed under second option
  to drop outside bunker ..................................................................................... 24-2b/5
- point where ball last crossed margin of lateral water hazard determined
  and ball dropped; point then proves to be wrong point; whether
  player may change relief option when re-dropping ........................................ 26-1/16

dropped ball
- lifted and re-dropped when it should have been played as it lay;
  ball then lifted again and placed ..................................................................... 18-2a/10
- player drops ball after play suspended for dangerous situation .......................... 6-8b/8
- rolls out of prescribed dropping area; whether re-drop required ...................... 20-2c/1

explanation of "maximum available relief" from casual water in bunker .................. 25-1b/5
improving line of play when taking relief from abnormal ground conditions ............ 25-1b/3

Local Rule
- allowing free relief from damage made by insects ............................................ 33-8/21
- altering ground under repair relief procedure to require player to
  drop behind condition; whether authorized .................................................. 33-8/26

measuring
- across ground under repair in obtaining relief ................................................. 25-1b/15
- club to be used in measuring .................................................................................. 20/1
- borrowed club used for measuring purposes ........................................................... 20/2
- club-lengths directly through fence, tree or wall or across ditch ...................... 20-2b/2

obstruction causes mental interference ..................................................................... 24-2a/1

player entitled to relief without penalty from condition lifts ball
- chooses not to take relief and wishes to proceed under unplayable
  ball Rule ..................................................................................................... 18-2a/12.5
- player then replaces ball and plays it from original position ............................ 18-2a/12

player takes relief from area of casual water and ball comes to rest in
  position where another area of casual water interferes; whether
  re-drop required ................................................................................................... 20-2c/7

player's options when bunker completely covered by casual water ........................... 25-1b/8

relief from immovable obstruction incidentally results in relief from
  boundary fence .................................................................................................... 24-2b/6

relief from obstruction interfering with swing incidentally gives relief
  from intervention on line of play ........................................................................ 24-2b/7

stance interfered with by burrowing animal hole; unreasonable to
  play stroke because of other condition ............................................................... 25-1b/20

water hazard
- ball played from water hazard to unplayable lie outside water hazard;
  explanations of options under Rule 26-2b ...................................................... 26-2/1
- ball played from within water hazard comes to rest in same hazard
  after exiting hazard; explanation of relief options .......................................... 26-2/2
- marked as water hazard where ball last crosses margin and as
  lateral water hazard where ball comes to rest; relief options for player .......... 26-1/12
- opposite side of lateral water hazard defined as water hazard;
  relief options for player ................................................................................. 26-1/13
- procedures for relief from lateral water hazard ................................................. 26-1/15

whether player himself must lift ball ....................................................................... 20-1/0.5
whether player may drop ball into area from which play prohibited ........................... 20-7/3

**Repair**

*See also* Damage; Ground Under Repair
ball mark on putting green
- hole damage due to ball mark; whether player may repair .................................. 16-1a/6
- in position to assist player; whether player may prevent repair
  by opponent ............................................................................................................ 16-1c/2
- partially on and partially off putting green on player's line of play;
  whether repair permitted ...................................................................................... 16-1c/1.5
- repair by caddie; whether permitted .......................................................................... 6-4/10
- repaired second time .................................................................................................. 16-1c/1

club or clubs
- meaning of "repair" when club damaged in normal course of play ........................ 4-3/2
- rendered unfit for play by outside agency or opponent's side;
  whether repair or replacement permitted ............................................................ 4-3/9.5
- damaged in normal course of play breaks into pieces when repaired;
  whether replacement permitted ............................................................................ 4-3/3

damaged hole
- inside edge of damaged hole touched while repaired; whether permitted .......... 16-1a/5
- repair procedures; damage due to ball mark; damage due to other cause ............ 16-1a/6
- repaired after player holes out but before opponent, fellow-competitor
  or partner holes out .............................................................................................. 1-2/3.5

line of putt
- agreement to repair spike marks on one another's line of putt made
  by player and opponent or competitor and fellow-competitor ............................ 1-3/3
- damaged accidentally by opponent, fellow-competitor or their caddies;
  whether repair permitted ...................................................................................... 16-1a/13
- depression exposed when partially embedded acorn removed;
  whether repair permitted ...................................................................................... 16-1a/7
- old hole plug sunk or raised on line of putt; relief options available
  to player ................................................................................................................ 16-1c/3

old hole plugs and other turf plugs
- Local Rule permitting repair of turf plugs on putting green not
  4-1/4 inches in diameter ........................................................................................ 33-8/30
- repair by caddie; whether permitted .......................................................................... 6-4/10
- sunken or raised on line of putt; relief options available to player ........................ 16-1c/3

pitch-mark
- area of intended swing improved by repair of pitch-mark made by
  ball on previous stroke .......................................................................................... 13-2/21
- repaired in area where ball to be dropped ................................................................ 13-2/10

spike mark
- agreement to repair spike marks on one another's line of putt made
  by player and opponent or competitor and fellow-competitor ............................ 1-3/3
- damage around hole; whether repair permitted ...................................................... 16-1c/4
- pressed down when player repairs old hole plug .................................................... 16-1a/16.5
- repaired during repair of ball mark .......................................................................... 16-1a/16

**Roads and Paths**

*See also* Status of Object
ball breaks into pieces as result of striking paved cart path .................................... 5-3/4
Local Rule
- deeming ground under repair adjacent to artificially-surfaced cart
  paths to have same status as path ........................................................................ 33-8/25
- providing relief from unsurfaced road for tee shot only;
  whether authorized ................................................................................................ 33-8/20
- providing relief in all cases on fairway side of paved path, or ball drop
  (dropping zone), when nearest point of relief effectively gives no relief;
  whether authorized ................................................................................................ 33-8/19
meaning of "artificially-surfaced" .................................................................................. 24/9

nearest point of relief from cart path in casual water; nearest point of
    relief from casual water back on cart path ........................................................... 1-4/8
public road defined as out of bounds divides course; status of ball crossing road ........ 27/20
status of
   - gravel used to surface road ................................................................................... 23/14
   - paved area other than road or path ..................................................................... 24/10

## Roots

*See also* Tree or Bush

ball against root popped up by stroke; player swings at ball in disgust;
    whether action considered either exerting influence or stroke
    at moving ball ..................................................................................................... 14/6
divot lies substantially with all of its roots downward in divot hole;
    whether considered replaced ............................................................................ 13-2/7
Local Rule providing relief from tree roots; whether authorized ....................... 33-8/8
moving natural object enough to determine whether loose impediment
    or attached to roots; whether breach of Rule 13-2 ......................................... 13-2/26
moving raised tuft of grass on line of putt to determine if attached to
    roots; whether breach of Rule 13-2 ................................................................. 16-1a/11
player misses stroke at ball between tree roots then deems it unplayable;
    Rule 28a option discussed .................................................................................. 28/7
probing for tree roots or rocks near ball; whether permitted ........................... 13-2/27
status of roots outside area of ground under repair growing from
    tree inside area ............................................................................................... 25/10.7
unplayable ball between tree roots; whether relief available if obstruction
    interferes with player's swing ......................................................................... 24-2b/16

## Rough

*See also* Through The Green

ball in rough
   - found and then lost again; time permitted for search ...................................... 27/3
   - lifted by fellow-competitor at player's request; turns out to be player's
      ball in play ................................................................................................. 18-2a/16
   - moved accidentally and original lie altered; ball replaced in wrong
      place and played ..................................................................................... 18-2a/21.3
   - moved accidentally; ball placed instead of dropped when original
      spot not determinable ............................................................................ 18-2a/21.5
   - moved after practice swings taken near ball and grass behind
      ball touched ............................................................................................... 18-2a/30
   - moves downward when addressed; ball will not remain at rest
      when replaced ............................................................................................ 20-3d/3
   - touched and rotated for identification purposes ........................................... 12-2/2
casual water on putting green; nearest point of relief off green in rough .................. 25-1b/10
concealed ball in rough dislodged by
   - practice swing ........................................................................................................ 7-2/7
   - stroke at player's own ball in rough ..................................................................... 15/2
dropping from rough to fairway in obtaining relief under Rule;
    whether permitted ............................................................................................ 24-2b/8
lie improved due to relief from condition; whether ball must be
    re-dropped if condition interferes for stroke with different club ..................... 20-2c/0.8
Local Rule defining rough and unplayable areas adjacent to fairways
    (areas not meeting definition of lateral water hazard) as lateral
    water hazard; whether authorized ..................................................................... 33-8/35
pressed down due to removal of loose impediment .............................................. 13-2/13
when club grounded in grass ................................................................................. 18-2b/5
wrong ball played from rough
   - and lost when played by fellow-competitor; procedure for player
      to whom ball belonged ............................................................................... 15-3b/1
   - hole conceded prior to discovery ......................................................................... 2-4/9
   - then player wins hole with original ball; opponent does not lodge
      claim during hole; claim lodged next day ..................................................... 2-5/4

## Saliva

*See also* Loose Impediments
applying saliva to face of club .................................................................................... 4-2/4
status of saliva .................................................................................................................. 25/6

## Sand

*See also* Bunker
ball embedded in lip of bunker ..................................................................................... 13/4
ball overhanging edge of bunker ................................................................................... 13/3
hitting sand in bunker with club after failing to extricate ball
   - in breach of Rule 13-4 ......................................................................................... 13-4/35
   - in foursome match ..................................................................................................... 29/5
   - partner's ball in same bunker ............................................................................. 30-3f/2
hitting sand in bunker with club in frustration after stroke played from
      bunker onto grass bank but before ball rolls back into bunker ................. 13-4/35.5
in bunker club touches
   - casual water without touching sand ................................................................... 13-4/7
   - sand during backswing ......................................................................................... 13-4/31
   - sand when ball lies outside bunker ..................................................................... 13-4/1
lie on apron of green affected by sand from partner's, opponent's or
      fellow-competitor's stroke from bunker ......................................................... 13-2/8.5
lie through the green improved when sand behind ball removed by backswing ......... 13-2/9
Local Rule permitting re-dropping or placing when dropped ball
      embeds in bunker; whether authorized ............................................................ 33-8/28
pressed down behind ball through the green when addressed ............................. 13-2/12
removing sand or loose soil from dropping area ....................................................... 13-2/11
searching for ball covered by sand in bunker
   - with clubhead ............................................................................................................. 12-1/1
   - ball removed from buried lie during search ...................................................... 12-1/2
smoothing sand after ball played out of bunker; ball later returns to
      smoothed area ......................................................................................................... 13-4/38
spilling over margin of bunker; whether considered part of bunker ...................... 13/1

## Scores and Score Cards

*See also* Information as to Strokes Taken; Marker
all scores not to count
   - application of disqualification penalty in competition in which
      not all team members' scores count for each round ........................................ 33/8
   - competition in which competitors' best of two of four scores used to
      determine winner; competitor returns score card with higher handicap ......... 6-2b/5
Committee error
   - score cards not returned promptly due to Committee failure to advise competitors
      where to return score cards ................................................................................. 6-6b/4
   - winner's score not posted due to Committee error ....................................... 34-1b/6
   - wrong ball penalty not included in competitor's score due to
      incorrect Committee ruling; during subsequent round error
      discovered and penalty applied retroactively; competitor objects ................ 34-3/1
   - wrong handicap applied by Committee results in player not
      receiving prize ........................................................................................................... 33-5/2
   - wrong handicap recorded on score card by Committee;
      error discovered before competition closed ............................................... 6-2b/3.5
four-ball play
   - competitor records score for hole not completed ........................................... 31-7a/1
   - gross score of partner with better net score omitted from score card ....... 31-4/1
   - lower gross score attributed to wrong partner .............................................. 31-7a/2
   - side's scores transposed at hole but not to side's advantage
      in handicap four-ball Stableford competition ................................................. 32-2a/1
   - side's scores transposed at hole to side's advantage in handicap
      four-ball Stableford competition ......................................................................... 32-2a/2

guidelines for determining which ball counts when player
    proceeds under Rule 3-3 .................................................................................. 3-3/0.5
handicap
  - competition in which best two of four scores used to determine
    winner; competitor returns score card with higher handicap ............................. 6-2b/5
  - competitor records incorrect handicap for partner in foursome
    stroke play competition; error discovered after competition closed ................. 6-2b/2.5
  - recording of lower gross score affects result at hole in handicap
    Stableford competition ................................................................................. 32-2a/3
  - recording of lower gross score does not affect result of hole in
    handicap Stableford competition .................................................................. 32-2a/4
  - recording of lower gross score does not affect result of hole in
    handicap Bogey or Par competition ............................................................... 32-2a/5
  - side's scores transposed at hole but not to side's advantage in
    handicap four-ball Stableford competition .................................................... 32-2a/1
  - side's scores transposed at hole to side's advantage in handicap
    four-ball Stableford competition ................................................................... 32-2a/2
  - wrong handicap applied by Committee results in player not receiving prize ...... 33-5/2
  - wrong handicap recorded on score card by Committee; error
    discovered before competition closed ........................................................... 6-2b/3.5
hole scores
  - competitor's scores recorded on fellow-competitor's score card
    and vice versa .............................................................................................. 6-6d/4
  - entered in wrong boxes; marker corrects error by altering hole
    numbers on card .......................................................................................... 6-6a/3
  - for first nine holes recorded in boxes for second nine and vice versa .................. 6-6d/3
  - no score entered for one hole but total correct .................................................... 6-6d/1
making competitors responsible for adding scores; whether permitted ........................ 33-1/7
marker
  - and competitor sign score card in wrong places .................................................. 6-6b/1
  - attests wrong score knowingly; competitor aware score wrong ............................. 1-3/6
  - attests wrong score knowingly; competitor unaware score wrong ......................... 6-6a/5
  - competitor plays several holes without marker .................................................... 6-6a/2
  - disappears with competitor's score card .............................................................. 6-6b/3
  - lone competitor appoints own marker ................................................................. 6-6a/1
  - not appointed by Committee signs score cards .................................................... 6-6b/5
  - refuses to sign competitor's card after dispute resolved in
    favor of competitor ....................................................................................... 6-6a/4
  - score corrected by competitor after marker leaves area in which
    score card returned ...................................................................................... 6-6b/7
match play
  - player and opponent agree hole halved; after match result posted
    player realizes he won hole and should have won match; player
    then makes claim .......................................................................................... 2-5/9
  - player concedes match after winning it when opponent lodges
    invalid claim regarding strokes taken ........................................................... 2-4/15
  - player concedes match due to misconception as to opponent's
    score at last hole .......................................................................................... 2-4/14
  - player reporting wrong score causes opponent with chance for
    half to pick up ball ........................................................................................ 9-2/6
  - player reports wrong score for hole; error discovered several holes later ................ 9-2/9
  - wrong score on score card in qualifying round discovered during
    match play ................................................................................................. 34-1b/7
  - wrong score on score card in qualifying round discovered; player
    disqualified has advanced in match play; Committee options
    regarding opponents beaten by player ........................................................ 34-1b/8
minus or zero net score ................................................................................................ 2-1/2
modifying disqualification penalty for returning wrong score .......................................... 33-7/4

**Scores and Score Cards** (continued)
penalty strokes
- breach of 14-club Rule; where penalty strokes applied ................................................. 4-4a/10
- competitor correctly advised he incurred penalty by fellow-competitor; competitor disagrees and fails to include penalty in returned score card; Committee advised of incident after close of competition .......... 34-1b/1.5
- competitor fails to include penalty in first round score due to incorrect Committee ruling; Committee corrects error during second round .................................................................................. 34-3/1
- competitor unaware of penalty returns wrong score; whether waiving or modifying disqualification penalty justified ...................... 33-7/4.5
- omitted from score card returned by player ........................................................ 34-1b/1

requirement that score be entered into computer ................................................... 6-6b/8
returning score card
- different score card returned when original lost or damaged .................... 6-6a/7
- requirement to return score card in sudden-death play-off ...................... 33-5/1
- score cards not returned promptly due to Committee failure to advise competitors where to return score cards ................................................. 6-6b/4
- when score card considered returned ........................................................ 6-6c/1
- with name of wrong player or no name on it .............................................. 6-6d/4

score card or pencil used to gauge distance ............................................................ 14-3/2
score may count with wrong ball in some circumstances
- ball thrown into bounds by outside agency and played; neither player nor caddie aware of action of outside agency ........................................... 15/10
- fellow-competitor lifts competitor's ball and sets it aside; competitor plays ball from where set aside .................................................................. 15-3b/3
- play of wrong ball in stroke play not rectified; error discovered after competition closed ............................................................................ 34-1b/3
- play of wrong ball not rectified on advice of committee member ........... 33-7/5

signing of score card
- competitor and marker sign score card in wrong places ........................... 6-6b/1
- competitor's failure to sign score card discovered after competition closed ........ 34-1b/2
- competitor records initials in space reserved for signature ...................... 6-6b/2
- competitor's failure to countersign score card blamed on lack of time provided by Committee ............................................................................ 33-7/3
- competitor's failure to sign first-round card discovered on completion of last round ............................................................................................. 6-6b/3
- in foursome stroke play .............................................................................. 29/6
- marker not appointed by Committee signs score cards ............................. 6-6b/5
- marker refuses to sign competitor's card after dispute resolved in favor of competitor ................................................................................. 6-6a/4
- requirement that alteration on score card be initialed ............................... 6-6a/6

spectators allege competitor's score incorrect ............................................................ 6-6d/5
total score recorded by competitor incorrect ........................................................... 6-6d/2

**Searching for and Identifying Ball**

*See also* Lost Ball

ball accidentally stepped on during search by opponent's caddie ........................... 18-3b/3
ball assumed in water hazard found outside hazard after another ball played under stroke-and-distance procedure ................................................... 26/6
ball changed during play of hole to aid identification .............................................. 15/6.5
ball covered by sand in bunker removed from buried lie during search ................ 12-1/2
ball dislodged from tree
- circumstances in which player not penalized .......................................... 18-2a/27
- circumstances in which player penalized ................................................ 18-2a/28

ball in casual water difficult to identify or retrieve without unreasonable effort ........ 25-1/1
ball in tree
- identified but not retrieved ....................................................................... 27/14
- visible but not identifiable ......................................................................... 27/15

ball thought lost found before another ball put into play ........................................ 27/16

caddie on own initiative lifts ball for identification ................................................................ 18-2a/14
continuation of play with provisional ball without searching for original ball ............ 27-2b/1
ground in bunker or water hazard touched with club while probing for
    ball believed covered by loose impediments ............................................................... 12-1/4
identifying ball
  - by brand and number only .............................................................................................. 12-2/1
  - player lifts ball with mud adhering for identification and rotates it
      when replaced ................................................................................................................ 21/5
  - through testimony of spectator ...................................................................................... 27/12
loose impediment affecting lie
  - moved when ball lifted for identification .................................................................... 23-1/7
  - removed while ball lifted for identification ................................................................. 23-1/8
meaning of "goes forward to search" ..................................................................................... 27-2a/1.5
opponent's caddie lifts player's ball
  - after player claims another ball ..................................................................................... 18-3b/4
  - which may or may not have been out of bounds ........................................................ 18-3b/5
original ball found; player wishes to ignore it and continue play with
    provisional ball ................................................................................................................ 27-2c/2
original ball found within five-minute search period, not identified until
    after period elapses ........................................................................................................ 27/5.5
player breaches two Rules with different penalties; more severe penalty applied ........ 1-4/15
player directs caddie not to search for ball until others can assist ..................................... 27/1
player kicks ball while probing for it in water in water hazard .......................................... 12-1/5
player searching for ball mistakes his ball for opponent's then discovers
    mistake after five-minute search period ..................................................................... 27/5
player unable to distinguish his ball from another ball ....................................................... 27/10
position of ball lifted for identification not marked, intention to lift not
    announced and ball cleaned beyond extent necessary to identify it ...................... 21/4
provisional ball
  - not distinguishable from original ball .......................................................................... 27/11
  - played solely in belief original ball might be in water hazard ................................ 27-2a/2
reasonable evidence
  - ball lost in abnormal ground condition or obstruction; drop made
      under applicable Rule; original ball then found within five minutes ............ 25-1c/2.5
  - ball in water hazard; drop made under water hazard Rule; original
      ball then found within five minutes ........................................................................ 26-1/3.5
refusal to identify ball ............................................................................................................... 27/13
searching with clubhead for ball covered by sand in bunker ............................................. 12-1/1
time permitted for search
  - after wrong ball played .................................................................................................... 27/2
  - for original ball and provisional ball ............................................................................. 27/4
  - if lost ball found and then lost again ............................................................................ 27/3
  - if play suspended during search ................................................................................... 27/1.5
top of ball in hazard covered by leaves but part of ball visible from
    another angle .................................................................................................................. 12-1/3
touching and rotating half-buried ball in rough for identification purposes
  - in hazard .......................................................................................................................... 12-2/3
  - in rough ............................................................................................................................ 12-2/2
two balls lie together in hazard; neither identifiable ............................................................ 1-4/6
unidentifiable ball played in water hazard and lost .............................................................. 26/5
when necessary to find and identify ball deemed unplayable ............................................ 28/1

### Second Ball

*See also* Doubt as to Procedure; Provisional Ball; Serious Breach of Rules
competitor and fellow-competitor unaware ball moved by fellow-competitor's
    ball until after completion of hole ............................................................................... 18-5/3
determining which ball counts when two balls played
  - guidelines for determining which ball counts when player proceeds
      under Rule 3-3 ............................................................................................................ 3-3/0.5
  - whether score with second ball counts if dropped in wrong place and played ...... 3-3/5

**Second Ball** (continued)
explanation of "any ball he has played" .................................................................. 18/7
match play
- Local Rule allowing play of second ball in match play; whether authorized ........ 33-8/3
- player invokes Rule 3-3 in match play; whether permitted ............................................ 3-3/9
- player with honor plays from outside teeing ground; order of play if opponent requires player to cancel stroke ................................................................................ 11-4a/1
meaning of "penalty strokes incurred solely by playing ball ruled not to count" when competitor plays second ball under Rule 20-7c ....................... 20-7c/5
moves after being addressed; whether penalty canceled if second ball never becomes ball in play ........................................................................................ 15/7
original ball strikes second ball or vice versa ................................................................ 3-3/7
player invokes Rule 3-3 (doubt as to procedure)
- and plays second ball despite adverse ruling by Committee member ....................... 3-3/2
- ball dropped in wrong place and played; second ball dropped in right place; both balls played out ........................................................................ 3-3/3
- ball dropped in wrong place but not played; second ball dropped in right place; both balls played out ........................................................................ 3-3/4
- ball played under water hazard Rule; original ball then found in hazard and holed out as second ball .................................................................. 26-1/5
- competitor announces intention to play two balls; plays original ball before dropping second ball; elects not to play second ball .......................... 3-3/7.5
- competitor drops one ball in accordance with two different Rules instead of playing second ball ........................................................................... 3-3/11
- competitor drops one ball in accordance with two different Rules instead of playing second ball; dropped ball rolls back into condition from which relief taken .......................................................................................... 3-3/12
- competitor invokes Rule 3-3; second ball played first from spot where original ball lay ............................................................................................... 3-3/14
- competitor lifts and drops original ball then places second ball where original ball lay and plays it .......................................................................... 3-3/13
- competitor picks up second ball, completes hole with original ball and plays from next tee ........................................................................................... 3-3/8
- competitor plays original ball then invokes Rule 3-3 and plays second ball ............. 3-3/6
- competitor plays second ball without announcing intention to invoke Rule 3-3 and fails to report facts to Committee ............................................ 3-3/6.5
- competitor plays three balls when doubtful of rights ................................................. 3-3/10
- in match play; whether permitted .................................................................................. 3-3/9
- provisional ball used as second ball when not determinable whether original ball out of bounds .......................................................................................... 3-3/1
player wishes provisional ball to serve as ball in play if original unplayable or in water hazard ........................................................................................................... 27-2/1
spectator claims ball moved by outside agency; player not sure; procedure for player if Committee decision not possible in reasonable time ....................... 18-1/4
wrong ball played in belief it is provisional or second ball ................................................. 15/7

**Serious Breach of Rules**

*See also* Agreement to Waive Rules; Etiquette
exerting influence
- application of Rule 1-2 disqualification penalty in team competition in which not all team members' scores count for each round .................................. 33/8
- ball deliberately deflected or stopped on putting green by fellow-competitor ...... 19-1/5
- opponent or fellow-competitor attending flagstick for player deliberately fails to remove it; ball strikes flagstick ...................................................... 17-3/2
meaning of "serious breach of etiquette" ............................................................................. 33-7/8
player placed at serious disadvantage due to incorrect Committee ruling ................. 34-3/3.3
player plays from wrong place as directed by Committee member; error discovered before player begins next hole; procedure when serious breach involved ................................................................................................ 34-3/3

Index **I-123**

playing from wrong place
- ball believed lost in bunker; competitor drops and plays substituted
 ball in bunker; then original ball found outside bunker ............................ 20-7c/3
- ball deemed unplayable in water hazard; dropped in hazard and played ............. 20-7/2
- ball dropped in area where original ball lost; ball then played....................... 27-1/3
- ball dropped outside bunker under option of unplayable ball Rule
 requiring drop in bunker................................................................................. 28/10
- ball dropped and played under ground under repair Rule in absence
 of reasonable evidence original ball lost in ground under repair ..................... 25-1c/2
- ball knocked out of bunker by fellow-competitor's stroke at own ball
 not replaced ................................................................................................... 18-4/2
- ball played from ground under repair abandoned and relief taken
 under ground under repair Rule................................................................... 18-2a/8.5
- ball played from putting green deflected by moving outside agency;
 stroke not replayed ......................................................................................... 19-1/3
- ball played from spot where original ball deflected out of bounds
 by maintenance vehicle.................................................................................. 20-7/1
- ball played under water hazard Rule; original ball then found
 outside hazard ................................................................................................ 26-1/3
- ball played under water hazard Rule without reasonable evidence
 original ball in hazard; original ball then found in hazard................................. 26-1/4
- competitor and fellow-competitor unaware ball moved by
 fellow-competitor's ball until after completion of hole ..................................... 18-5/3
- environmentally-sensitive area, playing from.................................................. 33-8/43
- environmentally-sensitive area; significant advantage gained when
 player plays stroke from ................................................................................. 33-8/44
- example of serious breach of lateral water hazard Rule ............................... 26-1/21
- lost ball treated as moved by outside agency in absence of reasonable
 evidence to that effect ................................................................................. 27-1/2.5
- player invokes Rule 3-3 (doubt as to procedure); guidelines for
 determining which ball counts ........................................................................ 3-3/0.5
- player plays second shot, deems ball unplayable and returns to tee.............................. 28/6
- water hazard treated as lateral water hazard ................................................ 26-1/11
wrong ball played in belief it was second ball played under Rule 20-7c .......................... 15/7

### Singles Match

advice
- sought by player then given by opponent ....................................................... 8-1/25
- whether partners may exchange advice on singles match after
 result of hole or match in concurrent four-ball match decided ......................... 30-3/1
ball at rest moved accidentally
- by golf cart shared by player and opponent ........................................................ 18/8
- player's ball knocked away by opponent after concession hits and
 moves opponent's ball ................................................................................. 18-2a/18
- player's stroke moves opponent's ball lying nearby ....................................... 18-3b/1
concurrent four-ball and singles matches
- player causes opponent's ball to move; whether penalty stroke
 applies to player's singles match with other opponent ................................... 30-3/1
- player causes partner's ball to move; whether penalty stroke applies
 to player's singles match ................................................................................ 30-3/1
- player starts round with 15 clubs; whether four-ball partner incurs
 penalty in singles match ................................................................................. 30-3/1
- player starts round with non-conforming club; whether player's
 partner disqualified in his singles match ........................................................ 30-3/1
- whether concessions made under various circumstances apply to
 only four-ball or singles match or both ........................................................... 30-3/1
- whether partners may exchange advice on singles match after
 result of hole or match in concurrent four-ball match decided ......................... 30-3/1

**S**

## Singles Match (continued)

concurrent match and stroke play
- player in singles match concurrently competes in stroke-play event ........................ 33-1/6
- players in singles match joined by competitor in stroke-play event
  needing marker; whether breach of combining match and stroke play ............ 33-1/5

golf cart shared by player and opponent deflects or stops player's ball in motion .......... 19/1
incorrect ruling by Committee places player at serious disadvantage;
  when ruling may be reversed .................................................................... 34-3/3.3
injury or physical problem
- discontinuing play due to physical problem .................................................. 6-8a/3
- postponement of final match due to injury of player ...................................... 6-3a/1

match-play finalists both disqualified ........................................................................... 33/3
order of play
- for provisional ball played other than from teeing ground ............................... 10/4
- player plays out of turn in match after play suspended by Committee
  and after opponent discontinues play ....................................................... 6-8b/3.5
- player with honor plays from outside teeing ground;
  order of play if opponent requires player to cancel stroke ........................... 11-4a/1

player invites third person to play along with singles match;
  opponent objects then plays match under protest .......................................... 2/1
players unable to arrange foursome match agree to singles match
  between one player from each side to decide which team will concede;
  whether permitted ...................................................................................... 2-4/21
referee reverses ruling
- made at last hole of match after players leave putting green ......................... 34-2/5
- made on previous hole after play of next hole begun .................................. 34-2/6
result of match when player dormie and opponent concedes .................................... 2-3/2
true state of match not determinable; recommendations to Committee .................. 34-3/5
when match result "officially announced" ................................................................ 2-5/14
when play of hole completed in singles match so players may practice
  between holes .......................................................................................... 7-2/1

## Snake

*See also* Burrowing Animal, Reptile or Bird; Status of Object

ball near rattlesnake ................................................................................................ 1-4/10
status of snake ........................................................................................................ 23/6.5

## Spectator

*See also* Outside Agency

alleges competitor's score incorrect ........................................................................ 6-6d/5
assistance in removing large loose impediment .................................................... 23-1/3
ball at rest kicked away from hole by spectator attending flagstick ..................... 18-1/10
ball dislodged in tree knocked down by outside agency ....................................... 18-1/9
ball falls into bunker when person walks nearby ..................................................... 18/10
deflects or stops ball
- deliberately, from putting green ................................................................... 19-1/4
- through the green .................................................................................... 19-1/4.1

identifying ball ........................................................................................................ 27/12
Local Rule declaring areas of extensive damage due to heavy rain and
  spectator traffic ground under repair ...................................................... 33-2a/3
marker not appointed by Committee signs score cards ....................................... 6-6b/5
player concedes match then spectator informs him of opponent's
  breach of Rule; player lodges claim ........................................................ 2-4/15
seeking information on whereabouts of another player's ball from spectator ....... 8-1/5
spectator says ball moved by outside agency but player not sure; procedure
  for player if Committee decision not possible in reasonable time ................ 18-1/4
wrong information given by mistake after play of last hole; claim made
  after result announced ............................................................................ 2-5/11

## Spike Mark(s)

*See also* Damage; Improving Area of Intended Stance or Swing, Position or Lie of Ball, or Line of Play or Putt; Line of Putt; Putting Green

agreement to repair spike marks made by player and opponent or by
      competitor and fellow-competitor ................................................................................. 1-3/3
competitor sanctions or tacitly approves repair of spike marks by
      fellow-competitor on line of putt ...................................................................... 13-2/36
line of putt
  - accidentally damaged by opponent, fellow-competitor or their caddies ............. 16-1a/13
  - purposely damaged or improved by opponent or fellow-competitor
      or their caddies ............................................................................................... 1-2/1
raised tuft of grass on line of putt
  - brushed to determine whether loose impediment or attached spike mark ........ 16-1a/11
  - pressed down when ball put down ahead of ball-marker and rolled
      back into original position to replace ball ..................................................... 16-1a/17
  - pressed down when ball-marker positioned in front of ball on
      putting green .................................................................................................. 20-1/19
repaired
  - around hole ................................................................................................................ 16-1c/4
  - during repair of ball mark .................................................................................... 16-1a/16
  - during repair of old hole plug ........................................................................... 16-1a/16.5

## Sportsmanship Code

*See also* Etiquette

Local Rule for breach of sportsmanship code; whether permitted .......................... US/33-8/101

## Stableford Competition

*See also* Bogey Competition; Four-Ball Stableford Competition

breach of Rule by both partners at same hole in four-ball Stableford ........................... 32-2b/1
competing simultaneously in Stableford competition and stroke-play
      competition .......................................................................................................... 32-1/1
determination of honor in handicap or Stableford competition ..................................... 32-1/3
in four-ball Stableford competition on handicap basis
  - side's scores transposed at hole but not to side's advantage ................................... 32-2a/1
  - side's scores transposed at hole to side's advantage ............................................... 32-2a/2
handicap and handicap competition
  - recording of lower gross score affects result of hole ................................................ 32-2a/3
  - recording of lower gross score does not affect result of hole .................................. 32-2a/4
minus or zero net score ............................................................................................................ 2-1/2
omitting holes in Bogey or Stableford competition .............................................................. 32-1/2
when practice between holes permitted ................................................................................. 7-2/1

## Stakes

*See also* Boundary Fence, Line, Wall or Stakes; Status of Object

ball lifted and dropped away from boundary stake under obstruction Rule ................ 18-2a/3
ball within natural margin of water hazard but outside stakes defining margin ............ 26/2
boundary altered by unauthorized removal of boundary stake ..................................... 33-2a/19
boundary stakes having no significance in play of hole being played ................................. 24/5
displaced boundary stake ...................................................................................................... 33-2a/20
dropped ball comes to rest and then rolls out of bounds ............................................... 20-2c/3.5
hole of removed stake defining water hazard ............................................................................ 25/18
lie of ball changed by removal of gallery-control stake ..................................................... 20-3b/3
Local Rule
  - allowing free relief from immovable water hazard stake for ball
      lying in water hazard; whether authorized ................................................. 33-8/15
  - deeming all stakes on course (except boundary stakes) immovable
      obstructions ................................................................................................... 33-8/16
outside agency removes immovable obstruction on player's line of play ..................... 13-2/33
player removes boundary post on line of play but replaces it before playing .............. 13-2/25
provisional ball played from point nearer hole than visible original ball;
      player erroneously thought original ball out of bounds ........................................ 27-2c/3

**Index**

**Stakes** *(continued)*
removal of boundary stake interfering with swing .................................................. 13-2/17
status of half of double green serving hole not being played ............................ 25-3/1
supporting tree broken in attempt to remove it .................................................... 13-2/16
where to place lines or stakes defining margin of water hazard ....................... 33-2a/4

**Stance**
*See also* Addressing the Ball; Improving Area of Intended Stance or Swing, Position or Lie of Ball, or Line of Play or Putt
ball dropped from ground under repair, rolls to position where same area
    interferes with stance; whether re-drop required .................................. 20-2c/0.5
ball moves
  - after player addresses it, steps away and re-takes stance
    without grounding club ........................................................................... 18-2b/7
  - after club grounded but before stance completed ....................................... 18-2b/4
  - after stance taken but before club grounded ............................................... 18-2b/1
  - after stance taken in hazard without club .................................................... 18-2b/2
  - after stance taken and club rested in heather where ball perched ......... 18-2b/6
  - while player in process of taking stance in bunker ..................................... 18-2b/3
building stance
  - kneeling on towel while playing stroke ......................................................... 13-3/2
  - knocking down side of bunker to get level stance ...................................... 13-3/3
  - player builds stance then corrects error before playing stroke ................ 13-3/5
  - standing on mat on teeing ground .................................................................. 13-3/1
environmentally-sensitive area; stance taken or stroke played from;
    explanation of penalties and procedures ............................................... 33-8/43
"fairly taking his stance"
  - meaning of "fairly taking his stance" ............................................................ 13-2/1
  - player allowed to play in any direction in "fairly taking his stance" ...... 13-2/1.5
  - player attempts to take stance fairly; improves line of play by
    moving growing object; stance abandoned and object returns
    to original position; stance then taken fairly without moving object ............ 13-2/1.1
  - player under tree, changes intended direction of play and fairly
    takes stance second time ...................................................................... 13-2/1.7
improving stance by
  - moving interfering growing object in attempting to take stance fairly ............... 13-2/1.1
  - moving loose impediment in hazard accidentally ....................................... 13-4/13
  - moving loose impediments when approaching ball in hazard .................. 13-4/13.5
  - taking stance fairly .............................................................................................. 13-2/1
  - taking stance fairly; player then changing direction of play .................... 13-2/1.7
in bunker or water hazard
  - ball moves after stance taken without club ................................................... 18-2b/2
  - ball moves while player in process of taking stance in bunker ................ 18-2b/3
  - loose impediment accidentally moved by player; stance not improved ............ 13-4/13
  - loose impediment accidentally kicked by player into bunker;
    does not interfere with player's stance or lie in bunker; player lifts it;
    whether permitted ................................................................................... 13-4/14
  - loose impediments touched and moved by player's feet when
    approaching ball in hazard ..................................................................... 13-4/13.5
  - player's lie changed by another player taking stance ................................. 20-3b/2
  - stance leveled by knocking down side of bunker; whether permitted .... 13-3/3
  - stance taken without club; whether permitted ............................................ 13-4/24
  - stance taken with club; player then decides to change clubs;
    whether permitted ................................................................................... 13-4/26
  - stance taken firmly some distance from where ball lies to
    simulate next stroke; whether permitted ............................................ 13-4/25
  - stance taken firmly; player then smoothes footprints after deciding
    to play different type of shot ................................................................. 13-4/27
  - when stance taken ............................................................................................... 13-4/23

interference with stance by
- artificial object lying out of bounds; whether movable without penalty ................ 24-1/3
- burrowing animal hole; unreasonable to play stroke because of
    other condition ........................................................................................... 25-1b/20
- crawfish mound ................................................................................................. 25-1b/18
- divot hole from stroke just made by another player ................................... 13-2/8.7
- loose impediment lying out of bounds; whether removal permitted ...................... 23-1/9
- tee-markers for first stroke with ball from teeing ground;
    player moves tee-markers ........................................................................... 11-2/2
Local Rule allowing free relief from condition (Committee should
    deny relief if interference occurs only with player's stance)
- damage made by insects ..................................................................................... 33-8/21
- edging grooves around putting green ................................................................. 33-8/24
- severe damage by non-burrowing animals ...................................................... 33-8/32.5
nearest point of relief
- player unable to take stance for intended stroke at nearest point of
    relief due to interference by something other than condition from
    which relief taken ...................................................................................... 24-2b/3
- diagram illustrating situations when player must estimate nearest
    point of relief because simulating stance for intended stroke
    not possible ............................................................................................. 24-2b/3.7
- relief taken properly from obstruction for stroke towards green;
    after taking proper relief same obstruction interferes with stance
    for necessary sideways stroke ................................................................. 24-2b/9.5
side-saddle putting; clarification of when player has taken stance and
    addressed ball ............................................................................................ 18-2b/5.7
standing astride or touching extension of line of putt behind ball
    inadvertently or to avoid other player's line while holing short putt ................ 16-1e/2
water visible as result of undue effort with feet ......................................................... 25/4

## Status of Object

acorn embedded in ground ............................................................................................ 23/9
aeration holes ................................................................................................................ 25/15
aeration plugs ................................................................................................................ 23/12
angled supports supporting boundary fence ................................................................ 24/2
ants and ant hills ........................................................................................................... 23/5
ball
- abandoned .................................................................................................................. 24-1/2
- artificially warmed .................................................................................................. 14-3/13.5
- broken piece of ball struck by player mistaking it for his ball lying
    in heavy grass ............................................................................................. 15/3
- completely embedded in lip of bunker ................................................................... 13/4
- containing electronic transmitter ......................................................................... 14-3/14
- crossing public road defined as out of bounds that divides course that
    comes to rest on another part of course ...................................................... 27/20
- embedded in ground (criteria for being embedded) ............................................. 25-2/0.5
- inside but touching boundary fence; when out of bounds .......................................... 27/19
- not on List of Conforming Golf Balls ................................................................... US/5-1/101
- on obstruction in bunker .......................................................................................... 13/5
- on edge of bunker overhanging sand .................................................................. 13/3
- placed behind ball-marker on putting green by caddie so player can
    assess line of putt ........................................................................................ 20-4/2
- to be removed from List of Conforming Golf Balls ............................................. US/5-1/102
- warming device ....................................................................................................... 14-3/13
bottled drink used as level ........................................................................................... 14-3/12.5
boundary stakes having no significance in play of hole being played ................................. 24/5
bridge in water hazard .................................................................................................. 13-4/30
bunker totally under repair ........................................................................................... 25/13
carts pulled by double caddie ....................................................................................... 6-4/6
calculator ....................................................................................................................... 14-3/16

## Status of Object *(continued)*

| | |
|---|---|
| chalk applied to face of club | 4-2/3 |
| chipper | 4-1/3 |
| clod of earth | 23/13 |
| club used as plumb line | 14-3/12 |
| compass used during round | 14-3/4 |
| concrete bases of boundary fence posts | 24/3 |
| dead land crab | 23/6 |
| dew or frost on line of putt | 16-1a/3 |
| dew or frost other than on line of putt | 13-2/35 |
| displaced boundary stake | 33-2a/20 |
| distance measuring device | 14-3/0.5 |
| distance meter attached to golf cart | 14-3/1 |
| divot undetached | 13-2/5 |
| electronic device | |
|     - containing distance measurements between various points | 14-3/5.5 |
|     - used during stipulated round | 14-3/16 |
| fence off course leaning across boundary | 13-2/20 |
| finely crushed shells | 33-8/40 |
| flagstick not positioned in hole moved to prevent another player's ball from striking it | |
|     - held away from hole prior to stroke; moved to prevent ball from striking it | 17-1/8 |
|     - removed after attendance during stroke, placed on ground then lifted | 17-1/6 |
|     - removed prior to stroke, lying on ground then lifted | 1-2/3 |
|     - removed prior to stroke, lying on ground within reach of player then lifted | 17-1/7 |
| fruit | |
|     - in which ball embeds | 23/10 |
|     - skins | 23/4 |
| gallery-control line or mark consisting of lime or paint | 24-2b/20 |
| gate in boundary fence or wall | 27/18 |
| glove used as indicating mark; whether equipment | 20-2a/7 |
| golf ball warmer | 14-3/13 |
| gradient measuring device | 14-3/0.5 |
| grass adhering to ball | 21/2 |
| grass cuttings | 25/11 |
| grass-covered ground within bunker | 13/2 |
| gravel used to surface road | 23/14 |
| guy wires supporting boundary fence | 24/2 |
| half of double green serving hole not being played | 25-3/1 |
| hand-held computer | 14-3/16 |
| hand warmer | 14-3/13 |
| half-eaten pear | 23/3 |
| immovable artificial object situated out of bounds | 24-2b/21 |
| insect | |
|     - flying in water hazard | 13-4/16.5 |
|     - on ball | 23-1/5 |
|     - on ball in bunker | 23-1/5.5 |
| insect-like creatures | 23/5.5 |
| lava dust | 33-8/40 |
| lie changed by removal of gallery-control stake | 20-3b/3 |
| loose soil remaining when molehill swept flat | 23/11 |
| material similar to sand | 33-8/40 |
| mobile phone | 14-3/16 |
| moss or creepers in tree and on ground | 13-2/37 |
| motorized golf carts | 33-8/4 |
| movable artificial object lying out of bounds | 24-1/3 |
| movable part of drainage hose | 24-2b/15.3 |
| non-growing plants within area of ground under repair | 25/10.9 |
| original ball if another ball played under stroke-and-distance procedure | 27/17 |

Index **I-129**

| | |
|---|---|
| parked car | 24/8 |
| part of boundary fence within boundary line | 24/4 |
| partially embedded pine needle on backswing in bunker | 13-4/32 |
| paved area | 24/10 |

person
- in shared golf cart ... 19/2
- or person(s) other than caddie carry items, other than clubs, for player ... 6-4/5.3
- transporting player's clubs on motorized golf cart or trolley ... 6-4/2.5

| | |
|---|---|
| plumb line | 14-3/11 |

provisional ball played from point nearer hole than visible original ball; player
erroneously thought original ball out of bounds ... 27-2c/3

| | |
|---|---|
| radio | 14-3/16 |
| saliva | 25/6 |
| sand spilling over margin of bunker | 13/1 |
| snake | 23/6.5 |
| standard spectacles and field glasses | 14-3/3 |
| starting time fixed by players | 33-3/1 |
| stile attached to boundary fence | 24/1 |

stone
- broken away from retaining wall in water hazard ... 24/6
- serving as part of drain in bunker ... 24/7

| | |
|---|---|
| spiders and spider webs | 23/5.5 |
| stretching device | 14-3/10.5 |
| team captain or coach | 33-1/11.5 |
| tee-markers after first stroke | 11-2/1 |
| television | 14-3/16 |

tree
- basins ... 33-2a/10.5
- fallen ... 23/7
- fallen, attached to stump ... 25/9
- fallen, in process of being removed ... 25/7
- in bunker ... 13/2
- roots outside ground under repair growing from tree inside ground under repair ... 25/10.7
- stump ... 25/8

| | |
|---|---|
| turf raised by underground pipe | 24/14 |
| two holes on each green of nine-hole course | 16/7 |
| weighted headcover or "doughnut" on club | 14-3/10 |
| wind gauge | 14-3/0.5 |
| wooden or earthen steps | 24/12 |
| wooden planks | 24/11 |

worm
- casts ... 23-1/1
- partially underground ... 23/8

| | |
|---|---|
| "X-out" ball | 5-1/4 |

## Steps

*See also* Obstructions

| | |
|---|---|
| wooden or earthen steps; status | 24/12 |

## Stipulated Round

*See also* Artificial Devices and Unusual Equipment

| | |
|---|---|
| advice between rounds in 36-hole match | 8-1/19 |
| alteration of handicap stroke table | 33-4/1 |
| asking advice when play suspended | 8-1/20 |

ball played from teeing ground of hole to be played later in round lifted;
ball replaced at spot from which lifted and played out when that hole
subsequently reached ... 11-5/5

| | |
|---|---|
| ball-marker moved by wind or casual water during stipulated round | 20-1/10.5 |
| borrowing balls or towel from another player | 5-1/5 |

**S**

**Stipulated Round** (continued)

clubs
- changing between rounds in 36-hole match .................................................. 4-4a/2
- fellow-competitor's club put in competitor's bag by mistake during round used unintentionally by competitor ......................................... 4-4a/5
- replacement of club for stroke-play play-off ................................................. 4-3/12

competitors play two holes not included in stipulated round ........................... 3/2
discontinuance of play for refreshment .............................................................. 6-8a/2.5
hole(s) omitted in match
- by mistake .............................................................................................................. 2-1/3
- purposely ................................................................................................................ 2-1/4
number of holes reduced after play begins; whether permitted ........................ 33-1/2
player who has not yet played seeks advice from player who has finished round ......................................................................................... 8-1/18
players agree to consider hole halved during play of hole ................................. 2-1/1.5
playing characteristics
- changed while play suspended; error discovered before play resumed .......... 4-2/2
- modifying penalty for holing short putt with club whose playing characteristics changed other than in normal course of play ................ 4-3/4
practice
- competitor practices putting on 3rd green after finishing hole during first round of 36-hole stroke-play competition ................................. 7-1b/7
- competitor practices putting on 3rd green of 9-hole course during 18-hole stroke-play competition ................................................................ 7-2/9
- replaying match from beginning instead of resuming play where discontinued not practice .............................................................................. 2-1/6
starting players from 1st and 10th tees .................................................................. 33-1/3
three holes played out of sequence in match ...................................................... 2-1/5
two balls in play simultaneously at different holes ............................................ 1-1/1
wrong teeing ground; play from attributable to Committee failure to indicate hole numbers on teeing ground .............................................. 11-5/2

**Stone(s), Rock(s) or Gravel**

*See also* Loose Impediments; Status of Object; Wall

ball moved by stone dislodged by partner's or opponent's stroke ..................... 18-1/8
ball outside bunker; stone in bunker on line of play pressed down or removed ......... 13-2/31
bending grass in removal of loose impediments .............................................. 13-2/13
competitor correctly advised he incurred penalty for moving stone from water hazard by fellow-competitor; competitor disagrees and fails to include penalty in returned score card; Committee advised of incident after close of competition ............................................ 34-1b/1.5
gravel surfaced road or path; whether artificially-surfaced .............................. 24/9
improving line of play by removing stone from wall ........................................ 13-2/32
large stone movable only with much effort ....................................................... 23-1/2
specimen Local Rule deeming stones in bunkers movable obstructions ........ App I-B-4
player builds stance through use of object such as stone, brick, or golf cart; corrects error before playing stroke ............................................. 13-3/5
probing near ball for stones or tree roots; whether permitted .......................... 13-2/27
solidly embedded
- meaning of "solidly embedded" in definition of loose impediments ........... 23/2
- stone in hazard touched with club during backswing ................................... 13-4/6
status of
- gravel used to surface road or path .................................................................. 23/14
- stone broken away from retaining wall in water hazard ............................... 24/6
- stone serving as part of drain in bunker .......................................................... 24/7

# Index I-131

## Stroke

*See also* Artificial Devices and Unusual Equipment; Concession; Handicap Competition and Handicap Strokes; Practice; Practice Swing; Stroke-and-Distance; Stroke Canceled or Recalled; Wrong Ball

ball missed with stroke
- backward movement of club after stroke accidentally moves ball ........................ 18-2a/22
- in foursome play accidentally; which partner plays next stroke ................................ 29-1/6
- in foursome play purposely; whether stroke made and which partner
  plays next stroke ................................................................................................................ 29-1/7
- player then addresses ball and accidentally knocks it off tee ........................................ 11-3/1
- player then deems it unplayable; explanation of stroke-and-distance option ............ 28/7
- then discovered to be wrong ball ...................................................................................... 15/1

ball moves during backswing; struck while still moving ......................................................... 14-5/1

ball lying between tree roots popped up by stroke; in disgust player swings at
popped up ball; whether stroke made or any Rule breached ...................................... 14/6

concealed ball
- dislodged by practice swing ............................................................................................ 7-2/7
- dislodged by player's stroke at own ball........................................................................... 15/2

club damaged while making stroke, practice swing or practice stroke;
whether "damaged in normal course of play"............................................................... 4-3/1

flagstick held with one hand; short putt holed by stroke with club held in
other hand; whether breach of any Rule ...................................................................... 17-1/5

meaning of "strokes played in continuing the play of a hole" ............................................ 7-2/1.7

piece of broken ball lying in heavy rough mistaken by player as his ball;
player makes stroke at it; whether stroke with wrong ball........................................... 15/3

player holds umbrella over own head and makes stroke; whether breach
of Rule 14-2 ........................................................................................................................ 14-2/2

practice swing
- dislodges concealed ball.................................................................................................... 7-2/7
- moves ball accidentally prior to tee shot ...................................................................... 18-2a/19
- moves ball accidentally through the green ................................................................... 18-2a/20

whether ball struck more than once in course of stroke if
- ball adheres to face of club after stroke ........................................................................ 1-4/2
- ball falls on club face after stroke and sticks to mud thereon ...................................... 14-4/1
- ball strikes pipeline and on rebound deflects off face of club ..................................... 14-4/2

whether stroke made and/or ball fairly struck at if
- after nearly hit by ball played from following group; in anger, player
  strikes ball back toward group ....................................................................................... 1-4/4
- ball knocked aside after marking position instead of lifting ....................................... 20-1/22
- ball knocked from lip of hole in disgust ........................................................................ 18-2a/23
- ball played from outside teeing ground in stroke play ................................................. 11-4b/6
- ball played from wrong teeing ground in match play goes out of bounds;
  stroke not recalled by opponent ................................................................................... 11-5/3
- ball struck from environmentally-sensitive area .......................................................... 33-8/43
- ball struck with back of clubhead................................................................................... 14-1/1
- ball struck with billiard-type motion.............................................................................. 14-1/2
- ball struck with grip of putter ......................................................................................... 14-1/3
- ball struck with half-inch backswing.............................................................................. 14-1/4
- club breaks during backswing; swing completed ......................................................... 14/2
- club breaks during downswing; swing completed but misses ball;
  clubhead falls and moves ball ........................................................................................ 14/5
- club breaks during downswing; swing stopped short of ball;
  clubhead falls and moves ball ........................................................................................ 14/4
- club stopped or deflected on downswing by tree branch ............................................ 14/1
- clubhead separates from shaft on downswing .............................................................. 14/3
- in foursome match ball played from outside teeing ground ....................................... 29-1/1
- intent to strike ball ceases during downswing and player alters path
  of clubhead to avoid striking ball .................................................................................. 14/1.5
- lower part of branch struck at to dislodge ball beyond reach higher
  in branch .......................................................................................................................... 14/7

## Stroke (continued)
- more than one club used to swing at ball ............................................. 14-1/7
- other side of fence struck at to move ball lying against fence ................... 14-1/5
- player hits ball back to player who lost it ............................................. 7-2/5.5
- practice range ball hit back to range by player ...................................... 7-2/5
- swing discontinued after branch broken on backswing ........................... 13-2/14.5
- swing made in disgust at ball popped straight up after hitting tree root ...... 14/6
- when ball addressed, club held with one hand and shaft struck with other hand to move ball ............................................................... 14-1/6

## Stroke and Distance
ball deemed unplayable
- after player made stroke at ball lying through the green; player returns to teeing ground and plays ............................. 28/6
- after player missed stroke at ball lying in tree roots; player wishes to return to teeing ground ........................................... 28/7
- and dropped in another unplayable lie; ball deemed unplayable second time; player wishes to proceed under stroke and distance ............ 28/6.5
- in bunker; player lifts ball, announces intention to proceed under Rule 28a then smoothes irregularities; whether permitted ................ 13-4/35.8
- lying through the green; dropped in water hazard under Rule 28b or c; player wishes to proceed under water hazard Rule rather than playing dropped ball ................................................ 28/4.5
- place from which previous stroke played nearer hole; whether player may proceed under stroke-and-distance option (Rule 28a) ........ 28/8
- regression under unplayable ball Rule; when permitted ......................... 28/5
- when ball deemed unplayable must be found and identified ................... 28/1

ball moved, lifted or touched
- ball in bunker moves when rake removed; whether player may proceed under stroke-and-distance or any other option outside bunker or press ball into sand if not possible to replace or place in bunker not nearer hole ......................................................... 20-3d/2
- ball lifted without intention of proceeding under stroke and distance and without authority; player subsequently plays under stroke-and-distance .................................................................. 27-2b/1
- ball moved accidentally by practice swing prior to tee shot ..................... 18-2a/19
- ball moved into bounds by flow of water in lateral water hazard ............. 26-1/8
- ball moved out of bounds by flow of water in water hazard .................... 26-1/7
- stroke just touches ball which falls off tee; player lifts and re-tees it ......... 18-2a/2
- stroke misses teed ball; player then addresses and accidentally knocks ball off tee ................................................................. 11-3/1
- stroke misses teed ball; player then adjusts height of ball on tee ............. 18-2a/1
- tee shot wrongly thought out of bounds lifted; competitor returns to teeing ground and plays another ball ...................................... 18-2a/11

original ball not found
- ball believed lost in bunker; competitor drops and plays substituted ball in bunker; then original ball found outside bunker .................. 20-7c/3
- substituted ball dropped at spot of previous stroke; original ball then found within five minutes ............................................... 27-1/2
- substituted ball dropped at spot of previous stroke; original ball then found within five minutes and played ............................... 27-1/2.3
- substituted ball teed at spot of previous stroke; original ball then found within five minutes ................................................... 27-1/1
- substituted ball dropped where original ball thought lost and played ....... 27-1/3
- substituted ball played under procedure for ball lost in ground under repair (Rule 25-1c) after another ball played under stroke-and-distance procedure (Rule 27-1) ...................................... 15/8

- substituted ball played under procedure for ball lost in ground
  under repair (Rule 25-1c) in absence of reasonable evidence
  original ball lost in ground under repair.......................................................... 25-1c/2
- treated as moved by outside agency in absence of reasonable
  evidence to that effect; player substitutes ball under procedure
  in Rule 18-1 and plays it .................................................................................... 27-1/2.5
- unaware original ball holed out, player puts another ball into play .......................... 1-1/2

out of bounds
- ball dropped under stroke-and-distance strikes course through
  the green within inches of and not nearer hole than spot in
  bunker where previous stroke played ............................................................... 20-5/2
- ball moved into bounds by flow of water in lateral water hazard .......................... 26-1/8
- ball moved out of bounds by flow of water in water hazard ..................................... 26-1/7
- ball played from outside teeing ground goes out of bounds ................................... 11-4b/6
- ball played from spot where original ball deflected out of bounds
  by maintenance vehicle ........................................................................................... 20-7/1
- ball wrongly thought out of bounds lifted; competitor plays another
  ball from tee ................................................................................................................ 18-2a/11
- original ball out of bounds; ball re-teed under stroke-and-distance
  touched at address and falls off tee .................................................................... 11-3/3

spot from which previous stroke played not precisely known; explanation
  of how to determine "estimated spot" for dropping under
  stroke-and-distance ............................................................................................ 20-2c/1.5

status of original ball after substituted ball played under stroke-and-distance
  procedure ................................................................................................................ 27/17

stroke played out of turn from tee abandoned; another ball played
  in proper order .......................................................................................................... 10-2c/1

substituted ball played
- from where original ball thought lost ....................................................................... 27-1/3
- under procedure for ball lost in ground under repair (Rule 25-1c)
  after another ball played under stroke-and-distance procedure (Rule 27-1) .......... 15/8
- under procedure for ball lost in ground under repair (Rule 25-1c)
  in absence of reasonable evidence original ball lost in
  ground under repair .............................................................................................. 25-1c/2
- under water hazard Rule (Rule 26-1b or c); original ball then found
  outside hazard ........................................................................................................ 26-1/3
- under water hazard Rule (Rule 26-1b or c) without reasonable evidence
  original ball in hazard; original ball then found in hazard ..................................... 26-1/4

water hazard
- ball assumed in water hazard; reasonable evidence not established;
  player proceeds under stroke and distance; original ball found
  outside hazard .......................................................................................................... 26/6
- ball moved into bounds by flow of water in lateral water hazard .......................... 26-1/8
- ball moved out of bounds by flow of water in water hazard ..................................... 26-1/7
- ball played from within water hazard comes to rest in same hazard
  after exiting hazard ................................................................................................ 26-2/2
- ball substituted and played under water hazard Rule (Rule 26-1b or c);
  original ball then found outside hazard ................................................................. 26-1/3
- ball substituted and played under water hazard Rule (Rule 26-1b or c)
  without reasonable evidence original ball in hazard; original ball
  then found in hazard ............................................................................................. 26-1/4

wrong ball
- deemed unplayable played under stroke-and-distance procedure;
  original ball then found ........................................................................................ 28/14
- found out of bounds played under stroke-and-distance procedure;
  original ball then found in bounds ........................................................................ 15/12

## Stroke Canceled or Recalled

*See also* Ball Deflected or Stopped; Order of Play; Order of Play in Foursomes and Threesomes; Stroke-and-Distance; Teeing Ground

after stroke from putting green
- ball dropped accidentally by opponent or fellow-competitor strikes player's moving ball .................................................................................................. 19-5/1.7
- ball played from another hole deflects ball in motion ................................................ 19-1/10
- ball replaced while another ball in motion after stroke from putting green; ball in motion strikes replaced ball; procedures for accidental and deliberate acts .................................................................................. 16-1b/3
- ball strikes opponent's or fellow-competitor's ball set aside after being lifted ...... 19-5/1
- dog deflects or picks up ball in motion ........................................................................ 19-1/7
- fellow-competitor deliberately deflects or stops player's putt; procedure for player ................................................................................................ 19-1/5
- flagstick struck when purposely not removed by fellow-competitor asked to attend it; procedure for player ...................................................... 17-3/2
- hole-liner deflects ball when accidentally pulled by flagstick from hole .................. 17/8
- knob falls from top of flagstick as attendant removes flagstick and deflects ball ................................................................................................................. 17/9
- moving outside agency deflects ball; stroke not replayed as required by Rule 19-1b .................................................................................................... 19-1/3
- spectator deliberately deflects or stops ball in motion ............................................... 19-1/4

ball breaks into pieces after striking paved cart path; procedure for player ..................... 5-3/4

Committee in error directs player to play from wrong place; error discovered before player begins next hole; procedure when serious breach involved ............................................................................................................... 34-3/3

incorrect ruling by Committee places player at serious disadvantage; whether error may be corrected by canceling strokes played ............................. 34-3/3.3

Local Rule
- providing relief from temporary power lines and cables ...................................... App I-B-6b
- requiring cancelation and replay of stroke without penalty when ball deflected by power line, tower or pole ........................................................ 33-8/13

player's ball strikes opponent, opponent's caddie or equipment after stroke
- opponent struck accidentally while standing in bounds; ball comes to rest out of bounds ......................................................................................... 19-3/1
- opponent's trolley deflects player's ball which then strikes player's trolley .......... 19-3/3
- shared golf cart struck while opponent driving it ....................................................... 19/1

provisional ball played out of turn other than from teeing ground; when opponent may recall stroke .................................................................................. 10/4

stroke played from outside teeing ground or from wrong teeing ground in match play
- canceled by opponent; correct order of play ............................................................. 11-4a/1
- canceled by opponents in foursome match; which partner replays stroke ........... 29-1/1
- goes out of bounds; procedure if stroke not recalled by opponent ......................... 11-5/3

stroke played out of turn in match play
- after player's stroke, opponent claims player played out of turn; procedure for referee ........................................................................................... 10-1b/1
- bunker smoothed by player after playing out of turn; opponent recalls stroke and player must drop ball in smoothed area ................................ 13-4/39
- opponent requests player replay in correct order; opponent plays stroke, then withdraws request for player to replay stroke; procedure for player .............................................................................................. 10-1c/1
- partners both play out of turn from tee; opponents cancel stroke of one partner but not other; whether permitted .................................................... 30-1/1
- player putts instead of complying with opponent's request to lift ball due to interference .......................................................................................... 10-1c/2
- provisional ball nearer hole than opponent's ball tapped in by player to end opponent's search for player's original ball; whether opponent may recall stroke ............................................................... 27-2b/1
- three-ball match play; player plays out of turn; one opponent requests replay, other opponent does not ............................................................ 30-2/1

whether cancelation and replay of stroke allowed if
- flagstick stuck into green some distance from hole by practical joker ............... 1-4/3
- player mis-hits ball when distracted by ball dropped by another player ............... 1-4/1
- sprinkler head deflects ball ................................................................. 33-8/12

### Substituted Ball

*See also* Exchanging Balls

ball changed during play of hole to aid identification ............................................. 15/6.5
ball deemed unplayable in water hazard; substituted ball dropped in
 hazard without lifting original; error discovered before stroke played ............ 20-7/2.5
ball dropped away from obstruction immediately after resumption
 of play; whether player may lift and substitute for dropped ball
 under Rule 6-8d(ii) .......................................................................... 6-8d/3
ball fit for play deemed unfit during play of hole; player substitutes and
 plays another ball ............................................................................ 5-3/3
ball lifted and thrown into pond in anger .................................................... 18-2a/13.5
ball mistakenly substituted when dropped; correction of error .......................... 20-6/3
ball played from ground under repair abandoned and relief taken under
 ground under repair Rule ................................................................. 18-2a/8.5
ball played under Rule for ball lost in ground under repair after another
 ball played under stroke-and-distance procedure .................................... 15/8
balls inadvertently exchanged
- by competitors at unknown place ........................................................ 15-1/2
- by players after one ball strikes and moves other .................................... 15-1/2.5
- by players between holes ................................................................... 15-1/1
- by partners in four-ball Stableford competition ....................................... 32-2b/1
- competitor who lifts his and fellow-competitor's balls inadvertently
 exchanges them when replaced ..................................................... 15-2/4
- when recovered from water hazard ..................................................... 15-1/4
casual water mistaken for water hazard; substituted ball played under
 water hazard Rule .......................................................................... 25-1b/13
competitor mistakenly substitutes another ball on putting green; error
 discovered after stroke played from next teeing ground .......................... 15-2/3
competitor's ball lifted without authority by fellow-competitor's caddie
 who subsequently substitutes another ball which competitor plays ........... 20-1/5
competitor's ball played by fellow-competitor; competitor substitutes
 another ball at wrong place, plays it and then abandons it and
 plays out original ball from right place ............................................... 20-7c/4
original ball found within five-minute search period
- after substituted ball dropped at spot of previous stroke ........................... 27-1/2
- after substituted ball dropped at spot of previous stroke; dropped
 ball played ................................................................................ 27-1/2.3
- after substituted ball teed but not played .............................................. 27-1/1
player lifts ball on putting green; then throws it into lake and announces
 ball unfit for play ............................................................................. 5-3/3.5
player mistakenly substitutes another ball on putting green; error discovered
 before stroke played ........................................................................ 15-2/2
player substitutes another ball on putting green because original ball thrown
 to caddie for cleaning came to rest in lake ............................................ 15-2/1
players inadvertently exchange balls recovered from water hazard .................. 15-1/4
reasonable evidence
- ball lost in abnormal ground condition or obstruction; substituted
 ball dropped under applicable Rule; original ball then found within
 five minutes ............................................................................... 25-1c/2.5
- ball in water hazard; substituted ball dropped under water hazard Rule;
 original ball then found within five minutes ...................................... 26-1/3.5
re-drop required under Rule permitting substitution; whether player may
 substitute when re-dropping ............................................................ 20-6/4

### Substituted Ball (continued)
wrong ball
- dropped and played under stroke-and-distance procedure; original ball then found .................................................................................................. 28/14
- dropped under unplayable ball Rule but not played ...................................... 15/13
- dropped under unplayable ball Rule within two club-lengths and played before error discovered ..................................................................... 28/15
- in bunker deemed unplayable, dropped in bunker and played; ball then discovered to be wrong ball .................................................................. 15/14

### Tape
adhesive tape
- applied to clubhead to reduce glare during round ........................................ 4-2/1
- applying to golf glove .................................................................................. 14-3/8
- binding fingers together ............................................................................. 14-3/8

lead tape
- applied to clubhead or shaft before start of round ....................................... 4-1/4
- applied to clubhead or shaft during round ............................................. 4-2/0.5
- weight of club changed during round; breach discovered after competition closed ............................................................................. 34-1b/4

### Team Competition
advice
- given by team mate in another group in stroke play .................................. 8-1/21
- given by unauthorized team coach or captain ............................................ 8-1/24
- team captain gives advice while playing ......................................................... 8/2
- team mates playing as fellow-competitors exchange advice ...................... 8-1/22
- whether team captain authorized to give advice may be required to keep off putting greens ...................................................................... 8-2b/4

application of disqualification penalty in competition in which not all team members' scores count for each round ................................................ 33/8
conditions of team competition stipulate team captain or amateur authorized to give advice ............................................................................................... 8/1
player's team mate in gallery hits ball to green to show player whether green will hold .............................................................................................. 8-1/23
status of team captain or coach ........................................................................ 33-1/11.5

### Tee
*See also* Status of Object; Teeing Ground and Tee-Markers

ball falls off tee when stroke just touches it; player lifts, re-tees and plays ball .......... 18-2a/2
ball played out of bounds from wrong teeing ground in match not recalled ............... 11-5/3
original ball out of bounds; ball re-teed under stroke-and-distance touched at address and falls off tee ..................................................................................... 11-3/3
player who misses tee shot tees ball lower before playing next stroke ........................ 18-2a/1
probing with tee near ball for tree roots or rocks ........................................................ 13-2/27
stroke misses ball; ball then accidentally knocked off tee ............................................ 11-3/1
tee marking position of player's ball deflects opponent's ball .................................... 20-1/17
teed ball missed then hit out of bounds ........................................................................ 20-5/1

### Teeing Ground and Tee-Markers
*See also* Marking or Defining Course; Status of Object; Stroke-and-Distance; Tee

ball embeds in teeing ground ........................................................................................ 25-2/8
ball in or on movable obstruction within teeing ground .............................................. 25-2/8
ball played from outside teeing ground
- ball played from outside teeing ground goes out of bounds ................................. 11-4b/6
- ball played from outside teeing ground in foursome match .................................. 29-1/1
- competitor plays from outside teeing ground in foursome stroke play; partner replays stroke ........................................................................................... 29-1/2
- dispute as to whether competitor played from outside teeing ground ................. 34-3/4
- order of play when opponent requires player with honor to cancel stroke played from outside teeing ground ........................................................ 11-4a/1

## Index  I-137

ball played out of turn from teeing ground abandoned and another ball
    played in proper order ........................................................................................... 10-2c/1
ball moved, lifted or touched
    - ball moved accidentally by practice swing prior to tee shot .................................. 18-2a/19
    - stroke just touches ball which falls off tee; player lifts and re-tees it ................. 18-2a/2
    - stroke misses teed ball; player then addresses and accidentally
      knocks ball off tee ................................................................................................. 11-3/1
    - stroke misses teed ball; player then adjusts height of ball on tee ....................... 18-2a/1
    - tee shot wrongly thought out of bounds lifted; competitor returns to
      teeing ground and plays another ball .................................................................. 18-2a/11
branch interfering with backswing on teeing ground broken by player ...................... 13-2/14
casual water completely covers teeing ground; Committee options for
    match and stroke play ............................................................................................. 25-1b/4
foursome competition
    - changing partners after driving from first teeing ground ................................... 29/1
    - condition of competition stipulates which foursome partner must play
      from 1st teeing ground; whether permitted ..................................................... 33-1/3.5
    - player and partner both drive from same teeing ground in foursome play ......... 29-1/9
    - tee shot hit out of bounds in mixed foursome (different teeing grounds
      used by men and women); which teeing ground partner plays next
      stroke from .............................................................................................................. 29/2
grass behind ball on teeing ground pulled out or broken off by player ....................... 13-2/3
Local Rule
    - deeming area of adjoining hole out of bounds for play of particular hole
      but not for play of other holes .............................................................................. 33-2a/14
    - deeming area of adjoining hole out of bounds for stroke played from
      teeing ground only; whether authorized ............................................................. 33-2a/14
    - deeming area surrounding tee in bounds for tee shot and out of
      bounds thereafter; whether authorized ................................................................ 33-2a/13
original ball
    - found within five-minute search period after another ball teed
      but not played ....................................................................................................... 27-1/1
    - out of bounds; ball re-teed under stroke-and-distance touched at
      address and falls off tee ......................................................................................... 11-3/3
players agree not to play from teeing ground in prescribed order to
    save time; whether agreement to waive Rules ....................................................... 1-3/1
standing on mat on teeing ground ................................................................................ 13-3/1
starting players from 1st and 10th tees ......................................................................... 33-1/3
stroke misses teed ball
    - player presses down turf behind ball before next stroke ..................................... 13-2/2
    - player then addresses ball and accidentally knocks it off tee .............................. 11-3/1
    - player then pushes teed ball lower ...................................................................... 18-2a/1
    - next stroke hit out of bounds; whether ball for subsequent stroke
      may be teed anywhere within teeing ground ...................................................... 20-5/1
stroke made at ball lying through the green
    - in tree roots misses ball; player then deems it unplayable and wishes
      to return to teeing ground ..................................................................................... 28/7
    - player deems ball unplayable and returns to teeing ground .............................. 28/6
suspension of play declared by Committee
    - one competitor in group wishes to complete play of hole after other
      competitors discontinue play; whether permitted ............................................. 6-8b/3
    - options for players if one competitor in group has played from tee ................ 6-8b/2
tee-markers
    - competitors determine spot from which to play from tee when both
      tee-markers missing .............................................................................................. 11-4b/3
    - competitors estimate area of teeing ground when one tee-marker missing ........ 11-4b/2
    - moved and/or holes relocated during stroke-play round .................................. 33-2b/1
    - moved by player .................................................................................................... 11-2/2
    - status of after first stroke ..................................................................................... 11-2/1

## Teeing Ground and Tee-Markers (continued)

wrong teeing ground
- ball played from teeing ground of hole to be played later in round lifted; ball replaced at spot from which lifted and played out when that hole subsequently reached .................................................................. 11-5/5
- ball played from wrong teeing ground in stroke play; error corrected ................... 11-5/4
- ball played out of bounds not recalled ................................................................. 11-5/3
- meaning of "next teeing ground" after competitors have played from wrong teeing ground ............................................................................................. 11-5/1
- play from wrong teeing ground attributed to Committee failure to indicate hole numbers on teeing ground ............................................................. 11-5/2

## Terminology

"added," when club considered ................................................................................... 4-4a/1
"any ball he has played" ............................................................................................... 18/7
"artificially-surfaced" .................................................................................................... 24/9
"as soon as practicable" in Rule 9-2 .............................................................................. 9-2/1
"behind," as applied in Rule 26-1b ........................................................................... 26-1/1.5
"dangerous situation" .................................................................................................. 1-4/11
"directly attributable" in Rules 20-1 and 20-3a .......................................................... 20-1/15
"embedded," when ball considered embedded in ground ......................................... 25-2/0.5
"estimated spot;" explanation of how to determine ................................................. 20-2c/1.5
"fairly taking his stance"
- explanation of "fairly taking his stance" .................................................................. 13-2/1
- player allowed to play in any direction in "fairly taking his stance" ................... 13-2/1.5
- player attempts to take stance fairly but improves line of play by moving interfering growing object .................................................................... 13-2/1.1
- player under tree, changes intended direction of play and fairly takes stance second time ................................................................................. 13-2/1.7
"goes forward to search" ........................................................................................ 27-2a/1.5
"good reason to lift" when play suspended ................................................................ 6-8c/1
"grounded;" when club considered grounded in long grass ..................................... 18-2b/5
"hole made by greenkeeper" in definition of ground under repair ............................. 25/14
"immediately recoverable" .......................................................................................... 18/11
"immediately," when player makes stroke out of order in match play and opponent wishes to immediately cancel stroke so played ................................ 30-1/1
"line of putt" in context of "standing astride or on line of putt" ................................ 16-1e/1
"marking position of ball;" permissible methods ....................................................... 20-1/16
"maximum available relief" from casual water in bunker ......................................... 25-1b/5
"nearest point of relief," diagrams illustrating ......................................................... 25-1b/2
"next teeing ground" after competitors have played from wrong teeing ground .......... 11-5/1
"normal course of play" ............................................................................................... 4-3/1
"officially announced" ................................................................................................ 2-5/14
"opposite margin" as applied in Rule 26-1c ............................................................... 26-1/14
"penalty strokes incurred solely by playing ball ruled not to count" clarified for situations where competitor plays second ball under Rule 20-7c ............. 20-7c/5
point where ball "last entered" abnormal ground condition when ball lost in condition .................................................................................................. 25-1c/1.5
"reasonable evidence"
- ball lost in abnormal ground condition .................................................................. 25-1c/1
- ball lost in water hazard ........................................................................................ 26-1/1
- criteria to treat ball as moved by outside agency rather than lost ball ................ 18-1/1
- lost ball treated as moved by outside agency in absence of reasonable evidence ............................................................................................................ 27-1/2.5
"repair" ....................................................................................................................... 4-3/2
"serious breach of etiquette" .................................................................................... 33-7/8
"separate Rules," for purpose of determining whether multiple penalties apply ......... 1-4/12
"solidly embedded" ..................................................................................................... 23/2
"specific directions" .................................................................................................... 6-4/1
"stands near the hole" ................................................................................................ 17-1/1

# Index    i-139

"strokes played in continuing play of a hole" ............................................................. 7-2/1.7
"time of starting" ......................................................................................................... 6-3a/2.5
"valid claim," procedure for ...................................................................................... 2-5/2

## Test or Testing
bunker or water hazard
- ball played from bunker either out of bounds or lost; player tests condition of bunker or smoothes footprints before dropping another ball in bunker .................................................................................................. 13-4/37
- condition of bunker tested before player decides whether to play through it .... 13-2/30
- player in bunker takes firm stance and then smoothes footprints after deciding to play different type of shot ......................................................... 13-4/27
- player uses cane or club to enter or leave hazard when ball lies in hazard ........ 13-4/3.5
- rake handle stuck in bunker before stroke ......................................................... 13-4/22
- rake thrown into bunker before stroke .............................................................. 13-4/21
- smoothing irregularities in bunker after stroke but before ball extricated ........... 13-4/36
- stance in bunker taken without club .................................................................. 13-4/24
- taking firm stance in bunker some distance from where ball in bunker lies to simulate next stroke ................................................................................. 13-4/25
- taking stance in bunker and then changing clubs ............................................... 13-4/26
- touching grass with club during practice swing in water hazard ......................... 13-4/4
- umbrella or rake placed in hazard before stroke ................................................. 13-4/20

putting green
- caddie practices on or tests putting green surfaces of course before stroke-play round ................................................................................................ 7-1b/5
- caddie roughens surface of putting green but player does not benefit ................. 16-1d/6
- knocking ball aside after marking position instead of lifting ............................... 20-1/22
- player concedes opponent's next stroke and knocks ball away along own line of putt .................................................................................................. 16-1d/2
- player concedes opponent's next stroke and rolls or knocks ball to opponent ........................................................................................................ 16-1d/1
- player returns ball to spot from which it was lifted by rolling it with putter ..................................................................................................... 16-1d/3
- rubbing ball on putting green for cleaning purposes ......................................... 16-1d/5
- tested for wetness surface of putting green behind ball ...................................... 16-1d/4

## Three-Ball Match Play
player concedes hole after which one opponent plays wrong ball .................................... 2-4/10
player plays out of turn from tee in three-ball match; one opponent requests replay and other does not ........................................................................................... 30-2/1

## Through the Green
*See also* Fairway and Closely Mown Areas; Rough
ball deemed unplayable through the green
- dropped in bunker or water hazard ........................................................................... 28/4
- dropped in water hazard; player elects not to play ball and wishes to proceed under water hazard Rule .................................................................... 28/4.5
ball enters burrowing animal hole
- in bounds and comes to rest out of bounds ........................................................ 25-1b/24
- in bunker and comes to rest underneath putting green ...................................... 25-1b/25
- out of bounds and comes to rest in bounds ....................................................... 25-1b/23
ball hit out of bounds from bunker; player's drop under Rule 20-5 strikes course through the green within inches of and not nearer hole than spot in bunker where previous stroke played .................................................. 20-5/2
ball in drainpipe under course; entrance to drainpipe out of bounds ....................... 24-2b/12
ball touched accidentally in removing loose impediments .............................................. 18-2a/31
dropping from rough to fairway in obtaining relief from obstruction .......................... 24-2b/8
embedded ball
- ball on steep bank driven straight into ground ............................................................ 25-2/6
- in ground under repair in closely mown area ............................................................... 25-2/4

## Through the Green (continued)

ground under repair or casual water through the green
- ball dropped from ground under repair area rolls to position where area interferes with stance; whether re-drop required .................... 20-2c/0.5
- ball embedded in ground under repair in closely mown area ................ 25-2/4
- ball in tree in ground under repair ........................................ 25/10.5
- bunker totally under repair; Committee options ........................... 25/13
- Local Rule declaring accumulations of leaves (at specified holes) through the green as ground under repair ............................. 33-8/31
- measuring across ground under repair in obtaining relief .................. 25-1b/15
- player takes relief from area of casual water and ball comes to rest in position where another area of casual water interferes; whether re-drop required .......................................................... 20-2c/7
- two equidistant nearest points of relief meet requirements of ground under repair Rule ............................................... 25-1b/16

loose impediments
- affecting lie removed while ball lifted ................................... 23-1/8
- competitor asks fellow-competitor to remove loose impediment near ball to avoid penalty ................................................. 33-7/7
- removal of insect on ball .............................................. 23-1/5
- removal of loose impediments from area in which ball to be dropped ........ 23-1/6
- removing grass adhering to ball ........................................ 21/2

natural object interfering with swing moved to determine whether loose impediment or attached .................................................. 13-2/26

pitch-mark through the green
- ball returns to pitch-mark from prior stroke ............................. 25-2/3
- made by partner's, opponent's or fellow-competitor's ball affects player's lie or line of play ........................................... 13-2/8
- repaired in dropping area before ball dropped ............................ 13-2/10

probing near ball for tree roots or rocks ................................... 13-2/27

sand or loose soil through the green
- behind ball pressed down during address ................................ 13-2/12
- behind ball removed by backswing ...................................... 13-2/9
- removed from dropping area ............................................ 13-2/11

spectator deliberately deflects or stops ball through the green ................ 19-1/4.1

treating ocean and beach as through the green ................................. 33-2a/8

tree falls onto fairway during stipulated round; options for Committee ........ 25/9.5

whether ball lies through the green
- ball completely embedded in lip of bunker .............................. 13/4
- ball within natural margin of water hazard but outside stakes defining margin ....................................................... 26/2

## Time of Starting

*See also* Course Unplayable or Closed; Groups and Grouping

"time of starting," meaning of ............................................. 6-3a/2.5

absent player joins partner after fellow-competitor plays from teeing ground but before partner plays ........................................ 31-2/1

all competitors must be present ............................................ 6-3a/2

application of Rule 6-3a disqualification penalty in team competition in which not all team members' scores count for each round ............... 33/8

course closed
- match begun by players unaware course closed .......................... 33-2d/4
- player not present at time of starting .................................. 33-3/2

groupings and starting times determined by competitors; whether Committee may permit ..................................................... 33-3/3

note to Rule 6-3 in effect
- absent player joins partner after fellow-competitor plays from teeing ground but before partner plays ...................................... 31-2/1
- all competitors must be present ....................................... 6-3a/2
- both players in match late ............................................ 6-3a/3

# Index I-141

player unable to meet match-play schedule defaults; match schedule
    subsequently changed; player requests reinstatement .................................... 2-4/20
player(s) not present at time of starting
  - arrives at 9:00:45 for 9:00 tee time ........................................................................ 6-3a/2.5
  - both players in match late .......................................................................................... 6-3a/3
  - circumstances which warrant waiving disqualification penalty
    for lateness ................................................................................................................. 6-3a/1.5
  - course closed at that time ......................................................................................... 33-3/2
  - group unable to start due to delay ......................................................................... 6-3a/4
  - listed as third to play in group arrives in time to do so ................................... 6-3a/2
  - time agreed to by players as authorized by Committee ................................. 33-3/1
postponement of final match due to injury of player ................................................. 6-3a/1
status of starting time fixed by players ........................................................................... 33-3/1
when play resumed after suspension of play
  - competitor refuses to start or picks up because of weather conditions;
    round subsequently canceled ............................................................................. 33-2d/3
  - player unable to resume match at scheduled time .......................................... 6-8b/4
  - when players must be present ............................................................................... 6-8b/9

## Towel

borrowed from another player; whether permitted ..................................................... 5-1/5
covering player's clubs removed by another player to determine club used ..... 8-1/11
kneeled on to play stroke ..................................................................................................... 13-3/2
moves ball when dropped by player and blown onto ball ..................................... 18-2a/17
used to remove loose impediments
  - by Committee ................................................................................................................. 33/1
  - by player .......................................................................................................................... 16-1a/8
used to remove casual water
  - by Committee ................................................................................................................. 33/1
  - by player .......................................................................................................................... 16-1a/1
waved to make insect in bunker move ......................................................................... 23-1/5.5

## Trademark

aimed along line of putt when ball replaced ............................................................. 20-3a/2
rotating ball on putting green without marking position ................................... 18-2a/33

## Tree or Bush

*See also* Leaves; Pine Needles; Status of Object
ball dislodged from tree
  - circumstances in which player not penalized ................................................ 18-2a/27
  - circumstances in which player penalized ........................................................ 18-2a/28
  - knocked down by outside agency ........................................................................ 18-1/9
  - replacement of ball not possible ........................................................................ 18-2a/29
  - when player climbs tree to play stroke ............................................................ 18-2a/26
ball in tree or bush
  - ball lost in ground under repair ............................................................................ 25/10
  - branch struck at to move ball lodged beyond reach higher in branch ...... 14/7
  - in fork of tree moves in relation to ground but not in relation to fork ...... 18/3
  - in ground under repair ............................................................................................ 25/10.5
  - identified but not retrieved ................................................................................... 27/14
  - more than one club used to make stroke at ball in bush ............................. 14-1/7
  - unplayable; player opts to drop within two club-lengths ........................... 28/11
  - visible but not identifiable .................................................................................... 27/15
ball interfered with by abnormal ground condition
  - sideways stroke behind tree reasonable ............................................................ 25-1b/22
  - tree prevents stroke towards green ..................................................................... 25-1b/21
  - tree within area interferes with stroke at ball outside area ...................... 25-1a/1
  - unreasonable to play stroke due to bush .......................................................... 25-1b/19
  - unreasonable to play stroke because of tree .................................................... 25-1b/20

## Tree or Bush *(continued)*

branch
- area of original intended swing improved by breaking branch; area of intended swing finally used not affected by branch ............ 13-2/24
- broken during backswing; swing discontinued .......... 13-2/14.5
- broken off part of larger branch fallen from tree .......... 23-1/4
- held back by caddie to prevent it from deflecting ball when dropped .......... 20-2a/5
- moved by competitor improving or worsening fellow-competitor's line of play while discussing with Committee member whether fellow-competitor entitled to free relief .......... 1-2/1.5
- player breaks off branch interfering with backswing on teeing ground .......... 13-2/14

breaching two Rules with different penalties; whether multiple penalties apply .......... 1-4/15

cast of burrowing animal interferes with stroke toward green; tree prevents such stroke .......... 25-1b/21

dropped ball
- never strikes ground .......... 20-2b/1
- strikes tree branch then ground; whether re-drop required .......... 20-2c/1.3

"fairly taking his stance"
- diagram illustrating player unable to determine nearest point of relief .......... 24-2b/3.7
- explanation of "fairly taking his stance" .......... 13-2/1
- player allowed to play in any direction in "fairly taking his stance" .......... 13-2/1.5
- player attempts to take stance fairly but improves line of play by moving interfering growing object .......... 13-2/1.1
- player determines nearest point of relief but physically unable to play intended stroke .......... 24-2b/3
- player under tree, changes intended direction of play and fairly takes stance second time .......... 13-2/1.7

fallen tree
- attached to stump lying in fairway .......... 25/9
- in process of being removed .......... 25/7
- on fairway after round begun .......... 25/9.5
- status .......... 23/7

Local Rule
- providing relief from exposed tree roots; whether authorized .......... 33-8/8
- requiring player to take relief under penalty from tree nursery (or plantation) from which play prohibited; whether authorized .......... 33-8/29

opponent's stroke disturbs bushes causing player's ball to move .......... 18-3b/2

pine cone falls from tree and comes to rest behind ball lying in bunker .......... 13-4/18.5

probing near ball for tree roots or rocks .......... 13-2/27

provisional ball deemed unplayable and dropped but not played; original ball then found .......... 27-2b/6.5

roots outside ground under repair growing from tree inside ground under repair .......... 25/10.7

shaking water from tree branch interfering with backswing .......... 13-2/23

stake supporting tree broken in attempt to remove it .......... 13-2/16

status of
- moss or creepers in tree .......... 13-2/37
- non-growing plants within area of ground under repair .......... 25/10.9
- tree basins .......... 33-2a/10.5
- tree in bunker .......... 13/2
- tree stump .......... 25/8

taking stance under tree .......... 13-2/1

## Trolley

*See also* Equipment; Golf Cart

player's ball strikes opponent's or fellow-competitor's trolley then strikes own trolley .......... 19-3/3

status of
- individual who transports player's clubs on motorized golf cart or trolley .......... 6-4/2.5
- carts pulled by double caddie .......... 6-4/6

Index  **I-143**

## Tumbleweed

| | |
|---|---|
| ball at rest moved by blowing tumbleweed | 18-1/6 |
| interfering with swing moved to determine whether loose impediment or attached | 13-2/26 |

## Umbrella

| | |
|---|---|
| player holds umbrella over own head when making stroke | 14-2/2 |
| umbrella carrier employed in addition to caddie | 6-4/5 |
| umbrella or rake placed in hazard before stroke | 13-4/20 |

## Undue Delay

*See also* Pace of Play

| | |
|---|---|
| caddie swings club to show player how to play shot | 8-1/15 |
| Committee does not penalize player in breach of pace of play condition believing player had already lost hole | 34-3/2 |
| competitor practices putting on 3rd green after finishing hole during first round of 36-hole stroke-play competition | 7-1b/7 |
| discontinuance of play for refreshment | 6-8a/2.5 |
| four-ball stroke play | |
| - extent to which side may play in order it considers best | 31-5/2 |
| - player waives turn to play; circumstances under which he may complete hole | 31-5/1 |
| player walks off green under mistaken impression partner halved hole returns and putts for half | 30/4 |
| watching television for 45 minutes after nine holes | 6-8a/1 |
| whether Rule 6-7 prohibiting undue delay breached if | |
| - player ascertains whereabouts of opponent's ball before playing | 9-2/16 |
| - player enters clubhouse or half-way house for refreshment during round | 6-8a/2.7 |
| - player requests another player to lift player's ball in absence of reasonable possibility that ball might interfere or assist | 22/3 |
| - player returns to tee to retrieve forgotten club | 6-7/1 |
| - player searches for lost ball after putting another ball into play | 27/9 |
| - player searches ten minutes for lost ball | 6-7/2 |
| - removal of large loose impediment delays play | 23-1/2 |
| - second ball played despite adverse ruling | 3-3/2 |
| window of clubhouse opened and ball played through window | 24-2b/14 |

## Unplayable Ball

*See also* Ball Unfit for Play

| | |
|---|---|
| after declaring ball unplayable and lifting it, player discovers ball was in ground under repair | 28/13 |
| at base of cliff, player wishes to drop within two club-lengths of point above ball | 28/12 |
| ball deemed unplayable | |
| - and dropped, then deemed unplayable second time, player wishes to proceed under stroke-and-distance | 28/6.5 |
| - in bunker; player lifts ball, announces intention to proceed under Rule 28a then smoothes irregularities; whether permitted | 13-4/35.8 |
| - in bunker; player lifts ball and then removes loose impediment from bunker | 13-4/35.7 |
| - place from which previous stroke played nearer hole | 28/8 |
| - through the green dropped in hazard | 28/4 |
| - through the green dropped in water hazard; player elects not to play ball and wishes to proceed under water hazard Rule | 28/4.5 |
| - in water hazard; ball dropped in hazard and played | 20-7/2 |
| - in water hazard; substituted ball dropped in hazard without lifting original; error discovered before stroke played | 20-7/2.5 |
| ball dislodged from tree | |
| - circumstances in which player not penalized | 18-2a/27 |
| - replacement of ball not possible | 18-2a/29 |

**Unplayable Ball** *(continued)*

ball dropped
- outside bunker under option of unplayable ball Rule requiring drop in bunker .................................................................................................. 28/10
- under option 28c of unplayable ball Rule strikes player; whether player may change relief option when re-dropping ............................... 20-2a/6

ball in tree
- identified but not retrieved ....................................................................... 27/14
- player opts to drop within two club-lengths............................................. 28/11

ball lying on grass-covered ground within bunker deemed unplayable ............ 28/9

ball played from water hazard to unplayable lie outside water hazard; explanations of options under Rule 26-2b .................................................... 26-2/1

caddie on own initiative lifts ball considering it unplayable.......................... 18-2a/15

changing relief option
- dropped ball first strikes course outside where applicable Rule requires; whether player may change relief option when re-dropping............... 20-6/2
- dropped ball first strikes course outside where applicable Rule requires; whether player may replace ball in original location ........................... 20-6/5
- dropped ball rolls to position requiring re-drop; whether player may change relief option when re-dropping...................................... 20-2c/5
- dropped ball strikes player; whether player may change relief option when re-dropping ............................................................................... 20-2a/6
- player drops ball in bunker under first option of Rule 25-1b(ii); player then wishes to proceed under second option to drop outside bunker......................................................................................... 25-1b/9
- player lifts ball from bunker intending to drop under first option of Rule 24-2b(ii); player then wishes to proceed under second option to drop outside bunker............................................................... 24-2b/5
- point where ball last crossed margin of lateral water hazard determined and ball dropped; point then proves to be wrong point; whether player may change relief option when re-dropping................ 26-1/16

comes to rest back in original position or another unplayable position ........... 28/3

competitor drops one ball in accordance with two different Rules instead of playing second ball........................................................................ 3-3/11

competitor drops one ball in accordance with two different Rules instead of playing second ball; dropped ball rolls back into condition from which relief taken................................................................................... 3-3/12

dropped ball comes to rest and then rolls out of bounds............................... 20-2c/3.5

dropped in ground under repair from which play prohibited; ball then dropped under ground under repair Rule........................................ 25-1b/14.5

Local Rule allowing drop within water hazard behind point where ball lies unplayable in hazard; whether authorized....................................... 33-8/37

obstruction interferes but ball unplayable due to some other condition ................... 24-2b/16

player entitled to relief without penalty from condition lifts ball; chooses not to take relief and wishes to proceed under unplayable ball Rule........................................................................................................... 18-2a/12.5

player misses ball and deems it unplayable; wishes to return to tee under stroke-and-distance ......................................................................... 28/7

player plays second shot, deems ball unplayable and returns to tee ................. 28/6

procedure for dropping and re-dropping on ball drop (dropping zone) established by Local Rule............................................................................ 33-8/34

provisional ball
- deemed unplayable; player lifts and drops ball; original ball then found ........ 27-2b/6.5
- player wishes provisional ball to serve as ball in play if original unplayable or in water hazard ............................................................... 27-2/1
- played from tee then player deems original ball unplayable while still at tee and plays third ball; claims third ball lies three........................ 28/2

re-drop required when proceeding under unplayable ball Rule; whether player may substitute when re-dropping ....................................... 20-6/4

regression under unplayable ball Rule .................................................................. 28/5
suggesting fellow-competitor deem ball unplayable ..................................... 8-1/16
when necessary to find and identify ball deemed unplayable............................. 28/1
wrong ball
- dropped within two club-lengths and played; error then discovered ....... 28/15
- in bunker deemed unplayable, dropped in bunker and played;
  error then discovered ................................................................................. 15/14
- lifted and dropped under unplayable ball Rule but not played ................. 15/13
- played under stroke-and-distance procedure; original ball then found ................... 28/14

## Wall

*See also* Boundary Fence, Line, Wall or Stakes; Fence; Integral Part of Course; Obstructions; Status of Object

club-length measured directly through wall; whether permitted .................................. 20-2b/2
deeming ball in bounds until beyond boundary wall........................................ 33-2a/16
diagram illustrating player unable to determine nearest point of
  relief because of boundary wall .................................................................. 24-2b/3.7
earthen wall of bunker touched on backswing; whether breach of Rule 13-4 ............. 13-4/34
status of
- artificial wall encircling tree basin ................................................................ 33-2a/10.5
- stone broken away from retaining wall in water hazard ................................. 24/6
stone removed from wall; whether line of play improved ..................................... 13-2/32

## Water Hazards

*See also* Marking or Defining Course; Provisional Ball; Reasonable Evidence

ball assumed in water hazard found outside hazard after another ball
  played under stroke-and-distance procedure .............................................. 26/6
ball at rest moves
- after loose impediment outside hazard moved.............................................. 18-2a/5
- after stance taken in hazard without club..................................................... 18-2b/2
- in water in water hazard after address; played while still moving .................. 14-6/1
- into bounds by flow of water in lateral water hazard .................................... 26-1/8
- out of bounds by flow of water in water hazard ........................................... 26-1/7
- when kicked while probing for it in water in water hazard .......................... 12-1/5
- when loose impediment removed................................................................. 13-4/15
- while player in process of taking stance ....................................................... 18-2b/3
ball deemed unplayable
- through the green dropped in water hazard ................................................ 28/4
- through the green dropped in water hazard; player elects not to
  play ball and wishes to proceed under water hazard Rule ........................ 28/4.5
- in water hazard; ball dropped in hazard and played .................................... 20-7/2
- in water hazard; substituted ball dropped in hazard without lifting
  original; error discovered before stroke played ......................................... 20-7/2.5
ball dropped in another hazard when proceeding under water hazard Rule................. 26-1/2
ball lost in either water hazard or casual water overflowing hazard .................. 1-4/7
ball played after relief taken under water hazard Rule
- original ball then found in hazard and holed out as second ball ............................. 26-1/5
- original ball then found outside hazard......................................................... 26-1/3
- without reasonable evidence original ball in hazard; original ball
  then found in hazard..................................................................................... 26-1/4
ball played back into water hazard from putting green side of hazard............................ 26-1/6
balls exchanged when recovered from water hazard....................................... 15-1/4
burrowing animal hole relief taken by player unaware ball in water
  hazard; error discovered before ball played ............................................... 25-1b/26
caddie lifts ball in water hazard without player's authority................................. 26-1/9
casual water mistaken for water hazard
- original ball played under water hazard Rule .............................................. 25-1b/12
- substituted ball played under water hazard Rule ........................................ 25-1b/13

**Water Hazards** *(continued)*

changing relief option
- dropped ball first strikes course outside where applicable Rule requires; whether player may change relief option when re-dropping .................. 20-6/2
- dropped ball first strikes course outside where applicable Rule requires; whether player may replace ball in original location ............... 20-6/5
- dropped ball rolls to position requiring re-drop; whether player may change relief option when re-dropping .............. 20-2c/5
- dropped ball strikes player; whether player may change relief option when re-dropping ............... 20-2a/6
- player drops ball in bunker under first option of Rule 25-1b(ii); player then wishes to proceed under second option to drop outside bunker ............... 25-1b/9
- player lifts ball from bunker intending to drop under first option of Rule 24-2b(ii); player then wishes to proceed under second option to drop outside bunker ............... 24-2b/5
- point where ball last crossed margin of lateral water hazard determined and ball dropped; point then proves to be wrong point; whether player may change relief option when re-dropping ............... 26-1/16

club accidentally touches ball in water hazard; ball does not move ............... 13-4/12
embedded ball in water hazard lifted to determine whether unfit for play ............... 5-3/5
environmentally-sensitive area
- entering to retrieve ball ............... 33-8/42
- marking and defining; recommendations for Committee ............... 33-8/41
- significant advantage gained when player plays stroke from environmentally-sensitive area defined as water hazard ............... 33-8/44
- stroke played from environmentally-sensitive water hazard ............... 33-8/43

explanation of options under Rule 26-2 (ball played within water hazard)
- ball played from water hazard comes to rest in same hazard after exiting hazard ............... 26-2/2
- stroke played from water hazard; ball either not extracted from hazard or comes to rest out of bounds or in unplayable lie outside hazard ............... 26-2/1

grounding club
- cane or club used to enter or leave hazard when ball lies in hazard ............... 13-4/3.5
- cleaning clubhead in water hazard when ball lies in hazard ............... 13-4/40
- leaning on club in hazard while waiting to play ............... 13-4/2
- moving loose impediments and improving area of intended swing in hazard ............... 13-4/28
- on bridge in water hazard ............... 13-4/30
- several practice swings touch ground in water hazard ............... 13-4/3
- touching grass with club during practice swing in water hazard ............... 13-4/4
- touching ground in hazard with club while probing for ball believed covered by leaves ............... 12-1/4
- touching solidly embedded stone in hazard with club during backswing ............... 13-4/6

identifying ball
- half-buried ball in water hazard touched or rotated for identification purposes ............... 12-2/3
- two balls lie together in water hazard; neither identifiable; procedure for players ............... 1-4/6

insect flying in water hazard ............... 13-4/16.5
lateral water hazard
- allowing drop opposite to spot where ball comes to rest in lateral water hazard; whether authorized ............... 26-1/20
- ball dropped within 2 club-lengths of hazard margin comes to rest almost 4 club-lengths from margin; whether re-drop required ............... 20-2c/1
- ball moved into bounds by flow of water in lateral water hazard ............... 26-1/8
- clarification of "opposite margin" in Rule 26-1c ............... 26-1/14
- deeming part of body of water as water hazard and remainder as lateral water hazard ............... 33-2a/7

Index **i-147**

- deeming water hazard as lateral water hazard in play from forward
  tee by Local Rule .................................................................................................. 33-2a/6
- defined as water hazard ........................................................................................... 26/3.5
- defining rough and unplayable areas adjacent to fairways (areas not
  meeting definition of lateral water hazard) as lateral water hazard ................. 33-8/35
- example of serious breach of lateral water hazard Rule ............................................ 26-1/21
- hazard marked as water hazard where ball last crosses margin and
  as lateral water hazard where ball comes to rest; relief options for player ...... 26-1/12
- impossible to drop not nearer hole than point where ball last
  crossed margin of lateral water hazard ............................................................... 26-1/18
- opposite side of lateral water hazard defined as water hazard;
  relief options for player ........................................................................................ 26-1/13
- part of lateral water hazard where impossible to drop not nearer hole ................ 33-2a/9
- permissible dropping area under lateral water hazard Rule so
  narrow player has difficulty dropping within it .................................................. 26-1/19
- point where ball last crossed margin of lateral water hazard determined
  and ball dropped; point then proves to be wrong point .................................... 26-1/16
- point where ball last crossed margin of lateral water hazard determined,
  ball dropped and played; point then proves to be wrong point ........................ 26-1/17
- procedures for relief from lateral water hazard ...................................................... 26-1/15
- water hazard treated as lateral water hazard ......................................................... 26-1/11

Local Rule
- allowing drop on green side of water hazard when ball fails to
  clear hazard; whether authorized ........................................................................ 33-8/2
- allowing drop within water hazard behind point where ball lies
  unplayable in same hazard; whether authorized ................................................ 33-8/37
- allowing free relief for ball in water hazard within limits of fairway;
  whether authorized .............................................................................................. 33-8/36
- allowing free relief from immovable water hazard stake for ball
  lying in water hazard; whether authorized ......................................................... 33-8/15
- deeming water hazard as lateral water hazard in play from forward tee ............ 33-2a/6
- defining rough and unplayable areas adjacent to fairways
  (areas not meeting definition of lateral water hazard) as lateral
  water hazard; whether authorized ...................................................................... 33-8/35
- for water hazard with bunker adjacent .............................................................. US/33-8/100
- procedure for dropping and re-dropping on ball drop (dropping zone)
  established by Local Rule ..................................................................................... 33-8/34

loose impediment
- accidentally moved in hazard ................................................................................... 13-4/13
- affecting opponent's lie in hazard removed by player .............................................. 1-2/6
- ball in hazard moves when loose impediment removed ........................................... 13-4/15
- removal of obstruction in hazard would move loose impediment ............................ 1-4/5
- removed from water hazard; player then decides not to play from hazard ............ 13-4/17
- removed in water hazard partially covering wrong ball ........................................... 13-4/16
- top of ball in hazard covered by leaves but part of ball visible from
  another angle ......................................................................................................... 12-1/3

marking and defining
- ball within natural margin of water hazard but outside stakes defining margin .. 26/2
- deeming water hazard as lateral water hazard in play from forward
  tee by Local Rule .................................................................................................. 33-2a/6
- defining part of body of water as water hazard and remainder as
  lateral water hazard .............................................................................................. 33-2a/7
- environmentally-sensitive areas; recommendations for Committee ...................... 33-8/41
- island green ................................................................................................................ 33-2a/10
- part of lateral water hazard where impossible to drop not nearer hole ................ 33-2a/9
- river or other body of water adjacent to hole but off club property .................... 33-2a/11
- treating ocean and beach as through the green ...................................................... 33-2a/8
- unmarked water hazard with margin out of bounds ................................................. 26/3
- where to place lines or stakes defining margin of water hazard ........................... 33-2a/4

**W**

**Water Hazards** *(continued)*

meaning of
- "behind" in Rule 26-1 .................................................................................................. 26-1/1.5
- "opposite margin" in Rule 26-1c ............................................................................... 26-1/14
- "reasonable evidence" in Rule 26-1 ........................................................................... 26-1/1

order of play
- when two balls lost in lateral water hazard ............................................................... 10/3
- when two balls lie in lateral water hazard and both players take relief ..................... 10/2

overflow from water hazard .............................................................................................. 25/2

placing ball
- instead of dropping when obvious dropped ball will roll into
  water hazard requiring re-drop .................................................................................. 20-2c/3
- on bank of water hazard instead of dropping to prevent ball
  rolling into water ....................................................................................................... 26-1/10

player tells opponent he will proceed under water hazard Rule;
  changes mind after opponent plays ........................................................................... 9-2/13

provisional ball
- played solely in belief original ball might be in water hazard ................................... 27-2a/2
- played in belief original might be lost outside water hazard;
  player then discovers no possibility ball lost outside water hazard .......................... 27-2a/2.5
- possibility that original ball in water hazard may not preclude
  play of provisional ball ............................................................................................. 27-2c/1
- serving as ball in play if original unplayable or in water hazard ............................... 27-2/1

re-drop required when proceeding under water hazard Rule; whether
  player may substitute when re-dropping ................................................................... 20-6/4

reasonable evidence original ball in water hazard; substituted ball
  dropped under water hazard Rule; original ball then found
  within five minutes .................................................................................................... 26-1/3.5

serious breach
- ball deemed unplayable in water hazard; dropped in hazard and played ................. 20-7/2
- example of serious breach of lateral water hazard Rule ............................................ 26-1/21
- significant advantage gained when player plays stroke from
  environmentally-sensitive area defined as water hazard .......................................... 33-8/44
- stroke played from environmentally-sensitive water hazard ..................................... 33-8/43
- water hazard treated as lateral water hazard ............................................................. 26-1/11

status of
- hole of removed stake defining water hazard ............................................................ 25/18
- insect flying in water hazard ..................................................................................... 13-4/16.5
- man-made reservoir ................................................................................................... 26/4
- movable part of drainage hose .................................................................................. 24-2b/15.3
- stone broken away from retaining wall in water hazard ........................................... 24/6
- water overflowing margin of water hazard ............................................................... 25/2

testing condition of water hazard
- player uses cane or club to enter or leave hazard when ball lies in hazard ........ 13-4/3.5
- touching grass with club during practice swing in water hazard ............................. 13-4/4
- umbrella placed in water hazard before stroke ......................................................... 13-4/20

unidentifiable ball in water hazard played and lost .......................................................... 26/5

when ball considered in water hazard ............................................................................... 26/1

whether player entitled to ascertain whereabouts of opponent's
  ball that may be in water hazard before playing ....................................................... 9-2/16

wrong ball
- player concedes hole after which opponent's last stroke discovered
  played with wrong ball from hazard ......................................................................... 2-4/9.5
- removal of loose impediment in water hazard partially covering wrong ball .... 13-4/16

## Weather Conditions

*See also* Course Unplayable or Closed; Discontinuance and Resumption of Play

ball visible from tee prior to suspension of play disappears or moved by
    outside agency during suspension .................................................................. 6-8d/4
competitor refuses to start or picks up because of weather conditions;
    round subsequently canceled .......................................................................... 33-2d/3
guidelines for Committee on whether to cancel round ....................................... 33-2d/1
lightning
    - condition requiring immediate discontinuance of play; guidelines
        for waiving or modifying disqualification penalty for failure to
        discontinue play immediately ................................................................... 6-8b/7
    - player claiming danger from lightning refuses to resume play
        when resumption ordered by Committee ................................................ 6-8b/5
Local Rule
    - permitting competitors to discontinue play by agreement in bad
        weather; whether authorized .................................................................. 33-8/5
    - permitting use of wind gauge; whether permitted .................................... 14-3/0.5
player not present at time of starting; course closed at that time ..................... 33-3/2
rain
    - extensive damage due to heavy rain and traffic ......................................... 33-2a/3
    - match discontinued by agreement; one player subsequently wishes
        to resume; opponent refuses although course playable ......................... 6-8a/5
    - match discontinued by agreement; one player subsequently wishes
        to resume; opponent refuses on ground course unplayable.................. 6-8a/6
    - number of holes reduced after start of competition due to rain ............... 33-1/2
    - player holds umbrella over own head when making stroke ...................... 14-2/2
    - resuming play from where discontinued; lie altered by rainfall ................ 6-8d/1
    - taking shelter while waiting to play ........................................................... 6-8a/2
wind
    - ball at rest moved by blowing tumbleweed ................................................ 18-1/6
    - ball in plastic bag moves when bag blown to new position by wind ........ 18-1/7
    - ball moved by wind or casual water while play suspended ....................... 18-1/11
    - ball moved by wind replaced instead of played as lies ............................. 18-2a/7
    - ball moves after player grounds club but before stance completed ........ 18-2b/4
    - ball oscillating in wind pressed into surface of putting green ................. 18-2a/6
    - ball replaced and at rest thereafter moved by wind ................................. 18-1/12
    - ball replaced on putting green but ball-marker not removed;
        ball then moves ......................................................................................... 20-4/1
    - ball-marker moved by wind or casual water during stipulated round ...... 20-1/10.5
    - ball-marker moved off green by wind or casual water while play suspended ...... 20-1/10
    - resuming play from where discontinued; lie altered by wind .................. 6-8d/1
    - shielding line of putt from wind ................................................................. 1-2/2
    - towel dropped by player blown onto ball causing it to move ................... 18-2a/17

## Worm

ball played from putting green, deflected by moving worm;
    whether stroke should be replayed ................................................................. 19-1/3
means by which worm casts may be removed from line of play and line of putt ........ 23-1/1
status of worm partially underground ................................................................... 23/8

## Wrong Ball

ball lifted
    - by player from putting green then placed by caddie behind ball-marker; whether
        wrong ball if played ................................................................................... 20-4/2
    - by player, set aside and played from where set aside ............................... 15/4
    - competitor's ball mistaken for wrong ball picked up by fellow-competitor
        at competitor's request ............................................................................. 18-2a/16
    - fellow-competitor lifts competitor's ball and sets it aside; competitor
        plays ball from where set aside ................................................................ 15-3b/3

**Wrong Ball** (continued)
- from putting green without its position being marked in mistaken belief it is wrong ball ........ 20-1/1
- player wins hole with wrong ball and partner picks up; error discovered at next hole ........ 30-3d/2
- players on opposite sides exchange balls during play of hole and their partners pick up; error discovered at next hole ........ 30-3d/3
- provisional ball lifted subsequently becomes ball in play after wrong ball played ........ 27-2b/9

ball moved accidentally by player in playing wrong ball in bunker ........ 18-2a/21
balls inadvertently exchanged by players between holes ........ 15-1/1
competitor plays second ball under Rule 20-7c; clarification of "penalty strokes incurred solely by playing the ball ruled not to count" ........ 20-7c/5
competitor's ball played by fellow-competitor
- in bunker not replaced ........ 18-4/1
- balls inadvertently exchanged by competitors at unknown place ........ 15-1/2
- balls inadvertently exchanged by players after one ball strikes and moves other ........ 15-1/2.5
- competitor substitutes another ball at wrong place, plays it and then abandons it and plays out original ball from right place ........ 20-7c/4

deemed unplayable
- dropped in bunker then played; ball then discovered to be wrong ball ........ 15/14
- dropped under unplayable ball Rule but not played ........ 15/13
- dropped within two club-lengths and played before error discovered ........ 28/15
- played under stroke-and-distance procedure; original ball then found ........ 28/14

hole at which wrong ball played unknown ........ 15-1/3
in anger, player strikes ball played by player in following group ........ 1-4/4
loose impediment removed in water hazard covering wrong ball ........ 13-4/16
lost ball, provisional ball or ball out of bounds
- ball thrown into bounds by outside agency and played; caddie aware of action of outside agency ........ 15/9
- ball thrown into bounds by outside agency and played; neither player nor caddie aware of action of outside agency ........ 15/10
- competitor plays wrong ball and loses it; wrong ball may have been fellow-competitor's ball ........ 15-3b/1
- lost ball found after search exceeding five minutes; ball then played ........ 27/8
- original ball found and played after another ball put into play ........ 15/5
- original ball found within five-minute search period after another ball dropped; original ball played ........ 27-1/2.3
- original ball played after provisional ball played from point nearer hole than original ball likely to be ........ 27-2b/5
- player unable to find his ball because another player has played it ........ 27/6
- provisional ball played from point nearer hole than visible original ball; player erroneously thought original ball out of bounds ........ 27-2c/3
- stroke played with ball lying out of bounds ........ 15/6
- time permitted for search for lost ball after wrong ball played ........ 27/2
- wrong ball found out of bounds played under stroke-and-distance procedure; original ball then found in bounds ........ 15/12
- wrong ball hit out of bounds; another ball played under Rule 27-1; original ball then found nearby ........ 15/11
- wrong ball played in belief it is provisional or second ball ........ 15/7
- wrong ball played; provisional ball lifted subsequently becomes ball in play ........ 27-2b/9

match play
- after playing wrong ball, player wins hole with original ball; opponent does not lodge claim during hole; claim lodged next day ........ 2-5/4
- balls inadvertently exchanged by players after one ball strikes and moves other ........ 15-1/2.5

- implied concession of hole withdrawn after player plays stroke
with wrong ball .................................................................................................. 2-4/13
- opponent's misreading of number on player's ball results in
agreement that player lost hole for playing wrong ball ........................... 9-2/11
- player concedes hole after which opponent discovered to have
played wrong ball prior to concession ...................................................... 2-4/9
- player concedes hole after which opponent discovered to have
played wrong ball with previous stroke from hazard .............................. 2-4/9.5
- player concedes hole after which opponent plays wrong ball .................... 2-4/10
- player plays partner's ball in four-ball match ................................................ 30-3d/1
- player plays partner's ball; error discovered after opponents have
played next strokes ...................................................................................... 30-3d/3.5
- player unaware original ball holed plays wrong ball; opponent
claims hole; claim not disputed ................................................................. 2-5/5
- player wins hole with wrong ball and partner picks up; error
discovered at next hole ............................................................................... 30-3d/2
- player wins hole with wrong ball; error discovered at next hole,
opponent claims previous hole ................................................................. 9-2/8
- player's ball moved by wrong ball played by opponent .............................. 18-5/1
- players on opposite sides exchange balls during play of hole and
their partners pick up; error discovered at next hole ............................. 30-3d/3
- second ball played in match play; whether permitted; status of
original and second balls ............................................................................ 3-3/9
order of play in foursome stroke play when wrong ball played .......................... 29-1/8
penalty for playing wrong ball not included in competitor's score due
to incorrect Committee ruling; during subsequent round error
discovered and penalty applied retroactively; competitor objects ........................ 34-3/1
play of two different wrong balls between strokes with ball in play ............................. 15-3b/2
play of wrong ball not rectified in stroke play
- error discovered after competition closed ................................................... 34-1b/3
- on advice of Committee member ................................................................. 33-7/5
played from environmentally-sensitive area ........................................................ 33-8/43
player discovers own ball in hole after playing wrong ball ................................. 1-1/4
player plays stroke at part of abandoned ball which had broken into pieces .................. 15/3
player's stroke at own ball dislodges concealed ball ............................................. 15/2
practice swing dislodges concealed ball ................................................................. 7-2/7
searching for and identifying ball by brand and number only .......................... 12-2/1
score may count with wrong ball in some circumstances
- ball thrown into bounds by outside agency and played; neither player
nor caddie aware of action of outside agency ......................................... 15/10
- fellow-competitor lifts competitor's ball and sets it aside; competitor
plays ball from where set aside ................................................................. 15-3b/3
- play of wrong ball in stroke play not rectified; error discovered after
competition closed ...................................................................................... 34-1b/3
- play of wrong ball not rectified on advice of committee member ............ 33-7/5
stroke misses wrong ball ........................................................................................... 15/1

## Wrong Information

*See also* Claims and Disputes; Incorrect Information on the Rules; Information as to the Strokes Taken

breach of 14-club Rule discovered after match concluded but before
result officially announced ................................................................................ 2-5/5.5
conscious failure to correct opponent's misunderstanding of state of match ............... 9-2/12
four-ball match play
- player wins hole with wrong ball and partner picks up; error discovered
at next hole .................................................................................................... 30-3d/2
- player lifts ball resting against flagstick before being holed; others
in match pick up mistakenly believing player won hole ....................... 30-3f/3
- player out of contention on hole gives wrong information; whether
partner also penalized ................................................................................. 30-3f/4

**Wrong Information** (continued)
- player plays partner's ball; error discovered after opponents have
  played next strokes .................................................................................. 30-3d/3.5
- players on opposite sides exchange balls during play of hole and
  their partners pick up; error discovered at next hole .......................................... 30-3d/3
foursome side drives for three holes in wrong order; opponents
  make claim during third hole ........................................................................ 29-2/2
handicap information
- handicap stroke wrongly claimed at hole; error discovered before
  hole completed ............................................................................................. 6-2a/3
- wrong handicap used by mistake; error discovered after result
  officially announced .................................................................................... 6-2a/5
- wrong handicap used due to Committee misinformation ............................... 33-1/12
incorrect information
- causes opponent mistakenly to think he has putt for half; opponent
  holes putt and then error discovered ......................................................... 9-2/14
- causes opponent to lift ball-marker ............................................................... 9-2/5
- given after play of hole; when penalty applicable ......................................... 9-2/15
- given by caddie or partner ............................................................................. 9-2/2
- given by player; corrected after opponent concedes player's
  putt but before opponent plays next stroke ............................................... 9-2/7
- on penalty applicable to player given by opponent; error discovered
  after match result announced; player then makes claim .......................... 2-5/10
- on Rules given to player ................................................................................... 9/1
- on strokes, given voluntarily by player to opponent ....................................... 9-2/3
invalid claim not disputed................................................................................... 2-5/5
match conceded by player after winning it when opponent lodges
  invalid claim regarding strokes taken............................................................ 2-4/15
misunderstandings
- opponent's misreading of number on player's ball results in
  agreement that player lost hole for playing wrong ball ........................... 9-2/11
- player and opponent agree hole halved; after match result posted
  player realizes he won hole and should have won match; player then
  makes claim ................................................................................................. 2-5/9
- player and opponent mistakenly believe match all square after
  18 holes and play extra hole without making claim ..................................... 2-5/6
- players leave last green under impression match over later realize
  it was all square; whether late claim valid .................................................. 2-3/1
opponent asks player number of strokes taken
- player refuses to answer ........................................................................... 9-2/3.5
- player withholds information until opponent's turn to play............................. 9-2/4
player lifts ball before holing out; opponent then picks up his ball
  claiming player loses hole............................................................................... 2-5/3
player tells opponent he will proceed under water hazard Rule;
  changes mind after opponent plays............................................................ 9-2/13
player wins hole
- with original ball after playing wrong ball; opponent does not
  lodge claim during hole; claim lodged next day ......................................... 2-5/4
- with wrong ball and partner picks up; error discovered at next hole ............ 30-3d/2
- with wrong ball; error discovered at next hole; opponent
  claims previous hole .................................................................................... 9-2/8
referee imposes penalty for previous hole after play of next hole
  begun; whether permitted ........................................................................ 2-5/12
rightful winner of match makes no claim and agrees to play extra holes......... 2-5/7
stroke play
- competitor gives fellow-competitor incorrect information in
  sudden-death play-off.................................................................................... 9-3/1
- incorrect information on Rules given .............................................................. 9/1

wrong score for hole given by player
- causes opponent with chance for half to pick up ball ........................................... 9-2/6
- error discovered several holes later ...................................................................... 9-2/9
- penalty stroke omitted by player when advising opponent of
  score for hole; error discovered after match conceded by opponent ................... 9-2/10
- upon completion of last hole; claim made after result announced ....................... 2-5/11

## Wrong Place

*See also* Serious Breach of Rules

ball deemed unplayable
- ball dropped outside bunker under option of unplayable ball
  Rule requiring drop in bunker .............................................................................. 28/10
- ball dropped under option 28c of unplayable ball Rule strikes
  player; whether player may change relief option when re-dropping ................. 20-2a/6
- in water hazard; ball dropped in hazard and played ........................................... 20-7/2
- player plays second shot, deems ball unplayable and returns to tee............................ 28/6

ball dropped
- in improper manner and in wrong place................................................................ 20-2a/3
- in wrong place when proceeding under Rule permitting substitution;
  whether player may substitute when re-dropping ............................................... 20-6/4
- with reasonable evidence original lost in abnormal ground
  condition or obstruction; whether re-drop required if finding
  original demonstrates drop made in wrong place ............................................... 25-1c/2.5

ball stepped on accidentally and original lie altered; player places ball
  in wrong place and plays ........................................................................................ 18-2a/21.3

borrowing club for measuring purposes ....................................................................... 20/2

changing relief option
- dropped ball first strikes course outside where applicable Rule requires;
  whether player may change relief option when re-dropping.............................. 20-6/2
- dropped ball first strikes course outside where applicable Rule requires;
  whether player may replace ball in original location .......................................... 20-6/5
- dropped ball rolls to position requiring re-drop; whether player may
  change relief option when re-dropping ................................................................ 20-2c/5
- dropped ball strikes player; whether player may change relief option
  when re-dropping .................................................................................................. 20-2a/6
- player drops ball in bunker under first option of Rule 25-1b(ii); player
  then wishes to proceed under second option to drop outside bunker ............. 25-1b/9
- player lifts ball from bunker intending to drop under first option
  of Rule 24-2b(ii); player then wishes to proceed under second option
  to drop outside bunker .......................................................................................... 24-2b/5
- point where ball last crossed margin of lateral water hazard determined
  and ball dropped; point then proves to be wrong point; whether
  player may change relief option when re-dropping ............................................ 26-1/16

competitor's ball played by fellow-competitor in bunker not replaced.......................... 18-4/1

competitor's ball moved by fellow-competitor's ball; both players unaware
  until after completion of hole ................................................................................. 18-5/3

competitor's ball played by fellow-competitor; competitor substitutes
  another ball at wrong place, plays it and then abandons it and
  plays out original ball from right place ................................................................. 20-7c/4

environmentally-sensitive area
- ball played from environmentally-sensitive area .................................................. 33-8/43
- significant advantage gained when player plays stroke from
  environmentally-sensitive area defined as water hazard ................................... 33-8/44

player does not follow recommended procedure in determining
  nearest point of relief............................................................................................... 24-2b/2

player invokes Rule 3-3 (doubt as to procedure)
- ball dropped and played; Rule 3-3 then invoked and second ball
  dropped in right place; both balls played out....................................................... 3-3/3
- ball dropped but not played; Rule 3-3 then invoked and second ball
  dropped in right place; both balls played out....................................................... 3-3/4

**Wrong Place** *(continued)*
- guidelines for determining which ball counts when player proceeds under Rule 3-3 .................................................................... 3-3/0.5
- whether score with second ball counts if ball dropped in wrong place and played .................................................................... 3-3/5

player plays from wrong place as directed by Committee member
- based on available facts; subsequent facts prove ruling incorrect ............. 34-3/7
- based on player's version of facts; player's version later found incorrect ........ 34-3/8
- based on incorrect ruling; procedure for player when error discovered ........ 34-3/3

provisional ball lifted by competitor subsequently becomes ball in play;
ball played from tee instead of replaced at spot from which lifted ................ 27-2b/10

putting green
- ball putted from wrong place lifted and putted from right place ................. 20-7c/2
- ball replaced at wrong place on putting green and holed ........................ 20-7c/1
- ball replaced then player makes several strokes on wrong putting green ............. 25-3/2
- ball resting against flagstick moves away from hole when flagstick removed by player; ball not placed on lip of hole ........................... 17-4/4
- fellow-competitor lifts competitor's ball from putting green and sets it aside; competitor plays ball from where set aside ................ 15-3b/3
- penalty for repeatedly replacing ball nearer hole on green ...................... 33-7/6
- valid timely claim made after concession of match when player determines opponent putted from wrong place on last hole .................. 2-4/16

serious breach of Rule 20-7c may be involved
- ball believed lost in bunker; competitor drops and plays substituted ball in bunker; then original ball found outside bunker ................ 20-7c/3
- ball deemed unplayable in water hazard; dropped in hazard and played ............. 20-7/2
- ball dropped and played under ground under repair Rule in absence of reasonable evidence original ball lost in ground under repair ...... 25-1c/2
- ball dropped in area where original ball lost; ball then played.................... 27-1/3
- ball dropped outside bunker under option of unplayable ball Rule requiring drop in bunker................................................................ 28/10
- ball played from ground under repair abandoned and relief taken under ground under repair Rule .................................................. 18-2a/8.5
- ball played from spot where original ball deflected out of bounds by maintenance vehicle .................................................................... 20-7/1
- ball played under water hazard Rule without reasonable evidence original ball in hazard; original ball then found in hazard................... 26-1/4
- competitor's ball knocked out of bunker by fellow-competitor's stroke at own ball not replaced ............................................................ 18-4/2
- competitor plays second ball under Rule 20-7c; clarification of "penalty strokes incurred solely by playing the ball ruled not to count"........................................................................................ 20-7c/5
- example of serious breach of lateral water hazard Rule .......................... 26-1/21
- lost ball treated as moved by outside agency in absence of reasonable evidence to that effect........................................................ 27-1/2.5
- player plays second shot, deems ball unplayable and returns to tee............ 28/6
- significant advantage gained when player plays stroke from environmentally-sensitive area defined as water hazard ...................... 33-8/44

water hazard and lateral water hazard
- ball deemed unplayable in water hazard; dropped in hazard and played ............. 20-7/2
- ball played under water hazard Rule original ball then found outside hazard .................................................................................. 26-1/3
- ball played under water hazard Rule without reasonable evidence original ball in hazard; original ball then found in hazard................... 26-1/4
- casual water mistaken for water hazard; original ball played under water hazard Rule .................................................................... 25-1b/12
- casual water mistaken for water hazard; substituted ball played under water hazard Rule .................................................................... 25-1b/13
- example of serious breach of lateral water hazard Rule .......................... 26-1/21

- player unaware ball in water hazard takes relief from interference
  by burrowing animal hole; error discovered before ball played ........................ 25-1b/26
- point where ball last crossed margin of lateral water hazard
  determined and ball dropped; point then proves to be wrong point ................. 26-1/16
- point where ball last crossed margin of lateral water hazard determined,
  ball dropped and played; point then proves to be wrong point ........................... 26-1/17
- water hazard treated as lateral water hazard ................................................................. 26-1/11

## Wrong Putting Green

ball dropped on wrong putting green in taking relief under a Rule;
  whether permitted............................................................................................................. 20-7/3
double green; status of portion serving hole not being played ........................................... 25-3/1
Local Rule deeming wrong putting green to include apron to
  prohibit dropping on and play from............................................................................. 33-8/33
recommended procedure for determining nearest point of relief not
  used by player when taking relief from wrong putting green ............................. 24-2b/2
several strokes made on wrong putting green; explanation of penalties;
  subsequent relief procedure in stroke play .................................................................. 25-3/2

## Wrong Teeing Ground

*See also* Teeing Ground and Tee-Markers
match play; ball played from wrong teeing ground goes out of bounds;
  stroke not recalled by opponent ...................................................................................... 11-5/3
stroke play
  - competitor plays from teeing ground of hole to be played later in round;
    when hole subsequently reached competitor replaces ball at spot
    from which original tee shot lifted and plays out hole ............................................ 11-5/5
  - group plays from wrong teeing ground; corrects error ................................................ 11-5/4
  - group plays from wrong teeing ground; attributes Committee
    failure to indicate hole numbers on teeing grounds as reason;
    whether Committee should waive penalties ................................................................ 11-5/2
  - meaning of "next teeing ground" after competitors have played
    from wrong teeing ground ................................................................................................ 11-5/1

## "X-out" Ball

status .................................................................................................................................................. 5-1/4

In the Rules of Golf and Decisions on the Rules of Golf, the gender used in relation to any person is understood to include both genders.

# SECTION I ETIQUETTE; BEHAVIOR ON THE COURSE

## Introduction

This Section provides guidelines on the manner in which the game of golf should be played. If they are followed, all players will gain maximum enjoyment from the game. The overriding principle is that consideration should be shown to others on the course at all times.

## The Spirit of the Game

Unlike many sports, golf is played, for the most part, without the supervision of a *referee* or umpire. The game relies on the integrity of the individual to show consideration for other players and to abide by the *Rules*. All players should conduct themselves in a disciplined manner, demonstrating courtesy and sportsmanship at all times, irrespective of how competitive they may be. This is the spirit of the game of golf.

## Safety

Players should ensure that no one is standing close by or in a position to be hit by the club, the ball or any stones, pebbles, twigs or the like when they make a *stroke* or practice swing.

Players should not play until the players in front are out of range.

Players should always alert greenstaff nearby or ahead when they are about to make a *stroke* that might endanger them.

If a player plays a ball in a direction where there is a danger of hitting someone, he should immediately shout a warning. The traditional word of warning in such situations is "fore."

## Consideration for Other Players

### No Disturbance or Distraction

Players should always show consideration for other players on the *course* and should not disturb their play by moving, talking or making unnecessary noise.

Players should ensure that any electronic device taken onto the *course* does not distract other players.

On the *teeing ground,* a player should not tee his ball until it is his turn to play.

Players should not stand close to or directly behind the ball, or directly behind the *hole,* when a player is about to play.

### On the Putting Green

On the *putting green,* players should not stand on another player's *line of putt* or, when he is making a *stroke,* cast a shadow over his *line of putt.*

Players should remain on or close to the *putting green* until all other players in the group have *holed* out.

## Scoring

In stroke play, a player who is acting as a *marker* should, if necessary, on the way to the next tee, check the score with the player concerned and record it.

## Pace of Play

### Play at Good Pace and Keep Up

Players should play at a good pace. The *Committee* may establish pace of play guidelines that all players should follow.

It is a group's responsibility to keep up with the group in front. If it loses a clear hole and it is delaying the group behind, it should invite the group behind to play through, irrespective of the number of players in that group.

### Be Ready to Play

Players should be ready to play as soon as it is their turn to play. When playing on or near the *putting green,* they should leave their bags or carts in such a position as will enable quick movement off the green and towards the next tee. When the play of a hole has been completed, players should immediately leave the *putting green.*

### Lost Ball

If a player believes his ball may be *lost* outside a *water hazard* or is *out of bounds,* to save time, he should play a *provisional ball.*

Players searching for a ball should signal the players in the group behind them to play through as soon as it becomes apparent that the ball will not easily be found. They should not search for five minutes before doing so. Having allowed the group behind to play through, they should not continue play until that group has passed and is out of range.

## Priority on the Course

Unless otherwise determined by the *Committee*, priority on the *course* is determined by a group's pace of play. Any group playing a whole round is entitled to pass a group playing a shorter round.

## Care of the Course

### Bunkers

Before leaving a *bunker,* players should carefully fill up and smooth over all holes and footprints made by them and any nearby made by others. If a rake is within reasonable proximity of the *bunker,* the rake should be used for this purpose.

### Repair of Divots, Ball-Marks and Damage by Shoes

Players should carefully repair any divot holes made by them and any damage to the *putting green* made by the impact of a ball (whether or not made by the player himself). On completion of the hole by all players in the group, damage to the *putting green* caused by golf shoes should be repaired.

### Preventing Unnecessary Damage

Players should avoid causing damage to the *course* by removing divots when taking practice swings or by hitting the head of a club into the ground, whether in anger or for any other reason.

Players should ensure that no damage is done to the *putting green* when putting down bags or the *flagstick*.

In order to avoid damaging the *hole,* players and *caddies* should not stand too close to the *hole* and should take care during the handling of the *flagstick* and the removal of a ball from the *hole*. The head of a club should not be used to remove a ball from the *hole.*

Players should not lean on their clubs when on the *putting green,* particularly when removing the ball from the *hole.*

The *flagstick* should be properly replaced in the *hole* before the players leave the *putting green.*

Local notices regulating the movement of golf carts should be strictly observed.

### Conclusion; Penalties for Breach

If players follow the guidelines in this Section, it will make the game more enjoyable for everyone.

If a player consistently disregards these guidelines during a round or over a period of time to the detriment of others, it is recommended that the *Committee* consider taking appropriate disciplinary action against the offending player. Such action may, for example, include prohibiting play for a limited time on the *course* or in a certain number of competitions. This is considered to be justifiable in terms of protecting the interest of the majority of golfers who wish to play in accordance with these guidelines.

In the case of a serious breach of etiquette, the *Committee* may disqualify a player under Rule 33-7.

# SECTION II  DEFINITIONS

### Abnormal Ground Conditions

An "*abnormal ground condition*" is any *casual water, ground under repair* or hole, cast or runway on the *course* made by a *burrowing animal*, a reptile or a bird.

### Addressing the Ball

A player has "*addressed the ball*" when he has taken his *stance* and has also grounded his club, except that in a *hazard* a player has *addressed the ball* when he has taken his *stance.*

### Advice

"*Advice*" is any counsel or suggestion that could influence a player in determining his play, the choice of a club or the method of making a *stroke.*

Information on the *Rules* or on matters of public information, such as the position of *hazards* or the *flagstick* on the *putting green*, is not *advice*.

**Ball Deemed to Move**

See "*Move* or *Moved*."

**Ball Holed**

See "*Holed*."

**Ball Lost**

See "*Lost Ball*."

**Ball in Play**

A ball is "*in play*" as soon as the player has made a *stroke* on the *teeing ground*. It remains *in play* until it is *holed*, except when it is *lost, out of bounds* or lifted, or another ball has been *substituted* whether or not the substitution is permitted; a ball so *substituted* becomes the *ball in play*.

If a ball is played from outside the *teeing ground* when the player is starting play of a hole, or when attempting to correct this mistake, the ball is not *in play* and Rule 11-4 or 11-5 applies. Otherwise, *ball in play* includes a ball played from outside the *teeing ground* when the player elects or is required to play his next *stroke* from the *teeing ground*.

**Exception in match play:** *Ball in play* includes a ball played by the player from outside the *teeing ground* when starting play of a hole if the opponent does not require the *stroke* to be canceled in accordance with Rule 11-4a.

**Best-Ball**

See "*Matches*."

**Bunker**

A "*bunker*" is a *hazard* consisting of a prepared area of ground, often a hollow, from which turf or soil has been removed and replaced with sand or the like.

Grass-covered ground bordering or within a *bunker,* including a stacked turf face (whether grass-covered or earthen), is not part of the *bunker*. A wall or lip of the *bunker* not covered with grass is part of the *bunker*.

The margin of a *bunker* extends vertically downwards, but not upwards. A ball is in a *bunker* when it lies in or any part of it touches the *bunker*.

**Burrowing Animal**

A "*burrowing animal*" is an animal that makes a hole for habitation or shelter, such as a rabbit, mole, groundhog, gopher or salamander.

**Note:** A hole made by a non-burrowing animal, such as a dog, is not an *abnormal ground condition* unless marked or declared as *ground under repair*.

**Caddie**

A "*caddie*" is one who assists the player in accordance with the *Rules*, which may include carrying or handling the player's clubs during play.

When one *caddie* is employed by more than one player, he is always deemed to be the *caddie* of the player whose ball is involved, and *equipment* carried by him is deemed to be that player's *equipment*, except when the *caddie* acts upon specific directions of another player, in which case he is considered to be that other player's *caddie*.

### Casual Water
"*Casual water*" is any temporary accumulation of water on the *course*, that is visible before or after the player takes his *stance*, and is not in a *water hazard*. Snow and natural ice, other than frost, are either *casual water* or *loose impediments*, at the option of the player. Manufactured ice is an *obstruction*. Dew and frost are not *casual water*. A ball is in *casual water* when it lies in or any part of it touches the *casual water*.

### Committee
The "*Committee*" is the committee in charge of the competition or, if the matter does not arise in a competition, the committee in charge of the *course*.

### Competitor
A "*competitor*" is a player in a stroke play competition. A "*fellow-competitor*" is any person with whom the *competitor* plays. Neither is *partner* of the other.

In stroke play *foursome* and *four-ball* competitions, where the context so admits, the word "*competitor*" or "*fellow-competitor*" includes his *partner*.

### Course
The "*course*" is the whole area within any boundaries established by the *Committee* (see Rule 33-2).

### Equipment
"*Equipment*" is anything used, worn or carried by or for the player except any ball he has played at the hole being played and any small object, such as a coin or a *tee*, when used to mark the position of a ball or the extent of an area in which a ball is to be dropped. *Equipment* includes a golf cart, whether or not motorized. If such a cart is shared by two or more players, the cart and everything in it are deemed to be the *equipment* of the player whose ball is involved except that, when the cart is being moved by one of the players sharing it, the cart and everything in it are deemed to be that player's *equipment*.

**Note:** A ball played at the hole being played is *equipment* when it has been lifted and not put back into play.

### Fellow-Competitor
See "*Competitor*."

### Flagstick
The "*flagstick*" is a movable straight indicator, with or without bunting or other material attached, centered in the *hole* to show its position. It must be circular in cross-section. Padding or shock absorbent material that might unduly influence the movement of the ball is prohibited.

### Forecaddie
A "*forecaddie*" is one who is employed by the *Committee* to indicate to players the position of balls during play. He is an *outside agency*.

## Four-Ball
See "*Matches*."

## Foursome
See "*Matches*."

## Ground Under Repair
"*Ground under repair*" is any part of the *course* so marked by order of the *Committee* or so declared by its authorized representative. It includes material piled for removal and a hole made by a greenkeeper, even if not so marked.

All ground and any grass, bush, tree or other growing thing within the *ground under repair* is part of the *ground under repair*. The margin of *ground under repair* extends vertically downwards, but not upwards. Stakes and lines defining *ground under repair* are in such ground. Such stakes are *obstructions*. A ball is in *ground under repair* when it lies in or any part of it touches the *ground under repair*.

**Note 1:** Grass cuttings and other material left on the *course* that have been abandoned and are not intended to be removed are not *ground under repair* unless so marked.

**Note 2:** The *Committee* may make a Local Rule prohibiting play from *ground under repair* or an environmentally-sensitive area defined as *ground under repair*.

## Hazards
A "*hazard*" is any *bunker* or *water hazard*.

## Hole
The "*hole*" must be 4¼ inches (108 mm) in diameter and at least 4 inches (101.6 mm) deep. If a lining is used, it must be sunk at least 1 inch (25.4 mm) below the *putting green* surface unless the nature of the soil makes it impracticable to do so; its outer diameter must not exceed 4¼ inches (108 mm).

## Holed
A ball is "*holed*" when it is at rest within the circumference of the *hole* and all of it is below the level of the lip of the *hole*.

## Honor
The player who is to play first from the *teeing ground* is said to have the "*honor*."

## Lateral Water Hazard
A "*lateral water hazard*" is a *water hazard* or that part of a *water hazard* so situated that it is not possible or is deemed by the *Committee* to be impracticable to drop a ball behind the *water hazard* in accordance with Rule 26-1b.

That part of a *water hazard* to be played as a *lateral water hazard* should be distinctively marked. A ball is in a *lateral water hazard* when it lies in or any part of it touches the *lateral water hazard*.

**Note 1:** Stakes or lines used to define a *lateral water hazard* must be red.

When both stakes and lines are used to define *lateral water hazards,* the stakes identify the *hazard* and the lines define the *hazard* margin.

**Note 2**: The *Committee* may make a Local Rule prohibiting play from an environmentally-sensitive area defined as a *lateral water hazard.*

**Note 3**: The *Committee* may define a *lateral water hazard* as a *water hazard.*

### Line of Play

The "*line of play*" is the direction that the player wishes his ball to take after a *stroke*, plus a reasonable distance on either side of the intended direction. The *line of play* extends vertically upwards from the ground, but does not extend beyond the *hole.*

### Line of Putt

The "*line of putt*" is the line that the player wishes his ball to take after a *stroke* on the *putting green.* Except with respect to Rule 16-1e, the *line of putt* includes a reasonable distance on either side of the intended line. The *line of putt* does not extend beyond the *hole.*

### Loose Impediments

"*Loose impediments*" are natural objects including:

- stones, leaves, twigs, branches and the like,
- dung, and
- worms and insects and casts or heaps made by them,

provided they are not:

- fixed or growing,
- solidly embedded, or
- adhering to the ball.

Sand and loose soil are *loose impediments* on the *putting green*, but not elsewhere.

Snow and natural ice, other than frost, are either *casual water* or *loose impediments*, at the option of the player.

Dew and frost are not *loose impediments.*

### Lost Ball

A ball is deemed "*lost*" if:

a. It is not found or identified as his by the player within five minutes after the player's *side* or his or their *caddies* have begun to search for it; or

b. The player has made a *stroke* at a *substituted ball*; or

c. The player has made a *stroke* at a *provisional ball* from the place where the original ball is likely to be or from a point nearer the *hole* than that place.

Time spent in playing a *wrong ball* is not counted in the five-minute period allowed for search.

### Marker

A "*marker*" is one who is appointed by the *Committee* to record a *competitor's* score in stroke play. He may be a *fellow-competitor*. He is not a *referee*.

**Matches**

Single: A match in which one plays against another.

Threesome: A match in which one plays against two, and each *side* plays one ball.

Foursome: A match in which two play against two, and each *side* plays one ball.

Three-Ball: A match-play competition in which three play against one another, each playing his own ball. Each player is playing two distinct matches.

Best-Ball: A match in which one plays against the better ball of two or the best ball of three players.

Four-Ball: A match in which two play their better ball against the better ball of two other players.

**Move or Moved**

A ball is deemed to have "*moved*" if it leaves its position and comes to rest in any other place.

**Nearest Point of Relief**

The "*nearest point of relief*" is the reference point for taking relief without penalty from interference by an immovable *obstruction* (Rule 24-2), an *abnormal ground condition* (Rule 25-1) or a *wrong putting green* (Rule 25-3).

It is the point on the *course* nearest to where the ball lies:

(i) that is not nearer the *hole,* and

(ii) where, if the ball were so positioned, no interference by the condition from which relief is sought would exist for the *stroke* the player would have made from the original position if the condition were not there.

**Note:** In order to determine the *nearest point of relief* accurately, the player should use the club with which he would have made his next *stroke* if the condition were not there to simulate the *address* position, direction of play and swing for such a *stroke*.

**Observer**

An "*observer*" is one who is appointed by the *Committee* to assist a *referee* to decide questions of fact and to report to him any breach of a *Rule*. An *observer* should not attend the *flagstick*, stand at or mark the position of the *hole*, or lift the ball or mark its position.

**Obstructions**

An "*obstruction*" is anything artificial, including the artificial surfaces and sides of roads and paths and manufactured ice, except:

a. Objects defining *out of bounds*, such as walls, fences, stakes and railings;

b. Any part of an immovable artificial object that is *out of bounds*; and

c. Any construction declared by the *Committee* to be an integral part of the *course*.

An *obstruction* is a movable *obstruction* if it may be moved without unreasonable effort, without unduly delaying play and without causing damage. Otherwise it is an immovable *obstruction*.

**Note:** The *Committee* may make a Local Rule declaring a movable *obstruction* to be an immovable *obstruction*.

### Out of Bounds

"*Out of bounds*" is beyond the boundaries of the *course* or any part of the *course* so marked by the *Committee*.

When *out of bounds* is defined by reference to stakes or a fence or as being beyond stakes or a fence, the *out of bounds* line is determined by the nearest inside points of the stakes or fence posts at ground level excluding angled supports.

Objects defining *out of bounds* such as walls, fences, stakes and railings, are not *obstructions* and are deemed to be fixed.

When *out of bounds* is defined by a line on the ground, the line itself is *out of bounds*.

The *out of bounds* line extends vertically upwards and downwards.

A ball is *out of bounds* when all of it lies *out of bounds*.

A player may stand *out of bounds* to play a ball lying within bounds.

### Outside Agency

An "*outside agency*" is any agency not part of the match or, in stroke play, not part of the *competitor's side*, and includes a *referee*, a *marker*, an *observer* and a *forecaddie*. Neither wind nor water is an *outside agency*.

### Partner

A "*partner*" is a player associated with another player on the same *side*.

In a *threesome*, *foursome*, *best-ball* or *four-ball* match, where the context so admits, the word "player" includes his *partner* or *partners*.

### Penalty Stroke

A "*penalty stroke*" is one added to the score of a player or *side* under certain *Rules*. In a *threesome* or *foursome*, *penalty strokes* do not affect the order of play.

### Provisional Ball

A "*provisional ball*" is a ball played under Rule 27-2 for a ball that may be lost outside a *water hazard* or may be *out of bounds*.

### Putting Green

The "*putting green*" is all ground of the hole being played that is specially prepared for putting or otherwise defined as such by the *Committee*. A ball is on the *putting green* when any part of it touches the *putting green*.

### Referee
A "*referee*" is one who is appointed by the *Committee* to accompany players to decide questions of fact and apply the *Rules*. He must act on any breach of a *Rule* that he observes or is reported to him.

A *referee* should not attend the *flagstick*, stand at or mark the position of the *hole*, or lift the ball or mark its position.

### Rub of the Green
A "*rub of the green*" occurs when a ball in motion is accidentally deflected or stopped by any *outside agency* (see Rule 19-1).

### Rule or Rules
The term "*Rule*" includes:

    a. The Rules of Golf and their interpretations as contained in "Decisions on the Rules of Golf";

    b. Any Conditions of Competition established by the *Committee* under Rule 33-1 and Appendix I;

    c. Any Local Rules established by the *Committee* under Rule 33-8a and Appendix I; and

    d. The specifications on clubs and the ball in Appendices II and III.

### Side
A "*side*" is a player, or two or more players who are *partners*.

### Single
See "*Matches*."

### Stance
Taking the "*stance*" consists in a player placing his feet in position for and preparatory to making a *stroke*.

### Stipulated Round
The "*stipulated round*" consists of playing the holes of the *course* in their correct sequence unless otherwise authorized by the *Committee*. The number of holes in a *stipulated round* is 18 unless a smaller number is authorized by the *Committee*. As to extension of *stipulated round* in match play, see Rule 2-3.

### Stroke
A "*stroke*" is the forward movement of the club made with the intention of striking at and moving the ball, but if a player checks his downswing voluntarily before the clubhead reaches the ball he has not made a *stroke*.

### Substituted Ball
A "*substituted ball*" is a ball put into play for the original ball that was either *in play, lost, out of bounds* or lifted.

### Tee
A "*tee*" is a device designed to raise the ball off the ground. It must not be longer than 4 inches (101.6 mm) and it must not be designed or manufactured in such a way that it could indicate the *line of play* or influence the movement of the ball.

## Teeing Ground

The "*teeing ground*" is the starting place for the hole to be played. It is a rectangular area two club-lengths in depth, the front and the sides of which are defined by the outside limits of two tee-markers. A ball is outside the *teeing ground* when all of it lies outside the *teeing ground*.

## Three-Ball

See "*Matches*."

## Threesome

See "*Matches*."

## Through the Green

"*Through the green*" is the whole area of the *course* except:

a. The *teeing ground* and *putting green* of the hole being played; and

b. All *hazards* on the *course*.

## Water Hazard

A "*water hazard*" is any sea, lake, pond, river, ditch, surface drainage ditch or other open water course (whether or not containing water) and anything of a similar nature on the *course*.

All ground or water within the margin of a *water hazard* is part of the *water hazard*. The margin of a *water hazard* extends vertically upwards and downwards. Stakes and lines defining the margins of *water hazards* are in the *hazards*. Such stakes are *obstructions*. A ball is in a *water hazard* when it lies in or any part of it touches the *water hazard*.

**Note 1:** Stakes or lines used to define a *water hazard* must be yellow. When both stakes and lines are used to define *water hazards,* the stakes identify the *hazard* and the lines define the *hazard* margin.

**Note 2:** The *Committee* may make a Local Rule prohibiting play from an environmentally-sensitive area defined as a *water hazard*.

## Wrong Ball

A "*wrong ball*" is any ball other than the player's:

- *ball in play*,
- *provisional ball*, or
- second ball played under Rule 3-3 or Rule 20-7c in stroke play;

and includes:

- another player's ball,
- an abandoned ball, and
- the player's original ball when it is no longer *in play*.

**Note:** *Ball in play* includes a ball *substituted* for the *ball in play* whether or not the substitution is permitted.

## Wrong Putting Green

A "*wrong putting green*" is any *putting green* other than that of the hole being played. Unless otherwise prescribed by the *Committee*, this term includes a practice *putting green* or pitching green on the *course*.

# SECTION III  THE RULES OF PLAY

## 1 THE GAME

## Rule 1. The Game

### Definitions
All defined terms are in *italics* and are listed alphabetically in the Definitions section — see pages 3-11.

### 1-1. General
The Game of Golf consists of playing a ball with a club from the *teeing ground* into the *hole* by a *stroke* or successive *strokes* in accordance with the *Rules*.

### 1-2. Exerting Influence on Ball
A player or *caddie* must not take any action to influence the position or the movement of a ball except in accordance with the *Rules*.

(Removal of movable obstruction — see Rule 24-1.)

**PENALTY FOR BREACH OF RULE 1-2:**
*Match play* — Loss of hole; *Stroke play* — Two strokes.

**Note:** In the case of a serious breach of Rule 1-2, the *Committee* may impose a penalty of disqualification.

### 1-3. Agreement to Waive Rules
Players must not agree to exclude the operation of any *Rule* or to waive any penalty incurred.

**PENALTY FOR BREACH OF RULE 1-3:**
*Match play* — Disqualification of both sides;
*Stroke play* — Disqualification of *competitors* concerned.

(Agreeing to play out of turn in stroke play — see Rule 10-2c.)

### 1-4. Points Not Covered by Rules
If any point in dispute is not covered by the *Rules*, the decision should be made in accordance with equity.

### 1-1/1  Two Balls in Play Simultaneously at Different Holes

**Q.** Two players on the 8th hole play their approach shots to the 8th green. They agree to tee off at the 9th hole and then putt out on the 8th green. This is to avoid having to walk back up a hill to the 9th tee and to save time. What is the ruling?

**A.** In match play, the players are disqualified under Rule 1-3 for excluding the operation of Rule 2-1 by failing to play the stipulated round.

In stroke play, the competitors are disqualified under Rule 3-2 for failing to hole out on the 8th hole before making a stroke from the 9th tee. (Revised)

### 1-1/2  Player Unaware He Has Holed Out Puts Another Ball into Play

**Q.** A player, unable to find his ball, puts another ball into play. He then discovers that his original ball is in the hole. What is the ruling?

**A.** The score with the original ball counts. The play of the hole was completed when the player holed that ball.

### 1-1/3  Player Discovers Original Ball in Hole After Searching Five Minutes and Then Continuing Play with Provisional Ball

**Q.** At a par-3 hole, a player, believing his original ball may be lost, plays a provisional ball. He searches five minutes for the original ball and then plays the provisional ball onto the green. At that point, the original ball is found in the hole. What is the ruling?

**A.** The player's score is 1. The play of the hole was completed when the player holed the original ball (Rule 1-1).

### 1-1/4  Player Discovers Own Ball Is in Hole After Playing Wrong Ball

**Q.** A player played to a blind green and putted what he thought was his ball. He then discovered that his own ball was in the hole and that the ball he had putted was a wrong ball. What is the ruling?

**A.** Since the play of the hole was completed when the original ball was holed (Rule 1-1), the player was not in breach of Rule 15 for subsequently playing a wrong ball.

**Player with Lost Ball Concedes Hole; Ball Then Found in Hole — See 2-4/11.**

**Player Discovers Own Ball in Hole After Playing Wrong Ball; Opponent Claims Hole and Claim Not Disputed — See 2-5/5.**

### 1-2/1  Line of Putt Altered Purposely by Opponent or Fellow-Competitor by Stepping on It

**Q.** An opponent or a fellow-competitor purposely steps on the player's line of putt with the intention either of improving the line (e.g., by pressing down a raised tuft of grass) or of damaging it (e.g., by making spike marks). What is the ruling?

**A.** In either case, the opponent or the fellow-competitor was in breach of Rule 1-2. The penalty is loss of hole in match play or two strokes in stroke play, unless the Committee decides to impose a penalty of disqualification — see Note under Rule 1-2.

In stroke play if the line of putt has been damaged, the player, in equity

(Rule 1-4), may restore the line of putt to its previous condition. A player is entitled to the lie and line of putt he had when his ball came to rest. The line of putt may be restored by anyone.

**Competitor Sanctions Repair of Spike Damage on His Line of Putt by Fellow-Competitor — See 13-2/36.**

**Loose Impediments Brushed Along Line of Putt Rather Than to Side — See 16-1a/10.**

**Line of Putt Damaged Accidentally by Opponent, Fellow-Competitor or Their Caddies— See 16-1a/13.**

**Ball Lifted on Putting Green Placed Ahead of Ball-Marker and Then Moved Back to Original Position — See 16-1a/17.**

**Ball Mark in Position to Assist Opponent Repaired by Player — See 16-1c/2.**

**Placing Object Marking Position of Ball in Front of Ball — See 20-1/19.**

### 1-2/1.5 Competitor Alters Line of Play of Fellow-Competitor

**Q.** In stroke play, A's ball is under a partially detached tree branch from which he believes he is entitled to relief without penalty. A calls for a ruling. B, A's fellow-competitor, argues A's case to a member of the Committee and, during the conversation, lifts the branch and improves or worsens A's line of play. What is the ruling?

**A.** As B's actions were not made with the intention of improving or worsening A's line of play, he is not in breach of Rule 1-2. The branch may be replaced, but A is not required to do so. (New)

### 1-2/2 Shielding Line of Putt from Wind

**Q.** May a player lay his golf bag parallel to the line of putt to shield the line from the wind?

**A.** No. Such procedure would be a breach of Rule 1-2.

### 1-2/3 Flagstick Lying on Putting Green Removed by Player to Prevent Another Player's Ball from Striking It

**Q.** B removes the flagstick, places it on the putting green behind the hole and putts. A, believing that B's ball will strike the flagstick, picks up the flagstick, allowing B's ball to roll beyond where the flagstick had been placed. What is the ruling?

**A.** In match play, A loses the hole for removing an obstruction which might influence the movement of the ball while the player's ball was in motion — Rule 1-2 or 24-1.

In stroke play, A incurs a penalty of two strokes — Rule 1-2 or 24-1.

B incurs no penalty.

**Adjustment of Flagstick; Player's Rights — See 17/4.**

**Attended Flagstick Placed on Ground Subsequently Lifted — See 17-1/6.**

**Removed Flagstick Placed on Ground Subsequently Lifted — See 17-1/7.**

**Removed Flagstick Being Held by Opponent or Fellow-Competitor Subsequently Moved — See 17-1/8.**

**Opponent or Fellow-Competitor Attending Flagstick for Player Deliberately Fails to Remove It; Player's Ball Strikes Flagstick — See 17-3/2.**

**Ball Deliberately Deflected or Stopped on Putting Green by Fellow-Competitor — See 19-1/5.**

**Removal of Loose Impediments Affecting Player's Play — See 23-1/10.**

**Opponent or Fellow-Competitor Removes Obstruction Affecting Player's Play — See 24/16.**

### 1-2/3.5 Player Repairs Hole After Holing Out But Before Opponent, Fellow-Competitor or Partner Holes Out

**Q.** After holing out, a player observes that the edge of the hole is ragged. He pats the ragged edge with his hand and smoothes it. Does the player incur a penalty under Rule 1-2 if his opponent, fellow-competitor or partner has not holed out?

**A.** If the player smoothed the edge of the hole as a courtesy to following players, which seems likely, there is no penalty under Rule 1-2. However, he incurs a penalty under Rule 1-2 if he smoothed the edge of the hole for the express purpose of influencing the movement of the opponent's, fellow-competitor's or partner's ball.

Since the player had holed out, he is not subject to penalty under Rule 16-1a.

If a four-ball competition was involved and the player's partner had not completed the hole, the partner is subject to penalty under Rule 16-1a — See Definition of "Partner."

### 1-2/3.8 Player Jumps Close to Hole to Cause Ball to Drop; Ball Does Not Move

**Q.** A ball at rest overhangs the lip of the hole. The player jumps close to the hole in the hope of jarring the ground and causing the ball to fall into the hole. The ball does not move. What is the ruling?

**A.** There is no penalty. Rule 1-2 does not apply to a situation where the player takes an action that does not result in a change in the position of a ball at rest. If the ball had moved, see Decision 1-2/4. (New)

### 1-2/4 Player Jumps Close to Hole to Cause Ball to Drop; Ball Moves

**Q.** A ball overhangs the lip of the hole. The player jumps close to the hole in the hope of jarring the earth and causing the ball to fall into the hole, which it does. Is this permissible?

**A.** No.

If the ball was still moving when the player jumped, the player took action to influence the movement of the ball in breach of Rule 1-2. In match play, he lost the hole. In stroke play, he incurred a penalty of two strokes, and the ball was holed.

If the ball was at rest when the player jumped, it should be assumed that the player caused the ball to move, and he incurred a penalty of one stroke in both match and stroke play under Rule 18-2a and was required to replace the ball.

If it is not possible to determine whether the ball was still moving, it should be presumed to be moving unless it was deemed to be at rest under Rule 16-2.

### 1-2/4.5 Player Leaves Putt Short and Instinctively Throws Putter at Ball

**Q.** A player putts and the ball comes to rest just short of the hole. The player then instinctively throws his putter toward the ball, but misses. Should the player incur a penalty for a breach of Rule 1-2 which prohibits taking action to influence the position of a ball?

**A.** No. See Decision 14/6 which deals with a similar case.

If the putter had moved the ball, the player would have incurred a penalty stroke under Rule 18-2a, and would be required to replace the ball.

### 1-2/5 Player Putts with One Hand and Catches Ball in Hole with Other Hand

**Q.** A player whose ball is on the lip of the hole putts with one hand and catches the ball with his other hand after the ball is below the level of the lip of the hole. What is the ruling?

**A.** The player purposely stopped his moving ball.

In match play, he lost the hole — Rule 1-2.

In stroke play, he incurred a penalty of two strokes and was required to place his ball on the lip of the hole and hole out — Rule 1-2. If he did not do so, he was disqualified under Rule 3-2 for failing to hole out.

In order for a ball to be holed (see Definition of "Holed"), it must be at rest within the circumference of the hole.

### 1-2/5.5 Player Purposely Stops or Deflects Ball; Where Next Stroke Must Be Played From

**Q.** A player's ball lies through the green. After playing a pitch shot up a slope, the player sees his ball start to roll back towards him. He places his club in front of the ball and stops it. The ball would have rolled only a few yards more and remained through the green. What is the ruling?

**A.** Since the player purposely stopped the ball, he is in breach of Rule 1-2. As the breach was not serious, he would lose the hole in match play or incur a two-stroke penalty in stroke play. In stroke play, he must play the ball from the point where he stopped it with his club.

If the player had purposely deflected the ball but not stopped it, in match play, he would lose the hole. In stroke play, if a serious breach has not occurred, he would incur a two-stroke penalty and must then play the ball from its new position. In stroke play, if a serious breach has occurred, the player is disqualified. (Revised)

**Ball Popped Up Swung at in Disgust — See 14/6.**

**Ball Overhanging Hole Knocked Away by Opponent Before Player Determines Status — See 16-2/2.**

**Casting Shadow on Ball Overhanging Hole — See 16-2/3.**

**Ball Moved by Another Ball After Being Addressed — See 18-2b/11.**

**Ball Moves Prior to Address and Is Accidentally Stopped by Player's Club; Player Removes Club and Ball Rolls Away — See 19-2/1.5.**

### 1-2/6 Player Removes Loose Impediment Affecting Lie of Opponent or Fellow-Competitor in Hazard

**Q.** As a gesture of sportsmanship, a player removes a loose impediment from a hazard, thus improving the lie in the hazard of the ball of his opponent or fellow-competitor. What is the ruling?

**A.** Under Rule 1-2, the player loses the hole in match play or incurs a penalty of two strokes in stroke play. The opponent or fellow-competitor is not required to replace the loose impediment. (Revised)

### 1-2/7 Player Purposely Deflects Partner's Ball in Motion on Putting Green

**Q.** In four-ball match play, A and B are playing C and D. All four balls lie on the putting green in five strokes. A lies four feet from the hole and B lies 30 feet from the hole. Player A is standing near and behind the hole with respect to B's line of putt while B putts. B's ball goes past the hole and is rolling towards where A is standing. Without waiting for B's ball to come to rest, A knocks B's ball back to B. What is the ruling?

**A.** A and B abandoned B's right to complete the hole when A returned B's ball to him after his failure to hole his putt. Such a casual action by A is not contemplated by Rule 1-2 and, in such circumstances, is not a breach of Rule 1-2 or any other Rule. Although Side A-B abandoned B's right to complete the hole, A may continue to represent the side without penalty. (New)

Waiving Turn to Putt in Four-Ball Match — See 30-3c/2.

Player Waives Turn to Play; Circumstances Under Which He May Complete Hole — See 31-5/1.

### Other Decisions relating to Rule 1-2:

Ball Lifted from Putting Green; Ball Replaced While Another Ball in Motion Subsequently Deflects Moving Ball — See 16-1b/3.

Caddie Holds Back Tree Branch to Prevent Branch from Deflecting Dropped Ball — See 20-2a/5.

Caddie Stops Dropped Ball Before It Comes to Rest; When Penalty Incurred — See 20-2c/4.

### *1-3/1 Players Agree Not to Tee Off in Prescribed Order to Save Time*

**Q.** In match play, a player wins a hole. On his way to the next tee, the player returns to retrieve a club left at the last green and suggests that the opponent play first to save time. The opponent does so. Are the players in breach of Rule 1-3?

**A.** Yes, because they agreed to exclude the operation of Rule 10-1a. However, in these particular circumstances, the Committee would be justified in waiving the disqualification penalty under Rule 33-7. If the players subsequently agreed to exclude the operation of Rule 10-1a, they should be disqualified.

Competitors in Stroke Play Agree to Play Out of Turn But Not for Purpose of Giving One of Them an Advantage — See 10-2c/2.

### *1-3/2 Agreement to Concede Short Putts*

**Q.** In a match, the two players agree in advance to concede all putts within a specified length. Is this contrary to Rule 1-3?

**A.** Yes. The players agreed to exclude the operation of Rule 1-1 and should be disqualified under Rule 1-3. Under Rule 2-4, the only stroke which may be conceded is the "next stroke" and it cannot be conceded in advance.

### *1-3/3 Player and Opponent or Fellow-Competitor Agree to Repair Spike Marks on One Another's Line of Putt*

**Q.** A player and his opponent or fellow-competitor agree that they will repair spike marks on one another's line of putt. Is this a breach of Rule 1-3?

**A.** Yes. Both would be subject to disqualification for agreeing to waive Rule 16-1a (Touching Line of Putt).

### 1-3/4  Failure of Players to Apply Known Penalty

**Q.** In a match, a player discovers at the 2nd hole that he has 15 clubs in his bag contrary to Rule 4-4a, but his opponent refuses to apply the penalty. The extra club is declared out of play and the match continues. The Committee disqualifies both players. Is this correct?

**A.** Yes. Since the players agreed to waive the penalty, they should be disqualified under Rule 1-3.

### 1-3/5  Players Unaware Penalty Incurred

**Q.** In a match, A incurred a penalty stroke under Rule 12-2 for lifting his ball for identification without announcing his intention to B, his opponent. A did not penalize himself and B did not make a claim because neither A nor B was aware a penalty had been incurred. Should the Committee disqualify A and B under Rule 1-3 for agreeing to waive a penalty?

**A.** No. Since the players were not aware a penalty had been incurred, there could have been no agreement between them to waive the penalty.

**Players Unable to Resolve Rules Problem Agree to Consider Hole Halved — See 2-1/1.**

**Player's Obligation Re: Lodging Claim — See 2-5/1.**

**Player and Opponent Agree on Incorrect Procedure; Whether Valid Claim May Be Made After Procedure Followed — See 2-5/8.5.**

### 1-3/6  Marker Attests Wrong Score Knowingly and Competitor Aware Score Wrong

**Q.** In stroke play, B failed to hole out at a hole. A few holes later he realized he had erred. A, B's marker and fellow-competitor, was aware both that B had infringed the Rules and that B knew this, but nevertheless he signed B's card. B was disqualified under Rule 3-2 (Failure to Hole Out). Should A, who knowingly overlooked the breach, be penalized?

**A.** A should have been disqualified for a breach of Rule 1-3.

**Marker Attests Wrong Score Knowingly But Competitor Unaware Score Wrong — See 6-6a/5.**

**Competitor Seeks Help from Fellow-Competitor to Avoid Penalty — See 33-7/7.**

### 1-3/7  Agreement That Side Losing After 18 Holes of 36-Hole Match Will Concede Match

**Q.** Prior to a 36-hole match, the players agree that they will play only 18 holes and whoever is behind at that point will concede the match. Is this permissible?

**A.** No. Both players should be disqualified under Rule 1-3 for agreeing to exclude the operation of a condition of the competition (Rule 33-1).

**Wrong Form of Play Used to Decide Which Side Concedes Match — See 2-4/21.**

**Wrong Form of Play Used in Match-Play Event — See 6-1/1.**

**Match Decided by Wrong Form of Play by Agreement — See 33-1/4.**

**Other Decisions relating to Rule 1-3:**

**Players Agree to Consider Hole Halved During Play of Hole — See 2-1/1.5.**

**Two Holes Purposely Omitted in Match — See 2-1/4.**

**Discontinued Match Replayed Instead of Being Resumed from Where Play Stopped — See 2-1/6.**

**Handicap Stroke Given at Incorrect Hole in Error — See 6-2a/2.**

**Competitor Requests That Ball in Position to Assist Him Should Not Be Lifted — See 22/6.**

**Competitor Refuses to Lift Ball Assisting Play — See 22/7.**

**Player Who Has Reached Third Round of Match Play Disqualified for Agreeing to Waive Rules in First-Round Match — See 34-1a/1.**

### *1-4/1 Player Distracted by Ball Dropped by Another Player Mis-Hits Ball*

**Q.** As A was making his backswing, B accidentally dropped a ball, which rolled within six inches of A's ball. The appearance of the dropped ball startled A, causing him to top his shot. In equity, should A be permitted to replay his stroke?

**A.** No. Distractions are a common occurrence which players must accept.

### *1-4/2 Ball Adhering to Face of Club After Stroke*

**Q.** A player plays a stroke from wet sand or soil and the ball adheres to the face of the club. What is the ruling?

**A.** In equity (Rule 1-4), the ball should be dropped, without penalty, as near as possible to the spot where the club was when the ball stuck to it. But see also Decision 14-4/1.

### *1-4/3 Flagstick Stuck into Green Some Distance from Hole by Practical Joker*

**Q.** A practical joker removes the flagstick from the hole and sticks it into the putting green some distance from the hole. The players approaching the green are unaware of this action and they play towards the flagstick and not the hole. Do the players have the option to replay?

**A.** No. In equity (Rule 1-4), the players must accept the resultant advantage or disadvantage.

**Other Decisions relating to Rule 1-4:**

**Player Lifts Ball in Mistaken Belief That Next Stroke Conceded — See 2-4/3.**

**Putting Out After Concession of Stroke Assists Partner — See 2-4/6.**

**Player Concedes Opponent's Next Stroke and Plays Before Opponent Has Opportunity to Lift Ball — See 2-4/8.**

**Ball-Marker Moved by Opponent's Caddie Accidentally — See 20-1/7.**

**Player Plays Away from Hole to Assist Partner — See 30-3f/6.**

## 1-4/4 In Anger Player Strikes Ball Played by Player in Following Group

**Q.** A is nearly struck by a ball played by a player in the following group. In anger, A hits the ball back towards the group. Has A played a practice stroke or a wrong ball?

**A.** No. However, in equity (Rule 1-4), A should incur the general penalty of loss of hole in match play or two strokes in stroke play.

## 1-4/5 Removal of Obstruction in Hazard Would Move Loose Impediment

**Q.** In a hazard, a player's ball lies against a movable obstruction. A loose impediment lies on top of the obstruction in such a position that the player cannot remove the obstruction without also moving the loose impediment. The player is entitled to move the movable obstruction under Rule 24-1 but is not entitled to move the loose impediment under Rule 23. What is the procedure?

**A.** The player may remove the obstruction as authorized by Rule 24-1. As the loose impediment will be moved in the process, in equity (Rule 1-4), the player incurs no penalty and must place the loose impediment as near as possible to the spot where it originally lay. If the player fails to place the loose impediment as required, in equity (Rule 1-4) and in view of the purpose of Rule 13-4, he would lose the hole in match play or incur a penalty of two strokes in stroke play. (Revised)

## 1-4/6 Two Balls Lie Together in Hazard and Neither Is Identifiable

**Q.** Two balls lie together in a hazard. Both balls are playable. The ball nearer the hole would interfere with a stroke at the other ball, and vice versa. It appears likely that one of the balls is the player's ball. However, neither ball is identifiable because the markings on both balls are obscured by mud. What is the proper procedure if the other ball is (a) probably the ball of an opponent or a fellow-competitor or (b) an abandoned ball?

**A.** The Rules of Golf do not contemplate such a situation. In equity (Rule 1-4), the player may lift the ball farther from the hole following the procedure prescribed in Rule 12-2, and clean it to the extent necessary for identification.

In situation (a), if the lifted ball is a ball in play, it must be replaced. Before playing, the owner of the ball which had been lifted would be entitled to have the other ball lifted by its prospective owner under Rule 22.

In situation (b), if the lifted ball is an abandoned ball, the player may discard it and play the other ball.

**Other Decisions relating to Rule 1-4:**

**Ball in Bunker Moves Closer to Hole When Obstruction Removed and Ball Will Not Remain at Rest When Replaced; All Other Parts of Bunker Are Nearer Hole — See 20-3d/2.**

**Loose Impediment Affecting Lie Moved When Ball Lifted — See 23-1/7.**

**Loose Impediment Affecting Lie Removed While Ball Lifted — See 23-1/8.**

### 1-4/7 Ball Lost in Either Water Hazard or Casual Water Overflowing Hazard

**Q.** A ball is lost. It is either in a water hazard or in casual water overflowing the hazard. What is the proper procedure?

**A.** In equity (Rule 1-4), the player must proceed under the water hazard Rule.

### 1-4/8 Nearest Point of Relief from Cart Path Is in Casual Water; Nearest Point of Relief from Casual Water Is Back on Cart Path

**Q.** A player's ball lies on a paved cart path from which he wishes to take relief under Rule 24-2b(i). It appears that the nearest point of relief will be in a large area of casual water which adjoins the cart path and the nearest point of relief from the casual water under Rule 25-1b(i) would be back on the cart path. What are the player's options?

**A.** The player may proceed in accordance with Rule 24-2 and then, if applicable, Rule 25-1. He is not entitled to take relief from both the immovable obstruction and the casual water in a single procedure, unless after proceeding under these Rules, the player is essentially back where he started and it is evident that such a procedure is necessary to obtain relief from both conditions.

Therefore, the player should proceed as follows:

(1) He may lift and drop the ball in accordance with Rule 24-2b(i) in the casual water.

(2) He may play the ball as it lies or take relief from the casual water, in which case he would lift and drop the ball in accordance with Rule 25-1b(i).

(3) If the ball when dropped comes to rest in such a position that there is interference by the cart path, he may play the ball as it lies or proceed in accordance with Rule 24-2b(i). If the nearest point of relief is in the casual water, as an additional option, the player may, in equity (Rule 1-4), obtain relief without penalty as follows:

Using the new position of the ball on the cart path, the nearest point of relief from both the cart path and the casual water shall be determined which is not in a hazard or on a putting green. The player shall lift the ball and drop it within one club-length of and not nearer the hole than the nearest point of relief, on a part of the course which avoids interference by the cart path and the casual water and is not in a hazard or on a putting green.

If the dropped ball rolls into a position where there is interference by either the cart path or the casual water, Rule 20-2c applies.

The same principle would apply if there was interference from any two conditions, e.g., casual water, a hole made by a burrowing animal, an immovable obstruction, from which relief without penalty was available and taking relief from one condition resulted in interference from the second condition.

## 1-4/9 Bird's Nest Interfering with Stroke

**Q.** A player's ball came to rest in a bird's nest or so close to the nest that he could not play a stroke without damaging it. Is he entitled to relief without penalty?

**A.** Yes. In equity (Rule 1-4), the player may, without penalty, drop the ball at the nearest spot not nearer the hole which would allow him to make his stroke without damaging the nest. If the ball lies in a hazard, it must be dropped in the hazard.

### Other Decisions relating to Rule 1-4:

**Lie or Line of Play Affected by Pitch-Mark Made by Partner's, Opponent's or Fellow-Competitor's Ball — See 13-2/8.**

**Player's Lie Affected by Sand from Partner's, Opponent's or Fellow-Competitor's Stroke from Bunker — See 13-2/8.5.**

**Extension of Line of Play Affected When Opponent or Fellow-Competitor Creates Footprints in Bunker — See 13-2/29.5.**

**Partner's, Opponent's or Fellow-Competitor's Divot Comes to Rest Near Player's Ball in Bunker — See 13-4/18.**

**Lie in Bunker Changed by Another Player Taking His Stance — See 20-3b/2.**

**Lie Changed by Removal of Gallery-Control Stake — See 20-3b/3.**

## 1-4/10 Dangerous Situation; Rattlesnake or Bees Interfere with Play

**Q.** A player's ball comes to rest in a situation dangerous to the player, e.g., near a live rattlesnake or a bees' nest. Does the player have any options in addition to playing the ball as it lies or, if applicable, proceeding under Rule 26 or 28?

**A.** Yes. It is unreasonable to expect the player to play from such a dangerous situation and unfair to require the player to incur a penalty under Rule 26 (Water Hazards) or Rule 28 (Ball Unplayable).

In equity (Rule 1-4), as an additional option the player should be permitted, without penalty, to drop a ball on the nearest spot not nearer the hole which is not dangerous.

If the ball lay in a hazard, it should be dropped, if possible, in the same hazard and, if not, in a similar nearby hazard, but in either case not nearer the hole. If it is not possible for the player to drop the ball in a hazard, he may drop it, under penalty of one stroke, outside the hazard, keeping the point where the original ball lay between the hole and the spot on which the ball is dropped.

If it is clearly unreasonable for the player to play a stroke because of interference by anything other than the dangerous situation he may not take relief as prescribed above, but he is not precluded from proceeding under Rule 26 or 28.

**Danger from Fire Ants — See 33-8/22.**

### 1-4/11 Meaning of "Dangerous Situation"

**Q.** According to Decision 1-4/10, a ball lying near a live rattlesnake or bees' nest is a "dangerous situation" and relief should be granted in equity.

If a player's ball comes to rest in or near an area of plants such as poison ivy, cacti or stinging nettles, should the provisions of Decision 1-4/10 apply?

**A.** No. The player must either play the ball as it lies or, if applicable, proceed under Rule 26 (Water Hazards) or Rule 28 (Ball Unplayable).

Decision 1-4/10 contemplates a situation which is unrelated to conditions normally encountered on the course. Unpleasant lies are a common occurrence which players must accept.

### 1-4/12 Player Breaches Rules More Than Once Prior to Stroke; Whether Multiple Penalties Applied

Prior to making a stroke, there may be circumstances where a player breaches a Rule more than once, or breaches different Rules and it would seem that a penalty should be applied to each separate breach. However, in the majority of cases and based on equity (Rule 1-4), it would not be appropriate to apply multiple penalties.

For the purpose of applying the principles in this Decision, Rules 4-3a, 4-3b, 4-3c, 13-4a, 13-4b, 13-4c, 14-2a, 14-2b, 17-3a, 17-3b, 17-3c, 18-2a and 18-2b should be considered as separate Rules.

Below are the specific principles to be applied when determining whether multiple penalties are appropriate when more than one breach has occurred prior to a player making a stroke:

**(1) Single Act Results in One Rule Being Breached More Than Once — Single Penalty Applied**
Example: In stroke play, a competitor's ball on the putting green strikes a fellow-competitor's ball in breach of Rule 19-5 and then strikes another fellow-competitor's ball, also in breach of Rule 19-5. The ruling would be a single two-stroke penalty (see Decision 19-5/3).

**(2) Single Act Results in Two Rules Being Breached — Single Penalty Applied**
Example: In stroke play, a competitor is considering putting his ball from a bunker and rakes a footprint in the bunker on his line of play. Both Rule 13-2 and Rule 13-4a have been breached. The ruling would be a single two-stroke penalty.

**(3) Multiple Occurrences of the Same or Similar Acts Result in One Rule Being Breached More Than Once — Single Penalty Applied**
Example 1: In stroke play, a competitor takes several practice swings in a hazard, touching the ground each time. The ruling would be a single two-stroke penalty (see Decision 13-4/3).

Example 2: In stroke play, a player removes sand on his line of play through the green and presses down a replaced divot which is also on his line of play. The ruling would be a single two-stroke penalty.

**(4) Different Acts Result in Two Rules Being Breached, but Breach of Second Rule Is a Direct Consequence of the Initial Breach — Single Penalty Applied**
Example: In stroke play, a competitor's ball moves prior to address and while it is in motion it is accidentally stopped by the competitor's club in breach of Rule 19-2b. The competitor then moves the club and, therefore, moves his ball, normally a penalty stroke under Rule 18-2a. This would result in a single two-stroke penalty under Rule 19-2b (see Decision 19-2/1.5). If the ball is not replaced before the competitor makes his next stroke, the failure to replace the ball is considered a separate act and he incurs an additional penalty of two strokes under Rule 18-2a.

**(5) Different Acts Result in Two Rules Being Breached — Multiple Penalties Applied**
Example: In stroke play, a competitor (1) lifts his ball in play and (2) substitutes another ball, both acts without authority, and plays the substituted ball. The ruling would be a one-stroke penalty under Rule 18-2a (lifting the ball in play) and a further penalty of two strokes under Rule 15-2 and the applicable Rule (substitution without correction), giving a total penalty of three strokes (see Decision 15/6.5).

### (6) Different Acts Result in One Rule Being Breached More Than Once — Multiple Penalties Applied

Example: In stroke play, a competitor (1) purposely steps on another player's line of putt with the intention of improving the line, and then (2) purposely stops his own ball in motion after it began moving without apparent cause before address. The ruling would be two separate penalties, each of two strokes, for breaches of Rule 1-2, giving a total penalty of four strokes.

The following chart summarizes the principles of this Decision:

| Rules Breach | Action of Player | | |
|---|---|---|---|
| | Single Act | Multiple Occurrence of Same or Similar Act | Different Acts |
| **One Rule Breached More Than Once** | Single Penalty See Principle 1 | Single Penalty See Principle 3 | Multiple Penalty See Principle 6 |
| **Two or More Rules Breached** | Single Penalty See Principle 2 | X | Multiple Penalty See Principle 5 |
| **Two or More Rules Breached, but Second and Subsequent Breaches Only as Direct Consequence of First Breach** | X | Single Penalty See Principle 4 | Single Penalty See Principle 4 |

(Revised)

### 1-4/13 Player Advised of Breach of Rule; Player Breaches Same Rule Prior to Stroke

**Q.** In stroke play, a competitor, whose ball lies in a bunker, makes a practice swing and touches the ground in the bunker with his club. His fellow-competitor advises him that his action may be a breach of the Rules. The competitor disagrees and makes several more practice swings prior to making his stroke, touching the sand each time. What is the penalty?

**A.** As the competitor was correctly advised that touching the ground in the bunker with his club during a practice swing was a breach of the Rules (Rule 13-4b), the third principle in Decision 1-4/12 is not applicable. Therefore, the competitor is penalized four strokes — two strokes for the initial breach and two strokes for all subsequent breaches when the additional practice swings were made.

### 1-4/14 Player Breaches Same Rule Before and After Stroke

**Q.** In stroke play, a competitor whose ball lies in a bunker makes a practice swing, touching the ground in the bunker with his club in breach of Rule 13-4. He makes the stroke, but the ball remains in the bunker. Before his next stroke, he makes another practice swing, again touching the ground in the bunker. What is the penalty?

**A.** The competitor incurs two separate penalties, each of two strokes, for breaches of Rule 13-4, giving a total penalty of four strokes. The third principle in Decision 1-4/12 does not apply in this case as the player made a stroke between the two breaches.

## 1-4/15 Player Breaches Two Rules with Different Penalties; More Severe Penalty Applied

**Q.** In stroke play, a competitor is searching for his ball under a tree. He accidentally moves his ball with his foot in breach of Rule 18-2a and, at the same time, breaks a branch, improving the area of his intended swing in breach of Rule 13-2. What is the ruling?

**A.** The competitor has breached two Rules as a result of a single act. In accordance with the second principle in Decision 1-4/12, the competitor only incurs a single penalty. However, in this case, the Rules that have been breached by the competitor give different penalties (i.e., Rule 18-2a carries a one-stroke penalty and Rule 13-2 carries a two-stroke penalty). In such circumstances, in equity (Rule 1-4), the more severe of the two penalties must be applied and, therefore, the competitor is penalized two strokes under Rule 13-2.

If the same circumstances arose in match play, the player would lose the hole for the breach of Rule 13-2.

### Other Decisions relating to Rule 1-4:

**Player Lifts Opponent's Ball-Marker** — See 2-4/5.

**Playing Characteristics of Club Changed While Play Suspended; Error Discovered Before Play Resumed** — See 4-2/2.

**Club Rendered Unfit for Play by Outside Agency or Opponent's Side** — See 4-3/9.5.

**Time of Starting; Both Players in Match are Late** — See 6-3a/3.

**Match Discontinued by Agreement Cannot Be Resumed Until Three Days Later; One Player Wishes to Play on Competition Course Prior to Resumption** — See 7-2/10.

**Match Discontinued by Agreement on 13th Tee Cannot be Resumed Until Following Day; May Players Play First Twelve Holes Prior to Resuming Match** — See 7-2/11.

**Player's Team Mate in Gallery Hits Ball to Green to Show Player Whether Green Will Hold** — See 8-1/23.

**Advice Given by Team Coach or Captain** — See 8-1/24.

**Player Places Mark to Indicate Distance for Pitch Shot** — See 8-2a/3.

**Determination of Honor at Hole Following Disputed Hole** — See 10-1a/2.

**Competitors Estimate Area of Teeing Ground When One Tee-Marker Missing** — See 11-4b/2.

**Divots Replaced and Pressed Down In Area in Which Ball Is to Be Dropped** — See 13-2/4.5.

**Player's Area of Intended Stance Affected by Another Player's Stroke** — See 13-2/8.7.

**Flying Insect in Water Hazard** — See 13-4/16.5.

**Player Deems Ball Unplayable in Bunker, Announces His Intention to Proceed Under Rule**

28a Outside Bunker and Then Rakes Bunker on New Line of Play — See 13-4/35.8.

Ball Thrown into Bounds by Outside Agency and Played; Neither Player Nor Caddie Aware of Action of Outside Agency — See 15/10.

Hole at Which Wrong Ball Played Unknown — See 15-1/3.

Opponent or Fellow-Competitor Attending Flagstick for Player Fails to Remove It; Player's Ball Strikes Flagstick — See 17-3/2.

Ball Stolen by Outside Agency from Unknown Spot — See 18-1/5.

Ball Lodged in Tree Knocked Down by Outside Agency — See 18-1/9.

Ball Dislodged from Tree; Replacement of Ball Not Possible — See 18-2a/29.

Ball Moved by Fellow-Competitor's Ball, Neither Competitor Nor Fellow-Competitor Aware of Movement Until After Completion of Hole — See 18-5/3.

Ball Deliberately Deflected or Stopped on Putting Green by Spectator — See 19-1/4.

Ball Deliberately Deflected or Stopped Through the Green by Spectator — See 19-1/4.1.

Ball Deliberately Deflected or Stopped on Putting Green by Fellow-Competitor — See 19-1/5.

Ball Deflected by Player's Golf Cart Being Pulled by Opponent or Fellow-Competitor Without Player's Knowledge — See 19-2/6.

Status of Saliva — See 25/6.

Tree Falls onto Fairway During Stipulated Round — See 25/9.5.

Lifting Ball to Determine Whether It Lies in Burrowing Animal Hole — See 25/21.

Ball Dropped from Casual Water in Bunker at Point of Maximum Relief Rolls Elsewhere — See 25-1b/6.

Dropped Ball Embeds; Procedure If Ball Again Embeds When Re-Dropped — See 25-2/2.5.

Lifting Ball to Determine Whether It Is Embedded — See 25-2/7.

Player Makes Several Strokes on Wrong Putting Green — See 25-3/2.

Provisional Ball Not Distinguishable from Original Ball — See 27/11.

Gate in Boundary Fence — See 27/18.

Original Ball Found Within Five-Minute Search Period After Another Ball Dropped; Dropped Ball Played — See 27-1/2.3.

Continuation of Play With Provisional Ball Without Searching for Original Ball — See 27-2b/1.

Caddie Shared by Opponents' Side in Four-Ball Match Moves Player's Ball — See 30/2.

Relocating Hole After Ball Already Positioned Nearby on Putting Green — See 33-2b/2.

Player Who Has Reached Third Round of Match Play Disqualified for Agreeing to Waive Rules in First-Round Match — See 34-1a/1.

Player Who Has Advanced in Match Play Is Disqualified for Wrong Score in Qualifying Round — See 34-1b/8.

# Rule 2. Match Play

## Definitions
All defined terms are in *italics* and are listed alphabetically in the Definitions section — see pages 3-11.

## 2-1. General
A match consists of one *side* playing against another over a *stipulated round* unless otherwise decreed by the *Committee*.

In match play the game is played by holes.

Except as otherwise provided in the *Rules*, a hole is won by the *side* that *holes* its ball in the fewer *strokes*. In a handicap match the lower net score wins the hole.

The state of the match is expressed by the terms: so many "holes up" or "all square," and so many "to play."

A *side* is "dormie" when it is as many holes up as there are holes remaining to be played.

## 2-2. Halved Hole
A hole is halved if each *side holes* out in the same number of *strokes*.

When a player has *holed* out and his opponent has been left with a *stroke* for the half, if the player subsequently incurs a penalty, the hole is halved.

## 2-3. Winner of Match
A match is won when one *side* leads by a number of holes greater than the number remaining to be played.

If there is a tie, the *Committee* may extend the *stipulated round* by as many holes as are required for a match to be won.

## 2-4. Concession of Next Stroke, Hole or Match
A player may concede his opponent's next *stroke* at any time provided the opponent's ball is at rest. The opponent is considered to have *holed* out with his next *stroke* and the ball may be removed by either *side*.

A player may concede a hole at any time prior to the start or conclusion of that hole.

A player may concede a match at any time prior to the start or conclusion of that match.

A concession may not be declined or withdrawn.

(Ball overhanging hole — see Rule 16-2.)

## 2-5. Doubt as to Procedure; Disputes and Claims

In match play, if a doubt or dispute arises between the players, a player may make a claim. If no duly authorized representative of the *Committee* is available within a reasonable time, the players must continue the match without delay. The *Committee* may consider a claim only if the player making the claim notifies his opponent (i) that he is making a claim, (ii) of the facts of the situation and (iii) that he wants a ruling. The claim must be made before any player in the match plays from the next *teeing ground* or, in the case of the last hole of the match, before all players in the match leave the *putting green*.

A later claim may not be considered by the *Committee* unless it is based on facts previously unknown to the player making the claim and he had been given wrong information (Rules 6-2a and 9) by an opponent.

Once the result of the match has been officially announced, a later claim may not be considered by the *Committee* unless it is satisfied that the opponent knew he was giving wrong information.

## 2-6. General Penalty

The penalty for a breach of a *Rule* in match play is loss of hole except when otherwise provided.

### 2/1 Players in Singles Match Accompanied by Third Party

**Q.** Prior to a singles match between A and B, A stated to B that a third player, C, would be playing with them. B played the match under protest and lost. What ruling should the Committee give?

**A.** A single is a match in which one plays against another. Since B made a timely claim, the Committee should have awarded the match to B. If B had not protested, i.e., had agreed that C accompany the match, the result of the match would stand as played.

**Wrong Form of Play Used in Match-Play Event — See 6-1/1.**

**Match Decided by Wrong Form of Play by Agreement — See 33-1/4.**

### 2-1/1 Players Unable to Resolve Rules Problem Agree to Consider Hole Halved

**Q.** In a match, A putted to within three inches of the hole and then knocked his ball away. B, the opponent, objected. He stated that he wanted A's ball left by the hole. A and B were uncertain how to resolve the matter, so they agreed to consider the hole halved. Should A and B be disqualified under Rule 1-3?

**A.** No. There was no agreement to waive the Rules. Rather, the players were ignorant of the Rules.

### 2-1/1.5 Players Agree to Consider Hole Halved During Play of Hole

**Q.** In a match, a player and his opponent play their second shots on a par-5 hole. Unexpectedly, neither ball can be found. Rather than proceeding under Rule 27-1, both players agree to a half. Is this permitted?

**A.** Yes. An agreement to halve a hole being played does not of itself constitute an agreement to waive the Rules.

However, if the players agree to consider a hole halved without either player making a stroke, they should be disqualified under Rule 1-3 for agreeing to exclude the operation of Rule 2-1 by failing to play the stipulated round. (Revised)

**Hole Not Completed by Either Player — See 2-5/3.**

### 2-1/2 Minus or Zero Net Score

**Q.** In a handicap match, a player entitled to two handicap strokes at a par-3 hole scores a 2 or a hole-in-one. What would be his net score in each case?

**A.** The player's net score would be zero (0) if he scored a 2 or minus one (-1) if he had a hole-in-one.

The same would be true in a four-ball stroke play or Stableford competition since scores are calculated on a hole-by-hole basis.

**Determination of Honor in Handicap Match — See 10-1a/1.**

### 2-1/3 Hole Inadvertently Omitted in Match; Error Discovered After Match Concluded

**Q.** The players in a match inadvertently omitted playing a hole. The error was discovered after the match had been played to a conclusion. What is the ruling?

**A.** The result should stand. (Revised — Formerly 2-3/2)

### 2-1/4 Two Holes Purposely Omitted in Match

**Q.** The players in a match agreed to omit two holes, i.e., agreed to settle the match over 16 holes. Is this permitted?

**A.** No. The players are disqualified under Rule 1-3 for excluding the operation of Rule 2-1 by failing to play the stipulated round. (Revised – Formerly 2-3/3)

### 2-1/5 Three Holes Played Out of Sequence in Match

**Q.** In an 18-hole match, the players by mistake play three holes out of sequence. The error is discovered before the match concludes. What is the ruling?

**A.** The holes played out of sequence should be disregarded and the match resumed at the proper hole. However, if such procedure would delay the competition, both players should be disqualified unless one of them concedes the match to the other. (Revised — Formerly 2-3/4)

### 2-1/6 Replaying Match When Play Discontinued Instead of Resuming from Where Play Stopped

**Q.** A match which was all square after 16 holes was discontinued by agreement due to darkness. The match should have been resumed at the 17th hole. However, the players, thinking it was in accordance with the Rules, replayed the match starting at the 1st tee. The result was posted. At that point the Committee became aware of the improper procedure. What is the ruling?

**A.** The result of the match as replayed should stand. The players were not subject to disqualification under Rule 1-3 because they were unaware that their procedure was contrary to the Rules. (Revised — Formerly 2-3/5)

### 2-2/1 Player Putting for Half Is Given Advice by Opponent

The following is an example of the application of the second paragraph of Rule 2-2:

In a match, A has holed out. As B, A's opponent, is preparing to putt for a half, A gives B advice as to his line of putt. A would normally lose the hole for a breach of Rule 8-1, but Rule 2-2 becomes operative in these circumstances and the hole is halved.

**Player Incorrectly Believing He Has Won a Hole Lifts Opponent's Ball-Marker; Opponent Had Putt for Half — See 2-4/5.**

**Player Reporting Wrong Score Causes Opponent with Chance for Half to Pick Up — See 9-2/6.**

### 2-3/1 Players Under Impression Match Is Over Later Realize It Was All Square

**Q.** In a match, A and B left the 18th green under the impression that A had won. They later realized that in fact the match was all square. The matter was referred to the Committee. What is the ruling?

**A.** Since there was no indication that wrong information had been given, the match stands as played, with A the winner.

**Players Mistakenly Believing Match Is All Square After 18 Holes Play Extra Hole Without Claim Being Made — See 2-5/6.**

**Rightful Winner of Match Makes No Claim and Agrees to Play Extra Holes — See 2-5/7.**

**Match-Play Finalists Both Disqualified — See 33/3.**

**True State of Match Not Determinable — See 34-3/5.**

## 2-3/2 Result of Match When Player Dormie and Opponent Concedes

**Q.** In a match between A and B, A is one up playing the last hole. In the following situations and considering B's actions, does A win by one hole or two holes?

  (i) B is on the green in three strokes but a long way from the hole. A plays his third stroke from the edge of the green and it comes to rest about one foot from the hole. B goes over and shakes hands with A.

  (ii) B is on the green in two strokes. A holes his third stroke and B shakes hands with A.

  (iii) A plays his second shot from the fairway onto the green. B's second shot misses the green and plugs in a bunker. B immediately walks over to A and shakes his hand.

  (iv) B is on the green in six strokes but a long way from the hole. A plays his third stroke from the edge of the green and it comes to rest about one foot from the hole. B goes over and shakes hands with A.

  (v) A is on the green in two strokes. B plays his third stroke from the fairway onto the green and the ball comes to rest about one foot from the hole. B goes over and shakes hands with A.

**A.** The handshake between the players is deemed to represent an agreement to concede each player's next stroke. Accordingly, in situations (i) to (iii), A wins the match by one hole. In situations (iv) and (v), A has won the final hole and wins the match by two holes. (Formerly 2-3/6)

## 2-4/1 Player Concedes Opponent's Next Stroke and Then Knocks Opponent's Ball into Hole

**Q.** A player conceded his opponent's next stroke and then, in attempting to knock the opponent's ball back to him, he inadvertently knocked the ball into the hole. The opponent, who had played three strokes prior to the concession, claimed a 3 for the hole. Was the claim valid?

**A.** No. The player conceded the opponent a 4 for the hole and, at that point, the opponent had completed the hole. It is irrelevant that the player subsequently knocked the opponent's ball into the hole, whether he did so inadvertently or otherwise.

**Opponent's Ball Knocked Away by Player After Concession Moves Player's Ball — See 18-2a/18.**

### 2-4/2 Ball Falls into Hole After Concession of Next Stroke

**Q.** A player's ball overhung the edge of the hole. After elapse of the time allowed in Rule 16-2, the opponent conceded the player's next stroke for a 5, after which the player's ball fell into the hole. What was the player's score for the hole?

**A.** The player's score was 5. It is immaterial that the player's ball fell into the hole after the opponent had conceded the player's next stroke. If the opponent had not conceded the next stroke, the player's score would also be 5 because in those circumstances the player would be deemed to have holed out with his last stroke and he would incur a penalty stroke — Rule 16-2.

**Ball Overhanging Hole Knocked Away by Opponent Before Player Determines Status — See 16-2/2.**

### 2-4/3 Player Lifts Ball in Mistaken Belief That Next Stroke Conceded

**Q.** In a match between A and B, B made a statement which A interpreted to mean that his (A's) next stroke was conceded. Accordingly, A lifted his ball. B then said that he had not conceded A's next stroke. What is the ruling?

**A.** If B's statement could reasonably have led A to think his next stroke had been conceded, in equity (Rule 1-4) A should replace his ball as near as possible to where it lay, without penalty.

Otherwise, A would incur a penalty stroke for lifting his ball without marking its position — Rule 20-1 — and he must replace his ball as near as possible to where it lay.

**In Four-Ball Match Player with Putt for Half Picks Up in Error at Suggestion of Opponent Based on Misunderstanding — See 30/5.**

### 2-4/4 Whether Picking Up Opponent's Ball Is Concession of Next Stroke

**Q.** In match play, A holes a putt and, thinking he has won the match, picks up B's ball. B then advises A that he (B) had a putt to win the hole. Did A concede B's next stroke when he picked up B's ball?

**A.** No. A incurred a penalty stroke under Rule 18-3b; B must replace his ball and now has two putts to win the hole.

### 2-4/5 Whether Lifting Opponent's Ball-Marker Is Concession of Next Stroke

**Q.** In a match, A, believing he has won a hole, picks up the coin marking the position of his opponent B's ball. In fact B had a putt to halve the hole. Should the picking up of B's ball-marker be considered a concession of B's next stroke?

**A.** No. In equity (Rule 1-4), A should be penalized one stroke. Therefore, under the second paragraph of Rule 2-2 the hole is automatically halved.

## 2-4/6 Putting Out After Concession of Stroke

Rule 2-4 does not cover the question of whether a player may putt out after his next stroke has been conceded. A player incurs no penalty for holing out in such circumstances. However, if the act would be of assistance to a partner in a four-ball or best-ball match, the partner is, in equity (Rule 1-4), disqualified for the hole.

**Agreement to Concede Short Putts — See 1-3/2.**

## 2-4/7 Concession of Stroke Refused by Player and Withdrawn by Opponent; Player Then Putts and Misses

**Q.** In a match between A and B, A putts and his ball comes to rest near the hole. B concedes A's next stroke. A says: "No. I haven't holed out yet." B says: "OK. Go ahead and putt." A putts and misses. In such circumstances, is the concession invalidated?

**A.** No. When B conceded A's next stroke, A had completed the hole. Concession of a stroke may not be declined or withdrawn — see Rule 2-4.

## 2-4/8 Player Concedes Opponent's Next Stroke and Plays Before Opponent Has Opportunity to Lift Ball

**Q.** In a match between A and B, A chips and his ball comes to rest about one foot from the hole. B concedes A's next stroke. A states that he wishes to lift his ball. However, B proceeds to play his next stroke before A has an opportunity to lift his ball and B's ball strikes A's ball. What is the ruling?

**A.** B deprived A of his right to lift his ball after his next stroke was conceded. In equity (Rule 1-4), B lost the hole, whether or not his ball struck A's ball.

**Ball Resting Against Flagstick; Putt Conceded and Ball Removed Before Player Can Remove Flagstick — See 17-4/2.**

## 2-4/9 Player Concedes Hole After Which It Is Discovered Opponent Had Played Wrong Ball

**Q.** In a match between A and B, A has played two strokes and the ball with which he played his second stroke out of the rough is on the green. B, having played five, concedes the hole to A. A then discovers that he has played a wrong ball to the green. What is the ruling?

**A.** Since A did not play the wrong ball from a hazard, he lost the hole (Rule 15-3a) before B conceded it to him. Therefore, B's concession was irrelevant.

### 2-4/9.5 Player Concedes Hole After Which It Is Discovered Opponent's Last Stroke Was Played with a Wrong Ball from a Hazard

**Q.** In a match between A and B, B has played four strokes and his ball lies three feet from the hole. A, who has played two strokes, plays a stroke out of a bunker to the edge of the hole. B concedes the hole.

A and B pick their balls up, whereupon A discovers that he has played a wrong ball from the bunker, but has incurred no penalty for doing so (Rule 15-3a, second paragraph).

What is the ruling?

**A.** The concession stands — see Rule 2-4.

### 2-4/10 Player Concedes Hole After Which Opponent Plays Wrong Ball

**Q.** In a three-ball match, A loses his ball and concedes the hole to B and C. Subsequently, B plays a wrong ball. Is A's concession to B binding?

**A.** Yes.

**Player Concluding He Played Wrong Ball When Opponent Misread Number on Player's Ball Concedes Hole — See 9-2/11.**

### 2-4/11 Player with Lost Ball Concedes Hole; Ball Then Found in Hole

**Q.** In a match, A played his second shot towards the green but he could not find his ball. He conceded the hole to B, whose second shot was on the green. The following players then found A's ball in the hole. What is the ruling?

**A.** Since a player may not concede a hole after conclusion of the hole — Rule 2-4 — A holed out in two strokes and won the hole if he made a claim before B played from the next teeing ground (Rule 2-5). If A did not do so, he lost the hole.

### 2-4/12 Player Concedes Hole on Basis of Invalid Claim

**Q.** In a match between A and B, A putts out of turn. B incorrectly claims that A loses the hole for putting out of turn. A protests but concedes the hole. Later, A, having consulted the Rule book, lodges an official protest with the Committee. How should the Committee rule?

**A.** Although B's claim was invalid — see Rule 10-1c — A lost the hole when he conceded it — Rule 2-4.

**Handicap Stroke Claimed After Hole Conceded — See 6-2a/4.**

### 2-4/13 Implied Concession of Hole Withdrawn

**Q.** A, unable to find his ball after a two-minute search, suggests to B, his opponent, that they move on to the next hole. A's ball is then found. A withdraws his suggestion to move on to the next hole and play is resumed. Before A plays his ball, B plays a stroke with a wrong ball. What is the ruling?

**A.** A's suggestion amounted to a concession of the hole and B won the hole. Concession of a hole may not be withdrawn — Rule 2-4. B's actions after A's concession could not deprive him of a hole already won.

## 2-4/14 Player Concedes Match Due to Misconception as to Opponent's Score at Last Hole

**Q.** In a match, A and B were all square playing the last hole. A had a short putt for a 4. B holed a putt for a 4. A, mistakenly believing that B had holed out in three strokes, shook hands with B, conceded the match and lifted his ball. At that point B told A that he (B) had scored a 4. What is the ruling?

**A.** A conceded the match. Even if A had not conceded the match, he lost it when he lifted his ball without marking its position and thereby incurred a penalty stroke under Rule 20-1.

## 2-4/15 Player Concedes Match After Winning It When Opponent Lodges Invalid Claim Regarding Strokes Taken

**Q.** In a match, A and B were all square playing the last hole. A incurred a penalty without knowing it, and accordingly did not advise B of the penalty. B was aware of what had happened but did not realize it was a breach of the Rules either.

A won the hole and the match, and the result was posted.

Subsequently, a spectator informed B that A had incurred a penalty at the 18th hole. B then claimed the hole and the match, and A conceded the match to B.

Who was the rightful winner?

**A.** A won the match because a match can only be conceded prior to its conclusion (Rule 2-4).

A gave wrong information when he did not advise B that he had incurred a penalty and would have lost the hole had a timely claim been made — Rule 9-2b(i). However, a belated claim by B was not valid for two reasons:

(1) it was not based on facts previously unknown to B, and

(2) the claim was made after the result of the match was announced — see Rule 2-5.

**Agreement That Side Losing After 18 Holes of 36-Hole Match Will Concede Match — See 1-3/7.**

**Conceding Match to Avoid Disqualification — See 2-1/5 and 33-1/6.**

### 2-4/16 Valid Timely Claim Made After Concession of Match

**Q.** In a match, A and B are playing the last hole. B is 1 up. A holes out for a 4. B putts from a wrong place and holes the putt for a 4. A congratulates B and concedes the match. Before leaving the putting green, A asks B if he (B) had putted from a wrong place. B acknowledges that he did so. A claims that B loses the hole under Rule 20-7b. Is the claim valid?

**A.** Yes. Concession of a match is not binding if subsequently a valid claim is timely made. A's valid claim was made within the time limit in Rule 2-5.

**Player Omits Penalty Stroke When Advising Opponent as to Score for Hole; Error Discovered After Match Conceded by Opponent — See 9-2/10.**

### 2-4/17 Player in Erroneous Belief Match Is Over Shakes Opponent's Hand and Picks Up Opponent's Ball

**Q.** In match play, A holes a putt and, thinking he has won the match, shakes hands with B and picks up B's ball. The referee advises B that he had a putt to win the hole and keep the match alive. Has B conceded the match by his acquiescence in A's action of shaking hands and picking up B's ball?

**A.** No. B was entitled to replace his ball and hole out. Since A incurred a one-stroke penalty under Rule 18-3b, B now had two putts to win the hole.

**Player's Conscious Failure to Correct Opponent's Misunderstanding of State of Match Results in Opponent Conceding Match When in Fact Player Is Dormie — See 9-2/12.**

### 2-4/18 Defaulting Player Plays Informal Match with Opponent and Wins

**Q.** B concedes a match to A. A and B then play an informal match and B wins it, 5 and 4. Should the Committee post A as the winner by default or B as the winner by 5 and 4?

**A.** A should be posted as the winner by default.

### 2-4/19 Winner of Match Wishes to Default to Beaten Opponent

**Q.** In match play, A defeats B and then concedes the match to B because he (A) cannot continue in the competition. Is this permissible?

**A.** No. A won the match. A beaten player may not be reinstated in such circumstances. A should be posted as the winner and, since A cannot continue, A's opponent in the next round would win by default.

Under Rule 2-4, a side may concede a match at any time prior to conclusion of the match, but not thereafter.

### 2-4/20 Player Unable to Meet Match-Play Schedule Defaults; Schedule Then Changed and Player Requests Reinstatement

**Q.** The final matches in a competition were to be played on a Saturday. A was to play B in one match. On Thursday, A defaulted to B, saying that he would be out of town on Saturday.

On Saturday, the course was unplayable and the matches were postponed until the following Saturday. On Monday, A requested that he be reinstated. Should the Committee reinstate A?

**A.** No. A conceded the match as provided for in Rule 2-4. In the circumstances concession is irrevocable.

### 2-4/21 Wrong Form of Play Used to Decide Which Side Concedes Match

**Q.** In a foursome match, the players are unable to arrange a date to play their match within the prescribed time limit for the round. As a result, the players agree to play a singles match between one player from each side in order to decide which side would concede the match in accordance with Rule 2-4. Is this permissible?

**A.** There is nothing in the Rules of Golf to prohibit players from agreeing to a method of determining which side will concede a match. However, in view of the intention of Rule 1-3 (Agreement to Waive Rules), if players agree to play a match other than in the form prescribed in the conditions of the competition in order to decide which side will concede, both sides should be disqualified under Rule 1-3 for agreeing to exclude the operation of a condition of competition (Rule 33-1).

If the players agree to use some other method which does not involve playing a match to determine which side will concede, such as a putting competition, tossing a coin, etc., they are not considered to be in breach of Rule 1-3.

**Agreement that Side Losing After 18 Holes of 36-Hole Match Will Concede Match — See 1-3/7.**

**Wrong Form of Play Used in Match-Play Event — See 6-1/1.**

**Match Decided by Wrong Form of Play by Agreement of Players — See 33-1/4.**

### 2-5/1 Player's Obligation Re: Lodging Claim

In match play, a player may disregard a breach of the Rules by his opponent, provided there is no agreement between the players. There is a difference between overlooking an opponent's breach and agreement with the opponent to waive a penalty. Rule 1-3 prohibits the latter.

### 2-5/2 Procedure for a Valid Claim

For a claim to be valid, the claimant must notify his opponent (i) that he is making a claim, (ii) of the facts of the situation and (iii) that he wants a ruling. He must do so within the time required by Rule 2-5. For example, Rule 16-1e prohibits putting from a stance astride an extension of the line of putt behind the ball. In a match between A and B, if A putts from a stance astride an extension of the line and B states "that is not allowed, you are penalized" or "I'm making a claim because of that stroke," the Committee should consider the claim.

Statements by B such as "I'm not sure that's allowed" or "I don't think you can do that" do not by themselves constitute a valid claim because each statement does not contain the notice of a claim, the facts of the situation and an indication that he wants a ruling.

### 2-5/3 Player Lifts Ball Before Holing Out; Opponent Then Picks Up His Ball Claiming Player Loses Hole

**Q.** In match play, A's ball was resting against the flagstick but it was not holed. A, believing he had holed out, lifted his ball without first marking its position. In doing so, A incurred a penalty stroke under Rule 20-1. Since A was not aware that he had incurred a penalty, he did not inform B. B, who had not witnessed A's actions, played his next stroke. A's actions were then brought to the attention of B and he picked up his ball, claiming that A's lifting of his ball entailed a penalty of loss of hole. A and B agreed to continue the match and refer B's claim to the Committee later. How should the Committee have ruled?

**A.** The Committee should have ruled that B won the hole. B's claim was valid since he notified his opponent that he was making a claim, of the facts that gave rise to the claim (A's lifting of the ball) and that he wanted a ruling (A and B agreed to refer B's claim to the Committee). Although the penalty for A's lifting of the ball without first marking its position is one stroke, he lost the hole for giving wrong information (Rule 9-2b) when he failed to inform B before he (B) played his next stroke that he (A) had incurred the penalty stroke.

### 2-5/4 Player Wins Hole with Own Ball After Playing Wrong Ball; Opponent Lodges Belated Claim

**Q.** In a match, A and B are all square playing the last hole. A plays a wrong ball in the rough and discovers the error before his next stroke. A and B go back to look for A's ball without any question being raised as to whether A had incurred a penalty. A's ball is found. A plays out the hole with his original ball and wins the hole and the match. Several days later B claims the last hole and the match by virtue of the fact that A played a wrong ball.

Is the claim valid?

**A.** No. A gave wrong information when he did not advise B that he (A) had incurred a penalty — Rule 9-2b(i). However, a belated claim by B was not valid for two reasons:

(1) it was not based on facts previously unknown to B, and

(2) the claim was made after the result of the match was announced — See Rule 2-5.

**Player Wins Hole with Wrong Ball; Error Discovered at Next Hole; Opponent Claims Previous Hole — See 9-2/8.**

**Player Wins Hole with Wrong Ball and Partner Picks Up; Error Discovered at Next Hole; Opponents Claim Hole — See 30-3d/2.**

## 2-5/5 Invalid Claim Not Disputed

**Q.** In a match, A played a wrong ball to a green and then found his own ball in the hole. His own ball had been holed in three strokes, which was fewer strokes than B had taken. However, B claimed the hole on the ground that A had played a wrong ball. A did not dispute the claim. A lost the match.

Later, A learned that, because he had completed the hole when his own ball was holed and before play of a wrong ball, the play of the wrong ball was irrelevant and he was the rightful winner of the hole in question. A then lodged a claim with the Committee. Was the claim valid?

**A.** No. Since A did not dispute B's invalid claim before B played from the next teeing ground, B's claim stands and B won the hole in question — Rule 2-5.

**Player Concedes Hole on Basis of Invalid Claim — See 2-4/12.**

**Player Concedes Match After Winning It When Opponent Lodges Invalid Claim Regarding Strokes Taken — See 2-4/15.**

## 2-5/5.5 Breach of 14-Club Rule Discovered After Match Concluded But Before Result Officially Announced

**Q.** On completion of the 14th hole in a match between A and B, A wins by 5 and 4. The players continue the round. After the 16th hole, it is discovered by the players that A has 15 clubs in his bag.

Before the result of the match has been officially announced, B reports the facts to the Committee and asks for a ruling. Is the claim valid?

**A.** Yes. Although the players had left the putting green of the last hole of the match, B's claim is based on facts previously unknown to him and he is deemed to have been given wrong information by A (Rule 9-2b(i)). The players must return to the 15th hole and resume the match. A is penalized under Rule 4-4a and is three up with four holes to play.

### 2-5/6 Players Mistakenly Believe Match Is All Square After 18 Holes and Play Extra Hole Without Claim Being Made

**Q.** In a match between A and B, A is 1 up after the prescribed 18 holes. However, both A and B believe the match is all square. So they play extra holes and B wins at the 20th hole. The error is then discovered. What is the ruling?

**A.** Since A did not make a claim before either player played from the tee at the 19th hole, the match must be considered all square at that point. Thus, B was the winner.

**Players Under Impression Match Is Over Later Realize It Was All Square — See 2-3/1.**

### 2-5/7 Rightful Winner of Match Makes No Claim and Agrees to Play Extra Holes

**Q.** In a match, A and B are all square going to the 18th hole. On completion of the 18th hole, B states that he has scored 7; A states that he (A) has scored 6. A and B go into the clubhouse under the impression that A has won the match. At that point B tells A that, on reflection, he (B) believes A scored 7 at the 18th hole. On recounting, A acknowledges that he had a 7.

By agreement, A and B resume the match; A wins it at the 20th hole and the result is posted.

That night, B discovers that, because A gave wrong information after completion of the 18th hole, under Rule 9-2b(iii) he (B) was rightfully the winner of the 18th hole and the match. B reports the matter to the Committee and claims the match. What is the ruling?

**A.** The match stands as played, with A the winner.

B's claim was not made within the time limit in Rule 2-5. B's claim would have been valid if he had refused to play extra holes or had played the extra holes under protest.

### 2-5/8 Status of Valid Claim If Players Accept Wrong Ruling from Someone Not on Committee and Continue Match

**Q.** In an 18-hole match between A and B, A's ball strikes the flagstick which was attended by B. A and B believe that a loss-of-hole penalty is incurred but they are in doubt as to which one of them incurs the penalty. Accordingly, before teeing off at the next hole, they agree to refer the matter to the Committee later.

At the conclusion of 18 holes, A and B agree that if B incurred a loss-of-hole penalty at the hole in question, the match is all square; if A incurred it, B has won the match by two holes. A and B seek a ruling from X, who is not on the Committee. X incorrectly advises A and B that B incurred the penalty and that the match is therefore all square.

A and B accept X's ruling, play extra holes and A wins.

Subsequently, the incident was brought to the attention of the Committee. What should the Committee do?

**A.** When A and B accepted X's incorrect ruling, they, in effect, settled the doubt themselves and, after A and B began playing extra holes, the Committee was no longer entitled to consider a claim. The match stands as played, with A the winner.

**Valid Timely Claim Made After Concession of Match — See 2-4/16.**

### 2-5/8.5 Player and Opponent Agree on Incorrect Procedure; Whether Valid Claim May Be Made After Procedure Followed

**Q.** In a match, a player's ball comes to rest on an artificially-surfaced road. He is uncertain if the road is to be treated as an immovable obstruction or an integral part of the course. He asks his opponent and they agree that the player should treat the road as an immovable obstruction. The player drops the ball in accordance with the procedure under Rule 24-2b and plays it. Prior to playing from the next tee, the opponent discovers that he and the player were wrong as the Committee had introduced a Local Rule declaring the road to be an integral part of the course and, therefore, the player was not entitled to take relief under Rule 24-2b. The player should have incurred a loss of hole penalty under Rule 18 for lifting his ball without authority and failing to replace it. May the opponent claim the hole?

**A.** No. The claim must not be considered by the Committee because the opponent and the player agreed that the player was entitled to relief under Rule 24-2b. When this agreement was reached, there was no longer a doubtful or disputed point and there was no basis under Rule 2-5 for making a claim.

The players were not in breach of Rule 1-3 as they believed at the time they were proceeding properly.

**Players Unaware Penalty Incurred — See 1-3/5.**

**Extra Stroke Taken by Mistake in Handicap Match; Status of Late Claim — See 2-5/13.**

### 2-5/9 Player Agreeing with Opponent That Hole Was Halved Later Realizes He Has Won Hole; Player Then Makes Claim

**Q.** In a match between A and B, at the 16th hole A scored 6 and B scored 5. When leaving the putting green, B commented to A: "A half?" and A replied: "Yes."

A won the match at the 20th hole and the result was posted. Later, B realized that he had won the 16th hole and, if the mistake had not been made, he would have won the match 1 up.

A admitted that he had made a mistake. B reported the matter to the Committee and claimed the match. Is the claim valid?

**A.** No. The match stands as played, with A the winner. After the result of the match was posted, the claim by B could have been considered only if A had knowingly given wrong information as to the number of strokes he (A) had taken at the 16th hole — see Rule 2-5.

### 2-5/10 Player Accepting Erroneous Claim Disputes It After Result Announced

**Q.** In a match, A was in breach of a Rule. Although the penalty for a breach of the Rule in question was only one stroke, B, his opponent, claimed that A lost the hole. A did not dispute the claim. B won the match and the result was posted. Three days later, A protested to the Committee that B had misinformed him with respect to the Rules. What is the ruling?

**A.** The match stands as played. Under Rule 2-5, no claim may be considered after the result of a match has been announced unless the opponent knowingly gave wrong information. Incorrect information on the Rules is not wrong information. It is up to each player to know the Rules.

### 2-5/11 Wrong Information Given After Play of Last Hole; Claim Made After Result Announced

**Q.** In a match, A and B came to the last hole all square. After completion of the hole, A stated that he had scored 9 and B stated that he (B) had scored 8, making B the winner, 1 up. The result was recorded by the Committee.

A few minutes later, a spectator told A that B had scored 9 at the last hole. B reviewed the hole and acknowledged that he had made a mistake and that his actual score was 9. What is the ruling?

**A.** The match stands as played, with B the winner. Under Rule 2-5 no claim may be considered after the result of a match is announced unless wrong information has been given knowingly.

### 2-5/12 Imposition of Penalty by Referee After Any Player in Match Has Played from Next Tee

**Q.** In match play, may a referee penalize a player for a breach of a Rule at a hole if he does not become aware of the breach until someone in the match has played from the next teeing ground?

**A.** Yes, unless the facts giving rise to the penalty were known to the opponent.

## 2-5/13 Extra Stroke Taken by Mistake in Handicap Match; Status of Late Claim

**Q.** Prior to the start of a handicap match, the two players correctly advised one another as to the handicaps to which they were entitled. However, during the match, A, by mistake, took a stroke to which he was not entitled at a certain hole. The error was discovered several holes later. Could B, the opponent, then claim the hole in question?

**A.** No. A late claim would not be valid unless it was based on facts previously unknown to B and B had been given wrong information by A. In this case A did not give B wrong information as to the number of strokes to which he was entitled during the round, and it was B's responsibility to know the holes at which handicap strokes were to be given (see Note under Rule 6-2). The hole in question stands as played.

**Player and Opponent Agree on Incorrect Procedure; Whether Valid Claim May Be Made After Procedure Followed — See 2-5/8.5.**

## 2-5/14 When Match Result "Officially Announced"

**Q.** Rule 2-5 prohibits a Committee from considering a claim after the result of a match has been "officially announced," except in cases where a player knowingly gave wrong information. When is the result of a match "officially announced?"

**A.** It is a matter for the Committee to decide when the result of the match has been "officially announced" and it will vary depending on the nature of the competition. When an official scoreboard exists, Rule 2-5 should be interpreted so that the recording of the winner of the match on the official scoreboard is the official announcement of the result of the match. In such cases where a referee has been assigned by the Committee to accompany a match, any announcement of the result of the match by the referee on the final putting green is not the official announcement. However, there may be cases where an official scoreboard is not used, in which case the Committee must clarify when it considers the result "officially announced."

In some cases the official scoreboard will be a prominent structure and in other cases it might be a sheet of paper in the golf shop or locker room. The Committee is generally responsible for recording the winner's name on the scoreboard, but there may be times when the Committee charges the players with this responsibility.

### Other Decisions relating to Rule 2-5:

**Player with Lost Ball Concedes Hole; Ball Then Found in Hole and Player Claims Hole — See 2-4/11.**

**Second Ball Played in Match Play; No Claim Made — See 3-3/9.**

**Wrong Handicap Used in Match by Mistake; Error Discovered After Result Officially Announced; Status of Claim by Opponent — See 6-2a/5.**

**Match Discontinued by Agreement Due to Rain; One Player Subsequently Wishes to Resume; Opponent Refuses on Ground Course Unplayable and Makes Claim** — See 6-8a/6.

**Player Omits Penalty Stroke When Advising Opponent as to Score for Hole; Error Discovered After Match Conceded by Opponent; Opponent Lodges Claim** — See 9-2/10.

**Doubt Whether Ball Moved by Outside Agency; Opponent Lodges Claim** — See 18-1/4.

**In Foursome Side Drives for Three Holes in Wrong Order and Then Claim Is Made** — See 29-2/2.

**Committee Does Not Penalize Player in Breach of Pace of Play Condition Believing Player Had Already Lost Hole** — See 34-3/2.

# Rule 3. Stroke Play

**Definitions**
All defined terms are in *italics* and are listed alphabetically in the Definitions section — see pages 3-11.

### 3-1. Winner
The *competitor* who plays the *stipulated round* or rounds in the fewest *strokes* is the winner.

In a handicap competition, the *competitor* with the lowest net score for the *stipulated round* or rounds is the winner.

### 3-2. Failure to Hole Out
If a *competitor* fails to *hole* out at any hole and does not correct his mistake before he makes a *stroke* on the next *teeing ground* or, in the case of the last hole of the round, before he leaves the *putting green*, he is disqualified.

### 3-3. Doubt as to Procedure
#### a. Procedure
In stroke play, if a *competitor* is doubtful of his rights or the correct procedure during the play of a hole he may, without penalty, complete the hole with two balls.

After the doubtful situation has arisen and before taking further action, the *competitor* must announce to his *marker* or a *fellow-competitor* that he intends to play two balls and which ball he wishes to count if the *Rules* permit. If he fails to do so, the provisions of Rule 3-3b(ii) apply.

The *competitor* must report the facts of the situation to the *Committee* before returning his score card. If he fails to do so, he is disqualified.

#### b. Determination of Score for Hole
(i) If the ball that the *competitor* selected in advance to count has been played in accordance with the *Rules*, the score with that ball is the *competitor's* score for the hole. Otherwise, the score with the other ball counts if the *Rules* allow the procedure adopted for that ball.

(ii) If the *competitor* fails to announce in advance his decision to complete the hole with two balls, or which ball he wishes to count, the score with the original ball counts, provided it has been played in accordance with the *Rules*. If the original ball is not one of the balls being played, the first ball put into play counts, provided it has been played in accordance with the *Rules*. Otherwise, the score with the other ball counts if the *Rules* allow the procedure adopted for that ball.

**Note 1:** If a *competitor* plays a second ball under Rule 3-3, the *strokes* made after this Rule has been invoked with the ball ruled not to count and *penalty strokes* incurred solely by playing that ball are disregarded.

**Note 2:** A second ball played under Rule 3-3 is not a *provisional ball* under Rule 27-2.

### 3-4. Refusal to Comply with a Rule

If a *competitor* refuses to comply with a *Rule* affecting the rights of another *competitor*, he is disqualified.

### 3-5. General Penalty

The penalty for a breach of a *Rule* in stroke play is two strokes except when otherwise provided.

#### 3/1 Disqualification in Play-Off

**Q.** A competitor in a stroke-play play-off incurs a penalty of disqualification. Does the disqualification apply to the play-off only or to the entire competition?

**A.** The disqualification applies only to the play-off.

#### 3/2 Competitors Play Two Holes Not Included in Stipulated Round

**Q.** In stroke play, the stipulated round was 16 holes, i.e., the 13th and 14th holes were omitted. After play of the 12th hole, one group elected to play the 13th and 14th holes without counting their scores for those holes. They then completed the round. What is the ruling?

**A.** The stipulated round consists of playing the holes of the course in the sequence prescribed by the Committee — see Definition of "Stipulated Round." These competitors were in breach of the conditions of the competition and the Committee should in this case impose a penalty of disqualification under Rule 33-7.

#### 3-2/1 Fellow-Competitor's Ball Knocked from Lip of Hole by Competitor Not Replaced

**Q.** In stroke play, a competitor concedes his fellow-competitor a short putt and knocks the ball away. The fellow-competitor lifts his ball, does not replace it as required by Rule 18-4 and plays from the next tee. What is the ruling?

**A.** The fellow-competitor is disqualified — Rule 3-2.

Ball Played from Putting Green Deflected by Moving Outside Agency; Stroke Not Replayed — See 19-1/3.

### 3-2/2 Ball Blown into Hole by Competitor Not Replaced and Holed Out

**Q.** In stroke play, a competitor's ball stopped on the lip of the hole and on impulse he blew the ball into the hole. He did not replace the ball, as required by Rule 18-2a, and hole out. He played from the next tee. Is the competitor disqualified under Rule 3-2 for failing to hole out?

**A.** Yes.

**Player Who Putts with One Hand and Catches Ball in Hole with Other Hand Does Not Place Ball on Lip of Hole and Hole Out — See 1-2/5.**

### 3-2/3 Competitor in Error Does Not Hole Out; Error Corrected Before Playing from Next Tee

**Q.** In four-ball stroke play, A holed out in 4. B, A's partner, who was lying 3 and had marked and lifted his ball, forgot he had a handicap stroke. He did not replace his ball and hole out or pick up his ball-marker. On the way to the next teeing ground, B remembered his stroke, returned to the green, replaced his ball where it previously lay and holed out for a net 3. Was this in order?

**A.** Yes, since B had not played from the next teeing ground (Rule 3-2).

**Competitor Picks Up Second Ball — See 3-3/8.**

**Modifying Penalty for Not Holing Out — See 33-7/2.**

### 3-3/0.5 Guidelines for Determining Which Ball Counts When Player Proceeds Under Rule 3-3

The purpose of Rule 3-3 is to allow a competitor to avoid a penalty when he is in doubt as to the proper procedure. The following are guidelines for determining the ball with which the competitor scores in various situations:

(1) If both balls are played in accordance with the Rules, the ball selected counts if the competitor announces in advance his decision to invoke this Rule and announces in advance the ball with which he wishes to score. If the competitor does not announce or select in advance, the score with the original ball counts if played in accordance with the Rules. Otherwise the score with the second ball counts if played in accordance with the Rules.

(2) If the procedure with the ball selected in advance is not in accordance with the Rules, the other ball must count (see Decision 3-3/5).

(3) If neither ball is played in accordance with the Rules, the following applies:

(a) In a case where the competitor plays both balls from a wrong place but is not guilty of a serious breach with either ball, the score with the original ball counts, with an additional penalty under the applicable Rule (see Rule 20-7c).

(b) In a case where the competitor is guilty of a serious breach with one ball and not guilty of a serious breach with the other ball, the score with the other ball counts, with an additional penalty under the applicable Rule (see Rule 20-7c).

(c) In a case where the competitor is guilty of a serious breach with both balls, the competitor is disqualified.

(4) If the original ball is played and then Rule 3-3 is invoked, the score with the original ball must count, even if the Rules do not allow the procedure adopted for that ball, i.e., Rule 3-3 is not applicable in such circumstances. (Revised)

### 3-3/1 Provisional Ball Used as Second Ball When Not Determinable Whether Original Ball Is Out of Bounds

**Q.** In stroke play, a player is in doubt as to whether his drive may be out of bounds. He plays a provisional ball under Rule 27-2. He finds the original ball and cannot determine whether it is out of bounds or not. The player wishes to consider the provisional ball as his second ball under Rule 3-3 and complete the play of the hole with both balls. Is this permissible?

**A.** Yes. In invoking Rule 3-3 after playing a provisional ball, the player must treat the provisional ball as a second ball. Although Note 2 to Rule 3-3 provides: "A second ball played under Rule 3-3 is not a provisional ball under Rule 27-2," the reverse is not true in the present case.

### 3-3/2 Second Ball Played Despite Adverse Ruling

**Q.** In stroke play, a competitor believes he is entitled to relief under a Rule, but a member of the Committee disagrees. In spite of the ruling by the Committee member, the competitor invokes Rule 3-3 and opts to score with the second ball. He plays his original ball as it lies and the second ball under the Rule he believes is applicable.

May a competitor invoke Rule 3-3 in such circumstances?

**A.** The answer depends upon whether or not the Committee has given authority to make final decisions to its individual members.

If the Committee member concerned has not been given authority to make final decisions, the competitor is entitled to invoke Rule 3-3.

If, on the other hand, the Committee member has been given authority to make final decisions, he may, despite his own view that the competitor is not entitled to relief, permit the competitor to invoke Rule 3-3. However, if the Committee member exercises his authority and gives the competitor a final decision that he is not entitled to the relief he claims, there is then no justification for the competitor invoking Rule 3-3, and he will incur a penalty of two strokes for undue delay (Rule 6-7) if he, nevertheless, goes ahead and invokes Rule 3-3. The score with his original ball, including this two-stroke penalty, must count.

### 3-3/3 Ball Dropped in Wrong Place and Played; Rule 3-3 Then Invoked and Second Ball Dropped in Right Place; Both Balls Played Out

**Q.** In stroke play, a competitor's ball comes to rest through the green on a paved path. He lifts the ball, drops it off the path at a point almost two club-lengths from the nearest point of relief (i.e., he drops in a wrong place) and plays it. The competitor's marker advises the competitor that he (the marker) believes the ball must be dropped within one club-length of the nearest point of relief. The competitor, in doubt, invokes Rule 3-3, drops a second ball within one club-length of the nearest point of relief and otherwise in accordance with Rule 24-2b(i) and opts to score with the second ball. The competitor holes out with both balls. What is the ruling?

**A.** Rule 20-7c states in part: "If a competitor makes a stroke from a wrong place, he incurs a penalty of two strokes under the applicable Rule. He must play out the hole with the ball played from the wrong place..." Thus, the competitor's score with the original ball, with a penalty of two strokes added, must count.

Rule 20-7c does not permit the second ball to count. However, the competitor incurs no penalty for having played the second ball.

### 3-3/4 Ball Dropped in Wrong Place But Not Played; Rule 3-3 Then Invoked and Second Ball Dropped in Right Place; Both Balls Played Out

**Q.** With reference to Decision 3-3/3, what would have been the ruling if the marker had advised the competitor of his possible error before the ball dropped in a wrong place was played and the competitor had invoked Rule 3-3 at that point?

**A.** Rule 20-7c would not have applied because Rule 3-3 was invoked before the ball dropped in a wrong place was played.

The score with the second ball would have counted and no penalty would have been incurred.

The competitor, had he not been in doubt, could have lifted the ball dropped in the wrong place, without penalty -- Rule 20-6.

### 3-3/5 Whether Score with Second Ball Counts If Ball Dropped in Wrong Place and Played

**Q.** In stroke play, a competitor's ball came to rest on an artificially-surfaced road which had not been declared an integral part of the course. The competitor, not sure whether the road was an obstruction or an integral part of the course, invoked Rule 3-3 and announced that he wished his score with the second ball to count. He played his original ball as it lay and dropped and played a second ball under Rule 24-2b(i). He met all the requirements of that Rule, except that he dropped the second ball almost two club-lengths from the nearest point of relief, instead of within one club-length. Does the score with the second ball count?

**A.** No. Rule 3-3b(i) states in part: "If the ball that the competitor selected in advance to count has been played in accordance with the Rules, the score with that ball is the competitor's score for the hole." In this case, the ball selected in advance to count (i.e., the second ball) was not played in accordance with the Rules since it was dropped almost two club-lengths from the nearest point of relief. Accordingly, the score with the original ball counts.

### 3-3/6 Competitor Plays Original Ball After Doubtful Situation Has Arisen and Then Invokes Rule 3-3

**Q.** In stroke play, a competitor's ball lies in a water hazard. A movable stake defining the margin of the hazard interferes with the area of his intended swing. He plays his next stroke, avoiding the stake. It then occurs to him that he may have been entitled to remove the stake. The competitor informs his marker that he is invoking Rule 3-3 and elects to score with a second ball. He removes the stake and drops a second ball at the spot from which his original ball was played. He holes out with both balls. What is the ruling?

**A.** The situation which caused the doubt arose when the competitor's ball lay in the water hazard and the stake interfered with his swing. Since the competitor took further action, i.e., played the original ball, after the situation which caused the doubt had arisen, the score with the original ball must count — see last paragraph of Rule 3-3b.

However, the competitor incurs no penalty for having played the second ball.

### 3-3/6.5 Competitor Plays Second Ball Without Announcing Intention to Invoke Rule 3-3 and Fails to Report Facts to Committee

**Q.** In stroke play, a competitor's ball came to rest on an artificially-surfaced road which had not been declared an integral part of the course. Without announcing his decision to invoke Rule 3-3 or the ball with which he would score if the Rules permitted, the competitor dropped and played a second ball in accordance with Rule 24-2b. The competitor then played the original ball as it lay and completed play of the hole with both balls, scoring 4 with the original ball and 5 with the dropped ball.

The competitor returned his score card to the Committee with a score of 4 on the hole in question and failed to report the facts to the Committee.

What is the ruling?

**A.** Although the competitor did not announce his decision to invoke Rule 3-3, it is clear from the facts that he intended to invoke such Rule. As the competitor did not report the facts of the situation to the Committee before returning his score card, he is disqualified under Rule 3-3a.

### 3-3/7 Original Ball Strikes Second Ball or Vice Versa

**Q.** A competitor invokes Rule 3-3 and plays a second ball. Subsequently, the competitor makes a stroke at one ball and it strikes and moves the other ball. What is the ruling?

**A.** If both balls lay on the putting green prior to the stroke, the competitor incurs a penalty of two strokes if the score with the striking ball ultimately becomes the competitor's score for the hole — Rule 19-5. Otherwise, there is no penalty.

The striking ball must be played as it lies — Rule 19-5.

The moved ball must be replaced — Rule 18-5.

### 3-3/7.5 Competitor Announces Intention to Play Two Balls; Plays Original Ball Before Dropping Second Ball; Elects Not to Play Second Ball

**Q.** A competitor's ball comes to rest in a rut made by a maintenance vehicle. Believing the Committee might declare the rut to be ground under repair, he announces that he will invoke Rule 3-3 and play a second ball in accordance with Rule 25-1b and that he wishes his score with the second ball to count if the Rules permit. He hits his original ball from the rut to one foot from the hole and then states he will not play a second ball. He completes the hole with his original ball. On completion of the round, the facts are reported to the Committee. What is the ruling?

**A.** The answer depends on whether the Committee declares the rut to be ground under repair. If the Committee declares the rut to be ground under repair, the competitor is disqualified for failing to hole out (Rule 3-2) since the score with the second ball would have counted — see Rule 3-3 and Decision 3-3/8. Otherwise, the score with the original ball counts.

If a player declares his intention to invoke Rule 3-3, he may change his mind at any time before he takes further action, such as making another stroke at his original ball or putting a second ball into play. Once he invokes the Rule and takes further action, he is bound by the procedures in Rule 3-3.

### 3-3/8 Competitor Picks Up Second Ball

**Q.** In stroke play, a competitor, uncertain whether the road his ball lies on is an obstruction or not, invokes Rule 3-3. He plays his original ball as it lies on the road and a second ball under Rule 24-2b(i), telling his marker he wishes his score with the second ball to count if the Rules permit. Having hit his original ball onto the green and the second ball into a bunker, the competitor picks up the second ball, holes out with the original ball and plays from the next tee. At this point the matter is referred to the Committee, which establishes that the road on which the competitor's ball lay was an obstruction. What is the ruling?

**A.** Since the road on which the competitor's ball lay was an obstruction and therefore Rule 24-2b(i) allowed the procedure selected by the competitor, the score with the second (or selected) ball would have counted if it had been holed out. However, since the competitor did not hole out with that ball, he is disqualified — Rule 3-2.

If, on the other hand, the road had not been an obstruction, there would have been no penalty. In that case, since the Rules would not have allowed the selected procedure, a score with the second ball would not have counted, and the competitor's score with his original ball would have been his score for the hole. There is no penalty for picking up a ball played under Rule 3-3 if that ball cannot count.

### 3-3/9 Second Ball Played in Match Play

**Q.** In a match between A and B, A was unsure of his rights at a hole. Neither A nor B was aware that Rule 3-3 applies only in stroke play, so A played a second ball and holed out with both balls. At the end of the round, the matter was referred to the Committee. What is the ruling?

**A.** A second ball played in match play is a wrong ball — See Definition of "Wrong Ball." Accordingly, A would have lost the hole had B claimed it under Rule 2-5 before either player had played from the next tee. However, B made no claim. Therefore, the score with A's original ball counts.

**Local Rule Allowing Play of Second Ball in Match Play — See 33-8/3.**

### 3-3/10 Competitor Plays Three Balls When Doubtful of Rights

**Q.** Are there any circumstances under which a competitor in stroke play, who is doubtful of his rights or procedure, may play a third ball under Rule 3-3?

**A.** No. If a competitor so proceeds, the score with the original ball or, if the original ball is not one of the balls being played, the first ball put into play shall count. If the Rules do not allow the procedure adopted for the original ball or the first ball put into play, the competitor incurs the penalty prescribed for the improper procedure.

### 3-3/11 Competitor Drops One Ball in Accordance with Two Different Rules Instead of Playing Second Ball

**Q.** In stroke play, a competitor's ball comes to rest through the green in a deep rut which has not been defined as ground under repair by the Committee. The ball is not playable due to the rut. The competitor believes that the Committee might declare the rutted area to be ground under repair. He announces to his marker or a fellow-competitor that he will drop the ball at a spot which conforms to the procedures prescribed in both Rule 25-1b(i) (Ground Under Repair) and Rule 28c (Ball Unplayable), seek a ruling from the Committee before returning his score card, and accept the penalty stroke in Rule 28 if the Committee does not declare the rutted area to be ground under repair. Is such a procedure permissible?

**A.** Yes. Although it would have been advisable for the competitor to proceed under Rule 3-3 in this situation, the Rules do not prohibit such a procedure — see also Decision 3-3/12.

### 3-3/12 Competitor Drops One Ball in Accordance with Two Different Rules Instead of Playing Second Ball; Dropped Ball Rolls Back into the Condition from Which Relief Taken

**Q.** In the circumstances described in Decision 3-3/11, what is the ruling if the competitor drops the ball and it rolls and comes to rest where there is still interference from the same rutted area?

**A.** If this occurred it would be advisable for the competitor to obtain a ruling from the Committee before proceeding further or invoke Rule 3-3.

If the Committee determines that the area is ground under repair, the ball must be re-dropped (Rule 20-2c(v)). Otherwise, the dropped ball is in play and the competitor must either play the ball as it lies or, for a second time, proceed under the unplayable ball Rule (Rule 28) incurring an additional penalty stroke.

### 3-3/13 Competitor Invokes Rule 3-3; Lifts and Drops Original Ball

**Q.** A competitor's ball comes to rest in an area that he feels should be marked as ground under repair. Believing the Committee might declare the area to be ground under repair, he announces that he will invoke Rule 3-3 and play a second ball in accordance with Rule 25-1b and that he wishes his score with the ball played under Rule 25-1b to count if the Rules permit. He marks the position of and lifts the original ball, drops it in accordance with Rule 25-1b and plays it. He then places a second ball where the original lay and plays it. Is the competitor's procedure correct?

**A.** Yes. Rule 3-3 does not require the original ball to be played as it lies and, therefore, the competitor's procedure was acceptable. However, it would also have been correct for the competitor to play his original ball as it lay and play a second ball in accordance with Rule 25-1b.

### 3-3/14 Competitor Invokes Rule 3-3; Second Ball Played First

**Q.** A competitor accidentally causes his ball to move after he has addressed it in breach of Rule 18-2b. He is unsure whether the ball must be replaced or played from its new position. He announces that he will invoke Rule 3-3, places a second ball on the spot from which the original ball was moved and states that he wishes the second ball to count if the Rules permit. He plays the second ball first and then plays the original ball. Is the competitor's procedure correct in terms of the order in which the balls were played?

**A.** Yes. Rule 3-3 does not require the original ball to be played first and, therefore, the competitor's procedure was acceptable.

#### Other Decisions relating to Rule 3-3:

**Wrong Ball Played in Belief It Is Second Ball — See 15/7.**

**Ball Dropped from Ground Under Repair Area Rolls to Position Where Area Interferes with Stance; Whether Re-Drop Required — See 20-2c/0.5.**

**Ball Dropped and Played Under Water Hazard Rule; Original Ball Then Found in Hazard and Holed Out as Second Ball — See 26-1/5.**

### 3-4/1 Competitor Not Given Opportunity to Lift Ball Assisting Fellow-Competitor

**Q.** In stroke play, A's ball lies near the hole in a position to assist B, whose ball lies off the green. A states his intention to lift his ball under Rule 22-1. However, B says that he does not want A's ball lifted. B plays before A has an opportunity to lift his ball. Should B be penalized?

**A.** Yes. B is disqualified under Rule 3-4.

## CLUBS AND THE BALL

The United States Golf Association (USGA) reserves the right, at any time, to change the Rules relating to clubs and balls (see Appendices II and III) and make or change the interpretations relating to these Rules.

# Rule 4. Clubs

A player in doubt as to the conformity of a club should consult the USGA.

A manufacturer should submit to the USGA a sample of a club to be manufactured for a ruling as to whether the club conforms with the *Rules*. If a manufacturer fails to submit a sample or to await a ruling before manufacturing and/or marketing the club, the manufacturer assumes the risk of a ruling that the club does not conform with the *Rules*. Any sample submitted to the USGA becomes its property for reference purposes.

## Definitions
All defined terms are in *italics* and are listed alphabetically in the Definitions section — see pages 3-11.

## 4-1. Form and Make of Clubs
### a. General
The player's clubs must conform with this Rule and the provisions, specifications and interpretations set forth in Appendix II.

### b. Wear and Alteration
A club that conforms with the *Rules* when new is deemed to conform after wear through normal use. Any part of a club that has been purposely altered is regarded as new and must, in its altered state, conform with the *Rules*.

## 4-2. Playing Characteristics Changed and Foreign Material
### a. Playing Characteristics Changed
During a *stipulated round*, the playing characteristics of a club must not be purposely changed by adjustment or by any other means.

### b. Foreign Material
Foreign material must not be applied to the club face for the purpose of influencing the movement of the ball.

**PENALTY FOR BREACH OF RULE 4-1 or -2: Disqualification.**

## 4-3. Damaged Clubs: Repair and Replacement
### a. Damage in Normal Course of Play
If, during a *stipulated round*, a player's club is damaged in the normal course of play, he may:

(i) use the club in its damaged state for the remainder of the *stipulated round*; or

(ii) without unduly delaying play, repair it or have it repaired; or

(iii) as an additional option available only if the club is unfit for play, replace the damaged club with any club. The replacement of a club must not unduly delay play and must not be made by borrowing any club selected for play by any other person playing on the *course*.

PENALTY FOR BREACH OF RULE 4-3a:
See Penalty Statement for Rule 4-4a or b, and c.

**Note:** A club is unfit for play if it is substantially damaged, e.g., the shaft is dented, significantly bent or broken into pieces; the clubhead becomes loose, detached or significantly deformed; or the grip becomes loose. A club is not unfit for play solely because the club's lie or loft has been altered, or the clubhead is scratched.

### b. Damage Other Than in Normal Course of Play

If, during a *stipulated round*, a player's club is damaged other than in the normal course of play rendering it non-conforming or changing its playing characteristics, the club must not subsequently be used or replaced during the round.

### c. Damage Prior to Round

A player may use a club damaged prior to a round provided the club, in its damaged state, conforms with the *Rules*.

Damage to a club that occurred prior to a round may be repaired during the round, provided the playing characteristics are not changed and play is not unduly delayed.

PENALTY FOR BREACH OF RULE 4-3b or c: Disqualification.

(Undue delay — see Rule 6-7.)

## 4-4. Maximum of 14 Clubs

### a. Selection and Addition of Clubs

The player must start a *stipulated round* with not more than 14 clubs. He is limited to the clubs thus selected for that round except that, if he started with fewer than 14 clubs, he may add any number provided his total number does not exceed 14.

The addition of a club or clubs must not unduly delay play (Rule 6-7) and the player must not add or borrow any club selected for play by any other person playing on the *course*.

### b. Partners May Share Clubs

*Partners* may share clubs, provided that the total number of clubs carried by the *partners* so sharing does not exceed 14.

PENALTY FOR BREACH OF RULE 4-4a or b,
REGARDLESS OF NUMBER OF EXCESS CLUBS CARRIED:

Match play — At the conclusion of the hole at which the breach is discovered, the state of the match is adjusted by deducting one hole for each hole at which a breach occurred. Maximum deduction per round: Two holes.

Stroke play — Two strokes for each hole at which any breach occurred; maximum penalty per round: Four strokes.

Bogey and par competitions — Penalties as in match play.

Stableford competitions — see Note 1 to Rule 32-1b.

### c. Excess Club Declared Out of Play
Any club or clubs carried or used in breach of Rule 4-3a(iii) or Rule 4-4 must be declared out of play by the player to his opponent in match play or his *marker* or a *fellow-competitor* in stroke play immediately upon discovery that a breach has occurred. The player must not use the club or clubs for the remainder of the *stipulated round*.

PENALTY FOR BREACH OF RULE 4-4c: Disqualification.

## 4-1/1 Non-Conforming Club Carried But Not Used

**Q.** If a player unwittingly carries a non-conforming club but does not use it, would the Committee be justified, under Rule 33-7, in waiving or modifying the disqualification penalty?

**A.** No.

## 4-1/2 Material in Head of Metal Wood Club Broken Away from Shell

**Q.** A piece of material in the head of a metal wood club, which conformed with the Rules when manufactured, has broken away from the shell due to use, and it rattles around in the head. Appendix II, 1a states in part: "All parts of the club must be fixed so that the club is one unit." Is this metal wood club now non-conforming because of the loose piece of material?

**A.** No, because Rule 4-1b states in part: "A club that conforms with the Rules when new is deemed to conform after wear through normal use." The piece of material in the metal wood club in question broke loose from the shell due to wear through normal use.

**Attachment to Grip or Shaft of Club of Player with Artificial Arm — See 14-3/15.**

### 4-1/3 Status of a Chipper

**Q.** What Rules apply to "chippers"?

**A.** A "chipper" is an iron club designed primarily for use off the putting green, generally with a loft greater than ten degrees. As most players adopt a "putting stroke" when using a chipper, there can be a tendency to design the club as if it was a putter. To eliminate confusion, the Rules which apply to "chippers" include:

(1) The club must not be designed to be adjustable except for weight (Appendix II, 1b);

(2) The shaft must be attached to the clubhead at the heel (Appendix II, 2c);

(3) The grip must be circular in cross-section (Appendix II, 3(i)) and only one grip is permitted (Appendix II, 3(v));

(4) The clubhead must be generally plain in shape (Appendix II, 4a) and have only one striking face (Appendix II, 4c); and

(5) The face of the club must conform to specifications with regard to hardness, surface roughness, material and markings in the impact area (Appendix II, 5).

### 4-1/4 Lead Tape Applied to Clubhead or Shaft Before Start of Round

**Q.** Before the start of a round, may a player attach lead tape to a clubhead or shaft for the purpose of adjusting weight?

**A.** Yes. The use of lead tape is an exception to Appendix II, 1b(ii).

### 4-2/0.5 Lead Tape Applied to Clubhead or Shaft During Round

**Q.** With regard to Decision 4-1/4, may a player remove, add or alter lead tape during a round?

**A.** No. However, lead tape that becomes detached from the club in the normal course of play may be placed back onto the club in the same location. If the lead tape will not remain on the club in the same location, new tape may be used. Every effort should be made to restore the club, as nearly as possible, to its previous condition. Alternatively, the club may be used in its damaged state (without the lead tape) for the remainder of the round (Rule 4-3a).

If the tape is altered or damaged other than in the normal course of play, the club may not be used for the remainder of the round, under penalty of disqualification (see Rules 4-2a and 4-3).

### 4-2/1 Material Applied to Top of Clubhead to Reduce Glare

**Q.** During a round, may a player put a BAND-AID® or a strip of tape on the top of a clubhead to reduce glare?

**A.** No. This would change the playing characteristics of the club in breach of Rule 4-2.

**Caddie Shields Player from Sun During Stroke — See 14-2/3.**

**Competitor Changes Weight of Club During Round; Breach Discovered After Competition Closed — See 34-1b/4.**

### 4-2/2 Playing Characteristics of Club Changed While Play Suspended; Error Discovered Before Play Resumed

**Q.** While play is suspended, a player changes the lie of four of his clubs. Before play is resumed, he becomes aware that Rule 4-2a prohibits changing the playing characteristics of a club purposely during a round. If the original lie of the four clubs is restored, or if the player discards them before play is resumed, can he avoid the disqualification penalty prescribed by Rule 4-2?

**A.** Rule 4-2a is intended to ensure that, apart from damage sustained in the normal course of play, the playing characteristics of the clubs with which the player starts the stipulated round shall not be altered until he has finished it. Accordingly, although the stipulated round has been suspended and the player did not technically change the playing characteristics during the round, in equity (Rule 1-4):

(1) the player incurs no penalty if he discards the clubs in question before play is resumed and, assuming he started the round with 14 clubs, finishes the round with the remaining ten clubs, or

(2) if the player resumes play carrying the four clubs, whether or not he has attempted to restore the original playing characteristics, he should be disqualified, in view of the purpose of Rule 4-2a. If the lie of a club has been changed, it would be impossible exactly to restore the original lie.

### 4-2/3 Applying Chalk to Club Face

**Q.** During a round, may a player apply chalk to the face of an iron club in order to obtain more backspin?

**A.** No.

### 4-2/4 Applying Saliva to Face of Club

**Q.** A player spat on the face of his club and did not wipe the saliva off before playing his next stroke. Is this permissible?

**A.** If the purpose of doing this was to influence the movement of the ball, the player was in breach of Rule 4-2b as saliva is "foreign material."

### 4-3/1 Meaning of Damage Sustained in "Normal Course of Play"

**Q.** In Rule 4-3a, what is meant by the term "normal course of play"?

**A.** The term "normal course of play" is intended to cover all reasonable acts but specifically excludes cases of abuse.

In addition to making a stroke, practice swing or practice stroke, examples of acts that are in the "normal course of play" include the following:

- removing or replacing a club in the bag;
- using a club to search for or retrieve a ball;
- leaning on a club while waiting to play, teeing a ball or removing a ball from the hole; or
- accidentally dropping a club.

Examples of acts that are not in the "normal course of play" include the following:

- throwing a club in anger or otherwise;
- 'slamming' a club into a bag; or
- intentionally striking something (e.g., the ground or a tree) with the club other than during a stroke, practice swing or practice stroke. (Revised)

**Leaning on Club in Hazard While Waiting to Play — See 13-4/2.**

### 4-3/2 Meaning of "Repair"

**Q.** During a round, a player may repair a club damaged in the normal course of play, or he may have it repaired by someone else. What does the term "repair" mean within the context of Rule 4-3a(ii)?

**A.** The term "repair" in Rule 4-3a(ii) means to restore the club, as nearly as possible, to its condition prior to the incident which caused the damage.

### 4-3/3 Club Damaged in Normal Course of Play Breaks into Pieces When Repaired

**Q.** The shaft of a player's club is bent in the normal course of play. The player, in attempting to repair the damaged club as permitted by Rule 4-3a(ii), breaks the shaft into pieces. What is the ruling?

**A.** Since the player was entitled to repair the damaged club, the further damage to the club, which has rendered it unfit for play, is also considered to have occurred in the normal course of play. Thus, Rule 4-3a permits the player to use the club in its damaged state, repair it or have it repaired, or replace it with any club.

### 4-3/4 Modifying Penalty for Holing Short Putt with Club Whose Playing Characteristics Changed Other Than in Normal Course of Play

**Q.** A player leaves a putt about an inch short of the hole. In disgust, he hits his shoe with the head of his putter. The impact bends the neck of the putter, changing its playing characteristics. The player then holes the one-inch putt with the putter.

Rule 4-3b states in part: "If, during a stipulated round, a player's club is damaged other than in the normal course of play... changing its playing characteristics, the club must not subsequently be used or replaced during the round." The penalty for breach of Rule 4-3b is disqualification. Would the Committee be justified in waiving or modifying the disqualification penalty in these circumstances, provided the player does not subsequently use the altered putter during the round?

**A.** No.

### 4-3/5 Changing Clubs Because of Wet Grips

**Q.** May a player change clubs during a round if the grips become wet?

**A.** No. A club is "unfit for play" if it is substantially damaged, but not if the grip becomes slippery — see Note to Rule 4-3a.

### [4-3/6 Reserved]

### 4-3/7 Club Broken While Used as Cane

**Q.** A player uses one of his clubs as a cane while climbing a hill and the shaft breaks. May he replace the club during the round?

**A.** Yes. A club broken in such circumstances is considered to have become "damaged in the normal course of play" as its use as a cane is considered a reasonable act — see Decision 4-3/1. (Revised)

### 4-3/8 Player Starting with 13 Clubs Breaks Putter in Anger and Replaces It

**Q.** A player who started a round with 13 clubs broke his putter in anger, i.e., other than in the normal course of play, during the first nine holes. He bought another putter in the pro shop after the first nine holes and used it for the remainder of the round. Rule 4-3a(iii) permits replacing a club only if it becomes unfit for play in the normal course of play. Was the player subject to penalty?

**A.** No. Since he started with 13 clubs, he was entitled to add another club under Rule 4-4a.

### 4-3/9 Club Broken Due to Habit of Hitting Head of Club on Ground

**Q.** Rule 4-3a states that a club may be replaced if it becomes "damaged in the normal course of play." A player has a habit of hitting the head of his putter on the ground as he walks to the next tee, especially after missing a putt. On one occasion, after missing a short putt, the player hit the head of his putter on the ground so hard that the putter broke. The player said that he often taps the putter on the ground, and that it was not done in anger or with the intention of breaking the club. Should he be allowed to replace the club?

**A.** No. A club broken by hitting it hard on the ground or tapping it on the ground is not considered to have become "damaged in the normal course of play" as such actions are not considered reasonable acts — see Decision 4-3/1. (Revised)

### 4-3/9.5 Club Rendered Unfit for Play By Outside Agency or Opponent's Side

**Q.** After reaching the putting green, a player places his clubs near the next tee. A greenkeeper's vehicle or an opponent's golf cart accidentally strikes the player's clubs, breaking several of them. What is the ruling?

**A.** Rule 4-3 does not contemplate a situation where the player's clubs are damaged by an outside agency or opponent. Therefore, in equity (Rule 1-4), the player may use the clubs in their damaged state, repair them or have them repaired, or replace them in accordance with Rule 4-3a(iii).

### 4-3/10 Replacement of Club Lost During Round

**Q.** A player who started a round with 14 clubs lost his putter. May he replace it during the round?

**A.** No. A lost club is not one which has become unfit for play in the normal course of play — see Rule 4-3.

### 4-3/11 Replacement of Club Broken on Practice Ground While Play Suspended

**Q.** Play has been suspended by the Committee. Prior to resuming play, a player is practicing on the practice ground. While hitting a ball, the shaft of his sand wedge breaks. In such circumstances, is the club considered to have become unfit for play in the normal course of play, in which case the player would be entitled to replace the broken club under Rule 4-3a(iii)?

**A.** Yes.

## 4-3/12 Replacing Club for Stroke-Play Play-Off

**Q.** In stroke play, a competitor broke a club in anger, finished the round with 13 clubs and then learned that he would be involved in a sudden-death play-off. May the competitor replace his broken club for the play-off?

**A.** The play-off constituted a new round — see Definition of "Stipulated Round." The competitor was therefore entitled to replace his broken club.

### Another Decision relating to Rule 4-3:

**Whether Player May Use Excess Club to Replace Club Damaged in Normal Course of Play — See 4-4c/2.**

## 4-4a/1 When Club Is Considered Added

**Q.** A player finds on the first green that he has no putter and is carrying only 13 clubs. He continues play but sends his caddie back to the clubhouse. The caddie fetches one of two putters which he finds and gives it to the player. May the player then tell the caddie to take it back and fetch the other one instead?

**A.** Yes, provided he did not play a stroke with any club when the first putter was in his possession.

## 4-4a/2 Changing Clubs Between Rounds in 36-Hole Match

**Q.** In a 36-hole match, may a player who started with 14 clubs change putters after play of the first 18 holes and before the start of the second 18 holes?

**A.** Yes. Rule 4-4a prohibits such procedure only during a stipulated round. A 36-hole match comprises two stipulated rounds of 18 holes each — Definition of "Stipulated Round."

## 4-4a/3 Competitor Withdraws During Round and Puts His Clubs in Fellow-Competitor's Bag

**Q.** In stroke play, B withdrew during a round, put his clubs in A's bag, making the total number of clubs in the bag exceed 14, and carried A's bag for the remainder of the round. Should A be penalized under Rule 4-4a?

**A.** No, provided he did not use any of B's clubs.

## 4-4a/4 Partners' Clubs Carried in One Bag

**Q.** In a foursome competition, is it permissible for partners to put both sets of clubs in one golf bag, provided each player uses only his own clubs?

**A.** Yes, provided each player's clubs are clearly identifiable.

### 4-4a/5 Fellow-Competitor's Club Put in Competitor's Bag by Mistake During Round Used Unintentionally by Competitor

**Q.** In stroke play, A and B both started with 14 clubs. They were using iron clubs of the same model. At one hole, B's caddie inadvertently put one of B's clubs into A's bag. At a subsequent hole, A played a stroke with B's club by mistake. What is the ruling?

**A.** Rule 4-4a states: "The player must start a stipulated round with not more than 14 clubs. He is limited to the clubs thus selected..." A complied with the first sentence and therefore incurred no penalty for carrying B's club. However, when A played a stroke with B's club, he did not comply with the second sentence and was subject to penalty under Rule 4-4a.

### 4-4a/5.5 Player's Club Put in Another Player's Bag by Mistake During Suspension of Play

**Q.** A and B both began the stipulated round with 14 clubs. During a suspension of play, one of B's clubs was placed accidentally into A's bag. After play resumed, A noticed B's club in his (A's) bag but he did not play a stroke with B's club. What is the ruling?

**A.** Both players complied with Rule 4-4a as they began the stipulated round with not more than 14 clubs. Since A did not play a stroke with B's club, there is no penalty to either player and B may have his club returned to him — but see also Decision 4-4a/5.

### 4-4a/6 Excess Club Put in Player's Golf Bag After Player Has Counted His Clubs at 1st Tee; Error Discovered After Player Has Started Round

**Q.** A arrives at the 1st tee, counts his clubs and confirms that he is carrying 14. He then removes his driver from his golf bag, leaves the bag beside the tee and checks in with the starter. At this point, X, a player in another match or group, by mistake puts his putter in A's golf bag, which was identical to X's bag. A then drives from the 1st tee. During play of the 1st hole, A discovers that X's club has been put in his (A's) golf bag. Does A incur a penalty for starting the round with more than 14 clubs?

**A.** Yes.

### 4-4a/7 Carrying Weighted Training Club

**Q.** May a player carry a weighted training club in addition to the 14 clubs selected for the round?

**A.** No, but a weighted training club may be selected as one of 14 clubs carried by a player, provided it conforms with Rule 4-1. Rule 4 does not regulate the weight of the golf club.

## 4-4a/8 Retrieving Another Player's Lost Club

**Q.** A player carrying 14 clubs found another player's club on the course. He picked up the lost club, put it in his bag but did not use it, and handed it in at the pro shop when the round was completed. Was the player in breach of Rule 4-4a for carrying 15 clubs?

**A.** No.

## 4-4a/9 Clarification of Match-Play Penalty

**Q.** Please confirm that the following is a correct interpretation of Rule 4-4a in a match between A and B:

(1) After the 1st hole, it is discovered that B has more than 14 clubs:

    (a) If B won the hole — the match is all square.

    (b) If the hole was halved — A is 1 up.

    (c) If A won the hole — A is 2 up.

(2) After the 2nd hole, it is discovered that B has more than 14 clubs:

    (a) If B won both holes — the match is all square.

    (b) If B was 1 up — A is 1 up.

    (c) If the match was all square — A is 2 up.

    (d) If A was 1 up — A is 3 up.

    (e) If A was 2 up — A is 4 up.

(3) Later in the match, but before the players leave the last green, it is discovered that B has more than 14 clubs:

    (a) If B was more than 2 up — 2 "ups" are deducted.

    (b) If B was 2 up — the match is all square.

    (c) If B was 1 up — A is 1 up.

    (d) If the match was all square — A is 2 up.

    (e) If A was 1 up — A is 3 up.

    (f) If A was 2 up — A is 4 up.

    (g) If A was more than 2 up — 2 "ups" are added to his "ups."

**A.** As the loss of hole penalty for a breach of Rule 4-4a is not applied to a specific hole, but to the state of the match at the conclusion of the hole at which the breach is discovered, your interpretation is correct.

**Breach of 14-Club Rule Discovered After Match Concluded But Before Result Announced — See 2-5/5.5.**

### 4-4a/10 Breach of 14-Club Rule in Stroke Play Discovered at 8th Hole; Where Penalty Strokes Applied

**Q.** In stroke play, A discovers during play of the 8th hole that he has 15 clubs in his bag and thus has incurred a penalty of four strokes under Rule 4-4a. How should the four-stroke penalty be applied?

**A.** A must add penalties of two strokes to his scores for the 1st and 2nd holes.

In four-ball stroke play, both A and his partner would add penalties of two strokes to their scores for the 1st and 2nd holes — see Rule 31-3.

### 4-4a/11 Excess Club Discovered Before Player Plays from 2nd Tee But After Opponent or Fellow-Competitor Has Played

**Q.** A player starts a round with 15 clubs. He discovers his error at the 2nd tee after his opponent or a fellow-competitor has played but before he has played. Does the player incur the maximum penalty of (a) deduction of two holes in match play or (b) four strokes in stroke play?

**A.** No. Since the player has not started play of the 2nd hole, he incurs a penalty of (a) deduction of one hole in match play or (b) two strokes in stroke play.

### 4-4a/12 Competitor Who Misplaces Putter Borrows Fellow-Competitor's Putter

**Q.** In stroke play, A, who had mistakenly left his putter at the previous green, borrows a putter from B, a fellow-competitor, and uses it. At the next tee, the Committee is advised of the situation. What is the ruling?

**A.** A was not entitled to borrow a club selected for play by any other person on the course — Rule 4-4a. A incurs a penalty of two strokes for a breach of Rule 4-4a and must immediately declare B's putter out of play as prescribed in Rule 4-4c. If A recovers his own putter, he may use it.

B may have his putter returned to him and use it for the remainder of the round.

### 4-4a/13 Player Practices with Another Player's Club

**Q.** A player starts a round with 14 clubs. Between the play of two holes he borrows another player's putter and makes several practice putts on the putting green of the hole last played. What is the ruling?

**A.** There is no penalty. Such practice putting is permitted by Rule 7-2. The borrowing of the putter does not breach Rule 4-4a since the putter was not used to make a stroke that counted in the player's score. (Revised)

## 4-4a/14 Player Carries Pieces of Broken Club

**Q.** A player starts a round with 14 clubs as well as a club that had been broken into pieces prior to the start of the round, but had not yet been removed from his bag. What is the ruling?

**A.** The Rules do not contemplate such a situation. In these circumstances, in equity (Rule 1-4), there is no penalty provided the broken club is not used during the stipulated round. (New)

## 4-4b/1 Borrowing Partner's Putter

**Q.** Neither A nor B, who were partners in a four-ball match, had 14 clubs, but between them they had more than 14 clubs. Several times during the round A borrowed B's putter. Is this permissible?

**A.** No. A and B should have had two holes deducted. The penalty would be applied to the state of the match at the conclusion of the hole at which it became known that a breach had occurred.

**Whether Player May Borrow Balls from Another Player — See 5-1/5.**

**Borrowing Club for Measuring Purposes — See 20/2.**

## 4-4c/1 Excess Club Declared Out of Play Before Round and Placed on Floor of Golf Cart

**Q.** Before the start of a round, a player discovers that there are 15 clubs in his golf bag. He declares one of the clubs out of play, removes it from his bag, places it on the floor of his golf cart and begins the round. Is the player subject to penalty?

**A.** Yes, for starting the round with more than 14 clubs. Rule 4-4c has to do with declaring an excess club out of play on discovery of a breach after a round has started. There is nothing in the Rules to permit carrying, during a round, an excess club declared out of play before the round.

## 4-4c/2 Whether Player May Use Excess Club to Replace Club Damaged in Normal Course of Play

**Q.** A player begins a round with 15 clubs. On discovering his error, he applies the appropriate penalty under Rule 4-4a and declares a club out of play in accordance with Rule 4-4c. Later in the round, the player damages one of his remaining clubs in the normal course of play to the extent that it is unfit for play. May the player replace the damaged club with the excess club he declared out of play in accordance with Rule 4-4c?

**A.** Yes. Rule 4-3a(iii), which states in part that a player may replace a club that is unfit for play as a result of damage that occurred in the normal course of play "with any club" overrides Rule 4-4c, which prohibits the use of a club declared out of play as a result of a breach of Rule 4-4a or b.

# Rule 5. The Ball

### Definitions
All defined terms are in *italics* and are listed alphabetically in the Definitions section — see pages 3-11.

### 5-1. General
The ball the player uses must conform to requirements specified in Appendix III.

**Note:** The *Committee* may require, in the conditions of a competition (Rule 33-1), that the ball the player plays must be named on the current List of Conforming Golf Balls issued by the United States Golf Association.

### 5-2. Foreign Material
Foreign material must not be applied to a ball for the purpose of changing its playing characteristics.

**PENALTY FOR BREACH OF RULE 5-1 or -2: Disqualification.**

### 5-3. Ball Unfit for Play
A ball is unfit for play if it is visibly cut, cracked or out of shape. A ball is not unfit for play solely because mud or other materials adhere to it, its surface is scratched or scraped or its paint is damaged or discolored.

If a player has reason to believe his ball has become unfit for play during play of the hole being played, he may lift the ball without penalty to determine whether it is unfit.

Before lifting the ball, the player must announce his intention to his opponent in match play or his *marker* or a *fellow-competitor* in stroke play and mark the position of the ball. He may then lift and examine it provided that he gives his opponent, *marker* or *fellow-competitor* an opportunity to examine the ball and observe the lifting and replacement. The ball must not be cleaned when lifted under Rule 5-3.

If the player fails to comply with all or any part of this procedure, he incurs a penalty of one stroke.

If it is determined that the ball has become unfit for play during play of the hole being played, the player may *substitute* another ball, placing it on the spot where the original ball lay. Otherwise, the original ball must be replaced. If a player *substitutes* a ball when not permitted and he makes a *stroke* at the wrongly *substituted ball*, he incurs the general penalty for a breach of Rule 5-3, but there is no additional penalty under this Rule or Rule 15-1.

If a ball breaks into pieces as a result of a *stroke*, the *stroke* is canceled and the player must play a ball without penalty as nearly as possible at the spot from which the *original* ball was played (see Rule 20-5).

Rule 5

**\*PENALTY FOR BREACH OF RULE 5-3:**
Match play — Loss of hole; Stroke play — Two strokes.
\*If a player incurs the general penalty for breach of Rule 5-3, there is no additional penalty under this Rule.

**Note:** If the opponent, *marker* or *fellow-competitor* wishes to dispute a claim of unfitness, he must do so before the player plays another ball.

(Cleaning ball lifted from putting green or under any other Rule — see Rule 21.)

### 5-1/1  Use of Ball Not Conforming with Prescribed Specifications

**Q.** If a player unwittingly plays one stroke with a ball which does not meet the prescribed specifications, would the Committee be justified, under Rule 33-7, in waiving or modifying the disqualification penalty?

**A.** No — but see Decision 5-1/3 with regard to a provisional ball.

### 5-1/2  Condition Requiring Use of Ball on List of Conforming Golf Balls; Penalty for Breach

**Q.** If it is a condition of a competition that players must play a brand of ball on the current List of Conforming Golf Balls, may the Committee provide that the penalty for breach of the condition is loss of hole in match play or two strokes in stroke play for each hole at which a breach occurs rather than disqualification?

**A.** Yes, unless the ball obviously does not meet the prescribed specifications — see Decision 5-1/1.

### 5-1/3  Condition Requiring Use of Ball on List of Conforming Golf Balls; Ball Not on List Played as Provisional Ball

**Q.** It is a condition of the competition that players must play a brand of ball on the current List of Conforming Golf Balls. A player, believing his ball may be lost or out of bounds, plays a provisional ball. He subsequently finds his original ball and then discovers that the ball he played as his provisional ball was not on the List. What is the ruling?

**A.** The player incurs no penalty as the provisional ball was never the ball in play.

### 5-1/4  Status of an 'X-out' Ball

**Q.** 'X-out' is the common name used for a golf ball which a manufacturer considers to be imperfect and has, therefore, crossed out the brand name on the golf ball. What is the status of an 'X-out' ball?

**A.** The vast majority of 'X-out' balls are rejected for aesthetic reasons only, i.e., paint or printing errors. In the absence of strong evidence to suggest that an 'X-out' ball does not conform to the Rules, it is permissible for such a ball to be used. However, in a competition where the Committee has adopted the condition that the ball the player uses must be named on the List of Conforming Golf Balls (see Note to Rule 5-1), an 'X-out' ball may not be used, even if the ball in question (without the X's) does appear on the List.

### 5-1/5 Whether Player May Borrow Balls from Another Player

**Q.** During a stipulated round, a player runs out of balls. May he borrow one or more balls from another player?

**A.** Yes. Rule 4-4a prohibits a player from borrowing a club from another player playing on the course but the Rules do not prevent a player from borrowing other items of equipment (balls, towels, gloves, tees, etc.) from another player or an outside agency.

If the "One Ball" Condition in Appendix I is in effect, the player would need to obtain the same brand and type of ball as required by that condition.

**Borrowing Partner's Putter — See 4-4b/1.**

**Another Decision relating to Rule 5-1:**

**Golf Ball Artificially Warmed — See 14-3/13.5.**

### 5-3/1 Ball Internally Damaged

**Q.** A player hit his tee shot and expressed the view that the ball behaved erratically in flight. Before his next shot he examined the ball but he could find no external damage and the ball was not out of shape. He commented that the ball must have been damaged internally by his last stroke and claimed the right to substitute another ball under Rule 5-3. Was the player entitled to invoke Rule 5-3?

**A.** No.

### 5-3/2 Ball Declared Unfit for Play Played at Later Hole

**Q.** A player damaged his ball at a certain hole, declared it unfit for play and substituted another ball. At a subsequent hole he played the damaged ball. What is the ruling?

**A.** There is no penalty. However, the player may not again declare the ball (in the same condition) unfit for play.

### 5-3/3 Ball Not Unfit for Play Deemed Unfit

**Q.** In stroke play, a competitor, after announcing his intention of doing so, lifted his ball to check for damage, showed it to his marker and claimed that it was unfit for play. The marker disputed this claim, but the competitor insisted on substituting and playing another ball. Before completion of the hole, however, a Committee member was consulted and ruled that the ball taken out of play by the competitor was not, after all, unfit for play. What is the ruling?

**A.** The competitor should be penalized two strokes for a breach of Rule 5-3 and must hole out with the substituted ball.

In similar circumstances in match play, the player would lose the hole for a breach of Rule 5-3.

### 5-3/3.5 Player Lifts Ball on Putting Green, Throws Ball into Lake and Then Announces That Ball Is Unfit for Play

**Q.** A player mis-hits his approach shot but the ball comes to rest on the putting green. The player marks the position of his ball, inspects it and throws it into an adjacent lake from which it cannot be retrieved.

The player then announces to his opponent, marker or fellow-competitor that the ball was unfit for play and that he is substituting another ball. The player did not, as required by Rule 5-3, announce his intention in advance to his opponent in match play or his marker or a fellow-competitor in stroke play and give his opponent, marker or fellow-competitor an opportunity to examine the ball.

What is the ruling?

**A.** The player was entitled under Rule 16-1b to lift his ball without announcing his intentions. However, when he threw the ball into the lake, he deprived his opponent, marker or fellow-competitor of the opportunity to examine the ball and dispute the claim of unfitness, and he made it impossible to replace the original ball should such a dispute be resolved against him. Accordingly, he incurs a penalty of loss of hole in match play or two strokes in stroke play for a breach of Rule 5-3, but he may substitute another ball to complete the hole.

### 5-3/4 Ball Breaks into Pieces as a Result of Striking Paved Cart Path

**Q.** A player plays a stroke and the ball strikes a paved cart path. As a result of the impact with the cart path, the ball breaks into pieces. Should the ball be considered to have broken into pieces "as a result of a stroke," in which case the player must replay the stroke without penalty under the last paragraph of Rule 5-3?

**A.** Yes.

### 5-3/5 Ball Embedded in Hazard Lifted to Determine Whether Unfit for Play

**Q.** Under Rule 5-3, a ball in a hazard may be lifted to determine whether it is unfit for play. If a ball embedded in a bunker is lifted to determine whether it is unfit for play and the lie is altered in the lifting process,

Rule 20-3b seems to make it clear that the original lie must be re-created and the ball must be placed in that lie. However, if the ball is embedded in a water hazard and the lie is altered in the lifting process, it would appear that, under Rule 20-3b, the ball must be placed in the nearest lie most similar to that which it originally occupied, not more than one club-length from the original lie. Is this correct?

**A.** No. Rule 5-3 states: "If it is determined that the ball has become unfit for play during play of the hole being played, the player may substitute another ball, placing it on the spot where the original ball lay. Otherwise, the original ball must be replaced." Therefore, if a ball is embedded in a bunker or in a water hazard and Rule 5-3 is invoked, the original ball or a substituted ball must be embedded in the original lie to the extent that the original ball was embedded before Rule 5-3 was invoked. Rule 20-3b does not apply in such cases.

### 5-3/6 Ball Thought to Be Unfit for Play Lifted Under Another Rule and Cleaned; Ball Then Determined to Be Unfit for Play

**Q.** A player believes that his ball may have become unfit for play as a result of his previous stroke, but he is unable to determine whether the ball is unfit due to a large piece of mud adhering to it. He lifts his ball to take relief from an area of ground under repair. He then cleans the ball as permitted under Rule 25-1b and determines that the ball is unfit for play. Is the player subject to penalty under Rule 5-3 which prohibits cleaning the ball?

**A.** No. The player is entitled to clean the ball as provided in Rule 25-1b.

### 5-3/7 Ball Thought to Be Unfit for Play; Committee Involvement When Opponent, Marker or Fellow-Competitor Not Readily Available

**Q.** A player wishes to lift his ball to determine if it is unfit for play, but his opponent, marker or fellow-competitor is not readily available. May a referee or a member of the Committee fulfill the responsibilities of the opponent, marker or fellow-competitor in the relief procedure under Rule 5-3?

**A.** Yes. However, every effort should be made to have the opponent, marker or fellow-competitor fulfill his responsibilities under Rule 5-3. A referee or a member of the Committee should only become involved if the opponent, marker or fellow-competitor is not readily available.

The same ruling would apply if a player wishes to lift his ball for identification (Rule 12-2) or to determine if it is in a hole made by a burrowing animal (Rule 25-1) or if it is embedded (Rule 25-2).

## 5-3/8 Opponent or Fellow-Competitor Disputes Player's Claim That Ball Is Unfit for Play

**Q.** A player considers his ball unfit for play. His opponent or fellow-competitor disagrees. There is no referee or Committee member available for a ruling. In spite of the opponent's or fellow-competitor's disagreement, may the player substitute another ball?

**A.** Yes, subject to the following considerations.

In match play, if the opponent then makes a claim (Rule 2-5) and the Committee, after examination of the original ball, upholds the opponent's claim, the player would lose the hole. Otherwise, the result of the hole would stand as played.

In stroke play, the player may also play a second ball in accordance with Rule 3-3.

In either form of play, the player must ensure that the condition of the ball he considered unfit for play is preserved until the Committee examines it. Otherwise, the Committee should rule against the player and in match play the player would lose the hole and in stroke play the player incurs a penalty of two strokes.

**PLAYER'S RESPONSIBILITIES**

# Rule 6. The Player

**Definitions**
All defined terms are in *italics* and are listed alphabetically in the Definitions section — see pages 3-11.

**6-1. Rules**
The player and his *caddie* are responsible for knowing the *Rules*. During a *stipulated round*, for any breach of a *Rule* by his *caddie*, the player incurs the applicable penalty.

**6-2. Handicap**
   **a. Match Play**
Before starting a match in a handicap competition, the players should determine from one another their respective handicaps. If a player begins a match having declared a handicap higher than that to which he is entitled and this affects the number of strokes given or received, he is disqualified; otherwise, the player must play off the declared handicap.

   **b. Stroke Play**
In any round of a handicap competition, the *competitor* must ensure that his handicap is recorded on his score card before it is returned to the *Committee*. If no handicap is recorded on his score card before it is returned (Rule 6-6b), or if the recorded handicap is higher than that to which he is entitled and this affects the number of strokes received, he is disqualified from the handicap competition; otherwise, the score stands.

**Note:** It is the player's responsibility to know the holes at which handicap strokes are to be given or received.

**6-3. Time of Starting and Groups**
   **a. Time of Starting**
The player must start at the time established by the *Committee*.

   **b. Groups**
In stroke play, the *competitor* must remain throughout the round in the group arranged by the *Committee* unless the *Committee* authorizes or ratifies a change.

PENALTY FOR BREACH OF RULE 6-3: Disqualification.

(Best-ball and four-ball play — see Rules 30-3a and 31-2.)

**Note:** The *Committee* may provide in the conditions of a competition (Rule 33-1) that, if the player arrives at his starting point, ready to play, within five minutes after his starting time, in the absence of circumstances that warrant waiving the penalty of disqualification as provided in Rule 33-7, the penalty for failure to start on time is loss of the first hole in match play or two strokes at the first hole in stroke play instead of disqualification.

## 6-4. Caddie

The player may be assisted by a *caddie*, but he is limited to only one *caddie* at any one time.

PENALTY FOR BREACH OF RULE 6-4:

Match play — At the conclusion of the hole at which the breach is discovered, the state of the match is adjusted by deducting one hole for each hole at which a breach occurred; maximum deduction per round — Two holes.

Stroke play — Two strokes for each hole at which any breach occurred; maximum penalty per round—Four strokes.

Match or stroke play — In the event of a breach between the play of two holes, the penalty applies to the next hole.

A player having more than one caddie in breach of this Rule must immediately upon the discovery that a breach has occurred ensure that he has no more than one caddie at any one time during the remainder of the stipulated round. Otherwise, the player is disqualified.

Bogey and par competitions — Penalties as in match play.

Stableford competitions — see Note 2 to Rule 32-1b.

**Note:** The *Committee* may, in the conditions of a competition (Rule 33-1), prohibit the use of *caddies* or restrict a player in his choice of *caddie*.

## 6-5. Ball

The responsibility for playing the proper ball rests with the player. Each player should put an identification mark on his ball.

## 6-6. Scoring in Stroke Play

### a. Recording Scores

After each hole the *marker* should check the score with the *competitor* and record it. On completion of the round the *marker* must sign the score card and hand it to the *competitor*. If more than one *marker* records the scores, each must sign for the part for which he is responsible.

### b. Signing and Returning Score Card

After completion of the round, the *competitor* should check his score for each hole and settle any doubtful points with the *Committee*. He must ensure that the *marker* or *markers* have signed the score card, sign the score card himself and return it to the *Committee* as soon as possible.

PENALTY FOR BREACH OF RULE 6-6b: Disqualification.

### c. Alteration of Score Card
No alteration may be made on a score card after the *competitor* has returned it to the *Committee*.

### d. Wrong Score for Hole
The *competitor* is responsible for the correctness of the score recorded for each hole on his score card. If he returns a score for any hole lower than actually taken, he is disqualified. If he returns a score for any hole higher than actually taken, the score as returned stands.

**Note 1:** The *Committee* is responsible for the addition of scores and application of the handicap recorded on the score card — see Rule 33-5.

**Note 2:** In *four-ball* stroke play, see also Rules 31-4 and -7a.

## 6-7. Undue Delay; Slow Play
The player must play without undue delay and in accordance with any pace of play guidelines that the *Committee* may establish. Between completion of a hole and playing from the next *teeing ground*, the player must not unduly delay play.

PENALTY FOR BREACH OF RULE 6-7:
Match play — Loss of hole; Stroke play — Two strokes.
Bogey and par competitions — See Note 3 to Rule 32-1a.
Stableford competitions — See Note 3 to Rule 32-1b.
For subsequent offense — Disqualification.

**Note 1:** If the player unduly delays play between holes, he is delaying the play of the next hole and except for bogey, par and Stableford competitions (Rule 32), the penalty applies to that hole.

**Note 2:** For the purpose of preventing slow play, the *Committee* may, in the conditions of a competition (Rule 33-1), establish pace of play guidelines including maximum periods of time allowed to complete a *stipulated round*, a hole or a *stroke*.

In stroke play only, the *Committee* may, in such a condition, modify the penalty for a breach of this Rule as follows:

First offense — One stroke;
Second offense — Two strokes.
For subsequent offense — Disqualification.

## 6-8. Discontinuance of Play; Resumption of Play
### a. When Permitted
The player must not discontinue play unless:

(i) the *Committee* has suspended play;
(ii) he believes there is danger from lightning;

(iii) he is seeking a decision from the *Committee* on a doubtful or disputed point (see Rules 2-5 and 34-3); or

(iv) there is some other good reason such as sudden illness.

Bad weather is not of itself a good reason for discontinuing play.

If the player discontinues play without specific permission from the *Committee*, he must report to the *Committee* as soon as practicable. If he does so and the *Committee* considers his reason satisfactory, there is no penalty. Otherwise, the player is disqualified.

**Exception in match play**: Players discontinuing match play by agreement are not subject to disqualification unless by so doing the competition is delayed.

**Note**: Leaving the *course* does not of itself constitute discontinuance of play.

### b. Procedure When Play Suspended by Committee

When play is suspended by the *Committee*, if the players in a match or group are between the play of two holes, they must not resume play until the *Committee* has ordered a resumption of play. If they have started play of a hole, they may discontinue play immediately or continue play of the hole, provided they do so without delay. If the players choose to continue play of the hole, they are permitted to discontinue play before completing it. In any case, play must be discontinued after the hole is completed.

The players must resume play when the *Committee* has ordered a resumption of play.

PENALTY FOR BREACH OF RULE 6-8b: Disqualification.

**Note**: The *Committee* may provide in the conditions of a competition (Rule 33-1) that, in potentially dangerous situations, play must be discontinued immediately following a suspension of play by the *Committee*. If a player fails to discontinue play immediately, he is disqualified unless circumstances warrant waiving the penalty as provided in Rule 33-7.

### c. Lifting Ball When Play Discontinued

When a player discontinues play of a hole under Rule 6-8a, he may lift his ball without penalty only if the *Committee* has suspended play or there is a good reason to lift it. Before lifting the ball the player must mark its position. If the player discontinues play and lifts his ball without specific permission from the *Committee*, he must, when reporting to the *Committee* (Rule 6-8a), report the lifting of the ball.

If the player lifts the ball without a good reason to do so, fails to mark the position of the ball before lifting it or fails to report the lifting of the ball, he incurs a penalty of one stroke.

**d. Procedure When Play Resumed**
Play must be resumed from where it was discontinued, even if resumption occurs on a subsequent day. The player must, either before or when play is resumed, proceed as follows:

(i) If the player has lifted the ball, he must, provided he was entitled to lift it under Rule 6-8c, place a ball on the spot from which the original ball was lifted. Otherwise, the original ball must be placed on the spot from which it was lifted;

(ii) If the player entitled to lift his ball under Rule 6-8c has not done so, he may lift, clean and replace the ball, or substitute a ball on the spot from which the original ball was lifted. Before lifting the ball he must mark its position; or

(iii) If the player's ball or ball-marker is moved (including by wind or water) while play is discontinued, a ball or ball-marker must be placed on the spot from which the original ball or ball-marker was moved.

**Note:** If the spot where the ball is to be placed is impossible to determine, it must be estimated and the ball placed on the estimated spot. The provisions of Rule 20-3c do not apply.

*PENALTY FOR BREACH OF RULE 6-8c or d:
Match play — Loss of hole; Stroke play — Two strokes.
*If a player incurs the general penalty for a breach of Rule 6-8d, there is no additional penalty under Rule 6-8c.

### 6-1/1 Wrong Form of Play Used in Match-Play Event

**Q.** In a foursome match-play competition, four players begin their match on a four-ball match-play basis. The error is discovered after play of the 9th hole. What is the ruling?

**A.** It would be improper to decide any match by a form of play other than the prescribed form.

If the wrong form of play is used as a result of a Committee error, the match should be replayed. If the wrong form of play is used unintentionally by players, the match should be replayed; if, however, this would delay the competition, both sides should be disqualified unless one side concedes the match to the other — see Rules 2-4 and 6-1. If the wrong form of play is used intentionally by players, they should be disqualified — Rule 1-3.

**Wrong Form of Play Used to Decide Which Side Concedes Match — See 2-4/21.**

**Wrong Handicap Allowance Used in Match — See 6-2a/6.**

## Other Decisions relating to Rule 6-1:

**Agreement to Waive Condition** — See 1-3/7.

**Responsibility for Knowing Stipulated Round** — See 11-5/2.

### 6-2a/1 Failure to Determine Handicaps Prior to Start of Match

There is no penalty if players fail to determine one another's handicaps before starting a match. If this results in one of them not receiving a handicap stroke at a hole at which he is entitled to receive one, the hole stands as played.

### 6-2a/2 Handicap Stroke Given at Incorrect Hole in Error

**Q.** In a match between A and B, under the Handicap Stroke Table A was to receive a handicap stroke at the 9th hole. However, both A and B mistakenly believed that A should receive a handicap stroke at the 7th hole, and the match was played on this basis. Subsequently, the Committee became aware of the error. What should the Committee do?

**A.** The Committee should take no action. Since the players did not agree to deviate from the Handicap Stroke Table and did so by mistake, there was no breach of Rule 1-3. The match should stand as played. See Note under Rule 6-2.

### 6-2a/3 Handicap Stroke Wrongly Claimed at Hole; Error Discovered Before Hole Completed

**Q.** In match play, on the tee of a hole A states in error that he is to receive a handicap stroke at that hole. When A is preparing to putt, his opponent, B, recalls that A does not receive a handicap stroke. B so advises A and claims the hole on the ground that A gave wrong information. What is the ruling?

**A.** The hole should have been completed without a stroke being given to A, and with no penalty to either side. A did not give wrong information. It is up to each player to know the holes at which handicap strokes are to be given or received — see Note under Rule 6-2.

**Extra Stroke Taken by Mistake in Handicap Match; Error Discovered Several Holes Later** — See 2-5/13.

### 6-2a/4 Handicap Stroke Claimed After Hole Conceded

**Q.** In a handicap match, A holed out in 3. B, having a putt for a gross 4 and forgetting that he was entitled to a handicap stroke at the hole, conceded the hole to A. Before A or B played from the next teeing ground, B remembered that he had a handicap stroke at the last hole. What is the ruling?

**A.** A won the hole when B conceded it — Rule 2-4. It was B's responsibility to know the holes at which he received handicap strokes — see Note under Rule 6-2. Since B forgot about his handicap stroke, he must suffer the consequences.

### 6-2a/5 Wrong Handicap Used in Match by Mistake; Error Discovered After Result Officially Announced

**Q.** In a handicap match between A and B, A stated by mistake before the match began that his handicap was ten strokes, whereas in fact his handicap was nine strokes. The match was played on the basis that A's handicap was ten strokes. A won the match. The error was discovered after the result had been officially announced. What is the ruling?

**A.** The match stands as played. No claim by B could be considered unless A had known he was giving wrong information about his handicap — See Rules 2-5, 6-2a and 34-1a.

**Wrong Handicap Used Due to Committee Misinformation — See 33-1/12.**

### 6-2a/6 Wrong Handicap Allowance Used in Match

**Q.** In a handicap match-play competition, the conditions provided that, where handicaps were different, an allowance of ¾ of the difference would be used. In one match, however, the players, unaware of this condition, used the full difference, and the higher handicapped player won. How should the Committee rule?

**A.** The Committee should rule that the match stands as played. The players failed to take note of the conditions of the competition (Rule 6-1) and have only themselves to blame.

**Determination of Handicap Allowances in Four-Ball Match If One Player Unable to Compete — See 30-3a/3.**

### 6-2b/1 Wrong Handicap Used in Stroke Play by Mistake; Error Discovered After Competition Closed

**Q.** In a stroke-play competition, A believed that his handicap was ten strokes, which he recorded on his score card. In fact his handicap was nine strokes. He won the event because of the error. The result of the competition was announced and the error was then discovered.

What is the ruling?

**A.** The competition should stand as played. Under Rule 34-1b, a penalty under Rule 6-2b may not be imposed after a handicap stroke-play competition has closed unless the competitor has knowingly played off a handicap higher than that to which he was entitled.

### 6-2b/2 Wrong Handicap Knowingly Used in Stroke Play; Error Discovered After Competition Closed

**Q.** In late June, A submitted an entry form for a handicap stroke-play competition to be held on July 10 and stated therein that his handicap was seven strokes, which was his correct handicap. On July 1, A's handicap was reduced to six strokes and he was aware of the reduction.

On July 10, he played in the stroke-play competition and returned his score card with a handicap of seven strokes recorded thereon. Under the conditions for the event he should have recorded his up-to-date handicap of six strokes. After the competition was closed, it was discovered that A had played off seven, instead of six.

The Committee questioned A, and A stated that he had assumed he should play off the handicap recorded on his entry form. What should the Committee do?

**A.** A should not have assumed he should play off seven. Under Rule 34-1b, he should be disqualified for knowingly playing off a handicap higher than that to which he was entitled.

### 6-2b/2.5 Competitor Records Incorrect Handicap for Partner in Foursome Stroke-Play Competition; Error Discovered After Competition Closed

**Q.** A and B were partners in a foursome stroke-play competition. At the conclusion of the round, A recorded on the score card that his handicap was eight strokes but, mistakenly and without B's knowledge, recorded B's handicap as ten strokes, whereas B knew that his handicap was nine. The mistake affected the number of strokes received by the side, but was not discovered until after the competition had closed. What is the ruling?

**A.** The side should be disqualified for returning a score card on which B's recorded handicap was higher than that to which he was entitled and this affected the number of strokes received (Rule 6-2b). Since B knew that his handicap was nine, the fact that the competition had closed makes no difference — see Rule 34-1b(ii).

### 6-2b/3 Competitor Wins Competition with Handicap Which Was Incorrect Due to Committee Error; Error Discovered Several Days Later

**Q.** The Committee incorrectly calculated a competitor's handicap and posted it on the notice board as 17 when it should have been 16. The competitor won an 18-hole stroke-play event as a result of the error. May the Committee correct the error several days later and retract the prize?

**A.** Yes. There is no time limit on correcting such an error. Rule 34-1b is not applicable since it deals with penalties, not with Committee errors.

The competitor should not be disqualified but his net score should be increased by one stroke.

### 6-2b/3.5 Wrong Handicap Recorded on Score Card by Committee; Error Discovered Before Competition Closed

**Q.** In a stroke-play competition, the Committee issues the score cards containing the competitor's handicap in addition to his name and the date.

The Committee mistakenly records a competitor's handicap as seven instead of six and this affects the number of strokes received. The error remains unnoticed until after the card is returned, but before the competition has closed. What is the ruling?

**A.** The competitor should be disqualified under Rule 6-2b. It is the responsibility of the competitor to ensure that his correct handicap is recorded on his score card before it is returned to the Committee.

### 6-2b/4 Competitors in Foursome Competition Fail to Record Individual Handicaps on Score Card

**Q.** In a foursome stroke-play competition, partners A and B correctly calculated their combined handicap allowance and recorded it on their score card, rather than their individual handicaps.

A and B were disqualified. Was the ruling correct?

**A.** Yes. In any round of a handicap stroke-play competition, it is the responsibility of the competitor to ensure that his handicap is recorded on his score card before it is returned to the Committee (Rule 6-2b).

The word "competitor" includes his partner in a stroke-play foursome competition — see Definition of "Competitor." Therefore, the individual handicaps of A and B should have been recorded on the score card. As only the combined handicap allowance was recorded, A and B were correctly disqualified.

### 6-2b/5 Competition in Which Best Two of Four Scores Used to Determine Winner; Competitor Returns Score Card with Higher Handicap

**Q.** A handicap competition is based on the best two of four scores. In the first round, a competitor returns his score card with a handicap higher than that to which he is entitled and it affects the number of strokes received. What is the ruling?

**A.** The competitor is disqualified only from the first round of the competition and now has three rounds in which to determine his best two net scores.

**Application of Disqualification Penalty in Competition in Which Not All Scores Used to Determine Winner — See 33/8.**

## 6-3a/1 Postponement of Final Match Due to Injury of Player

If a player who reaches the final of a match-play event suffers an injury and is unable to play at the time arranged, the Committee may, with the concurrence of the opponent, postpone the match for a reasonable period. This applies in all forms of match play.

## 6-3a/1.5 Circumstances Which Warrant Waiving of Disqualification Penalty Under Rule 6-3a

**Q.** A Committee may in exceptional circumstances waive the penalty of disqualification under Rule 6-3a for failure to start on time (Rule 33-7). With reference to the following examples, what circumstances are considered exceptional such that the Committee would be justified in waiving the penalty if the player failed to start at the time established:

(1) The player gets lost on the way to the course.

(2) Heavy traffic results in the journey to the course taking longer than expected.

(3) A major accident results in the journey to the course taking longer than expected.

(4) The player's car breaks down on the way to the course.

(5) The player was present at the scene of an accident and provided medical assistance or was required to give a statement as a witness and otherwise would not have failed to start on time.

**A.** There is no hard-and-fast Rule. The proper action depends on the circumstances in each case and must be left to the judgment of the Committee.

Generally, only example (5) constitutes exceptional circumstances which might justify waiving the disqualification penalty under Rule 6-3a.

It is the player's responsibility to ensure that he allows enough time to reach the course and he must make allowances for possible delays.

## 6-3a/2 Time of Starting; All Competitors Must Be Present

**Q.** In a stroke-play competition, A, B and C were drawn by the Committee to play together starting at 9 a.m. A and B were present at the appointed time. C arrived at 9:02 a.m. after A and B had played from the teeing ground, but just in time to play in the correct order.

What is the ruling?

**A.** C is disqualified for failure to start at the time established by the Committee (Rule 6-3a) unless circumstances warrant waiving the penalty under Rule 33-7.

All competitors in a group must be present and ready to play at the time established by the Committee, in this case 9 a.m. The order of play is not relevant.

If the Committee had adopted the Note to Rule 6-3 as a condition of the competition, the five-minute period would have started at the time established by the Committee. Therefore, in this case the time started at 9 a.m. and C would incur a penalty of two strokes, rather than be subject to disqualification.

### 6-3a/2.5  Meaning of "Time of Starting"

**Q.** A player's starting time is listed on the official starting sheet as 9:00 a.m. He does not arrive at the 1st tee until 9:00:45 a.m. and claims that, as it is still 9:00 a.m., he is not late for his starting time. What is the ruling?

**A.** When a starting time is listed as 9:00 a.m., the starting time is deemed to be 9:00:00 a.m. and the player is subject to penalty under Rule 6-3a if he is not present and ready to play at 9:00:00 a.m. Therefore, the player is disqualified unless circumstances warrant waiving the penalty under Rule 33-7.

### 6-3a/3  Time of Starting; Both Players in Match are Late

**Q.** In a match-play competition with the Note to Rule 6-3 in effect, A and B were to start their match at 9 a.m. A arrives at the 1st tee at 9:01 a.m., but before B, who arrives at 9:03 a.m. What is the ruling?

**A.** If neither player had circumstances which would warrant waiving the penalty for failure to start on time, each player would incur a penalty of loss of the 1st hole (Note to Rule 6-3). Therefore, in equity (Rule 1-4), the 1st hole is deemed halved and the match would commence on the 2nd hole.

### 6-3a/4  Time of Starting; Player is Late but Group Unable to Play Due to Delay

**Q.** A player is assigned by the Committee to a group with a 9 a.m. starting time. He arrives at the first tee at 9:06 a.m. but for whatever reason (e.g., weather, slow play or a ruling) the starting time has been delayed until after he arrives (e.g., 9:10 a.m.). What is the ruling?

**A.** As the group was unable to start at the time originally established by the Committee and the player arrived before it could do so, the player is not in breach of Rule 6-3a.

## Other Decisions relating to Rule 6-3a:

**Absent Player Joins Partner After Fellow-Competitor Plays from Teeing Ground But Before Partner Plays — See 31-2/1.**

**Competitor Refuses to Start Because of Weather Conditions; Round Subsequently Canceled — See 33-2d/3.**

**Status of Starting Time Fixed by Players — See 33-3/1.**

**Player Not Present at Time of Starting; Course Closed at the Time — See 33-3/2.**

### 6-4/1 Meaning of "Specific Directions" in Definition of "Caddie"

**Q.** A and B are sharing a caddie. A asks the caddie to bring him a club. The caddie removes A's club from his bag, places both bags behind the green and walks towards A to give him his club. At that point B plays and his ball strikes one of the bags. What is the ruling?

**A.** B incurred a penalty under Rule 19-2 (Ball in Motion Deflected or Stopped by Player's Equipment).

The Definition of "Caddie" (second paragraph) provides that, when a caddie is shared by two players, the equipment he carries is deemed to belong to the player whose ball is involved in any incident (in this case, B).

The only exception to the above provision occurs when the shared caddie is acting upon the specific directions of another player. In this case, although A asked the caddie to bring him a club, he did not instruct the caddie, when complying with his request, to place the two bags in a particular position. In placing the bags where he did, therefore, the caddie was not acting on "specific directions" of A within the meaning of that term in the Definition of "Caddie." Before playing, B could have asked the caddie to move the bags if he thought his ball might strike them.

**Player's Ball Strikes Opponent's or Fellow-Competitor's Bag Left Ahead by Shared Caddie — See 19-2/8.**

### [6-4/2 Reserved]

### 6-4/2.5 Status of Individual Who Transports Player's Clubs on Motorized Golf Cart or Trolley

**Q.** During a round, a player's clubs are transported on a motorized golf cart or trolley by a friend who performs no other functions of a caddie. Is the friend considered to be the player's caddie?

**A.** Yes. By driving the cart or pulling the trolley, the friend is deemed to be carrying the player's clubs — see Definition of "Caddie."

**Breach of Transportation Condition by Caddie — See 33-1/9.5.**

### 6-4/3 Player Whose Clubs Are Transported on Motorized Golf Cart Hires Individual to Perform All Other Functions of a Caddie

**Q.** A player whose clubs are transported on a motorized golf cart hires an individual to perform all the other duties of a caddie. Is this permissible, and is the individual considered to be a caddie?

**A.** The individual is considered to be a caddie.

This arrangement is permissible provided the player has not engaged someone else to drive the cart. In such a case, the cart driver, since he is transporting the player's clubs, is also a caddie. Rule 6-4 prohibits a player from having two caddies at any one time.

Thus, the arrangement is permissible (a) if the player and an opponent or a fellow-competitor are sharing the cart, even if the player walks and the opponent or fellow-competitor drives the cart, or (b) if the cart is not being shared with an opponent or a fellow-competitor and the player drives the cart.

### 6-4/4 Caddie Hires Boy to Carry All of Player's Clubs Except Putter

**Q.** A player's caddie hires a young boy to carry all of the player's clubs except his putter, which the caddie carries. The caddie assists the player in other ways, i.e., attends the flagstick and gives advice. The young boy does not so assist. Is this permissible?

**A.** No. The player would be considered to have two caddies in contravention of Rule 6-4.

### 6-4/4.5 Another Caddie or Friend Carries Clubs While Player's Caddie Returns to Tee with Player's Glove

**Q.** A player walks from the putting green of the previous hole to the next tee with his driver while his caddie walks ahead with the clubs in order to save time. The caddie realizes he has his player's glove and gives the clubs to another player's caddie or friend to be carried while he takes the player his glove.

Did the player have two caddies in breach of Rule 6-4?

**A.** No. The casual act of someone assisting the player or his caddie in these circumstances does not constitute a breach of Rule 6-4.

### 6-4/5 Umbrella Carrier Employed in Addition to Caddie

**Q.** May a player employ both a caddie and a second person to carry his umbrella and hold it over his head (except when a stroke is being made) to protect him from the sun or rain?

**A.** Yes. The second person would be an outside agency. However, the Committee may prohibit the employment of an umbrella carrier in the conditions of the competition.

### 6-4/5.3 Additional Persons Carry Items for Player

**Q.** May a player have a caddie carry his clubs and additional persons carry other items (e.g., a rainsuit, umbrella, food and drink) for the player, but not the clubs he has selected for the round?

**A.** Yes. The additional persons would be outside agencies. However, the Committee may prohibit the use of such persons in the conditions of the competition. (New)

### 6-4/5.5 Application of Penalty When Player Has Multiple Caddies

**Q.** During play of the 1st hole a player has two caddies in breach of Rule 6-4. He does not correct his breach before holing out at the 1st hole. What is the ruling?

**A.** The player is penalized at both the 1st and 2nd holes. Since he did not correct his error prior to holing out at the 1st hole he was also in breach of Rule 6-4 between the play of two holes, which results in a penalty at the next hole. The player must immediately correct his breach and ensure that he has no more than one caddie at any one time for the remainder of the stipulated round.

In match play, the state of the match is adjusted by deducting two holes at the conclusion of the 2nd hole.

In stroke play, the player incurs a penalty of two strokes at both the 1st and 2nd holes.

### 6-4/6 Status of Carts Pulled by Double Caddie

**Q.** A and B are sharing a caddie who is pulling A's bag on one cart and B's on another. A plays a stroke and his ball strikes B's cart. With reference to the Definition of "Caddie," since B's cart was not being carried by the caddie, would it be considered B's equipment?

**A.** No. The cart is considered A's equipment in these circumstances. The word "carried" in the Definition should not be taken so literally as to exclude the pulling of a cart by a caddie.

### 6-4/7 Changing Caddies During Round

**Q.** May a player have more than one caddie during a round? If so, may each caddie give the player advice?

**A.** A player may have more than one caddie during a round, provided he has only one at a time. He is entitled to receive advice from whoever is his caddie at the time — see Definition of "Caddie."

### 6-4/8 Player in Competition Caddies for Another Player in Same Event

**Q.** Two players playing in the same competition at different times on the same day caddie for each other. Is this permissible?

**A.** Yes.

### 6-4/9 Competitor Withdraws During Round and Carries Fellow-Competitor's Clubs for Remainder of Round

**Q.** In stroke play, A, B's fellow-competitor and marker, withdrew during a round and ceased to play. He continued to mark B's card, and also carried B's clubs for the rest of the round. Is this permissible?

**A.** Yes. A became B's caddie as well as his marker when he started carrying B's clubs.

### 6-4/10 Acts Which Caddie May Perform

While the Rules do not expressly so state, the following are examples of acts which the caddie may perform for the player without the player's authority:

1. Search for the player's ball as provided in Rule 12-1.

2. Place the player's clubs in a hazard — Exception 1 under Rule 13-4.

3. Repair old hole plugs and ball marks — Rules 16-1a(vi) and -1c.

4. Remove loose impediments on the line of putt or elsewhere — Rules 16-1a and 23-1.

5. Mark the position of a ball, without lifting it — Rule 20-1.

6. Clean the player's ball — Rule 21.

7. Remove movable obstructions — Rule 24-1.

**Competitor's Caddie Practices on or Tests Putting Green Surfaces of the Course Before Stroke-Play Round — See 7-1b/5.**

**Caddie Attending Flagstick Advises Player to Aim at his Foot — See 8-2b/2.**

**Ball Thrown into Bounds by Outside Agency and Played; Caddie Aware of Action of Outside Agency — See 15/9.**

**Caddie Roughens Surface of Putting Green But Player Does Not Benefit — See 16-1d/6.**

**Caddie on Own Initiative Lifts Ball Considering It Unplayable — See 18-2a/15.**

**Caddie Lifts Ball in Water Hazard Without Player's Authority — See 26-1/9.**

## 6-6a/1  Lone Competitor Appoints Own Marker

**Q.** In a stroke-play competition, a lone competitor had no marker. No member of the Committee was present to appoint one. So the competitor played with two players playing a friendly game, and one of them served as his marker. Should the Committee accept the card?

**A.** Yes. Since the Committee failed to provide a marker, the Committee should give retrospective authority to the player who acted as the competitor's marker.

**Retrospective Appointment of Marker by Committee — See 33-1/5.**

## 6-6a/2  Competitor Plays Several Holes Without Marker

**Q.** A plays three holes by himself while his marker, B, rests. B then resumes play and marks A's scores for the holes he (A) played alone as well as his scores for the remainder of the holes. Should A's card be accepted?

**A.** No. A should have insisted on B accompanying him or have discontinued play and reported to the Committee. Since A was not accompanied by a marker for three holes, he did not have an acceptable score.

## 6-6a/3  Hole Scores Entered in Wrong Boxes; Marker Corrects Error by Altering Hole Numbers on Card

**Q.** In stroke play, a marker recorded some of the competitor's hole scores in the wrong boxes. He altered the hole numbers on the card to correct the error. Should the card be accepted?

**A.** Yes.

**Hole Scores for First Nine Holes Recorded in Boxes for Second Nine and Vice Versa — See 6-6d/3.**

## 6-6a/4  Marker Refuses to Sign Competitor's Card After Dispute Resolved in Favor of Competitor

**Q.** In stroke play, B, who was A's fellow-competitor and marker, refused to sign A's score card on the grounds that A had played outside the teeing ground at the 15th hole. A claimed that he played from within the teeing ground.

The Committee decided in favor of A. Despite the Committee's decision, B continued to refuse to sign A's card. Should B be penalized?

**A.** No. A marker is not obliged to sign a card he believes to be incorrect, notwithstanding the determination of the Committee. However, the marker must report the facts and authenticate those scores which he considers correct.

The Committee should accept certification of A's score at the 15th hole by anyone who witnessed the play of the hole. If no witness is available, the Committee should accept A's score without certification.

### 6-6a/5 Marker Attests Wrong Score Knowingly But Competitor Unaware Score Wrong

**Q.** In stroke play, a competitor returned a wrong score because his score card did not include a penalty he had incurred. The competitor was unaware that he had incurred the penalty. The competitor's marker (a fellow-competitor) was aware of the penalty but nevertheless signed the card. The facts were discovered before the result of the competition was officially announced.

The competitor is, of course, disqualified — Rule 6-6d. Is the marker also subject to disqualification?

**A.** Yes. The Committee should disqualify the marker under Rule 33-7.

**Marker Attests Wrong Score Knowingly and Competitor Aware Score Wrong — See 1-3/6.**

### 6-6a/6 Requirement That Alteration on Score Card Be Initialed

**Q.** May a Committee require that alterations made on score cards be initialed?

**A.** No. Nothing is laid down in the Rules of Golf as to how alterations should be made on a score card.

### 6-6a/7 Different Score Card Returned

**Q.** At the end of a round in stroke play, a competitor returns to the Committee a score card different from the one issued by the Committee at the start of the round (e.g., because the original score card was lost or illegible due to wet weather). The new score card contained the competitor's name and scores and was signed by both him and his marker. Should the score card be accepted?

**A.** Yes. (Revised)

### 6-6b/1 Competitor and Marker Sign Score Card in Wrong Places

There is no penalty if a marker signs the competitor's score card in the space provided for the competitor's signature, and the competitor then signs in the space provided for the marker's signature.

### 6-6b/2 Competitor Records Initials in Space Reserved for Signature

**Q.** Instead of recording his usual signature on his score card, a competitor records his initials. Has the competitor met the requirements of Rule 6-6b?

**A.** Yes.

## 6-6b/3 Competitor Fails to Sign First-Round Card; Error Discovered on Completion of Last Round

**Q.** In a 36-hole stroke-play event, it was discovered just before the results were announced that a competitor had omitted to sign his score card at the end of the first round. In all other respects the cards for both rounds were correct. Should he be disqualified?

**A.** Yes, because he was in breach of Rule 6-6b.

**Signing of Score Card in Foursome Stroke Play — See 29/6.**

**Competitor's Failure to Countersign Card Blamed on Lack of Time Provided by Committee — See 33-7/3.**

**Competitor's Failure to Countersign Card Discovered After Competition Closed — See 34-1b/2.**

## 6-6b/4 Score Cards Not Returned Promptly Due to Committee Failure to Advise Competitors Where to Return Cards

It is a duty of the Committee to inform competitors where and to whom to return their score cards. If the Committee fails to do so, and as a result some competitors delay in returning cards, a penalty of disqualification under Rule 6-6b or any other Rule would not be justified.

## 6-6b/5 Marker Not Appointed by Committee Signs Cards

**Q.** In stroke play, A and B were appointed by the Committee as markers for one another. During the round, C joined them as a spectator; from that point, C marked the cards of both A and B, signed them at the end of the round and returned them to A and B. A and B checked their respective cards, signed them and returned them to the Committee. Before the competition closed, the Committee became aware that A had not signed B's card and vice versa. What is the ruling?

**A.** Since C had not been appointed as a marker by the Committee and there were no exceptional circumstances, A and B should be disqualified under Rule 6-6b.

## 6-6b/6 Marker Disappears with Competitor's Score Card

**Q.** In a stroke-play event, competitors were instructed to return their score cards at the scoreboard. Unbeknownst to a competitor, his marker leaves the course hastily at the end of the round and does not report to the scoreboard. He takes the competitor's score card with him. What should the Committee do?

**A.** The Committee should make every effort to reach the marker. If unsuccessful, the Committee should accept certification of the score by someone else who witnessed the round, perhaps the marker's caddie or the competitor's caddie. If no one other than the marker witnessed the round, the score should be accepted without attestation by a marker.

### 6-6b/7 Score Corrected by Competitor After Marker Leaves Area in Which Card Returned

**Q.** A marker signed a competitor's score card, gave it to the competitor and left the area. The competitor discovered an error in his score for the 14th hole; the marker had recorded a 5 when, in fact, the competitor had scored 4. Without consulting the Committee, the competitor corrected the card, signed it and handed it in to the Committee. Later, the Committee heard what had happened, interviewed the competitor and his marker and established that the competitor did, in fact, score 4 at the 14th hole. Was the competitor in breach of Rule 6-6b and thus disqualified?

**A.** Yes. When the competitor altered the score card, he invalidated the attestation of his score by the marker. Therefore, he effectively returned a score card which was not signed by the marker.

If the competitor had informed the Committee, before returning his card, that he was correcting the error, he would not have been subject to penalty.

### 6-6b/8 Requirement That Score Be Entered into Computer

**Q.** May a Committee, as a condition of competition, provide that a competitor must enter his score into a computer?

**A.** No. Such a condition would modify Rule 6-6b.

However, while it is not permissible to penalize a player under the Rules of Golf for failing to enter his score into a computer, a Committee may, in order to assist in the administration of the competition, introduce a "club regulation" to this effect and provide disciplinary sanctions (e.g., ineligibility to play in the next club competition(s)) for failure to act in accordance with the regulation.

**Making Competitors Responsible for Adding Scores — See 33-1/7.**

### 6-6c/1 When Score Card Considered Returned

**Q.** Rule 6-6c prohibits alterations to the score card "after the competitor has returned it to the Committee." When is a score card considered returned?

**A.** This is a matter for the Committee to decide and it will vary depending on the nature of the competition. The Committee should designate a "scoring area" where competitors are to return their score cards (e.g., in a tent, a trailer, the golf shop, by the scoreboard, etc.). When it has done so, Rule 6-6c should be interpreted in such a way that a competitor within the "scoring area" is considered to be in the process of returning his score card. Alterations may be made on the score card even if the competitor has handed the score card to a member of the Committee. He is considered to have returned his score card when he has left the scoring area.

Alternatively, the Committee may require a competitor to return his score card by placing it in a box and thus consider it returned when it is dropped into the box, even if he has not left the scoring area.

### 6-6d/1  No Score Entered for One Hole But Total Correct

**Q.** In stroke play, A returned his score card. The Committee discovered that no score had been entered for the 17th hole; however, A's total score for the round as recorded on the card by A or his marker was correct. What is the ruling?

**A.** A should be disqualified for a breach of Rule 6-6d.

**Gross Score of Partner with Better Net Score Omitted from Card — See 31-4/1.**

### 6-6d/2  Total Score Recorded by Competitor Incorrect

**Q.** In stroke play, a competitor returns his score card to the Committee. The hole-by-hole scores are correct, but the competitor records a total score which is one stroke lower than his actual total score. Is the competitor subject to penalty?

**A.** No. The competitor is responsible only for the correctness of the score recorded for each hole — Rule 6-6d. The Committee is responsible for the addition of scores — Rule 33-5. If the competitor records a wrong total score, the Committee must correct the error, without penalty to the competitor.

### 6-6d/3  Hole Scores for First Nine Holes Recorded in Boxes for Second Nine and Vice Versa

**Q.** A competitor who started at the 10th hole returns a card with scores for the first nine holes recorded in the boxes for the second nine holes, and vice versa. Should he be disqualified since the scores for some holes were lower than actually taken?

**A.** Yes.

**Hole Scores Entered in Wrong Boxes; Marker Corrects Error by Altering Hole Numbers on Card — See 6-6a/3.**

### 6-6d/4 Competitor's Scores Recorded on Score Card with Fellow-Competitor's Name and Vice Versa

**Q.** A and B are playing together in stroke play. A is B's marker and B is A's marker. A score card is distributed to each player by the starter. When the score cards are returned, the score card with A's name printed on it contains the correct scores of B and vice versa. Each score card contains the signature of the competitor whose scores are recorded together with the signature of his marker.

The mismatch of the competitors' printed names with the reported scores is discovered after the score cards are returned. What is the ruling?

**A.** Assuming that each competitor himself has signed the score card on which his scores were recorded and that his marker has also signed this score card, the Committee should strike the name printed on the score card, enter the name of the competitor whose scores are recorded on the score card and accept the score card without penalty to either player. Administrative errors of this specific nature are not contemplated by the Rules and the Committee should correct such an error. There is no time limit for correcting such an administrative error. Rule 6-6b implies that the competitor is responsible only for the correctness of the scores recorded for each hole, ensuring that the marker has signed the score card and that the competitor has signed the score card himself.

The same principle would also apply in the case of a score card returned without a name recorded on it. (Revised)

### 6-6d/5 Spectators Allege Competitor's Score Incorrect

**Q.** All strokes played by A at the 18th hole were observed by spectators, but when the card was returned the recorded score for that hole was lower than that which the spectators alleged had been taken. What should the Committee do?

**A.** If any doubt arises as to the correctness of a card, the Committee should consult with the competitor and marker and also take into account the testimony of other witnesses.

If the evidence indicates that the recorded score for the 18th hole was lower than actually taken, the Committee should disqualify A — Rule 6-6d. Otherwise, no penalty should be applied.

**Other Decisions relating to Rule 6-6d:**

**Competitor in Four-Ball Stroke Play Records Score for Hole Not Completed — See 31-7a/1.**

**Competitor in Four-Ball Stroke Play Attributes Lower Gross Score to Wrong Partner — See 31-7a/2.**

Handicap Stableford Competition; Recording of Lower Gross Score Affects Result of Hole — See 32-2a/3.

Handicap Stableford Competition; Recording of Lower Gross Score Does Not Affect Result of Hole — See 32-2a/4.

Handicap Bogey or Par Competition; Recording of Lower Gross Score Does Not Affect Result of Hole — See 32-2a/5.

Modifying Penalty for Returning Wrong Score — See 33-7/4.

Competitor Unaware of Penalty Returns Wrong Score; Whether Waiving or Modifying Disqualification Penalty Justified — See 33-7/4.5.

Omission of Penalty Stroke When Score Returned — See 34-1b/1.

Omission of Penalty Strokes When Score Returned Is Due to Incorrect Ruling — See 34-3/1.

## 6-7/1 Player Returns to Tee to Retrieve Forgotten Club

**Q.** A player arrives at a green and discovers that he has left his putter at the tee. He returns to the tee to retrieve the putter. If this delays play, is the player subject to penalty?

**A.** Yes. Rule 6-7 (Undue Delay; Slow Play) and not Rule 6-8a (Discontinuance of Play) applies in this case.

## 6-7/2 Searching Ten Minutes for Lost Ball

**Q.** If a player searches for a lost ball for 10 minutes, is he subject to penalty under Rule 6-7 for undue delay?

**A.** Yes.

### Other Decisions relating to Rule 6-7:

Second Ball Played Despite Adverse Ruling — See 3-3/2.

Entering Clubhouse or Half-Way House for Refreshment During Round — See 6-8a/2.7.

Ascertaining Whereabouts of Opponent's Ball Before Playing — See 9-2/16.

Player Requests Another Player to Lift His Ball in Absence of Reasonable Possibility That Ball Might Interfere or Assist — See 22/3.

Removal of Large Loose Impediment Delays Play — See 23-1/2.

Player Searches for Lost Ball After Putting Another Ball into Play — See 27/9.

Committee Does Not Penalize Player in Breach of Pace of Play Condition Believing Player Had Already Lost Hole — See 34-3/2.

## 6-8a/1 Watching Television for 45 Minutes After Nine Holes

**Q.** In stroke play, a group went into the clubhouse after nine holes and watched the final round of a golf tournament on television for 45 minutes. Then the group resumed play. Should the members of the group be penalized under Rule 6-7 (Undue Delay; Slow Play) or Rule 6-8 (Discontinuance of Play)?

**A.** The competitors should be disqualified under Rule 6-8a.

### 6-8a/2  Taking Shelter While Waiting to Play

**Q.** In stroke play, a group preparing to start a hole is waiting for the group ahead to get out of range. May the group take shelter from the rain in a rain shelter close to the tee?

**A.** Yes, but the group must leave the shelter and resume play as soon as the group in front is out of range.

### 6-8a/2.5  Discontinuing Play for Refreshment

The Committee may not permit players to discontinue play for refreshment for an extended period during a stipulated round. Such a condition would modify Rule 6-8a.

The Committee may, however, in the conditions of a competition, permit players to discontinue play for a short period of time (e.g., up to five minutes), if it considers there to be good reason (e.g., a danger of dehydration or heat exhaustion in hot climates or a need to warm up in cold climates).

However, since the Rules make specific provision for players to play without undue delay (Rule 6-7) and continuously (Rule 6-8a), such a condition is not recommended.

### 6-8a/2.7  Entering Clubhouse or Half-Way House for Refreshment During Round

**Q.** May a player, between the play of two holes, enter the clubhouse or a "half-way house" to obtain a refreshment if he then proceeds immediately to the next tee and consumes the food and/or drink while continuing his round?

**A.** Yes. A player may enter the clubhouse or a half-way house without penalty (see Note to Rule 6-8a).

However, the player must not unduly delay either his own play or that of his opponent or any other competitor (Rule 6-7).

### 6-8a/3  Discontinuing Play Due to Physical Problem

**Q.** During a round, a player is incapacitated by heat exhaustion, a bee sting or because he has been struck by a golf ball. The player reports his problem to the Committee and requests the Committee to allow him some time to recuperate. Should the Committee comply with the request?

**A.** The matter is up to the Committee. Rule 6-8a(iv) permits a player to discontinue play because of sudden illness and the player incurs no penalty if he reports to the Committee as soon as practicable and the

Committee considers his reason satisfactory. It would seem reasonable for a Committee to allow a player 10 or 15 minutes to recuperate from such a physical problem but ordinarily allowing more time than that would be inadvisable.

### 6-8a/4 Discontinuing Play Due to Inoperable Motorized Cart

**Q.** In stroke play, two competitors are sharing a motorized golf cart. During the round the cart becomes inoperable. The competitors discontinue play and return to the clubhouse to obtain another cart. Should the competitors be penalized for discontinuing play?

**A.** If the competitors reported to the Committee as soon as practicable after discontinuing play (as required by Rule 6-8a), it is recommended that, since it may not always be reasonable to expect players to carry their own bags, the Committee may consider the reason for discontinuance satisfactory, in which case there would be no penalty provided the competitors resume play when directed to do so by the Committee.

### 6-8a/5 Match Discontinued by Agreement Due to Rain; One Player Subsequently Wishes to Resume; Opponent Refuses Although Course Playable

**Q.** In accordance with the Exception under Rule 6-8a, A and B discontinue a match due to rain. Subsequently, although the rain continues to fall, A wishes to resume play. B refuses because he does not want to play in the rain, not because he considers the course unplayable. What is the ruling?

**A.** B is disqualified — Rule 6-8a. The Exception to Rule 6-8a permits discontinuance of a match by mutual agreement. However, when A decided that he wanted to resume play, there was no longer an agreement and B was obliged to resume play.

### 6-8a/6 Match Discontinued by Agreement Due to Rain; One Player Subsequently Wishes to Resume; Opponent Refuses on Ground Course Unplayable

**Q.** In accordance with the Exception under Rule 6-8a, A and B discontinue a match due to rain. Subsequently, A wishes to resume play. B refuses on the ground that the course is unplayable. What is the ruling?

**A.** B is entitled to refer the dispute to a representative of the Committee if one is available within a reasonable time. If a Committee member is not available within a reasonable time, B is obliged to continue the match without delay — Rule 2-5. If B does not do so, he is disqualified under Rule 6-8a, which allows a player to discontinue play for a decision on a disputed point, but only within the limits prescribed in Rule 2-5.

However, before continuing the match B is entitled to make a claim that the course is unplayable — Rule 2-5. If B does so, (a) the match should be resumed at the spot at which it was discontinued if the Committee subsequently upholds B's claim, or (b) the match should stand as played if the Committee subsequently rejects B's claim.

**Replaying Match When Play Discontinued Instead of Resuming from Where Play Stopped — See 2-1/6.**

**Player Returns to Tee to Retrieve Forgotten Club — See 6-7/1.**

**Discontinuing Play Because Hole-Liner Not Sunk Deep Enough — See 16/4.**

**Discontinuing Play Due to Raised or Sunken Hole Plug on Line of Putt — See 16-1c/3.**

**Competitor Discontinues Play Because of Weather Conditions; Round Subsequently Canceled — See 33-2d/3.**

## 6-8b/1 Competitors Playing Hole When Play Suspended Discontinue Play Immediately But Then Complete Hole Before Committee Orders Resumption of Play

**Q.** In stroke play, a group was playing a hole when it was announced that play was suspended. The group discontinued play for 10 to 15 minutes and then decided to complete the hole, even though the Committee had not yet announced resumption of play. Is this permissible?

**A.** No. Competitors playing a hole when play is suspended may only continue play of that hole if they do so without delay — Rule 6-8b. The group in question was in breach of Rule 6-8b. The penalty is disqualification.

## 6-8b/2 Options If Play Suspended After One Competitor in Group Has Played from Tee

**Q.** In stroke play, A plays a stroke from the teeing ground and the competition is at that point suspended. May B, A's fellow-competitor, also play from the teeing ground, even though play has been suspended?

**A.** Yes. When A played from the teeing ground, play had commenced for that hole and thus A and B may continue play of the hole provided they do so without delay and then discontinue play either before or immediately after completing it.

## 6-8b/3 Completion of Hole by One Competitor in Group After Play Suspended During Play of Hole

**Q.** In stroke play, A plays a stroke from the teeing ground and play is at that point suspended. B, A's marker and fellow-competitor, decides not to play the hole until play is officially resumed. May A play alone and complete the hole?

**A.** Yes, provided B accompanies A until the hole is completed. Otherwise, A would have no marker for the hole and thus would not have an acceptable score for the round.

### 6-8b/3.5 Player Plays Out of Turn in Match Play After Play Suspended by Committee and After Opponent Discontinues Play

**Q.** In match play, A and B are opponents. They are in the process of playing a hole when play is suspended by the Committee due to darkness. A states that he does not wish to continue, but B wants to complete the hole being played. What is the ruling?

**A.** Although Rule 6-8b suggests that one of the players in the match may complete the hole (see analogous Decision 6-8b/3), the Rules contemplate that opponents will play together and have the opportunity to observe each other's play.

Therefore, when A states that he does not wish to continue the match after play has been suspended by the Committee, the players must discontinue play.

When play is discontinued in this manner, if either player continues play, Rule 6-8b prescribes a penalty of disqualification. However, in the exceptional circumstances described, if B were to continue play of the hole, a penalty of disqualification would be too severe. Accordingly, the Committee should modify the disqualification penalty to loss of the hole concerned (Rule 33-7).

### 6-8b/4 Player Unable to Resume Suspended Match at Scheduled Time

**Q.** During a match-play competition, the course becomes unplayable and play is suspended. The Committee announces that the suspended matches will be completed the next day. One player states that he is unable to play the next day. What is the ruling?

**A.** The player is disqualified under Rule 6-8b.

### 6-8b/5 Player Claiming Danger from Lightning Refuses to Resume Play When Resumption Ordered by Committee

**Q.** In a stroke-play competition, the Committee, after having suspended play because of lightning, orders play to be resumed. Must a player resume play if he considers that there is still danger from lightning?

**A.** Rule 6-8a authorizes a player to discontinue play if he considers that there is danger from lightning. This is one of the rare occasions on which the player is virtually the final judge. The safety of players is paramount, especially as there is a common natural fear of lightning. Committees should not risk exposing players to danger.

However, if the Committee has used all reasonable means to ascertain the weather prospects and has concluded that no danger from lightning exists, it has the power to order resumption of play and to disqualify under Rule 6-8b any player who refuses to comply.

### 6-8b/6 Play Suspended by Committee; Competitor Does Not Resume Play at Time Ordered by Committee

**Q.** In stroke play, the Committee suspends play. Subsequently, the Committee advises all competitors that a siren will signify resumption of play at a specific time.

A competitor in one group resumed play about two minutes before the siren sounded, because he saw a group of competitors walking down an adjacent fairway. Should the competitor be disqualified under Rule 6-8b?

**A.** No. Due to the exceptional nature of resumption of play, such minor errors are inevitable, and a penalty of disqualification is too severe. Accordingly, if the Committee has ordered a resumption of play and a competitor is no more than five minutes late (or five minutes early) in resuming play, the Committee would be justified in modifying the disqualification penalty to two strokes or, if circumstances warrant, waiving it entirely under Rule 33-7.

In this case, modifying the penalty to two strokes would be appropriate.

### 6-8b/7 Condition Requiring Immediate Discontinuance of Play; Guidelines for Waiving or Modifying Disqualification Penalty for Failure to Discontinue Play Immediately

**Q.** It is a condition of the competition (Note under Rule 6-8b) that players must discontinue play immediately following a suspension of play by the Committee in a potentially dangerous situation. In what circumstances should the Committee consider waiving or modifying the disqualification penalty under Rule 33-7?

**A.** The intent of the condition is to enable the course to be cleared as quickly as possible when a potentially dangerous situation, such as lightning, exists. A player who breaches this condition may place others at serious risk by creating the impression that no danger exists. Therefore, it is generally recommended that the penalty of disqualification should not be waived or modified and that any doubt on this matter should be resolved against the player.

However, if a player plays a stroke after play has been suspended by the sounding of a siren, the Committee must consider all of the relevant facts in determining if the player should be disqualified or if the penalty should be waived or modified.

The following are examples of Committee decisions that are justified in light of the circumstances:

After the siren has sounded:

(a) a player finished assessing his shot, selects a club and plays his stroke, taking approximately 30 seconds to do so — disqualification.

(b) a player approaches the ball and taps in a short putt, all within a few seconds — disqualification.

(c) a player, having addressed the ball, steps away momentarily, addresses the ball again and then completes his stroke within a few seconds — disqualification.

(d) a player, having addressed the ball, completes his stroke without hesitation — no penalty.

### 6-8b/8 Player Drops Ball After Play Suspended for Dangerous Situation

**Q.** It is a condition of the competition (Note under Rule 6-8b) that players must discontinue play immediately following a suspension of play by the Committee in a potentially dangerous situation. After such a suspension is signaled by the Committee, may a player proceed under a Rule by dropping a ball or determining an appropriate reference point, e.g., the nearest point of relief?

**A.** In view of the purpose of this type of suspension of play, it is recommended that all players take shelter immediately without taking such further actions. However, discontinuing play in the context of this condition means making no further strokes and, therefore, there is no penalty for taking actions such as those described.

### 6-8b/9 Resumption of Play; When Players Must Be Present

**Q.** In a stroke-play competition, A, B and C are fellow-competitors. When the group is on the 3rd fairway, the Committee suspends play. The group elects to complete play of the 3rd hole. The Committee schedules the resumption of play for 8 a.m. on the following day and the group will be the third group to play from the 4th tee when play is resumed. When is the group required to be at the 4th tee?

**A.** The group must be present at the 4th tee and ready to play when it becomes possible for the group to play. Any player not present at that time is disqualified under Rule 6-8b. (New)

**Time of Starting; All Competitors Must Be Present — See 6-3a/2.**

### Other Decisions relating to Rule 6-8b:

**Player's Club Put in Another Player's Bag by Mistake During Suspension of Play —** See 4-4a/5.5.

**Play Suspended by Committee; Player Wishes to Practice After Resumption —** See 7-2/12.

**Ball Moved Accidentally by Player During Suspension of Play —** See 18-2a/25.

**Time Permitted for Search for Lost Ball if Play Suspended During Search —** See 27/1.5.

### 6-8c/1 Explanation of "Good Reason to Lift"

When play has been suspended by the Committee under Rule 6-8a(i) and a player discontinues play of a hole, he is entitled to lift his ball without penalty. If a player discontinues play of a hole under Rule 6-8a(ii), (iii) or (iv) he is not entitled to lift his ball unless there is a "good reason" to lift it (Rule 6-8c). It is a matter for the Committee to decide in each case whether a "good reason" exists.

Generally, the ball should not be lifted unless the player is required to leave the area where his ball is located and it is likely that the ball may be moved or taken by an outside agency in his absence.

If the player lifts his ball without a "good reason" to do so, the player is penalized one stroke under Rule 6-8c, unless he was proceeding under another Rule which entitled him to lift the ball, such as Rule 16-1b.

### 6-8d/1 Resuming Play from Where It Was Discontinued; Lie Altered by Natural Causes

**Q.** Rule 6-8d states that following a discontinuance of play under Rule 6-8d, play must be resumed "from where it was discontinued" and a ball must be placed on the spot where it lay prior to the discontinuance. Does this requirement mean the player is always entitled to the lie he had prior to discontinuance?

**A.** No. The original lie or the conditions around the ball may be altered through natural causes (e.g., wind, rain and water) and the player must accept those conditions, whether they worsen or improve the lie of the ball, area of intended stance or swing or the line of play.

### 6-8d/2 Lie in Bunker Altered Prior to Resumption of Play

**Q.** After play is suspended by the Committee, a player marks the position of and lifts his ball from a bunker as permitted by Rule 6-8c. When play is resumed and the ball is to be replaced, what is the correct procedure given that the lie of the ball may have been altered by the greenkeeping staff?

**A.** If the bunker has been prepared by the greenkeeping staff, regardless of whether the ball-marker has been moved, the original lie must be recreated as nearly as possible and a ball must be placed in that lie (Rule

20-3b). The obligation to re-create the original lie is limited to what is practical in the circumstances. For example, a buried lie or footprints around the ball must be re-created whereas the player is not required to replace loose impediments or restore conditions such as washed out areas or casual water that have been eliminated by the greenkeeping staff or have changed naturally.

However, if the bunker has not been prepared by the greenkeeping staff, the player is not necessarily entitled to the lie he had prior to the discontinuance of play (see Decision 6-8d/1). The player must place a ball on the spot from which the original ball was lifted (Rule 6-8d). If the ball-marker is missing when play is resumed (e.g., moved by wind or water), and the spot where the ball is to be placed is impossible to determine, it must be estimated and the ball placed on the estimated spot — see Note to Rule 6-8d(iii) and Exception to Rule 20-3c. (Revised)

**Ball Visible from Tee Disappears or Is Moved While Play Suspended — See 6-8d/4.**

**Ball Moved by Wind or Casual Water While Play Suspended — See 18-1/11.**

**Ball-Marker Moved Off Green by Wind or Casual Water While Play Suspended — See 20-1/10.**

### 6-8d/3  Player Who Drops Ball Immediately After Committee Has Ordered Resumption of Play Subsequently Lifts Ball Under Rule 6-8d(ii)

**Q.** A player's ball lies on an immovable obstruction when play is suspended by the Committee. Immediately after the Committee orders a resumption of play and before the player makes a stroke, he takes relief from the obstruction under Rule 24-2b. Prior to playing the dropped ball, may he lift it under Rule 6-8d(ii) and either clean and replace the ball or substitute another ball?

**A.** Yes. When the player discontinued play under Rule 6-8a, he was entitled to lift his ball without penalty under Rule 6-8c. When he resumed play under Rule 6-8d, he was entitled to follow the provisions of that Rule, despite the fact that he initially proceeded under Rule 24-2b after the Committee ordered a resumption of play. Resuming play in the context of Rule 6-8d means making a stroke and, therefore, Rule 6-8d(ii) applies to the player's situation. It is not the intent of the Rules to limit the player's options under Rule 6-8d(ii) simply because he did not take relief until the Committee ordered a resumption of play (see analogous Decision 6-8b/8). (New)

### 6-8d/4  Ball Visible from Tee Disappears While Play Suspended

**Q.** A player's tee shot came to rest and was visible from the tee by all players in the match or group. At that point play was suspended. The player took cover and did not lift the ball. When play was resumed, the player's ball was missing or was found some distance from where it was seen to come to rest. What is the procedure?

**A.** As the player's ball was moved while play was suspended, the player must place a ball on the spot from which his ball was moved, without penalty (Rule 6-8d(iii)). If this spot is not determinable, it must be estimated and a ball placed on the estimated spot — see Note to Rule 6-8d(iii) and the Exception to Rule 20-3c. (Revised — Formerly 18-1/2)

# Rule 7. Practice

**Definitions**
All defined terms are in *italics* and are listed alphabetically in the Definitions section — see pages 3-11.

## 7-1. Before or Between Rounds

### a. Match Play
On any day of a match-play competition, a player may practice on the competition *course* before a round.

### b. Stroke Play
Before a round or play-off on any day of a stroke-play competition, a *competitor* must not practice on the competition *course* or test the surface of any *putting green* on the *course* by rolling a ball or roughening or scraping the surface.

When two or more rounds of a stroke-play competition are to be played over consecutive days, a *competitor* must not practice between those rounds on any competition *course* remaining to be played, or test the surface of any *putting green* on such *course* by rolling a ball or roughening or scraping the surface.

**Exception:** Practice putting or chipping on or near the first *teeing ground* before starting a round or play-off is permitted.

**PENALTY FOR BREACH OF RULE 7-1b: Disqualification.**

**Note:** The *Committee* may, in the conditions of a competition (Rule 33-1), prohibit practice on the competition *course* on any day of a match-play competition or permit practice on the competition *course* or part of the *course* (Rule 33-2c) on any day of or between rounds of a stroke-play competition.

## 7-2. During Round

A player must not make a practice *stroke* during play of a hole.

Between the play of two holes, a player must not make a practice *stroke*, except that he may practice putting or chipping on or near:

(a) the *putting green* of the hole last played,

(b) any practice *putting green*, or

(c) the *teeing ground* of the next hole to be played in the round, provided a practice *stroke* is not made from a *hazard* and does not unduly delay play (Rule 6-7).

*Strokes* made in continuing the play of a hole, the result of which has been decided, are not practice *strokes*.

**Exception:** When play has been suspended by the *Committee*, a player may, prior to resumption of play, practice (a) as provided in this Rule, (b) anywhere other than on the competition course and (c) as otherwise permitted by the *Committee*.

PENALTY FOR BREACH OF RULE 7-2:
Match play — Loss of hole; Stroke play — Two strokes.
In the event of a breach between the play of two holes, the penalty applies to the next hole.

**Note 1:** A practice swing is not a practice stroke and may be taken at any place, provided the player does not breach the *Rules*.

**Note 2:** The *Committee* may, in the conditions of a competition (Rule 33-1), prohibit:

(a) practice on or near the *putting green* of the hole last played, and

(b) rolling a ball on the *putting green* of the hole last played.

### *7-1b/1  One Practice Stroke Played on Course Before Stroke-Play Round*

**Q.** On the day of a stroke-play competition, a competitor, before starting his round, played one practice stroke from a forward tee at the first hole into an out-of-bounds area. What is the ruling?

**A.** The competitor infringed Rule 7-1b and was subject to disqualification. However, the Committee would be justified, in the circumstances, in modifying the penalty to two strokes under Rule 33-7. If the competitor played more than one such stroke, modification of the disqualification penalty would not be appropriate.

### *7-1b/2  Waiving Penalty for Practice on Course*

**Q.** A 36-hole stroke-play competition was scheduled over consecutive days. After completing his first round, a competitor who was a member of the club at which the event was being held played several more holes and thus was subject to disqualification under Rule 7-1b.

Would the Committee be justified in waiving or modifying the penalty?

**A.** No.

### *7-1b/3  Competitor Who Practices on Competition Course After Qualifying Round Subsequently Is in Play-Off on Same Day*

**Q.** After early completion of a stroke-play qualifying round for a match-play event, a competitor practiced on the competition course after the last group in the competition had teed off. After the conclusion of play, the competitor was tied for the last place in the match-play event. Such a tie was to be decided by a sudden-death play-off which was scheduled to be played immediately. Was the competitor subject to disqualification from the play-off under Rule 7-1b? If so, would the Committee have been justified in waiving the penalty under Rule 33-7?

**A.** The competitor was subject to disqualification. Waiving the penalty is not recommended in such circumstances.

### 7-1b/4 Stroke Play Over 36 Holes on Two Courses; Player Completes First Round, Practices on Same Course and Is Later in Play-Off on That Course

**Q.** Stroke play to determine the qualifiers for match play was scheduled over 36 holes on consecutive days. Eighteen holes were to be played on the East Course and 18 on the North Course. Any play-off was to be held on the East Course.

Several competitors who played their first qualifying round on the East Course wanted to play more golf. They knew that they would be in breach of Rule 7-1b if they played the North Course, so they played the East Course again.

After the second qualifying round, one of the competitors was tied for the last qualifier's place. Should he be disqualified from the play-off on the East Course under Rule 7-1b?

**A.** Yes.

### 7-1b/5 Competitor's Caddie Practices on or Tests Putting Green Surfaces of the Course Before Stroke Play Round

**Q.** In stroke play, a competitor's caddie practices on or tests the putting green surfaces of the course before the competitor tees off. Is the competitor disqualified under Rule 7-1b?

**A.** No. A competitor is responsible for the actions of his caddie only during a stipulated round (Rule 6-1). (Revised)

### 7-1b/6 Stroke Play Over 54 Holes on Consecutive Days; Second Round Canceled and Competitor Practices on Course Following Cancelation

**Q.** A 54-hole stroke-play competition was scheduled to be played on consecutive days. The second round was canceled when the course became unplayable, and the competition was reduced to 36 holes. A competitor practiced on the course on the day of the second round after that round was canceled. Was the competitor subject to disqualification for a breach of Rule 7-1b?

**A.** Yes, because the competition was scheduled to be played over consecutive days. It is irrelevant that at the time the competitor practiced the competition was no longer to be played over consecutive days.

However, the Committee may in such circumstances permit practice on the course between rounds — see Note under Rule 7-1b.

### 7-1b/7 Competitor Practices Putting on 3rd Green After Finishing Hole During First Round of 36-Hole Stroke-Play Competition

**Q.** A 36-hole stroke-play competition was scheduled to be played on one day. During the first round a competitor, having holed out at the 3rd hole, plays a practice putt on the 3rd green. Is the competitor disqualified under Rule 7-1b for practicing on the course before his second round?

**A.** No. A competitor is entitled to do anything which the Rules permit him to do during a stipulated round. Rule 7-2 permits a player between the play of two holes to practice putting or chipping on or near the putting green of the hole last played, any practice putting green or the teeing ground of the next hole to be played in the round, provided such practice stroke is not played from a hazard and does not unduly delay play (Rule 6-7).

**Competitor Practices Putting on 18th Green Immediately After Finishing First Round of Stroke-Play Competition Played Over Consecutive Days — See 7-2/8.**

**Competitor Practices Putting on 3rd Green of 9-Hole Course During 18-Hole Stroke-Play Round — See 7-2/9.**

### 7-2/1 When Practice Between Holes Permitted

**Q.** When is play of a hole completed by a player so that he may practice as permitted in Rule 7-2?

**A.**

*Match play:*

   *Singles* — When he has holed out, his next stroke has been conceded or the hole has been conceded by either player.

   *Four-ball* — When both he and his partner have holed out, their next strokes have been conceded or either side has conceded the hole.

*Stroke play:*

   *Individual* — When he has holed out.

   *Four-ball* — When both he and his partner have holed out or picked up.

   *Bogey, Par and Stableford* — When he has holed out or picked up.

### 7-2/1.5 Continuing Play of Hole in Match Play After Result of Hole Decided

**Q.** In a match between A and B, A holes out for a 4. B has played four strokes and his ball lies in a bunker. Thus, the hole has been decided. If B plays from the bunker, would the stroke be considered a practice stroke?

**A.** No. Strokes played in continuing play of a hole, the result of which has been decided, are not practice strokes — see Rule 7-2.

### 7-2/1.7  Explanation of "Strokes Played in Continuing the Play of a Hole"

**Q.** Rule 7-2 states that strokes played in continuing the play of a hole, the result of which has been decided, are not practice strokes. What is meant by "continuing the play of a hole"?

**A.** This phrase covers situations in which a player plays the remainder of the hole with one ball in play. Its interpretation is not restricted to continuing the play of the hole in accordance with the Rules and includes, for example, situations where a player plays a ball from a spot close to where his original ball went out of bounds or in the area where it was lost.

### 7-2/2  Putting on Fairway While Waiting to Play to Green

**Q.** While waiting to play to the putting green, a player dropped a ball on the fairway and struck it several times with his putter. When questioned, he stated that he was not practicing but was "killing time." What is the ruling?

**A.** The player was in breach of Rule 7-2.

**In Anger Player Hits Ball Played by Player in Following Group — See 1-4/4.**

### 7-2/3  Player Practices Putting Off Green While Waiting to Putt

**Q.** A player lifted his ball on the putting green and, while waiting for his opponent or a fellow-competitor to play, dropped his ball off the green and played a few practice putts. What is the penalty?

**A.** Under Rule 7-2 the player lost the hole in match play or incurred a penalty of two strokes in stroke play.

### 7-2/4  Hitting Plastic Ball Before Playing Ball in Play

**Q.** During play of a hole, a player plays a stroke with a plastic ball before playing his ball in play. Is he in breach of Rule 7-2?

**A.** Yes.

### 7-2/5  Hitting Practice Range Ball Back to Range

**Q.** During play of a hole, a player saw some balls from the adjoining practice range lying on the course and flicked one back to the range with his club. Is there a penalty under Rule 7-2?

**A.** In some circumstances the hitting of a practice range ball back towards the range during the play of a hole would be a breach of

Rule 7-2, but the casual flicking of a range ball, apparently only for the purpose of tidying up the course, is not a breach.

### 7-2/5.5 Player Finds Ball and Hits It to Player Who Lost It

**Q.** As A was playing the 13th hole, X, who was playing the adjoining 14th, was searching for his ball on the 13th fairway. X could not find his ball and walked off down the 14th. A then found X's ball plugged in the 13th fairway and called to him. X requested that the ball be returned to him. As X was out of throwing range, A hit the ball to him with a short iron.

In doing so, should A be considered to have played a practice stroke in contravention of Rule 7-2?

**A.** No. Since A was acting out of courtesy, there is no penalty.

### [7-2/6 Reserved]

### 7-2/7 Practice Swing Dislodges Concealed Ball

**Q.** A player makes a practice swing in the rough and dislodges a concealed ball. Is there any penalty?

**A.** No. Since the player had no intention of striking the concealed ball, his swing remained a practice swing and was not a stroke. Consequently, there is no question of his having played either a practice stroke (Rule 7-2) or a stroke with a wrong ball (Rule 15).

**Ball Moved Accidentally by Practice Swing — See 18-2a/19 and 18-2a/20.**

### 7-2/8 Competitor Practices Putting on 18th Green Immediately After Finishing First Round of Stroke-Play Competition Played Over Consecutive Days

**Q.** In a 72-hole stroke-play competition held over four consecutive days, a competitor, immediately after holing out at the 18th hole of the first round, plays a practice putt on the 18th green. Is the competitor disqualified under Rule 7-1b for practicing on the course between rounds?

**A.** No. Rule 7-2 permits practice putting or chipping on or near the putting green of the hole last played between the play of two holes. It follows that the same privilege applies immediately after completion of the last hole of the round, even though technically such practice would be between rounds, not during a round.

Rule 7-1b would apply if a competitor, after holing out at the 18th hole, left the course and later returned and played a practice putt on the 18th green.

## 7-2/9 Competitor Practices Putting on 3rd Green of 9-Hole Course During 18-Hole Stroke-Play Competition

**Q.** An 18-hole stroke-play competition is played on a 9-hole course. A competitor, having holed out at the 3rd hole, plays a practice putt on the 3rd green. Since the stipulated round requires that the competitor play the 3rd hole as the 12th hole later in the round, is the competitor penalized for practicing?

**A.** No. Rule 7-2 permits a player between the play of two holes to practice putting or chipping on or near the putting green of the hole last played.

**Penalty Strokes Incurred by Playing Ball Ruled Not to Count — See 20-7c/5.**

## 7-2/10 Match Discontinued by Agreement Cannot Be Resumed Until Three Days Later; One Player Wishes to Play on Competition Course Prior to Resumption

**Q.** In accordance with the Exception under Rule 6-8a, a match is discontinued due to fading light. The players establish that the only mutually convenient time for play to be resumed, which will not delay the competition, is three days later.

They agree to resume play at that time, but one of them wishes to take part in another competition on the course the following day. What is the ruling?

**A.** Rule 7-2 does not contemplate such a case and as it is unreasonable to prohibit a player from playing on the competition course in such circumstances, in equity (Rule 1-4), either player may play on the course at any time prior to the resumption of play.

## 7-2/11 Match Discontinued by Agreement on 13th Tee Cannot Be Resumed Until Following Day; May Players Play First 12 Holes Prior to Resuming Match

**Q.** In accordance with the Exception under Rule 6-8a, a match is discontinued at the 13th tee due to fading light. The players agree to resume the match the following afternoon. However, the next day, it is not possible for the players to resume play on the competition course at the 13th tee, due to heavy play on the course.

The players wish to play the first 12 holes and resume the match at the 13th tee. What is the ruling?

**A.** Rule 7-2 does not contemplate such a case. In equity (Rule 1-4), the players may play the first 12 holes and resume the match at the 13th tee.

### 7-2/12 Play Suspended by Committee; Player Wishes to Practice After Resumption

**Q.** In a stroke-play competition, the Committee suspends play and schedules the resumption for 8 a.m. on the following day. A player, whose group will be the third group to play from a particular tee, wishes to continue practicing on the designated practice area after play has been resumed at 8 a.m. because his group will not be able to play at that time. What is the ruling?

**A.** When play is resumed at 8 a.m., the Exception to Rule 7-2 no longer applies. Accordingly, the player is restricted to practicing in accordance with Rule 7-2.

#### Other Decisions relating to Rule 7-2:

Player Practices With Another Player's Club — See 4-4a/13.

Competitor Practices Putting on 3rd Green After Finishing Hole During First Round of 36-Hole Stroke-Play Competition — See 7-1b/7.

Player in Foursome Match Practices Putts on Previous Green After Partner Has Driven from Next Tee — See 29/3.

Player After Picking Up Drops Ball Where Partner's Ball Lies and Plays Practice Stroke — See 30-3f/7.

In Four-Ball Match Player Disqualified for Next Hole Plays That Hole; Whether Strokes Played on That Hole Were Practice Strokes — See 30-3f/8.

# Rule 8.
# Advice; Indicating Line of Play

**Definitions**
All defined terms are in *italics* and are listed alphabetically in the Definitions section — see pages 3-11

### 8-1. Advice

During a *stipulated round,* a player must not:

(a) give *advice* to anyone in the competition playing on the *course* other than his *partner,* or

(b) ask for *advice* from anyone other than his *partner* or either of their *caddies.*

### 8-2. Indicating Line of Play

#### a. Other Than on Putting Green

Except on the *putting green,* a player may have the *line of play* indicated to him by anyone, but no one may be positioned by the player on or close to the line or an extension of the line beyond the *hole* while the *stroke* is being made. Any mark placed by the player or with his knowledge to indicate the line must be removed before the *stroke* is made.

**Exception:** *Flagstick* attended or held up — see Rule 17-1.

#### b. On the Putting Green

When the player's ball is on the *putting green,* the player, his *partner* or either of their *caddies* may, before but not during the *stroke,* point out a line for putting, but in so doing the *putting green* must not be touched. A mark must not be placed anywhere to indicate a line for putting.

**PENALTY FOR BREACH OF RULE:**
Match play — Loss of hole; Stroke play — Two strokes.

**Note:** The *Committee* may, in the conditions of a team competition (Rule 33-1), permit each team to appoint one person who may give *advice* (including pointing out a line for putting) to members of that team. The *Committee* may establish conditions relating to the appointment and permitted conduct of that person, who must be identified to the *Committee* before giving *advice.*

---

### 8/1 Conditions of Team Competition Stipulate Who Is Authorized to Give Advice

**Q.** A condition of a team competition stipulates that only the Team Captain may give advice or that the person to be appointed by each team to give advice must be an amateur. Is this permitted?

**A.** Yes — see Note to Rule 8.

### 8/2 Team Captain Gives Advice While Playing

**Q.** If the Committee has adopted the Note to Rule 8 as a condition of the competition, may a Team Captain, while playing in the competition, give advice to a team mate other than his partner?

**A.** No.

**Advice Given by Team Mate in Another Group in Stroke Play — See 8-1/21.**

### 8-1/1 Seeking Information About Length of Hole

**Q.** A player asks his opponent or fellow-competitor the length of the hole about to be played. This information was not displayed on the teeing ground. Was the player in breach of Rule 8-1 which prohibits asking for advice?

**A.** No. Information as to the length of a hole is not advice within the meaning of the term in the Rules. This is factual information normally available to all players through score cards, tee signs, etc.

### 8-1/2 Exchanging Distance Information

Information regarding the distance between two objects is public information and not advice. It is therefore permissible for players to exchange information relating to the distance between two objects. For example, a player may ask anyone, including his opponent, fellow-competitor or either of their caddies, the distance between his ball and the hole. (Revised)

### 8-1/3 Asking If Distance Marker Accurate

**Q.** A player inquires of another player as to the accuracy of a 150-yard marker. Was the player in breach of Rule 8-1?

**A.** No.

### [8-1/4 Reserved]

### 8-1/5 Seeking Information on Whereabouts of Another Player's Ball

**Q.** A player preparing to play to a putting green asks a spectator to advise him how far his opponent's or fellow-competitor's ball, which is on the green, lies from the flagstick. Was the player in breach of Rule 8-1?

**A.** No.

### 8-1/6 Asking Opponent or Fellow-Competitor What Club He Used at Previous Hole

**Q.** During play of the 6th hole, A asked B what club he had used for a shot at the 4th hole. Was A in breach of Rule 8-1?

**A.** No.

### 8-1/7 After Player Has Played to Green He Asks Opponent or Fellow-Competitor What Club He Used in Playing to Green

**Q.** A plays his second shot which lands on the green. B does likewise. A then asks B what club he used for his second shot. Was A in breach of Rule 8-1?

**A.** No.

### 8-1/8 Comment About Club Selection After Stroke

**Q.** After playing a stroke, a player says: "I should have used a 5-iron." Was the player in breach of Rule 8-1?

**A.** If the statement was made casually, there was no breach. If the statement was made to another player who had a shot to play from about the same position, there was a breach.

### 8-1/9 Misleading Statement About Club Selection

**Q.** A made a statement regarding his club selection which was purposely misleading and was obviously intended to be overheard by B, who had a similar shot. What is the ruling?

**A.** A was in breach of Rule 8-1 and lost the hole in match play or incurred a two-stroke penalty in stroke play.

### 8-1/10 Looking into Another Player's Bag to Determine Club Used

**Q.** A looks into B's bag to determine which club B used for his last stroke. Is this the equivalent of asking for advice?

**A.** No. Information obtained by observation is not advice. But see also Decision 8-1/11.

### 8-1/11 Removing Towel Covering Another Player's Clubs to Determine Club Used

**Q.** Decision 8-1/10 states that it is not a breach of Rule 8-1 for A to look into B's golf bag to determine which club B used for his last stroke. Suppose a towel was covering B's clubs and A removed the towel in order to determine which club B had used, would that be a breach of Rule 8-1?

**A.** Yes. A player is prohibited from obtaining such information through a physical act.

### 8-1/12 Double Caddie Informs One Employer About Club Used by Other

**Q.** When one caddie is employed by two players, A and B, who are not partners, is it permissible for A, who is about to play, to ask the caddie which club B used for a stroke from a nearby position?

**A.** Yes. A is entitled to seek from the caddie any information the caddie might possess.

### 8-1/13 Player Giving Opponent or Fellow-Competitor Instruction During Round

**Q.** During a round a player tells an opponent or a fellow-competitor that he is overswinging. Is this giving advice in breach of Rule 8-1?

**A.** Yes.

### 8-1/14 Competitor, After Finishing Hole, Demonstrates to Fellow-Competitor How to Play Shot

**Q.** In individual stroke play, A, who had holed out, demonstrated to B, whose ball was just off the green, how he should play his chip shot. What is the ruling?

**A.** B incurred no penalty as he did not seek advice. A incurred a penalty of two strokes for giving advice to B. As both competitors had not completed the hole, the penalty would be applied to the hole being played.

### 8-1/15 Caddie Swings Club to Show Player How to Play Shot

**Q.** A player's caddie takes one of his clubs and swings it to show him how to play a certain shot. Is this permissible?

**A.** Yes, provided there is no undue delay. A player may always seek and accept advice from his caddie — Rule 8-1.

### 8-1/16 Suggesting to Competitor That He Deem His Ball Unplayable

**Q.** B's ball was lying badly. B was deliberating what action to take when A, his fellow-competitor, said: "You have no shot at all. If I were you, I would deem the ball unplayable." Was A giving advice, contrary to Rule 8-1?

**A.** Yes. A's suggestion could have influenced B "in determining his play." Thus, it constituted advice — see Definition of "Advice." It did not constitute "information on the Rules," which is not advice.

### 8-1/17 Request for Advice Made in Error to Opponent's Caddie Withdrawn Before Advice Given

**Q.** While surveying his putt, A sought advice from B's caddie, whom he mistook for his own caddie. A immediately realized his mistake and told B's caddie not to answer. The caddie said nothing. What is the ruling?

**A.** There should be no penalty.

### 8-1/18 Player Who Has Not Yet Played Seeks Advice from Player Who Has Finished Round

**Q.** May a player about to start his round seek advice as to clubs used at various holes from a player who has just finished?

**A.** Yes. Rule 8-1 applies only during the play of a round.

### 8-1/19 Advice Between Rounds in 36-Hole Match

**Q.** May a player seek advice, other than from his partner or caddie, after 18 holes in a 36-hole match?

**A.** Yes. Rule 8-1 applies only during a stipulated round. A 36-hole match consists of two 18-hole stipulated rounds — see Definition of "Stipulated Round."

### 8-1/20 Asking Advice When Play Suspended

**Q.** A is about to play the 6th hole, a par-3, when play is suspended by the Committee. Prior to the resumption of play, A asks X, who had already played the 6th, what club he used for his tee shot. Is A penalized under Rule 8-1?

**A.** No. The prohibition against giving or asking for advice applies only during a stipulated round. In this case, the stipulated round had been suspended.

### 8-1/21 Advice Given by Team Mate in Another Group in Stroke Play

**Q.** Individual and team competitions are being played concurrently in stroke play. A competitor is given advice by a team mate who is playing in another group. What is the ruling?

**A.** The team mate would be penalized two strokes.

### 8-1/22  Team Mates Playing as Fellow-Competitors Exchange Advice

**Q.** The format for a competition between two teams is as follows: Individual stroke play, with the winner being the team with the lowest aggregate score. Play is in groups of four, with two players from each team in each group.

In such an event, may two team members playing in the same group give each other advice?

**A.** No. The team mates are fellow-competitors and not partners in this type of event, which is not the same as four-ball stroke play (Rule 31-1), and they would be penalized for each breach of Rule 8-1.

### 8-1/23  Player's Team Mate in Gallery Hits Ball to Green to Show Player Whether Green Will Hold

**Q.** In a team competition, A, a member of one team, is playing against B, a member of the opposing team. X, a team mate of A, is in the gallery. X drops a ball close to A's ball and hits it to the green to show A whether or not the green will hold. What is the ruling?

**A.** In equity (Rule 1-4), if A did nothing to stop X's irregular action, he should lose the hole in view of the purpose of Rule 8-1.

### 8-1/24  Advice Given by Team Coach or Captain

**Q.** A team competition is being played, and in the conditions the Committee has not authorized captains or coaches to give advice under the Note to Rule 8. A non-playing coach or captain gives advice during a round to one of the members of his team. What is the ruling?

**A.** There is no penalty. However, the player should take action to stop this irregular procedure. If he does not do so, he should, in equity (Rule 1-4), incur a penalty of loss of hole in match play or two strokes in stroke play in view of the purpose of Rule 8-1.

**Conditions of Team Competition Stipulate Who Is Authorized to Give Advice — See 8/1.**

**Team Captain Authorized to Give Advice; Whether Advice May Be Given While Playing — See 8/2.**

**Status of Team Captain or Coach — See 33-1/11.5.**

### 8-1/25  Advice Given on Request; Penalties in Various Forms of Play

In singles match play, if A asks for advice from B, it is irrelevant whether B gives advice because A lost the hole as soon as he asked.

In a four-ball match, A and B versus C and D, if A asks for advice from C and C gives advice, A and C are disqualified for the hole. The penalties do not apply to their partners — Rule 30-3f.

In stroke play, if A asks for advice from B, a fellow-competitor, A incurs a penalty of two strokes. If B gives advice, he also incurs a penalty of two strokes.

**Penalty Strokes Incurred by Playing the Ball Ruled Not to Count — See 20-7c/5.**

**Absent Partner Gives Advice Before Joining Four-Ball Match — See 30-3a/2.**

### 8-2a/1  Club Placed on Ground to Align Feet

**Q.** A player places a club on the ground parallel to the line of play to assist him in aligning his feet properly. Is this permissible?

**A.** Yes, provided the player removes the club before playing his stroke. Otherwise, a breach of Rule 8-2a would occur.

### 8-2a/2  Object Placed Beside or Behind Ball to Indicate Line of Play

**Q.** May a player place his pipe or a club beside his ball, or an object behind his ball, to indicate the line of play and leave the object there while playing a stroke?

**A.** No. Such action would be a breach of Rule 8-2a.

### 8-2a/3  Player Places Mark to Indicate Distance for Pitch Shot

**Q.** A player who has a pitch shot places a club on the ground off his line of play to indicate the distance he would like his ball to carry and leaves the club there during the stroke. What is the ruling?

**A.** In view of the purpose of Rule 8-2a, in equity (Rule 1-4), the player incurs the general penalty of loss of hole in match play or two strokes in stroke play.

### 8-2b/1  Caddie Casts Shadow to Indicate Line of Putt

**Q.** A caddie cast his shadow on the putting green for the purpose of indicating to the player a line for putting. Is this permissible?

**A.** No. Such action is a breach of Rule 8-2b if the shadow remains in position while the stroke is being played.

### 8-2b/2  Caddie Attending Flagstick Advises Player to Aim at His Foot

**Q.** A player's ball lies on the putting green and his caddie attends the flagstick for him. The caddie suggests, before the stroke, that the player aim at the caddie's left foot. Is the player in breach of Rule 8-2b?

**A.** If the caddie had placed his foot in position for the purpose of pointing out the line for putting, the player was in breach of Rule 8-2b as soon as the caddie placed his foot in that position. The breach could not be corrected by the caddie subsequently moving his foot.

If the caddie did not initially place his foot in such a position for the purpose of pointing out the line for putting but subsequently suggested the player aim at his left foot, the player would be in breach of Rule 8-2b if the caddie did not move that foot to another position that does not indicate a line for putting prior to the stroke.

The same answer would apply if a player's partner attends the flagstick for him. (New)

### 8-2b/3 Caddie Touches Putting Green to Indicate Line of Play Before Player Chips from Off Green

**Q.** The caddie of a player who is preparing to play a chip shot from off the putting green touches the green with a club to indicate the line of play. What is the ruling?

**A.** There is no penalty. The prohibition against touching the putting green to indicate the line of play applies only if the player's ball lies on the putting green.

### 8-2b/4 Whether Team Captain Who Is Authorized to Give Advice May Be Required to Keep Off Putting Greens

**Q.** In a team competition, the Committee wishes to introduce a condition of competition permitting a team captain to give advice to members of his team, including pointing out a line for putting. However, it wishes to stipulate that he must keep off the putting greens. Is such a condition permitted?

**A.** Yes — see Note to Rule 8.

**Other Decisions relating to Rule 8-2b:**

**Ball-Marker in Position to Assist Another Player — See 20-1/11.**

**Trademark Aimed Along Line of Putt When Ball Replaced — See 20-3a/2.**

**Player Touches Putting Green in Pointing Out Line for Putting for Partner and Incidentally Touches Own Line of Putt — See 30/2.5.**

# Rule 9.
# Information as to Strokes Taken

**Definitions**
All defined terms are in *italics* and are listed alphabetically in the Definitions section — see pages 3-11.

### 9-1. General

The number of *strokes* a player has taken includes any *penalty strokes* incurred.

### 9-2. Match Play

#### a. Information as to Strokes Taken

An opponent is entitled to ascertain from the player, during the play of a hole, the number of *strokes* he has taken and, after play of a hole, the number of *strokes* taken on the hole just completed.

#### b. Wrong Information

A player must not give wrong information to his opponent. If a player gives wrong information, he loses the hole.

A player is deemed to have given wrong information if he:

(i) fails to inform his opponent as soon as practicable that he has incurred a penalty, unless (a) he was obviously proceeding under a *Rule* involving a penalty and this was observed by his opponent, or (b) he corrects the mistake before his opponent makes his next *stroke*; or

(ii) gives incorrect information during play of a hole regarding the number of *strokes* taken and does not correct the mistake before his opponent makes his next *stroke*; or

(iii) gives incorrect information regarding the number of *strokes* taken to complete a hole and this affects the opponent's understanding of the result of the hole, unless he corrects the mistake before any player makes a *stroke* from the next *teeing ground* or, in the case of the last hole of the match, before all players leave the *putting green*.

A player has given wrong information even if it is due to the failure to include a penalty that he did not know he had incurred. It is the player's responsibility to know the *Rules*.

### 9-3. Stroke Play

A *competitor* who has incurred a penalty should inform his *marker* as soon as practicable.

---

### 9/1 Incorrect Information on Rules

A player incurs no penalty for giving incorrect information on the Rules (see Definition of "Rules"); this is not wrong information as that term is used in Rule 9. It is up to each player to know the Rules (Rule 6-1). However, if it is established that a player has knowingly given incorrect information on the Rules, the Committee would be justified in imposing a penalty of disqualification under Rule 33-7.

### 9-2/1 Meaning of "As Soon as Practicable" in Rule 9-2

Rule 9-2b(i) requires a player who has incurred a penalty to inform his opponent "as soon as practicable." This phrase is purposely broad so as to allow for consideration of the circumstances in each situation, especially the proximity of the player to his opponent. Thus, informing the opponent "as soon as practicable" of a penalty incurred does not, in all circumstances, mean that the player must do so before the opponent plays his next stroke.

### 9-2/2 Incorrect Information Given by Caddie or Partner

**Q.** If incorrect information as to the number of strokes a player has taken is given to an opponent, not by the player himself, but by the player's partner or caddie, is the player liable to a penalty under Rule 9-2?

**A.** Yes, provided the error is not corrected before the opponent makes his next stroke. (Revised)

### 9-2/3 Wrong Information on Strokes Taken Given Voluntarily

**Q.** In a match between A and B, A voluntarily told B during play of a hole that he had played three strokes, whereas in fact he had played four strokes. A did not correct the error before B played his next stroke. Was A subject to penalty under Rule 9-2?

**A.** Yes. When a player gives incorrect information, it is irrelevant whether the error is contained in a response to a question from the player's opponent or in a voluntary statement by the player. Such an error must be corrected before the opponent's next stroke is made. (Revised)

### 9-2/3.5 Player Refuses to Tell Opponent How Many Strokes He Has Taken

**Q.** In a match, B asks A how many strokes he (A) has taken during play of a hole or on a hole just completed. A refuses to give B the information requested. What is the ruling?

**A.** A incurs the general penalty of loss of hole (Rule 2-6) for failing to act in accordance with the requirements of Rule 9-2a. The penalty applies to the hole being played or, if the hole has been completed, the penalty applies to the last hole played. (New)

### 9-2/4 Withholding Information on Strokes Taken Until Opponent's Turn to Play

**Q.** In a match between A and B, A asks B during play of a hole how many strokes he (B) has taken. B, whose turn it is to play, withholds

Rule 9   125

the information until he has played his next stroke. Is B subject to penalty under Rule 9-2?

**A.** No, provided B gave the information before A played his next stroke.

### 9-2/5 Incorrect Information Causes Opponent to Lift His Ball-Marker

**Q.** Rule 9-2 provides that, if during play of a hole a player gives incorrect information to the opponent and does not correct the error before the opponent makes his next stroke, the player loses the hole. During play of a hole, a player gives incorrect information to his opponent and the incorrect information results in the opponent lifting the coin marking the position of his ball. Is the lifting of the coin by the opponent the equivalent of the opponent making his next stroke?

**A.** Yes; the player loses the hole. (Revised)

### 9-2/6 Player Reporting Wrong Score Causes Opponent with Chance for Half to Pick Up Ball

**Q.** In match play, A holed out and stated to B, his opponent, that he had scored a 4. B, having played four strokes, picked up assuming he had lost the hole. A then realized that he had scored a 5. He immediately told B. What is the ruling?

**A.** A gave wrong information as to the number of strokes taken and, under the principle of Rule 9-2, A would normally lose the hole. However, since A had holed out for no worse than a half, the hole was halved — see Rule 2-2.

**Player Lifts Ball Before Holing Out; Opponent Then Picks Up His Ball and Claims Player Loses Hole — See 2-5/3.**

**In Four-Ball Match Player with Putt for Half Picks Up at Suggestion of Opponent Due to Misunderstanding — See 30/5.**

**Player's Ball Resting Against Flagstick Lifted Before Being Holed; Others in Four-Ball Match Pick Up Mistakenly Believing Player Won Hole — See 30-3f/3.**

**Wrong Information Given by Player Out of Contention in Four-Ball Match — See 30-3f/4.**

### 9-2/7 Incorrect Information Given by Player Corrected Before Opponent Makes Next Stroke But After Opponent Has Conceded Player's Putt

**Q.** In a match, A's ball was a few inches from the hole. B asked A, "How many will that be in the hole?" A answered "6," whereupon B, lying 5, conceded A's next stroke. Before B putted, A informs B that he (A) had actually scored 5. What is the ruling?

**A.** A loses the hole under Rule 9-2 for giving wrong information.

The principle of Rule 9-2 applies if, after receiving incorrect information, a player picks up his ball, concedes his opponent's next stroke or takes some similar action before the mistake is corrected.

In this case, the answer does not turn on how close A's ball was to the hole or on the fact that B could not have done any better. (Revised)

### 9-2/8 Player Wins Hole with Wrong Ball; Error Discovered at Next Hole; Opponent Claims Previous Hole

**Q.** In a match, A holed out in 3 at the 5th hole. His opponent, B, holed out in 4. After driving from the next tee, it was discovered that A had played a wrong ball at the 5th hole. B claimed the 5th hole. What is the ruling?

**A.** Since A failed to inform B as soon as practicable that he had incurred a penalty for playing a wrong ball, he is deemed to have given wrong information even though he was not aware he had incurred a penalty (Rule 9-2). Thus, B's belated claim was valid (Rule 2-5) and the Committee should have ruled that B won the 5th hole.

**Player Wins Hole with Own Ball After Playing Wrong Ball; Opponent Lodges Belated Claim — See 2-5/4.**

**Player Wins Hole with Wrong Ball and Partner Picks Up; Error Discovered at Next Hole — See 30-3d/2.**

**Players on Opposite Sides Exchange Balls During Play of Hole and Their Partners Pick Up; Error Discovered at Next Hole — See 30-3d/3.**

**Player Plays Partner's Ball; Error Discovered After Opponents Have Played Next Strokes — See 30-3d/3.5.**

### 9-2/9 Player Reports Wrong Score for Hole; Error Discovered Several Holes Later

**Q.** In match play, after completion of a hole, A inadvertently reports to B, his opponent, that he scored a 5, whereas in fact he scored a 6. This results in the hole being halved or won by A. A realizes his mistake several holes later. What is the ruling?

**A.** In either case, A loses the hole and the state of the match must be adjusted accordingly (Rule 9-2).

### 9-2/10 Player Omits Penalty Stroke When Advising Opponent as to Score for Hole; Error Discovered After Match Conceded by Opponent

**Q.** In a match, A and B were all square after 18 holes and were playing the 19th hole. A incurred a penalty stroke but was unaware of that fact. A holed out and told B that he had scored a 6. B played his sixth shot, missed the hole and conceded the match to A.

When returning to the clubhouse, A learned that he had incurred a penalty stroke and that his score had been 7, not 6. B claimed the match on the ground that A gave wrong information. What is the ruling?

**A.** B's claim was valid since the result had not been announced — see Rule 2-5. A lost the hole for giving wrong information, even though he may not have been aware that he had incurred a penalty — Rule 9-2.

**Player Concedes Match After Winning It When Opponent Lodges Invalid Claim Regarding Strokes Taken — See 2-4/15.**

**Player Wins Match; Breach of 14-Club Rule Discovered Before Result Announced — See 2-5/5.**

**Winner of Match Due to Wrong Information by Opponent Makes No Claim and Loses in Extra Holes — See 2-5/7.**

### 9-2/11 Opponent's Misreading of Number on Player's Ball Results in Agreement That Player Lost Hole

**Q.** In a match, A and B are playing the same brand of ball (Brand X). The identification number on A's ball is "3" and A's name is imprinted on his ball. The identification number on B's ball is "5."

On completion of the 2nd hole, which A won, B picks up both balls and says, "Both 5's — which is yours?" A states that he was playing a "3" and therefore he must have played a wrong ball. A and B agree that A lost the hole for playing a wrong ball.

B wins the match and then discovers he has in his possession a Brand X ball with the identification number "3" and A's name imprinted on it. A and B conclude that B misread the number at the 2nd hole. Did B give A wrong information?

**A.** No. Wrong information as the term is used in Rule 9 refers to the number of strokes taken.

The agreement of A and B that A lost the 2nd hole must stand and the match must stand as played. It would have been advisable for A to inspect the two balls at the 2nd hole.

### 9-2/12 Conscious Failure to Correct Opponent's Misunderstanding of State of Match; What Constitutes Wrong Information

**Q.** In a match, B is 1 up on A playing the 14th hole. A and B take 6's at the 14th hole, but B, assuming A scored a 5, says: "We are now all square." A says nothing although he knows that both have scored 6 and he is still 1 down.

At the end of the 17th hole, B, believing he is 2 down, concedes the match, although in fact he is only 1 down. Is A subject to penalty under Rule 9-2 for giving wrong information?

**A.** No. Rule 9-2 deals with giving wrong information as to the number of strokes taken at a hole and would include acquiescence by the player (whether oral or tacit) in a misstatement by his opponent of the number of strokes taken by the player. Wrong information does not include acquiescence by the player in a misstatement by his opponent of the result of a hole or the state of the match.

However, A's conscious failure to correct B's misunderstanding of the state of the match is so contrary to the spirit of the game that the Committee should disqualify A under Rule 33-7 and reinstate B.

### 9-2/13 Player Who Told Opponent He Would Proceed Under Water Hazard Rule Changes Mind After Opponent Plays

**Q.** In a match, B hit his tee shot short of a water hazard and A hit his into the hazard. Before B played his second shot he asked A what he was going to do. A said he was going to drop out and take a one-stroke penalty. B then played his second shot, after which A changed his mind and played his ball out of the hazard. Did A give wrong information, contrary to Rule 9-2?

**A.** No. A could have refused to answer B's question or replied that he would await B's play before deciding his own tactics. The fact that A did tell B what he planned to do does not preclude A from changing his mind.

### 9-2/14 Incorrect Information Causes Opponent Mistakenly to Think He Has Putt for Half; Opponent Holes Putt and Then Error Discovered

**Q.** In a match between A and B, A's ball was a few inches from the hole. B conceded A's next stroke and then asked, "How many strokes did you take?" A answered, "6." B, lying 5, then holed a putt for a 6 and assumed that he had halved the hole. At that point, A told B that he (A) had actually scored 5. The Committee ruled that A won the hole. Was this correct?

**A.** Yes. The hole was over when A's putt was conceded and he had won the hole with a 5. Since A corrected the error before either player played from the next tee, no penalty was incurred — see Rule 9-2. (Revised)

### 9-2/15 Wrong Information After Play of Hole; When Penalty Applicable

**Q.** Decision 9-2/14 implies that, if A had not corrected the error before playing from the next tee, he would have lost the hole under Rule 9-2. However, it would seem that A would not incur a penalty because he won the hole, and therefore the incorrect information did not affect the result of the hole. Which answer is correct?

**A.** There is a penalty for giving incorrect information after play of a hole that is not corrected before play from the next teeing ground unless the incorrect information does not affect the opponent's understanding of the result of the hole just completed. Incorrect information would not affect the opponent's understanding of the result of the hole in the following circumstances: A and B are playing a match. After play of a hole, A states that he scored 5 and B states that he (B) scored 7. After teeing off at the next hole, A states that he was incorrect in saying that he scored 5 and that, in fact, he scored 6.

In Decision 9-2/14, the incorrect information caused B to believe that the hole in question had been halved, when in fact B lost the hole. Accordingly, if A had not corrected the error before playing from the next tee, under Rule 9-2 the hole would have been awarded to B. (Revised)

## 9-2/16 Ascertaining Whereabouts of Opponent's Ball Before Playing

**Q.** In a match, B's tee shot may be lost, out of bounds or in a water hazard. In view of the wording in Rule 9-2a, under which an opponent is entitled to ascertain from the player the number of strokes he has taken, may A go forward to determine the status of B's ball before he (A) plays from the tee?

**A.** No. A would be in breach of Rule 6-7 (Undue Delay; Slow Play) if he did so. A player may make such a determination only if it can be done without unduly delaying play.

### Another Decision relating to Rule 9-2:

**In Foursome Match Side Drives for Three Holes in Wrong Order and Then Claim Is Made —
See 29-2/2.**

## 9-3/1 Competitor in Sudden-Death Play-Off Gives Wrong Information

**Q.** In a stroke play sudden-death play-off, B has completed the hole in 5 strokes. A, who has a putt for a 5, inquires as to B's score for the hole, and B wrongly states that he (B) has holed out in 4 strokes. A picks up his ball without marking its position. B then corrects his mistake. What is the ruling?

**A.** B incurs no penalty. Rule 9 imposes no penalty for giving wrong information as to the number of strokes taken in stroke play.

A incurs a penalty of one stroke under Rule 20-1 for lifting his ball at rest without marking its position. Since this leaves A with a putt for a 6, he loses the play-off.

**ORDER OF PLAY**

# Rule 10. Order of Play

**Definitions**
All defined terms are in *italics* and are listed alphabetically in the Definitions section — see pages 3-11.

### 10-1. Match Play

#### a. When Starting Play of Hole

The *side* that has the *honor* at the first *teeing ground* is determined by the order of the draw. In the absence of a draw, the *honor* should be decided by lot.

The *side* that wins a hole takes the *honor* at the next *teeing ground*. If a hole has been halved, the *side* that had the *honor* at the previous *teeing ground* retains it.

#### b. During Play of Hole

After both players have started play of the hole, the ball farther from the *hole* is played first. If the balls are equidistant from the *hole* or their positions relative to the *hole* are not determinable, the ball to be played first should be decided by lot.

**Exception:** Rule 30-3c (*best-ball* and *four-ball* match play).

**Note:** When the original ball is not to be played as it lies and the player is required to play a ball as nearly as possible at the spot from which the original ball was last played (see Rule 20-5), the order of play is determined by the spot from which the previous *stroke* was made. When a ball may be played from a spot other than where the previous *stroke* was made, the order of play is determined by the position where the original ball came to rest.

#### c. Playing Out of Turn

If a player plays when his opponent should have played, there is no penalty, but the opponent may immediately require the player to cancel the *stroke* so made and, in correct order, play a ball as nearly as possible at the spot from which the original ball was last played (see Rule 20-5).

### 10-2. Stroke Play

#### a. When Starting Play of Hole

The *competitor* who has the *honor* at the first *teeing ground* is determined by the order of the draw. In the absence of a draw, the *honor* should be decided by lot.

The *competitor* with the lowest score at a hole takes the *honor* at the next *teeing ground*. The *competitor* with the second lowest score plays next and so on. If two or more *competitors* have the same score at a hole, they play from the next *teeing ground* in the same order as at the previous *teeing ground*.

#### b. During Play of Hole

After the *competitors* have started play of the hole, the ball farthest from the *hole* is played first. If two or more balls are equidistant from the *hole* or their positions relative to the *hole* are not determinable, the ball to be played first should be decided by lot.

**Exceptions:** Rules 22 (ball assisting or interfering with play) and 31-5 (*four-ball* stroke play).

**Note:** When the original ball is not to be played as it lies and the player is required to play a ball as nearly as possible at the spot from which the original ball was last played (see Rule 20-5), the order of play is determined by the spot from which the previous *stroke* was made. When a ball may be played from a spot other than where the previous *stroke* was made, the order of play is determined by the position where the original ball came to rest.

### c. Playing Out of Turn

If a *competitor* plays out of turn, there is no penalty and the ball is played as it lies. If, however, the *Committee* determines that *competitors* have agreed to play out of turn to give one of them an advantage, they are disqualified.

(Playing stroke while another ball in motion after stroke from putting green — see Rule 16-1f.)

(Incorrect order of play in threesomes and foursomes stroke play — see Rule 29-3.)

### 10-3. Provisional Ball or Second Ball from Teeing Ground

If a player plays a *provisional ball* or a second ball from a *teeing ground*, he must do so after his opponent or *fellow-competitor* has played his first *stroke*. If a player plays a *provisional ball* or a second ball out of turn, Rule 10-1c or -2c applies.

## 10/1 *Order of Play When Two Balls Lie in Ground Under Repair and Both Players Take Relief*

**Q.** A and B hit their balls into ground under repair. The balls are approximately 18 inches apart. A's ball is farther from the hole. Both players decide to take relief. Is the order of play for the next shot determined by the relative positions of the balls before relief is taken, or after?

**A.** The order of play is determined by the relative positions of the balls before relief is taken. A should play before B — see Note to Rules 10-1b and -2b.

## 10/2 *Order of Play When Two Balls Lie in Lateral Water Hazard and Both Players Take Relief*

**Q.** A and B hit their balls into a lateral water hazard. The balls are approximately 18 inches apart. A's ball is farther from the hole but B's ball last crossed the hazard margin farther from the hole than A's ball. Both players decide to take relief from the hazard. What is the proper procedure?

**A.** Since A's ball lies farther from the hole, under the Note to Rule 10-1b or -2b A should play before B.

### 10/3 Order of Play When Two Balls Are Lost in Lateral Water Hazard

**Q.** A and B hit their balls into the same general area of a lateral water hazard. Both balls are lost in the hazard and therefore it is not known which ball is farther from the hole. However, B's ball last crossed the hazard margin farther from the hole than A's ball. What is the proper procedure?

**A.** The ball to be played first should be decided by lot, just as would be the case if the balls were equidistant from the hole — see Rules 10-1b and -2b.

### 10/4 Order of Play for Provisional Ball Other Than from Teeing Ground

**Q.** In a match between A and B, A hits his approach shot towards an area of trees. As the ball might be lost outside a water hazard, he announces to B that he intends to play a provisional ball. What is the order of play for A's provisional ball?

**A.** Except when playing a provisional ball from the teeing ground (Rule 10-3), the order of play for a provisional ball is for the player playing the provisional ball to do so immediately. Therefore, A would play his provisional ball before B's next stroke.

If A allows B to play before he (A) states his intention to play a provisional ball, A has abandoned his right to recall B's stroke under Rule 10-1c, but he may still play the provisional ball. (New)

### 10-1a/1 Determination of Honor in Handicap Match

**Q.** A and B are playing a match on a handicap basis. B has the honor at the 1st hole.

Both players score 5's at the 1st hole but A receives a handicap stroke and therefore has a net 4. Does A take the honor at the 2nd hole?

**A.** Yes. See Rules 2-1 and 10-1a.

### 10-1a/2 Determination of Honor at Hole Following Disputed Hole

**Q.** A dispute arises in a match between A and B, and A lodges a claim. A and B agree to continue the match and get a ruling later. Which player has the honor at the next hole?

**A.** In equity (Rule 1-4), the honor should be decided by lot, except that, if A's claim was to gain a half, B would retain the honor if he had it at the previous hole.

**Other Decisions relating to Rule 10-1a:**

**Players Agree Not to Tee Off in Prescribed Order to Save Time — See 1-3/1.**

**Determination of Honor in Four-Ball Match in Which Points Awarded for Both Better-Ball and Aggregate Scores** — See 30/3.

## 10-1b/1 Procedure for Referee in Determining Ball Farther from Hole

**Q.** In a match, A's ball is on one side of the fairway and B's ball is on the other side. Both balls are about 100 yards from the hole. A plays and B questions whether A played out of turn. Is the referee obliged to pace off the distances to the hole to resolve the question?

**A.** No. In view of the distances involved, the referee would be justified in resolving the question by eye. If he could not do so, he would be justified in deciding by lot which player should have played first. If it was decided by lot that B should have played first, B would have the option of recalling A's stroke under Rule 10-1c.

### Other Decisions relating to Rule 10-1b:

**Player Who Walks Off Green Under Mistaken Impression Partner Halved Hole Returns and Putts for Half** — See 30/5.

**Waiving Turn to Putt in Four-Ball Match** — See 30-3c/2.

## 10-1c/1 Request for Player to Replay Stroke Withdrawn After Opponent Plays

**Q.** In a match between A and B, A played his tee shot out of turn. B requested A to abandon the ball and play in the correct order. However, after B played, he told A not to bother playing another ball. What is the ruling?

**A.** A was not obliged to comply with B's instruction to continue with the original ball. B incurred no penalty for giving the instruction.

Whether A continued with his original ball or played another ball in correct order as was his right, the result of the hole should stand as played.

## 10-1c/2 Player Requested to Lift Ball Due to Interference Plays Out of Turn Instead

**Q.** In match play, A's ball is on B's line of putt. B requests A to lift his ball under Rule 22-2. Instead of complying with the request, A putts out of turn. Does A lose the hole for a breach of Rule 22-2 or does Rule 10-1c apply, in which case there would be no penalty but B would have the right to require A to replay the stroke in correct order?

**A.** Rule 10-1c governs.

### Other Decisions relating to Rule 10-1c:

**Player Plays Out of Turn in Match Play After Play Suspended by Committee and After Opponent Discontinues Play** — See 6-8b/3.5.

**Player Smoothes Irregularities in Bunker After Playing Out of Turn; Opponent Then Recalls Stroke and Player Must Drop Ball in Smoothed Area** — See 13-4/39.

**Player Wishing to Render Original Ball Lost Plays Provisional Ball Out of Turn** — See 27-2b/1.

**In Four-Ball Match Side Plays Out of Turn from Tee; Opponents Require One Member of Side to Replay But Not Other** — See 30-1/1.

**Player Plays Out of Turn from Tee in Three-Ball Match; One Opponent Requests Replay and Other Does Not** — See 30-2/1.

### *10-2a/1 Determination of Honor in Handicap Stroke Play*

**Q.** In a stroke-play competition on a handicap basis, the handicap is deducted at the end of the round and not at individual holes. In such a competition, how is the honor determined?

**A.** According to gross scores.

**Determination of Honor in Handicap Stableford Competition** — See 32-1/3.

### *10-2b/1 Competitor Objects to Fellow-Competitor Putting Out of Turn*

**Q.** In stroke play, A's ball is 40 feet from the hole and B's is 30 feet away. A putts and his ball comes to rest four feet from the hole. A prepares to hole out before B putts. B objects and claims that under the Rules (Rule 10-2b) he is entitled to putt before A.

Although putting out of turn in stroke play is generally condoned, should the Committee allow A to putt out of turn in these circumstances?

**A.** If A had lifted his ball when the objection was lodged, the Committee should rule that A is not entitled to putt out of turn, in view of Rule 10-2b.

If A had not lifted his ball at the time the objection was lodged, the answer depends on whether B would require A to lift his ball under Rule 22 (Ball Interfering with or Assisting Play) before he (B) putts. If so, the Committee should rule that A is entitled to play out of turn, provided he does so without first lifting his ball, i.e., Rule 22-2 permits a competitor in stroke play who is required to lift his ball because of interference to "play first rather than lift."

If B would not require A to lift his ball before he (B) putts, the Committee should rule that A is not entitled to putt out of turn.

Although condoning putting out of turn in stroke play may be questionable in view of the explicit language of Rule 10-2b, there is no penalty for doing so (Rule 10-2c), it is not in conflict with the intent of Rule 10-2b, and it may tend to speed play.

Accordingly, it is considered that the practice should not be discouraged.

### Other Decisions relating to Rule 10-2b:

Waiving Turn to Play in Four-Ball Stroke Play — See 31-5/1.

Extent to Which Side May Play in Order It Considers Best — See 31-5/2.

### *10-2c/1 Ball Played Out of Turn from Tee Abandoned and Another Ball Played in Proper Order*

**Q.** In stroke play, a competitor played out of turn from the teeing ground and, although he should have continued play with the ball played out of turn without penalty, he abandoned the ball and played another ball in proper order. What is the ruling?

**A.** When the competitor played another ball from the tee, the original ball was lost and the other ball was in play under penalty of stroke and distance — see Decision 27/17.

### *10-2c/2 Competitors in Stroke Play Agree to Play Out of Turn But Not for Purpose of Giving One of Them an Advantage*

**Q.** In stroke play, A and B agree to play out of turn at the 10th hole to save time. There is no penalty under Rule 10-2c because they did not do so in order to give one of them an advantage. However, are they liable to disqualification under Rule 1-3 for agreeing to exclude the operation of Rule 10-2a or 10-2b as the case may be?

**A.** No. Rule 10-2c specifically governs and permits the procedure in stroke play. Accordingly, Rule 1-3 does not apply. As to match play, see Decision 1-3/1.

### Decision relating to Rule 10-3:

Player With Honor Plays from Outside Teeing Ground; Order of Play if Opponent Requires Player to Cancel Stroke — See 11-4a/1.

**TEEING GROUND**

# Rule 11. Teeing Ground

**Definitions**
All defined terms are in *italics* and are listed alphabetically in the Definitions section — see pages 3-11.

## 11-1. Teeing

When the player's ball is to be teed within the *teeing ground*, it must be placed on:

- the surface of the *teeing ground* including an irregularity of surface (whether or not created by the player), or
- a *tee* placed in or on the surface of the *teeing ground*, or
- sand or other natural substance placed on the surface of the *teeing ground*.

A player may stand outside the *teeing ground* to play a ball within it.

In teeing, if a player uses a non-conforming *tee* or any other object to raise the ball off the ground, he is disqualified.

## 11-2. Tee-Markers

Before a player makes his first *stroke* with any ball on the *teeing ground* of the hole being played, the tee-markers are deemed to be fixed. In these circumstances, if the player moves or allows to be moved a tee-marker for the purpose of avoiding interference with his *stance*, the area of his intended swing or his *line of play*, he incurs the penalty for a breach of Rule 13-2.

## 11-3. Ball Falling Off Tee

If a ball, when not *in play*, falls off a *tee* or is knocked off a *tee* by the player in *addressing* it, it may be re-teed without penalty. However, if a *stroke* is made at the ball in these circumstances, whether the ball is moving or not, the *stroke* counts but there is no penalty.

## 11-4. Playing from Outside Teeing Ground

### a. Match Play

If a player, when starting a hole, plays a ball from outside the *teeing ground* there is no penalty, but the opponent may immediately require the player to cancel the *stroke* and play a ball from within the *teeing ground*.

### b. Stroke Play

If a *competitor*, when starting a hole, plays a ball from outside the *teeing ground*, he incurs a penalty of two strokes and must then play a ball from within the *teeing ground*.

If the *competitor* plays a *stroke* from the next *teeing ground* without first correcting his mistake or, in the case of the last hole of the round, leaves the *putting green* without first declaring his intention to correct his mistake, he is disqualified.

The *stroke* from outside the *teeing ground* and any subsequent *strokes* by the *competitor* on the hole prior to his correction of the mistake do not count in his score.

### 11-5. Playing from Wrong Teeing Ground
The provisions of Rule 11-4 apply.

**Decisions relating to Rule 11-1:**

**Player Who Misses Tee Shot Presses Down Irregularities Before Next Stroke — See 13-2/2.**

**Breaking Off Grass Behind Ball on Teeing Ground — See 13-2/3.**

**Breaking Branch Interfering with Backswing on Teeing Ground — See 13-2/14.**

**Standing on Mat on Teeing Ground — See 13-3/1.**

**Player Who Misses Tee Shot Tees Ball Lower Before Playing Next Stroke — See 18-2a/1.**

**Teed Ball Missed Then Hit Out of Bounds — See 20-5/1.**

**Casual Water Covering Teeing Ground — See 25-1b/4.**

**Mixed Foursome in Which Different Tees Used by Men and Women; Tee Shot Out of Bounds — See 29/2.**

### 11-2/1 Status of Tee-Markers After First Stroke

**Q.** Under Rule 11-2, tee-markers are deemed to be fixed when playing the first stroke with any ball from the teeing ground. Are tee-markers obstructions thereafter?

**A.** Yes.

### 11-2/2 Tee-Marker Moved by Player

Rule 11-2 states that before a player plays his first stroke with any ball from the teeing ground, the tee-markers are deemed to be fixed. Thereafter, Decision 11-2/1 clarifies that they are obstructions and if movable, may be moved (see Definition of "Obstruction").

In view of the fact that tee-markers are initially fixed, and when moved can have a significant effect on the competition, the following are examples of the appropriate ruling in various circumstances. In all cases a moved tee-marker should be replaced. In some cases, the replacement of the tee-marker may affect the penalty to the player.

(a) A player moves a tee-marker before playing his first stroke with any ball from the teeing ground because the tee-marker interferes with the lie of the ball, his stance or his area of intended swing — loss of hole in match play or two strokes in stroke play for breach of Rule 13-2.

(b) A player moves a tee-marker before or after playing a stroke from the teeing ground because, in his view, the tee-markers are too close together, too far back, aimed in the wrong direction or some similar reason — disqualification under Rule 33-7, unless the tee-marker is replaced before the player or any other player plays from the teeing ground, in which case the penalty is modified to loss of hole in match play or two strokes in stroke play.

(c) A player moves a tee-marker before or after playing a stroke from the teeing ground as a result of falling over the marker — no penalty and the tee-marker should be replaced.

(d) A player moves a tee-marker before or after playing a stroke from the teeing ground as a result of intentionally kicking it or striking it with a club — no penalty and the tee-marker should be replaced.

(e) A player lifts a tee-marker before or after playing a stroke from the teeing ground for no apparent reason and without authority under the Rules — no penalty and the tee-marker should be replaced.

### 11-3/1 Stroke Misses Ball; Ball Then Accidentally Knocked Off Tee

**Q.** A player teed his ball within the teeing ground. He made a stroke at the ball but missed it. He addressed the ball again and accidentally knocked it off the tee. What is the ruling?

**A.** When the player made a stroke at the ball, it was in play and Rule 11-3 no longer applied. When the ball in play moved after it was addressed, the player incurred a penalty stroke and was obliged to replace the ball (Rule 18-2b).

**Ball Falling Off Tee When Stroke Just Touches It Is Picked Up and Re-Teed — See 18-2a/2.**

### [11-3/2 Reserved]

### 11-3/3 Original Ball Out of Bounds; Ball Played Under Stroke-and-Distance Procedure Falls Off Tee at Address

**Q.** A player played his original ball out of bounds from the teeing ground. Under Rule 27-1, he teed up another ball. When addressing the ball, he touched it and it fell off the tee. What is the ruling?

**A.** There is no penalty, because a teed ball is not in play until a stroke has been made at it (see Definition of "Ball in Play"). The ball may be re-teed (Rule 11-3).

### 11-4a/1 Player With Honor Plays from Outside Teeing Ground; Order of Play if Opponent Requires Player to Cancel Stroke

**Q.** In match play, the player with the honor plays from outside the teeing ground. His opponent immediately requires the player to cancel his stroke in accordance with Rule 11-4a. Does the player retain the honor?

**A.** Yes. The player's next stroke from the tee is not considered a second ball as the term is used in Rule 10-3.

#### Other Decisions relating to Rule 11-4a:

Ball Played Out of Bounds from Wrong Teeing Ground not Recalled — See 11-5/3.

Ball Played from Outside Teeing Ground in Foursome Match — See 29-1/1.

### [11-4b/1 Reserved]

### 11-4b/2 Competitors Estimate Area of Teeing Ground When One Tee-Marker Missing

**Q.** In stroke play, competitors in a group, finding one tee-marker missing from a teeing ground, determine for themselves the area of the teeing ground based on the position of the remaining tee-marker and the shape of the tee. What is the ruling?

**A.** The correct procedure is to discontinue play until the Committee resolves the problem.

However, if the Committee is satisfied that the competitors did not gain an advantage by playing from the place they judged to be the teeing ground, it would be appropriate for the Committee, in equity (Rule 1-4), to accept their scores, without penalty. Otherwise, they incur the penalty prescribed in Rule 11-4b.

### 11-4b/3 Competitors Determine Spot from Which to Play from Tee When Both Tee-Markers Are Missing

**Q.** In stroke play, the competitors in a group, finding no tee-markers on a particular hole, determine for themselves the spot from which to begin play on the hole, and tee off. What is the ruling?

**A.** It would be appropriate for the Committee to accept without penalty the scores of the competitors in question if there was evidence as to where the tee-markers were intended to be and the competitors determined the teeing ground from such evidence and played from within such teeing ground. Sufficient evidence might include spots of paint established to show where the tee-markers were to be installed or, if the tee-markers were removed during a round, depressions or other marks on the ground indicating where the tee-markers had been located.

In the absence of such evidence, the competitors should be disqualified under Rule 11-4b unless, before playing from the next tee, they discontinue play, get the Committee to establish tee-markers and replay the hole from within the established teeing ground. Any competitor so replaying would incur a penalty of two strokes — Rule 11-4b.

*[11-4b/4  Reserved]*

*[11-4b/5  Reserved]*

### 11-4b/6  Ball Played from Outside Teeing Ground Goes Out of Bounds

**Q.** In stroke play, A played from outside the teeing ground and his ball came to rest out of bounds. He played another ball from within the teeing ground. Is he penalized stroke and distance under Rule 27-1, as well as two strokes under Rule 11-4b?

**A.** No. A is penalized only two strokes under Rule 11-4b. The ball played from outside the teeing ground was not in play. Therefore, the fact that it came to rest out of bounds was irrelevant and the stroke itself did not count.

**Competitor Plays from Outside Teeing Ground in Foursome Stroke Play; Partner Replays Stroke — See 29-1/2.**

### 11-5/1  Explanation of "Next Teeing Ground" When Competitors Have Played from Wrong Teeing Ground

**Q.** In stroke play, two competitors, having completed the 11th hole, played from the 15th tee, completed the hole and played from the 16th tee. Before playing their second shots they realized their mistake, returned to the 12th tee and completed the round. On reporting the incident the competitors were each penalized two strokes, as the Committee interpreted the "next teeing ground" referred to in Rule 11-4b to be that of the 12th hole. Was this correct?

**A.** No. When the competitors played from the 16th tee, they had played from the "next teeing ground" and could not correct their error. Therefore, they should have been disqualified.

### 11-5/2  Use of Wrong Teeing Ground Attributable to Committee Failure to Indicate Hole Numbers on Teeing Ground

**Q.** In a stroke-play competition, the Committee failed to place a sign at each teeing ground indicating the hole number. As a result, a group which had just finished the 4th hole played from the teeing ground of the 12th hole, rather than the 5th hole. Should the members of the group be penalized under Rule 11-4b in the circumstance?

**A.** Yes.

The Committee was remiss in not placing a sign at each teeing ground. However, each player is responsible for knowing the stipulated round, this being one of the conditions of the competition.

## 11-5/3 Ball Played Out of Bounds from Wrong Teeing Ground Not Recalled

**Q.** A played B in a match. A drove out of bounds from the wrong teeing ground. B did not recall the stroke. What is the ruling?

**A.** As A played from the wrong teeing ground and B did not require him to cancel the stroke and play a ball from within the correct teeing ground, A's ball has been put into play (See Definition of "Ball in Play").

Therefore, under Rule 27-1 A must drop a ball, under penalty of one stroke, as nearly as possible at the spot from which the original ball was played, i.e., on the wrong teeing ground. He could not tee the ball because the original ball was not played from the teeing ground of the hole being played (Rule 20-5).

**Ball Played from Outside Teeing Ground in Foursome Match — See 29-1/1.**

## 11-5/4 Ball Played From Wrong Teeing Ground in Stroke Play; Error Corrected

**Q.** In stroke play, after finishing the 10th hole, A and B played from the teeing ground of the 15th hole instead of the 11th hole. They realized their error before completing the 15th hole, returned to the 11th tee and completed the round. What is the ruling?

**A.** A and B each incurred a penalty of two strokes under Rule 11-4b. They were correct in discontinuing play at the 15th hole and returning to the 11th hole. Strokes played at the 15th hole, when it was played out of order, did not count.

## 11-5/5 Ball Played from Teeing Ground of Hole to Be Played Later in Round Lifted; Ball Replaced at Spot from Which Lifted and Played Out When That Hole Subsequently Reached

**Q.** In stroke play, after playing the 8th hole, A, by mistake, played from the teeing ground of the 18th hole, instead of the 9th hole. A marked the position of the ball, lifted it and played from the teeing ground of the 9th hole. He added a two-stroke penalty to his score for the 9th hole under Rule 11-4b for playing from the wrong teeing ground, i.e., playing from the 18th tee. A played the holes from the 10th to the 17th. He then replaced his ball at the spot on the 18th hole from which he had lifted it, played out the hole and returned his score card. Did A proceed correctly?

**A.** No. A should have disregarded the original stroke played from the 18th tee and replayed from that tee after completion of the 17th hole. In failing to do so, A did not play the stipulated round — see Definition of "Stipulated Round" — and thus did not have an acceptable score.

## PLAYING THE BALL

# Rule 12. Searching for and Identifying Ball

**Definitions**
All defined terms are in *italics* and are listed alphabetically in the Definitions section — see pages 3-11.

### 12-1. Searching for Ball; Seeing Ball

In searching for his ball anywhere on the *course*, the player may touch or bend long grass, rushes, bushes, whins, heather or the like, but only to the extent necessary to find and identify it, provided that this does not improve the lie of the ball, the area of his intended *stance* or swing or his *line of play*.

A player is not necessarily entitled to see his ball when making a *stroke*.

In a *hazard*, if a ball is believed to be covered by *loose impediments* or sand, the player may remove by probing or raking with a club or otherwise, as many *loose impediments* or as much sand as will enable him to see a part of the ball. If an excess is removed, there is no penalty and the ball must be re-covered so that only a part of the ball is visible. If the ball is *moved* during the removal, there is no penalty; the ball must be replaced and, if necessary, re-covered. As to removal of *loose impediments* outside a *hazard*, see Rule 23.

If a ball lying in an *abnormal ground condition* is accidentally *moved* during search, there is no penalty; the ball must be replaced, unless the player elects to proceed under Rule 25-1b. If the player replaces the ball, he may still proceed under Rule 25-1b if applicable.

If a ball is believed to be lying in water in a *water hazard*, the player may probe for it with a club or otherwise. If the ball is *moved* in probing, it must be replaced, unless the player elects to proceed under Rule 26-1. There is no penalty for causing the ball to *move* provided the movement of the ball was directly attributable to the specific act of probing. Otherwise, the player incurs a *penalty stroke* under Rule 18-2a.

PENALTY FOR BREACH OF RULE 12-1:
Match play — Loss of hole; Stroke play — Two strokes.

### 12-2. Identifying Ball

The responsibility for playing the proper ball rests with the player. Each player should put an identification mark on his ball.

Except in a *hazard*, if a player has reason to believe a ball is his, he may lift the ball without penalty to identify it.

Before lifting the ball, the player must announce his intention to his opponent in match play or his *marker* or a *fellow-competitor* in stroke play and mark the position of the ball. He may then lift the ball and identify it provided that he gives his opponent, *marker* or *fellow-competitor* an opportunity to observe the lifting and replacement. The ball must not be cleaned beyond the extent necessary for identification when lifted under Rule 12-2. If the player fails to comply with all or any part of this procedure, or if he lifts his ball for identification in a *hazard*, he incurs a penalty of one stroke.

If the lifted ball is the player's ball he must replace it. If he fails to do so, he incurs the general penalty for a breach of Rule 12-2, but there is no additional penalty under this Rule.

*PENALTY FOR BREACH OF RULE 12-2:
Match play — Loss of hole; Stroke play — Two strokes.
*If a player incurs the general penalty for a breach of Rule 12-2, there is no additional penalty under this Rule.

### 12-1/1  Searching with Clubhead for Ball Covered by Sand in Bunker

**Q.** If a ball is covered by sand in a bunker, may a clubhead be used in searching?

**A.** Yes.

### 12-1/2  Ball Covered by Sand in Bunker Removed from Buried Lie During Search

**Q.** A ball buried in sand in a bunker is removed from the buried lie during search. The player replaces and re-covers it as required by Rule 12-1, third paragraph. May the player then remove as much sand as will enable him to see a part of the ball?

**A.** Yes.

### 12-1/3  Top of Ball in Hazard Covered by Leaves But Part of Ball Visible from Another Angle

**Q.** The top of a ball in a hazard is covered by leaves so that it is not visible when the player addresses it. However, a portion of the ball is visible from another angle. Is it permissible for the player to remove enough leaves to see the ball when addressing it?

**A.** No. A player is entitled to remove loose impediments covering a ball in a hazard only if the ball is not visible from any angle.

### 12-1/4  Player Touches Ground in Hazard When Searching for Ball Believed to Be Covered by Loose Impediments in Hazard

**Q.** A player's ball is believed to be in a bunker covered by leaves. The player probes for the ball with a club which touches the ground in the bunker. What is the ruling?

**A.** There is no penalty. Rule 12-1 specifically authorizes touching ground in the hazard while probing. Such permission overrides any prohibitions in Rule 13-4.

### 12-1/5 Player Kicks Ball While Probing for It in Water in Water Hazard

**Q.** A player is probing for his ball in the water in a water hazard and accidentally kicks the ball which is in fact lying in long grass on the bank within the hazard. What is the ruling?

**A.** As the movement of the ball was not directly attributable to the specific act of probing for the ball, the player incurs a penalty stroke under Rule 18-2a for moving his ball in play. The player may replace the ball and play it or, under an additional penalty of one stroke, proceed under Rule 26-1. If the player proceeds under Rule 26-1, he is not required to replace the ball. (Revised)

**Ball Accidentally Kicked by Player Asked to Lift It Due to Interference — See 20-1/13.**

### 12-2/1 Identifying Ball by Brand and Number Only

**Q.** In the area in which his ball presumably came to rest, a player finds a ball of the same brand and identification number as the ball he is playing. The player assumes it is his ball, even though it does not carry an identification mark as suggested in Rule 12-2, and plays it. Should the player be considered to have played a wrong ball?

**A.** No, unless (1) there is reasonable evidence that, because of the ball's condition, it is not the player's ball or (2) subsequently it is established that another ball of the same brand and identification number was lying in the area at the time the player played and either ball, from a condition standpoint, could be the player's ball.

**Player Unable to Distinguish His Ball from Another Ball — See 27/10.**

**Provisional Ball Not Distinguishable from Original Ball — See 27/11.**

**Identification of Ball Through Testimony of Spectator — See 27/12.**

**Refusal to Identify Ball — See 27/13.**

### 12-2/2 Touching and Rotating Half-Buried Ball in Rough for Identification Purposes

**Q.** A ball is half buried in the rough. Having announced his intention in advance to his opponent, marker or fellow-competitor, the player, for the purpose of identifying the ball, touches the ball and rotates it. By so doing he identifies the ball as his ball. Is there a penalty?

**A.** Yes, for touching the ball other than as provided for in the Rules — Rule 18-2a. Under Rules 12-2 and 20-1, a ball may be lifted (or touched and rotated) for identification purposes after its position has been marked. If the player had marked the position of the ball before rotating it, there would have been no penalty, assuming the rotating did not result in the ball being cleaned beyond the extent necessary to identify it.

## 12-2/3 Touching and Rotating Half-Buried Ball in Hazard for Identification Purposes

**Q.** A ball is half buried in a water hazard and is not identifiable. Having announced his intention in advance to his opponent, marker or fellow-competitor, the player touches the ball and rotates it. By so doing he is able to identify the ball as his ball. Is such procedure permissible?

**A.** No. Neither Rule 12-2 nor any other Rule permits a player to touch his ball in a hazard for identification purposes. Accordingly, the player was in breach of Rule 18-2a for touching his ball purposely and incurred a penalty of one stroke.

**Two Balls Lie Together in Hazard and Neither Is Identifiable — See 1-4/6.**

**Caddie on Own Initiative Lifts Ball for Identification — See 18-2a/14.**

**Ball Dislodged from Tree for Identification Purposes by Shaking Tree or Throwing Club — See 18-2a/27.**

**Position of Ball Lifted for Identification Not Marked, Intention to Lift Not Announced and Ball Cleaned Beyond Extent Necessary to Identify It — See 21/4.**

**Ball in Tree Identified But Not Retrieved — See 27/14.**

**Ball in Tree Visible But Not Identifiable — See 27/15.**

## Rule 13. Ball Played as It Lies

**Definitions**
All defined terms are in *italics* and are listed alphabetically in the Definitions section — see pages 3-11.

### 13-1. General

The ball must be played as it lies, except as otherwise provided in the *Rules*.

(Ball at rest *moved* — see Rule 18.)

### 13-2. Improving Lie, Area of Intended Stance or Swing or Line of Play

A player must not improve or allow to be improved:

- the position or lie of his ball,
- the area of his intended *stance* or swing,
- his *line of play* or a reasonable extension of that line beyond the *hole*, or
- the area in which he is to drop or place a ball,

by any of the following actions:

- moving, bending or breaking anything growing or fixed (including immovable *obstructions* and objects defining *out of bounds*),
- creating or eliminating irregularities of surface,
- removing or pressing down sand, loose soil, replaced divots or other cut turf placed in position, or
- removing dew, frost or water.

However, the player incurs no penalty if the action occurs:

- in fairly taking his *stance*,
- in making a *stroke* or the backward movement of his club for a *stroke* and the *stroke* is made,
- on the *teeing ground* in creating or eliminating irregularities of surface (Rule 11-1), or
- on the *putting green* in removing sand and loose soil or in repairing damage (Rule 16-1).

The club may be grounded only lightly and must not be pressed on the ground.

**Exception:** Ball in *hazard* — see Rule 13-4.

### 13-3. Building Stance

A player is entitled to place his feet firmly in taking his *stance*, but he must not build a *stance*.

### 13-4. Ball in Hazard; Prohibited Actions

Except as provided in the *Rules*, before making a *stroke* at a ball that is in a *hazard* (whether a *bunker* or a *water hazard*) or that, having been lifted from a *hazard*, may be dropped or placed in the *hazard*, the player must not:

  a. Test the condition of the *hazard* or any similar *hazard*;
  b. Touch the ground in the *hazard* or water in the *water hazard* with his hand or a club; or
  c. Touch or move a *loose impediment* lying in or touching the *hazard*.

**Exceptions:**

  1. Provided nothing is done that constitutes testing the condition of the *hazard* or improves the lie of the ball, there is no penalty if the player (a) touches the ground in any *hazard* or water in a *water hazard* as a result of or to prevent falling, in removing an *obstruction*, in measuring or in retrieving, lifting, placing or replacing a ball under any *Rule* or (b) places his clubs in a *hazard*.
  2. After making the *stroke*, the player or his *caddie* may smooth sand or soil in the *hazard*, provided that, if the ball is still in the *hazard* or has been lifted from the *hazard* and may be dropped or placed in the *hazard*, nothing is done that improves the lie of the ball or assists the player in his subsequent play of the hole.

**Note:** At any time, including at *address* or in the backward movement for the *stroke*, the player may touch with a club or otherwise any *obstruction*, any construction declared by the *Committee* to be an integral part of the *course* or any grass, bush, tree or other growing thing.

PENALTY FOR BREACH OF RULE:
Match play — Loss of hole; Stroke play — Two strokes.

(Searching for ball — see Rule 12-1.)
(Relief for ball in water hazard — see Rule 26.)

## 13/1 Sand Spilling Over Margin of Bunker

**Q.** If sand spills over the margin of a bunker, is the sand part of the bunker?

**A.** No.

## 13/2 Status of Tree in Bunker

**Q.** Is a tree in a bunker part of the bunker?

**A.** No. Grass-covered ground within a bunker is not part of the bunker. The same principle applies to a tree. The margin of a bunker does not extend upward.

## 13/3 Ball on Edge of Bunker Overhanging Sand

**Q.** Is a ball in a bunker if it lies on the edge of the bunker overhanging, but not touching, the sand?

**A.** No. The margin of a bunker, unlike that of a water hazard, does not extend vertically upward.

### 13/4 Ball Completely Embedded in Lip of Bunker

**Q.** A player's ball is completely embedded in the vertical lip of a bunker. The lip is not grass-covered, so it is part of the bunker. Is the ball considered to be lying through the green? If so, the player would be entitled to drop the ball behind the bunker if he deems it unplayable.

**A.** No. An embedded ball is considered to be lying in the part of the course where it entered the ground.

**Ball Embedded in Grass Bank or Face of Bunker — See 25-2/5.**

### 13/5 Ball Lying on Obstruction in Bunker

**Q.** If a ball is lying on either a movable or an immovable obstruction in a bunker, is the ball considered to be in the bunker?

**A.** Yes. Although the margin of a bunker does not extend upward, a ball lying on an obstruction in a bunker is in the bunker.

**Decisions relating to Rule 13-1:**

**Ball Played from Ground Under Repair Abandoned and Relief Taken Under Ground Under Repair Rule — See 18-2a/8.5.**

**Competitor's Ball Played by Fellow-Competitor; Competitor Substitutes Another Ball at Wrong Place, Plays It and Then Abandons It and Plays Out Original Ball from Right Place — See 20-7c/4.**

### 13-2/1 Explanation of "Fairly Taking His Stance"

**Q.** Rule 13-2 states that a player must not improve the position or lie of his ball, the area of his intended stance or swing or his line of play or a reasonable extension of that line beyond the hole by moving, bending or breaking anything growing or fixed (including immovable obstructions and objects defining out of bounds). An exception permits a player to do so in "fairly taking his stance." What is the significance of "fairly"?

**A.** Without "fairly," the exception would permit improvement of position or lie, area of intended stance or swing or line of play by anything that could be said to be taking a stance. The use of "fairly" is intended to limit the player to what is reasonably necessary to take a stance for the selected stroke without unduly improving the position of the ball, his lie, area of intended stance or swing or line of play. Thus, in taking his stance for the selected stroke the player should select the least intrusive course of action which results in the minimum improvement in the position or lie of the ball, area of intended stance or swing or line of play. The player is not entitled to a normal stance or swing. He must accommodate the situation in which the ball is found and take a stance as normal as the circumstances permit. What is fair must be determined in the light of all circumstances.

Examples of actions which do constitute fairly taking a stance are:

- backing into a branch or young sapling if that is the only way to take a stance for the selected stroke, even if this causes the branch to move out of the way or the sapling to bend or break.
- bending a branch of a tree with the hands in order to get under the tree to play a ball.

Examples of actions which do not constitute fairly taking a stance are:

- deliberately moving, bending or breaking branches with the hands, a leg or the body to get them out of the way of the backswing or stroke.
- standing on a branch to prevent it from interfering with the backswing or stroke.
- hooking one branch on another or braiding two weeds for the same purpose.
- bending with a hand a branch obscuring the ball after the stance has been taken.
- bending an interfering branch with the hands, a leg or the body in taking a stance when the stance could have been taken without bending the branch.

### 13-2/1.1 Player Attempts to Take Stance Fairly But Improves Line of Play by Moving Interfering Growing Object

**Q.** A player's ball lies under the branch of a tree. In attempting to take his stance fairly, the player improves his line of play by moving the branch with his body. Before playing, he realizes he could have taken his stance without moving the branch. He abandons his stance and the branch returns to its original position or is returned to its original position by the player. The player then approaches the ball from a different direction, takes his stance without disturbing the branch and makes his stroke. What is the ruling?

**A.** There is no penalty. When fairly taking his stance the player is required to take his stance in the least intrusive manner that results in the minimum improvement in the position or lie of the ball, area of intended stance or swing or line of play. However, as the branch moved as a result of the player's attempt to take his stance fairly and was returned to its original position before the stroke was made, there is no penalty. Any doubt as to whether the branch returned to its original position should be resolved against the player.

The same principle would apply to fixed artificial objects (e.g., a boundary stake) if the position or lie of the ball, area of intended stance or swing or line of play is improved as a result of the player's attempt to take his stance fairly but the object is returned to its original position before the player makes a stroke.

**Player Removes Boundary Post on Line of Play But Replaces It Before Playing — See 13-2/25.**

### 13-2/1.5 Player Allowed to Play in Any Direction in Fairly Taking His Stance

**Q.** Decision 13-2/1 clarifies what is meant by a player "fairly taking his stance" and states that a player is not entitled to a normal stance or swing and he must accommodate the situation in which the ball is found. Does the requirement to fairly take a stance restrict the player in the stroke or direction of play he adopts?

**A.** No. It is a matter for the player to decide on the stroke and direction of play he wishes to adopt and he is entitled to fairly take his stance for that stroke and direction of play.

**Player Determines Nearest Point of Relief But Physically Unable to Play Intended Stroke — See 24-2b/3.**

### 13-2/1.7 Player Having Fairly Taken Stance Changes Direction of Play

**Q.** A player's ball lies under a tree. The player fairly takes his stance by backing into the branches of the tree. He then decides to adopt a different direction of play and fairly takes his stance for a second time by backing into the branches of the tree from a different angle. Is this permissible?

**A.** Yes. A player may change his intended direction of play and re-take his stance with respect to the new stroke. However, if the taking of the original stance improved the position or lie of his ball, the area of his new stance or swing or line of play for the new stroke beyond what occurred in fairly taking the stance for the second time, he is in breach of Rule 13-2.

### 13-2/2 Player Who Misses Tee Shot Presses Down Irregularities Before Next Stroke

**Q.** In playing a tee shot A misses the ball. Before playing his next stroke, A presses down turf behind the ball. Is this permissible, since the ball is in play?

**A.** Yes. Rule 13-2 permits eliminating irregularities of surface on the teeing ground, whether or not the ball is in play.

### 13-2/3 Breaking Off Grass Behind Ball on Teeing Ground

**Q.** Under Rule 13-2, it is permissible to eliminate irregularities of surface on the teeing ground. Is it also permissible to break off or pull out grass growing behind a ball on the teeing ground?

**A.** Yes.

### 13-2/4 Greenkeeping Staff Member Rakes Bunker When Player's Ball Lies Therein

**Q.** If a member of the greenkeeping staff rakes a bunker when the player's ball lies therein and the raking improves the lie of the ball or the line of play, is the player penalized under Rule 13-2?

**A.** If the staff member raked the bunker on the instructions, or with the sanction, of the player, the player would incur a penalty. Otherwise, there would be no penalty.

### 13-2/4.5 Divots Replaced in Area in Which Ball Is to Be Dropped

**Q.** A player makes a stroke. He replaces his divot and other divots nearby. He then discovers that his ball is lost or out of bounds. The player must now drop a ball as nearly as possible at the spot from which his previous stroke was made — Rule 27-1. In these circumstances, is the player in breach of Rule 13-2, which prohibits improving the area in which a ball is to be dropped by eliminating irregularities of surface by replacing a divot?

**A.** No. When the player replaced the divots, he was unaware that he would be required to drop a ball in the area. Therefore, in equity (Rule 1-4), he is not penalized.

However, if the player wished to play a provisional ball because he thought his original ball might be lost outside a water hazard or out of bounds, he would be prohibited from replacing his or other divots in the area where he would be dropping the provisional ball.

### 13-2/5 Replacing or Removing Undetached Divot

**Q.** A player's ball comes to rest in front of a divot which is folded over but not completely detached. The divot interferes with his backswing. May the player replace or remove the divot before playing?

**A.** No. A divot which is not completely detached is not a loose impediment. It is something fixed and therefore its removal or replacement would be a breach of Rule 13-2 as the lie and area of intended swing would be improved.

### 13-2/6 Replacing Divot in Divot Hole on Line of Play

**Q.** A player's ball comes to rest close to the putting green and he wishes to use his putter for his next stroke. However, there is a divot hole just in front of his ball on his line of play. May the player replace the divot before playing his next stroke?

**A.** No. Rule 13-2 prohibits a player from improving his line of play by eliminating an irregularity of surface.

### 13-2/7 When Divot Replaced

**Q.** Under Rule 13-2 a player may not remove or press down a replaced divot. When is a divot considered replaced?

**A.** When substantially all of it, with the roots downward, lies in a divot hole. The hole need not be the one from which the divot was extracted.

### 13-2/8 Player's Lie or Line of Play Affected by Pitch-Mark Made by Partner's, Opponent's or Fellow-Competitor's Ball

**Q.** A player's lie or line of play through the green is affected by a pitch-mark made by his partner's, his opponent's or a fellow-competitor's ball. Is the player entitled to relief?

**A.** If the pitch-mark was there before the player's ball came to rest, he is not entitled to relief without penalty.

If the pitch-mark was created after the player's ball came to rest, in equity (Rule 1-4) he may repair the pitch-mark. A player is entitled to the lie which his stroke gave him.

### 13-2/8.5 Player's Lie Affected by Sand from Partner's, Opponent's or Fellow-Competitor's Stroke from Bunker

**Q.** A's ball is on the apron between the green and a bunker. A's partner, opponent or fellow-competitor (B) plays from the bunker and deposits sand on and around A's ball. Is A entitled to any relief?

**A.** Yes. A is entitled to the lie and line of play he had when his ball came to rest. Accordingly, in equity (Rule 1-4) he is entitled to remove the sand deposited by B's stroke and lift his ball and clean it, without penalty.

### 13-2/8.7 Player's Area of Intended Stance Affected by Another Player's Stroke

**Q.** The balls of A and B lie near each other through the green. A plays and in doing so affects B's area of intended stance (e.g., by creating a divot hole). What is the ruling?

**A.** B may play the ball as it lies. In addition, if the original area of intended stance could be easily restored, in equity (Rule 1-4), the area of intended stance may be restored as nearly as possible, without penalty.

If the original area of intended stance could not be easily restored, in equity (Rule 1-4), the player may place his ball, without penalty, on the nearest spot within one club-length of the original lie that provides the most similar lie and area of intended stance to the original lie and area of intended stance. This spot must not be nearer the hole and must not be in a hazard. (New)

## 13-2/9 Lie Through the Green Improved When Sand Behind Ball Removed by Backswing

**Q.** A player's ball lies in a sandy area through the green and there is a mound of sand a few inches behind his ball. The player makes his stroke and in the process he removes the mound of sand with the clubhead on his backswing, improving his lie. Is the player subject to penalty?

**A.** No, provided that he did not ground his club other than lightly and that he took a normal backswing.

## 13-2/10 Pitch-Mark in Dropping Area Repaired Before Ball Dropped

**Q.** Through the green, a player's ball was embedded in its own pitch-mark in a closely mown area. He lifted the ball under Rule 25-2 but, before dropping it, repaired the pitch-mark. Is such repair permissible?

**A.** No. The player was in breach of Rule 13-2 when he improved the area in which his ball was to be dropped by eliminating an irregularity of surface.

## 13-2/11 Removing Sand or Loose Soil from Dropping Area

**Q.** Through the green, may a player remove or brush away sand or loose soil from the area in which he is preparing to drop a ball?

**A.** No. Rule 13-2 prohibits improving the area in which a ball is to be dropped by removing sand or loose soil. Sand and loose soil are loose impediments only on the putting green.

**Ball Played from Bunker Is Out of Bounds or Lost; Player Tests Condition of Bunker or Smoothes Footprints Before Dropping Another Ball in Bunker — See 13-4/37.**

## 13-2/12 Player Presses Down Sand Behind Ball in Grounding Club

**Q.** In addressing his ball through the green, a player grounded his club on sand behind the ball and in so doing pressed down the sand, thereby improving the lie of the ball. What is the ruling?

**A.** Except in a hazard, Rule 13-2 permits a player to ground his club lightly behind the ball. If the club was grounded only lightly, there is no breach of Rule 13-2 or any other Rule. However, if the club was pressed on the ground, the player was in breach of Rule 13-2. (New)

**When Club Grounded in Grass — See 18-2b/5**

## 13-2/13 Bending Grass in Removal of Loose Impediments

**Q.** A player whose ball was in long grass rolled a stone away from the ball, pressing down some of the long grass in the process. Was he in breach of Rule 13-2?

**A.** Yes, if the pressing down of the grass improved the position or lie of his ball, the area of his intended swing or his line of play.

### 13-2/14  Breaking Branch Interfering with Backswing on Teeing Ground

**Q.** On the teeing ground, a player broke off a branch of a tree which was interfering with his swing. The player maintained that such action was not a breach of Rule 13-2 because his ball was not yet in play. Was the player correct?

**A.** No. The player was in breach of Rule 13-2 for improving the area of his intended swing. Although Rule 13-2 allows a player to eliminate irregularities of surface on the teeing ground, it does not allow him to break a branch interfering with his swing. The penalty would apply even if the player, before playing his next stroke, re-teed elsewhere on the teeing ground — see Decision 13-2/24.

### 13-2/14.5  Branch Broken on Backswing and Swing Discontinued

**Q.** A player's ball lies under a tree. The player fairly takes his stance and starts his backswing with the intention of making a stroke. Near the top of his backswing his club strikes a branch and breaks it. At that point he discontinues his swing.

Rule 13-2 states in part: "... a player must not improve ... the area of his intended stance or swing ... except ... in making a stroke or the backward movement of his club for a stroke." Is the player exempt from penalty under this exception?

**A.** No, because the swing was discontinued, the backward movement of the club was not in fact the backward movement for a stroke.

### 13-2/15  Area of Intended Swing Improved by Removing Immovable Obstruction

**Q.** A player's swing is interfered with by an immovable obstruction. The player and his caddie, with great effort, remove the obstruction. Is the player subject to penalty?

**A.** Yes, for a breach of Rule 13-2. An immovable obstruction is something fixed. Rule 13-2 prohibits a player from improving the area of his intended swing by moving anything fixed.

### 13-2/15.5  Position of Ball Worsened When Obstruction Removed; Player Replaces Obstruction

**Q.** A player's ball comes to rest near a tree. A branch of the tree is being held back by a rope installed for gallery control. The player removes the rope (movable obstruction). This releases the branch and worsens the position of the ball. The player then re-installs the rope which results in the branch being held back as before. Was the player in breach of Rule 13-2 when he re-installed the rope?

**A.** Yes.

If an outside agency had removed the rope without the player's authority or sanction, the player would be entitled to re-install the rope without penalty.

**Grounding Club, Removing Leaves and Improving Area of Intended Swing in Water Hazard — See 13-4/28.**

**Lie Altered by Act of Marking Position of Ball — See 20-1/15.5.**

## 13-2/16 Stake Supporting Tree Broken in Attempt to Remove It

**Q.** A stake supporting a young tree interferes with a player's stroke. He tries to remove it, but it cannot readily be removed and it breaks. What is the ruling?

**A.** The player was in breach of Rule 13-2 for breaking the stake. However, as the stake was not readily removable, it was an immovable obstruction and relief could have been taken, without penalty, under Rule 24-2b.

## 13-2/17 Removal of Boundary Stake Interfering with Swing

**Q.** A player removes a stake defining out of bounds which interferes with his swing. Is this permissible?

**A.** No. Objects defining out of bounds are fixed. Improving the position of a ball by moving anything fixed is a breach of Rule 13-2.

**Boundary Post on Line of Play Removed But Replaced Before Stroke — See 13-2/25.**

## 13-2/18 Improving Position of Ball by Bending Boundary Fence

**Q.** Part of a boundary fence is bowed towards the course so that it is inside the out of bounds line formed by the fence posts. A player's ball comes to rest against this part of the fence. Decision 24/4 states that the player is not entitled to drop the ball away from the fence under Rule 24-2b. May the player push back the bowed section of the fence to obtain a measure of relief?

**A.** No. Such action would be a breach of Rule 13-2, which prohibits improving the position or lie of his ball or the area of his intended stance or swing by moving or bending anything fixed (including objects defining out of bounds).

**Part of Boundary Fence Within Boundary Line — See 24/4.**

**Gate in Boundary Fence — See 27/18.**

### 13-2/19 Improving Area of Intended Swing by Moving Growing or Fixed Object Situated Out of Bounds

**Q.** A young tree or a fixed artificial object situated out of bounds interferes with a player's swing. May the player move, bend or break the tree or fixed artificial object without penalty?

**A.** No. Such action would be a breach of Rule 13-2.

### 13-2/20 Part of Fence Off Course Leans Across Boundary and Interferes with Swing

**Q.** Part of a fence which is beyond white stakes defining out of bounds, and therefore not a boundary fence, leans onto the course and interferes with a player's swing. May the player push the fence back into an upright position or treat it as an obstruction?

**A.** Rule 13-2 prohibits improving the position of the ball by moving anything fixed, even if such thing is off the course. Therefore, the player may not push the fence back. However, that part of the fence leaning onto the course is an immovable obstruction and the player is entitled to relief under Rule 24-2b.

### 13-2/21 Area of Intended Swing Improved by Repairing Pitch-Mark Made by Ball on Previous Stroke

**Q.** A pitch-mark made by the ball as a result of the previous stroke interferes with a player's backswing. Before playing his next stroke, the player steps on the pitch-mark, improving the area of his intended swing. Is this permissible?

**A.** No. The player was in breach of Rule 13-2 which prohibits improving the area of the intended swing by eliminating irregularities of surface.

### 13-2/22 Knocking Down Leaves with Practice Swing

**Q.** A player's ball lies near a tree or bush. The player takes a practice swing near his ball and knocks down leaves in the area of his intended swing. Is this a breach of Rule 13-2?

**A.** The answer depends on whether the area of the intended swing is improved. In some cases, the knocking down of a number of leaves would not improve the area of the intended swing as the player still has to swing through a number of remaining leaves when making his stroke. In such circumstances, there would be no breach of the Rules. In other cases, the knocking down of one leaf might improve the area of the intended swing, in which case there would be a breach of Rule 13-2.

If a player has improved the area of his intended swing by knocking down a leaf or a number of leaves, he cannot avoid penalty under Rule

13-2 by subsequently changing the area of his swing when he actually makes the stroke.

### 13-2/23 Shaking Water from Tree Branch Interfering with Backswing

**Q.** After heavy rain, a player plays a stroke that comes to rest under a tree. A branch of the tree interferes with the player's backswing. Before playing his next stroke, the player shakes the water off this branch in order to eliminate the possibility of dislodged water distracting him. Is this a breach of Rule 13-2?

**A.** Yes. In moving the branch, the player removed water which could have caused a distraction and thereby improved the area of his intended swing in breach of Rule 13-2.

### 13-2/24 Area of Originally Intended Swing Improved by Breaking Branch; Area of Swing Finally Used Not Affected by Branch

**Q.** A player, intending to play in a certain direction, took a practice backswing for a stroke in that direction and broke a branch impeding his backswing. The player then decided to play in a different direction. The area of his intended swing for a stroke in this new direction was not improved by the breaking of the branch. In such circumstances, would the player incur a penalty under Rule 13-2?

**A.** Yes. The player was in breach of Rule 13-2 as soon as he improved the area of the originally intended swing. The penalty is not avoided if he subsequently plays in another direction, even if the breaking of the branch had no effect on the area of the swing for a stroke in the new direction.

### 13-2/25 Player Removes Boundary Post on Line of Play But Replaces It Before Playing

**Q.** A player removes a post defining out of bounds on his line of play. He realizes he has made a mistake and replaces it before playing his next stroke. What is the ruling?

**A.** The player was in breach of Rule 13-2 the moment he moved the post and there was nothing he could do to avoid the penalty. The replacement of the post before the next stroke was irrelevant.

**Player Attempts to Take Stance Fairly But Improves Line of Play by Moving Interfering Growing Object — See 13-2/1.1.**

### 13-2/26 Natural Object Interfering with Swing Moved to Determine Whether It Is Loose

**Q.** A player cannot determine whether a long blade of grass, a twig, a tumbleweed or some similar natural object interfering with his swing through the green is loose or is attached. The player moves the object to the extent necessary to make a determination and discovers that the object is attached. What is the ruling?

**A.** A player is entitled to move a natural object for the specific purpose of determining whether the object is loose, provided that if the object is found not to be loose, (1) it has not become detached and (2) it is returned to its original position before the next stroke if failure to do so would result in a breach of Rule 13-2.

Except as otherwise permitted in Rule 13-2 (e.g., in fairly taking the stance), if a player moves a natural object other than to determine whether it is loose and it is found to be attached, the player cannot avoid a breach of Rule 13-2 by returning the object to its original position. (Revised)

### 13-2/27 Probing Near Ball for Tree Roots or Rocks

**Q.** A player's ball comes to rest through the green in such a position that he believes tree roots or rocks may be just below the surface of the ground. May he, without penalty, probe the area around his ball with a tee to see if his club would strike a root or rock in the course of making a stroke?

**A.** Yes, provided there is a reasonable possibility that there are roots or rocks in the area and the lie of the ball, the area of intended stance or swing or the line of play is not improved (Rule 13-2) and the ball is not moved (Rule 18-2). The same principles would apply if the player wished to probe to determine the presence of an immovable obstruction.

### 13-2/28 Smoothing Irregularities in Bunker Situated Between Ball and Hole

**Q.** There is a bunker between A's ball and the hole. Before playing, A smoothes footprints and other irregularities in the bunker on his line of play. Was A in breach of Rule 13-2?

**A.** Yes, such action would improve the line of play, contrary to Rule 13-2.

**Player Smoothes Irregularities in Bunker After Playing Out Backward; Smoothed Area on Line of Play — See 13-4/37.5.**

### 13-2/29 Worsening and Then Restoring Line of Play

**Q.** There is a bunker between a player's ball and the hole. The player walks through the bunker, for example, to remove a rake on his line of play or determine the distance to the hole. On his way back to the ball, he smoothes the footprints he made, restoring his line of play to its original condition. Is such smoothing permissible?

**A.** No. If a player worsens the lie of his ball, the area of his intended stance or swing, his line of play or a reasonable extension of that line beyond the hole, or the area in which he is to drop or place a ball, he is not entitled to restore that area to its original condition. If he does so, he is in breach of Rule 13-2 and incurs a penalty of loss of hole in match play or two strokes in stroke play (but see Decision 13-2/29.3). (Revised)

### 13-2/29.3 Creating Footprints in Bunker on Line of Play When Required to Enter Bunker to Retrieve Ball

**Q.** With reference to Decision 13-2/29, would a player be prohibited from smoothing footprints if he had been required to enter the bunker to retrieve a ball (e.g., a ball that had rolled into the bunker after having been dropped)?

**A.** No. In such circumstances, the player is entitled to restore the bunker to the condition it was in before he entered it.

### 13-2/29.5 Extension of Line of Play Affected When Opponent or Fellow-Competitor Creates Footprints in Bunker

**Q.** A's ball lies behind the green. The ball of his opponent or fellow-competitor (B) lies in a bunker in front of the green, which is on an extension of A's line of play.

It is A's turn to play but before he does so, B walks into the bunker to assess his next stroke, thereby creating footprints. A believes that his ball might come to rest in the bunker. Is A entitled to have the bunker restored to the condition which existed when A's ball came to rest?

**A.** Yes. In equity (Rule 1-4), A may have the bunker restored to its former condition because the footprints were created by B after A's ball came to rest. The bunker may be restored by anyone.

### 13-2/30 Testing Condition of Bunker Before Deciding Whether to Play Through It

**Q.** A player's ball lies behind a bunker. May he test the condition of the bunker to determine whether it is feasible to putt through it?

**A.** The Rules do not prohibit a player from testing the condition of a hazard except when his ball lies in or touches the hazard — see Rule 13-4. However, if such testing improved the line of play, the player would be in breach of Rule 13-2.

### 13-2/31 Ball Outside Bunker; Stone in Bunker on Line of Play Pressed Down or Removed

**Q.** A player's ball is lying behind a bunker and he decides to putt through the bunker. There is a small stone (loose impediment) in the bunker on his line of play. May he push the stone down into the sand or remove it?

**A.** Sand may not be pressed down if the act would improve the line of play — Rule 13-2. However, Rule 23-1 permits the removal of a loose impediment in a hazard when the ball is not lying in the hazard.

### 13-2/32  Improving Line of Play by Removing Stone from Wall

**Q.** A stone wall on the course (immovable obstruction) is on A's line of play. A removes a stone from the top of the wall. Is this permissible?

**A.** No. An immovable obstruction is fixed. In removing part of an immovable obstruction, A was in breach of Rule 13-2. The same ruling would apply if the wall had been declared an integral part of the course.

### 13-2/32.5  Improving Line of Play by Removing Part of Fence

**Q.** A fence which is not a boundary fence does not interfere with a player's swing but it is on his line of play. May the player remove a part of the fence, which is readily movable, in order to improve his line of play?

**A.** No. A fence is an immovable obstruction and thus is something fixed. If a player removes a part of something fixed and in so doing improves his line of play, he is in breach of Rule 13-2.

### 13-2/33  Outside Agency Removes Immovable Obstruction on Player's Line of Play

**Q.** A stake supporting a young tree has been deemed an immovable obstruction by the Committee. A player's ball comes to rest in such a position that the stake intervenes on his line of play but does not interfere with his swing or stance. At that point, an outside agency removes the stake. What is the ruling?

**A.** If the player allowed the outside agency to remove the stake, the player loses the hole in match play or incurs a penalty of two strokes in stroke play for a breach of Rule 13-2.

If the player did not know the stake had been removed, or if he knew it but was not in a position to prevent it, there is no penalty and the player may replace the stake, but he is not required to do so.

**Relief from Obstruction Incidentally Gives Relief from Intervention on Line of Play — See 24-2b/7.**

**Window of Clubhouse Opened and Ball Played Through Window — See 24-2b/14.**

**Opening Barn Doors to Play Shot Through Barn — See 24-2b/15.**

**Improving Line of Play When Taking Relief from Abnormal Ground Condition — See 25-1b/3.**

### 13-2/34  Mopping Up Casual Water on Line of Play

**Q.** A pool of casual water was on the putting green between the player's ball, which was lying short of the green, and the hole. The player's caddie mopped up the water. Was this permissible?

**A.** No. When the player's caddie improved the line of play by removing the water, the player was in breach of Rule 13-2 and incurred a penalty of loss of hole in match play or two strokes in stroke play.

**Brushing Aside or Mopping Up Casual Water on Line of Putt — See 16-1a/1.**

**Ball Mark Partially on and Partially Off Putting Green Is on Line of Play — See 16-1c/1.5.**

## 13-2/35  Removal of Dew or Frost

The removal of dew or frost from the area immediately behind or to the side of a player's ball is not permitted. Such action is deemed to improve the position or lie of the ball or the area of the player's intended swing and is a breach of Rule 13-2, unless it occurs incidentally to some other action permitted under the Rules, such as in addressing the ball or removing loose impediments.

Additionally, the removal of dew or frost from the player's line of play or line of putt is not permitted. Such action is deemed to improve the line and is a breach of Rule 13-2 or, on the putting green, Rule 16-1a, unless it occurs incidentally to some other action permitted under the Rules, such as in removing loose impediments, repairing ball marks on the putting green or addressing the ball.

**Removing Dew or Frost from Line of Putt — See 16-1a/3.**

## 13-2/36  Competitor Sanctions Repair of Spike Damage on His Line of Putt by Fellow-Competitor

**Q.** If a fellow-competitor purposely improves the competitor's line of putt by repairing spike damage, the fellow-competitor is penalized under Rule 1-2. If the fellow-competitor's action is sanctioned, tacitly or otherwise, by the competitor, is the competitor also subject to penalty?

**A.** Yes, under Rule 13-2, for allowing his line of play to be improved.

**Repair of Spike Mark Damage Around Hole — See 16-1c/4.**

## 13-2/37  Status of Moss or Creepers in Tree

**Q.** May moss, or a creeper, in a tree be removed if its removal would improve the line of play?

**A.** No. Trees are the natural habitat of some mosses and creepers. Accordingly, such plants growing in a tree may not be moved — see Rule 13-2.

Moss or a creeper which has fallen to the ground, and is not growing there, is a loose impediment and may be removed, without penalty — see Rule 23-1.

### 13-3/1  Standing on Mat on Teeing Ground

**Q.** Is it permissible for a player to carry a mat and stand on it when playing from the teeing ground?

**A.** No. The player would be building a stance in breach of Rule 13-3.

### 13-3/2  Playing Stroke While Kneeling on Towel

**Q.** A player's ball was under a tree in such a position that he found it expedient to play his next stroke while on his knees. Because the ground was wet, the player placed a towel on the ground at the spot where his knees would be situated so that the knees of his trousers would not get wet. He then knelt on the towel and played his stroke. Was the player subject to penalty under Rule 13-3 for building a stance?

**A.** Yes.

### 13-3/3  Knocking Down Side of Bunker to Get Level Stance

**Q.** A player knocks down the side of a bunker with his foot in an effort to get his feet on the same level. Is this permissible?

**A.** No. Such action constitutes building a stance in breach of Rule 13-3.

### [13-3/4  Reserved]

### 13-3/5  Player Builds Stance But Corrects Error Before Playing Stroke

**Q.** A player's ball is lodged in the branch of a tree just beyond his reach with a club. The player positions his motorized golf cart under the tree, stands on the cart and prepares to make a stroke at his ball. At that point, the player is advised that he is building a stance, contrary to Rule 13-3. If the player removes the cart and does not play a stroke while standing on it, does he nevertheless incur a penalty for a breach of Rule 13-3?

**A.** No. If a player builds a stance through use of an object such as a golf cart, stone or brick, he incurs no penalty if he removes the object before playing his next stroke.

However, if a player builds a stance through alteration of the ground on which he is taking his stance, it is impossible for him to restore the ground to its original state. Accordingly, a player who builds a stance in such manner incurs the penalty prescribed in Rule 13-3, whether or not he attempts to restore the ground to its original state before playing his next stroke.

### 13-4/1 Touching Sand in Bunker When Ball Lies Outside Bunker

**Q.** A ball lies just outside a bunker. The player takes his stance in the bunker. May the player ground his club on the sand in the bunker or touch the sand during his backswing?

**A.** Yes. Since the ball was not in or touching the bunker, Rule 13-4 does not apply. However, the player may ground his club only lightly — see Rule 13-2.

### 13-4/2 Leaning on Club in Hazard While Waiting to Play

**Q.** A, whose ball lies in a hazard, casually leans on his club in the hazard while waiting for B to play. What is the ruling?

**A.** A was in breach of Rule 13-4b for touching the ground in the hazard with his club before making a stroke. The Exceptions to Rule 13-4 do not apply.

### 13-4/3 Touching Ground in Hazard with Several Practice Swings

**Q.** In stroke play, a competitor in ignorance of the Rules took several practice swings in a hazard, touching the ground each time. What is the penalty?

**A.** Two strokes for a breach of Rule 13-4.

**Player Breaches Rules More Than Once Prior to Stroke; Whether Multiple Penalties Applied — See 1-4/12.**

### 13-4/3.5 Player Uses Cane or Club to Enter or Leave Hazard When Ball Lies in Hazard

**Q.** A player, to prevent falling, uses a cane or club to enter or leave a hazard when his ball lies in the hazard. Is the player in breach of Rule 13-4?

**A.** No, provided nothing is done which constitutes testing the condition of the hazard or improves the lie of the ball — see Exception 1 to Rule 13-4.

### 13-4/4 Touching Grass with Club During Practice Swing in Hazard

**Q.** A player takes a practice swing in a water hazard without grounding his club, but his club touches some long grass. Is there a penalty?

**A.** No, provided the player did not improve his lie or test the condition of the hazard — see Note to Rule 13-4.

**When Club Grounded in Grass — See 18-2b/5.**

### 13-4/5 Touching Mound Made by Burrowing Animal with Backswing in Bunker

**Q.** A player's ball and a mound made by a burrowing animal are in a bunker. The mound interferes with the player's backswing, but the player elects not to take relief under Rule 25-1b(ii). During his backswing, the player's club touches the mound. Is the player in breach of Rule 13-4?

**A.** Yes. Rule 13-4 prohibits touching the ground in a hazard with a club before making a stroke, which is the forward movement of the club. In a hazard, a mound made by a burrowing animal is ground in the hazard.

### 13-4/6 Touching Solidly Embedded Stone in Hazard with Club During Backswing

**Q.** A player's ball lies in a hazard. In making his backswing for the stroke, the player's club touches a solidly embedded stone in the hazard. Is the stone considered "ground in the hazard"?

**A.** Yes.

### 13-4/7 Touching Casual Water in Bunker with Club

**Q.** A player's ball lies in casual water in a bunker. The player elects to play his ball as it lies and touches the casual water with his club when addressing the ball. The player's club does not touch the sand in the bunker except in making the stroke. What is the ruling?

**A.** The player incurs no penalty as he did not touch the ground in the bunker with his club prior to making his stroke — see Rule 13-4b.

### [13-4/8 Reserved]

### [13-4/9 Reserved]

### [13-4/10 Reserved]

### 13-4/11 Smoothing Footprints Made in Search for Ball in Bunker Before Playing Stroke from Bunker

**Q.** A player searches for his ball in a bunker and in the process makes numerous footprints. He subsequently finds his ball. Before playing his stroke, may the player or his caddie smooth the footprints?

**A.** No, such action would be a breach of Rule 13-4.

### 13-4/12 Ball Touched Accidentally with Club in Hazard But Not Moved

**Q.** A player, when addressing his ball which was lying in a bunker or was partially submerged in water in a water hazard, accidentally touches the ball with his club, but without moving it. Does this constitute touching the ground in a hazard or water in a water hazard in breach of Rule 13-4?

**A.** No.

### 13-4/13 Accidentally Moving Loose Impediment in Hazard

**Q.** A player accidentally moves a loose impediment in a hazard. Does the player incur a penalty?

**A.** No, provided the loose impediment was not moved in making the backswing and the lie of the ball or area of the intended stance or swing was not improved.

### 13-4/13.5 Player Moves Loose Impediments When Approaching Ball in Hazard

**Q.** A player's ball lies in a bunker that is covered with many loose twigs and leaves. In approaching the ball and taking his stance, the player touches and moves loose impediments with his feet. Does he incur a penalty?

**A.** There is no penalty provided the lie of the ball or area of intended stance or swing is not improved.

### 13-4/14 Player Accidentally Kicks Pine Cone into Bunker and Picks It Up

**Q.** A player's ball went into a bunker. The player accidentally kicked a pine cone, and it rolled into the bunker. He picked up the pine cone which was not interfering with his stance or the area of his intended swing. Did he incur a penalty?

**A.** Yes. A pine cone is a loose impediment — see Definition of "Loose Impediments" — and may not be removed when both the impediment and the ball lie in a hazard (Rule 13-4c). By removing the pine cone from the bunker, the player incurred a penalty of loss of hole in match play or two strokes in stroke play for a breach of Rule 13-4c.

### 13-4/15 Ball in Hazard Moves When Loose Impediment Removed

**Q.** In stroke play, a competitor's ball is in a hazard. He removes a loose impediment in the hazard that causes his ball to move. What is the ruling?

**A.** As a single act resulted in two Rules being breached (Rule 13-4 and Rule 18-2a), in equity (Rule 1-4), a single penalty is applied. Therefore, the competitor incurs a two-stroke penalty under Rule 13-4 and the ball must be replaced (Rule 18-2a). If the ball is not replaced before the competitor makes his next stroke, the failure to replace the ball is considered a separate act and he incurs an additional penalty of two strokes under Rule 18-2a.

**Player Breaches Rules More Than Once Prior to Stroke; Whether Multiple Penalties Applied — See 1-4/12.**

**Ball in Hazard Moves After Loose Impediment Outside Hazard Moved — See 18-2a/5.**

### 13-4/16 Removal of Loose Impediment in Water Hazard Covering Wrong Ball

**Q.** A player plays his ball into a water hazard. He finds a ball in the hazard and removes a loose impediment partially covering it. He discovers that the ball is not his ball. He searches for his ball but does not find it. He proceeds under Rule 26-1. Is the player subject to penalty under Rule 13-4 for removing the loose impediment?

**A.** Yes.

**Removal of Obstruction in Hazard Would Move Loose Impediment — See 1-4/5.**

### 13-4/16.5 Flying Insect in Water Hazard

**Q.** A player's ball is in a water hazard. The player is being distracted by an insect (a loose impediment) flying in the hazard. May the player swat away the insect?

**A.** Although the margin of a water hazard extends vertically upward such that the insect is in the hazard, the Rules do not contemplate such a case. Thus, in equity (Rule 1-4), the player may swat away the insect whether it be flying or on the player.

**Removal of Insect on Ball — See 23-1/5.**

**Status of Insect on Ball in Bunker — See 23-1/5.5.**

### 13-4/17 Loose Impediment Removed from Water Hazard; Player Then Decides Not to Play from Hazard

**Q.** A player whose ball was in a water hazard removed a loose impediment from the hazard. He then decided not to play from the hazard. He proceeded under Rule 26-1. Was the player absolved from the penalty incurred under Rule 13-4 for removing the loose impediment in view of the fact that he subsequently invoked Rule 26-1 and did not play his ball from the hazard?

**A.** No.

**Player Removes Loose Impediment Affecting Opponent's Lie in Hazard — See 1-2/6.**

**Player Lifts Loose Impediment in Bunker When His Ball and Partner's Ball in Bunker — See 30-3f/1.**

**Competitor Lifts Loose Impediment in Bunker When His Ball and Partner's Ball in Bunker — See 31-8/1.**

### 13-4/18 Partner's, Opponent's or Fellow-Competitor's Divot Comes to Rest Near Player's Ball in Bunker

**Q.** A player's partner, opponent or fellow-competitor plays a stroke from near a bunker and the divot comes to rest near the player's ball lying in the bunker. May the divot be removed?

**A.** A player is entitled to the lie which his stroke gave him. Accordingly, in equity (Rule 1-4) the divot may be removed without penalty.

The same would apply if the player's ball was lying in a water hazard.

### 13-4/18.5 Pine Cone Falls from Tree and Comes to Rest Behind Ball Lying in Bunker

**Q.** A pine cone falls from a tree and comes to rest behind a ball which is lying in a bunker. Under the principle in Decision 13-4/18, may the player remove the pine cone without penalty?

**A.** No. The principle in Decision 13-4/18 is applied only in cases in which the lie of a ball has been altered as a result of an act by another player or caddie, or by a spectator or other animate outside agency. In this case, the lie was altered through natural causes.

### 13-4/19 Player Preparing to Play from Bunker Requests Another Player Who Has Just Played from Bunker to Smooth His Footprints

**Q.** In a match between A and B, both balls lie in a bunker and B's ball is farther from the hole. B plays out of the bunker. A then asks B to rake the bunker in case A's ball rolls backwards into B's footprints if A fails to get out of the bunker. What is the ruling?

**A.** B was entitled to rake the bunker under Exception 2 to Rule 13-4. A incurs no penalty for having asked B to rake the bunker.

### 13-4/20 Umbrella or Rake Placed in Hazard Before Stroke

**Q.** May a player place an umbrella or a rake in a bunker before playing a stroke from the bunker?

**A.** Placing an umbrella or rake in a hazard is equivalent to placing clubs in the hazard — see Exception 1 to Rule 13-4. There is no penalty, providing nothing is done which may constitute testing the soil or improving the lie of the ball. But see Decision 13-4/22.

### 13-4/21 Rake Thrown into Bunker Before Stroke

**Q.** A player's ball lies in a bunker. He casually throws a rake into the bunker for use after his stroke. The rake does not move his ball or improve the lie of the ball. Does the player incur a penalty?

**A.** No. Placing a rake in a bunker is permissible. In this case, throwing the rake into the bunker was the equivalent of placing it.

If the rake had moved the ball, the player would incur a penalty of one stroke for causing his ball to move; and the ball would have to be replaced — Rule 18-2a.

### 13-4/22  Rake Handle Stuck in Bunker Before Stroke

**Q.** A takes a rake into a bunker so that he can smooth his footprints after playing from the bunker. He sticks the handle of the rake into the sand prior to playing his stroke. Is this permissible?

**A.** No. A was in breach of Rule 13-4 which prohibits testing the condition of a hazard when the ball lies in the hazard.

### 13-4/23  When Stance Taken in Bunker

**Q.** In a bunker, when is a player deemed to have taken his stance and thus to have addressed the ball?

**A.** Whether a stance has been taken is a question of fact to be determined in the light of the circumstances in each case. In a bunker, some "digging in" with the feet would normally precede the completion of the stance.

### 13-4/24  Stance in Bunker Taken Without Club

**Q.** A player whose ball was in a bunker entered it without a club, dug in with his feet and simulated a stroke. He then left the bunker, got a club, dug in again with his feet at the same place and made a stroke.

The Committee asked the player why he had gone through this exercise. He replied that he had wanted to get the "feel" of the shot he was about to make and that the purpose of the simulated stroke was to determine which club to use and what kind of stroke to make. He stated that he was not testing the condition of the hazard or building a stance when he dug his feet in for the simulated stroke.

How should the Committee have ruled?

**A.** The Committee should have ruled that no penalty was incurred.

Rule 13-3 states: "A player is entitled to place his feet firmly in taking his stance."

The Definition of "Stance" states: "Taking the 'stance' consists in a player placing his feet in position for and preparatory to making a stroke."

On the first occasion, the player was "placing his feet in position for and preparatory to making a stroke," even though he had no club in his hands. If it were ruled otherwise, a player would be in breach of Rule

13-4 if he selected a club for a bunker shot, took his stance with the club in hand and then decided to play the stroke with another club.

**Ball Moves After Stance Taken in Hazard Without Club — See 18-2b/2.**

### 13-4/25 Taking Firm Stance in Bunker Some Distance from Where Ball Lies in Bunker to Simulate Next Stroke

**Q.** While waiting to play a bunker shot, a player went to another part of the bunker, took a firm stance and simulated the bunker shot, with or without using a club. Was he in breach of Rule 13-4?

**A.** Yes. The player tested the condition of the bunker in breach of Rule 13-4a. (Revised)

### 13-4/26 Taking Stance in Bunker and Then Changing Clubs

**Q.** A player takes his stance in a bunker and firmly places his feet in the sand. He then leaves his position to change clubs and thereafter takes his stance a second time. Is the player considered to have tested the condition of the hazard, contrary to Rule 13-4?

**A.** No. Rule 13-3 allows a player to place his feet firmly in taking his stance in a bunker or elsewhere. There is nothing in the Rules to prohibit changing clubs or taking a stance twice in a bunker.

**Ball Moves While Player in Process of Taking Stance in Bunker — See 18-2b/3.**

### 13-4/27 Player in Bunker Takes Firm Stance and Then Smoothes Footprints When He Decides to Play Different Type Shot

**Q.** A player places his feet firmly in the sand in a bunker, intending to play an explosion shot. He then changes his mind and decides to play a chip shot. He takes a different club and, before playing, smoothes out his original footprints because he does not want his feet so firmly implanted for a chip shot. Is this permissible?

**A.** No. The player incurs a penalty under Rule 13-4a for testing the condition of the hazard. Rule 13-3 allows him to place his feet firmly in taking his stance. However, there is nothing in the Rules to permit the player to place his feet firmly and then smooth the footprints before the stroke, even if the smoothing is due to the player having changed his mind as to the type of stroke. If it were otherwise, the way would be open for a player to test the condition of a bunker with his feet beyond any testing incidental to taking his stance.

### 13-4/28 Grounding Club, Moving Loose Impediments and Improving Area of Intended Swing in Hazard

**Q.** In stroke play, a competitor's ball is in a hazard. He takes a practice swing and in so doing moves loose impediments and touches the ground in the hazard. He also bends a shrub with his hand, improving the area of his intended swing. What is the penalty?

**A.** As a single act (i.e., the practice swing) resulted in two Rules being breached (Rule 13-4b and Rule 13-4c), in equity (Rule 1-4), a single penalty of two strokes is applied. However, the competitor also incurs a penalty of two strokes for improving the area of his intended swing by bending a shrub (Rule 13-2).

The practice swing and the bending of the shrub are different acts that resulted in the breach of two Rules and both penalties are applied giving a total penalty of four strokes.

**Player Breaches Rules More Than Once Prior to Stroke; Whether Multiple Penalties Applied — See 1-4/12.**

### 13-4/29 Grounding Club Outside Water Hazard When Playing Stroke at Ball in Hazard

**Q.** A player's ball touches a line defining the margin of a water hazard. So the ball is in the hazard. In addressing the ball for his next stroke, may the player's club be grounded outside the hazard?

**A.** Yes.

### 13-4/30 Grounding Club on Bridge in Water Hazard

**Q.** A player's ball lies on a bridge over a water hazard within the margins of the hazard when extended upward. May the player ground his club?

**A.** Yes. A bridge is an obstruction. In a hazard, the club may touch an obstruction at address or in the backward movement for the stroke — see Note under Rule 13-4. Touching the bridge prior to address is also permissible, since an obstruction in a water hazard is not "ground in the hazard."

This applies even if the bridge has been declared an integral part of the course.

### 13-4/31 Touching Sand in Bunker During Backswing

**Q.** A player playing a shot in a bunker accidentally touched the sand when making his backswing. What is the ruling?

**A.** The player was in breach of Rule 13-4b when he touched the ground in the bunker with his club before making the stroke — see Definition of "Stroke."

## 13-4/32 Club Touches Partially-Embedded Pine Needle on Backswing in Bunker

**Q.** A player whose ball lies in a bunker touches a partially embedded pine needle with his club on his backswing. What is the ruling?

**A.** The player is in breach of Rule 13-4c. A partially embedded pine needle is not solidly embedded and is not considered to be fixed; therefore, it is a loose impediment (see Definition of "Loose Impediments").

## 13-4/33 Bunker Covered by Leaves; Player Touches Leaves During Backswing

**Q.** A player hits a ball into a bunker which is covered by leaves (loose impediments). The player removes as many leaves as will enable him to see a part of the ball in accordance with Rule 12-1. If the player then touches some of the leaves on his backswing, is he in breach of the Rules?

**A.** Yes. If the player touches leaves on his backswing, he is in breach of Rule 13-4c which prohibits a player from touching a loose impediment in a hazard before making a stroke in the hazard. A stroke does not begin until after the completion of the player's backswing — see Definition of "Stroke."

If fallen leaves in bunkers seasonally create an abnormal problem, the Committee may make a Local Rule declaring accumulations of leaves in bunkers to be ground under repair. Rule 25-1b(ii) would then apply.

## 13-4/34 Touching Bare Earth Wall of Bunker on Backswing

**Q.** In playing from a bunker, a player touches a bare earth wall of the bunker with his club on his backswing. What is the ruling?

**A.** The player touched the ground in the hazard in breach of Rule 13-4b. The Note to Rule 13-4 permits a player's club to touch an obstruction (such as an artificial wall) on his backswing. However, an earth wall of a bunker is not an artificial wall.

**Local Rule for Bunker Faces Consisting of Stacked Turf — See 33-8/39.**

## 13-4/35 Hitting Sand in Bunker with Club After Failing to Extricate Ball

**Q.** A played a stroke in a bunker and failed to get the ball out. He then swung his club into the sand, but his action did not affect his new lie in the bunker. However, since A had to play another stroke in the bunker, was he in breach of Rule 13-4?

**A.** Yes. Neither of the Exceptions under Rule 13-4 applies to A's action.

**Hitting Sand in Bunker with Club After Failing to Extricate Ball; Foursome Match — See 29/5.**

**Hitting Sand in Bunker with Club After Failing to Extricate Ball; Partner's Ball in Same Bunker — See 30-3f/2.**

### 13-4/35.5 Ball Played from Bunker onto Grass Bank; Player Hits Sand with Club; Ball Then Rolls Back into Bunker

**Q.** A player plays from a bunker and the ball lands on the grass bank of the bunker. Before the ball comes to rest, the player swings his club into the sand, after which the ball rolls back into the bunker.

Rule 13-4b prohibits touching the ground in a hazard with a club when the ball lies in the hazard. Does the player incur a penalty under this Rule even though the ball was outside the bunker when the club was swung into the sand?

**A.** No. However, if the club was still touching the sand when the ball rolled back into the bunker, a breach of Rule 13-4 occurred, and any doubt on this point should be resolved against the player.

### 13-4/35.7 Player Deems Ball Unplayable in Bunker, Lifts Ball and Then Removes Loose Impediment from Bunker

**Q.** A player's tee shot comes to rest in a bunker. He lifts his ball from the bunker after deeming it unplayable. Before selecting an option under Rule 28, he removes a loose impediment from the bunker. Since this action took place while his ball was lifted, i.e., it was not lying in the hazard, was the player in breach of Rule 13-4?

**A.** Yes. The prohibitions of Rule 13-4 apply when a ball is in a hazard or when a ball, having been lifted from a hazard, may be dropped or placed in the hazard. Under the unplayable ball Rule, two of the player's options require him to drop a ball in the bunker. The player would incur the penalty even if he subsequently elected to put a ball into play outside the bunker under Rule 28a. However, the player would not incur the penalty if, before removing the loose impediment, he had indicated that he would put a ball into play outside the bunker under Rule 28a and subsequently did so. (Revised)

**Loose Impediments Affecting Lie Removed While Ball Lifted — See 23-1/8.**

### 13-4/35.8 Player Deems Ball Unplayable in Bunker, Announces His Intention to Proceed Under Rule 28a Outside Bunker and Then Rakes Bunker on New Line of Play

**Q.** A player's tee shot comes to rest in a bunker in front of the putting green. He lifts the ball after deeming it unplayable and announces his intention to proceed under Rule 28a. Before walking back to play from the teeing ground again, the player smoothes his footprints in the bunker, which are on his line of play from the teeing ground. He then plays from the teeing ground. What is the ruling?

**A.** In equity (Rule 1-4), and by analogy to Exception 2 to Rule 13-4, once a player has indicated he will proceed under a Rule that requires him to make his next stroke from outside the hazard, he may smooth sand or soil in the hazard.

The fact that the smoothing improved the player's line of play for his next stroke from the teeing ground is irrelevant as the right to smooth in these circumstances overrides any conflicting provisions in Rule 13-2.

However, if the player changed his mind and proceeded under Rule 28b or c, he would be in breach of Rule 13-4 for smoothing the bunker. (New)

### 13-4/36 Smoothing Irregularities in Bunker After Stroke But Before Ball Extricated

**Q.** A makes a stroke in a bunker but fails to extricate his ball from the bunker. He smoothes irregularities in the area where the stroke was made. The smoothing does not improve the new lie of the ball. However, B claims that the smoothing assisted A in his subsequent play of the hole because it constituted testing the consistency of the sand. Is B right?

**A.** No. Exception 2 to Rule 13-4 permits smoothing, provided that the lie of the ball is not improved and the player is not assisted in his subsequent play of the hole. The claim that A's smoothing of the sand assisted him in his subsequent play of the hole would only be valid if, as a result of a subsequent stroke in the bunker, A's ball came to rest in the smoothed area. (Revised)

### 13-4/37 Ball Played from Bunker Is Out of Bounds or Lost; Player Tests Condition of Bunker or Smoothes Footprints Before Dropping Another Ball in Bunker

**Q.** A player plays from a bunker and his ball comes to rest out of bounds or is lost. He smoothes his footprints in the bunker at the place where he must drop a ball under Rule 27-1 or, before dropping a ball under Rule 27-1, he takes a few practice swings touching the sand in the bunker. Is the player in breach of Rule 13-4?

**A.** No. The prohibitions in Rule 13-4 apply only when the player's ball is in the hazard or when it has been lifted from a hazard and may be dropped or placed in the hazard. In this case, the player's ball has been played from the hazard rather than lifted.

Furthermore, Exception 2 under Rule 13-4 allows a player, after playing his ball out of a hazard, to smooth sand or soil in the hazard, without restriction. This right overrides any conflicting provisions in other Rules, including Rule 13-2.

### 13-4/37.5 Player Smoothes Irregularities in Bunker After Playing Out Backwards; Smoothed Area on Line of Play

**Q.** A player plays out of a bunker backwards and smoothes his footprints. He then discovers that the smoothed area of the bunker is on his line of play. Is he in breach of Rule 13-2?

**A.** No. Exception 2 to Rule 13-4 allows a player, after playing his ball out of a hazard, to smooth sand in the hazard without restriction. This right overrides any conflicting provisions in other Rules, including Rule 13-2.

**Smoothing Irregularities in Bunker Situated Between Ball and Hole — See 13-2/28.**

**Creating and Then Smoothing Footprints in Bunker on Line of Play — See 13-2/29.**

**Creating Footprints in Bunker on Line of Play When Required to Enter Bunker to Retrieve Ball — See 13-2/29.3.**

### 13-4/38 Sand Smoothed After Ball Played Out of Bunker; Ball Later Returns to Smoothed Area

**Q.** After playing his ball out of a greenside bunker, the player smoothes his footprints. He then discovers that his ball is in another bunker on the other side of the green. He plays out of the second bunker and the ball comes to rest in the smoothed area of the first bunker. What is the ruling?

**A.** No penalty was incurred. The player did not smooth his footprints in the first bunker while his ball still lay in that bunker — see Exception 2 to Rule 13-4.

If, however, the player had failed to extricate his ball from the first bunker with his first stroke and had smoothed his footprints while his ball still lay in that bunker, he would have incurred a penalty if, as a result of a subsequent stroke in the bunker, his ball had rolled back into the smoothed area.

### 13-4/39 Player Smoothes Irregularities in Bunker After Playing Out of Turn in Match Play; Opponent Then Recalls Stroke and Player Must Drop Ball in Smoothed Area

**Q.** In a match between A and B, A's ball lay in a bunker near the green and B's ball was on the green. B's ball was farther from the hole but A played first. B recalled the stroke under Rule 10-1c. In the meantime A had raked his footprints. Did A incur a penalty?

**A.** If A's ball played out of turn came to rest outside the bunker, there was no breach of Rule 13-4b because A's ball was not lying in the bunker when he raked the footprints, i.e., the prohibitions in Rule 13-4 apply only when the player's ball lies in or touches the hazard.

If A's ball still lay in the bunker, he was in breach of Rule 13-4 because it must be assumed that the smoothing assisted him in his subsequent play of the hole. Exception 2 to Rule 13-4 exempts the player from penalty for assisting himself in the subsequent play of a hole by smoothing footprints if the ball lies outside the hazard when the smoothing takes place, but not if the ball still lies in the hazard.

### 13-4/40 Player Cleans Clubhead in Water Hazard When Ball Lies in Hazard

**Q.** A player plays a stroke from within a water hazard but does not extricate the ball from the hazard. The player sees the ball land in deep water and it is clearly unreasonable for him to play a stroke at the ball from its new position. Before leaving the hazard, the player cleans mud off his clubhead by rinsing it in the water. Is the player in breach of Rule 13-4?

**A.** No, provided that there is no doubt or it is reasonable to assume from the player's actions or statements that he will play his next stroke from outside the hazard.

**Other Decisions relating to Rule 13-4:**

Player Touches Ground in Hazard When Searching for Ball Believed to Be Covered by Loose Impediments in Hazard — See 12-1/4.

Greenkeeping Staff Member Rakes Bunker When Player's Ball Lies Therein — See 13-2/4.

Smoothing Irregularities in Bunker Situated Between Ball and Hole — See 13-2/28.

Extension of Line of Play Affected When Opponent or Fellow-Competitor Creates Footprints in Bunker — See 13-2/29.5.

Testing Condition of Bunker Before Deciding Whether to Play Through It — See 13-2/30.

Ball Outside Bunker; Stone in Bunker on Line of Play Pressed Down or Removed — See 13-2/31.

Ball Lying on Grass-Covered Ground in Bunker Deemed Unplayable — See 28/9.

Ball Unplayable in Bunker Dropped Outside Bunker Under Option Requiring Drop in Bunker — See 28/10.

# Rule 14. Striking the Ball

**Definitions**
All defined terms are in *italics* and are listed alphabetically in the Definitions section — see pages 3-11.

### 14-1. Ball to Be Fairly Struck At

The ball must be fairly struck at with the head of the club and must not be pushed, scraped or spooned.

### 14-2. Assistance

In making a *stroke,* a player must not:

    **a.** Accept physical assistance or protection from the elements; or

    **b.** Allow his *caddie*, his *partner* or his *partner's caddie* to position himself on or close to an extension of the *line of play* or the *line of putt* behind the ball.

PENALTY FOR BREACH OF RULE 14-1 or -2:
Match play — Loss of hole; Stroke play — Two strokes.

### 14-3. Artificial Devices and Unusual Equipment

The United States Golf Association (USGA) reserves the right, at any time, to change the Rules relating to artificial devices and unusual equipment and make or change the interpretations relating to these Rules.

A player in doubt as to whether use of an item would constitute a breach of Rule 14-3 should consult the USGA.

A manufacturer may submit to the USGA a sample of an item to be manufactured for a ruling as to whether its use during a *stipulated round* would cause a player to be in breach of Rule 14-3. The sample becomes the property of the USGA for reference purposes. If a manufacturer fails to submit a sample before manufacturing and/or marketing the item, the manufacturer assumes the risk of a ruling that use of the item would be contrary to the *Rules*.

Except as provided in the *Rules*, during a *stipulated round* the player must not use any artificial device or unusual equipment:

    a. That might assist him in making a *stroke* or in his play; or

    b. For the purpose of gauging or measuring distance or conditions that might affect his play; or

    c. That might assist him in gripping the club, except that:

        (i) plain gloves may be worn;

        (ii) resin, powder and drying or moisturizing agents may be used; and

        (iii) a towel or handkerchief may be wrapped around the grip.

PENALTY FOR BREACH OF RULE 14-3: Disqualification.

### 14-4. Striking the Ball More than Once

If a player's club strikes the ball more than once in the course of a *stroke*, the player must count the *stroke* and add a *penalty stroke*, making two *strokes* in all.

## 14-5. Playing Moving Ball

A player must not make a *stroke* at his ball while it is moving.

**Exceptions:**
- Ball falling off *tee* — Rule 11-3.
- Striking the ball more than once — Rule 14-4.
- Ball moving in water — Rule 14-6.

When the ball begins to *move* only after the player has begun the *stroke* or the backward movement of his club for the *stroke*, he incurs no penalty under this Rule for playing a moving ball, but he is not exempt from any penalty under the following Rules:

- Ball at rest *moved* by player — Rule 18-2a.
- Ball at rest moving after *address* — Rule 18-2b.

(Ball purposely deflected or stopped by player, partner or caddie — see Rule 1-2.)

## 14-6. Ball Moving in Water

When a ball is moving in water in a *water hazard*, the player may, without penalty, make a *stroke*, but he must not delay making his *stroke* in order to allow the wind or current to improve the position of the ball. A ball moving in water in a *water hazard* may be lifted if the player elects to invoke Rule 26.

**PENALTY FOR BREACH OF RULE 14-5 or -6:**
Match play — Loss of hole; Stroke play — Two strokes.

### 14/1 Club Stopped on Downswing by Agency Other Than Player

**Q.** If a player starts his downswing and his clubhead is deflected or stopped by an agency other than himself, e.g., the branch of a tree, is he deemed to have made a stroke?

**A.** Yes.

### 14/1.5 Intent to Strike Ball Ceases During Downswing; Club Not Stopped But Path of Clubhead Altered to Avoid Striking Ball

**Q.** A player begins his downswing with the intention of striking the ball but decides during the downswing not to strike the ball. The player is unable to stop the club before it reaches the ball, but he is able to swing intentionally over the top of the ball. Is the player deemed to have made a stroke?

**A.** No. The player has checked his downswing voluntarily by altering the path of his downswing and missing the ball even though the swing carried the clubhead beyond the ball.

However, any doubt in such a case must be resolved against the player. If, for example, the clubhead struck the ball there would be insufficient evidence to support a claim that the player had not made a stroke.

### 14/2 Club Breaks During Backswing; Swing Completed

**Q.** The head of a player's club separated from the shaft during his backswing. The player completed the swing but missed the ball. Is the player deemed to have made a stroke?

**A.** No. A stroke is "the forward movement of the club..." A shaft by itself is not a club — see Rule 4-1a.

### 14/3 Clubhead Separates from Shaft on Downswing

**Q.** A player starts his downswing and the clubhead separates from the shaft. The player continues his swing but no contact is made with the ball. Did the player make a stroke?

**A.** Yes.

### 14/4 Club Breaks During Downswing; Swing Stopped Short of Ball; Clubhead Falls and Moves Ball

**Q.** The shaft of a player's club broke during his downswing. The player stopped his swing short of the ball, but the clubhead fell and moved the ball. What is the ruling?

**A.** The player did not make a stroke — see Definition of "Stroke."

If the ball was not in play, i.e., the incident involved a tee shot, no penalty was incurred, and a ball must be played from the teeing ground.

If the ball was in play, the player would incur a one-stroke penalty under Rule 18-2a or -2b and the ball must be replaced.

### 14/5 Club Breaks During Downswing; Swing Completed But Misses Ball; Clubhead Falls and Moves Ball

**Q.** The shaft of a player's club broke during his downswing. The player continued his swing and missed the ball. However, the clubhead fell and moved the ball. What is the ruling?

**A.** The stroke counts but the player incurs no penalty. The ball must be played as it lies.

### 14/6 Ball Popped Up Swung at in Disgust

**Q.** A player's ball is lying against a root. He makes a stroke and the ball pops up into the air. In disgust, he swings at it on the way down, but misses. Was the swing in disgust a stroke?

**A.** No. Such an instinctive swing in anger is not a stroke. Nor should the player be considered to have taken action to influence the movement of the ball in breach of Rule 1-2. However, if the player had struck the ball accidentally while it was in motion, he would have incurred a penalty of loss of hole in match play or two strokes in stroke play — Rules 19-2a and -2b.

**Ball Knocked from Lip of Hole in Disgust — See 18-2a/23.**

## 14/7 Striking at Tree Branch to Move Ball Lodged Higher in Branch

**Q.** A player's ball is lodged in a tree branch beyond the reach of a club. The player swings at a lower part of the branch with a club for the purpose of dislodging the ball, and the ball falls to the ground. Has the player made a stroke?

**A.** No, because the player did not strike at the ball — see Definition of "Stroke." The player incurred a one-stroke penalty under Rule 18-2a (Ball at Rest Moved by Player) and must replace the ball.

Since the spot where the ball lay is unreachable and the ball therefore cannot be replaced, the player must proceed under the unplayable ball Rule, incurring an additional penalty stroke — see Decisions 18-1/9 and 18-2a/29.

**Meaning of Damage Sustained in "Normal Course of Play" — See 4-3/1.**

**Other Decisions relating to Rule 14:**

**Stroke at Own Ball Dislodges Concealed Ball — See 15/2.**

**Ball Moved Accidentally by Practice Swing Prior to Tee Shot — See 18-2a/19.**

**Ball Moved Accidentally by Practice Swing Through the Green — See 18-2a/20.**

**Ball Moved Accidentally by Backward Movement of Club After Stroke Misses — See 18-2a/22.**

**Player Misses Ball Purposely in Foursome So Partner Would Play Ball Over Water — See 29-1/7.**

## 14-1/1 Playing Stroke with Back of Clubhead

**Q.** May a player play a left-handed stroke with the back of the head of a right-handed club?

**A.** Yes. A player may play a stroke with any part of the clubhead, provided the ball is fairly struck at (Rule 14-1) and the club conforms with Rule 4-1.

## 14-1/2 Striking Ball with Billiard-Type Motion

**Q.** A player holed a short putt by squatting behind the ball (but not on an extension of the line of putt behind the ball) and striking the ball with the bottom of the clubhead, using a motion similar to that used in playing a shot in billiards or shuffleboard. Was the player in breach of Rule 14-1?

**A.** Yes. Such a manner of moving the ball constitutes a push in golf.

### 14-1/3  Putting with Wrong End of Putter

**Q.** A player misses a short putt and hastily holes the ball with the wrong (handle) end of his putter. What is the ruling?

**A.** The player incurs a penalty of loss of hole in match play or two strokes in stroke play for a breach of Rule 14-1, which requires that the ball be struck at with the head of the club. In stroke play, the stroke with the wrong end of the putter counts, and, since the ball was holed, the player had completed play of the hole.

### 14-1/4  Striking Ball with Half an Inch Backswing

**Q.** A player's ball lies close to an out of bounds fence, but there is room behind the ball to insert an iron club or a putter and leave a space of half an inch between the ball and the face of the club. If the player plays a stroke with such a limited backswing, is he in breach of Rule 14-1?

**A.** It is possible to strike a ball fairly with a half inch backswing. However, in most such cases the player would be pushing the ball, contrary to Rule 14-1. In the absence of strong evidence to the contrary, it should be ruled that the player has pushed the ball.

In order to strike the ball fairly, it must be swung at with the clubhead. If the ball is moved by any other method, it has been pushed, scraped or spooned.

If a ball is fairly struck at, there is only momentary contact between the clubhead and the ball or whatever intervenes between the clubhead and the ball.

### 14-1/5  Moving Ball Lying Against Fence by Striking Other Side of Fence

**Q.** A player's ball lies against a board at the base of an out of bounds fence. He swings a club from the out of bounds side of the fence against the board, i.e., swings at the ball with the board intervening between the club and the ball. The stroke moves the board which causes the ball to move away from the fence. Is such a stroke permissible?

**A.** Yes. The player fairly struck at the ball even though other material intervened between the club and the ball. The Definition of "Out of Bounds" allows a player to "stand out of bounds to play a ball lying within bounds."

### 14-1/6  Player Holds Club with Left Hand and Moves Ball by Striking Shaft with Other Hand

**Q.** A player addresses his ball lying in high grass on a steep bank. His ball does not move, but the player believes it will move if he takes a backswing. Accordingly, the player holds the club with his left hand

and strikes the shaft of the club with his right hand, thereby moving the ball. Is this permissible?

**A.** No. The player pushed the ball, contrary to Rule 14-1.

### 14-1/7 Using More Than One Club to Make Stroke

**Q.** A player, whose ball was lodged in a bush, swung at the ball with three clubs to minimize the chance of missing it. Is this permissible?

**A.** No. Rule 14-1 requires that the ball be struck at with the "head of the club;" the word "club" is in the singular. The player was in breach of this Rule when he swung at the ball with three clubs.

### 14-2/1 Player Aligns Partner's Club Before Stroke

**Q.** A player aligns his partner's putter and then moves away before his partner plays. Is this permissible?

**A.** Yes. Rule 14-2 (Assistance) does not apply prior to making a stroke.

### 14-2/2 Player Holds Umbrella Over Own Head When Playing Stroke

**Q.** A player playing in the rain holds an umbrella over his head with one hand while holing a very short putt, gripping the putter with the other hand. Is this permissible?

**A.** Yes. Rule 14-2 prohibits a player, while making a stroke, from accepting protection from the elements from someone other than himself. However, it does not prohibit him from protecting himself.

### 14-2/3 Caddie Shields Player from Sun During Stroke

**Q.** May a player's caddie purposely stand between the player and the setting sun so that the sun's glare is not in the player's face while he is playing a stroke?

**A.** No. Such procedure is a breach of Rule 14-2.

**Material Applied to Top of Clubhead to Reduce Glare — See 4-2/1.**

### 14-2/4 Caddie Inadvertently Stands on Extension of Line of Play Behind Ball

**Q.** A player's caddie inadvertently stood on an extension of the player's line of play behind the ball when the player made a stroke. The caddie was watching another player play from the next tee. Neither the player nor his caddie was aware that the caddie was so located. Was the player subject to penalty under Rule 14-2b?

**A.** No. The purpose of Rule 14-2b is to prohibit a caddie from positioning himself behind the player while the player makes a stroke in order to advise the player on alignment or otherwise assist him. In this case, the caddie was not so positioned.

The same ruling would apply if the player's caddie inadvertently stood on an extension of the line of putt behind the ball during the stroke. (Revised)

### 14-3/0.5 Local Rule Permitting Use of Distance-Measuring Device

**Q.** May a Committee, by Local Rule, permit the use of distance-measuring devices?

**A.** Yes. A Committee may establish a Local Rule allowing players to use devices that measure distance only. However, the use of devices that gauge or measure other conditions that might affect a player's play (e.g., wind or gradient) is not permitted.

In the absence of such a Local Rule, the use of a distance-measuring device would be contrary to Rule 14-3. (New)

**Reflector on Flagstick — See 17/3.5**

### 14-3/1 Distance Meter Attached to Golf Cart

**Q.** May a player attach a meter to his golf cart for the purpose of measuring the distances of shots?

**A.** Use of such a meter during a stipulated round would be a breach of Rule 14-3. However, see also Decision 14-3/0.5. (Revised)

### 14-3/2 Pencil or Score Card Used to Assist in Gauging Distance

**Q.** It is possible to gauge distance to a putting green by holding a score card or pencil at arm's length and comparing it with the height of the flagstick. Is such a practice permissible?

**A.** Yes, provided the score card or pencil has not been specially marked. Use of anything specially marked to gauge distance is a breach of Rule 14-3. However, see also Decision 14-3/0.5. (Revised)

### 14-3/3 Standard Spectacles and Field Glasses

Neither standard spectacles nor field glasses that have no range-finder feature are artificial devices within the meaning of the term in Rule 14-3. However, see also Decision 14-3/0.5. (Revised)

### 14-3/4 Use of Compass During Round

**Q.** A player uses a compass during a round to assist him in determining wind direction or the direction of the grain in the greens or for some other similar reason. Is the player in breach of Rule 14-3?

**A.** Yes.

### 14-3/5 Booklet Providing Distances Between Various Points

**Q.** A booklet contains illustrations of the holes on a course, including isolated trees, bunkers, etc. Superimposed on each illustration is a yardage scale in increments of 10 yards. Thus, a player using such a booklet can estimate how far his ball lies from a putting green or a tee. Is use of such a booklet during a round contrary to Rule 14-3?

**A.** No.

### 14-3/5.5 Electronic Device Providing Distances Between Various Points

**Q.** With regard to Decision 14-3/5, may a player use an electronic device containing the same information?

**A.** Yes, although a player must not use a device with a distance measuring or distance calculating function. However, see also Decision 14-3/0.5. (Revised)

### 14-3/6 Holding Ball in Hand Against Grip When Putting

**Q.** A player putts with a golf ball held in his left hand against the grip. He claims the pressure transmitted to the grip through the ball assists him in putting. Is such use of a ball permissible?

**A.** No. A ball is an artificial device when used in such a manner.

### 14-3/7 Player with Injured Right Wrist Inserts Left Thumb Under Elastic Bandage on Right Wrist and Hand

**Q.** A player, who wore an elastic bandage around his right wrist and hand because of an injury, inserted his left thumb under the bandage where it crosses his right palm, and played a number of strokes with his left thumb so located. Is this permissible?

**A.** No. Because of the injury, the player was entitled to wear the elastic bandage. However, when he inserted his left thumb under the bandage, he was in breach of Rule 14-3.

### 14-3/8 Adhesive Tape

**Q.** May a player bind certain fingers together with adhesive tape or apply such tape to a golf glove?

**A.** The use of adhesive tape for any medical reason, e.g., to reduce blisters or to eliminate the possibility of skin splits between the fingers, is not contrary to the Rules. However, if a player binds fingers together with tape solely to aid himself in gripping the club, he is in breach of Rule 14-3.

Applying tape to a golf glove to prevent the glove from slipping or to reduce wear is not a breach of Rule 14-3.

### 14-3/9  Player Putts with One Hand and Steadies Himself with Club Held in Other Hand

**Q.** A player, while putting with one hand, uses another club to lean on and steady himself. In the circumstances, is the club the player leans on an artificial device, contrary to Rule 14-3?

**A.** Yes.

**Player Uses Cane or Club to Enter or Leave Hazard When Ball Lies in Hazard — See 13-4/3.5.**

### 14-3/10  Use of Training or Swing Aid During Round

**Q.** During a round, may a player make a stroke or a practice swing using a club with a weighted headcover or "donut" on it, or use any other device designed as a training or swing aid?

**A.** No — but see also Decision 4-4a/7 for the use of a weighted training club. (Revised)

### 14-3/10.5  Use of Stretching Devices

**Q.** Rule 14-3a prohibits a player, during a stipulated round, from using any artificial device or unusual equipment that "might assist him in making a stroke or in his play." Would the use of a stretching device during a stipulated round be a breach of Rule 14-3?

**A.** During a stipulated round, it is permissible to use a device designed for stretching unless the device is designed specifically to be used in a golf swing and is used during a golf swing (see Decision 14-3/10). For example, the following stretching devices may be used:

- Items designed specifically for golf but not used in a golf swing (e.g., a bar to place across the shoulders);
- Items designed for general stretching (e.g., rubber tubing); and
- Items not originally designed for stretching (e.g., a section of pipe).

(New)

### 14-3/11  Plumb-Line

**Q.** Is a plumb-line, i.e., a weight suspended on a string, an artificial device within the meaning of the term in Rule 14-3?

**A.** Yes.

### 14-3/12  Club Used as Plumb-Line

**Q.** May a player use his putter as a plumb-line to assist him in determining the slope on a putting green?

**A.** Yes. Such a practice is not a breach of Rule 14-3.

### 14-3/12.5 Bottled Drink Used as a Level

**Q.** A player places a bottled drink on the putting green in order to gauge the slope of the green. Is the player in breach of Rule 14-3?

**A.** Yes. However, if the placing of the bottle on the putting green was not for the purpose of gauging the slope, the player would not be in breach of Rule 14-3.

### 14-3/13 Hand Warmer

**Q.** A player uses a device to warm his hands during a round. Is the player in breach of Rule 14-3?

**A.** No.

### 14-3/13.5 Golf Ball Artificially Warmed

**Q.** Is the use of a golf ball that was purposely warmed during a stipulated round with a golf ball warmer, hand warmer or any such device a breach of Rule 14-3?

**A.** Yes. However, it would not be a breach of Rule 14-3 to use a ball that was artificially warmed prior to the stipulated round. (Revised)

### 14-3/14 Electronic Instrument Used to Find Ball

**Q.** A transmitter has been embedded in a golf ball. When used with a special radio receiver, a player may find such a ball readily because the transmitter emits a signal that grows louder as the receiver moves closer to the ball. Is the use of such a ball and receiver permissible?

**A.** No. Use of such a ball in conjunction with the receiver is a breach of Rule 14-3.

However, use of such a ball without the receiver is permissible, provided the ball conforms to the Rules and its use is in accordance with any conditions of competition that may have been adopted (e.g., the List of Conforming Golf Balls Condition). (Revised)

### 14-3/15 Artificial Limbs

An artificial leg or arm is not an artificial device within the meaning of the term in Rule 14-3, even if an artificial leg has been modified to aid a player in playing the game or an artificial arm has a fitting specially designed for gripping a golf club. However, if the Committee believes that an artificial limb so modified would give the player an undue advantage over other players, the Committee has authority to deem it to be an artificial device contrary to Rule 14-3.

Clubs used by a player with an artificial arm must conform with Rule 4-1 except that an attachment may be fitted to the grip or shaft to assist the player to hold the club. However, if the Committee believes that the use of a club modified in this way would give the player an undue advantage over other players, it should deem the attachment an artificial device contrary to Rule 14-3.

### 14-3/16 Use of Electronic Devices

As provided in the Etiquette Section, players should ensure that any electronic device taken onto the course does not distract other players.

The use of an electronic device such as a mobile phone, hand-held computer, calculator, television or radio is not itself a breach of Rule 14-3. For example, the following uses of an electronic device during a stipulated round are not a breach of the Rules:

- Using the device for matters unrelated to golf (e.g., to call home);

- Using the device to access information on advice-related matters that were published prior to the start of the player's round (e.g., an electronic yardage book, swing tips); or

- Using the device to obtain information related to the competition being played (e.g., the leader board or projected "cut").

However, examples of uses of an electronic device during a stipulated round that are a breach of Rule 14-3, for which the penalty is disqualification, include:

- Using the device (e.g., a television or radio) to watch or listen to a broadcast of the competition being played;

- Using the device to ask for or give advice in breach of Rule 8-1 (e.g., calling a swing coach at home); or

- Using the device to access information on advice-related matters that were not published prior to the start of his round (e.g., analysis of strokes made during that round). (Revised)

### 14-4/1 Ball Falls on Club Face After Stroke and Sticks to Mud Thereon

**Q.** A player, playing a stroke at his ball on the bank of a bunker, hit the ball straight up. The ball came down and adhered to mud on the face of the club. Was the player in breach of Rule 14-4?

**A.** No. However, the player stopped his ball and was in breach of Rule 19-2.

In match play, the player loses the hole — Rule 19-2a.

In stroke play, the player incurs a penalty of two strokes and must drop the ball as near as possible to the spot where the ball adhered to the club — Rule 19-2b.

But see Decision 1-4/2.

### 14-4/2 Ball Strikes Pipeline and on Rebound Is Deflected by Face of Club

**Q.** A player's ball strikes a pipeline and on the rebound hits the face of his club. Is the player considered to have struck the ball more than once in breach of Rule 14-4?

**A.** No. The player did not strike the ball more than once. He struck it once and it rebounded and hit the face of his club. Rule 19-2 applies.

### 14-5/1 Ball Moving During Backswing Struck While Still Moving

**Q.** A player's ball starts moving during his backswing and he strikes the ball while it is still moving. What is the ruling?

**A.** There is no penalty under Rule 14-5 because the ball began to move after the player had begun his backswing. However, if the player had caused the ball to move or had addressed it, he incurred a penalty stroke — Rule 18-2a or -2b.

### 14-6/1 Ball Moves in Water in Water Hazard After Address

**Q.** A ball was at rest in shallow, rapidly-running water in a water hazard. After the player had carefully entered the water, walked to the ball and addressed it, the ball moved, presumably due to the current. What is the ruling?

**A.** There is no penalty, and the player must play the ball from its new position. Rule 14-6 overrides Rule 18-2b (Ball Moving After Address) in such a case.

When a ball is in water and it is not clear whether the player's actions caused the ball to move, he should be given the benefit of the doubt and no penalty should be applied. However, if the player's actions clearly caused the ball to move, he would be subject to a penalty stroke under Rule 18-2a and required to replace the ball. For example, if a player were to jump into the water close to the ball and in so doing create a splash that moved the ball, he would be subject to penalty under Rule 18-2a.

# Rule 15.
# Substituted Ball; Wrong Ball

**Definitions**
All defined terms are in *italics* and are listed alphabetically in the Definitions section — see pages 3-11.

### 15-1. General

A player must hole out with the ball played from the *teeing ground* unless the ball is *lost, out of bounds* or the player *substitutes* another ball, whether or not substitution is permitted (see Rule 15-2). If a player plays a *wrong ball,* see Rule 15-3.

### 15-2. Substituted Ball

A player may *substitute* a ball when proceeding under a *Rule* that permits the player to play, drop or place another ball in completing the play of a hole. The *substituted ball* becomes the *ball in play*.

If a player *substitutes* a ball when not permitted to do so under the *Rules,* that *substituted ball* is not a *wrong ball*; it becomes the *ball in play*. If the mistake is not corrected as provided in Rule 20-6 and the player makes a *stroke* at a wrongly *substituted ball,* he incurs the penalty prescribed by the applicable *Rule* and in stroke play, must play out the hole with the *substituted ball*.

(Playing from Wrong Place — see Rule 20-7.)

### 15-3. Wrong Ball

#### a. Match Play

If a player makes a *stroke* at a *wrong ball* that is not in a *hazard,* he loses the hole.

There is no penalty if a player makes a *stroke* at a *wrong ball* in a *hazard*. Any *strokes* made at a *wrong ball* in a *hazard* do not count in the player's score.

If the *wrong ball* belongs to another player, its owner must place a ball on the spot from which the *wrong ball* was first played.

If the player and opponent exchange balls during the play of a hole, the first to make a *stroke* at a *wrong ball* that is not in a *hazard,* loses the hole; when this cannot be determined, the hole must be played out with the balls exchanged.

#### b. Stroke Play

If a *competitor* makes a *stroke* or *strokes* at a *wrong ball* that is not in a *hazard,* he incurs a penalty of two strokes.

There is no penalty if a *competitor* makes a *stroke* at a *wrong ball* in a *hazard*. Any *strokes* made at a *wrong ball* in a *hazard* do not count in the *competitor's* score.

The *competitor* must correct his mistake by playing the correct ball or by proceeding under the *Rules*. If he fails to correct his mistake before making a *stroke* on the next *teeing ground,* or in the case of the last hole of the round, fails to declare his intention to correct his mistake before leaving the *putting green,* he is disqualified.

*Strokes* made by a *competitor* with a *wrong ball* do not count in his score.

If the *wrong ball* belongs to another *competitor,* its owner must place a ball on the spot from which the *wrong ball* was first played.

(Lie of ball to be placed or replaced altered — see Rule 20-3b.)

(Spot not determinable — see Rule 20-3c.)

### 15/1 Stroke Misses Wrong Ball

**Q.** A player swings at and misses a wrong ball. What is the ruling?

**A.** Since the player made a stroke with a wrong ball, he lost the hole in match play (Rule 15-3a) or incurred a two-stroke penalty in stroke play (Rule 15-3b).

### 15/2 Player's Stroke at Own Ball Dislodges Concealed Ball

**Q.** A player plays a stroke with his own ball in the rough and also hits an old abandoned ball which was hidden beneath his ball. Since he struck the hidden ball, did he play a wrong ball?

**A.** No. The player played a stroke with his own ball, not with the hidden ball. Since he did not play a stroke with the hidden ball, Rule 15-3 is not applicable. The player must play his ball as it lies.

**Practice Swing Dislodges Concealed Ball — See 7-2/7.**

**Ball Moved Accidentally by Player in Playing Wrong Ball — See 18-2a/21.**

### 15/3 Player Plays Stroke at Part of Abandoned Ball Which Had Broken into Pieces

**Q.** A ball had broken into pieces and had been abandoned. Part of it was lying in heavy grass. A player mistook the part for his ball in play and played a stroke with it. The player asserts that part of a ball is not a ball and, therefore, that he has not played a wrong ball. Is the player correct?

**A.** No. Since the player made a stroke with a wrong ball, he lost the hole in match play (Rule 15-3a) or incurred a two-stroke penalty in stroke play (Rule 15-3b).

### 15/4 Player Lifts Ball, Sets It Aside and Plays It from Where Set Aside

**Q.** A player marks the position of his ball on the putting green, lifts the ball and sets it aside. By mistake, he putts the ball from the spot at which he set it aside. What is the ruling?

**A.** When a ball is lifted under Rule 20-1, it is out of play — see Definition of "Ball in Play." When the player played a stroke with his ball while it was out of play, he played a wrong ball (Rule 15-3).

In match play, the player lost the hole — Rule 15-3a.

In stroke play, he incurred a penalty of two strokes and was required to correct the error before playing from the next tee; otherwise, he would be disqualified — Rule 15-3b.

**Ball Lifted by Player from Putting Green Replaced by Caddie Behind Ball-Marker — See 20-4/2.**

### 15/5 Original Ball Found and Played After Another Ball Put into Play

**Q.** A player unable to find his ball after a brief search drops another ball (Ball B) under Rule 27-1 and plays it. His original ball is then found within five minutes after search for it began. The player lifted Ball B and continued to play with the original ball. Was this correct?

**A.** No. When the player put the substituted ball into play at the spot of the previous stroke with the intent to play a ball under Rule 27-1, he proceeded under an applicable Rule. Therefore, Rule 20-6 does not apply, and he must continue with the substituted ball (see Decision 27-1/2). The original ball was lost when Ball B was played under Rule 27-1 (see Definition of "Lost Ball").

When the player lifted Ball B, he incurred a penalty of one stroke under Rule 18-2a. When he made a stroke with the original ball after it was out of play, he played a wrong ball (see Definitions of "Ball in Play" and "Wrong Ball") and incurred a penalty of loss of hole in match play or an additional penalty of two strokes in stroke play (Rule 15-3). In stroke play, the player would be disqualified if, before playing from the next teeing ground, he did not correct his error (Rule 15-3b). (Revised)

**Ball Found After Search Exceeding Five Minutes Is Then Played — See 27/8.**

**Original Ball Found Within Five-Minute Search Period After Another Ball Dropped; Dropped Ball Played — See 27-1/2.3.**

**Original Ball Played After Provisional Ball Played from Point Nearer Hole Than Original Ball Likely to Be — See 27-2b/5.**

**Provisional Ball Played from Point Nearer Hole Than Original Ball Because Player Erroneously Thought Original Ball, Which Was Visible, Was Out of Bounds — See 27-2c/3.**

### 15/6 Stroke Played with Ball Lying Out of Bounds

**Q.** A player plays a stroke at his ball which is lying out of bounds. What is the ruling?

**A.** A ball lying out of bounds is no longer in play and thus is a wrong ball — see Definitions of "Ball in Play" and "Wrong Ball." Accordingly, in match play, the player loses the hole. In stroke play, he incurs a two-stroke penalty and must proceed under Rule 27-1, incurring the additional one-stroke penalty prescribed in that Rule.

**Stroke Played from Environmentally-Sensitive Area Defined as Out of Bounds — See 33-8/43.**

## 15/6.5 Ball Changed During Play of Hole to Aid Identification

**Q.** A and B realized after playing their tee shots on a par-5 hole that they were playing balls with identical markings. Based on the location of both tee shots, A knew which ball was his. To avoid subsequent confusion, A lifted his ball before playing his second shot, substituted a ball with different markings and played out the hole. Is this permissible?

**A.** No. A was not entitled to substitute a ball.

In match play, A loses the hole — Rule 15-2.

In stroke play, A incurs a total penalty of three strokes — two strokes under Rule 15-2 and one stroke under Rule 18-2a for lifting his ball in play without authority.

**Player Breaches Rules More Than Once Prior to Stroke; Whether Multiple Penalties Applied — See 1-4/12.**

**Second Ball Played in Match Play — See 3-3/9.**

## 15/7 Wrong Ball Played in Belief It Is Provisional or Second Ball

**Q.** A player, thinking his original ball may be lost or out of bounds, plays a provisional ball under Rule 27-2a. Before reaching the place where his original ball is likely to be, he plays a wrong ball, believing it is his provisional ball. He then finds his original ball in bounds and, correctly, abandons the provisional ball. Does the player incur a penalty under Rule 15-3 for playing a wrong ball, even though that wrong ball was played in mistake for a provisional ball which never became the ball in play?

**A.** Yes. Although a penalty incurred in play of a provisional ball is normally canceled if the provisional ball has to be abandoned under Rule 27-2c (e.g., a one-stroke penalty under Rule 18-2b if the provisional ball moves after being addressed), this does not apply when the penalty is for playing a wrong ball.

The same ruling would apply if a competitor played a wrong ball in the belief that it was a second ball played under Rule 3-3 (Doubt as to Procedure in Stroke Play) or Rule 20-7c (Serious Breach of Playing from a Wrong Place in Stroke Play). However, in similar circumstances, there would have been no penalty under Rule 15-3b if the competitor had first holed out with his ball in play and then played a stroke with a wrong ball when proceeding under Rule 3-3 or Rule 20-7c.

**Penalty Strokes Incurred by Playing the Ball Ruled Not to Count — See 20-7c/5.**

### 15/8 Ball Played Under Rule for Ball Lost in Ground Under Repair After Another Ball Played Under Stroke-and-Distance Procedure

**Q.** A player's ball was lost in ground under repair. He played another ball under the lost ball Rule (Rule 27-1). The player then realized that Rule 25-1c provides for relief without penalty for a ball lost in ground under repair. He decided to proceed under that Rule, lifted the ball played under Rule 27-1, dropped another ball in accordance with Rule 25-1c and played out the hole. What is the ruling?

**A.** The ball played under Rule 27-1 was the player's ball in play and he should have continued with that ball. The player, having put another ball into play under Rule 27-1, was no longer entitled to proceed under Rule 25-1c. Therefore, when he lifted his ball in play, dropped another ball elsewhere under Rule 25-1c and played it, he was in breach of Rule 18 (for lifting his ball in play and failing to replace it) and Rule 15-2 (for wrongly substituting a ball).

In match play, he loses the hole — Rule 15-2 or Rule 18.

In stroke play, in addition to the stroke-and-distance penalty incurred when he proceeded under the lost ball Rule (Rule 27-1), he incurs a penalty of two strokes under Rule 18 and an additional two-stroke penalty for a breach of Rule 15-2.

**Ball Played from Ground Under Repair Abandoned and Relief Taken Under Ground Under Repair Rule — See 18-2a/8.5.**

**Ball Dropped and Played Under Ground Under Repair Rule in Absence of Reasonable Evidence Original Ball Lost in Ground Under Repair — See 25-1c/2.**

**Ball Played Under Water Hazard Rule; Original Ball Then Found Outside Hazard — See 26-1/3.**

**Ball Played Under Water Hazard Rule Without Reasonable Evidence Original Ball in Hazard; Original Ball Then Found in Hazard — See 26-1/4.**

**Lost Ball Treated as Moved by Outside Agency in Absence of Reasonable Evidence to That Effect — See 27-1/2.5.**

### 15/9 Ball Thrown into Bounds by Outside Agency and Played; Caddie Aware of Action of Outside Agency

**Q.** A's ball was found lying in bounds and A played a shot towards the green. Then a man appeared and said that A's ball had come to rest out of bounds in his garden. He said he had thrown it onto the course and had told A's caddie what he had done. The caddie had not reported this to A. What is the ruling?

**A.** Under Rule 6-1, A is responsible for his caddie's failure to tell him what the man had said.

A's ball was no longer the ball in play when it came to rest out of bounds. Therefore, it was a wrong ball — see Definitions of "Ball in

Play" and "Wrong Ball." When A made a stroke with the wrong ball, he incurred the penalty prescribed in Rule 15-3 and, in stroke play, was obliged to proceed under Rule 27-1. (Revised)

### 15/10 Ball Thrown into Bounds by Outside Agency and Played; Neither Player Nor His Caddie Aware of Action of Outside Agency

**Q.** Decision 15/9 states that, if an outside agency throws a player's ball back onto the course from out of bounds and advises the player's caddie to this effect, the player is penalized for playing a wrong ball if he plays the ball from its position in bounds. What would be the ruling if neither the player nor his caddie knew the player's ball had been thrown back onto the course?

**A.** In match play, in equity (Rule 1-4), there would be no penalty for playing a wrong ball (Rule 15-3). If the player learns of the actions of the outside agency after playing the wrong ball, but before the opponent makes another stroke or takes some action (e.g. picks up or concedes the player's next stroke) that the opponent might not have taken if the wrong ball had not been played, then the player must correct his mistake and proceed correctly. If the player learns of the mistake later than this, he must proceed with the wrong ball without penalty and the score with the wrong ball must count.

In stroke play, in equity (Rule 1-4), there would be no penalty for playing a wrong ball (Rule 15-3). If the player discovers before playing from the next teeing ground that the original ball was out of bounds, he must go back and proceed under Rule 27-1. If the discovery is not made until later than this, the score with the wrong ball stands.

### 15/11 Wrong Ball Hit Out of Bounds; Another Ball Played Under Rule 27-1; Original Ball Then Found Nearby

**Q.** A player plays what he believes to be his ball and hits it out of bounds. He plays another ball under Rule 27-1 and then discovers that the ball he hit out of bounds was a wrong ball and that his original ball is lying in bounds. What is the ruling?

**A.** In match play, the player loses the hole for playing a wrong ball (Rule 15-3a).

In stroke play, the ball the player hit out of bounds was a wrong ball, and the ball played under Rule 27-1 was a continuation of the play of that wrong ball.

The player incurred a penalty of two strokes under Rule 15-3b and he was obliged to hole out with his original ball.

### 15/12 Wrong Ball Found Out of Bounds Played Under Stroke-and-Distance Procedure; Original Ball Then Found in Bounds

**Q.** A player finds a ball out of bounds, thinks it is his original ball, plays it at the spot from which the original ball was played and then finds his original ball in bounds. What is the ruling?

**A.** The original ball is lost and the ball found out of bounds is in play under penalty of stroke and distance. See Decision 27/17.

### 15/13 Stray Ball Dropped Under Unplayable Ball Rule But Not Played

**Q.** A player finds a ball he believes is his original ball, deems it unplayable and drops it under Rule 28b or c. He then discovers that the ball is not his but is, in fact, a stray ball. What is the ruling?

**A.** When the player dropped the stray ball, it became a substituted ball. However, the player was not entitled to proceed under Rule 28b or c without finding the original ball. Since a stroke has not been made with the substituted ball, the player is entitled to correct his error under Rule 20-6 by abandoning the substituted ball and resuming search for the original ball. If the player's ball is lost, the player must proceed under Rule 27-1. (Revised)

**Wrong Ball Declared Unplayable Played Under Stroke-and-Distance Procedure; Original Ball Then Found — See 28/14.**

**Wrong Ball Declared Unplayable, Dropped Within Two Club-Lengths and Played Before Error Discovered — See 28/15.**

### 15/14 Ball in Bunker Deemed Unplayable, Dropped in Bunker and Played; Ball Then Discovered to Be Wrong Ball

**Q.** A player, believing that a ball lying very badly in a bunker is his ball, deems it unplayable, drops it in the bunker and plays it out. He then discovers that the ball he has played is not his original ball. Has he played a wrong ball?

**A.** No. The procedures in Rules 28b and 28c may not be applied except with reference to the position of the player's ball in play, and this must first be found and identified (see Decision 28/1). Before proceeding under option b or c of Rule 28, the player should ensure he is doing so with reference to his ball in play and may lift the ball to inspect it when proceeding under Rule 28, even if the ball lies in a bunker. In this case, the ball dropped and played by the player was not his original ball; it was a substituted ball. Since the location of the original ball was not known at the time the substituted ball was dropped, he was required to proceed under Rule 27-1. As the substituted ball was not dropped at the spot required by Rule 27-1, he played from a wrong place (see Decision 28/15).

In match play, he incurred a penalty of loss of hole (Rule 20-7b).

In stroke play, he incurred a penalty of one stroke under Rule 27-1 and an additional penalty of two strokes under Rule 20-7c for playing from a wrong place. If the breach was a serious one, he is subject to disqualification unless he corrected his error as provided in Rule 20-7c.

#### Other Decisions relating to Rule 15:

**Player Discovers Own Ball in Hole After Playing Wrong Ball — See 1-1/4.**

**In Anger Player Hits Ball Played by Player in Following Group — See 1-4/4.**

**Player Wins Hole with Wrong Ball; Error Discovered at Next Hole — See 9-2/8.**

**Competitor's Ball Played by Fellow-Competitor in Bunker Not Replaced — See 18-4/1.**

**Ball Moved by Wrong Ball Played by Opponent — See 18-5/1.**

**Competitor's Ball Played by Fellow-Competitor; Competitor Substitutes Another Ball at Wrong Place, Plays It and Then Abandons It and Plays Out Original Ball from Right Place — See 20-7c/4.**

**Casual Water Mistaken for Water Hazard; Substituted Ball Played Under Water Hazard Rule — See 25-1b/13.**

**Time Permitted for Search for Lost Ball After Wrong Ball Played — See 27/2.**

**Order of Play in Foursome Stroke Play When Wrong Ball Played — See 29-1/8.**

**Player Plays Partner's Ball — See 30-3d/1.**

**Player Wins Hole with Wrong Ball and Partner Picks Up; Error Discovered at Next Hole — See 30-3d/2.**

**Players on Opposite Sides Exchange Balls During Play of Hole and Their Partners Pick Up; Error Discovered at Next Hole — See 30-3d/3.**

**Player Plays Partner's Ball; Error Discovered After Opponents Have Played Next Strokes — See 30-3d/3.5.**

### *15-1/1  Balls Inadvertently Exchanged by Players Between Holes*

**Q.** After completion of a hole, the balls of A and B were inadvertently exchanged and A played B's ball from the next teeing ground. Did A play a wrong ball?

**A.** No. A ball played from the teeing ground into the hole is not a wrong ball, even if it does not belong to the player — see Definitions of "Ball in Play" and "Wrong Ball."

### *15-1/2  Balls Inadvertently Exchanged by Competitors at Unknown Place*

**Q.** In stroke play, it was discovered after play of a hole that A had holed out with B's ball and vice versa. Both A and B were certain that they had holed out at this hole with the balls they played from the teeing ground. Thus, it was concluded that they had exchanged balls during play of a previous hole or between two holes. What is the ruling?

**A.** If it cannot be established that the balls were exchanged during play of a hole, A and B should be given the benefit of the doubt and it should be assumed that the balls were inadvertently exchanged between play of two holes, in which case no penalty would be imposed.

### 15-1/2.5 Balls Inadvertently Exchanged by Players After One Ball Struck and Moved the Other

**Q.** A plays to the green and his ball strikes and moves B's ball which was lying on the green. Both balls come to rest on the green. B, acting under Rules 18-5 and 20-3c, lifts A's ball by mistake and places it as near as possible to where his (B's) ball lay before it was moved. B then holes out with A's ball after which A, by mistake, holes out with B's. What is the ruling?

**A.** In both forms of play, A has played a "wrong ball," whereas B has, in effect, substituted another ball when not so permitted.

In match play, B lost the hole when he played A's ball (Rule 15-2). A's subsequent play of a wrong ball is irrelevant.

In stroke play, A incurs a penalty of two strokes, must retrieve his ball from B, replace it on the spot from which B had lifted it and hole out with it before playing from the next tee; otherwise A is disqualified (Rule 15-3b).

B incurs a penalty of two strokes under Rule 15-2, which must be added to his score for the hole.

### 15-1/3 Hole at Which Wrong Ball Played Unknown

**Q.** A player discovers after the 6th hole that he is not playing the ball with which he started the round. He does not know when he first played the different ball. What is the ruling in:

(a) stroke play?

(b) match play when:

    (i) he has won every hole?

    (ii) he has lost every hole?

    (iii) he has won 4 holes, lost 1 hole and halved 1 hole?

    (iv) he has lost 4 holes, won 1 hole and halved 1 hole?

**A.** The Committee must determine whether the different ball is a wrong ball or not and give the player the benefit of any doubt — see Decision 15-1/2. Thus, if the different ball might have been put into play under a Rule or if the player might have put the different ball into play at the start of a hole, the Committee should rule in favor of the player and the player incurs no penalty in either match play or stroke play.

If, however, the conclusion is that a wrong ball has been played:

(a) in stroke play, the player is disqualified, unless the conclusion is that the wrong ball was played at the 6th hole and the player rectifies his mistake as prescribed in Rule 15-3b.

(b) in match play, the Committee must determine on a balance of probabilities the hole at which the wrong ball was played and the player loses that hole, the state of the match being adjusted accordingly, if necessary. If it is impossible to determine the hole at which the wrong ball was played, in equity (Rule 1-4):

  (i) the player loses one of the holes which he had won and becomes 4 up instead of 6 up.

  (ii) the player remains 6 down.

  (iii) the player becomes one hole worse off, i.e., he becomes 2 up instead of 3 up.

  (iv) as in (iii), i.e., he becomes 4 down instead of 3 down.

### 15-1/4  Players Inadvertently Exchange Balls Recovered from Water Hazard

**Q.** A and B played into a water hazard at approximately the same spot. One caddie was authorized to retrieve both balls and he handed A's ball to B and B's ball to A. Each player dropped the ball handed to him behind the hazard under Rule 26-1b and played to the green. On reaching the green, they discovered the exchange of balls. Should they be penalized under Rule 15-2?

**A.** No. Rule 26-1b authorizes the player to drop "a ball." Accordingly, the substitution of another ball is permissible.

### 15-2/1  Player Substitutes Another Ball on Putting Green Because Original Ball Thrown to Caddie for Cleaning Came to Rest in Lake

**Q.** A player, whose ball was on the putting green, marked the ball's position, lifted it and threw it to his caddie for cleaning. The caddie failed to catch the ball and it went into a lake and could not be retrieved. The player holed out with another ball. Should he be penalized under Rule 15-2?

**A.** Yes. Rule 16-1b, under which the ball was lifted, does not permit substitution of another ball. Accordingly, the player incurred a penalty of loss of hole in match play or two strokes in stroke play.

**Ball Lifted and Thrown into Pond in Anger — See 18-2a/13.5.**

### 15-2/2 Player Mistakenly Substitutes Another Ball on Putting Green; Error Discovered Before Stroke Played

**Q.** A player marks the position of his ball on the putting green and lifts the ball. By mistake he places another ball on the spot from which his original ball was lifted. He discovers his error before playing his next stroke, places his original ball on the spot from which it was lifted and holes out with it. What is the ruling?

**A.** There is no penalty. The player corrected the error and did not make a stroke with the other ball. Therefore, a penalty under Rule 15-2 was not applicable. Further, the other ball effectively marked the position of his original ball. So a penalty under Rule 20-1 was not applicable.

**Ball Not Unfit for Play Deemed Unfit — See 5-3/3.**

**Ball Mistakenly Substituted When Dropped; Correction of Error — See 20-6/3.**

### 15-2/3 Competitor Mistakenly Substitutes Another Ball on Putting Green; Error Discovered After Stroke Played from Next Teeing Ground

**Q.** A competitor in stroke play lifted his ball on the putting green and by mistake replaced it with another ball. He holed out and drove off the next tee. What is the ruling?

**A.** The competitor incurs a penalty of two strokes — Rule 15-2.

### 15-2/4 Competitor Who Lifts His Ball and Fellow-Competitor's Ball Inadvertently Exchanges Balls When Replacing Them

**Q.** In stroke play, A's ball and B's ball are in the same area on the putting green. A marks the position of, and lifts, both balls with B's consent. When A replaces them, they are inadvertently exchanged and A putts out, from the right place, with B's ball and vice versa. What is the ruling?

**A.** Each player is penalized two strokes under Rule 15-2.

Because he authorized A to lift his ball, B cannot be exempted from penalty (Rule 20-1).

**Competitor's Ball Lifted Without Authority by Fellow-Competitor's Caddie Who Subsequently Substitutes Another Ball Which Competitor Plays — See 20-1/5.**

**Another Decision relating to Rule 15-2:**

**Ball Played from Ground Under Repair Abandoned and Relief Taken Under Ground Under Repair Rule — See 18-2a/8.5.**

**Other Decisions relating to Rule 15-3a:**

**Player Concedes Hole After Which It Is Discovered That Opponent Had Played Wrong Ball — See 2-4/9.**

**Player Concedes Hole After Which Opponent Plays Wrong Ball — See 2-4/10.**

**Player Wins Hole with Own Ball After Playing Wrong Ball; Opponent Lodges Belated Claim —**
See 2-5/4.

**Player Wins Hole with Wrong Ball; Error Discovered at Next Hole — See 9-2/8.**

**Ball Moved by Wrong Ball Played by Opponent — See 18-5/1.**

### 15-3b/1 Competitor Plays Wrong Ball and Loses It; Wrong Ball May Have Been Fellow-Competitor's Ball

**Q.** In stroke play, A and B drive into the same area in the rough. B finds a ball and hits it into the middle of a deep water hazard. A finds a ball that turns out to be B's ball. No other ball is found in the area, so presumably B played A's ball. B incurs a penalty of two strokes under Rule 15-3b and he must play his own ball. What is the proper procedure for A?

**A.** Since there was reasonable evidence that B played A's ball, A should place another ball at the spot from which B played the wrong ball, without penalty — Rule 15-3b.

### 15-3b/2 Play of Two Different Wrong Balls Between Strokes with Ball in Play

**Q.** In stroke play, a competitor plays a wrong ball to a putting green. He discovers his error and returns to the spot from which the wrong ball was played. He finds another ball and plays it to the green. He then discovers that he has played another wrong ball. Is the penalty two strokes or four strokes?

**A.** Two strokes for a breach of Rule 15-3b. A penalty of four strokes for playing two wrong balls in succession before a stroke with the correct ball would not be justified.

**Player Breaches Rules More Than Once Prior to Stroke; Whether Multiple Penalties Applied — See 1-4/12.**

### 15-3b/3 Fellow-Competitor Lifts Competitor's Ball and Sets It Aside; Competitor Plays Ball from Where Set Aside

**Q.** In stroke play, B marked the position of A's ball on the putting green, lifted it and placed it nearby on the green. A failed to replace the ball. He putted it from where it lay and holed out. The error was then discovered. What is the ruling?

**A.** When a ball is lifted, it is out of play — see Definition of "Ball in Play." When A played a stroke with his ball which was out of play, he played a wrong ball.

If A knew that B had lifted his ball, he incurred a penalty of two strokes under Rule 15-3b and was required to replace his ball on the correct spot and play out the hole.

If A did not know that B had lifted his ball, A could not be penalized for playing a wrong ball. If he became aware of the mistake before playing from the next tee, he was required to replace his ball on the correct spot, without penalty, and complete the hole. If he learned of the mistake after playing from the next tee, the score with the wrong ball would stand and there would be no penalty.

**Other Decisions relating to Rule 15-3:**

**Play of Wrong Ball Not Rectified on Advice of Committee Member — See 33-7/5.**

**Play of Wrong Ball Not Rectified; Error Discovered After Competition Closed — See 34-1b/3.**

## THE PUTTING GREEN

# Rule 16. The Putting Green

**Definitions**
All defined terms are in *italics* and are listed alphabetically in the Definitions section — see pages 3-11.

### 16-1. General

**a. Touching Line of Putt**

The *line of putt* must not be touched except:

(i) the player may remove *loose impediments*, provided he does not press anything down;

(ii) the player may place the club in front of the ball when *addressing* it, provided he does not press anything down;

(iii) in measuring — Rule 18-6;

(iv) in lifting the ball — Rule 16-1b;

(v) in pressing down a ball-marker;

(vi) in repairing old *hole* plugs or ball marks on the *putting green* — Rule 16-1c; and

(vii) in removing movable *obstructions* — Rule 24-1.

(Indicating line for putting on putting green — see Rule 8-2b.)

**b. Lifting and Cleaning Ball**

A ball on the *putting green* may be lifted and, if desired, cleaned. The position of the ball must be marked before it is lifted and the ball must be replaced (See Rule 20-1).

**c. Repair of Hole Plugs, Ball Marks and Other Damage**

The player may repair an old *hole* plug or damage to the *putting green* caused by the impact of a ball, whether or not the player's ball lies on the *putting green*. If a ball or ball-marker is accidentally *moved* in the process of the repair, the ball or ball-marker must be replaced. There is no penalty provided the movement of the ball is directly attributable to the specific act of repairing an old *hole* plug or damage to the *putting green* caused by the impact of a ball. Otherwise, the player incurs a penalty stroke under Rule 18-2a.

Any other damage to the *putting green* must not be repaired if it might assist the player in his subsequent play of the hole.

**d. Testing Surface**

During the play of a hole, a player must not test the surface of the *putting green* by rolling a ball or roughening or scraping the surface.

**e. Standing Astride or on Line of Putt**

The player must not make a *stroke* on the *putting green* from a *stance* astride, or with either foot touching, the *line of putt* or an extension of that line behind the ball.

**f. Making Stroke While Another Ball in Motion**

The player must not make a *stroke* while another ball is in motion after a *stroke* from the *putting green*, except that, if a player does so, there is no penalty if it was his turn to play.

(Lifting ball assisting or interfering with play while another ball in motion — see Rule 22.)

PENALTY FOR BREACH OF RULE 16-1:
Match play — Loss of hole; Stroke play — Two strokes.

(Position of caddie or partner — see Rule 14-2.)

(Wrong putting green — see Rule 25-3.)

### 16-2. Ball Overhanging Hole

When any part of the ball overhangs the lip of the *hole*, the player is allowed enough time to reach the *hole* without unreasonable delay and an additional ten seconds to determine whether the ball is at rest. If by then the ball has not fallen into the *hole*, it is deemed to be at rest. If the ball subsequently falls into the *hole*, the player is deemed to have *holed* out with his last *stroke*, and he must add a *penalty stroke* to his score for the hole; otherwise, there is no penalty under this Rule.

(Undue delay — see Rule 6-7.)

### 16/1 Mud on Ball Touches Putting Green But Ball Itself Does Not Touch Green

**Q.** A player's ball lies off the putting green, overhanging but not touching the green. A clump of mud adhering to the ball touches the green. Is the ball considered to be on the green?

**A.** No. However, if a ball lies on the green but does not actually touch the green because it is perched on mud, the ball is considered to be on the green.

**Status of Half of Double Green Serving Hole Not Being Played — See 25-3/1.**

### 16/2 Ball Embedded in Side of Hole; All of Ball Below Lip of Hole

**Q.** A player's ball embeds in the side of a hole. All of the ball is below the level of the lip of the hole. What is the ruling?

**A.** The ball should be considered holed even though all of the ball is not within the circumference of the hole as required by the Definition of "Holed."

### 16/3 Ball Embedded in Side of Hole; All of Ball Not Below Lip of Hole

**Q.** A player's ball embeds in the side of a hole. Part of the ball is above the level of the lip of the hole. What is the ruling?

**A.** The ball is not holed — see Definition of "Holed." The player may play the ball as it lies or lift the ball under Rule 16-1b, repair the damage under Rule 16-1c and place the ball on the lip of the hole.

## 16/4 Hole-Liner Not Sunk Deep Enough

**Q.** Players discover that a hole-liner is not sunk at least one inch below the putting green surface as prescribed in the Definition of "Hole." What should they do?

**A.** The players should call the matter to the attention of a Committee member if one is present. If feasible, the Committee member should attempt to have the fault corrected.

However, the players must not discontinue play in the meantime, because correction might not be possible and, if possible, might take considerable time.

## 16/5 Ball Strikes Edge of Hole-Liner and Bounces Out of Hole

**Q.** A player's ball struck the rim of a hole-liner, which had not been sunk deep enough, and bounced out of the hole. Should the ball be considered holed in such circumstances?

**A.** No. Under the Definition of "Holed," the ball must be at rest within the circumference of the hole.

## 16/5.5 Player Holes Short Putt and Allegedly Removes Ball from Hole Before It Is at Rest

**Q.** A player strikes a short putt into the hole and removes the ball from the hole. His opponent or a fellow-competitor claims he heard the ball bouncing in the bottom of the hole-liner at the time the player was removing the ball from the hole, and therefore the ball cannot be considered holed in view of the Definition of "Holed" which states: "A ball is holed when it is at rest within the circumference of the hole ..." What is the ruling?

**A.** The ball is holed. The words "at rest" are in the Definition of "Holed" to make it clear that if a ball falls below the lip and thereafter bounces out, it is not holed.

## [16/6 Reserved]

## 16/7 Two Holes on Each Green of Nine-Hole Course

**Q. 1.** Is it permissible for a Committee to make two holes on each green of a nine-hole course, one (A) for use in play of the first nine holes and the other (B) for use in play of the second nine?

**Q. 2.** If so, what is the status of hole B on each green when hole A is in use, and vice versa?

**A. 1.** Yes.

**A. 2.** The hole not in use on each green is a hole made by a greenkeeper — see Definition of "Ground Under Repair" — and Rule 25-1 is applicable.

**Other Decisions relating to Rule 16:**

Player Putts with One Hand and Catches Ball in Hole with Other Hand — See 1-2/5.

Marking Position of Ball on Putting Green — See Decisions under Rule 20-1.

### 16-1a/1 Brushing Aside or Mopping Up Casual Water on Line of Putt

**Q.** May a player whose ball lies on a putting green brush aside casual water on his line of putt, or mop it up with a towel?

**A.** No. Such action would be a breach of Rule 16-1a (Touching Line of Putt).

Mopping Up Casual Water on Line of Play — See 13-2/34.

### [16-1a/2 Reserved]

### 16-1a/3 Removing Dew or Frost from Line of Putt

**Q.** May a player brush dew or frost from his line of putt?

**A.** No. Rule 16-1a prohibits touching the line of putt except in removal of loose impediments, repair of ball marks, etc. Dew or frost is not a loose impediment — see Definition of "Loose Impediments." Accordingly, such action would be a breach of Rule 16-1a.

Removal of Dew or Frost Other Than from Line of Putt — See 13-2/35.

### 16-1a/4 Removing Casual Water from Hole

**Q.** A player, whose ball lies on the putting green, removes casual water from the hole without touching the inside of the hole. Is this permissible?

**A.** As the player has not touched the line of putt, he is not in breach of Rule 16-1a. However, the player is in breach of Rule 13-2 which prohibits improving the line of play by removing water. The player incurs a penalty of loss of hole in match play or two strokes in stroke play.

### 16-1a/5 Touching Inside of Hole

**Q.** Prior to putting, a player touched the inside of the hole. Should he be considered to have touched his line of putt in breach of Rule 16-1a?

**A.** Yes, unless the hole was materially damaged and the player was entitled to repair it — see Decision 16-1a/6. The line of putt includes the hole except in the unusual case when a player makes a stroke from the putting green away from the hole.

**Player Repairs Hole After Holing Out But Before Opponent, Fellow-Competitor or Partner Holes Out — See 1-2/3.5.**

## 16-1a/6  Damaged Hole; Procedure for Player

**Q.** Prior to putting, a player discovers that the hole has been damaged. What is the proper procedure?

**A.** If the damage is not clearly identifiable as a ball mark, then:

(a) If the damage is such that the proper dimensions of the hole have not been changed materially, the player should continue play without repairing the hole. If he touches the hole in such circumstances, a breach of Rule 16-1a occurs.

(b) If the proper dimensions of the hole have been changed materially, the player should request the Committee to have the hole repaired. If a Committee member is not readily available, the player may repair the damage, without penalty.

If a player repairs a materially damaged hole when a Committee member is readily available, he incurs a penalty for a breach of Rule 16-1a.

**Relocating Hole After Ball Already Positioned Nearby on Putting Green — See 33-2b/2.**

## 16-1a/7  Player Repairs Depression on Line of Putt Created When Partially Embedded Acorn Removed

**Q.** A player removed with his hand an embedded acorn on his line of putt. The acorn was not solidly embedded, so it was a loose impediment. The player then repaired the depression in which the acorn lay. Was the repair of the depression a breach of Rule 16-1a?

**A.** Yes.

## 16-1a/8  Loose Impediments Removed from Line of Putt with Cap or Towel

**Q.** A player touches his line of putt in brushing aside loose impediments with his cap or with a towel. Is this permissible?

**A.** Yes, provided he did not press anything down.

**Worm Partially Underground on Line of Putt — See 23/8.**

## 16-1a/9  Brushing Loose Impediments Off Line of Putt with Palm of Hand

**Q.** A player, with about one dozen strokes with the whole palm of his hand, attempted to remove small leaves, which are difficult to remove by any method, from his line of putt. Is this permissible under Rule

16-1a?

**A.** The action described exceeded that authorized by Rule 16-1a and was a breach of the Rule.

### 16-1a/10 Loose Impediments Brushed Along Line of Putt Rather Than to Side

**Q.** In removing loose impediments from his line of putt by brushing with a putter, a player brushed along the line for about one foot before brushing the impediments to the side. Did the player infringe Rule 16-1?

**A.** Under Rule 16-1a, a player is allowed to brush aside loose impediments on his line of putt. The casual movement of the putter along the line of putt would not be a breach of the Rules unless in the process the player did something to the putting green which might influence the movement of his ball when played (Rule 1-2).

### 16-1a/11 Raised Tuft of Grass on Line of Putt Brushed to Determine Whether It Is Loose

**Q.** A player cannot determine whether a raised tuft of grass on his line of putt is loose or is attached to its roots. The player brushes the raised tuft lightly with his hand to make a determination and discovers that the tuft is attached. What is the ruling?

**A.** A player is entitled to touch and move a natural object on his line of putt for the specific purpose of determining whether the object is loose, provided that if the object is found not to be loose, (1) it has not become detached and (2) it is returned to its original position before the next stroke if failure to do so would result in a breach of Rule 13-2. The touching of the line of putt in these circumstances is not a breach of Rule 16-1a.

Except as otherwise permitted in the Rules (e.g., in repairing a ball mark), if a player touches or moves a natural object on his line of putt other than to determine whether it is loose and it is found to be attached, the player cannot avoid a breach of Rule 16-1a by returning the object to its original position. (Revised)

### 16-1a/12 Player Walks on Line of Putt

**Q.** A player walked on his line of putt. Did he incur a penalty for a breach of Rule 16-1a?

**A.** Yes, if he did so intentionally. No, if he did so accidentally and the act did not improve the line.

## 16-1a/13 Line of Putt Damaged Accidentally by Opponent, Fellow-Competitor or Their Caddies

**Q.** An opponent, fellow-competitor or one of their caddies accidentally steps on and damages the player's line of putt. What is the ruling?

**A.** There is no penalty. Rule 1-2 is not applicable.

In equity (Rule 1-4), the player may have the line of putt restored to its original condition.

The player is entitled to the lie and line of putt he had when his ball came to rest. The line of putt may be restored by anyone.

If it is not possible to restore the line of putt, the player would be justified in requesting the Committee to grant relief. If the damage is severe enough, the Committee may declare the area to be ground under repair, in which case the competitor may take relief under Rule 25-1b(iii).

**Line of Putt Altered Purposely by Opponent or Fellow-Competitor by Stepping on It — See 1-2/1.**

## [16-1a/14 Reserved]

## 16-1a/15 Mushroom Growing on Line of Putt

**Q.** A mushroom is growing on a player's line of putt. Is the player entitled to relief?

**A.** The player would be justified in discontinuing play and requesting the Committee to remove the mushroom. The Committee should comply.

If such an abnormal condition is a recurring problem on a course, the Committee should make a Local Rule to the effect that mushrooms on the putting green are to be treated as ground under repair.

## 16-1a/16 Spike Mark on Line of Putt Repaired During Repair of Ball Mark

**Q.** A player stepped on a ball mark in the act of repairing it and incidentally pressed down a spike mark on his line of putt. Did the player incur a penalty under Rule 16-1a?

**A.** Yes, unless the spike mark was so close to the ball mark that it was impractical to repair the ball mark without affecting the spike mark.

### 16-1a/16.5 Spike Mark on Line of Putt Pressed Down When Player Repairs Old Hole Plug

**Q.** An old hole plug is raised on the player's line of putt. The player steps on the hole plug to make it level with the surface of the putting green. In so doing he presses down a spike mark within the hole plug. Was the player in breach of Rule 16-1a when he pressed down the spike mark?

**A.** No. Rule 16-1a permits touching the line of putt "in repairing old hole plugs."

If the spike mark had been near but not within the old hole plug, the ruling would be different. In these circumstances, the player would have been able to step on the hole plug without affecting the spike mark.

### 16-1a/17 Ball Lifted on Putting Green Placed Ahead of Ball-Marker and Then Moved Back to Original Position

**Q.** When replacing his ball on the putting green, a player has a habit of placing the ball ahead of his ball-marker and then rolling or sliding the ball to its original position. Is such a procedure permissible?

**A.** Such a procedure is not recommended but is not a breach of Rule 16-1a which permits touching the line of putt in lifting (or replacing) the ball. However, if in the process the player does something to the putting green which might influence the movement of the ball when played, e.g., presses down a raised tuft of grass, he is in breach of Rule 1-2.

#### Other Decisions relating to Rule 16-1a:

**Shielding Line of Putt from Wind — See 1-2/2.**

**Player and Opponent or Fellow-Competitor Agree to Repair Spike Marks on One Another's Line of Putt — See 1-3/3.**

**Caddie Touches Putting Green to Indicate Line of Play Before Player Chips from Off Green — See 8-2b/3.**

**Competitor Sanctions Repair of Spike Damage on His Line of Putt by Fellow-Competitor — See 13-2/36.**

**Placing Ball-Marker on Line of Putt — See 20-1/19.**

**Player Touches Putting Green in Pointing Out Line for Putting for Partner and Incidentally Touches Own Line of Putt — See 30/2.5.**

**Player Putting First When Partner's Ball Farther from Hole Stands on Partner's or Opponent's Line of Putt — See 30-3c/1.**

### 16-1b/1 Ball on Putting Green Lifted Because Player Feared Ball Might Move

**Q.** A player lifted his ball on the putting green under Rule 16-1b, cleaned it and replaced it. As the player approached the ball to play his next stroke, he feared the ball might move. So he lifted the ball again, replaced it and played. What is the ruling?

**A.** There is no penalty, provided the player marked the position of his ball both times. Rule 16-1b permits the lifting of a ball on the putting green for any reason.

### 16-1b/2 Ball Lifted from Putting Green; Ball Replaced While Another Ball in Motion But Then Lifted Because Moving Ball Might Strike It

**Q.** A's ball comes to rest on the putting green 20 feet from the hole. He marks the position of and lifts his ball so that B, whose ball is also on the putting green, but farther from the hole, can play first. While B's ball is in motion, A replaces his ball. He then realizes that B's ball might strike his ball. A re-marks the position of and lifts his ball to ensure the balls will not collide. What is the ruling?

**A.** There is no penalty. The replacing and subsequent lifting of A's ball is considered to be an extension of his initial authority to lift the ball under Rule 16-1b. Rule 22 does not apply in this case because the ball was initially lifted under Rule 16-1b.

### 16-1b/3 Ball Lifted from Putting Green; Ball Replaced While Another Ball in Motion Subsequently Deflects Ball

**Q.** A's ball comes to rest on the putting green 20 feet from the hole. He marks the position of and lifts his ball so that B, whose ball is also on the putting green, but farther from the hole, can play first. While B's ball is in motion, A replaces his ball. B's ball strikes A's ball. What is the ruling?

**A.** If A's action was unintentional, i.e., not for the purpose of deflecting B's ball, Rule 19-5a applies. There is no penalty to either player since A had lifted his ball and it was not lying on the putting green immediately prior to B's stroke. A must replace his ball, and B must play his ball as it lies.

If A's actions were for the purpose of deflecting B's ball, A is in breach of Rule 1-2 (Exerting Influence on Ball). In equity (Rule 1-4), B must replay his stroke, without penalty — see Note under Rule 19-1. (Revised)

**Rotating Ball on Putting Green Without Marking Position — See 18-2a/33.**

**Ball Replaced on Putting Green But Ball-Marker Not Removed; Ball Then Moves — See 20-4/1.**

Rule 16

**Ball Lifted by Player from Putting Green Replaced by Caddie Behind Ball-Marker — See 20-4/2.**

**Ball Replaced at Wrong Place on Putting Green and Holed — See 20-7c/1.**

### 16-1c/1  Repair of Ball Mark a Second Time

**Q.** A ball mark has been repaired by a player. The ball mark is on the line of putt of a following player. May the following player further repair the ball mark?

**A.** Yes, provided it is still clearly identifiable as a ball mark.

### 16-1c/1.5  Ball Mark Partially On and Partially Off Putting Green Is on Line of Play

**Q.** If a player's ball lies just off the putting green and there is a ball mark on his line of play, he is entitled to repair the ball mark if it is on the green (Rule 16-1c), but not if it is off the green (Rule 13-2). What is the ruling if a ball mark on the line of play is partially on and partially off the green?

**A.** Since it is impracticable to allow the repair of only that part of the ball mark which is on the putting green, the player may repair the entire ball mark.

### 16-1c/2  Ball Mark in Position to Assist Opponent

**Q.** A and B are playing a match. At a par-3 hole, both are on the green with their tee shots. A's ball comes to rest four feet from the hole. B's ball is fifteen feet from the hole. Upon reaching the green, A prepares to repair his ball mark. B tells A not to do so until he (B) has putted because A's ball mark is so situated that B's ball might be deflected into the hole by it. A objects, stating that he wishes to repair his ball mark immediately. May A do so?

**A.** No. If A were to repair the ball mark, he would lose the hole under Rule 1-2. A has no right to repair a ball mark affecting B's play if B requests A not to repair it, unless the ball mark also physically affects A's play and it is A's turn to play.

### 16-1c/3  Old Hole Plug Sunk or Raised on Line of Putt

**Q.** A player's ball lies on the green. An old hole plug is sunk or raised on the player's line of putt. What relief is available to the player?

**A.** The player may attempt to raise or lower the plug to make it level with the surface of the putting green — Rule 16-1c. If this is impossible, he may discontinue play and request the Committee to raise or lower the plug. If the Committee cannot level the plug without unduly delaying play, the Committee should declare the plug to be ground under repair, in which case the player would be entitled to relief under Rule 25-1b(iii).

**Whether Sunken Hole Plug Is "Hole Made by Greenkeeper" — See 25/17.**

**Local Rule Permitting Repair of Turf Plugs on the Putting Green That are Not 4¼ Inches in Diameter — See 33-8/30.**

### 16-1c/4  Repair of Spike Mark Damage Around Hole

**Q.** A player's ball lies on or near the putting green. Before playing his next stroke, he taps down spike marks in the vicinity of the hole. Is this permissible?

**A.** No. Such action would be a breach of Rule 16-1c since repair of spike marks in the vicinity of the hole might assist the player in his subsequent play of the hole.

### 16-1d/1  Player Concedes Opponent's Next Stroke and Rolls or Knocks Ball to Opponent

**Q.** A player concedes his opponent's next stroke and either picks up the opponent's ball and rolls it to the opponent or knocks it back to him with a club. The player did so only for the purpose of returning the opponent's ball to him, not to test the surface of the putting green. Was the player in breach of Rule 16-1d (Testing Surface)?

**A.** No. Such casual action is not a breach of Rule 16-1d.

### 16-1d/2  Player Concedes Opponent's Next Stroke and Knocks His Ball Away Along Own Line of Putt

**Q.** A player concedes his opponent's next stroke and knocks his ball away on the same line on which he (the player) must subsequently putt. Is this a breach of Rule 16-1d?

**A.** It is a question of fact whether or not the player's action was for the purpose of testing the surface of the putting green. The manner and apparent purpose of the action would be the determining factors in each individual case.

### 16-1d/3  Player Returns Ball to Spot from Which It Was Lifted by Rolling It with Putter

**Q.** A player marks the position of his ball on the putting green, lifts the ball and sets it aside. When it is his turn to putt, he rolls the ball with his putter back to the spot from which it was lifted. Was the player in breach of Rule 16-1d (Testing Surface)?

**A.** No, provided the action of rolling the ball was not for the purpose of testing the surface of the green. This method of replacing a ball is not recommended, but it is not a breach of the Rules.

### 16-1d/4  Testing for Wetness Surface of Putting Green Behind Ball

**Q.** A player placed the palm of his hand on the putting green behind his ball to determine if the green was wet. He did not roughen or scrape the surface. Was the player in breach of Rule 16-1d (Testing Surface)?

**A.** No. Rule 16-1d only prohibits rolling a ball or roughening or scraping the putting surface for testing purposes. Since the line of putt was not touched, Rule 16-1a also was not infringed.

### 16-1d/5  Rubbing Ball on Putting Green for Cleaning Purposes

**Q.** May a player clean his ball by rubbing it on the putting green?

**A.** Yes, provided the act is not for the purpose of testing the surface of the putting green. It is recommended that a ball be cleaned in other ways to eliminate any question as to the player's intentions.

### 16-1d/6  Caddie Roughens Surface of Putting Green But Player Does Not Benefit

**Q.** A player's caddie tests the surface of the putting green by roughening the grass. The player tells him immediately that he is not allowed to do that under the Rules. The player receives no information from the caddie about the condition of the green. Is the player penalized under Rule 16-1d?

**A.** Yes. The reference to the player in Rule 16-1d includes his caddie. Thus, the Rule prohibits the caddie, as well as the player, from testing the surface of the putting green. Under Rule 6-1, the player incurs the applicable penalty for a breach of a Rule by his caddie. (Revised)

### 16-1e/1  Meaning of "Line of Putt" in Context of "Standing Astride or On Line of Putt"

**Q.** With reference to the sketch above, the broken line is a direct line from the ball to the hole and the solid line is the line on which the player intends his ball to travel. Which line is "the line of putt" for purposes of application of Rule 16-1e (Standing Astride or on Line of Putt)? If the broken line is "the line of putt," the player will be in breach of Rule 16-1e. If the solid line is the "line of putt," he will not be in breach of the Rule.

**A.** The solid line is "the line of putt."

### 16-1e/2 Player Plays from Stance Astride Extension of Line of Putt Behind Ball

**Q.** A player holes a short putt from a stance astride, or with either foot touching, an extension of his line of putt behind the ball. The act was inadvertent or to avoid standing on another player's line of putt or prospective line of putt. Is the player subject to penalty under Rule 16-1e?

**A.** No. The purpose of Rule 16-1e is to prevent a "croquet" style of putting. In this case the player did not use the stance for that purpose. (New)

### 16-2/0.5 Ball Overhanging Hole Is Lifted, Cleaned and Replaced; Ball Then Falls into Hole

**Q.** After an approach shot, a player's ball is overhanging the hole. The player walks up to the hole without unreasonable delay and notices that there is mud on the ball. The player marks the position of the ball and lifts it. He then cleans the ball and replaces it. The ball remains on the lip of the hole for about five seconds and then, as the player is preparing to tap it into the hole, the ball falls into the hole. What is the ruling?

**A.** Under Rule 16-2, if a ball falls into the hole after it is deemed to be at rest, the player is deemed to have holed out with his last stroke and he shall add a penalty stroke to his score for the hole. In this case, when the player marked the position of the ball it must have been at rest. The ball must be considered to have been at rest when it was replaced; otherwise, it would have to be replaced again (Rule 20-3d).

Accordingly, the player is deemed to have holed out with his last stroke and must add a penalty stroke to his score for the hole.

### 16-2/1 Ball Overhanging Hole Falls into Hole After Player Waits 40 Seconds

**Q.** A player's ball overhangs the edge of the hole. The player walks up to the hole. He then waits about 40 seconds, after which the ball falls into the hole. Is the player subject to penalty?

**A.** Yes. The player incurs a penalty of one stroke — Rule 16-2.

### 16-2/2 Ball Overhanging Hole Knocked Away by Opponent Before Player Determines Status

**Q.** In a match between A and B, A putts and his ball apparently comes to rest, but is overhanging the hole. Within five seconds, B concedes A's next stroke and knocks his ball away. Was B entitled to knock A's ball away?

**A.** No. Under Rule 16-2, A is allowed a reasonable time to reach the hole and an additional 10 seconds to determine whether his ball is at rest. Since B infringed A's rights, B was in breach of Rule 1-2 (Exerting Influence on Ball) and lost the hole, assuming that Rule 2-2 (Halved Hole) did not apply.

**Player Jumps Close to Hole to Cause Ball Overhanging Hole to Drop — See 1-2/4.**

**Ball Falls into Hole After Concession of Next Stroke — See 2-4/2.**

**Ball Blown into Hole by Competitor Not Replaced and Holed Out — See 3-2/2.**

**Ball Overhanging Hole Falls into Hole After Being Addressed — See 18-2b/10.**

### 16-2/3 Casting Shadow on Ball Overhanging Hole

**Q.** A player's ball came to rest overhanging the edge of the hole. The player walked up to the hole and cast his shadow on the ball, believing that this would cause the grass to wilt and his ball to fall into the hole. Was the player in breach of Rule 1-2 (Exerting Influence on Ball) when he cast his shadow on the ball?

**A.** No.

### 16-2/4 Ball Overhanging Lip of Hole Moves When Flagstick Removed

**Q.** After a stroke from just off the putting green, a player's ball comes to rest overhanging the lip of the hole but not resting against the unattended flagstick. The player reaches the hole without unreasonable delay and removes the flagstick. The ball either rolls away from the hole or falls into the hole. What is the ruling?

**A.** It is a question of fact whether the player's actions caused the ball to move and any doubt should be resolved against the player.

The flagstick is a movable obstruction. If the movement of the ball was directly attributable to the removal of the flagstick, the ball must be replaced on the lip of the hole without penalty (Rule 24-1a). If the player caused the ball to move but the movement of the ball was not directly attributable to the removal of the flagstick, the ball must be replaced on the lip of the hole, and the player incurs a penalty stroke under Rule 18-2a.

If the player's actions did not cause the ball to move and the ball fell into the hole, the provisions of Rule 16-2 apply, whether the removal of the flagstick occurs before or after the lapse of time contemplated by Rule 16-2.

If the player's actions did not cause the ball to move and the ball moved to another position, the player must play the ball from that new position.

If an opponent or fellow-competitor were to remove the flagstick, without the player's authority, before the ball is deemed to be at rest under Rule 16-2 and as a result of this action causes the ball to move, the opponent or fellow-competitor has infringed the player's rights as, under Rule 16-2, the player is allowed a reasonable time to reach the hole and an additional 10 seconds to determine whether his ball is at rest. In such a case, the opponent or fellow-competitor is in breach of Rule 1-2 (Exerting Influence on Ball) and loses the hole in match play or incurs a penalty of two strokes in stroke play. The player incurs no penalty and, in stroke play, must place the ball on the lip of the hole. (New)

## 16-2/5 Ball Overhanging Lip of Hole Moves and Strikes Flagstick During Removal of Flagstick

**Q.** After a stroke from off the putting green, a player's ball overhangs the lip of the hole. While the player is removing the flagstick, the ball falls into the hole, striking the flagstick. The player's actions did not cause the ball to move. What is the ruling?

**A.** In equity (Rule 1-4), there is no penalty under Rule 17. If the ball came to rest within the circumference of the hole with all of it below the level of the lip of the hole, the ball is holed. If, after striking the flagstick, the ball is deflected out of the hole, the ball must be placed on the lip of the hole without penalty.

The answer with regard to Rule 17 is not affected by how much time elapses before the ball falls into the hole after the player reaches the hole.

There would be a penalty stroke under Rule 16-2 if the ball falls into the hole after it is deemed to be at rest under that Rule. (New)

# Rule 17. The Flagstick

**Definitions**
All defined terms are in *italics* and are listed alphabetically in the Definitions section — see pages 3-11.

### 17-1. Flagstick Attended, Removed or Held Up

Before making a *stroke* from anywhere on the *course*, the player may have the *flagstick* attended, removed or held up to indicate the position of the *hole*.

If the *flagstick* is not attended, removed or held up before the player makes a *stroke*, it must not be attended, removed or held up during the *stroke* or while the player's ball is in motion if doing so might influence the movement of the ball.

**Note 1:** If the *flagstick* is in the *hole* and anyone stands near it while a *stroke* is being made, he is deemed to be attending the *flagstick*.

**Note 2:** If, prior to the *stroke*, the *flagstick* is attended, removed or held up by anyone with the player's knowledge and he makes no objection, the player is deemed to have authorized it.

**Note 3:** If anyone attends or holds up the *flagstick* while a *stroke* is being made, he is deemed to be attending the *flagstick* until the ball comes to rest.

### 17-2. Unauthorized Attendance

If an opponent or his *caddie* in match play or a *fellow-competitor* or his *caddie* in stroke play, without the player's authority or prior knowledge, attends, removes or holds up the *flagstick* during the *stroke* or while the ball is in motion, and the act might influence the movement of the ball, the opponent or *fellow-competitor* incurs the applicable penalty.

*PENALTY FOR BREACH OF RULE 17-1 or 17-2:

Match play — Loss of hole; Stroke play — Two strokes.

*In stroke play, if a breach of Rule 17-2 occurs and the *competitor's* ball subsequently strikes the *flagstick*, the person attending or holding it or anything carried by him, the *competitor* incurs no penalty. The ball is played as it lies except that, if the *stroke* was made on the *putting green*, the *stroke* is canceled and the ball must be replaced and replayed.

### 17-3. Ball Striking Flagstick or Attendant

The player's ball must not strike:

    **a.** The *flagstick* when it is being attended, removed or held up;

    **b.** The person attending or holding up the *flagstick*; or

    **c.** The *flagstick* in the *hole*, unattended, when the *stroke* has been made on the *putting green*.

**Exception:** When the *flagstick* is attended, removed or held up without the player's authority — see Rule 17-2.

PENALTY FOR BREACH OF RULE 17-3:
Match play — Loss of hole; Stroke play — Two strokes and the ball must be played as it lies.

### 17-4. Ball Resting Against Flagstick

When the *flagstick* is in the *hole* and a player's ball when not *holed* rests against it, the player or another person authorized by him may move or remove the *flagstick,* and if the ball falls into the *hole,* the player is deemed to have *holed* out with his last *stroke;* otherwise, the ball, if *moved*, must be placed on the lip of the *hole,* without penalty.

### 17/1 Attachment to Flagstick to Indicate Position of Hole on Green

**Q.** A thin disc or sleeve is attached to the flagstick to indicate the distance of the hole from the front of the green. If the disc is placed near the bottom of the flagstick it means that the hole is at the front of the green; if it is placed near the top of the flagstick it means that the hole is at the back of the green. Is this permitted?

**A.** Yes, provided the attachment is circular in cross-section.

### 17/2 Different Colored Flags Used to Indicate Position of Hole on Green

**Q.** May a Committee use flagsticks with flags of two different colors, one color being used when the hole is at the front of the green and the other when the hole is at the back?

**A.** Yes.

### 17/3 Flagstick Tapered or of Varying Diameters

**Q.** May a flagstick be tapered or have a slender metal ferrule at the base?

**A.** Yes. The Definition does not prohibit sections of varying diameters. The Definition requires that the flagstick be circular in cross-section. This is to prohibit non-circular features in the lower part of the flagstick.

### 17/3.5 Reflector on Flagstick

**Q.** To aid in the use of distance-measuring devices, a course has reflectors on its flagsticks. However, the reflectors are not circular in cross-section. Is the use of such reflectors permissible?

**A.** Yes. The use of small non-circular reflectors is an exception to the requirement in the Definition of "Flagstick" that a flagstick and any attachment to it must be circular in cross-section. (New)

**Local Rule Permitting Use of Distance Measuring Device — See 14-3/0.5**

### 17/4 Adjustment of Flagstick; Player's Rights

**Q.** A player playing from off the green and wishing to leave the flagstick in the hole may find that the flagstick is leaning towards his ball (a disadvantage) or away from his ball (an advantage). What are the player's rights in such a situation?

**A.** The flagstick may be left as it is or centered in the hole, as contemplated by the Definition of "Flagstick."

The flagstick may not be adjusted to a more favorable position than centered. To do so would infringe Rule 1-2 (Exerting Influence on Ball).

An opponent or fellow-competitor who centers the flagstick incurs no penalty, but the player may have it restored to its original position.

### [17/5 Reserved]

### 17/6 Ball Lodged in Flag Attached to Flagstick

**Q.** A player's ball lodges in the flag attached to a flagstick. What is the procedure?

**A.** A flagstick is a movable obstruction and Rule 24-1 applies. However, in taking relief the player may not place the ball in the hole. Therefore, in equity (Rule 1-4), the player must place the ball on the lip of the hole when taking relief.

### 17/7 Hole-Liner Pulled Out by Flagstick Attendant and Ball Falls into Unlined Hole

**Q.** A flagstick attendant removes the flagstick and, in the process, pulls out the hole-liner. The player's ball rolls into the unlined hole. What is the ruling?

**A.** The player incurs no penalty and the ball is holed. A hole need not contain a lining — see Definition of "Hole."

### 17/8 Ball Strikes Hole-Liner Pulled Out with Flagstick

**Q.** A player played a stroke from the putting green. The ball struck the hole-liner, which had stuck to the bottom of the flagstick and had come out of the hole when the person attending the flagstick removed the flagstick. Is there any penalty?

**A.** No. A hole-liner is an outside agency. Accordingly, if the hole-liner was moving when the ball struck it, the stroke is canceled and the ball must be replaced — Rule 19-1b. If the hole-liner was not moving, the ball must be played as it lies — Rule 19-1. In case of doubt, the ball must be played as it lies.

### 17/9 Attendant Removes Flagstick Whereupon Knob Falls from Top of Flagstick and Deflects Ball

**Q.** After a player putts, the flagstick attendant removes the flagstick and a knob attached to the top of the flagstick falls off. The knob strikes the player's moving ball and deflects it. What is the ruling?

**A.** Once detached the knob was no longer a part of the flagstick. It was an outside agency. Therefore, the stroke is canceled and the ball must be replaced — Rule 19-1b.

### Other Decisions relating to Rule 17:

**Flagstick Lying on Putting Green Removed by Player to Prevent Another Player's Ball from Striking It — See 1-2/3.**

**Flagstick Stuck into Green Some Distance from Hole by Practical Joker — See 1-4/3.**

**Ball Overhanging Lip of Hole Moves When Flagstick Removed — See 16-2/4.**

**Ball Overhanging Lip of Hole Moves and Strikes Flagstick During Removal of Flagstick — See 16-2/5.**

**Ball Moved by Flagstick Accidentally Dropped on Ball — See 18-2a/24.**

### 17-1/1  Meaning of "Stands Near the Hole"

**Q.** Note 1 to Rule 17-1 states that, if anyone "stands near the hole," he is deemed to be attending the flagstick. Is such a person considered to be standing "near the hole" if he is close enough to touch the flagstick?

**A.** Yes.

### 17-1/2  Opponent or Fellow-Competitor Declines to Attend Flagstick

**Q.** Does a player have any redress if he requests his opponent or a fellow-competitor to attend the flagstick for him and the opponent or fellow-competitor declines?

**A.** No.

### 17-1/3  Flagstick Attended by Referee, Observer or Marker at Player's Request

**Q.** A player requests a referee, observer or marker to attend the flagstick and the referee, observer or marker does so. Is the player subject to penalty?

**A.** A referee or observer should not attend the flagstick — see Definitions of "Referee" and "Observer." However, a player incurs no penalty if he makes such a request and the referee or observer complies. A marker may attend the flagstick, even if he is not a fellow-competitor.

### 17-1/4  Flagstick Attendant Stands Behind Hole

**Q.** May a person attending the flagstick stand directly behind the hole, instead of to the side of it?

**A.** Yes. A flagstick attendant might have to stand behind the hole to avoid standing on the line of putt of another player.

### 17-1/4.5 Flagstick Attendant Removes Flagstick and Holds It Upright Behind Hole; End of Flagstick Touches Green

**Q.** A player preparing to putt asks his caddie to attend the flagstick. The caddie removes the flagstick from the hole and holds it upright two or three inches directly behind the hole, with the end of the flagstick touching the putting green. He attends the flagstick in this manner to eliminate the risk of the flagstick sticking in the hole. Is such a procedure a breach of the Rules?

**A.** No, but such a practice is not recommended because of the possibility of damage to the putting green.

### 17-1/5 Holding Flagstick with One Hand and Putting with Other Hand

**Q.** A player holds the flagstick with one hand and holes a short putt, gripping the putter with his other hand. Is this permissible?

**A.** Yes, provided the flagstick has been removed from the hole and the ball therefore does not strike it. If the ball were to strike the flagstick, a breach of Rule 17-3a would occur.

### 17-1/6 Attended Flagstick Placed on Ground Subsequently Lifted

**Q.** After a stroke is made, the person attending the flagstick removes it and places it on the ground. He then realizes the ball might strike the flagstick, so he picks it up. What is the ruling?

**A.** There is no penalty. The flagstick is deemed to be attended by the person attending it until the ball comes to rest and it may be moved by the attendant to a position where the ball will not strike it.

### 17-1/7 Removed Flagstick Placed on Ground Subsequently Lifted

**Q.** A, the opponent or fellow-competitor of B, removes the flagstick from the hole and places it on the ground. B putts and A, who is standing within reach of the removed flagstick, realizes that B's ball might strike the removed flagstick, so he picks the flagstick up. What is the ruling?

**A.** A loses the hole in match play or incurs a penalty of two strokes in stroke play for removing an obstruction which might influence the movement of the ball — Rule 1-2 or 24-1.

The provisions of Note 3 to Rule 17-1 do not apply because the flagstick was not being attended or held up to indicate the position of the hole when the stroke was made.

## 17-1/8 Removed Flagstick Being Held by Opponent or Fellow-Competitor Subsequently Moved

**Q.** A, the opponent or fellow-competitor of B, removes the flagstick from the hole and, while holding it, steps aside. B putts and A realizes that B's ball may strike him or the flagstick, so he moves out of the way while still holding the flagstick. What is the ruling?

**A.** Although the flagstick is not being attended and is not the equipment of either player, in equity (Rule 1-4), A incurs no penalty for moving the flagstick while B's ball was in motion as he was already holding it.

The answer would be the same if A had the flagstick leaning against his body with part of the flagstick touching the ground.

**Flagstick Lying on Putting Green Removed by Player to Prevent Another Player's Ball from Striking It — See 1-2/3.**

## 17-2/1 Opponent or Fellow-Competitor Attends Flagstick Without Authority But Ceases Attendance on Instruction of Player

**Q.** While a player is preparing to play from near the putting green, his opponent or fellow-competitor attends the flagstick without the player's authority or prior knowledge. The player makes the stroke, looks up and sees the flagstick being attended. While the ball is in motion, the player tells the opponent or fellow-competitor to leave the flagstick in the hole and step away, which he does. What is the ruling?

**A.** Since the unauthorized attendance might have influenced the movement of the ball, the opponent or fellow-competitor was in breach of Rule 17-2. The opponent or fellow-competitor does not avoid the penalty under Rule 17-2 by ceasing his attendance of the flagstick.

In match play, the opponent loses the hole (Rule 17-2).

In stroke play, the fellow-competitor is penalized two strokes and the ball is played as it lies. If the player's ball strikes the flagstick, the player incurs no penalty (Rule 17-2).

## 17-2/2 Flagstick Attended by Opponent or Fellow-Competitor Without Authority While Player's Ball in Motion

**Q.** A player plays from just off the putting green with the flagstick in the hole. While the ball is in motion, an opponent or fellow-competitor, without the authority of the player, removes the flagstick either because he believes the ball will not reach the hole or it has gone past the hole. What is the ruling?

**A.** The opponent or fellow-competitor is not penalized if the removal of the flagstick could not have influenced the movement of the ball.

If there is any doubt as to whether the ball could have reached the hole or, having gone past the hole, returned to the hole (e.g., as a result of the slope of the putting green, wind, etc.), the opponent loses the hole in match play or the fellow-competitor incurs a penalty of two strokes in stroke play for a breach of Rule 17-2.

### 17-3/1 Holing Out Without Ball Touching Flagstick

**Q.** A player plays a stroke from the putting green without having the flagstick attended. The ball stops momentarily on the lip of the hole and then falls into the hole. The player claims that the ball fell into the hole without striking the flagstick and therefore he incurs no penalty under Rule 17-3. Is the claim valid?

**A.** No. A ball is not holed until it is at rest in the hole — Definition of "Holed." If the flagstick is in the hole, it is impossible for a ball to come to rest in the hole without striking the flagstick.

### 17-3/2 Opponent or Fellow-Competitor Attending Flagstick for Player Fails to Remove It; Player's Ball Strikes Flagstick

**Q.** A requests B, his opponent or a fellow-competitor, to attend the flagstick, and B complies. A putts too firmly and B fails to remove the flagstick. A's ball strikes the flagstick. What is the ruling?

**A.** If B failed to remove the flagstick for the purpose of causing A to incur a penalty, B is disqualified in both match play and stroke play for a serious breach of Rule 1-2. In stroke play, in equity (Rule 1-4) A must replay the stroke without penalty.

If B's failure to remove the flagstick was for the purpose of preventing A's ball from going beyond the flagstick and not for the purpose of causing A to incur a penalty, in match play B lost the hole under Rule 1-2 when he failed to remove the flagstick before A's ball reached the hole. The fact that A's ball subsequently struck the flagstick (a breach of Rule 17-3a) is irrelevant since B had already lost the hole. In stroke play, B incurs a penalty of two strokes under Rule 1-2, and A incurs the same penalty under Rule 17-3a.

If B's failure to remove the flagstick was not deliberate, e.g., the flagstick stuck in the socket or B was distracted and did not see A putt, A incurs a penalty of loss of hole in match play or two strokes in stroke play under Rule 17-3. B incurs no penalty.

### 17-3/3 Ball Strikes Flagstick Lying on Ground

**Q.** Generally, the player's ball must not strike the flagstick when removed from the hole (Rule 17-3). What is the ruling in the following situations:

(a) A player putts too strongly and his ball strikes the flagstick which has been removed by someone in his match or group and placed on the ground behind the hole.

(b) A player plays his second shot to the green and the ball strikes the flagstick, which had been blown down by the wind and was lying on the ground.

(c) A player, not believing he can reach the green which is occupied by the preceding match or group, plays his second shot at a par-5 hole and the ball rolls onto the green and strikes the flagstick which has been removed from the hole and placed on the ground by someone in the preceding match or group.

**A.** (a) The player incurs a penalty of loss of hole in match play or two strokes in stroke play under Rule 17-3a.

(b) and (c) No penalty is incurred. Rule 17-3a is not applicable in either case. It applies only when the flagstick has been removed with the player's authority or prior knowledge by someone in the player's match or group.

### 17-3/4 Flagstick Attended by Partner Without Express Authority of Player; Ball Strikes Flagstick or Partner

**Q.** In four-ball play, A is preparing to play from off the putting green. B, A's partner, attends the flagstick without A's knowledge or express authority. A plays and his ball strikes B or the flagstick. What is the ruling?

**A.** If the flagstick is attended by the player's caddie, his partner or his partner's caddie, i.e., by a member of the player's side, it is deemed to be attended with the player's knowledge and authority.

Accordingly, in match play A is disqualified from the hole (Rule 17-3b), but B incurs no penalty (Rule 30-3f).

In stroke play, A incurs a penalty of two strokes and must play the ball as it lies (Rule 17-3b), but B incurs no penalty (Rule 31-8).

### 17-3/5 Flag Struck by Ball When Flagstick Attended

**Q.** While the flagstick was being attended, a player's ball struck the flag attached to the flagstick. Did the player incur a penalty under Rule 17-3a?

**A.** Yes. The flag is part of the flagstick.

### 17-3/6 Marking Position of Hole with Club

**Q.** The flagstick has been removed. A wants the position of the hole marked but he does not want to waste time retrieving the flagstick. So A asks B to place the grip end of his putter in the hole. Is this permissible?

**A.** Yes, but a putter used to mark the position of the hole must be treated as a flagstick for the purposes of applying the Rules.

**Ball at Rest Kicked Away from Hole by Spectator Attending Flagstick — See 18-1/10.**

**Player Attending Flagstick for Opponent Struck by Ball of Opponent's Partner Who Played Out of Turn — See 30-3f/5.**

### 17-4/1 Ball Resting Against Flagstick Lifted Before Being Holed

**Q.** A player's ball is resting against the flagstick, but it is not holed because all of it is not below the level of the lip of the hole. However, the player, believing the ball is holed, picks it up. What is the ruling?

**A.** The player incurs a penalty stroke under Rule 20-1 for lifting his ball without marking its position. The player must replace the ball against the flagstick and may then apply Rule 17-4.

**Player's Ball Resting Against Flagstick Lifted Before Being Holed; Others in Four-Ball Match Pick Up Mistakenly Believing Player Won Hole — See 30-3f/3.**

### 17-4/2 Ball Resting Against Flagstick; Putt Conceded and Ball Removed Before Player Can Remove Flagstick

**Q.** In a match, A plays a stroke from off the green and his ball comes to rest against the flagstick. B, A's opponent, concedes A's next stroke and removes A's ball. Despite B's concession, is A entitled to have the ball replaced to enable him to exercise his rights under Rule 17-4?

**A.** Yes. When A's ball was resting against the flagstick, Rule 17-4 applied and A was entitled to have the flagstick moved or removed to see whether the ball would fall into the hole. B had no right to remove the ball and concede the next stroke until A had an opportunity to proceed under Rule 17-4. By removing A's ball, B was in breach of Rule 18-3b and incurred a penalty stroke; A should then have replaced his ball against the flagstick and applied Rule 17-4.

### 17-4/3 Ball Resting Against Flagstick Moves Away from Hole When Flagstick Removed by Opponent or Fellow-Competitor

**Q.** A player's ball is resting against the flagstick. Without the player's authority, his opponent or a fellow-competitor removes the flagstick and the ball moves away from the hole. What is the ruling?

**A.** In match play, the opponent incurs a penalty stroke and the ball must be replaced against the flagstick — Rule 18-3b.

In stroke play, the ball must be replaced against the flagstick without penalty to anyone — Rule 18-4.

In either form of play, the player may then move or remove the flagstick as prescribed in Rule 17-4.

### 17-4/4 Ball Resting Against Flagstick Moves Away from Hole When Flagstick Removed by Player; Ball Not Placed on Lip of Hole

**Q.** A player's ball is resting against the flagstick. The player removes the flagstick and the ball moves away from the hole. The player plays the ball from its new position, holing the putt. What is the ruling?

**A.** The player was required to place the ball on the lip of the hole (Rule 17-4).

In match play, the player loses the hole — Rules 17-4 and 2-6.

In stroke play, the player incurs a penalty of two strokes and the ball is holed — Rules 17-4 and 3-5.

#### Other Decisions relating to Rule 17

**Ball Overhanging Lip of Hole Moves When Flagstick Removed — See 16-2/4.**

**Ball Overhanging Lip of Hole Moves and Strikes Flagstick During Removal of Flagstick — See 16-2/5.**

**BALL MOVED, DEFLECTED OR STOPPED**

# Rule 18. Ball at Rest Moved

## Definitions
All defined terms are in *italics* and are listed alphabetically in the Definitions section — see pages 3-11.

### 18-1. By Outside Agency
If a ball at rest is *moved* by an *outside agency*, there is no penalty and the ball must be replaced.

(Player's ball at rest *moved* by another ball — see Rule 18-5.)

### 18-2. By Player, Partner, Caddie or Equipment
#### a. General
When a player's ball is *in play*, if:

(i) the player, his *partner* or either of their *caddies* lifts or *moves* it, touches it purposely (except with a club in the act of *addressing* it) or causes it to *move* except as permitted by a *Rule*, or

(ii) *equipment* of the player or his *partner* causes the ball to *move*,

the player incurs a penalty of one stroke. If the ball is moved, it must be replaced unless the movement of the ball occurs after the player has begun the *stroke* or the backward movement of the club for the *stroke* and the *stroke* is made.

Under the *Rules* there is no penalty if a player accidentally causes his ball to *move* in the following circumstances:

- In searching for a ball in a *hazard* covered by *loose impediments* or sand, for a ball in an *abnormal ground condition* or for a ball believed to be in water in a *water hazard* — Rule 12-1
- In repairing a *hole* plug or ball mark — Rule 16-1c
- In measuring — Rule 18-6
- In lifting a ball under a *Rule* — Rule 20-1
- In placing or replacing a ball under a *Rule* — Rule 20-3a
- In removing a *loose impediment* on the *putting green* — Rule 23-1
- In removing movable *obstructions* — Rule 24-1.

#### b. Ball Moving After Address
If a player's *ball in play moves* after he has *addressed* it (other than as a result of a *stroke*), the player is deemed to have *moved* the ball and incurs a penalty of one stroke. The ball must be replaced unless the movement

of the ball occurs after the player has begun the *stroke* or the backward movement of the club for the *stroke* and the *stroke* is made.

## 18-3. By Opponent, Caddie or Equipment in Match Play

### a. During Search

If, during search for a player's ball, an opponent, his *caddie* or his *equipment moves* the ball, touches it or causes it to *move*, there is no penalty. If the ball is *moved*, it must be replaced.

### b. Other Than During Search

If, other than during search for a player's ball, an opponent, his *caddie* or his *equipment moves* the ball, touches it purposely or causes it to *move*, except as otherwise provided in the *Rules*, the opponent incurs a penalty of one stroke. If the ball is *moved*, it must be replaced.

(Playing a wrong ball — see Rule 15-3.)

(Ball moved in measuring — see Rule 18-6.)

## 18-4. By Fellow-Competitor, Caddie or Equipment in Stroke Play

If a *fellow-competitor*, his *caddie* or his *equipment moves* the player's ball, touches it or causes it to *move*, there is no penalty. If the ball is *moved*, it must be replaced.

(Playing a wrong ball — see Rule 15-3.)

## 18-5. By Another Ball

If a *ball in play* and at rest is *moved* by another ball in motion after a *stroke*, the *moved* ball must be replaced.

## 18-6. Ball Moved in Measuring

If a ball or ball-marker is *moved* in measuring while proceeding under or in determining the application of a *Rule*, the ball or ball-marker must be replaced. There is no penalty provided the movement of the ball or ball-marker is directly attributable to the specific act of measuring. Otherwise, the provisions of Rules 18-2a, 18-3b or 18-4 apply.

*PENALTY FOR BREACH OF RULE:
Match play — Loss of hole; Stroke play — Two strokes.
*If a player who is required to replace a ball fails to do so, he incurs the general penalty for breach of Rule 18. There is no additional penalty under Rule 18, except in the case of a wrongly *substituted ball* (Rule 15-2).

**Note 1:** If a ball to be replaced under this Rule is not immediately recoverable, another ball may be substituted.

**Note 2:** If the original lie of a ball to be placed or replaced has been altered, see Rule 20-3b.

**Note 3:** If it is impossible to determine the spot on which a ball is to be placed, see Rule 20-3c.

### 18/1 Ball Moves Vertically Downward

**Q.** A ball lying in long grass slips vertically downward. Or a ball is accidentally stepped on and pressed down, say a quarter of an inch, in the grass or into the ground. In each case, has the ball moved?

**A.** Yes, unless the ball returns to its original position. The direction of movement is immaterial.

### 18/2 Ball Oscillates During Address

**Q.** In addressing the ball, a player accidentally causes the ball to oscillate, but it returns to its original position. Has the ball "moved"?

**A.** No.

### 18/3 Ball in Fork of Tree Moves in Relation to Ground But Not in Relation to Fork

**Q.** A ball rests in the fork of a branch of a tree. The player climbs the tree to play his next stroke. The branch bends under his weight. Although the ball has moved relative to the ground, it has not moved relative to the fork. Is the ball deemed to have moved?

**A.** The ball is deemed not to have moved since it did not move in relation to the fork of the tree in which it was lodged.

### [18/4 Reserved]

### [18/5 Reserved]

### [18/6 Reserved]

### 18/7 Explanation of "Any Ball He Has Played"

**Q.** The Definition of "Equipment" excludes "any ball he (the player) has played at the hole being played." What does this mean?

**A.** The phrase means any ball the player has played at the hole being played except during any period when it has been lifted and has not been put back into play. Accordingly, the ball in play, a provisional ball, a second ball played under Rule 3-3 or Rule 20-7c and a ball being used for practice are not equipment.

**Player Lifts His Ball on Putting Green and Sets It Aside; Opponent's or Fellow-Competitor's Ball Played from Green Subsequently Strikes Player's Ball — See 19-5/1.**

### 18/7.5 Player's Ball Moved by Ball Accidentally Dropped by Opponent or Fellow-Competitor

**Q.** A lifts his ball on the putting green. He then accidentally drops the ball and it strikes and moves B's ball, which is in play and at rest. What is the ruling?

**A.** A ball which has been lifted and not put back into play is equipment — see the Note under Definition of "Equipment."

In match play, A incurs a penalty stroke and B must replace his ball — Rule 18-3b.

In stroke play, there is no penalty and B must replace his ball — Rule 18-4.

Rule 19-5 (Ball in Motion Deflected or Stopped by Another Ball) does not apply because A's ball was not "in motion after a stroke."

### 18/8 Ball Moved by Golf Cart Shared by Two Players

Under the Definition of "Equipment," equipment includes a golf cart, whether or not motorized. If two players share a golf cart, the cart and everything in it are deemed to be the equipment of the player whose ball is involved; except that, when the cart is being moved by one of the players, the cart and everything in it are deemed to be that player's equipment.

Thus, for example, in a singles match, if A and B are sharing a cart and the cart moves A's ball which was at rest, A would be penalized one stroke if he was driving or pulling the cart (Rule 18-2a). B would be penalized one stroke if he was driving or pulling the cart (Rule 18-3b), unless the incident occurred during search (Rule 18-3a).

### [18/9 Reserved]

### 18/10 Ball Falls into Bunker When Person Walks Nearby

**Q.** A ball at rest on the edge of a bunker falls into the bunker when X (a spectator, the player, an opponent or a fellow-competitor) walks nearby. Should the ball be replaced in accordance with Rules 18-1 or -4 or must the ball be played as it lies in the bunker?

**A.** The answer depends on whether X in any way caused the ball to move. If it is determined that X did not in any way cause the ball to move, there is no penalty and the ball must be played as it lies.

If it is determined that X caused the ball to move, it must be replaced. If X is the player, the player incurs a penalty stroke under Rule 18-2a; if X is an opponent, the opponent incurs a penalty stroke under Rule 18-3b. In all other cases, there is no penalty.

Whether X caused the ball to move is a question of fact to be determined in the light of all the circumstances. Relevant circumstances might include the distance between X and the ball and the nature of the ground. In the absence of evidence that X caused the ball to move, it should be concluded that the ball's movement was a coincidence.

### 18/11 Meaning of "Immediately Recoverable"

**Q.** With reference to Note 1 under Rule 18, when is a ball to be replaced deemed not to be "immediately recoverable"?

**A.** When it cannot be retrieved within a few seconds.

### 18-1/1 Treating Ball as Moved by Outside Agency Rather Than Lost

To treat a ball which cannot be found as moved by an outside agency rather than lost (Rule 27), there must be reasonable evidence to that effect. All available testimony should be considered. In the absence of such evidence, the ball must be treated as lost.

**Lost Ball Treated as Moved by Outside Agency in Absence of Reasonable Evidence to That Effect — See 27-1/2.5.**

### [18-1/2 Reserved]

### 18-1/3 Player Unaware Ball Moved by Outside Agency Does Not Replace Ball

**Q.** In stroke play, a player's ball was moved by an outside agency. Neither the player nor his caddie was aware that his ball had been moved, so the player did not replace the ball. He completed the hole, teed off at the next hole and then learned that his ball had been moved at the previous hole. What is the ruling?

**A.** It would be inequitable to impose a penalty for failure to replace a ball moved by an outside agency as required by Rule 18-1 if neither the player nor his caddie knew the ball had been moved. Accordingly, the score made with the moved ball would stand.

### 18-1/4 Spectator Says Ball Was Moved by Outside Agency But Player Not Sure

**Q.** A spectator tells a player that his ball has been moved by an outside agency. Neither the player nor his caddie was aware the ball had been moved. Is the player obliged to take the spectator's word and replace the ball on the spot from which the spectator said it was moved?

**A.** No. In stroke play, if it is impractical to get a decision from the Committee, the player should, under Rule 3-3, hole out both with the original ball and a second ball played from the spot from which the original ball is alleged to have been moved, and request the Committee to decide the matter at the end of the round. In reaching a decision, the Committee should interrogate the spectator, if possible.

In match play, if there is no referee or representative of the Committee available within a reasonable time, the player and his opponent should, if possible, agree on the place from which the player should play his next stroke. If agreement cannot be reached, the player must proceed as he thinks best, and if the opponent does not agree with the action taken, he should lodge a claim under Rule 2-5 so that the Committee may make a decision under Rule 34-3.

### *18-1/5  Ball Stolen by Outside Agency from Unknown Spot*

**Q.** At a par-3 hole, part of the green and the adjoining area cannot be seen from the tee. In this unseen area are a bunker, fairway and a dry water hazard.

A player plays towards this obscured area and cannot tell where the ball comes to rest. When the players are near the green, they see a boy running away with a ball in his hand. The boy throws the ball back and the player identifies it as his ball.

The player is unable to determine from where to play his next stroke under Rule 18-1. He does not know whether the ball was on the green, on the fairway or in one of the hazards.

How should he proceed?

**A.** As it was impossible to know where the ball should have been replaced under Rule 18-1, the player should, in equity (Rule 1-4), drop the ball in an area which was neither the most, nor the least, favorable of the various areas where it was equally possible that the ball originally lay.

### *18-1/6  Ball at Rest Moved by Blowing Tumbleweed*

**Q.** A tumbleweed blowing across the course strikes a ball at rest and knocks it into the hole. What is the procedure?

**A.** In the circumstances, a tumbleweed is an outside agency. Rule 18-1 applies and the ball must be replaced without penalty.

### *18-1/7  Ball in Plastic Bag Moves When Bag Blown to New Position by Wind*

**Q.** A player's ball comes to rest in a plastic bag that is lying on the ground. Before the player can invoke Rule 24-1b, a gust of wind blows the bag and the ball to a new position. In proceeding under Rule 24-1b, should the player drop the ball directly under the place where it originally lay in the bag or where it now lies in the bag?

**A.** Wind is not an outside agency. However, if an object being moved by the wind moves a ball, the object is an outside agency in the circumstances — see Decision 18-1/6.

In this case, the bag, not the wind, caused the ball to move. Accordingly, under Rules 18-1 and 24-1b, the player must drop the ball directly under the place where it originally lay in the bag.

### 18-1/8 Ball Moved by Stone Dislodged by Partner's or Opponent's Stroke

**Q.** In match play, a player played a stroke and dislodged a large stone. The stone struck his partner's or an opponent's ball which was lying about four yards ahead and moved it. What is the ruling?

**A.** The stone was an outside agency and Rule 18-1 applies. The partner or opponent must replace his ball.

In the circumstances, the player should not be held to have moved the ball. Accordingly, Rules 18-2a(i) and 18-3b are not applicable and no penalty is incurred.

### 18-1/9 Ball Lodged in Tree Knocked Down by Outside Agency

**Q.** A player's ball is lodged in a tree about eight feet off the ground. A spectator knocks the ball down from the tree. In complying with Rule 18-1, it is impossible to replace the ball in the prescribed manner in the tree because the spot where it lay in the tree is unknown or unreachable. What is the ruling?

**A.** Rules 20-3c and -3d cover cases in which the spot where a ball is to be placed or replaced is not determinable or a ball fails to come to rest on the spot on which it is placed. However, these Rules do not contemplate a case such as this one. Thus, in equity (Rule 1-4), if the position of the ball in the tree was such that the player could have made a stroke at it, the ball must be placed in the tree as near as possible to the spot from which it was moved, without penalty. Otherwise, the player must proceed under the unplayable ball Rule.

### 18-1/10 Ball at Rest Kicked Away from Hole by Spectator Attending Flagstick

**Q.** In stroke play, a competitor asked a spectator to attend the flagstick. The competitor putted and his ball stopped one inch short of the hole. The spectator then kicked the ball away. What is the ruling?

**A.** There was no infringement of Rule 17-3b because the competitor's ball had come to rest short of the hole. The spectator was not the competitor's caddie and so he was an outside agency. Under Rule 18-1 the competitor was required to replace his ball and hole out without penalty.

## 18-1/11 Ball Moved by Wind or Casual Water While Play Suspended

**Q.** While play is suspended, wind or casual water moves a ball. Since wind or water is not an outside agency, must the ball be played from its new position?

**A.** No. The ball must be replaced — see Rule 6-8d(iii). If the spot is not determinable, it must be estimated and the ball placed on the estimated spot — See Note to Rule 6-8d(iii) and Exception to Rule 20-3c.

**Ball Moved Accidentally by Player During Suspension of Play — See 18-2a/25.**

**Ball-Marker Moved Off Green by Wind or Casual Water — See 20-1/10.**

## 18-1/12 Ball Replaced and at Rest Is Thereafter Moved by Wind

**Q.** A player replaces his ball on the putting green and the ball is at rest. Before the player addresses the ball, a sudden gust of wind blows the ball farther from the hole. The player plays the ball from its new position. Is that correct?

**A.** Yes. Wind is not an outside agency — see Definition of "Outside Agency." Accordingly, Rule 18-1 does not apply.

## 18-2a/1 Player Who Misses Tee Shot Tees Ball Lower Before Playing Next Stroke

**Q.** A player playing from the teeing ground misses the ball completely. He pushes his tee further into the ground and plays. What is the ruling?

**A.** When the player made a stroke, the ball was in play (see Definition of "Ball in Play"). By pushing the tee further into the ground, he moved the ball and incurred a penalty of one stroke under Rule 18-2a and was required to replace it. However, when the player made a stroke at the ball without replacing it, he played under penalty of stroke and distance (see Decision 27/17). This procedure overrides Rule 18-2a and, therefore, the penalty under Rule 18-2a does not apply.

## 18-2a/2 Ball Falling Off Tee When Stroke Just Touches It Is Picked Up and Re-Teed

**Q.** A player making his first stroke on a hole just touched the ball and it fell off the tee. He picked up the ball, re-teed it and played out the hole. What is the ruling?

**A.** When the player made a stroke, the ball was in play (see Definition of "Ball in Play"). When he lifted the ball, he incurred a penalty of one stroke under Rule 18-2a and was required to replace it. However, when the player made a stroke at the re-teed ball, he played a ball under penalty of stroke and distance (see Decision 27/17). This procedure overrides Rule 18-2a and, therefore, the penalty under Rule 18-2a does not apply.

**Ball Putted from Wrong Place Lifted and Putted from Right Place — See 20-7c/2.**

### *18-2a/3 Ball Lifted and Dropped Away from Boundary Stake Under Obstruction Rule*

**Q.** A player's swing is interfered with by a stake defining out of bounds. The player mistakenly considers the stake an obstruction and he lifts his ball and drops it in the manner prescribed in Rule 24-2b. What is the ruling?

**A.** The player incurs a penalty of one stroke under Rule 18-2a and he must replace his ball before playing his next stroke. Otherwise, he loses the hole in match play or he incurs a total penalty of two strokes in stroke play — see penalty statement under Rule 18.

**Dropped Ball Comes to Rest and Then Rolls Out of Bounds — See 20-2c/3.5.**

### *18-2a/4 Ball Lifted and Dropped Away from Movable Obstruction*

**Q.** A player's ball comes to rest against a movable obstruction. The player lifts the ball and drops it away from the obstruction instead of removing the obstruction as provided in Rule 24-1. What is the ruling?

**A.** The player incurs a penalty of one stroke under Rule 18-2a and he must replace his ball before playing his next stroke. Otherwise, he loses the hole in match play or he incurs a total penalty of two strokes in stroke play — see penalty statement under Rule 18.

### *18-2a/5 Ball in Hazard Moves After Loose Impediment Outside Hazard Moved*

**Q.** A player's ball lies in a hazard. He moves a loose impediment which lies outside the hazard but is near the ball. Before the player addresses the ball, it moves. Is the player penalized?

**A.** It is a question of fact whether the player caused the ball to move. If he did so, he incurred a penalty stroke under Rule 18-2a and the ball must be replaced. Otherwise, the ball is played as it lies without penalty.

### *18-2a/6 Oscillating Ball Pressed into Surface of Putting Green*

**Q.** A ball lying on the putting green was oscillating due to wind. The player firmly pressed the ball into the surface of the green and the ball stopped oscillating. The player then holed out. Was the player in breach of the Rules?

**A.** Yes. The player incurred a penalty stroke under Rule 18-2a when he moved his ball by pressing on it. Since the original lie of the ball was altered when the ball was firmly pressed down, the player was obliged to proceed under Rule 20-3b. Since he did not do so, he lost the hole in match play and incurred a total penalty of two strokes in stroke play — see penalty statement under Rule 18.

### 18-2a/7  Ball Moved by Wind Replaced

**Q.** In stroke play, a competitor's ball was moved by wind. Since wind is not an outside agency (see Definition of "Outside Agency"), he should have played it from where it came to rest, but he replaced it. What is the ruling?

**A.** The competitor incurred one penalty stroke under Rule 18-2a, and, before playing his next stroke, he should have replaced the ball on the spot where it came to rest after being moved by the wind. If he did not do so, he incurred a total penalty of two strokes — see penalty statement under Rule 18.

### 18-2a/8  Ball Played from Ground Under Repair Picked Up and Relief Taken Under Ground Under Repair Rule

**Q.** A player, unaware that his ball was in ground under repair, played the ball as it lay. The player then learned that his ball had been in ground under repair, picked up the ball played from the ground under repair, dropped it in accordance with Rule 25-1b and played out the hole. What is the ruling?

**A.** When the player played from the ground under repair, which is permissible, relief under Rule 25-1b was no longer available and the ball was in play where it lay.

When the player picked up his ball in play, he incurred a penalty stroke — Rule 18-2a. Since he did not replace the ball, he incurred a penalty of loss of hole in match play or a total penalty of two strokes in stroke play — see penalty statement under Rule 18.

**Provisional Ball Lifted in Erroneous Belief Original Ball Is in Bounds — See 27-2b/8.**

**Provisional Ball Lifted Subsequently Becomes Ball in Play — See 27-2b/9.**

**Provisional Ball Lifted Subsequently Becomes Ball in Play; Competitor Then Plays from Wrong Place — See 27-2b/10.**

### 18-2a/8.5  Ball Played from Ground Under Repair Abandoned and Relief Taken Under Ground Under Repair Rule

**Q.** In Decision 18-2a/8, the player picked up the ball played from ground under repair and played it from another spot. What would be the ruling if the player abandoned the original ball by dropping and playing another ball under ground under repair procedures?

**A.** After the player played from ground under repair, which is permissible, relief under Rule 25-1b was no longer available and the player was required to play his ball as it lay (Rule 13-1). When he dropped the other ball, he was substituting a ball that became the ball in play (Rule 20-4).

If the location of the original ball was known at the time the substituted ball was dropped, the substitution was not permitted. When he did not correct his error as provided in Rule 20-6 and made a stroke at the wrongly substituted ball, he was in breach of Rule 15-2 as well as Rule 20-7 for playing from a wrong place and the applicable Rule is Rule 13-1. In match play, he incurred a penalty of loss of hole (Rule 15-2 or 20-7b). In stroke play, he incurred a total penalty of four strokes — two strokes for making a stroke at a wrongly substituted ball (Rule 15-2) and two strokes for playing from a wrong place (Rule 20-7c).

If the location of the original ball was not known at the time the substituted ball was dropped, he was required to proceed under Rule 27-1, in which case the substitution was permitted. Since the substituted ball was not dropped at the spot required by Rule 27-1, he played from a wrong place. In match play, he incurred a penalty of loss of hole (Rule 20-7b). In stroke play, he incurred a penalty of one stroke under Rule 27-1 and an additional penalty of two strokes under Rule 20-7c for playing from a wrong place. If the breach was a serious one, he is subject to disqualification unless he corrected his error as provided in Rule 20-7c.

**Ball Played Under Rule for Ball Lost in Ground Under Repair After Another Ball Played Under Stroke-and-Distance Procedure — See 15/8.**

**Ball Dropped and Played Under Ground Under Repair Rule in Absence of Reasonable Evidence That Original Ball Lost in Ground Under Repair — See 25-1c/2.**

### 18-2a/9  Ball Lifted Without Authority Dropped Instead of Being Replaced

**Q.** A player lifted his ball without being entitled to under the Rules and incurred a penalty stroke under Rule 18-2a. He then learned of his error, dropped the ball at the spot from which it was lifted instead of replacing it as required by Rule 18-2a, and played it. What is the ruling?

**A.** The player incurred a penalty of loss of hole in match play or a total of two strokes in stroke play — see penalty statement under Rule 18.

### 18-2a/10  Dropped Ball Lifted and Re-Dropped When It Should Have Been Played as It Lay; Ball Then Lifted Again and Placed

**Q.** In stroke play, a competitor whose ball was in a lateral water hazard elected to take relief under Rule 26-1c(i). When a ball was dropped, it rolled toward the hole but came to rest not more than two club-lengths from where it first struck the ground and not nearer the hole than the point where the original ball last crossed the margin of the water hazard.

Incorrectly believing that Rule 20-2c applied, the competitor lifted the ball and re-dropped it, whereupon the ball rolled toward the hole as before. The competitor again lifted the ball, placed it where it first struck the ground when re-dropped and played his next stroke. Is the competitor penalized two strokes or four strokes?

**A.** Two strokes. The ball when first dropped was in play — see Rule 20-4. The competitor was in breach of Rule 18-2a when he lifted it. Because the competitor failed to replace his ball at the spot at which it came to rest when first dropped, he incurred a total penalty of two strokes — see penalty statement under Rule 18.

**Player Breaches Rules More Than Once Prior to Stroke; Whether Multiple Penalties Applied — See 1-4/12.**

### *18-2a/11 Tee Shot Wrongly Thought to Be Out of Bounds Lifted; Competitor Plays Another Ball from Tee*

**Q.** In stroke play, a competitor hits his tee shot into a practice area. Thinking that the ball is out of bounds, he lifts it and plays another ball from the tee. He then discovers that the practice area is not out of bounds. What is the ruling?

**A.** When the player lifted his ball in play, he incurred a penalty of one stroke under Rule 18-2a and was required to replace it. However, when the player made a stroke from where the previous stroke was made (Rule 20-5), he played a ball under penalty of stroke and distance (see Decision 27/17). This procedure overrides Rule 18-2a and, therefore, the penalty under Rule 18-2a does not apply.

### *18-2a/12 Player Entitled to Relief from Condition Lifts Ball; Player Then Replaces Ball and Plays It from Original Position*

**Q.** A player elects to take relief from an immovable obstruction or abnormal ground condition and lifts his ball. He then realizes that the only area in which he may drop under the Rules is such that his ball, when dropped, will almost certainly be unplayable. He replaces his ball and plays it from its original position. What is the ruling?

**A.** The player was entitled to lift the ball to take relief under Rule 24 or 25. However, by subsequently deciding not to take relief, his right to lift the ball was negated and he incurred a penalty stroke under Rule 18-2a for having lifted his ball in play.

**Player Unaware Ball in Water Hazard Takes Relief from Interference by Burrowing Animal Hole — See 25-1b/26.**

### 18-2a/12.5 Player Entitled to Relief Without Penalty from Condition Lifts Ball; Chooses Not to Take Relief and Wishes to Proceed Under the Unplayable Ball Rule

**Q.** A player elects to take relief from an immovable obstruction or abnormal ground condition and lifts his ball. He then realizes that the only area in which he may drop under the Rules is such that his ball, when dropped, will almost certainly be unplayable. May the player deem the ball unplayable and proceed under Rule 28?

**A.** Yes. The player has the following options:

1. replace the ball in its original position under penalty of one stroke (Rule 18-2a) and then proceed under Rule 28, incurring an additional penalty of one stroke; or

2. proceed directly under Rule 28b or c, without replacing the ball and using the spot where the ball originally lay as the reference point for the relief procedure, incurring a penalty stroke under Rule 28 and an additional penalty stroke under Rule 18-2a; or

3. drop the ball in accordance with Rule 24 or 25 and then, using its new position as a reference point, proceed under Rule 28 incurring a penalty of one stroke; or

4. proceed directly under Rule 28a, without dropping the ball in accordance with Rule 24 or 25, incurring a penalty of one stroke under Rule 28 and no penalty under Rule 18-2a, as he does not need to establish a new reference point before proceeding under Rule 28a. (Revised)

### 18-2a/13 Ball Lifted Without Authority and Cleaned

**Q.** A player's ball comes to rest on the apron of a green. Mistakenly believing that the ball is on the green, the player marks, lifts and cleans it. The player incurs a penalty stroke under Rule 18-2a for lifting the ball without authority under the Rules. Does the player incur an additional penalty stroke under Rule 21 for cleaning the ball?

**A.** No. Rule 21 states that a ball may be cleaned when lifted except when it has been lifted in accordance with Rule 5-3, 12-2 or 22.

**Player Lifts Ball Without Authority Due to Misunderstanding Committee Member's Instructions — See 34-3/3.5.**

### 18-2a/13.5 Ball Lifted and Thrown into Pond in Anger

**Q.** A player played a poor shot and his ball came to rest through the green near a lake. In anger, the player lifted his ball and threw it into the lake from where it could not be retrieved. The player placed another ball on the spot from which the original ball was lifted and holed out. What is the ruling?

**A.** Although Note 1 to Rule 18 states "If a ball to be replaced under this Rule is not immediately recoverable, another ball may be substituted," as the player's ball became irrecoverable only due to the player's subsequent actions after his breach of Rule 18-2a, the Note is not applicable.

The player lost the hole in match play — Rule 15-2.

In stroke play, the player incurred a penalty of three strokes — one under Rule 18-2a for lifting his ball without authority under the Rules and two under Rule 15-2 for substituting a ball when not permitted.

**Player Substitutes Another Ball on Putting Green Because Original Ball Thrown to Caddie for Cleaning Came to Rest in Lake — See 15-2/1.**

### 18-2a/14 Caddie on Own Initiative Lifts Ball for Identification

**Q.** During search for A's ball, A's caddie found a ball and lifted it for identification without the authority of A and without A's announcing in advance his intention to do so. The ball was identified as A's. What is the ruling?

**A.** Since the ball was lifted other than in accordance with the Rules, Rule 18-2a applies and A incurs a penalty of one stroke. Rule 18-2a overrides Rule 12-2 in the circumstances. Accordingly, an additional penalty of one stroke under Rule 12-2 for failing to announce the intention to lift the ball for identification purposes is not applicable.

**Caddie Lifts Ball in Water Hazard Without Player's Authority — See 26-1/9.**

### 18-2a/15 Caddie on Own Initiative Lifts Ball Considering It Unplayable

**Q.** A player's caddie, considering the player's ball to be in an unplayable lie, lifted the ball before the player had an opportunity to inspect the lie. What is the ruling?

**A.** A player's caddie may not deem the player's ball to be unplayable (Rule 28). Therefore, the player incurred a penalty of one stroke under Rule 18-2a when the caddie lifted the ball. The player may replace the ball and play it or invoke the unplayable ball Rule (Rule 28). If the player invokes Rule 28, he may choose to estimate the original location of the ball rather than replace it, but in either case, by invoking Rule 28, the player incurs an additional penalty of one stroke under that Rule.

### 18-2a/16 Competitor's Ball Picked Up by Fellow-Competitor at Competitor's Request

**Q.** A competitor, mistakenly thinking his ball in play in the rough was a wrong ball, asked his fellow-competitor to pick up the ball. The fellow-competitor did so and then the error was discovered. Is the competitor subject to penalty under Rule 18-2a or exempt from penalty by virtue of Rule 18-4?

**A.** Because the lifting of the ball by the fellow-competitor was at the request of the competitor, it would not be correct to exonerate the competitor under Rule 18-4.

The competitor incurred a one-stroke penalty under Rule 18-2a and he was required to replace his ball.

### 18-2a/17 Towel Dropped by Player Is Blown onto and Moves Ball

**Q.** A player dropped a towel on the ground. The wind blew the towel onto the player's ball and moved it. What is the ruling?

**A.** As the player's equipment caused the ball to move, the player incurred a penalty stroke and must replace the ball — Rule 18-2a.

**Ball Blown into Hole by Competitor Not Replaced and Holed Out — See 3-2/2.**

### 18-2a/18 Opponent's Ball Knocked Away by Player After Concession Moves Player's Ball

**Q.** In singles match play, A concedes B's next stroke and knocks B's ball away. B's ball in motion moves A's ball. What is the ruling?

**A.** As A caused his own ball to move, he incurred a penalty of one stroke under Rule 18-2a, and he must replace his ball.

### 18-2a/19 Ball Moved Accidentally by Practice Swing Prior to Tee Shot

**Q.** Before playing from the teeing ground, a player took a practice swing, in the course of which he accidentally struck and moved the teed ball with his club. Did the player play a stroke or incur a penalty?

**A.** The player did not make a stroke — see Definition of "Stroke." Since the ball was not in play — see Definition of "Ball in Play" — he incurred no penalty under Rule 18-2a. The player must put a ball into play from the teeing ground.

### 18-2a/20 Ball in Play Moved Accidentally by Practice Swing

**Q.** A player makes a practice swing and accidentally moves his ball in play with his club. Has he made a stroke?

**A.** No. He had no intention of moving the ball — see Definition of "Stroke."

However, he incurs a penalty stroke under Rule 18-2a for moving his ball in play, and the ball must be replaced.

**Player Instinctively Throws Putter at Ball and Moves It — See 1-2/4.5.**

**Player Kicks Ball While Probing for it in Water in Water Hazard — See 12-1/5.**

**Club Breaks During Downswing; Swing Stopped But Clubhead Falls and Moves Ball — See 14/4.**

**Ball Accidentally Kicked by Player Asked to Lift It Due to Interference — See 20-1/13.**

**Ball Moved by Putter Dropped by Player Approaching Ball to Lift It — See 20-1/14.**

**Ball Moved by Ball-Marker Dropped Accidentally by Player — See 20-1/15.**

**Ball Moved in Removing Ball-Marker After Replacing Ball — See 20-3a/1.**

### 18-2a/21 Ball Moved Accidentally by Player in Playing Wrong Ball in Bunker

**Q.** In a bunker, A plays a wrong ball. In so doing, he accidentally moves a nearby ball which turns out to be his ball. While there is no penalty for playing a wrong ball in a hazard (Rule 15-3), does A incur a penalty for moving his ball in play (a) if the nearby ball was visible before A played the wrong ball or (b) if the nearby ball was not visible before A played the wrong ball?

**A.** If the nearby ball was visible before A played, he incurs a penalty of one stroke under Rule 18-2a and he must replace his ball on the spot from which it was moved. If the lie has been altered, it should be re-created as required by Rule 20-3b. As the nearby ball was likely to interfere with his stroke, the player would have been entitled to proceed in accordance with Decision 1-4/6.

If the nearby ball was not visible before A played, in equity (Rule 1-4), there would be no penalty under Rule 18-2a, but the ball must be replaced, and if necessary, the lie re-created.

**Ball Moved by Stone Dislodged by Partner's Stroke — See 18-1/8.**

**Caddie Shared by Members of Opposite Sides in Four-Ball Match Moves Ball — See 30/1.**

**Player's Ball Moved by Partner in Playing His Own Ball — See 30-3f/9.**

### 18-2a/21.3 Ball Moved Accidentally and Original Lie Altered; Player Places Ball in Wrong Place and Plays

**Q.** A player accidentally steps on his ball in the rough and pushes it into the ground, incurring a penalty stroke under Rule 18-2a. Instead of placing the ball in the nearest most similar lie within one club-length of the original lie as required by Rule 20-3b, the player places the ball almost two club-lengths away from the original lie and plays his next stroke.

In match play, it is clear that the player incurs the general penalty for a breach of Rule 18 or 20-3b, and loses the hole.

In stroke play, does the player incur an additional penalty of two strokes for a breach of Rule 20-3b or a total penalty of two strokes under Rule 18?

**A.** In stroke play, the player incurs a total penalty of two strokes under Rule 18.

Rule 18 requires replacement of a ball moved accidentally. If some other Rule — in this case Rule 20-3b — requires a moved ball to be placed somewhere else, the player is considered to be in breach of Rule 18 if he places the ball other than as prescribed by the other Rule.

### 18-2a/21.5 Ball Moved Accidentally; Spot Where Ball Originally Lay Not Determinable; Player Places Ball Instead of Dropping It

**Q.** A player accidentally moves his ball in the rough, incurring a penalty stroke under Rule 18-2a. The spot where the ball originally lay is not determinable. Instead of dropping the ball as near as possible to the spot where it originally lay as required by Rule 20-3c, the player places the ball as near as possible to that spot and plays his next stroke.

In match play, it is clear that the player incurs the general penalty for a breach of Rule 18 or 20-3c and loses the hole.

In stroke play, does the player incur an additional penalty of two strokes for a breach of Rule 20-3c or a total penalty of two strokes under Rule 18?

**A.** In stroke play, the player incurs a total penalty of two strokes under Rule 18 — see Decision 18-2a/21.3.

### 18-2a/22 Ball Moved Accidentally by Backward Movement of Club After Stroke Misses; Ball Comes to Rest Out of Bounds

**Q.** A player misses a shot completely and, in swinging his club back, he accidentally knocks his ball backwards. Was the backward swing a stroke? If the ball comes to rest out of bounds, how does the player proceed?

**A.** The backward swing was not a stroke. A stroke is the forward movement of the club made with the intention of striking at and moving the ball — see Definition of "Stroke."

In addition to counting the missed stroke, the player incurs a penalty stroke for moving his ball with the backward swing (Rule 18-2a), and the ball must be replaced. The fact that the ball lay out of bounds is irrelevant.

### 18-2a/23 Ball Knocked from Lip of Hole in Disgust

**Q.** In stroke play, a competitor's ball stops on the lip of the hole. In disgust the competitor knocks his ball off the green with the back of his putter. What is the ruling?

**A.** The competitor must replace the ball under penalty of one stroke — Rule 18-2a. The competitor is not considered to have made a stroke.

**Player Jumps Close to Hole to Cause Ball to Drop and Ball Drops — See 1-2/4.**

**Ball Stopped by Player's Foot Moves When Foot Removed — See 19-2/1.**

Rule 18

**Ball Moves Prior to Address and Is Accidentally Stopped by Player's Club; Player Removes Club and Ball Rolls Away — See 19-2/1.5.**

## 18-2a/24 Ball Moved by Flagstick When Measuring

**Q.** In measuring with the flagstick to determine the order of play, the player accidentally moves his ball in play with the flagstick. What is the ruling?

**A.** The answer depends on whether the movement of the ball was directly attributable to the specific act of measuring.

If the player was holding or touching the flagstick in the act of measuring when it touched and moved the ball, the movement of the ball was directly attributable to the specific act of measuring. There is no penalty and the ball must be replaced.

If the movement of the ball was not directly attributable to the specific act of measuring (e.g. the player dropped the flagstick on the ball), the player incurs a penalty stroke under Rule 18-2a and the ball must be replaced. (Revised)

**Rake Thrown into Bunker Before Stroke Moves Ball — See 13-4/21.**

**Ball Moved in Measuring to Determine If Re-Drop Required — See 18-6/1.**

## 18-2a/25 Ball Moved Accidentally by Player During Suspension of Play

**Q.** During a suspension of play, a player elects to leave his ball in position on the course. Prior to the resumption of play, the player accidentally causes his ball to move (e.g., he drops his club on the ball). What is the ruling?

**A.** Although play was suspended when the player accidentally moved his ball, the ball was in play (see Definition of "Ball in Play"). Therefore, the player incurred a penalty of one stroke under Rule 18-2a and the ball must be replaced.

**Ball Visible from Tee Disappears or Is Moved While Play Suspended — See 6-8d/4.**

**Ball Moved by Wind or Casual Water While Play Suspended — See 18-1/11.**

**Ball-Marker Moved Off Green by Wind or Casual Water While Play Suspended — See 20-1/10.**

## 18-2a/26 Ball Dislodged from Tree When Player Climbs Tree to Play Stroke

**Q.** As a player is climbing a tree to play a ball lodged in the tree, the ball falls to the ground. Does the player incur a penalty?

**A.** Yes, one stroke under Rule 18-2a, and the ball must be replaced.

### 18-2a/27  Ball Dislodged from Tree; Circumstances in Which Player Not Penalized

**Q.** A player whose ball is lodged high in a tree wishes to dislodge it by shaking the tree or throwing a club so that he can identify it and proceed under the unplayable ball Rule. Is this permissible?

**A.** Yes. The player should state his intention before taking such action to avoid any question being raised as to whether a penalty would be incurred under Rule 18-2a.

### 18-2a/28  Ball Dislodged from Tree; Circumstances in Which Player Penalized

**Q.** A player could not find his ball. Believing the ball might be lodged in a tree, he shook the tree and his ball fell to the ground. He played the ball from where it came to rest. What is the ruling?

**A.** The player incurred one penalty stroke under Rule 18-2a for moving his ball. He should have replaced the ball. Since he did not do so, in match play he lost the hole and in stroke play he incurred a total penalty of two strokes — see penalty statement under Rule 18.

### 18-2a/29  Ball Dislodged from Tree; Replacement of Ball Not Possible

**Q.** A player, believing his ball is lodged in a tree, shakes the tree in order to dislodge it. His ball falls to the ground. According to Decision 18-2a/28, the player incurs a penalty of one stroke under Rule 18-2a and must replace his ball. Suppose, however, that the player cannot replace his ball either:

(1) because the spot where it lay in the tree is not determinable, or

(2) because the ball fails to remain on the correct spot when replaced, or

(3) because the player cannot reach the spot where the ball lay.

How should the player proceed in each of these three circumstances?

**A.** Rules 20-3c and -3d would normally cover circumstances (1) and (2), but these Rules do not contemplate a situation such as the one described. Accordingly, in equity (Rule 1-4), in the first two circumstances the ball must be placed in the tree as near as possible to the spot from which it was moved, and in the third circumstance the player must proceed under the unplayable ball Rule, incurring an additional penalty stroke.

**Striking at Tree Branch to Move Ball Lodged Higher in Branch — See 14/7.**

### 18-2a/30  Ball Moves After Player Takes Several Practice Swings Near Ball and Touches Grass Behind Ball

**Q.** A player took several practice swings about one foot from his ball which was lying in light rough, and his club came in contact with the ground. He then took his stance, touched grass behind the ball with the clubhead but did not ground the club. At that point the ball moved.

The player claimed that no penalty was incurred because he had not addressed the ball. However, the Committee judged that the practice swings and the touching of the grass behind the ball caused the ball to move, and therefore the player incurred a penalty stroke under Rule 18-2a. Was the Committee correct?

**A.** It is a question of fact whether the player caused his ball to move and thus incurred a penalty under Rule 18-2a. Because of the practice swings and touching of the grass, the weight of evidence is against the player and therefore the Committee's decision was correct.

### 18-2a/30.5  Ball Moves After Removal of Loose Impediment Near Ball

**Q.** Through the green, a player's ball moves after the player removed a loose impediment near, but not touching, the ball. What is the ruling?

**A.** It is a question of fact whether the player caused his ball to move and thus incurred a penalty under Rule 18-2a. The Committee should evaluate all the evidence and make a decision based on the weight of that evidence. The Committee should consider a number of factors, including the proximity of the loose impediment to the ball, the force and means with which the loose impediment was removed, the presence of a strong wind and the delay, if any, between the removal of the loose impediment and the movement of the ball. Any doubt as to whether the player caused the ball to move should be resolved against the player. (New)

### 18-2a/31  Ball Touched Accidentally in Removing Loose Impediments

**Q.** In removing loose impediments from the vicinity of his ball lying through the green, the player accidentally touches the ball with his hand but does not move it. Is there any penalty?

**A.** No. Under Rule 18-2a there is only a penalty if the player, his partner or either of their caddies purposely touches the player's ball; it may be touched accidentally provided it does not move.

**Ball in Hazard Moves After Loose Impediment Outside Hazard Moved — See 18-2a/5.**

**Ball Moved Accidentally by Foot During Removal of Loose Impediment on Putting Green — See 23-1/11.**

**Holding Ball in Place While Removing Obstruction — See 24-1/4.**

### 18-2a/32 Ball Touched with Fir Cone or Stick to Prevent Movement When Loose Impediments Removed

**Q.** A player placed a fir cone or stick against his ball to prevent the ball from moving when he moved some loose impediments. Is this permissible?

**A.** No. The player purposely touched his ball in play, contrary to Rule 18-2a, and incurred a penalty of one stroke.

**Touching and Rotating Half-Buried Ball in Rough for Identification Purposes — See 12-2/2.**

**Touching and Rotating Half-Buried Ball in Hazard for Identification Purposes — See 12-2/3.**

### 18-2a/33 Rotating Ball on Putting Green Without Marking Position

**Q.** A player rotates his ball on the putting green to line up the trademark with the hole. He did not lift the ball, mark its position or change its position. Is there a penalty?

**A.** Yes, one stroke for touching the ball other than as provided for in the Rules — Rule 18-2a. Under Rules 16-1b and 20-1, a ball on the putting green may be lifted (or touched and rotated) after its position has been marked. If the player had marked the position of the ball before rotating it, there would have been no penalty.

### 18-2b/1 Ball Moves After Stance Taken But Before Address

**Q.** Outside a hazard, the player took his stance but did not ground his club. The ball moved. What is the ruling?

**A.** As the player had not addressed the ball, he did not incur a penalty under Rule 18-2b (see Definition of "Addressing the Ball").

If, however, the player caused the ball to move, he was subject to penalty and the ball should have been replaced — Rule 18-2a.

### 18-2b/2 Ball Moves After Stance Taken in Hazard Without Club

**Q.** A player enters a hazard without a club and positions his feet for the purpose of determining how he wishes to play the shot. Has he taken his stance (and thus addressed the ball) so that, if the ball thereafter moves, he is subject to penalty under Rule 18-2b?

**A.** Yes. See Decision 13-4/24.

### 18-2b/3 Ball Moves While Player in Process of Taking Stance in Bunker

**Q.** In a bunker, a player's ball moved when he was in the process of, but had not completed, taking his stance. What is the ruling?

**A.** Since the ball moved before the player had addressed it (see Definition of "Addressing the Ball"), the player incurred no penalty under Rule 18-2b.

If, however, the player's approach to the ball or the act of taking his stance caused the ball to move, the player incurred a penalty stroke under Rule 18-2a and the ball must be replaced.

**When Stance Taken in Bunker — See 13-4/23.**

**Ball Moving in Water Hazard After Address — See 14-6/1.**

### 18-2b/4 Ball Moves After Player Grounds Club But Before Stance Completed

**Q.** A player's routine prior to playing a stroke is as follows: He first grounds the club directly behind the ball with his feet together. Then he gradually widens his feet to shoulder width. At that point, he makes the stroke.

If the ball moves after he grounds the club but before he widens his stance to shoulder width, does he incur a penalty stroke under Rule 18-2b (Ball Moving After Address)?

**A.** No. A player has not addressed the ball until he completes taking his stance, i.e., his feet are essentially in the position in which he normally places them when making a stroke.

However, if the ball moved after the club was placed in position but before the player had completed taking his stance, he incurs a penalty stroke under Rule 18-2a for having caused the ball to move and must replace the ball, unless there is strong evidence that wind or some other agency caused the ball to move.

### 18-2b/5 When Club Grounded in Grass

**Q.** When is a club considered grounded in long grass?

**A.** When the grass is compressed to the point where it will support the weight of the club.

### 18-2b/5.5 Placing Clubhead on Ground in Front of Ball When Addressing

**Q.** A player takes his stance and places his clubhead on the ground in front of the ball without pressing anything down. Before the player grounds the club behind the ball, the ball moves. Has the player "addressed the ball" so that he is subject to penalty under Rule 18-2b?

**A.** Yes.

### 18-2b/5.7 When Player Who Putts "Side-Saddle" Has Addressed Ball

**Q.** A player who putts "side-saddle" usually stands directly behind the ball, places the clubhead on the ground behind the ball and aligns the clubhead. The player then moves to the side so as not to infringe Rule 16-1e and makes his stroke. When is the player deemed to have addressed the ball?

**A.** The player has addressed the ball when he moves to the side. The player has not placed his feet in position for a stroke, and therefore has not taken his stance, until he has moved to the side, and a ball is not addressed until a player has taken his stance.

### 18-2b/6 Ball Perched on Heather Moves When Club Rested on Heather

**Q.** A's ball is perched on a tuft of heather. He takes his stance and rests his club on the heather behind the ball. The ball moves. What is the ruling?

**A.** Resting the club on heather or grass behind the ball constitutes grounding it. Accordingly, A had addressed the ball and Rule 18-2b applies. A incurs a penalty stroke and must replace his ball.

### 18-2b/7 Ball Moves After Player Addresses It and Then Steps Away

**Q.** A player takes his stance and grounds his club. Realizing that the ball is precariously balanced and may move, he steps away from the ball and starts again. This time he does not ground his club, but before he strikes the ball, it moves. What is the ruling?

**A.** The player incurs a penalty stroke under Rule 18-2b, and the ball must be replaced.

### 18-2b/8 Player Addresses Ball, Steps Away, Lifts Ball and Replaces It; Ball Then Moves

**Q.** On the putting green, a player addressed the ball. He stepped away from the ball, marked its position and lifted it. He then replaced the ball and, before he addressed it, the ball moved. Since the ball was lifted and out of play after it was addressed, was the player subject to penalty under Rule 18-2b when it moved after it was put back into play?

**A.** No. The ball must be played as it lies. Once the ball has been lifted the presumption inherent in the Rule that the act of addressing the ball caused the ball to move is no longer valid.

**Ball Dropped in Improper Manner Moves When Addressed; Player Then Lifts Ball and Drops It in Proper Manner — See 20-2a/4.**

**After Ball Addressed on Putting Green Ball Moved in Removal of Loose Impediment — See 23-1/12.**

### 18-2b/9 Ball Moves After Address and Comes to Rest Out of Bounds

**Q.** A player's ball is lying on a slope. When he addresses the ball it moves and comes to rest out of bounds. What is the ruling?

**A.** If a ball moves after the player addresses it, he incurs a one-stroke penalty and the ball must be replaced — Rule 18-2b.

### 18-2b/10 Ball Falls into Hole After Being Addressed

**Q.** A player's ball overhangs the lip of the hole. He addresses the ball and it falls into the hole. What is the ruling?

**A.** The ball is not holed. The player incurs a penalty stroke and the ball must be replaced. Although Rule 16-2 applies when a player's ball overhangs the lip of the hole, Rule 18-2b, which specifically applies when a player's ball moves after he has addressed it, overrides Rule 16-2 in this case.

If the player does not replace the ball and hole out, in stroke play he is disqualified under Rule 3-2. (Revised)

### 18-2b/11 Ball Moved By Another Agency After Address

**Q.** After a player has addressed his ball in play, some other agency (e.g., a ball played by another player) strikes and moves the player's ball. What is the ruling?

**A.** The player incurs no penalty under Rule 18-2b. Whenever an agency directly causes a ball to move, the Rule applicable to that agency (e.g., Rule 18-1, 18-2a, 18-3, 18-4 or 18-5) overrides another Rule where a player is deemed to have moved the ball (e.g., Rule 18-2b).

### 18-2b/12 Ball Moves After Address and Is Stopped by Player's Club

**Q.** After a player addresses his ball, the ball moves backward. Before the player can remove his club, the ball is stopped by the clubhead. What is the ruling?

**A.** The player incurs a penalty stroke under Rule 18-2b and the ball must be replaced. Rule 19-2 does not apply in these circumstances.

**Player Purposely Stops Ball; Where Next Stroke Must be Played from — See 1-2/5.5.**

### Other Decisions relating to Rule 18-2b:

**Stroke Misses Ball Which Is Then Accidentally Knocked Off Tee After Being Addressed — See 11-3/1.**

**Ball Addressed; Club Breaks on Downswing; Swing Stopped But Clubhead Falls and Moves Ball — See 14/4.**

**Provisional Ball Moves After Being Addressed — See 15/7.**

**Ball in Rough Moves Downward When Addressed; Ball Will Not Remain at Rest When Replaced** — See 20-3d/3.

**Order of Play in Foursome Match If Player Accidentally Moves Ball After Address** — See 29-1/5.

**Player Proceeds on Basis of Ruling; Subsequent Facts Prove Ruling to be Incorrect** — See 34-3/7.

**Player Proceeds on Basis of Ruling; Player's Version of Facts Subsequently Found to be Incorrect** — See 34-3/8.

### 18-3b/1 Ball Moved Accidentally by Opponent in Playing His Own Ball

**Q.** In singles match play, A's ball is lying close to B's. It is B's turn to play. Although B has the right under Rule 22-2 to require A to mark and lift his ball, he fails to do so. In making a stroke at his ball, B causes A's ball to move. What is the procedure?

**A.** B incurs a penalty of one stroke under Rule 18-3b for moving A's ball and A must replace his ball. If A's lie has been altered, Rule 20-3b applies.

**Ball Moved by Stone Dislodged by Opponent's Stroke** — See 18-1/8.

### 18-3b/2 Opponent's Stroke Disturbs Bushes Causing Player's Ball to Move

**Q.** In playing a stroke, an opponent disturbed some bushes, causing the player's ball to move. What is the ruling?

**A.** The opponent incurs a penalty stroke (Rule 18-3b) and the player must replace his ball.

### 18-3b/3 Ball Accidentally Stepped on and Moved by Opponent's Caddie

**Q.** The opponent's caddie accidentally stepped on the player's ball and moved it. What is the ruling?

**A.** The opponent incurs a one-stroke penalty (Rule 18-3b) unless the caddie was searching for the ball, in which case there would be no penalty — Rule 18-3a.

### 18-3b/4 Opponent's Caddie Lifts Player's Ball After Player Claims Another Ball

**Q.** In a match, the player finds a ball and claims it as his. The opponent's caddie then finds another ball and lifts it. It is subsequently discovered that the ball the opponent's caddie lifted was the player's ball. Should the opponent incur a penalty under Rule 18-3b?

**A.** No. Rule 18-3b does not contemplate an opponent or his caddie moving a player's ball in such circumstances. In equity (Rule 1-4), the ball must be replaced without penalty to anyone.

### 18-3b/5 Opponent's Caddie Lifts Player's Ball Which May or May Not Have Been Out of Bounds

**Q.** An opponent's caddie lifted the player's ball and informed the player that the ball was out of bounds.

The player claimed that his ball might have been in bounds. What is the ruling?

**A.** If the Committee establishes that the ball was in bounds, the opponent incurs a penalty stroke under Rule 18-3b and the player must replace his ball.

If the ball was out of bounds, the opponent incurs no penalty.

If the position of the ball cannot be established, the benefit of the doubt should be given to the player.

#### Other Decisions relating to Rule 18-3b:

**Player Mistakenly Believing He Has Won Match Picks Up Opponent's Ball — See 2-4/4 and 2-4/17.**

**Ball Resting Against Flagstick; Putt Conceded and Ball Removed Before Player Can Remove Flagstick — See 17-4/2.**

**Ball Resting Against Flagstick Moves Away from Hole When Opponent Removes Flagstick — See 17-4/3.**

**Player's Ball Lifted by Opponent Without Authority — See 20-1/2.**

**Player's Ball Lifted by Opponent Without Authority; Player Lifts Ball-Marker, Claims Hole and Opponent Disputes Claim — See 20-1/3.**

**Caddie Shared by Members of Opposite Sides in Four-Ball Match Moves Ball — See 30/1.**

**Caddie Shared by Opponents' Side in Four-Ball Match Moves Player's Ball — See 30/2.**

**Player's Ball Lifted by Opponent Without Authority in Four-Ball Match — See 30-3f/10.**

### 18-4/1 Competitor's Ball Played by Fellow-Competitor in Bunker Not Replaced

**Q.** In stroke play, A's ball in a bunker was played by his fellow-competitor, B. B failed to get the ball out of the bunker and then discovered he had played a wrong ball. A played his ball from the spot to which B had played it and then learned that he should have replaced his ball. What is the ruling?

**A.** Rule 18-4 required A to replace his ball. A incurred a penalty of two strokes for a breach of Rule 18-4 when he played a stroke with his ball from the spot to which it had been played by B.

B incurred no penalty. There is no penalty for playing a stroke with a wrong ball in a hazard.

### 18-4/2 Competitor's Ball Knocked Out of Bunker by Fellow-Competitor's Stroke at Own Ball

**Q.** In stroke play, B, in playing a stroke at his ball in a bunker, accidentally hits A's ball that was also in the bunker. Both balls come to rest outside the bunker. A plays his ball from the spot to which it has been moved by B's stroke. What is the ruling?

**A.** A was required to replace his ball in the bunker — Rule 18-4. A's breach of Rule 18-4 was a serious one and he should have been disqualified under Rule 20-7c unless the serious breach was rectified as prescribed in the Rule. B incurred no penalty — Rule 18-4.

**Fellow-Competitor's Ball Knocked from Lip of Hole by Competitor Not Replaced — See 3-2/1.**

### 18-4/3 Fellow-Competitor Lifts Competitor's Ball Conceding Next Stroke in Stroke-Play Play-Off

**Q.** In a stroke-play play-off, B picks up A's ball, conceding A a 4. B then holed a putt for a 3 to win the play-off. Is B subject to penalty for conceding a putt in stroke play?

**A.** B incurs no penalty — Rule 18-4. If B had not holed in 3 to win the play-off, A would have been obliged to replace his ball and hole out (Rule 18-4).

**Other Decisions relating to Rule 18-4:**

**Ball Resting Against Flagstick Moves Away from Hole When Flagstick Removed by Fellow-Competitor — See 17-4/3.**

**Competitor's Ball Picked Up by Fellow-Competitor at Competitor's Request — See 18-2a/16.**

**Competitor's Ball Lifted Without Authority by Fellow-Competitor — See 20-1/4.**

### 18-5/1 Ball Moved by Wrong Ball Played by Opponent

**Q.** In match play, an opponent plays a wrong ball from a bunker and the wrong ball knocks the player's ball into the hole. What is the ruling?

**A.** No penalty is incurred and the player must replace his ball — Rule 18-5.

### 18-5/2 Original Ball Struck by Provisional Ball

**Q.** A player's provisional ball played from the tee strikes and moves his original ball. What is the ruling?

**A.** There is no penalty. The original ball must be replaced — Rule 18-5.

**Original Ball Strikes Second Ball or Vice Versa — See 3-3/7.**

**Provisional Ball Struck by Original Ball — See 19-5/5.**

## 18-5/3 Competitor and Fellow-Competitor Unaware Ball Moved by Fellow-Competitor's Ball Until After Completion of Hole

**Q.** In stroke play, A then B play their second strokes to the green but, due to the contours of the green, they cannot see where their balls come to rest. Both competitors complete the hole from about 12 feet with two putts each. On their way to the next tee, it was established that A's ball had come to rest about one foot from the hole, but that B's ball in motion had struck A's ball and moved it.

(a) How should A proceed?

(b) If A decided not to take any action because the hole had been completed, how should the Committee rule if the facts of the case come to its attention:

(i) before the card was returned?

(ii) after the card was returned but before the competition was closed?

**A.** (a) If A is certain that a serious breach of Rule 18-5 has not occurred, he should take no further action — see first paragraph of Rule 20-7c. The score with the original ball would be A's score for the hole. In equity (Rule 1-4), A would incur no penalty because he did not know that he had played from a wrong place until after he had completed the hole.

If A believes that he may have committed a serious breach of Rule 18-5, then he should rectify the situation as prescribed in Rule 20-7c. If the Committee determines that A is not guilty of a serious breach of the Rules, then his score with the original ball counts. If the Committee determines that A is guilty of a serious breach of the Rules, the score with the second ball counts. In equity (Rule 1-4), no penalty is incurred in either case — see first paragraph above.

(b) (i) and (ii) The answer depends on whether or not the Committee determines that A is guilty of a serious breach of playing from a wrong place. In making that determination, the Committee must consider all the facts. If the Committee rules that a serious breach of Rule 18-5 has not occurred, the score with the original ball will be A's score for the hole in both cases and, in equity (Rule 1-4), he incurs no penalty.

If, however, the Committee determines that A has committed a serious breach of Rule 18-5, he is disqualified in both cases — see Rule 20-7c.

**Player Unaware Ball Moved by Outside Agency Does Not Replace Ball — See 18-1/3.**

### Other Decisions relating to Rule 18-5:

**Ball Lifted from Putting Green; Ball Replaced While Another Ball in Motion But Then Lifted Because Moving Ball Might Strike It** — See 16-1b/2.

**Opponent's Ball Knocked Away by Player After Concession Moves Player's Ball** — See 18-2a/18.

**Ball Moved by Another Ball After Being Addressed** — See 18-2b/11.

**Competitor's Ball Played from Putting Green Moves Ball on Green Belonging to Competitor Playing in Another Group** — See 19-5/2.

### *18-6/1 Ball Moved in Measuring to Determine If Re-Drop Required*

**Q.** A player drops his ball in accordance with the Rules. The ball rolls and the player is uncertain whether it has come to rest more than two club-lengths from where it first struck a part of the course. The player measures to determine whether he must re-drop under Rule 20-2c(vi) and in doing so accidentally causes the ball to move. What is the ruling if (a) the ball had rolled more than two club-lengths or (b) the ball had not rolled more than two club-lengths?

**A.** The player incurs no penalty for causing his ball to move in either case (see Rule 18-6). If the ball had rolled more than two club-lengths, it must be re-dropped. If the ball had not rolled more than two club-lengths, it must be replaced.

# Rule 19. Ball in Motion Deflected or Stopped

**Definitions**
All defined terms are in *italics* and are listed alphabetically in the Definitions section — see pages 3-11.

**19-1. By Outside Agency**
If a ball in motion is accidentally deflected or stopped by any *outside agency*, it is a *rub of the green*, there is no penalty and the ball must be played as it lies except:

 a. If a ball in motion after a *stroke* other than on the *putting green* comes to rest in or on any moving or animate *outside agency*, the player must, *through the green* or in a *hazard*, drop the ball, or on the *putting green* place the ball, as near as possible to the spot where the *outside agency* was when the ball came to rest in or on it, and

 b. If a ball in motion after a *stroke* on the *putting green* is deflected or stopped by, or comes to rest in or on, any moving or animate *outside agency* except a worm or an insect, the *stroke* is canceled. The ball must be replaced and the *stroke* replayed.

If the ball is not immediately recoverable, another ball may be *substituted*.

(Player's ball deflected or stopped by another ball — see Rule 19-5.)

**Note:** If the *referee* or the *Committee* determines that a player's ball has been purposely deflected or stopped by an *outside agency*, Rule 1-4 applies to the player. If the *outside agency* is a *fellow-competitor* or his *caddie*, Rule 1-2 applies to the *fellow-competitor*.

**19-2. By Player, Partner, Caddie or Equipment**
 **a. Match Play**
 If a player's ball is accidentally deflected or stopped by himself, his *partner* or either of their *caddies* or *equipment*, he loses the *hole*.

 **b. Stroke Play**
 If a *competitor's* ball is accidentally deflected or stopped by himself, his *partner* or either of their *caddies* or *equipment*, the *competitor* incurs a penalty of two strokes. The ball must be played as it lies, except when it comes to rest in or on the *competitor's*, his *partner's* or either of their *caddies'* clothes or *equipment*, in which case the *competitor* must *through the green* or in a *hazard* drop the ball, or on the *putting green* place the ball, as near as possible to where the article was when the ball came to rest in or on it.

**Exception:** Dropped ball — see Rule 20-2a.

(Ball purposely deflected or stopped by player, *partner* or *caddie* — see Rule 1-2.)

### 19-3. By Opponent, Caddie or Equipment in Match Play

If a player's ball is accidentally deflected or stopped by an opponent, his *caddie* or his *equipment*, there is no penalty. The player may, before another *stroke* is made by either side, cancel the *stroke* and play a ball without penalty as nearly as possible at the spot from which the original ball was last played (see Rule 20-5) or he may play the ball as it lies. However, if the player elects not to cancel the *stroke* and the ball has come to rest in or on the opponent's or his *caddie's* clothes or *equipment*, the player must *through the green* or in a *hazard* drop the ball, or on the *putting green* place the ball, as near as possible to where the article was when the ball came to rest in or on it.

**Exception:** Ball striking person attending *flagstick* — see Rule 17-3b.

(Ball purposely deflected or stopped by opponent or caddie — see Rule 1-2.)

### 19-4. By Fellow-Competitor, Caddie or Equipment in Stroke Play

See Rule 19-1 regarding ball deflected by *outside agency*.

### 19-5. By Another Ball

#### a. At Rest

If a player's ball in motion after a *stroke* is deflected or stopped by a *ball in play* and at rest, the player must play his ball as it lies. In match play, there is no penalty. In stroke play, there is no penalty unless both balls lay on the *putting green* prior to the *stroke*, in which case the player incurs a penalty of two strokes.

#### b. In Motion

If a player's ball in motion after a *stroke* is deflected or stopped by another ball in motion after a *stroke*, the player must play his ball as it lies. There is no penalty unless the player was in breach of Rule 16-1f, in which case he incurs the penalty for breach of that Rule.

**Exception:** If the player's ball is in motion after a *stroke* on the *putting green* and the other ball in motion is an *outside agency* — see Rule 19-1b.

PENALTY FOR BREACH OF RULE:
Match play — Loss of hole; Stroke play — Two strokes.

---

### 19/1 Ball Deflected or Stopped by Golf Cart Shared by Two Players

Under the Definition of "Equipment," equipment includes a golf cart, whether or not motorized. If two players share a golf cart, the cart and everything in it are deemed to be the equipment of the player whose ball is involved; except that, when the cart is being moved by one of the players, the cart and everything in it are deemed to be that player's equipment.

Thus, for example, in a singles match, if A and B are sharing a cart and A's ball in motion is deflected or stopped by the cart, A loses the hole (Rule 19-2a) unless the cart is being driven or pulled by B when the incident occurs. If B is driving or pulling the cart, there is no penalty, and A would have the option of playing his ball as it lies or replaying the stroke (Rule 19-3).

### 19/2  Status of Person in Shared Golf Cart

**Q.** The Definition of "Equipment" refers to a shared cart and everything in it as being equipment of the player whose ball is involved or, if applicable, the player moving the cart. Does the phrase "and everything in it" include any person in the cart?

**A.** Yes.

**Local Rule for Events in Which Motorized Golf Carts Permitted — See 33-8/4.**

### 19-1/1  Ball Deflected by Direction Post

**Q.** A ball is deflected by a direction post. What is the ruling?

**A.** It is a rub of the green and the ball must be played as it lies, without penalty.

### 19-1/2  Player's Ball Deflected by Stroke of Player in Another Group

**Q.** A hit his ball over onto another fairway where, before it came to rest, it was struck by X in the course of striking his own ball. X's ball went 20 yards. A's ball could not be found. What is the ruling?

**A.** Each player was an outside agency in relation to the other.

Under Rule 19-1, A would have been obliged to play his ball as it lay, without penalty, if it had been found. Since it was not found, A must proceed under Rule 27-1, incurring a penalty of stroke and distance.

X must play his ball as it lies, without penalty.

**Ball Played from Spot Where Original Ball Deflected Out of Bounds by Maintenance Vehicle — See 20-7/1.**

### 19-1/3  Ball Played from Putting Green Deflected by Moving Outside Agency; Stroke Not Replayed

**Q.** In stroke play, a competitor putts and his ball is deflected by a moving outside agency other than a worm or an insect. The competitor did not replay the stroke as required by Rule 19-1b, holed out and then played from the next tee. What is the ruling?

**A.** The stroke that was deflected by the outside agency does not count in the competitor's score. When the competitor failed to replay the stroke he played from a wrong place. If the breach was a serious one, he is disqualified — Rule 20-7c. Otherwise, the score with the original ball counts and he incurs a penalty of two strokes for breach of Rule 19.

### 19-1/4 Ball Played from Putting Green Deliberately Deflected or Stopped by Spectator

**Q.** A player plays a stroke from the putting green and, while the ball is still in motion, a spectator deliberately deflects or stops it. What is the ruling?

**A.** The Committee must act in equity — see Note under Rule 19-1. The stroke should be canceled, the ball replaced and the stroke replayed, without penalty.

### 19-1/4.1 Ball Deliberately Deflected or Stopped Through the Green by Spectator

**Q.** A player overshoots a green. A spectator (X) who is standing behind the green deliberately deflects or stops the ball. According to the Note under Rule 19-1, equity (Rule 1-4) applies. What is the equitable procedure in this case?

**A.** In a case where the ball might have come to rest where X was situated if he had not deliberately deflected or stopped it, the player should be required to drop the ball at the spot where X was situated. For example, if another spectator (Y) had been behind X, the ball might have struck Y, if X had avoided it, and come to rest where X was situated.

If there is no question that the ball would have come to rest somewhere else if X had not deflected or stopped it, the Committee must make a judgment as to where the ball would have come to rest, giving the player the benefit of any doubt. For example, if no person or object had been behind X and without any doubt the ball would have come to rest either in a lateral water hazard behind the green or in the rough just short of the hazard, the Committee should require the player to drop the ball in the rough just short of the hazard.

### 19-1/5 Ball Deliberately Deflected or Stopped on Putting Green by Fellow-Competitor

**Q.** At the last hole of a stroke-play event, A has a putt to beat B by one stroke. A putts and B, seeing that A's ball might go into the hole, deliberately deflects it. What is the ruling?

**A.** In equity (Rule 1-4), A should replay his stroke, without penalty — see Note under Rule 19-1. B should be disqualified for a serious breach of Rule 1-2 (Exerting Influence on Ball).

### 19-1/6  Ball Picked Up or Deflected by Dog on Putting Green After Stroke from Off Green

**Q.** A ball played from off the green was about a foot from the hole and still in motion when it was moved by a dog to a spot about 10 feet from the hole. The ball was either deflected by the dog or the dog picked it up, ran with it and dropped it. What is the ruling?

**A.** If the ball was deflected, it would be played as it lay, without penalty, from the spot to which it was moved by the dog — Rule 19-1.

If the dog picked up the ball, the player should have placed the ball, without penalty, as near as possible to the spot where the original ball was when the dog picked it up — Rule 19-1a.

### 19-1/7  Ball Picked Up or Deflected by Dog on Putting Green After Stroke on Green

**Q.** A player plays a stroke on the putting green and, while the ball is still in motion, it is picked up and carried away, or is deflected, by a dog. What is the ruling?

**A.** In either case, the stroke is canceled and the ball must be replaced — Rule 19-1b.

### [19-1/8  Reserved]

### [19-1/9  Reserved]

### 19-1/10  Ball in Motion After Stroke on Putting Green Deflected by Ball Played at Another Hole

**Q.** A player plays a stroke on a putting green. While the ball is in motion, a ball played at another hole strikes the player's ball and knocks it into a bunker. What is the ruling?

**A.** Since the player's ball was deflected by a moving outside agency, the player's stroke is canceled and he must replace his ball — Rule 19-1b. Rule 19-5b does not apply — see Exception under that Rule.

**Ball Strikes Hole-Liner Pulled Out with Flagstick — See 17/8.**

**Attendant Removes Flagstick Whereupon Knob Falls from Top of Flagstick and Deflects Ball — See 17/9.**

### 19-2/1  Ball Stopped by Player's Foot Moves When Foot Removed

**Q.** A player making a stroke on the bank of a bunker hits the ball to the top of the bank. The ball then rolls back down the bank and comes to rest against the player's foot. The player removes his foot and the ball rolls into his footprint. What is the ruling?

**A.** In match play, the player loses the hole (Rule 19-2a).

In stroke play, the player incurs a penalty of two strokes (Rule 19-2b) and must replace the ball on the spot at which it came to rest against his foot. A further penalty under Rule 18-2a (Ball at Rest Moved by Player) would not be appropriate in the circumstances.

### 19-2/1.5 Ball Moves Prior to Address and Is Accidentally Stopped by Player's Club; Player Removes Club and Ball Rolls Away

**Q.** A player's ball lies on a steep slope through the green. The player takes his stance but, fearing the ball might move, does not ground his club and so has not addressed the ball. The ball rolls backwards and is stopped accidentally by the player's club. The player then removes his club and the ball rolls farther down the slope. Is the player subject to penalty under Rule 19-2?

**A.** Yes, and in stroke play the ball must be replaced on the spot at which it was stopped. A further penalty under Rule 18-2a (Ball at Rest Moved by Player) would not be appropriate in the circumstances provided the player replaces the ball. If the ball is not replaced before the competitor makes his next stroke, the failure to replace the ball is considered a separate act and he incurs an additional penalty of two strokes under Rule 18-2a. (Revised)

**Player Purposely Stops Ball; Where Next Stroke Must be Played from — See 1-2/5.5.**

**Player Breaches Rules More Than Once Prior to Stroke; Whether Multiple Penalties Applied — See 1-4/12.**

**Ball Moves After Address and Is Stopped by Player's Club — See 18-2b/12.**

### 19-2/2 Player's Ball Strikes Own Caddie and Comes to Rest Out of Bounds

**Q.** A player's ball accidentally strikes his caddie, who is standing in bounds, and the ball comes to rest out of bounds. What is the ruling?

**A.** In match play, the player loses the hole — Rule 19-2a.

In stroke play, the player incurs a penalty of two strokes (Rule 19-2b) and, since the ball lies out of bounds, he must proceed under Rule 27-1, incurring another penalty stroke.

### 19-2/3 Player's Ball Strikes Own Caddie Standing Out of Bounds and Comes to Rest on Course

**Q.** A player's ball accidentally strikes his caddie standing out of bounds and comes to rest in bounds. What is the ruling?

**A.** In match play, the player loses the hole — Rule 19-2a.

In stroke play, the player incurs a penalty of two strokes and, since the ball came to rest in bounds, it is in play — Rule 19-2b.

### 19-2/4 Player's Ball Strikes Own Caddie Standing Out of Bounds and Comes to Rest Out of Bounds

**Q.** A player's ball accidentally strikes his caddie standing out of bounds and comes to rest out of bounds. What is the ruling?

**A.** In match play, the player loses the hole — Rule 19-2a.

In stroke play, the player incurs a penalty of two strokes (Rule 19-2b) and, since the ball lies out of bounds, he must proceed under Rule 27-1, incurring another penalty stroke.

#### Other Decisions relating to Rule 19-2:

Ball Falls on Club Face After Stroke and Sticks to Mud Thereon — See 14-4/1.

Ball Strikes Pipeline and on Rebound Is Deflected by Face of Club — See 14-4/2.

Caddie Stops Dropped Ball Before It Comes to Rest; When Penalty Incurred — See 20-2c/4.

### 19-2/5 Ball Deflected or Stopped by Clubs Belonging to Different Side But Carried in Same Bag

**Q.** A had his bag of clubs on a golf cart. B had only a few clubs which A carried for him in his bag. B played a stroke which was deflected by the clubs. What is the ruling?

**A.** Under the principle in the Definition of "Caddie," the clubs should be deemed B's equipment.

In match play, B lost the hole — Rule 19-2a.

In stroke play, B incurred a penalty of two strokes and must play his ball as it lies — Rule 19-2b.

### 19-2/6 Ball Deflected or Stopped by Player's Golf Cart Being Pulled by Opponent or Fellow-Competitor

**Q.** A player's ball strikes his own golf cart while it is being pulled by an opponent or a fellow-competitor. What is the ruling?

**A.** Since the player is not sharing the cart with any other player, it remains his equipment even when it is being pulled by an opponent or a fellow-competitor.

If the player was aware that his cart was being pulled by an opponent or a fellow-competitor, in match play the player loses the hole — Rule 19-2a. In stroke play, he incurs a penalty of two strokes and must play the ball as it lies — Rule 19-2b.

But if he was not aware, in equity (Rule 1-4) no penalty is incurred, and the ball must be played as it lies.

### 19-2/7 Ball Strikes Competitor's Golf Bag and Then His Caddie

**Q.** In stroke play, a competitor's ball strikes his golf bag lying on the ground and then bounces off it and hits his caddie. Is the penalty two strokes or four strokes?

**A.** Two strokes — Rule 19-2b.

**Player Breaches Rules More Than Once Prior to Stroke; Whether Multiple Penalties Applied — See 1-4/12.**

**Ball Popped Up Swung at in Disgust and Hit — See 14/6.**

### 19-2/8 Player's Ball Strikes Opponent's or Fellow-Competitor's Bag Left Ahead By Shared Caddie

**Q.** A and B are either opponents in match play or fellow-competitors in stroke play and they are sharing a caddie. They are on the teeing ground and the caddie is positioned where their tee shots would be expected to come to rest. A's tee shot comes to rest well short of the caddie and B's tee shot comes to rest near the caddie. Without specific directions from either A or B, the caddie leaves B's bag near B's ball and returns with A's bag to A's ball. A's next stroke strikes B's bag. What is the ruling?

**A.** The Definition of "Caddie" states in part "When one caddie is employed by more than one player, he is always deemed to be the caddie of the player whose ball is involved, and equipment carried by him is deemed to be that player's equipment, except when the caddie acts upon specific directions of another player..." As no specific directions were given to the caddie by B, B's bag is deemed to be A's equipment in this case. It is irrelevant that the caddie was not carrying B's bag at the time A's ball struck it.

In match play, A lost the hole – Rule 19-2a.

In stroke play, A incurs a penalty of two strokes and must play his ball as it lies unless the ball has come to rest in or on B's bag – Rule 19-2b.

**Meaning of "Specific Directions" in Definition of "Caddie" — See 6-4/1.**

### 19-3/1 Ball Accidentally Strikes Opponent Standing Out of Bounds and Comes to Rest Out of Bounds

**Q.** In match play, a player's ball accidentally strikes his opponent, who is standing out of bounds. The ball comes to rest out of bounds. What is the ruling?

**A.** There is no penalty and the player is entitled to replay the stroke — Rule 19-3.

**Tee Marking Position of Player's Ball Deflects Opponent's Ball — See 20-1/17.**

### 19-3/2 Dropped Ball Accidentally Deflected by Opponent or His Caddie

**Q.** In match play, a player drops his ball under a Rule and the ball is accidentally deflected by the opponent or his caddie. What is the ruling?

**A.** The player has the option of playing his ball as it lies or re-dropping it — Rule 19-3.

### 19-3/3 Player's Ball Strikes Opponent's or Fellow-Competitor's Trolley Then Own Trolley

**Q.** A player's ball strikes his opponent's or fellow-competitor's trolley and then strikes his own trolley. What is the ruling?

**A.** In match play, because the ball first struck his opponent's equipment the player may replay the stroke, without penalty, regardless of what happens thereafter to the ball (Rule 19-3). The player may not play the ball as it lies, because after striking his opponent's equipment but before coming to rest, his ball struck his own equipment, the penalty for which is loss of hole (Rule 19-2a).

In stroke play, although the ball first struck a fellow-competitor's equipment, the competitor incurs a penalty of two strokes and must play the ball as it lies (Rules 19-4, -1, -2).

#### Decisions relating to Rule 19-4:

**Ball Deliberately Deflected or Stopped on Putting Green by Fellow-Competitor — See 19-1/5.**

**Player's Ball Strikes Opponent's or Fellow-Competitor's Trolley Then Own Trolley — See 19-3/3.**

### 19-5/1 Player Lifts His Ball on Putting Green and Sets It Aside; Opponent's or Fellow-Competitor's Ball Played from Green Subsequently Strikes Player's Ball

**Q.** B lifts his ball on the putting green and sets it aside elsewhere on the green. A then putts and his ball is deflected or stopped by B's ball. What is the ruling?

**A.** Since A's ball was deflected by B's equipment (see Note under Definition of "Equipment"), Rules 19-3 and -4 apply.

In match play, A incurs no penalty and has the option of playing his ball as it lies or canceling and replaying the stroke — Rule 19-3.

In stroke play, A incurs no penalty and must play his ball as it lies — Rules 19-4 and -1.

In either form of play, B must replace his ball on the spot from which it was lifted — Rule 20-3a.

Rule 19-5a does not apply because B's ball was not in play.

**Explanation of "Any Ball He Has Played" — See 18/7.**

### 19-5/1.7 Ball Dropped on Putting Green by Opponent or Fellow-Competitor Falls on Player's Moving Ball

**Q.** A plays a stroke on the putting green. B, A's opponent or a fellow-competitor, accidentally drops his ball, which he had lifted, and it falls on A's ball which is still in motion. What is the ruling?

**A.** In match play, since A's ball was deflected by B's equipment (see Note under Definition of "Equipment"), Rule 19-3 applies. A has the option of playing his ball as it lies or canceling and replaying the stroke. Neither A nor B incurs a penalty.

In stroke play, A's ball was deflected by a moving outside agency. Therefore, A must cancel and replay his stroke, without penalty, under Rule 19-1b. B incurs no penalty.

In either form of play, B must replace his ball on the spot from which it was lifted — Rule 20-3a.

Rule 19-5b does not apply because B's ball was not in motion after a stroke.

### 19-5/2 Competitor's Ball Played from Putting Green Strikes Ball on Green Belonging to Competitor Playing in Another Group

**Q.** In stroke play, C and D are playing together. A and B are playing immediately behind C and D. C's ball lies on the putting green and, since D is searching for his ball, C and D invite A and B to play through. Subsequently, A putts and his ball strikes C's ball. What is the ruling?

**A.** A incurs a penalty of two strokes and must play his ball as it lies — Rule 19-5. C must replace his ball without penalty — Rule 18-5.

### 19-5/3 Competitor's Ball Played on Putting Green Deflected by Balls of Two Fellow-Competitors

**Q.** In stroke play, a competitor plays a stroke on the putting green. His ball strikes a fellow-competitor's ball and is deflected. Before the competitor's ball comes to rest it strikes another fellow-competitor's ball. Under Rule 19-5, is the competitor penalized two strokes or four strokes?

**A.** Two strokes.

**Player Breaches Rules More Than Once Prior to Stroke; Whether Multiple Penalties Applied — See 1-4/12.**

## 19-5/4 Competitor's Ball Played from Putting Green Touches But Does Not Move Ball of Fellow-Competitor Lying on Green

**Q.** In stroke play, A putts and his ball comes to rest touching B's ball. B's ball did not move nor did B's ball prevent A's ball from rolling any farther. What is the ruling?

**A.** Since A's ball was not deflected or stopped by B's ball, A incurs no penalty under Rule 19-5 or any other Rule. However, if there is any doubt as to whether B's ball moved or prevented A's ball from rolling any farther, it should be resolved against A.

## 19-5/5 Provisional Ball Struck by Original Ball

**Q.** A player's original ball strikes and moves his provisional ball. What is the ruling?

**A.** Rule 19-5 does not apply because the provisional ball was not in play. Rule 19-2 does not apply because the provisional ball is not the equipment of the player — see Decision 18/7. In equity (Rule 1-4) and by analogy to Rule 19-5a, the player shall play the ball as it lies and no penalty is incurred except that, in stroke play, if both balls lay on the putting green prior to the stroke, the player incurs a penalty of two strokes.

### Other Decisions relating to Rule 19-5:

Original Ball Strikes Second Ball or Vice Versa — See 3-3/7.

Competitor Not Given Opportunity to Lift Ball Assisting Fellow-Competitor; Fellow-Competitor's Ball Strikes Competitor's Ball — See 3-4/1.

Ball Lifted from Putting Green; Ball Replaced While Another Ball in Motion but Then Lifted Because Moving Ball Might Strike It — See 16-1b/2.

Ball Lifted from Putting Green; Ball Replaced While Another Ball in Motion Subsequently Deflects Moving Ball — See 16-1b/3.

Explanation of "Any Ball He Has Played" — See 18/7.

Player's Ball Moved by Ball Accidentally Dropped by Opponent or Fellow-Competitor — See 18/7.5.

Provisional Ball Strikes Original Ball — See 18-5/2.

Competitor's Ball Moved by Fellow-Competitor's Ball — See 18-5/3.

**RELIEF SITUATIONS AND PROCEDURE**

# Rule 20.
# Lifting, Dropping and Placing; Playing From Wrong Place

### Definitions
All defined terms are in *italics* and are listed alphabetically in the Definitions section — see pages 3-11.

### 20-1. Lifting and Marking
A ball to be lifted under the *Rules* may be lifted by the player, his *partner* or another person authorized by the player. In any such case, the player is responsible for any breach of the *Rules*.

The position of the ball must be marked before it is lifted under a *Rule* that requires it to be replaced. If it is not marked, the player incurs a penalty of one stroke and the ball must be replaced. If it is not replaced, the player incurs the general penalty for breach of this Rule, but there is no additional penalty under Rule 20-1.

If a ball or ball-marker is accidentally *moved* in the process of lifting the ball under a *Rule* or marking its position, the ball or ball-marker must be replaced. There is no penalty provided the movement of the ball or ball-marker is directly attributable to the specific act of marking the position of or lifting the ball. Otherwise, the player incurs a penalty of one stroke under this Rule or Rule 18-2a.

**Exception:** If a player incurs a penalty for failing to act in accordance with Rule 5-3 or 12-2, there is no additional penalty under Rule 20-1.

**Note:** The position of a ball to be lifted should be marked by placing a ball-marker, a small coin or other similar object immediately behind the ball. If the ball-marker interferes with the play, *stance* or *stroke* of another player, it should be placed one or more clubhead-lengths to one side.

### 20-2. Dropping and Re-Dropping
#### a. By Whom and How
A ball to be dropped under the *Rules* must be dropped by the player himself. He must stand erect, hold the ball at shoulder height and arm's length and drop it. If a ball is dropped by any other person or in any other manner and the error is not corrected as provided in Rule 20-6, the player incurs a penalty of one stroke.

If the ball touches the player, his *partner*, either of their *caddies* or their *equipment* before or after it strikes a part of the *course*, the ball must be re-dropped, without penalty. There is no limit to the number of times a ball must be re-dropped in these circumstances.

(Taking action to influence position or movement of ball — see Rule 1-2.)

**b. Where to Drop**

When a ball is to be dropped as near as possible to a specific spot, it must be dropped not nearer the *hole* than the specific spot which, if it is not precisely known to the player, must be estimated.

A ball when dropped must first strike a part of the *course* where the applicable *Rule* requires it to be dropped. If it is not so dropped, Rules 20-6 and -7 apply.

**c. When to Re-Drop**

A dropped ball must be re-dropped without penalty if it:

  (i) rolls into and comes to rest in a *hazard*;

  (ii) rolls out of and comes to rest outside a *hazard*;

  (iii) rolls onto and comes to rest on a *putting green*;

  (iv) rolls and comes to rest *out of bounds*;

  (v) rolls to and comes to rest in a position where there is interference by the condition from which relief was taken under Rule 24-2b (immovable *obstruction*), Rule 25-1 (*abnormal ground conditions*), Rule 25-3 (*wrong putting green*) or a Local Rule (Rule 33-8a), or rolls back into the pitch-mark from which it was lifted under Rule 25-2 (*embedded ball*);

  (vi) rolls and comes to rest more than two club-lengths from where it first struck a part of the *course*; or

  (vii) rolls and comes to rest nearer the *hole* than:

  (a) its original position or estimated position (see Rule 20-2b) unless otherwise permitted by the *Rules*; or

  (b) the *nearest point of relief* or maximum available relief (Rule 24-2, 25-1 or 25-3); or

  (c) the point where the original ball last crossed the margin of the *water hazard* or *lateral water hazard* (Rule 26-1).

If the ball when re-dropped rolls into any position listed above, it must be placed as near as possible to the spot where it first struck a part of the *course* when re-dropped.

If a ball to be re-dropped or placed under this Rule is not immediately recoverable, another ball may be *substituted*.

**Note:** If a ball when dropped or re-dropped comes to rest and subsequently *moves*, the ball must be played as it lies, unless the provisions of any other *Rule* apply.

### 20-3. Placing and Replacing

#### a. By Whom and Where

A ball to be placed under the *Rules* must be placed by the player or his *partner*. If a ball is to be replaced, the player, his *partner* or the person who lifted or *moved* it must place it on the spot from which it was lifted or *moved*. In any such case, the player is responsible for any breach of the *Rules*.

If a ball or ball-marker is accidentally *moved* in the process of placing or replacing the ball, the ball or ball-marker must be replaced. There is no penalty provided the movement of the ball or ball-marker is directly attributable to the specific act of placing or replacing the ball or removing the ball-marker. Otherwise, the player incurs a *penalty stroke* under Rule 18-2a or 20-1.

#### b. Lie of Ball to Be Placed or Replaced Altered

If the original lie of a ball to be placed or replaced has been altered:

(i) except in a *hazard*, the ball must be placed in the nearest lie most similar to the original lie that is not more than one club-length from the original lie, not nearer the *hole* and not in a *hazard*;

(ii) in a *water hazard*, the ball must be placed in accordance with Clause (i) above, except that the ball must be placed in the *water hazard*;

(iii) in a *bunker*, the original lie must be re-created as nearly as possible and the ball must be placed in that lie.

#### c. Spot Not Determinable

If it is impossible to determine the spot where the ball is to be placed or replaced:

(i) *through the green*, the ball must be dropped as near as possible to the place where it lay but not in a *hazard* or on a *putting green*;

(ii) in a *hazard*, the ball must be dropped in the *hazard* as near as possible to the place where it lay;

(iii) on the *putting green*, the ball must be placed as near as possible to the place where it lay but not in a *hazard*.

**Exception:** When resuming play (Rule 6-8d), if the spot where the ball is to be placed is impossible to determine, it must be estimated and the ball placed on the estimated spot.

#### d. Ball Fails to Come to Rest on Spot

If a ball when placed fails to come to rest on the spot on which it was placed, there is no penalty and the ball must be replaced. If it still fails to come to rest on that spot:

(i) except in a *hazard*, it must be placed at the nearest spot where it can be placed at rest that is not nearer the *hole* and not in a *hazard*;

(ii) in a *hazard*, it must be placed in the *hazard* at the nearest spot where it can be placed at rest that is not nearer the *hole*.

If a ball when placed comes to rest on the spot on which it is placed, and it subsequently *moves*, there is no penalty and the ball must be played as it lies, unless the provisions of any other *Rule* apply.

PENALTY FOR BREACH OF RULE 20-1, -2 or -3:
Match play — Loss of hole; Stroke play — Two strokes.

## 20-4. When Ball Dropped or Placed is in Play

If the player's *ball in play* has been lifted, it is again in play when dropped or placed.

A *substituted ball* becomes the *ball in play* when it has been dropped or placed.

(Ball incorrectly substituted — see Rule 15-2.)

(Lifting ball incorrectly substituted, dropped or placed — see Rule 20-6.)

## 20-5. Making Next Stroke from Where Previous Stroke Made

When a player elects or is required to make his next *stroke* from where a previous *stroke* was made, he must proceed as follows:

(a) On the Teeing Ground: The ball to be played must be played from within the *teeing ground*. It may be played from anywhere within the *teeing ground* and it may be teed.

(b) Through the Green and in a Hazard: The ball to be played must be dropped.

(c) On the Putting Green: The ball to be played must be placed.

PENALTY FOR BREACH OF RULE 20-5:
Match play — Loss of hole; Stroke play — Two strokes.

## 20-6. Lifting Ball Incorrectly Substituted, Dropped or Placed

A ball incorrectly substituted, dropped or placed in a wrong place or otherwise not in accordance with the *Rules* but not played may be lifted, without penalty, and the player must then proceed correctly.

## 20-7. Playing from Wrong Place

### a. General

A player has played from a wrong place if he makes a *stroke* with his *ball in play*:

(i) on a part of the *course* where the *Rules* do not permit a *stroke* to be played or a ball to be dropped or placed; or

(ii) when the *Rules* require a dropped ball to be re-dropped or a *moved* ball to be replaced.

**Note:** For a ball played from outside the *teeing ground* or from a wrong *teeing ground* — see Rule 11-4.

### b. Match Play

If a player makes a *stroke* from a wrong place, he loses the hole.

### c. Stroke Play

If a *competitor* makes a *stroke* from a wrong place, he incurs a penalty of two strokes under the applicable *Rule*. He must play out the hole with the ball played from the wrong place, without correcting his error, provided he has not committed a serious breach (see Note 1). If a *competitor* becomes aware that he has played from a wrong place and believes that he may have committed a serious breach, he must, before making a *stroke* on the next *teeing ground,* play out the hole with a second ball dropped or placed in accordance with the *Rules.* If the hole being played is the last hole of the round, he must declare, before leaving the *putting green,* that he will play out the hole with a second ball dropped or placed in accordance with the *Rules.*

The *competitor* must report the facts to the *Committee* before returning his score card; if he fails to do so, he is disqualified. The *Committee* must determine whether the *competitor* has committed a serious breach of the applicable *Rule*. If he has, the score with the second ball counts and the *competitor* must add two *penalty strokes* to his score with that ball. If the *competitor* has committed a serious breach and has failed to correct it as outlined above, he is disqualified.

**Note 1:** A *competitor* is deemed to have committed a serious breach of the applicable *Rule* if the *Committee* considers he has gained a significant advantage as a result of playing from a wrong place.

**Note 2:** If a *competitor* plays a second ball under Rule 20-7c and it is ruled not to count, *strokes* made with that ball and *penalty strokes* incurred solely by playing that ball are disregarded. If the second ball is ruled to count, the *stroke* made from the wrong place and any *strokes* subsequently taken with the original ball including *penalty strokes* incurred solely by playing that ball are disregarded.

### *20/1 Club to Be Used in Measuring*

**Q.** A player, taking relief under a Rule, uses his driver to measure the one club-length or two club-lengths prescribed in the relevant Rule. He drops a ball correctly and the ball rolls less than two driver-lengths, but more than two putter-lengths, from where the ball first struck a part of the course when dropped.

Under Rule 20-2c, a dropped ball must be re-dropped if it rolls more than two club-lengths. If the ball comes to rest in a poor lie, may the player opt to use his putter to measure the distance his ball has rolled, in which case he would re-drop under Rule 20-2c and escape the poor lie?

**A.** No. The player must continue to use the club he originally used for measuring for all measuring in a given situation.

**Measuring Club-Lengths — See 20-2b/2.**

## 20/2 Borrowing Club for Measuring Purposes

For the purpose of measuring, a player may use any club he has selected for that round (Rule 4-4). If a player borrows a club to measure with, drops the ball in that area and plays it, he incurs no penalty if the spot on which the ball was dropped could have been reached with one of the player's own clubs selected for the round. If he could not have reached that spot by measuring with one of his own clubs, he incurs the penalty under the applicable Rule for playing from a wrong place (see Rule 20-7).

**Borrowing Partner's Putter — See 4-4b/1.**

## 20-1/0.5 Whether Player Himself Must Lift Ball

**Q.** Rule 20-1 states: "A ball to be lifted under the Rules may be lifted by the player, his partner or another person authorized by the player." On the other hand, other Rules, e.g., Rules 24-2b (i) and 25-1b (i), state that the player shall lift the ball. Does Rule 20-1 override other Rules which imply that the player himself must lift the ball?

**A.** Yes.

## 20-1/1 Ball Lifted from Putting Green in Mistaken Belief It Is Wrong Ball

**Q.** A player, mistakenly believing the ball he has played onto a putting green is a wrong ball, picks the ball up without marking its position. He then discovers that the ball is his ball in play. What is the ruling?

**A.** The player incurs a penalty stroke and he must replace his ball (Rule 20-1).

## 20-1/2 Player's Ball Lifted by Opponent Without Authority

**Q.** In a match between A and B, B, without A's authority, marked the position of, and lifted, A's ball on the putting green. Is B subject to penalty?

**A.** Yes. Under Rule 20-1, a player's ball may be lifted by his opponent only with the authority of the player. Since B was not entitled to lift A's ball, B incurred a penalty stroke — Rule 18-3b.

**Player's Ball Lifted Without Authority by Opponent in Four-Ball Match — See 30-3f/10.**

**Other Decisions relating to Rule 20-1:**

**Player Lifts Ball in Mistaken Belief That Next Stroke Conceded — See 2-4/3.**

**Player Concedes Match Due to Misconception as to Opponent's Score at Last Hole and Picks Up Ball — See 2-4/14.**

Player Lifts Ball, Sets It Aside and Plays It from Where Set Aside — See 15/4.

Ball Resting Against Flagstick Lifted Before Being Holed — See 17-4/1.

Ball Putted from Wrong Place Lifted and Putted from Right Place — See 20-7c/2.

Caddie Lifts Ball in Water Hazard Without Player's Authority — See 26-1/9.

Player's Ball Resting Against Flagstick Lifted Before Being Holed; Others in Four-Ball Match Pick Up Mistakenly Believing Player Won Hole — See 30-3f/3.

### 20-1/3 Ball Marked and Lifted by Opponent Without Player's Authority; Player Lifts Ball-Marker, Claims Hole and Opponent Disputes Claim

**Q.** In a match, B marks the position of A's ball and lifts it without A's authority. B holes out. A picks up the ball-marker with which B had marked the position of his (A's) ball and claims the hole. B disputes the claim. What is the ruling?

**A.** B incurs a penalty stroke — Rule 18-3b — for lifting A's ball without authority. A incurs a penalty stroke for lifting the ball-marker (Rule 20-1). A must replace his ball and hole out; otherwise, A loses the hole.

### 20-1/4 Competitor's Ball Lifted Without Authority by Fellow-Competitor

**Q.** In stroke play, a fellow-competitor lifts a competitor's ball on the putting green without the authority of the competitor. Such action is contrary to Rule 20-1. What is the ruling?

**A.** There is no penalty and the ball must be replaced — Rule 18-4.

Competitor Who Lifts His Ball and Fellow-Competitor's Ball Inadvertently Exchanges Balls When Replacing Them — See 15-2/4.

Fellow-Competitor Lifts Competitor's Ball and Sets It Aside; Competitor Plays Ball from Where Set Aside — See 15-3b/3.

### 20-1/5 Competitor's Ball Lifted Without Authority by Fellow-Competitor's Caddie Who Subsequently Substitutes Another Ball Which Competitor Plays

**Q.** A competitor's ball lying on the putting green is lifted by a fellow-competitor's caddie without the authority of the competitor. Subsequently, the fellow-competitor's caddie by mistake substitutes another ball and the competitor plays it. The error is then discovered. What is the ruling?

**A.** When a competitor authorizes another person to lift his ball, the competitor is responsible for any breach of the Rules (Rule 20-1). The converse is generally true, i.e., the competitor is not responsible for a breach of a Rule caused by the unauthorized lifting of his ball. Thus, in this case, the competitor should not be penalized under Rule 15-2. The competitor should hole out with the substituted ball, without penalty.

Player Mistakenly Substitutes Another Ball on Putting Green; Error Discovered Before Stroke Played — See 15-2/2.

## 20-1/5.5 Ball-Marker Moved Accidentally by Player

**Q.** A player marked the position of his ball on the putting green and lifted the ball. When it was the player's turn to play, he could not find his ball-marker. Subsequently, he found the ball-marker stuck to the sole of his shoe. He concluded that he had accidentally stepped on it while assisting his partner in lining up a putt. What is the ruling?

**A.** The player incurs a penalty stroke under Rule 20-1 which requires that the position of a ball be marked before it is lifted, and contemplates that the ball-marker will remain in position until the ball is replaced. The player must place the ball as near as possible to its original position but not nearer the hole — Rule 20-3c.

Under the last paragraph of Rule 20-1, a player is exempt from penalty if his ball-marker is accidentally moved in the process of lifting the ball or marking its position. In this case the ball-marker was not moved during such process.

## 20-1/6 Ball-Marker Moved Accidentally by Player in Process of Marking Position of Ball

**Q.** A player marked the position of his ball with a coin, lifted the ball and pressed down the coin with the sole of his putter. He walked to the edge of the green and then noticed that the coin had stuck to the sole of the putter. What is the ruling?

**A.** In this case, the movement of the ball-marker was directly attributable to the specific act of marking the position of the ball. Accordingly, no penalty is incurred and the ball or the ball-marker must be replaced. If the spot where the ball or ball-marker lay is not known, it must be placed as near as possible to where it lay but not nearer the hole (Rule 20-3c).

## 20-1/7 Ball-Marker Moved by Opponent's Caddie Accidentally

**Q.** A player's caddie accidentally kicked his opponent's ball-marker closer to the hole. What is the ruling?

**A.** In equity (Rule 1-4), the ball-marker should have been replaced as near as possible to the spot where it lay and the player should incur a penalty of one stroke.

**Whether Lifting Opponent's Ball-Marker Is Concession of Next Stroke — See 2-4/5.**

## 20-1/8 Ball-Marker Lifted by Player Who Mistakenly Believes He Has Won Hole

**Q.** A player, mistakenly believing he has won a hole, picks up his ball-marker. What is the ruling?

**A.** The player incurs a one-stroke penalty — Rule 20-1 — and must replace his ball.

**Wrong Information Causes Opponent to Lift His Ball-Marker — See 9-2/5.**

**Player Who Walks Off Green Under Mistaken Impression Partner Halved Hole Returns and Putts for Half — See 30/4.**

### 20-1/9 Ball-Marker Lifted by Outside Agency

**Q.** A marked the position of his ball on the putting green while a following match or group was playing through. After the following match or group had played through, A could not find his ball-marker. It apparently had been lifted by one of the players playing through. What is the ruling?

**A.** Under Rule 20-3c, A must place his ball as near as possible to where it lay on the green.

### 20-1/10 Ball-Marker Moved Off Green by Wind or Casual Water While Play Suspended

**Q.** While play is suspended due to a rainstorm, a player's ball-marker, which was made of a lightweight material, is moved off a putting green by wind or casual water. What is the procedure?

**A.** Under Rule 6-8d(iii), the player must place a ball or ball-marker on the spot from which it was moved. If the spot is not determinable, it must be estimated and the ball placed on the estimated spot — see Note to Rule 6-8d(iii) and Exception to Rule 20-3c.

The fact that the player used a lightweight ball-marker does not affect the result.

**Ball Moved by Wind or Casual Water While Play Suspended — See 18-1/11.**

**Ball Moved Accidentally by Player During Suspension of Play — See 18-2a/25.**

### 20-1/10.5 Ball-Marker Moved by Wind or Casual Water During Stipulated Round

**Q.** During a stipulated round, a player marked the position of and lifted his ball under a Rule. Prior to the player replacing his ball, wind or casual water moved his ball-marker. What is the procedure?

**A.** The ball or ball-marker must be replaced without penalty. If a ball has been lifted under a Rule which requires it to be replaced, it must be placed on the spot from which it was lifted (Rule 20-3a).

### 20-1/11 Ball-Marker in Position to Assist Another Player

**Q.** A player marks the position of his ball on the putting green and the ball-marker is so located that it might be of assistance to the opponent or a fellow-competitor in lining up his putt. Accordingly, the player prepares to move his ball-marker one or two clubhead-lengths to the side, but the opponent or fellow-competitor says he wants the ball-marker left where it is. What is the ruling?

**A.** The player is entitled to move his ball-marker to the side. The opponent or fellow-competitor may not insist on its being left where it is in view of the purposes of Rules 8-2b and 22-1.

### 20-1/12 Ball-Marker Moved Accidentally By Player After Having Moved Loose Impediments

**Q.** A player marked the position of his ball on the putting green with a coin and lifted the ball. He then placed his finger on the coin, while he brushed aside some loose impediments so that he did not move the coin. On lifting his finger the coin initially stuck to his finger before falling to the ground and coming to rest in a different position. What is the ruling?

**A.** The act of placing the finger on the coin is considered to be an extension of the marking process (see Decision 20-1/6). Therefore, as the movement of the coin was directly attributable to the specific act of marking the position of the ball, the player incurs no penalty and the ball or ball-marker must be replaced (Rule 20-1).

### 20-1/13 Ball Accidentally Kicked by Player Asked to Lift It Due to Interference

**Q.** A requests B to lift his (B's) ball because it interferes with A's play. As B is walking up to his ball to lift it, he accidentally kicks it. What is the ruling?

**A.** B incurs a penalty stroke under Rule 18-2a because the movement of the ball was not directly attributable to the specific act of marking the position of or lifting the ball. B must replace his ball.

**Player Kicks Ball While Probing for It in Water in Water Hazard — See 12-1/5.**

### 20-1/14 Ball Moved by Putter Dropped by Player Approaching Ball to Lift It

**Q.** A player, approaching his ball on the putting green to lift it, dropped his putter on his ball and moved it. Is it correct that there is no penalty in view of Rule 20-1 under which a player incurs no penalty if he accidentally moves his ball in the process of lifting it?

**A.** No. The player incurred a penalty stroke under Rule 18-2a because the movement of the ball was not directly attributable to the specific act of marking the position of or lifting the ball.

### 20-1/15 Meaning of "Directly Attributable" in Rules 20-1 and 20-3a

**Q.** What is meant by the phrase "directly attributable to the specific act" in Rules 20-1 and 20-3a?

**A.** In Rule 20-1 the phrase means the specific act of placing a ball-marker behind the ball, placing a club to the side of the ball, or lifting the ball such that the player's hand, the placement of the ball-marker or the club, or the lifting of the ball causes the ball or the ball-marker to move.

In Rule 20-3a the phrase means the specific act of placing or replacing a ball in front of a ball-marker, placing a club to the side of the ball-marker, or lifting the ball-marker such that the player's hand, the placement of the ball or the club, or the lifting of the ball-marker causes the ball or the ball-marker to move.

Under either Rule, any accidental movement of the ball or the ball-marker which occurs before or after this specific act, such as dropping the ball or ball-marker, regardless of the height from which it was dropped, is not considered to be "directly attributable" and would result in the player incurring a penalty stroke.

**Ball Moved in Removing Ball-Marker After Replacing Ball — See 20-3a/1.**

**Position of Ball Marked Before Obstruction Removed; Ball Moves When Ball-Marker Removed — See 24-1/5.**

### 20-1/15.5 Lie Altered by Act of Marking Position of Ball

**Q.** A player marks the position of his ball, and as a result of the act of marking, there is a change in the lie of the ball. Is the player required to restore the lie he had before marking the position of the ball?

**A.** No. The act of placing a marker may result in some change in the lie of the ball, for example, from grass being depressed by the weight of the marker, or grains of sand being moved in the placement or removal of a marker. Such occurrences may improve or worsen the lie of the ball, and the player must accept the result.

If the player attempted to restore the lie under these circumstances, or if the lie was improved from actions which exceeded what was necessary to the process of marking, he would be subject to penalty under Rule 13-2.

**Position of Ball Worsened When Obstruction Removed; Player Replaces Obstruction — See 13-2/15.5.**

### 20-1/16 Method Used to Mark Position of Ball

**Q.** The Note to Rule 20-1 provides that "the position of a ball to be lifted should be marked by placing a ball-marker, a small coin or other similar object immediately behind the ball." Is a player penalized if he uses an object which is not similar to a ball-marker or small coin to mark the position of his ball?

**A.** No. The provision in the Note to Rule 20-1 is a recommendation of best practice, but there is no penalty for failing to act in accordance with the Note.

Examples of methods of marking the position of a ball which are not recommended, but are permissible, are as follows:

- placing the toe of a club at the side of, or behind, the ball;
- using a tee;
- using a loose impediment;
- scratching a line, provided the putting green is not tested (Rule 16-1d) and a line for putting is not indicated (Rule 8-2b). As this practice may cause damage to the putting green, it is discouraged.

However, under Rule 20-1 it is necessary to physically mark the position of the ball. Reference to an existing mark on the ground does not constitute marking the position of a ball. For example, it is not permissible to mark the position with reference to a blemish on the putting green.

### 20-1/17 Tee Marking Position of Player's Ball Deflects Opponent's Ball

**Q.** In a match, B used a wooden tee to mark the position of his ball. A's ball was deflected by the tee. What is the ruling?

**A.** The tee was not B's equipment — see Definition of "Equipment." There is no penalty. A must play his ball as it lies.

A should have requested B to move the tee one or more clubhead-lengths to the side or to mark the position of his ball with a ball-marker, a small coin or other similar object — see Note under Rule 20-1.

### [20-1/18 Reserved]

### 20-1/19 Placing Object Marking Position of Ball Other Than Behind Ball

**Q.** When marking the position of a ball, must the ball-marker be placed behind the ball, or may it also be placed to the side of or in front of the ball?

**A.** There is no restriction. However, if a player positions his ball-marker in front of the ball on the putting green and in the process does something to the green which might influence the movement of the ball when played, e.g., presses down a raised tuft of grass, he is in breach of Rule 1-2.

Placing a ball-marker in front of the ball is not recommended but it is not a breach of Rule 16-1a because this Rule permits touching the line of putt in lifting a ball, and marking the position of the ball is part of the lifting process.

### 20-1/20  Player Places Ball-Marker Approximately Two Inches Behind Ball

**Q.** A player consistently places his ball-marker approximately two inches behind the ball on the green. He says that he does so to ensure that he does not accidentally move the ball. Does such a procedure comply with the Rules?

**A.** No. A player who places a ball-marker two inches behind his ball cannot be considered to have marked the position of the ball with sufficient accuracy. Accordingly, each time he does so, the player incurs a penalty of one stroke, as provided in Rule 20-1, and must place the ball as near as possible to the spot from which it was lifted — Rule 20-3c.

The player's action was unnecessary because Rule 20-1 states that no penalty is incurred if a ball is accidentally moved in the process of marking or lifting it under a Rule.

### [20-1/21  Reserved]

### 20-1/22  Knocking Ball Aside After Marking Position Instead of Lifting

**Q.** A player, whose ball is on the putting green, marks the position of his ball and knocks the ball aside with his putter instead of lifting it. What is the ruling?

**A.** Knocking the ball aside was the equivalent of lifting it under Rule 20-1. There would be no penalty unless the act was for the purpose of testing the putting surface (Rule 16-1d) or playing a practice stroke (Rule 7-2).

### 20-2a/1  Penalty When Ball Dropped in Other Than Prescribed Manner

**Q.** If a ball is dropped in a manner other than that prescribed in Rule 20-2a and the error is not corrected, it is stated in that Rule that the penalty is one stroke. However, the general penalty for a breach of Rule 20-2 is loss of hole in match play or two strokes in stroke play. Which penalty applies?

**A.** The one-stroke penalty specifically prescribed in Rule 20-2a applies.

### 20-2a/2  Spinning Ball When Dropping

**Q.** A player puts spin on a ball purposely when dropping it. What is the ruling?

**A.** The player incurs a penalty of one stroke under Rule 20-2a for dropping the ball in an improper manner, unless he corrects his mistake as permitted by Rule 20-6.

**Dropped Ball Accidentally Deflected by Opponent or His Caddie — See 19-3/2.**

### 20-2a/3  Ball Dropped in Improper Manner and in Wrong Place

**Q.** A player obtaining relief from ground under repair dropped a ball in a manner not conforming with Rule 20-2a and in a wrong place. What is the ruling?

**A.** If the player corrected the errors before playing his next stroke, there was no penalty — Rule 20-6.

If the player failed to correct the errors before playing his next stroke:

(a) In match play, he lost the hole for playing from a wrong place — Rule 20-7b.

(b) In stroke play, he incurred a penalty of three strokes — one stroke for dropping in an improper manner (Rule 20-2a) and two strokes for a breach of Rule 25-1b (see Rule 20-7c).

### 20-2a/4  Ball Dropped in Improper Manner Moves When Addressed; Player Then Lifts Ball and Drops It in Proper Manner

**Q.** A player drops his ball other than in the manner prescribed in Rule 20-2a. He addresses the ball and the ball moves. He then is advised that he dropped his ball improperly. So, as permitted by Rule 20-6, he lifts the ball, drops it properly and plays. According to Rule 20-6, the player incurs no penalty for the improper drop. Does he incur a penalty stroke under Rule 18-2b because the ball moved after it was addressed, even though the ball was subsequently lifted and re-dropped?

**A.** Yes. The ball was in play when it was first dropped, even though it was dropped in an improper manner (Rule 20-4). When it moved after being addressed, the penalty prescribed in Rule 18-2b was applicable.

#### Other Decisions relating to Rule 20-2a:

Pitch-Mark in Dropping Area Repaired Before Ball Dropped — See 13-2/10.

Removing Sand or Loose Soil from Dropping Area — See 13-2/11.

Removal of Loose Impediments from Area in Which Ball to Be Dropped — See 23-1/6.

Who Drops Ball in Foursome Competition — See 29/4.

### 20-2a/5  Caddie Holds Back Tree Branch to Prevent Branch from Deflecting Dropped Ball

**Q.** May a player have his caddie hold back a tree branch that is waist high and situated at the spot at which the player wishes to drop his ball under a Rule?

If the branch is not held back, the dropped ball might lodge in the branch or, in any case, the branch will be likely to deflect the dropped ball.

**A.** No. Such an act would be exerting influence on the position or movement of the ball, contrary to Rule 1-2.

**Dropped Ball Strikes Tree Branch Then Ground; Whether Re-Drop Required — See 20-2c/1.3.**

### 20-2a/6 Ball Dropped Under One Option of Unplayable Ball Rule Strikes Player; Player Wishes to Change Relief Option

**Q.** A player deems his ball unplayable and elects to proceed under Rule 28c, by dropping a ball within two club-lengths of the spot where it lay. The dropped ball strikes the player's foot, so he is required by Rule 20-2a to re-drop. May the player change his relief option and, for example, proceed under Rule 28b?

**A.** No. A player may not change his relief option when re-dropping a ball under Rule 20-2a.

**Changing Relief Option When Re-Dropping Required — See 20-2c/5.**

**Changing Relief Option After Ball Dropped in a Wrong Place — See 20-6/2.**

**Player Who Lifts Ball Under First Option of Rule 24-2b(ii) Then Wishes to Proceed Under Second Option — See 24-2b/5.**

**Player Who Invokes First Option of Rule 25-1b(ii) Then Wishes to Invoke Second Option — See 25-1b/9.**

**Player Deems Ball Unplayable a Second Time and Wishes to Proceed Under Stroke and Distance After Dropping a Ball Under Other Unplayable Option — See 28/6.5.**

### 20-2a/7 Whether Glove Used as Indicating Mark Is Equipment

**Q.** A player entitled to drop a ball marks with his glove the spot on which the ball is to be dropped or the outer limit of the area within which the ball is to be dropped. The dropped ball then strikes the glove.

If the glove is a "small object," it is not equipment of the player, and the ball would not be re-dropped. Otherwise, the glove is equipment and the ball must be re-dropped under Rule 20-2a.

What is the status of the glove?

**A.** A glove is not a "small object" within the meaning of that term in the Definition of "Equipment." Therefore, it is equipment and the ball must be re-dropped.

### 20-2b/1 Dropped Ball Never Strikes Ground

**Q.** A player drops a ball where the applicable Rule requires. It lodges in a bush without striking the ground. What is the ruling?

**A.** The ball is in play. It struck a part of the course where required by the applicable Rule and did not roll into a position requiring it to be re-dropped under Rule 20-2c.

### 20-2b/2 Measuring Club-Lengths

When measuring a distance of one club-length (Rules 24 or 25) or two club-lengths (Rules 26-1c or 28c), a player is entitled to measure directly across a ditch or through a fence, a tree or a wall made of earth or artificial materials.

**Club to Be Used in Measuring Club-Length — See 20/1.**

### 20-2c/0.5 Ball Dropped from Ground Under Repair Area Rolls to Position Where Area Interferes with Stance; Whether Re-Drop Required

**Q.** A player's ball lies in ground under repair through the green. The player elects to take relief and drops the ball in accordance with Rule 25-1b(i). The ball remains outside the ground under repair area but it rolls to a position where the player would have to stand in the area to play his stroke. Must the player re-drop the ball?

**A.** Yes. The ball has rolled and come to rest "in a position where there is interference by the condition from which relief was taken" — see Rule 20-2c(v). The same applies if a player is taking relief from an immovable obstruction.

**Competitor Drops One Ball in Accordance with Two Different Rules Instead of Playing Second Ball; Dropped Ball Rolls Back into the Condition from Which Relief Taken — See 3-3/12.**

### 20-2c/0.7 Ball Dropped from Immovable Obstruction Rolls Nearer Obstruction Than Nearest Point of Relief; Whether Re-Drop Required If Player Changes Clubs and Obstruction No Longer Interferes

**Q.** A player's ball lies behind a tree and he would play a low shot with a 4-iron, under the tree's branches, except that a protective fence interferes with the area of his intended swing. He determines the nearest point of relief using his 4-iron and measures a one club-length area within which to drop the ball. After he drops the ball in accordance with the Rules, the ball rolls and comes to rest nearer the fence than the nearest point of relief. Therefore, there is still interference by the fence for the intended stroke with the 4-iron. However, the ball is now in a position where it would be reasonable for the player to play his next shot over the tree with a pitching-wedge, and the fence would not interfere with this stroke. May the player play the dropped ball or must it be re-dropped?

**A.** The ball must be re-dropped because it came to rest at a point where the player still had interference from the fence for a stroke with the club used to determine the nearest point of relief — see Rule 20-2c(v).

**Club Used to Determine "Nearest Point" Not Used for Next Stroke — See 24-2b/4.**

### 20-2c/0.8 Player Takes Relief from an Area of Ground Under Repair; Whether Re-Drop Required If Condition Interferes for Stroke with Club Not Used to Determine "Nearest Point of Relief"

**Q.** A player finds his ball in heavy rough approximately 230 yards from the green. He selects a wedge to play his next shot and finds that his stance touches a line defining an area of ground under repair. He determines the nearest point of relief and drops the ball within one club-length of this point. The ball rolls into a good lie from where he believes he can play a 3-wood for his next stroke. If the player used a wedge for his next stroke he would not have interference from the ground under repair, but adopting a normal stance with the 3-wood, he again touches the ground under repair with his foot. Must the player re-drop his ball under Rule 20-2c?

**A.** No. The player proceeded in accordance with Rule 25-1b by determining his nearest point of relief using the club with which he expected to play his next stroke and he would only be required to re-drop the ball under Rule 20-2c if interference still existed for a stroke with this club — see analogous Decision 20-2c/0.7.

As it was expedient for the player to play his next stroke with another club, which resulted in interference from the condition, he would have the option of playing the ball as it lies or proceeding again under Rule 25-1b.

**Determining "Nearest Point of Relief" — See 24-2b/1.**

**Club Used to Determine Nearest Point of Relief Not Used for Next Stroke — See 24-2b/4.**

### 20-2c/1 Dropped Ball Rolling Out of Prescribed Dropping Area

**Q.** A player taking relief under the Rules sometimes appears to obtain more relief than he is entitled to because the relevant Rule allows him some latitude within which to drop and the dropped ball then rolls some distance from the place where it was dropped. When a Rule prescribes an area within which a ball must be dropped, e.g., within one or two club-lengths of a particular point, should it be re-dropped if it rolls outside the area so prescribed?

**A.** No, not necessarily. Provided the ball has been correctly dropped (Rule 20-2a) and does not roll into any of the positions listed in Rule 20-2c, it is in play and must not be re-dropped. In particular, under Rule 20-2c(vi), the ball may roll up to two club-lengths from the point where it first struck a part of the course when dropped, and this may result in its coming to rest an appreciable distance farther from the condition from which relief is being taken. For example:

> (a) a ball dropped within two club-lengths of the margin of a lateral water hazard may come to rest almost four club-lengths from the hazard margin without the player being required to re-drop it under Rule 20-2c; and

(b) a ball dropped away from an immovable obstruction within one club-length of the nearest point of relief may come to rest almost three club-lengths from the nearest point of relief without the player being required to re-drop it under Rule 20-2c.

## 20-2c/1.3 Dropped Ball Strikes Tree Branch Then Ground; Whether Re-Drop Required

**Q.** A player drops a ball within the area prescribed by the applicable Rule. It bounces off a tree branch and as a result strikes the ground outside that area. What is the ruling?

**A.** The ball struck a part of the course (the branch) where the applicable Rule requires (Rule 20-2b). Therefore, provided it does not roll into any of the positions listed in Rule 20-2c, it is in play and must not be re-dropped. In measuring the two club-lengths to determine if a re-drop is required under Rule 20-2c(vi), the point on the ground immediately below the spot where the ball first struck a part of the course (the branch) shall be used for measuring purposes.

## 20-2c/1.5 Ball Rolls Toward Hole When Dropped at Spot from Which Previous Stroke Played

**Q.** A player is required or elects to play his next stroke at the spot from which his previous stroke was played. He is able to identify that specific spot by reference to the divot hole which his previous stroke made. He drops a ball immediately behind that divot hole. The ball rolls nearer the hole than the spot from which the previous stroke was played, but not more than two club-lengths from where it first struck the ground. What is the ruling?

**A.** Rule 20-2c(vii)(a) requires a ball to be re-dropped if it rolls and comes to rest nearer the hole than "its original position or estimated position ... unless otherwise permitted by the Rules." The original position is the spot from which the previous stroke was played. Since the dropped ball rolled nearer the hole than that spot, it must be re-dropped.

However, in many such cases the player cannot determine exactly the spot from which his previous stroke was played. In those cases, the player has satisfied the requirements of the Rule if he uses his best endeavors to estimate the spot. The estimated spot is treated as the specific spot (see Rule 20-2b) and the ball must be re-dropped if it rolls nearer the hole than the estimated spot.

The same principle applies if the spot where a ball is to be placed is not determinable and the player is required, under Rule 20-3c, to drop the ball as near as possible to the spot where it lay.

### 20-2c/1.7 Whether Re-Drop Required If Ball Dropped Under Rule 24-2b Rolls Nearer Hole Than Nearest Point of Relief But Not Nearer Than Where It Originally Lay

**Q.** A player's ball comes to rest on a cart path such that his nearest point of relief is behind the obstruction. He properly determines this point and lifts and drops the ball in accordance with Rule 24-2b. The ball rolls and comes to rest nearer the hole than the nearest point of relief, but not nearer the hole than where it lay originally on the path. Must the ball be re-dropped?

**A.** Yes — see Rule 20-2c(vii)(b).

### 20-2c/2 Ball Dropped Third Time When Placement Required After Second Drop

**Q.** A player dropped his ball twice under a Rule and each time the ball rolled nearer the hole. He then dropped the ball a third time instead of placing it as required by Rule 20-2c. What is the ruling?

**A.** Before playing a stroke, the player may lift the ball and place it as prescribed in Rule 20-2c, without penalty (Rule 20-6). If he fails to do so and plays the ball, he incurs a penalty of loss of hole in match play or two strokes in stroke play for a breach of Rule 20-2c.

### 20-2c/3 Placing Ball Instead of Dropping When Obvious Dropped Ball Will Roll into Hazard, Etc.

**Q.** A player is required to drop a ball. However, it is obvious that the ball when dropped will roll into a hazard, more than two club-lengths, etc., in which case it must be re-dropped and then placed under Rule 20-2c. In such a case, is it permissible to waive the dropping requirement and allow the player initially to place the ball?

**A.** No. Dropping and then re-dropping are necessary to resolve any doubt as to whether the ball will roll into a hazard, etc., and to establish the spot at which the ball must be placed, if necessary.

### 20-2c/3.5 Dropped Ball Comes to Rest and Then Rolls Out of Bounds

**Q.** A player's ball comes to rest against a boundary stake. He deems the ball unplayable and drops it within two club-lengths of where the ball originally lay, as prescribed by Rule 28c. After the ball has been at rest, it rolls and comes to rest out of bounds. What is the ruling?

**A.** If a dropped ball comes to rest, but subsequently moves, the ball shall be played as it lies (see Note to Rule 20-2). In this case the ball is out of bounds and the player must proceed under Rule 27-1. Since the ball was at rest before moving, Rule 20-2c is not applicable.

## 20-2c/4 Caddie Stops Dropped Ball Before It Comes to Rest; When Penalty Incurred

**Q.** A player's caddie deliberately stops a ball dropped by the player. What is the ruling?

**A.** There is no penalty if the caddie stops the ball after it has rolled to a position from which the player would be required to re-drop it under Rule 20-2c, provided it is reasonable to assume that the ball would not return to a position at which Rule 20-2c would be inapplicable.

However, if a player's caddie acts prematurely and stops a dropped ball before it has reached such a position, the player incurs a penalty of loss of hole in match play or two strokes in stroke play under Rule 1-2 (see reference to Rule 1-2 under Rule 20-2a). In stroke play, he must play the ball as it lies where it was stopped. If the ball was lifted after it was stopped, the ball must be replaced.

The same principle would apply if the player's ball was deliberately stopped by the player, his partner, his partner's caddie or someone else authorized by the player (e.g., an opponent or fellow-competitor).

## 20-2c/5 Changing Relief Option When Re-Dropping Required

**Q.** A player deems his ball unplayable. Of the three options available under Rule 28, he elects Rule 28c and drops the ball within two club-lengths of the spot where it lay. The ball rolls and comes to rest nearer the hole than its original position, so the player is required by Rule 20-2c to re-drop. May the player now proceed under a different option, e.g., Rule 28b?

**A.** No. If the player did so, he would be in breach of Rule 20-2c. The same principles would apply when proceeding under Rule 26-1.

**Ball Dropped Under One Option of Unplayable Ball Rule Strikes Player; Player Wishes to Change Relief Option — See 20-2a/6.**

**Changing Relief Option After Ball Dropped in a Wrong Place — See 20-6/2.**

**Player Who Lifts Ball Under First Option of Rule 24-2b(ii) Then Wishes to Proceed Under Second Option — See 24-2b/5.**

**Player Who Invokes First Option of Rule 25-1b(ii) Then Wishes to Invoke Second Option — See 25-1b/9.**

**Player Deems Ball Unplayable a Second Time and Wishes to Proceed Under Stroke and Distance After Dropping a Ball Under Other Unplayable Option — See 28/6.5.**

## [20-2c/6 Reserved]

### 20-2c/7 Player Takes Relief from Area of Casual Water and Ball Comes to Rest in a Position Where Another Area of Casual Water Interferes; Whether Re-Drop Required

**Q.** Through the green, there are two areas of casual water which are close together. There is interference from one area and the player elects to take relief. He drops the ball in accordance with Rule 25-1b(i) and it rolls to a position where interference no longer exists from the first area of casual water, but there is interference from the second area. Does Rule 20-2c(v) require the player to re-drop the ball?

**A.** No, the ball is in play. The player may play the ball as it lies or take relief from the second area in accordance with Rule 25-1b(i).

The same procedure applies to ground under repair or a hole, cast or runway made by a burrowing animal, a reptile or a bird.

**Nearest Point of Relief from Cart Path Is in Casual Water; Nearest Point of Relief from Casual Water Is Back on Cart Path — See 1-4/8.**

**Other Decisions relating to Rule 20-2c:**

**Changing Relief Option After Ball Dropped in a Wrong Place — See 20-6/2.**

**After Relief Taken from Obstruction for Stroke Towards Green, Obstruction Interferes with Stance for Necessary Sideways Stroke — See 24-2b/9.5.**

**Ball Dropped from Casual Water in Bunker at Point of Maximum Relief Rolls Elsewhere — See 25-1b/6.**

**Permissible Dropping Area So Narrow Player Has Difficulty Dropping Within It — See 26-1/19.**

### 20-3a/0.5 Whether Player Himself Must Place or Replace Ball

**Q.** Rule 20-3a states: "A ball to be placed under the Rules must be placed by the player or his partner. If a ball is to be replaced, the player, his partner or the person who lifted or moved it must place it on the spot from which it was lifted or moved." On the other hand, other Rules, e.g., Rule 12-2, state that the player must place or replace the ball. Does Rule 20-3a override other Rules which imply that the player himself must place or replace the ball?

**A.** Yes.

### 20-3a/1 Ball Moved in Removing Ball-Marker After Replacing Ball

**Q.** A player replaces his ball under a Rule and, in the act of removing the object marking its position, accidentally moves the ball. What is the ruling?

**A.** Removal of the ball-marker is part of the replacement process. Accordingly, under Rule 20-3a, no penalty is incurred, and the ball must be replaced.

**Meaning of "Directly Attributable" in Rules 20-1 and 20-3a — See 20-1/15.**

### 20-3a/2  Trademark Aimed Along Line of Putt When Ball Replaced

**Q.** When a player is replacing his ball, is it permissible for him to position the ball so that the trademark is aimed along the line of putt to indicate the line of play?

**A.** Yes.

#### Other Decisions relating to Rule 20-3a:

Player Returns Ball to Spot from Which Lifted by Rolling It with Putter — See 16-1d/3.

Ball-Marker Moved by Wind or Casual Water During Stipulated Round — See 20-1/10.5.

Ball Replaced at Wrong Place on Putting Green and Holed — See 20-7c/1.

Player Lifts Ball Under Rule Not Permitting Cleaning and Rotates It when Replaced — See 21/5.

Removal of Loose Impediments from Spot on Which Ball to Be Placed — See 23-1/6.5.

Placing Ball on Bank of Water Hazard Instead of Dropping to Prevent Ball Rolling into Water — See 26-1/10.

Penalty for Repeatedly Replacing Ball Nearer Hole on Green — See 33-7/6.

### 20-3b/1  Lie of Lifted Ball in Bunker Altered by Another Player's Stroke

**Q.** The balls of A and B are in the same heel mark in a bunker. B's ball is farther from the hole. A lifts his ball under Rule 22-2, and B plays and obliterates the heel mark. What should A do?

**A.** Under Rule 20-3b, A is required to re-create his original lie as nearly as possible, including the heel mark, and place his ball in that lie.

### 20-3b/2  Lie in Bunker Changed by Another Player Taking His Stance

**Q.** In playing from a bunker, B, in taking his stance, pushed up a mound of sand behind A's ball, which had not been lifted. What is the ruling?

**A.** Since A's ball did not move when B took his stance, Rule 20-3b does not apply. In equity (Rule 1-4), A's original lie may be restored as nearly as possible by removing the mound of sand.

### 20-3b/3  Lie Changed by Removal of Gallery-Control Stake

**Q.** A ball comes to rest adjacent to a gallery-control stake. A marshal, without the sanction of the player, removes the stake and in so doing raises the turf in front of the ball. Is the player entitled to proceed under Rule 20-3b?

**A.** No. Since the ball did not move when the gallery-control stake was removed, Rule 20-3b does not apply.

However, if the original lie could be easily restored, in equity (Rule 1-4), the raised turf may be pressed down so that the original lie is restored as nearly as possible.

If the original lie could not be easily restored, in equity (Rule 1-4), the player may place his ball, without penalty, in the nearest lie most similar to that which it originally occupied, but not more than one club-length from the original lie, not nearer the hole and not in a hazard.

**Lie or Line of Play Affected by Pitch-Mark Made by Partner's, Opponent's or Fellow-Competitor's Ball — See 13-2/8.**

**Player's Lie Affected by Sand from Partner's, Opponent's or Fellow-Competitor's Stroke from Bunker — See 13-2/8.5.**

## [20-3b/4 Reserved]

## 20-3b/5 Lie of Ball to Be Replaced Altered and Spot Where Ball Originally Lay Not Determinable

**Q.** An outside agency accidentally steps on A's ball in tall grass through the green and presses the ball into the ground. The original lie of A's ball has been altered, and it is impossible to determine the spot where A's ball originally lay. Should A proceed under Rule 20-3b or Rule 20-3c?

**A.** If either the original lie or the spot where the ball lay is not known, Rule 20-3c overrides Rule 20-3b. The player must drop the ball as near as possible to where it lay but not in a hazard and not on a putting green.

If both the original lie and the spot where the ball lay are known, Rule 20-3b overrides Rule 20-3c. The ball must be placed in the nearest lie most similar to the original lie that is not more than one club-length from the original lie, not nearer the hole and not in a hazard. (Revised)

**Lie of Ball Embedded in Hazard Altered When Ball Lifted to Determine Whether Unfit for Play — See 5-3/5.**

**Lie Altered in Bunker Prior to Resumption of Play — See 6-8d/2.**

**Lie Altered When Player Presses Oscillating Ball into Surface of Putting Green — See 18-2a/6.**

**Ball Moved Accidentally and Original Lie Altered; Player Places Ball in Wrong Place and Plays — See 18-2a/21.3.**

### Decisions relating to Rule 20-3c:

**Lie Altered in Bunker Prior to Resumption of Play — See 6-8d/2.**

**Ball Lodged in Tree Knocked Down from Unknown Place by Outside Agency — See 18-1/9.**

**Ball Moved Accidentally; Spot Where Ball Originally Lay Not Determinable; Player Places Ball Instead of Dropping It — See 18-2a/21.5.**

**Ball Dislodged from Tree by Player; Spot Where Ball Lay Not Determinable — See 18-2a/29.**

**Ball-Marker Moved Accidentally by Player — See 20-1/5.5.**

**Ball-Marker Moved Accidentally by Player in Process of Marking Position of Ball — See 20-1/6.**

**Ball-Marker Lifted by Outside Agency — See 20-1/9.**

**Ball-Marker Moved Off Green by Wind or Casual Water — See 20-1/10.**

**Lie of Ball to Be Replaced Altered and Spot Where Ball Originally Lay Not Determinable —
See 20-3b/5.**

## 20-3d/1  Placed Ball Rolls into Hole

**Q.** A replaces his ball on the putting green three feet from the hole. As he is about to address the ball, it rolls into the hole. Should the ball be replaced or is A deemed to have holed out with his previous stroke?

**A.** The answer depends on whether the ball, when replaced, came to rest on the spot on which it was placed before it started rolling. If it did, A is deemed to have holed out with his previous stroke. If not, A is required to replace the ball (Rule 20-3d). However, if the ball had been overhanging the hole when it was lifted, the provisions of Rule 16-2 would override those of Rule 20-3d.

**Ball Overhanging Hole Is Lifted, Cleaned and Replaced; Ball Then Falls into Hole —
See 16-2/0.5.**

**Ball Dislodged from Tree by Player; Ball Fails to Remain on Correct Spot When Replaced —
See 18-2a/29.**

## 20-3d/2  Ball in Bunker Moves Closer to Hole When Obstruction Removed and Ball Will Not Remain at Rest When Replaced; All Other Parts of Bunker Are Nearer Hole

**Q.** A ball came to rest against a movable obstruction, a rake, in a bunker. When the rake was moved the ball rolled nearer the hole. According to Rule 24-1, the ball had to be replaced. Due to the slope and the fact that the sand was firm, the ball, when replaced, rolled closer to the hole.

Under Rule 20-3d, if a ball will not come to rest on the spot where it originally lay, it must be placed at the nearest spot not nearer the hole where it can be placed at rest. The spot where the ball originally lay was farther from the hole than any other part of the bunker. Thus, there was nowhere to place the ball at rest in the bunker which was not nearer the hole. What is the proper procedure if:

1. The only way the ball would remain at rest at the spot where it lay would be to press it lightly into the sand?

2. The sand is so hard that it is impossible to replace the ball?

**A.** There is nothing in the Rules permitting a player to press his ball lightly into the sand or ground to make it remain at rest. Accordingly, in either case, since the player could not place the ball in conformity with the Rules, he should proceed under the stroke-and-distance option of the unplayable ball Rule (Rule 28a) or, in equity (Rule 1-4), drop the ball, under penalty of one stroke, outside the bunker, keeping the point where the ball lay directly between the hole and the spot on which the ball is dropped.

The same principle would apply if a player is proceeding under any Rule and the ball will not come to rest in the bunker at a spot not nearer to the hole than the appropriate reference point.

**Whether Rakes Should Be Placed in or Outside Bunkers — See Misc./2.**

### 20-3d/3 Ball in Rough Moves Downward When Addressed; Ball Will Not Remain at Rest When Replaced

**Q.** A player's ball is sitting up in the rough about three inches above the ground. He addresses the ball. It moves downward about two inches and comes to rest at Point X. The player attempts to replace the ball as required by Rule 18-2b, but the ball falls downward to Point X. Under Rule 20-3d, he again attempts to replace the ball, with the same result. The player must now place the ball at the nearest spot not nearer the hole where it can be placed at rest — Rule 20-3d.

If the nearest spot where the ball will remain at rest is Point X, must the player place the ball there, even though that point is vertically below the original lie?

**A.** Yes.

### 20-4/1 Ball Replaced on Putting Green But Ball-Marker Not Removed; Ball Then Moves

**Q.** A player replaces his ball on the putting green but does not remove his ball-marker. Subsequently the wind moves his ball to a new position. What is the ruling?

**A.** Under Rule 20-4, a ball is in play when it is replaced, whether or not the object used to mark its position has been removed. Consequently the ball must be played from the new position — see Decision 18-1/12.

### 20-4/2 Ball Lifted by Player from Putting Green and Placed by Caddie Behind Ball-Marker

**Q.** A player marks the position of his ball on the putting green by placing a coin immediately behind the ball. He lifts the ball and gives it to his caddie to have it cleaned. The caddie then intentionally places the ball immediately behind the coin, i.e., not in the ball's original position, to allow the player to assess the line of putt from behind the hole. Is the ball in play when the caddie places the ball?

**A.** No. In these circumstances, the caddie's act in placing the ball on the putting green does not put the ball in play. The ball is not considered to be in play until the player repositions it with the intention of replacing the ball as required by Rule 16-1b. If the player played a stroke with his ball while it was out of play, he would be playing a wrong ball (Rule 15).

**Player Lifts Ball, Sets It Aside and Plays It from Where Set Aside — See 15/4.**

## Other Decisions relating to Rule 20-4:

**Original Ball Found Within Five-Minute Search Period After Another Ball Dropped — See 27-1/2.**

**Ball Dropped Under Unplayable Ball Rule Comes to Rest in Original Position or Another Position at Which Ball Is Unplayable — See 28/3.**

### 20-5/1 Teed Ball Missed Then Hit Out of Bounds

**Q.** A player plays a stroke from a teeing ground and misses the ball. He plays a second stroke and hits the ball out of bounds. In proceeding under Rule 27-1, may he tee a ball anywhere within the teeing ground or must he drop a ball where the original ball was teed?

**A.** The player may tee a ball anywhere within the teeing ground.

### 20-5/2 Player Proceeding Under Rule 20-5 Drops Ball on Different Part of Course

**Q.** A player whose ball lies in, and close to the edge of, a bunker hits the ball out of bounds. When proceeding under Rule 27-1, the player drops a ball within a few inches of, and not nearer the hole than, the spot where the original ball was last played, but the ball first strikes a part of the course through the green. What is the ruling?

**A.** The player must lift the ball under Rule 20-6 and drop it again so that, when dropped, it first strikes the bunker. If he fails to do so and plays the dropped ball, he has played from a wrong place (Rules 20-7 and 27-1).

Normally, the requirement of Rule 20-5 is satisfied if the ball strikes the ground within a few inches of the specific spot. However, through the green or in a hazard, when a player is required to play a ball "as nearly as possible at the spot from which the original ball was last played," he must drop the ball so that it first strikes the part of the course from which his original ball was last played. (New)

### 20-6/1 Ball Placed When Required to Be Dropped or Dropped When Required to Be Placed; Correction of Error

**Q.** A player placed a ball when he should have dropped it or dropped it when he should have placed it. Before playing a stroke, may the player lift the ball, without penalty, under Rule 20-6 and proceed correctly?

**A.** Yes. Otherwise the player would lose the hole in match play or incur a penalty of two strokes in stroke play for a breach of the applicable Rule.

**Ball Dropped Third Time When Placement Required After Second Drop; Correction of Error — See 20-2c/2.**

### 20-6/2 Changing Relief Option After Ball Dropped in a Wrong Place

**Q.** A player deems his ball unplayable and elects to take relief under Rule 28c. He drops the ball in a wrong place and is advised of this fact.

He then lifts his ball under Rule 20-6 and states that he wishes to proceed under Rule 28b. Is the player entitled to proceed under Rule 28b?

**A.** Yes. Decisions 20-2a/6 and 20-2c/5 suggest a different conclusion. However, in those cases Rules 20-2a and 20-2c are invoked and those Rules imply that a ball to be re-dropped must be re-dropped under the option originally invoked.

**Player Who Lifts Ball Under First Option of Rule 24-2b(ii) Then Wishes to Proceed Under Second Option — See 24-2b/5.**

**Player Who Invokes First Option of Rule 25-1b(ii) Then Wishes to Invoke Second Option — See 25-1b/9.**

**Player Unaware Ball in Water Hazard Takes Relief from Interference by Burrowing Animal Hole — See 25-1b/26.**

**Player Deems Ball Unplayable a Second Time and Wishes to Proceed Under Stroke and Distance After Dropping a Ball Under Other Unplayable Option — See 28/6.5.**

### 20-6/3 Ball Mistakenly Substituted When Dropped; Correction of Error

**Q.** A player's ball lies on a paved cart path. In taking relief from the obstruction, he mistakenly drops a ball other than the original ball. He discovers his error before playing his next stroke. How should he proceed?

**A.** The player is not entitled to substitute a ball when proceeding under Rule 24-2b, unless the ball is not immediately recoverable. Therefore, the player must lift the substituted ball, without penalty, and drop the original ball in accordance with the Rules.

### 20-6/4 Substituting Ball When Re-Dropping

**Q.** In taking relief from a water hazard, a player drops a ball in a wrong place but realizes his error before playing it. When he corrects the error under Rule 20-6, may he drop a different ball than the one originally dropped?

**A.** Yes. When correcting the error under Rule 20-6, the player is proceeding under the original Rule, in this case Rule 26-1. As the player is proceeding under a Rule that allows substitution (Rule 26-1), he may substitute balls. If he had been proceeding under a Rule that did not allow substitution (e.g., Rule 24-2b), he would have been required to drop the original ball, unless that ball is not immediately recoverable.

A player re-dropping a ball under Rule 20-2c may not substitute balls unless the ball that was originally dropped is not immediately recoverable. (New)

**Ball Dropped Under Water Hazard Rule with Reasonable Evidence; Original Ball Then Found — See 26-1/3.5**

### 20-6/5 Player Drops Ball Under Rules and Then Wishes to Replace Ball in Original Position

**Q.** A player's ball lies under a tree. The player deems the ball unplayable and drops a ball three club-lengths from where the ball originally lay. Before playing, he is informed that he dropped the ball in a wrong place. The player lifts the dropped ball under Rule 20-6 and realizes that, if he drops the ball within two club-lengths of the spot where the ball originally lay, it is likely to be unplayable. May the player replace the ball in its original position, incurring a penalty stroke under Rule 18-2a?

**A.** No. Once the player has put a ball into play under an applicable Rule, he must continue to proceed under that Rule until he has correctly put a ball into play. In this case, the player may change options under Rule 28 when correcting the error of dropping a ball in a wrong place (see Decision 20-6/2), but he may not proceed under another Rule or replace the ball in its original position.

After lifting a ball, a player is entitled to replace it in its original position only if he has not yet put it back into play under an applicable Rule. However, in that case, the player may incur a penalty of one stroke under Rule 18-2a for having lifted his ball without authority (see Decision 18-2a/12). (New)

### 20-7/1 Ball Played from Spot Where Original Ball Deflected Out of Bounds by Maintenance Vehicle

**Q.** A player's tee shot travels about 175 yards and, while still in motion, is deflected out of bounds by a golf course maintenance vehicle. The player, claiming the vehicle should not have been there, dropped a ball near the spot where the vehicle deflected the original ball, completed play of the hole and stated that he had incurred no penalty. Was the player correct?

**A.** No. A maintenance vehicle is an outside agency. The original ball would have been played as it lay, without penalty, if it had been in bounds — Rule 19-1. Since the ball was out of bounds, the player was obliged to proceed under Rule 27-1.

The player, in dropping a ball near where the original ball was deflected and playing it, played from a wrong place.

In match play, he incurred a penalty of loss of hole — Rule 20-7b.

In stroke play, he incurred the stroke-and-distance penalty prescribed by Rule 27-1 and an additional penalty of two strokes for a breach of that Rule. Since the breach was a serious one, he was subject to disqualification unless he corrected the error as prescribed in the second paragraph of Rule 20-7c.

**Ball Moved Accidentally and Original Lie Altered; Player Places Ball in Wrong Place and Plays — See 18-2a/21.3.**

**Casual Water Mistaken for Water Hazard; Original Ball Played Under Water Hazard Rule —
See 25-1b/12.**

**Player Plays Second Shot, Deems Ball Unplayable and Returns to Tee — See 28/6.**

**Player Plays from a Wrong Place on Basis of Incorrect Ruling — See 34-3/3.**

### 20-7/2 Ball Declared Unplayable in Water Hazard Is Dropped in Hazard and Played

**Q.** A player deems his ball unplayable in a water hazard and drops the ball in the water hazard, thinking that Rule 28b or c is applicable, and plays it. He then realizes that it is not permissible to deem a ball unplayable in a water hazard. What is the ruling?

**A.** The player played the ball from a wrong place, i.e., a place not permitted by Rule 26-1, the water hazard relief Rule.

In match play, the player loses the hole (Rule 20-7b).

In stroke play, if a serious breach of the water hazard Rule was not involved, the player, in addition to incurring the penalty stroke provided for in Rule 26-1, incurs a two-stroke penalty for playing from a wrong place and must play out the hole with the ball played out of the water hazard — see first paragraph of Rule 20-7c and Rule 26-1.

If a serious breach of the water hazard Rule was involved, the player must, before playing from the next teeing ground, play a ball in accordance with Rule 26-1 and add two penalty strokes to the score with that ball; otherwise the player is disqualified —see second and third paragraphs of Rule 20-7c.

### 20-7/2.5 Ball Deemed Unplayable in Water Hazard; Another Ball Is Dropped in Hazard But Player Realizes Error Before Playing

**Q.** A player deems his ball unplayable in a water hazard, does not lift the ball and drops another ball in the water hazard, thinking that Rule 28b or c is applicable. He realizes his error before playing the dropped ball. What is the ruling?

**A.** When the player dropped a ball under Rule 28, he proceeded under an inapplicable Rule. Under Rule 20-6 he must abandon the dropped ball and, without penalty, play the original ball or, under penalty of one stroke, proceed under the water hazard Rule (Rule 26-1) with respect to the original ball. (New)

**Player Proceeds Under an Inapplicable Rule; Committee's Decision — See 34-3/6**

## 20-7/3 Whether Player May Drop Ball into Area from Which Play Prohibited

**Q.** In proceeding under a Rule, a player wishes to drop a ball on a part of the course from which play is prohibited (e.g., a wrong putting green or an area of ground under repair from which play is prohibited). Is this permissible?

**A.** Yes. There is nothing in the Rules to prohibit a player from dropping a ball on a part of the course from which play is prohibited. However, the player must then take relief as prescribed by the applicable Rule. He would be penalized if he played the ball from such an area.

**Water Hazard Treated as Lateral Water Hazard — See 26-1/11.**

**Example of Serious Breach of Lateral Water Hazard Rule — See 26-1/21.**

**Ball Dropped in Area Where Original Ball Lost; Ball Then Played — See 27-1/3.**

**Significant Advantage Gained When Player Plays Stroke from Environmentally-Sensitive Area Defined as Water Hazard — See 33-8/44.**

## 20-7c/1 Ball Replaced at Wrong Place on Putting Green and Holed

**Q.** In stroke play, a competitor in replacing his ball on the putting green inadvertently put the ball in a wrong place nearby and holed out. The error was then discovered and the competitor put his ball in the right place and holed out. What is the ruling?

**A.** The score with the ball played from the wrong place counts and the competitor must add two penalty strokes to that score (Rule 16-1b or 20-3a and Rule 20-7c).

The competitor incurs no penalty for having putted from the right place after holing out from a wrong place.

## 20-7c/2 Ball Putted from Wrong Place Lifted and Putted from Right Place

**Q.** In stroke play, A mistakenly replaced his ball in front of B's ball-marker (which was near A's ball-marker) and putted. The ball came to rest about one foot from the hole. The error was then discovered and A lifted his ball without marking its position, placed it in front of his own ball-marker and finished the hole. What is the ruling?

**A.** When A replaced his ball in front of B's ball-marker and putted, he played from a wrong place and incurred a penalty of two strokes; the ball was in play — Rule 20-7c.

When A then lifted his ball from where it lay about one foot from the hole without marking its position and did not replace it, he incurred the general penalty (two strokes) for a breach of Rule 20-1 — see second paragraph of Rule 20-1.

Thus, A incurred a total penalty of four strokes.

### 20-7c/3 Ball Believed to Be Lost in Bunker; Competitor Drops Another Ball in Bunker and Plays It; Original Ball Then Found Outside Bunker

**Q.** In stroke play, A played a long shot to the green and the ball appeared to have come to rest in a bunker beside the green. The ball was not found in the bunker. A dropped a ball in the bunker and played it onto the green. A then discovered his original ball behind the green. What is the ruling?

**A.** When A dropped and played another ball in the bunker, it became the ball in play under penalty of stroke and distance and the original ball was lost — see Definition of "Lost Ball."

Since the place where the ball was dropped was well in advance of the spot from which the original ball was last played, A was guilty of a serious breach of the relevant Rule (Rule 27-1) in failing to go back to that spot. He should have been disqualified unless he rectified the breach as prescribed in Rule 20-7c, in which case he would incur an additional penalty of two strokes.

**Ball Knocked Out of Bunker by Fellow-Competitor's Stroke at Own Ball Not Replaced — See 18-4/2.**

**Ball Dropped Outside Bunker Under Option of Unplayable Ball Rule Requiring Drop in Bunker — See 28/10.**

### 20-7c/4 Competitor's Ball Played by Fellow-Competitor; Competitor Substitutes Another Ball at Wrong Place, Plays It and Then Abandons It and Plays Out Original Ball from Right Place

**Q.** In stroke play, A, B and C hit their tee shots into the same area. After B and C have played their second shots, A discovers that the remaining ball is not his and assumes that his ball has been played by B. The final paragraph of Rule 15-3b requires A to place a ball on the spot from which his ball was played. A places another ball on the spot from which B played his second shot and plays it to the green. There it is discovered that it was C, not B, who wrongly played A's ball and that A has therefore played the substituted ball from a wrong place. A accepts a two-stroke penalty under the applicable Rule (Rules 15-3b and 20-7c), but he then abandons the substituted ball, thinking he must correct his error. A picks up his original ball, goes back to the spot where C played his second shot, plays it from there onto the putting green and takes two putts to hole out. A then drives from the next tee. What is the ruling, and what did A score on the hole?

**A.** A's procedure was correct up to the point he abandoned the substituted ball. The substituted ball, albeit played from a wrong place, was now A's ball in play, and his original ball was out of play. Instead of abandoning the substituted ball, A should have played out the hole with it (Rule 13-1) in accordance with Rule 20-7c, adding to his score the two-stroke penalty he had correctly accepted under Rule 15-3b.

When A went back and played his original ball from the right place (i.e., from where C had wrongly played it), he was substituting a ball for his ball in play in breach of Rule 15-2 as well as playing from the wrong place. Therefore, he incurred an additional penalty of four strokes (Rules 13-1, 15-2 and 20-7c) for a total of six penalty strokes. A's score for the hole was 11. (Revised)

### 20-7c/5 Competitor Plays Second Ball Under Rule 20-7c; Clarification of "Penalty Strokes Incurred Solely by Playing the Ball Ruled Not to Count"

Note 2 under Rule 20-7c permits a player who has played a second ball to disregard penalty strokes incurred solely in playing a ball ruled not to count, such as accidentally causing the ball to move (Rule 18-2a) or proceeding under the water hazard Rule (Rule 26-1). However, a player cannot disregard a breach of the Rules which might apply to either ball, such as a breach of the practice Rule (Rule 7-2), the advice Rule (Rule 8-1) or playing a wrong ball (Rule 15-3).

**Wrong Ball Played in Belief It Is Provisional or Second Ball — See 15/7.**

### Other Decisions relating to Rule 20-7c:

**Guidelines for Which Ball Counts When Player Proceeds Under Rule 3-3 — See 3-3/0.5.**

**Ball Dropped in Wrong Place and Played; Rule 3-3 Then Invoked and Second Ball Dropped in Right Place; Both Balls Played Out — See 3-3/3.**

**Ball Dropped in Wrong Place But Not Played; Rule 3-3 Then Invoked and Second Ball Dropped in Right Place; Both Balls Played Out — See 3-3/4.**

**Whether Score with Second Ball Counts If Ball Dropped in Wrong Place and Played — See 3-3/5.**

**Ball Played from Ground Under Repair Abandoned and Relief Taken Under Ground Under Repair Rule — See 18-2a/8.5.**

**Competitor's Ball Moved by Fellow-Competitor's Ball Not Replaced — See 18-5/3.**

**Ball Dropped in Improper Manner and in Wrong Place — See 20-2a/3.**

**Point Where Ball Last Crossed Margin of Lateral Water Hazard Determined and Ball Dropped and Played; Point Then Proves to Be Wrong Point — See 26-1/17.**

**Provisional Ball Lifted Subsequently Becomes Ball in Play; Competitor Then Plays from Wrong Place — See 27-2b/10.**

# Rule 21. Cleaning Ball

**Definitions**
All defined terms are in *italics* and are listed alphabetically in the Definitions section — see pages 3-11.

A ball on the *putting green* may be cleaned when lifted under Rule 16-1b. Elsewhere, a ball may be cleaned when lifted except when it has been lifted:

    a. To determine if it is unfit for play (Rule 5-3);

    b. For identification (Rule 12-2), in which case it may be cleaned only to the extent necessary for identification; or

    c. Because it is assisting or interfering with play (Rule 22).

If a player cleans his ball during play of a hole except as provided in this Rule, he incurs a penalty of one stroke and the ball, if lifted, must be replaced.

If a player who is required to replace a ball fails to do so, he incurs the penalty for breach of Rule 20-3a, but there is no additional penalty under Rule 21.

**Exception:** If a player incurs a penalty for failing to act in accordance with Rule 5-3, 12-2 or 22, there is no additional penalty under Rule 21.

### 21/1 Removing Lime from Ball

**Q.** Lime has been used to mark lines on the ground for gallery-control purposes. A ball lands on such a line and some lime adheres to the ball. May the player remove the lime?

**A.** No, unless the ball is in a position from which it may be lifted under the Rules and cleaned under Rule 21.

### 21/2 Removing Grass Adhering to Ball

**Q.** Through the green, is it permissible to remove cut grass adhering to a ball?

**A.** No. Such action is prohibited by Rule 21. Anything adhering to a ball is not a loose impediment — see Definition of "Loose Impediments."

**Removal of Insect on Ball — See 23-1/5.**

### 21/3 Whether Ball Cleaned Through Act of Caddie Throwing It to Player

**Q.** A player is asked to lift his ball, which is lying through the green or in a hazard, because the ball interferes with the play of another player. The player authorizes the caddie to lift the ball and, having marked its position and lifted the ball, the caddie throws the ball to the player who catches it. Except when the ball lies on the putting green, it is not permissible to clean a ball lifted because of interference. Does the act of throwing and catching the ball constitute cleaning it?

**A.** Whether the ball is cleaned is a question of fact. The action described could result in a ball being cleaned. Any doubt should be resolved against the player. (Revised)

### 21/4 Position of Ball Lifted for Identification Not Marked, Intention to Lift Not Announced and Ball Cleaned Beyond Extent Necessary to Identify It

**Q.** A player lifted his ball for identification purposes without announcing his intention to his opponent, marker or a fellow-competitor. Thus, he was in breach of Rule 12-2. He also failed to mark the position of the ball before he lifted it in breach of Rule 20-1 and cleaned the ball more than was necessary for it to be identified, a breach of Rule 21. The penalty for breach of each of these Rules is one stroke. Does the player incur a penalty of three strokes?

**A.** No. The player incurs a penalty of one stroke for failing to act in accordance with Rule 12-2. An additional penalty under Rule 20-1 or Rule 21 is not justified — see Rule 12-2 and Exception under Rule 21.

### 21/5 Player Lifts Ball Under Rule Not Permitting Cleaning and Rotates It When Replaced

**Q.** A piece of mud adheres to a player's ball. The player lifts the ball under a Rule which does not permit cleaning. When he replaces the ball, may he place it facing another direction so that the mud would not interfere between the clubface and the ball?

**A.** Yes, provided the ball is replaced on the spot from which it was lifted. However, if the player rotated the ball in such a way so as to "tee" it on the mud, he would be in breach of Rule 20-3a.

#### Other Decisions relating to Rule 21:

Ball in Ground Under Repair Thought to Be Unfit for Play Lifted and Cleaned — See 5-3/6.

Ball Lifted Without Authority and Cleaned — See 18-2a/13.

# Rule 22.
# Ball Assisting or Interfering With Play

**Definitions**
All defined terms are in *italics* and are listed alphabetically in the Definitions section — see pages 3-11.

**22-1. Ball Assisting Play**
Except when a ball is in motion, if a player considers that a ball might assist any other player, he may:

(a) lift the ball if it is his ball, or

(b) have any other ball lifted.

A ball lifted under this Rule must be replaced (see Rule 20-3). The ball must not be cleaned unless it lies on the *putting green* (see Rule 21).

In stroke play, a player required to lift his ball may play first rather than lift the ball.

In stroke play, if the *Committee* determines that competitors have agreed not to lift a ball that might assist any other player, they are disqualified.

**22-2. Ball Interfering with Play**
Except when a ball is in motion, if a player considers that the ball of another player might interfere with his play, he may have it lifted.

A ball lifted under this Rule must be replaced (see Rule 20-3). The ball must not be cleaned unless it lies on the *putting green* (see Rule 21).

In stroke play, a player required to lift his ball may play first rather than lift the ball.

**Note:** Except on the *putting green*, a player may not lift his ball solely because he considers that it might interfere with the play of another player. If a player lifts his ball without being asked to do so, he incurs a penalty of one stroke for a breach of Rule 18-2a, but there is no additional penalty under Rule 22.

PENALTY FOR BREACH OF RULE:
Match play — Loss of hole; Stroke play — Two strokes.

### 22/1 Mental Interference by Another Ball

**Q.** In order for A to be entitled to have B's ball lifted because of interference, does B's ball have to be on or near A's line of play and thus in a position to interfere physically with A's ball? Or may A also have B's ball lifted if it is off his line of play but catches his eye and thus constitutes mental interference?

**A.** A player may, under Rule 22-2, have another ball lifted if the ball interferes either physically or mentally with his play.

## 22/2 Player Claims That Another Ball Lying 30 Yards Away Interferes with His Play

**Q.** B's ball is three feet from the green on a direct line to the hole with A's ball which is 30 yards from the green. May A require B to lift his ball, on the grounds that the ball interferes with his play?

**A.** Yes.

## 22/3 Player Requests Another Player to Lift His Ball in Absence of Reasonable Possibility Ball Might Interfere or Assist

**Q.** A's ball is on the putting green. B's ball is 100 yards from the green. B requests A to lift his ball under Rule 22-2 as it might interfere with his (B's) play. This happens several times during the round. Is such procedure permissible?

**A.** Rule 22 is intended to cover situations where there is a reasonable possibility that one ball might assist or interfere with another ball. If the Rule is being abused, as in this case, the Committee would be justified in penalizing B for undue delay — Rule 6-7.

## [22/4 Reserved]

## 22/5 Assisting Ball Lifted by Opponent Replaced on Request; Player's Ball Then Strikes Opponent's Ball and Opponent Lodges Claim

**Q.** In a match between A and B, A's ball is near the hole in a position to serve as a backstop for B's ball. A lifts his ball to clean it. B requests A to replace his ball before he (B) putts. A protests but B insists that, under the Rules, A must replace his ball immediately. A replaces his ball but disputes B's right to require him to do so and claims the hole. B putts and his ball strikes A's ball and stops very close to the hole. A replaces his ball and holes out for a 4. B then holes out for a 4. The match continues and the claim is later referred to the Committee. How should the Committee rule?

**A.** The hole stands as played. The Rules do not require A to replace his ball, but B was not in breach of the Rules by asking A to replace it — see Rule 22-1.

## 22/6 Competitor Requests That Ball in Position to Assist Him Should Not Be Lifted

**Q.** In stroke play, B's ball lies just off the putting green. A's ball lies near the hole in a position to serve as a backstop for B's ball. B requests A not to lift his ball. Is such a request proper?

**A.** No. If a competitor and a fellow-competitor were to agree to exclude the operation of Rule 22-1, both should be disqualified under Rule 1-3.

**Competitor Not Given Opportunity to Lift Ball Assisting Fellow-Competitor — See 3-4/1.**

**Player Requested to Lift Ball Due to Interference Plays Out of Turn Instead — See 10-1c/2.**

**Ball-Marker in Position to Assist Another Player — See 20-1/11.**

**Request to Lift Ball That Might Assist Partner Not Honored — See 30-3f/11.**

### 22/7 Ball Assisting Fellow-Competitor on Putting Green; Procedure for Committee Member If Competitor Does Not Lift Ball

**Q.** In stroke play, a competitor's ball is in a position to assist the play of a fellow-competitor and the competitor is in a position to lift the ball under Rule 22-1 without delaying the fellow-competitor's play. However, the competitor does not take any action to invoke the Rule. Would a Committee member be justified in intervening and requesting the competitor to invoke the Rule to protect himself and the rest of the field?

**A.** Yes. If the competitor were to object, there would be strong evidence of an agreement to exclude the operation of Rule 22-1 in contravention of Rule 1-3. The Committee member would be justified in so advising the competitors involved and warning that any further such evidence might result in disqualification of both under Rule 1-3.

#### Other Decisions relating to Rule 22:

**Two Balls Lie Together in Hazard and Neither Is Identifiable — See 1-4/6.**

**Ball Lifted from Putting Green; Ball Replaced While Another Ball in Motion but Then Lifted Because Moving Ball Might Strike It — See 16-1b/2.**

**Interfering Ball in Bunker Lifted; Lie Altered by Another Player's Stroke — See 20-3b/1.**

**Abandoned Ball Interferes with Play — See 24-1/2.**

# Rule 23. Loose Impediments

## Definitions
All defined terms are in *italics* and are listed alphabetically in the Definitions section — see pages 3-11.

## 23-1. Relief
Except when both the *loose impediment* and the ball lie in or touch the same *hazard*, any *loose impediment* may be removed without penalty.

If the ball lies anywhere other than on the *putting green* and the removal of a *loose impediment* by the player causes the ball to *move*, Rule 18-2a applies.

On the *putting green*, if the ball or ball-marker *moves* in the process of the player removing any *loose impediment*, the ball or ball-marker must be replaced. There is no penalty provided the movement of the ball or ball-marker is directly attributable to the removal of the *loose impediment*. Otherwise, if the player causes the ball to *move*, he incurs a penalty of one stroke under Rule 18-2a.

When a ball is in motion, a *loose impediment* that might influence the movement of the ball must not be removed.

**Note:** If the ball lies in a *hazard*, the player must not touch or move any *loose impediment* lying in or touching the same *hazard* — see Rule 13-4c.

PENALTY FOR BREACH OF RULE:
Match play — Loss of hole; Stroke play — Two strokes.

(Searching for ball in hazard — see Rule 12-1.)

(Touching line of putt — see Rule 16-1a.)

### 23/1 When Loose Impediment Transformed into Obstruction

Loose impediments may be transformed into obstructions through processes of construction or manufacturing. For example, a log (loose impediment) which has been split and had legs attached has been changed by construction into a bench (obstruction); or a piece of coal (loose impediment) is an obstruction when manufactured into a charcoal briquet.

### 23/2 Meaning of "Solidly Embedded" in Definition of "Loose Impediments"

**Q.** The Definition of "Loose Impediments" states that a stone is a loose impediment if it is not "solidly embedded." When is a stone solidly embedded?

**A.** If a stone is partially embedded and may be picked up with ease, it is a loose impediment. When there is doubt as to whether a stone is solidly embedded or not, it should not be removed.

### 23/3  Half-Eaten Pear

**Q.** A half-eaten pear lies directly in front of a ball in a bunker and there is no pear tree in the vicinity of the bunker. In the circumstances, is the pear an obstruction rather than a loose impediment, in which case the player could remove it without penalty?

**A.** No. A pear is a natural object. When detached from a tree it is a loose impediment. The fact that a pear has been half-eaten and there is no pear tree in the vicinity does not alter the status of the pear.

### 23/4  Fruit Skins

**Q.** Is a banana skin or other fruit skin a loose impediment?

**A.** Yes.

### 23/5  Ant Hill

**Q.** Is an ant hill a loose impediment?

**A.** Yes. A player is entitled to remove an ant hill under Rule 23-1.

### 23/5.5  Status of Insect-Like Creatures

For the purposes of the Rules of Golf, creatures that are similar to insects, such as spiders, are considered to be insects and are, therefore, loose impediments. A web made by a spider is considered to be a cast made by an insect and is also a loose impediment, even if attached to another object. (New)

### 23/6  Dead Land Crab

**Q.** A ball lodges against a dead land crab in a bunker. May the crab be removed without penalty?

**A.** No. A dead land crab is a natural object and thus a loose impediment and not an obstruction. Removal of the crab would be a breach of Rule 13-4.

### 23/6.5  Snake

**Q.** Is a snake an outside agency or a loose impediment?

**A.** A live snake is an outside agency. A dead snake is a loose impediment.

## 23/7 Fallen Tree

**Q.** Is a fallen tree a loose impediment?

**A.** If it is still attached to the stump, no; if it is not attached to the stump, yes.

## 23/8 Worm Partially Underground

**Q.** Is a worm, when half on top of the surface of the ground and half below, a loose impediment which may be removed? Or is it fixed or solidly embedded and therefore not a loose impediment?

**A.** A worm which is half underground is not "fixed or growing" or "solidly embedded" within the meaning of those terms in the Definition of "Loose Impediments." Accordingly, such a worm may be removed under Rule 16-1a(i) or Rule 23.

## 23/9 Embedded Acorn

**Q.** Is an embedded acorn a loose impediment?

**A.** Not if the acorn is solidly embedded — see Definition of "Loose Impediments."

**Club Touches Partially Embedded Pine Needle on Backswing in Bunker — See 13-4/32.**

**Player Repairs Depression on Line of Putt Created When Partially Embedded Acorn Removed — See 16-1a/7.**

## 23/10 Ball Embedded in Fruit

**Q.** A ball is embedded in an orange lying under an orange tree. What is the ruling?

**A.** The player must play the ball as it lies or deem it unplayable. Since the orange was adhering to the ball, it was not a loose impediment.

**Grass Adhering to Ball — See 21/2.**

## 23/11 Loose Soil from Cast of Hole Made by Burrowing Animal

**Q.** A player's ball lies through the green in the cast of a hole made by a burrowing animal. In addition to his relief options under Rule 25-1, may the player remove the loose soil, which forms the cast, from around his ball?

**A.** No — see Definition of "Loose Impediments."

## 23/12 Aeration Plugs

**Q.** Are plugs of compacted soil produced through aeration of fairways loose impediments?

**A.** Yes. Loose soil is not a loose impediment. However, such plugs, since they consist of compacted soil, are loose impediments.

### 23/13 Clod of Earth

**Q.** Is a loose clod of earth a loose impediment?

**A.** Yes. Loose soil is not a loose impediment except on the putting green. However, a clod of earth is not loose soil.

### 23/14 Gravel Used to Surface Road

**Q.** A player hits his ball onto a gravel-covered road. Even though he is entitled to relief from this obstruction, he prefers to play the ball from the road. May he remove gravel that might interfere with his stroke?

**A.** Yes. Gravel is a loose impediment and a player may remove loose impediments under Rule 23-1. This right is not canceled by the fact that, when a road is covered with gravel, it becomes an artificially-surfaced road and thus an obstruction.

**Other Decisions relating to Rule 23:**

Status of Moss or Creepers in Tree — See 13-2/37.

Status of Saliva — See 25/6.

Grass Cuttings — See 25/11.

### 23-1/1 Means by Which Loose Impediments May Be Removed

**Q.** Worm casts are loose impediments. By what means may such casts be removed?

**A.** Loose impediments may be moved by any means, except that, in removing loose impediments on the line of putt, the player must not press anything down (Rule 16-1a).

### 23-1/2 Large Stone Removable Only with Much Effort

**Q.** A player's ball lies in the rough directly behind a loose stone the size of a watermelon. The stone can be removed only with much effort. Is it a loose impediment which may be removed?

**A.** Yes. Stones of any size (not solidly embedded) are loose impediments and may be removed, provided removal does not unduly delay play (Rule 6-7).

### 23-1/3 Assistance in Removing Large Loose Impediment

**Q.** May spectators, caddies, fellow-competitors, etc., assist a player in removing a large loose impediment?

**A.** Yes.

## 23-1/4 Breaking Off Part of Large Loose Impediment

**Q.** If part of a large branch which has fallen from a tree (and thus is a loose impediment) interferes with a player's swing, may the player break off the interfering part rather than move the whole branch?

**A.** Yes.

Bending Grass in Removal of Loose Impediment — See 13-2/13.

Determining Whether Natural Object Interfering with Area of Intended Swing Is Loose Impediment — See 13-2/26.

## 23-1/5 Removal of Insect on Ball

**Q.** A live insect is stationary or crawling on a player's ball which is lying through the green. May the player remove the insect with his fingers or blow the insect off the ball?

**A.** Yes, in both cases, under Rule 23-1. A live insect is not considered to be adhering to the ball and therefore is a loose impediment — see Definition of "Loose Impediments."

## 23-1/5.5 Status of Insect on Ball in Bunker

**Q.** With regard to Decision 23-1/5, what is the ruling if the ball was in a bunker?

**A.** The insect is considered to be in the bunker and because it is, by definition, a loose impediment, the player may not touch or physically remove the insect from the ball (Rule 13-4c). However, as the insect is animate and capable of moving on its own, the player may take action, such as waving his hand or a club or towel, to encourage the insect to move. If the insect moves, there is no penalty provided the player has not touched the insect or the ground in the bunker, or moved another loose impediment in the bunker.

Flying Insect in Water Hazard — See 13-4/16.5.

## 23-1/6 Removal of Loose Impediments from Area in Which Ball to Be Dropped

**Q.** Through the green, is it permissible for a player to remove loose impediments from the area in which he is preparing to drop his ball?

**A.** Yes.

## 23-1/6.5 Removal of Loose Impediments from Spot on Which Ball to Be Placed

**Q.** A player taking relief under a Rule drops his ball and it rolls more than two club-lengths. He re-drops under Rule 20-2c, with the same result. He must now place the ball as near as possible to the spot where it first struck the ground when re-dropped — Rule 20-2c. Before he places the ball, may he remove loose impediments on or around the spot on which the ball is to be placed?

**A.** Yes.

### 23-1/7 Loose Impediment Affecting Lie Moved When Ball Lifted

**Q.** A loose impediment affecting a player's lie through the green is moved when the player lifts his ball under a Rule that requires him to replace the ball. In equity (Rule 1-4), should the player be required to replace the loose impediment?

**A.** Yes. If he fails to do so, in equity (Rule 1-4), the player incurs a penalty of one stroke. (Revised)

### 23-1/8 Loose Impediments Affecting Lie Removed While Ball Lifted

**Q.** A player's ball lies in an area through the green where there are a number of loose impediments, including a tree branch against which the ball has come to rest. It appears likely that the ball will move if the player moves the tree branch. The player wishes to lift the ball under Rule 5-3 (Ball Unfit for Play) or Rule 12-2 (Identifying Ball), or he is requested to lift it under Rule 22 (Ball Assisting or Interfering with Play). He lifts the ball but, before replacing it, he removes the loose impediments in the area, including the tree branch against which the ball was resting. Is this permissible?

**A.** No. Under Rule 18-2a, through the green a player incurs a penalty if he causes his ball to move as a result of moving a loose impediment. It would circumvent this Rule if, before a ball is replaced, it was permissible to remove loose impediments which affected the player's lie before the ball was lifted. In equity (Rule 1-4), the player should be penalized one stroke.

In such circumstances, if a player wishes to remove loose impediments affecting his lie, he should do so either before lifting the ball or after replacing it. If his ball then moves as a result of moving the loose impediments, the player incurs a penalty stroke under Rule 18-2a and must replace the ball.

**Removing Sand or Loose Soil from Dropping Area — See 13-2/11.**

**Ball Declared Unplayable in Bunker; Player Removes Loose Impediment from Bunker While Ball Lifted — See 13-4/35.7.**

### 23-1/9 Removal of Loose Impediment Lying Out of Bounds

**Q.** A loose impediment lying out of bounds interferes with a player's stance. May the player remove the impediment?

**A.** Yes.

Ball in Hazard Moves After Loose Impediment Outside Hazard Moved — See 18-2a/5.

### Other Decisions relating to Rule 23-1:

Player Removes Loose Impediments Affecting Opponent's Lie in Hazard — See 1-2/6.

Removal of Obstruction in Hazard Would Move Loose Impediment — See 1-4/5.

Replacing or Removing Undetached Divot — See 13-2/5.

Ball Outside Bunker; Stone in Bunker on Line of Play Pressed Down or Removed — See 13-2/31.

Accidentally Moving Loose Impediment in Hazard — See 13-4/13.

Player Accidentally Kicks Pine Cone into Bunker and Picks It Up — See 13-4/14.

Ball in Hazard Moves When Loose Impediment Removed — See 13-4/15.

Removal of Loose Impediment in Water Hazard Covering Wrong Ball — See 13-4/16.

Loose Impediment Removed from Water Hazard; Player Then Decides Not to Play from Hazard — See 13-4/17.

Ball Touched Accidentally in Removing Loose Impediment — See 18-2a/31.

Ball Touched with Fir Cone or Stick to Prevent Movement When Loose Impediment Removed — See 18-2a/32.

Pine Needles Piled for Removal Interfere with Line of Play After Ball Dropped Away — See 25-1b/17.

Player Lifts Loose Impediment in Bunker When His Ball and Partner's Ball in Bunker — See 30-3f/1.

Competitor Lifts Loose Impediment in Bunker When His Ball and Partner's Ball in Bunker — See 31-8/1.

## 23-1/10  *Removal of Loose Impediments Affecting Player's Play*

**Q.** A player with a downhill putt picks up loose impediments between his ball and the hole but leaves some behind the hole. The opponent or fellow-competitor wants to remove the impediments behind the hole as they may serve as a backstop, but the player objects. May the opponent or fellow-competitor remove the loose impediments behind the hole?

**A.** No. When it is the player's turn to play, his opponent or a fellow-competitor has no right to remove loose impediments affecting the player's play if the player requests the opponent or fellow-competitor not to do so. If the opponent or fellow-competitor ignores the request, he is in breach of Rule 1-2.

In the absence of a request not to remove loose impediments affecting the player's play, an opponent or fellow-competitor who does so incurs no penalty.

In either instance, if the player replaces the loose impediments he is in breach of Rule 1-2.

**Removal of Dew or Frost from Line of Putt — See 16-1a/3.**

**Loose Impediments Removed from Line of Putt with Cap or Towel — See 16-1a/8.**

**Brushing Loose Impediments Off Line of Putt with Palm of Hand — See 16-1a/9.**

**Loose Impediments Brushed Along Line of Putt Rather Than to Side — See 16-1a/10.**

**Determining Whether Natural Object on Line of Putt Is Loose Impediment — See 16-1a/11.**

**Opponent or Fellow-Competitor Removes Obstruction Affecting Player's Play — See 24/16.**

### 23-1/11 Ball Moved Accidentally by Foot During Removal of Loose Impediment on Putting Green

**Q.** A player in the process of removing a loose impediment on the putting green accidentally moved his ball with his foot. What is the ruling?

**A.** The player incurs a penalty stroke under Rule 18-2a, and the ball must be replaced.

Rule 23-1 provides that the player incurs no penalty if, on the putting green, his ball moves in the process of removing a loose impediment. However, this Rule applies only where the moving of a ball is directly attributable to removal of a loose impediment. In this case, removal of the loose impediment did not cause the ball to move.

### 23-1/12 After Ball Addressed on Putting Green Ball Moved in Removal of Loose Impediment

**Q.** After a player addresses his ball on the putting green, an insect alights on the ball. The player bends over without moving his feet and, in attempting to brush the insect off the ball, moves the ball several inches. Is the player subject to a penalty stroke under Rule 18-2b?

**A.** No. An insect is a loose impediment — See Definition of "Loose Impediments" and Decision 23-1/5.

Under Rule 23-1, a player incurs no penalty if a ball on the putting green moves while he is in the process of removing a loose impediment. Rule 23-1 overrides Rule 18-2b in this case.

**Other Decisions relating to Rule 23-1:**

**Ball Marker Moved Accidentally by Player After Having Moved Loose Impediments — See 20-1/12.**

**Competitor Seeks Help in Removal of Loose Impediment to Avoid Penalty — See 33-7/7.**

# Rule 24. Obstructions

## Definitions
All defined terms are in *italics* and are listed alphabetically in the Definitions section — see pages 3-11.

## 24-1. Movable Obstruction
A player may take relief without penalty from a movable *obstruction* as follows:

   a. If the ball does not lie in or on the *obstruction*, the *obstruction* may be removed. If the ball *moves*, it must be replaced, and there is no penalty provided that the movement of the ball is directly attributable to the removal of the *obstruction*. Otherwise, Rule 18-2a applies.

   b. If the ball lies in or on the *obstruction*, the ball may be lifted and the *obstruction* removed. The ball must *through the green* or in a *hazard* be dropped, or on the *putting green* be placed, as near as possible to the spot directly under the place where the ball lay in or on the *obstruction*, but not nearer the *hole*.

The ball may be cleaned when lifted under this Rule.

When a ball is in motion, an *obstruction* that might influence the movement of the ball, other than an attended *flagstick* or *equipment* of the players, must not be removed.

(Exerting influence on ball — see Rule 1-2.)

**Note:** If a ball to be dropped or placed under this Rule is not immediately recoverable, another ball may be *substituted*.

## 24-2. Immovable Obstruction
   ### a. Interference
   Interference by an immovable *obstruction* occurs when a ball lies in or on the *obstruction*, or when the *obstruction* interferes with the player's *stance* or the area of his intended swing. If the player's ball lies on the *putting green*, interference also occurs if an immovable *obstruction* on the *putting green* intervenes on his line of putt. Otherwise, intervention on the *line of play* is not, of itself, interference under this Rule.

   ### b. Relief
   Except when the ball is in a *water hazard* or a *lateral water hazard*, a player may take relief from interference by an immovable *obstruction* as follows:

   (i) Through the Green: If the ball lies *through the green*, the player must lift the ball and drop it without penalty within one club-length of and not nearer the *hole* than the *nearest point of relief*. The *nearest point of relief* must not be in a *hazard* or on a *putting green*. When the ball is dropped within one club-length of the *nearest point of relief*, the ball must first strike a part of the *course* at a spot that avoids interference by the immovable *obstruction* and is not in a *hazard* and not on a *putting green*.

(ii) In a Bunker: If the ball is in a *bunker*, the player must lift the ball and drop it either:

  (a) Without penalty, in accordance with Clause (i) above, except that the *nearest point of relief* must be in the *bunker* and the ball must be dropped in the *bunker*; or

  (b) Under penalty of one stroke, outside the *bunker* keeping the point where the ball lay directly between the *hole* and the spot on which the ball is dropped, with no limit to how far behind the *bunker* the ball may be dropped.

(iii) On the Putting Green: If the ball lies on the *putting green*, the player must lift the ball and place it without penalty at the *nearest point of relief* that is not in a *hazard*. The *nearest point of relief* may be off the *putting green*.

(iv) On the Teeing Ground: If the ball lies on the *teeing ground*, the player must lift the ball and drop it without penalty in accordance with Clause (i) above.

The ball may be cleaned when lifted under this Rule.

(Ball rolling to a position where there is interference by the condition from which relief was taken — see Rule 20-2c(v).)

**Exception:** A player may not take relief under this Rule if (a) it is clearly unreasonable for him to make a *stroke* because of interference by anything other than an immovable *obstruction* or (b) interference by an immovable *obstruction* would occur only through use of an unnecessarily abnormal *stance*, swing or direction of play.

**Note 1:** If a ball is in a *water hazard* (including a *lateral water hazard*), the player may not take relief from interference by an immovable *obstruction*. The player must play the ball as it lies or proceed under Rule 26-1.

**Note 2:** If a ball to be dropped or placed under this Rule is not immediately recoverable, another ball may be *substituted*.

**Note 3:** The *Committee* may make a Local Rule stating that the player must determine the *nearest point of relief* without crossing over, through or under the *obstruction*.

### 24-3. Ball Lost in Obstruction

It is a question of fact whether a ball lost after having been struck toward an *obstruction* is *lost* in the *obstruction*. In order to treat the ball as *lost* in the *obstruction*, there must be reasonable evidence to that effect. In the absence of such evidence, the ball must be treated as a *lost ball* and Rule 27 applies.

### a. Ball Lost in Movable Obstruction

If a ball is *lost* in a movable *obstruction*, a player may, without penalty, remove the *obstruction* and must *through the green* or in a *hazard* drop a ball, or on the *putting green* place a ball, as near as possible to the spot directly under the place where the ball last crossed the outermost limits of the movable *obstruction*, but not nearer the *hole*.

### b. Ball Lost in Immovable Obstruction

If a ball is *lost* in an immovable *obstruction*, the spot where the ball last crossed the outermost limits of the *obstruction* must be determined and, for the purpose of applying this Rule, the ball is deemed to lie at this spot and the player may take relief as follows:

(i) Through the Green: If the ball last crossed the outermost limits of the immovable *obstruction* at a spot *through the green*, the player may *substitute* another ball without penalty and take relief as prescribed in Rule 24-2b(i).

(ii) In a Bunker: If the ball last crossed the outermost limits of the immovable *obstruction* at a spot in a *bunker*, the player may *substitute* another ball without penalty and take relief as prescribed in Rule 24-2b(ii).

(iii) In a Water Hazard (including a Lateral Water Hazard): If the ball last crossed the outermost limits of the immovable *obstruction* at a spot in a *water hazard*, the player is not entitled to relief without penalty. The player must proceed under Rule 26-1.

(iv) On the Putting Green: If the ball last crossed the outermost limits of the immovable *obstruction* at a spot on the *putting green*, the player may *substitute* another ball without penalty and take relief as prescribed in Rule 24-2b(iii).

PENALTY FOR BREACH OF RULE:
Match play — Loss of hole; Stroke play — Two strokes.

## 24/1 Stile Attached to Boundary Fence

**Q.** Is a stile attached to a boundary fence an obstruction?

**A.** Yes, unless the Committee declares it to be an integral part of the course under Rule 33-2a(iv).

**Exposed Water Pipe Adjacent and Parallel to Boundary Fence — See 33-2a/1.**

### 24/2 Angled Supports or Guy Wires Supporting Boundary Fence

**Q.** Angled supports or guy wires support a boundary fence or a protective net above such a fence. If the angled supports or guy wires extend onto the course, are they obstructions?

**A.** Any part of such an angled support or guy wire which is in bounds is an obstruction.

### 24/3 Concrete Bases of Boundary Fence Posts

**Q.** Posts of a boundary fence have been set in concrete bases 14 inches in diameter. Are the parts of the bases within the boundary of the course obstructions?

**A.** No. Such a base is part of the fence and thus no part of it is an obstruction — see Definition of "Obstructions." If such bases are at or below ground level, the boundary line is the inside points of the fence posts at ground level. If they are above ground level, the Committee should clarify the location of the boundary line.

### 24/4 Part of Boundary Fence Within Boundary Line

**Q.** Part of a boundary fence is bowed towards the course so that it is inside the boundary line formed by the fence posts. A player's ball comes to rest against this part of the fence. Is the player entitled to relief under Rule 24-2b?

**A.** No. A fence defining out of bounds is not an obstruction even if part of it is inside the boundary line formed by the fence posts — see Definitions of "Obstructions" and "Out of Bounds."

**Improving Position of Ball by Bending Boundary Fence — See 13-2/18.**

**Gate in Boundary Fence — See 27/18.**

**Displaced Boundary Stake — See 33-2a/20.**

### 24/5 Boundary Stakes Having No Significance in Play of Hole Being Played

**Q.** White stakes installed between the 7th and 8th holes define out of bounds during play of the 7th hole, but they have no significance during play of the 8th hole. Are such stakes obstructions during play of the 8th hole?

**A.** No, the Definition of "Out of Bounds" states that such stakes are not obstructions. However, in this case it is recommended that, by Local Rule, the stakes be deemed immovable obstructions during play of the 8th hole.

**Removal of Boundary Stake Interfering with Swing — See 13-2/17.**

## 24/6 Stone Broken Away from Retaining Wall in Water Hazard

**Q.** A player's ball in a water hazard is in a playable lie but it is directly behind a stone which has broken away from a retaining wall in the hazard. The wall is an immovable obstruction from which the player is not entitled to relief without penalty. Is the stone which has broken away a movable obstruction, in which case the player may remove it before playing a stroke?

**A.** Yes.

## 24/7 Stone Serving as Part of Drain in Bunker

**Q.** A large stone has been placed at the entrance to a drain in a bunker to prevent sand from washing into the drain. What is the status of such a stone?

**A.** The stone is an immovable obstruction since it serves as part of the drain which is itself an immovable obstruction. The status of such a stone should be clarified by the Committee.

## 24/8 Parked Car

**Q.** A player's ball lies under a parked car. What is the procedure?

**A.** If the car is readily movable, it should be treated as a movable obstruction and moved — see Rule 24-1.

If the car is not readily movable, it should be treated as an immovable obstruction and the player is entitled to relief as provided in Rule 24-2b.

## 24/9 Artificially-Surfaced Road or Path

**Q.** An artificially-surfaced road or path is an obstruction. What constitutes artificial surfacing?

**A.** A road or path to which any foreign material, e.g., concrete, tar, gravel, wood chips, etc., has been applied is artificially-surfaced and thus an obstruction.

**Gravel Used to Surface Road — See 23/14.**

## 24/10 Paved Area

**Q.** Is a paved area, such as a paved car park or parking lot, an obstruction?

**A.** Yes. A paved area has the same status as an artificially-surfaced road.

## 24/11 Wooden Planks

**Q.** Is wood which has been manufactured into planks an obstruction?

**A.** Yes.

**Ball Lying on Obstruction in Bunker — See 13/5.**

**When Loose Impediment Transformed into Obstruction — See 23/1.**

**Half-Eaten Pear — See 23/3.**

**Tree Basins — See 33-2a/10.5.**

### 24/12  Wooden or Earthen Steps

Wooden steps which have been constructed on a steep bank are obstructions — see Decision 23/1.

Steps which have been cut into a steep bank but which have not been covered with any artificial material such as wooden planks are not obstructions.

### [24/13  Reserved]

### 24/14  Turf Raised by Underground Pipe

**Q.** A water pipe is partly underground and partly above ground. In some areas where the pipe is underground it has raised the turf. Is such turf, which has been raised by an obstruction, considered part of the obstruction?

**A.** No.

**Probing Near Ball for Immovable Obstruction — See 13-2/27.**

### [24/15  Reserved]

### 24/16  Opponent or Fellow-Competitor Removes Obstruction Affecting Player's Play

**Q.** An opponent or a fellow-competitor removes an obstruction which affects the player's play. What is the ruling?

**A.** If the obstruction was movable and the player had asked him not to remove it, the opponent loses the hole, or the fellow-competitor incurs a two-stroke penalty (Rule 1-2); otherwise, there is no penalty.

If the obstruction was immovable, the opponent loses the hole, or the fellow-competitor incurs a two-stroke penalty (Rule 1-2).

### [24-1/1  Reserved]

### 24-1/2  Abandoned Ball

**Q.** A player's ball comes to rest against an abandoned ball. What is the procedure?

**A.** An abandoned ball is a movable obstruction. The player may remove it under Rule 24-1.

Rule 22-2, which deals specifically with one ball interfering with another, does not apply. It applies only if a ball in play interferes with another ball in play.

### 24-1/3 Movable Artificial Object Lying Out of Bounds

**Q.** A movable artificial object lying out of bounds interferes with a player's stance. May the player remove it?

**A.** Yes. Rule 24-1 applies.

### 24-1/4 Holding Ball in Place While Removing Obstruction

**Q.** During removal of a movable obstruction, may a player hold his ball to prevent it from moving?

**A.** No. Such procedure would be a breach of Rule 18-2a. There is no penalty if a ball moves during removal of a movable obstruction provided the movement of the ball is directly attributable to the removal of the obstruction.

### 24-1/5 Position of Ball Marked Before Obstruction Removed; Ball Moves When Ball-Marker Removed

**Q.** A player's ball lies against a movable obstruction. Before removing the obstruction, the player marks the position of his ball so that he will be able to replace the ball precisely if the ball moves when the obstruction is removed. The player removes the obstruction and the ball does not move. However, the ball moves when the ball-marker is removed. What is the ruling?

**A.** The ball-marker is itself a movable obstruction. Accordingly, under Rule 24-1, the player incurs no penalty and he must replace the ball.

#### Other Decisions relating to Rule 24-1:

Flagstick Lying on Putting Green Removed by Player to Prevent Another Player's Ball from Striking It — See 1-2/3.

Removal of Obstruction in Hazard Would Move Loose Impediment — See 1-4/5.

Position of Ball Worsened When Obstruction Removed; Player Replaces Obstruction — See 13-2/15.5.

Attended Flagstick Placed on Ground Subsequently Lifted — See 17-1/6.

Ball in Plastic Bag Moves When Bag Blown to New Position by Wind — See 18-1/7.

Ball in Bunker Moves Closer to Hole When Obstruction Removed and Ball Will Not Remain at Rest When Replaced; All Other Parts of Bunker Are Nearer Hole — See 20-3d/2.

### 24-2a/1 Mental Interference by Obstruction

**Q.** A player's ball lies several inches to the side of a sprinkler head. The sprinkler head does not physically interfere with the player's stance or the area of his intended swing. However, the sprinkler head bothers the player mentally. Is the player entitled to relief under Rule 24-2b?

**A.** No. See Rule 24-2a.

### 24-2b/1 Determining "Nearest Point of Relief"

**Q.** The Note to the Definition of "Nearest Point of Relief" provides that the player should determine this point "by using the club with which he would have made his next stroke if the condition were not there to simulate the address position, direction of play and swing for such stroke." May the player use any club, address position, direction of play or swing in determining the nearest point of relief?

**A.** No. In determining the nearest point of relief accurately it is recommended that the player use the club, address position, direction of play and swing (right or left-handed) that he would have used had the obstruction or condition not been there. For example, the player has interference from an immovable obstruction and, were it not for the obstruction, he would have used a right-handed stroke with a 4-iron to play the ball from its original position towards the green. To determine the nearest point of relief accurately, he should use a right-handed stroke with a 4-iron and the direction of play should be towards the green. See also Decision 20-2c/0.7 and 20-2c/0.8.

### 24-2b/2 Player Does Not Follow Recommended Procedure in Determining Nearest Point of Relief

**Q.** A player's ball lies on an artificially surfaced path, which is an immovable obstruction, through the green. The ball is situated at the left edge of the obstruction and the player is right-handed. The player elects to take relief under Rule 24-2b(i) but does not go through the procedure recommended in the Note to the Definition of "Nearest Point of Relief" for determining the nearest point of relief. Instead, he lifts the ball and drops it within one club-length of the nearest edge of the obstruction, not nearer the hole than the ball's original position, and plays it. What is the ruling?

**A.** Provided the ball is dropped on a spot that satisfies the requirements of Rule 24-2b(i) and the ball did not roll into a position requiring a re-drop under Rule 20-2c, the player incurs no penalty.

Although there is a recommended procedure for determining the nearest point of relief, the Rules do not require a player to determine this point when proceeding under Rule 24-2, 24-3, 25-1 or 25-3. If a player does not determine a nearest point of relief accurately or identifies an incorrect nearest point of relief, a penalty only arises if, as a result, the player drops his ball at a spot which does not satisfy the requirements of the Rule under which he is proceeding and he then plays the ball (e.g., the spot is more than one club-length from the correct nearest point of relief or the ball is dropped nearer to the hole than the nearest point of relief). In such circumstances, the player would be penalized for playing from a wrong place (Rule 20-7).

**Diagrams Illustrating "Nearest Point of Relief" — See 25-1b/2.**

## 24-2b/3  Player Determines Nearest Point of Relief But Physically Unable to Play Intended Stroke

**Q.** In proceeding under Rule 24-2b(i) or Rule 25-1b(i), the Definition of "Nearest Point of Relief" provides that to determine the nearest point of relief accurately, the player should use the club, address position, direction of play and swing (right or left-handed) that he would have used to make his next stroke had the obstruction or condition not been there. What is the procedure if, having determined the stroke he would have used, he is unable physically to make such a stroke from, what would appear to be, the nearest point of relief because either (a) the direction of play is blocked by a tree, or (b) he is unable to take the backswing for the intended stroke due to a bush?

**A.** The point identified is the nearest point of relief. The fact that at this point the player cannot make the intended stroke due to something other than the obstruction or condition from which relief is being taken does not alter this result. The player must drop the ball within one club-length of the nearest point of relief, not nearer the hole. Once the ball is in play, the player must then decide what type of stroke he will make. This stroke may be different from the one he would have made from the ball's original position had the obstruction or condition not been there.

**Player Allowed to Play in Any Direction in Fairly Taking His Stance — See 13-2/1.5.**

## 24-2b/3.5  Player Unable Physically to Determine Nearest Point of Relief

**Q.** In proceeding under Rule 24-2b(i) or Rule 25-1b(i), the Definition of "Nearest Point of Relief" provides that to determine the nearest point of relief accurately, the player should use the club, address position, direction of play and swing (right or left-handed) that he would have used from the original position had the obstruction or condition not been there. What is the procedure if a player is unable physically to determine the nearest point of relief because, for example, that point is within the trunk of a tree or a boundary fence prevents the player from adopting the required address position?

**A.** The nearest point of relief in both cases must be estimated and the player must drop the ball within one club-length of the estimated point, not nearer the hole.

## 24-2b/3.7 Diagram Illustrating Player Unable to Determine Nearest Point of Relief

The following diagram illustrates the point raised in Decision 24-2b/3.5 where a player may be unable to determine the nearest point of relief from an immovable obstruction and will need to estimate this point under Rule 24-2b.

B1 = position of ball on cart path

P1 = nearest point of relief (determined)

▯▯— = notional stance used to determine nearest point of relief at P1 – results in player's stance being out of bounds

B2 = position of ball on cart path

P2 = nearest point of relief (estimated)

▯▯— = notional stance used to determine nearest point of relief at P2 – unable to take this stance because of boundary wall

B3 = position of ball on cart path

P3 = nearest point of relief (estimated)

▯▯— = notional stance used to determine nearest point of relief at P3 – unable to take this stance because of tree trunk

**Diagrams Illustrating "Nearest Point of Relief" — See 25-1b/2.**

## 24-2b/4 Club Used to Determine "Nearest Point of Relief" Not Used for Next Stroke

**Q.** The Note to the Definition of "Nearest Point of Relief" states: "In order to determine the nearest point of relief accurately, the player should use the club with which he would have made his next stroke if the condition were not there to simulate the address, direction of play and swing for such stroke." If the subsequent lie of the ball were such that it was expedient for the player to play his next stroke with some other club, may the player use the other club?

**A.** Yes.

**Dropped Ball Rolls Nearer Obstruction Than Nearest Point; Whether Re-Drop Required If Player Changes Clubs and Obstruction No Longer Interferes — See 20-2c/0.7.**

Player Takes Relief from an Area of Ground Under Repair; Whether Re-Drop Required If Condition Interferes for Stroke with Club Not Used to Determine "Nearest Point of Relief" — See 20-2c/0.8.

### 24-2b/5  Player Who Lifts Ball Under First Option of Rule 24-2b(ii) Then Wishes to Proceed Under Second Option

**Q.** A player elects to take relief from an immovable obstruction in a bunker. He lifts the ball to take relief without penalty under the first option of clause (ii) but realizes that where he will have to drop the ball will result in a very difficult shot. May he now elect to proceed under the second option of clause (ii) incurring the penalty stroke and drop outside the bunker?

**A.** Yes. The player lifted the ball to take relief from the immovable obstruction and is entitled to proceed under either of the options under Rule 24-2b(ii), irrespective of the fact that his original intention was to proceed under the first option. However, the player would be precluded from using the second option under Rule 24-2b(ii) if he had put the ball into play under the first option — see Decision 25-1b/9.

**Ball Dropped Under One Option of the Unplayable Ball Rule Strikes Player; Player Wishes to Change Relief Option — See 20-2a/6.**

**Changing Relief Option When Re-Dropping Required — See 20-2c/5.**

**Changing Relief Option After Ball Dropped in a Wrong Place — See 20-6/2.**

**Player Who Invokes First Option of Rule 25-1b(ii) Then Wishes to Invoke Second Option — See 25-1b/9.**

### 24-2b/6  Relief from Immovable Obstruction Incidentally Results in Relief from Boundary Fence

**Q.** A player's ball is in such a position that a boundary fence and an immovable obstruction near the fence both interfere with the area of the player's intended swing. It is reasonable for him to play the stroke despite the interference from the boundary fence. If the player takes relief from the obstruction under Rule 24-2b, he will incidentally get relief from the fence. Is the player entitled to invoke Rule 24-2b in such circumstances?

**A.** Yes.

### 24-2b/7  Relief from Obstruction Interfering with Swing Incidentally Gives Relief from Intervention on Line of Play

**Q.** A player's ball lies behind an immovable obstruction. The obstruction interferes with the player's swing and also intervenes on his line of play. In obtaining relief from interference with his swing, must the player drop the ball in such a position that intervention on the line of play is maintained?

**A.** No. Since the obstruction interferes with the player's swing, the player is entitled to relief under Rule 24-2b. If, in proceeding under this Rule, the player could drop the ball in a place which would also avoid intervention on his line of play, he is entitled to do so.

### 24-2b/8 Dropping from Rough to Fairway in Obtaining Relief from Obstruction

**Q.** A player whose ball lies in the rough close to the fairway is entitled to relief from an immovable obstruction. In obtaining relief under Rule 24-2b(i), may the player drop the ball on the fairway?

**A.** Yes. There is no distinction in the Rules between fairway and rough; both are covered by the term "through the green."

### 24-2b/9 After Relief from Obstruction Second Obstruction Interferes

**Q.** A player obtaining relief from an immovable obstruction drops his ball in such a position that another immovable obstruction interferes with his swing. What is the procedure?

**A.** The player is entitled to relief from the second obstruction as provided in Rule 24-2b.

**Player Takes Relief from Area of Casual Water and Ball Comes to Rest in a Position Where Another Area of Casual Water Interferes; Whether Re-Drop Required — See 20-2c/7.**

### 24-2b/9.5 After Relief Taken from Obstruction for Stroke Towards Green, Obstruction Interferes with Stance for Necessary Sideways Stroke

**Q.** With regard to the illustration above, Point X is the original position of the ball and Point A is the nearest point of relief from the obstruction (cart path). The player drops his ball within one club-length of Point A (within the shaded area) and it comes to rest on the cart path at Point B. He re-drops as required by Rule 20-2c, again dropping within one club-length of Point A and the ball comes to rest at Point C.

At Point C there is no interference by the cart path for a stroke towards the green. However, the player cannot play towards the green from Point C because of intervention by the tree. His only reasonable stroke is sideways to the fairway, and his stance for such a stroke would be on the cart path. Is the player now required to place the ball as near as possible to the spot where it first struck the ground when re-dropped under the penultimate paragraph of Rule 20-2c?

**A.** No. The player is not entitled to place the ball because at Point C there is no interference by the cart path for a stroke towards the green, the intended direction of play when relief was taken. However, as a result of the tree, the player has a new situation. He is entitled to take relief under Rule 24-2b(i) for the sideways stroke since this is not an unnecessarily abnormal direction of play — see Exception under Rule 24-2b — and his nearest point of relief would be Point D. After the ball is dropped within one club-length of Point D (within the shaded area) and it comes to rest at Point E, the player may play in any direction he wishes.

**Nearest Point of Relief from Cart Path Is in Casual Water; Nearest Point of Relief from Casual Water Is Back on Cart Path — See 1-4/8.**

**Ball Lying on Immovable Obstruction Is Dropped Away; Ball Rolls to Position Where Player Would Have to Stand on Obstruction; Whether Re-Drop Required — See 20-2c/0.5.**

### 24-2b/10  Obstruction in Ground Under Repair Interferes with Player's Swing

**Q.** An immovable obstruction situated within an area defined as ground under repair interferes with the area of the player's intended swing. May the player take relief from the obstruction under Rule 24-2b, drop his ball in the ground under repair and then have the option of playing the ball as it lies or proceeding under Rule 25-1b which provides relief from ground under repair?

**A.** Yes.

**Player Entitled to Relief from Obstruction Lifts Ball; Player Then Replaces Ball and Plays It from Original Position — See 18-2a/12.**

**Player Entitled to Relief Without Penalty from Condition Lifts Ball; Chooses Not to Take Relief and Wishes to Proceed Under the Unplayable Ball Rule — See 18-2a/12.5.**

**Ball in Casual Water Within Ground Under Repair; Whether Player Entitled to Take Relief from Both Conditions in Single Procedure — See 25-1b/11.5.**

### 24-2b/11  Ball Lying on Elevated Obstruction

**Q.** A ball comes to rest on a bridge over a deep hollow. What is the ruling?

**A.** Under Rule 24-2b, the player may drop the ball within one club-length of the point on the ground in the hollow directly beneath where the ball lay on the bridge, i.e., vertical distance is disregarded.

### 24-2b/12 Ball in Drainpipe Under Course; Entrance to Drainpipe Is Out of Bounds

**Q.** A ball enters an underground drainpipe the entrance to which is out of bounds. The ball is found in the drainpipe under an area which is through the green. What is the ruling?

**A.** Under Rule 24-2b(i), the player is entitled to drop the ball, without penalty, within one club-length of the spot on the ground immediately above its resting place in the drainpipe, but not nearer the hole and not in a hazard or on a putting green. A boundary line extends vertically upward and downward — see Definition of "Out of Bounds."

If the player cannot find or identify the ball and there is reasonable evidence that the ball is lost in the drainpipe within the boundaries of the course, the player may invoke Rule 24-3b. As that part of the drainpipe situated off the course is not an obstruction (see Definition of "Obstruction") the ball "last crossed the outermost limits of the immovable obstruction" where the underground drainpipe coincides with the boundary line. Therefore, as stated above, the player may drop a ball, without penalty, within one club-length of the spot on the ground immediately above where the drainpipe coincides with the boundary line, on a part of the course which is not nearer the hole, not in a hazard or on a putting green.

In the absence of reasonable evidence he must proceed under Rule 27-1.

**Ball Lost in Underground Drainpipe — See 24-3b/1.**

### [24-2b/13 Reserved]

### 24-2b/14 Window of Clubhouse Opened and Ball Played Through Window

**Q.** A competitor hit a ball into a clubhouse which was not out of bounds and had not been declared an integral part of the course. In order to play it out, he opened a window, claiming that it was a movable (or partially movable) obstruction. Was this permissible?

**A.** Yes. The clubhouse was an immovable obstruction. However, any part of it designed to be movable, such as a window or door, may be moved to any position if this can be done without undue delay.

The same principle would apply if the clubhouse had been declared an integral part of the course.

**Improving Line of Play by Removing Stone from Wall — See 13-2/32.**

**Improving Line of Play by Removing Part of Fence — See 13-2/32.5.**

**Outside Agency Removes Immovable Obstruction on Player's Line of Play — See 13-2/33.**

### 24-2b/15  Opening Barn Doors to Play Shot Through Barn

**Q.** May a player open the doors of a barn to enable him to play a shot through the barn?

**A.** Yes. A barn is an immovable obstruction, but the doors are movable and may be opened. See also Decision 24-2b/14.

### 24-2b/15.3  Status of Movable Part of Drainage Hose

**Q.** In a water hazard, a player's swing is interfered with by a drainage hose. One end of the hose is immovable, i.e., it is anchored in the ground. However, that part of the hose interfering with the player's swing can readily be moved to one side or the other. Is the player entitled to move the hose to the side so that it does not interfere with his swing?

**A.** Yes, since the part of the hose interfering with the player's swing is designed to be movable.

**Area of Intended Swing Improved by Removing Immovable Obstruction — See 13-2/15.**

**Stake Supporting Tree Broken in Attempt to Remove It — See 13-2/16.**

### 24-2b/16  Obstruction Interferes But Ball Unplayable Due to Some Other Condition

**Q.** A player's ball lies between two exposed tree roots. The ball is clearly unplayable due to the roots. An immovable obstruction is so located that it would interfere with the player's backswing if the player could play the ball. The player claims he is entitled to relief, without penalty, under Rule 24-2b(i). Is the player correct?

**A.** No. See Exception under Rule 24-2b. The player must invoke Rule 28.

### 24-2b/17  Obstruction Interferes with Abnormal Stroke; Abnormal Stroke Reasonable in Circumstances

**Q.** A right-handed player's ball is so close to a boundary fence on the left of a hole that the player, in order to play towards the hole, must play left-handed. In playing a left-handed stroke, the player's backswing would be interfered with by an immovable obstruction. Is the player entitled to relief from the obstruction?

**A.** The player is entitled to relief since employment of an abnormal (left-handed) stroke is necessary in the circumstances — see Exception under Rule 24-2b.

The proper procedure is for the player to take relief for a left-handed stroke in accordance with Rule 24-2b(i).

The player may then use a normal right-handed swing for his next stroke. If the obstruction interferes with the swing or stance for the right-handed stroke, the player may take relief for the right-handed stroke in accordance with Rule 24-2b(i).

### 24-2b/18 Obstruction Interferes with Abnormal Stroke; Abnormal Stroke Not Reasonable in Circumstances

**Q.** A right-handed player's ball is in a poor lie. A nearby immovable obstruction would not interfere with a normal right-handed swing but it would interfere with a left-handed swing. The player says he wishes to play his next stroke left-handed and, since the obstruction would interfere with such a stroke, he is entitled to proceed under Rule 24-2b. May the player invoke Rule 24-2b?

**A.** No. If the only reason for the player to use a left-handed stroke is to escape a poor lie, use of an abnormal (left-handed) stroke is not justifiable and the player is not entitled to invoke Rule 24-2b — see Exception under Rule 24-2b.

### 24-2b/19 Stroke at Ball Not Reasonable Due to Interference by Immovable Obstruction and Casual Water

**Q.** A player's ball lies against an immovable obstruction in casual water. It is clearly unreasonable for him to play a stroke because of interference by either of them. The Exceptions to Rule 24-2b and Rule 25-1b appear to preclude free relief from either because of interference by the other. Is this correct?

**A.** No. The player may take relief without penalty under either Rule 24-2b or Rule 25-1b. The purpose of the Exception to each of these Rules is to prevent the player from fortuitously obtaining free relief when it is clearly unreasonable for him to play a stroke because of interference by something from which free relief is not available.

### 24-2b/20 Interference by Line or Mark on Ground Consisting of Lime or Paint

**Q.** A ball comes to rest on a line or other mark on the ground consisting of lime or paint that has been drawn for gallery-control purposes or for providing fixed reference points relating to yardage. Is the player entitled to relief under Rule 24-2b?

**A.** No. Such lines or marks are not obstructions.

However, the Committee may, by Local Rule, declare such areas to be ground under repair. (Revised)

Rule 24

## 24-2b/21 Interference by Immovable Artificial Object Situated Out of Bounds

**Q.** An immovable artificial object situated out of bounds interferes with a player's swing. May the player obtain relief as provided in Rule 24-2b?

**A.** No. Immovable artificial objects off the course are not obstructions (see Definition of "Obstructions"); therefore, the Rules provide no relief without penalty.

**Part of Fence Off Course Leans Across Boundary and Interferes with Swing — See 13-2/20.**

## 24-3b/1 Ball Lost in Underground Drainpipe

**Q.** A player's ball goes into an underground drainpipe, but he cannot reach or identify it. What is the ruling?

**A.** An underground drainpipe or culvert is an obstruction. If there is reasonable evidence that the ball is lost in the immovable obstruction, the player may invoke Rule 24-3b. Under Rule 24-3b the ball is deemed to lie at the spot where it last crossed the outermost limits of the obstruction.

If the entrance to the underground drainpipe or culvert is in a water hazard, Rule 24-3b(iii) applies and the player is not entitled to relief without penalty and must proceed under Rule 26-1.

If the entrance to the underground drainpipe or culvert is out of bounds, in the absence of reasonable evidence that the ball is lost within the boundaries of the course, the player must proceed under Rule 27-1 — see Decision 24-2b/12.

### Other Decisions relating to Rule 24-3:

**Player Does Not Follow Recommended Procedure in Determining Nearest Point of Relief — See 24-2b/2.**

**Clarification of Point Where Ball "Last Crossed Outermost Limits" of Abnormal Ground Condition — See 25-1c/1.5.**

# Rule 25. Abnormal Ground Conditions, Embedded Ball and Wrong Putting Green

**Definitions**

All defined terms are in *italics* and are listed alphabetically in the Definitions section — see pages 3-11.

## 25-1. Abnormal Ground Conditions

### a. Interference

Interference by an *abnormal ground condition* occurs when a ball lies in or touches the condition or when the condition interferes with the player's *stance* or the area of his intended swing. If the player's ball lies on the *putting green*, interference also occurs if an *abnormal ground condition* on the *putting green* intervenes on his *line of putt*. Otherwise, intervention on the *line of play* is not, of itself, interference under this Rule.

**Note:** The *Committee* may make a Local Rule denying the player relief from interference with his *stance* by an *abnormal ground condition*.

### b. Relief

Except when the ball is in a *water hazard* or a *lateral water hazard*, a player may take relief from interference by an *abnormal ground condition* as follows:

(i) **Through the Green**: If the ball lies *through the green*, the player must lift the ball and drop it without penalty within one club-length of and not nearer the *hole* than the *nearest point of relief*. The *nearest point of relief* must not be in a *hazard* or on a *putting green*. When the ball is dropped within one club-length of the *nearest point of relief*, the ball must first strike a part of the *course* at a spot that avoids interference by the condition and is not in a *hazard* and not on a *putting green*.

(ii) **In a Bunker**: If the ball is in a *bunker*, the player must lift the ball and drop it either:

(a) Without penalty, in accordance with Clause (i) above, except that the *nearest point of relief* must be in the *bunker* and the ball must be dropped in the *bunker*, or if complete relief is impossible, as near as possible to the spot where the ball lay, but not nearer the *hole*, on a part of the *course* in the *bunker* that affords maximum available relief from the condition; or

(b) **Under penalty of one stroke**, outside the *bunker*, keeping the point where the ball lay directly between the *hole* and the spot on which the ball is dropped, with no limit to how far behind the *bunker* the ball may be dropped.

(iii) **On the Putting Green**: If the ball lies on the *putting green*, the player must lift the ball and place it without penalty at the *nearest point of relief* that is not in a *hazard*, or if complete relief is impossible, at the nearest position to where it lay that affords maximum available relief from the condition, but not nearer the *hole* and not in a *hazard*. The *nearest point of relief* or maximum available relief may be off the *putting green*.

(iv) **On the Teeing Ground**: If the ball lies on the *teeing ground*, the player must lift the ball and drop it without penalty in accordance with Clause (i) above.

The ball may be cleaned when lifted under Rule 25-1b.

(Ball rolling to a position where there is interference by the condition from which relief was taken — see Rule 20-2c(v).)

**Exception**: A player may not take relief under this Rule if (a) it is clearly unreasonable for him to make a *stroke* because of interference by anything other than an *abnormal ground condition* or (b) interference by an *abnormal ground condition* would occur only through use of an unnecessarily abnormal *stance*, swing or direction of play.

**Note 1**: If a ball is in a *water hazard* (including a *lateral water hazard*), the player is not entitled to relief without penalty from interference by an *abnormal ground condition*. The player must play the ball as it lies (unless prohibited by Local Rule) or proceed under Rule 26-1.

**Note 2**: If a ball to be dropped or placed under this Rule is not immediately recoverable, another ball may be *substituted*.

### c. Ball Lost

It is a question of fact whether a ball lost after having been struck toward an *abnormal ground condition* is lost in such a condition. In order to treat the ball as lost in the *abnormal ground condition*, there must be reasonable evidence to that effect. In the absence of such evidence, the ball must be treated as a *lost ball* and Rule 27 applies.

If a ball is lost in an *abnormal ground condition*, the spot where the ball last crossed the outermost limits of the condition must be determined and, for the purpose of applying this Rule, the ball is deemed to lie at this spot and the player may take relief as follows:

(i) **Through the Green**: If the ball last crossed the outermost limits of the *abnormal ground condition* at a spot *through the green*, the player may *substitute* another ball without penalty and take relief as prescribed in Rule 25-1b(i).

(ii) **In a Bunker**: If the ball last crossed the outermost limits of the *abnormal ground condition* at a spot in a *bunker*, the player may *substitute* another ball without penalty and take relief as prescribed in Rule 25-1b(ii).

(iii) **In a Water Hazard (including a Lateral Water Hazard):** If the ball last crossed the outermost limits of the *abnormal ground condition* at a spot in a *water hazard*, the player is not entitled to relief without penalty. The player must proceed under Rule 26-1.

(iv) **On the Putting Green:** If the ball last crossed the outermost limits of the *abnormal ground condition* at a spot on the *putting green*, the player may *substitute* another ball without penalty and take relief as prescribed in Rule 25-1b(iii).

## 25-2. Embedded Ball

A ball embedded in its own pitch-mark in the ground in any closely mown area *through the green* may be lifted, cleaned and dropped, without penalty, as near as possible to the spot where it lay but not nearer the *hole*. The ball when dropped must first strike a part of the *course through the green*. "Closely mown area" means any area of the *course*, including paths through the rough, cut to fairway height or less.

## 25-3. Wrong Putting Green

### a. Interference

Interference by a *wrong putting green* occurs when a ball is on the *wrong putting green*.

Interference to a player's *stance* or the area of his intended swing is not, of itself, interference under this Rule.

### b. Relief

If a player's ball lies on a *wrong putting green* he must not play the ball as it lies. He must take relief, without penalty, as follows:

The player must lift the ball and drop it within one club-length of and not nearer the *hole* than the *nearest point of relief*. The *nearest point of relief* must not be in a *hazard* or on a *putting green*. When dropping the ball within one club-length of the *nearest point of relief*, the ball must first strike a part of the *course* at a spot that avoids interference by the wrong *putting green* and is not in a *hazard* and not on a *putting green*. The ball may be cleaned when lifted under this Rule.

PENALTY FOR BREACH OF RULE:
Match play — Loss of hole; Stroke play — Two strokes.

### 25/1 Soft, Mushy Earth

**Q.** Is soft, mushy earth casual water?

**A.** No. Soft, mushy earth is not casual water unless water is visible on the surface before or after the player takes his stance — see Definition of "Casual Water."

## 25/2  Overflow from Water Hazard

**Q.** If a pond (water hazard) has overflowed, is the overflow casual water?

**A.** Yes. Any overflow of water from a water hazard which is outside the margin of the hazard is casual water.

**Ball Lost in Either Water Hazard or Casual Water Overflowing Hazard — See 1-4/7.**

## 25/3  Pitch-Mark Filled with Casual Water

**Q.** A player's ball plugged deeply in short rough. No casual water was visible on the surface, but the pitch-mark in which the ball came to rest is filled with water. Was the player's ball in casual water?

**A.** Yes.

## 25/4  Water Visible as Result of Undue Effort with Feet

**Q.** In a wet area, casual water is not visible before or after the player takes his normal stance. However, by pressing down hard with one foot, the player causes water to appear around the sole of his shoe. Is the player entitled to relief under Rule 25-1b?

**A.** No. Water visible through undue effort with the feet is not casual water — see Definition of "Casual Water."

## 25/5  Casual Water on Putting Green Visible When Player Walks Beside Line of Putt But Not Visible Elsewhere

**Q.** A player's ball lies on a putting green. Casual water is not visible on the green. However, when the player walks beside his line of putt, casual water is visible around the player's feet. Is the player entitled to relief?

**A.** Not unless there is casual water visible around the player's feet when he takes his stance — see Definition of "Casual Water."

## 25/6  Status of Saliva

**Q.** What is the status of saliva?

**A.** In equity (Rule 1-4), saliva may be treated as either an abnormal ground condition (Rule 25-1) or a loose impediment (Rule 23-1), at the option of the player.

### Other Decisions relating to Rule 25:

**Mopping Up Casual Water on Line of Play — See 13-2/34.**

**Brushing Aside or Mopping Up Casual Water on Line of Putt — See 16-1a/1.**

**Ball Moved by Wind or Casual Water While Play Suspended — See 18-1/11.**

**Ball-Marker Moved Off Green by Wind or Casual Water — See 20-1/10.**

**Removal of Casual Water on Putting Green by Committee — See 33/1.**

### 25/7 Fallen Tree in Process of Being Removed

**Q.** A greenkeeper is in the process of sawing up a fallen tree and stacking the wood. What is the status of such a tree?

**A.** The tree in its entirety is ground under repair as it constitutes "material piled for removal" — see Definition of "Ground Under Repair."

### 25/8 Tree Stump

**Q.** Do the Rules provide relief without penalty from a tree stump?

**A.** No, not unless it has been marked as ground under repair or it is in the process of being unearthed or cut up for removal, in which case it is "material piled for removal" and thus automatically ground under repair — see Definition of "Ground Under Repair."

A tree stump which the Committee intends to remove, but which is not in the process of being removed, is not automatically ground under repair.

### 25/9 Fallen Tree Attached to Stump

**Q.** A tree has fallen onto a fairway due to a windstorm and is still attached to the stump. Does it constitute ground under repair?

**A.** No. However, a player could request relief from the Committee and the Committee would be justified in declaring the area covered by the tree to be ground under repair.

### 25/9.5 Tree Falls onto Fairway During Stipulated Round

**Q.** A large tree falls onto a fairway during a stipulated round and cannot readily be removed. What should the Committee do?

**A.** The most appropriate course of action will depend on the circumstances in each case. The Committee has the following options:

(1) require play to continue, providing no additional relief from the fallen tree;

(2) suspend play and have the tree removed;

(3) declare the tree and the area covered by the tree to be ground under repair (Rule 25-1) and may, as an additional option, establish a dropping zone (or Ball Drop); or

(4) in equity (Rule 1-4), adopt the relief procedures under the Local Rule for Temporary Obstructions, thus providing intervention relief from the fallen tree.

**Other Decisions relating to Rule 25:**

Line of Putt Damaged Accidentally by Opponent, Fellow-Competitor or Their Caddies — See 16-1a/13.

Declaring Area as Ground Under Repair During Competition Round — See 33-2a/2.

Extensive Damage Due to Heavy Rain and Traffic — See 33-2a/3.

Referee's Authority to Declare Ground Under Repair — See 34-2/1.

## 25/10 Ball Lost in Tree in Ground Under Repair

**Q.** A ball is lost in a tree rooted in an area marked as ground under repair. Is the player entitled to relief without penalty under Rule 25-1c?

**A.** As all ground and any grass, bush, tree or other growing thing within ground under repair is considered to be part of the ground under repair (see Definition of "Ground Under Repair"), the ball is lost in ground under repair and the player is entitled to relief under Rule 25-1c.

In this case, the reference point for taking relief is the spot where the ball last crossed the outermost limits of the area of ground under repair.

## 25/10.5 Ball in Tree in Ground Under Repair

**Q.** A player's ball is found through the green in a tree rooted in an area marked as ground under repair. The spot on the ground directly under where the ball lies is outside the white-lined area defining the ground under repair. Is the player entitled to relief under Rule 25-1b(i)?

**A.** Yes, because the ball lies in or touches the ground under repair — see Definition of "Ground Under Repair." In this case, the reference point for taking relief is the spot on the ground immediately below the place where the ball lay in the tree.

## 25/10.7 Status of Roots Outside Ground Under Repair Growing from Tree Inside Ground Under Repair

**Q.** A player's ball comes to rest against a tree root. The tree is within ground under repair, but the ball is against a part of the root outside the ground under repair. Is the player entitled to relief without penalty under Rule 25-1?

**A.** No. The margin of ground under repair extends vertically downward, so part of a growing thing within ground under repair that extends beyond the area at or below ground level is not ground under repair.

**Ball Outside Ground Under Repair Area But High Grass Within Area Interferes with Swing — See 25-1a/1.**

### 25/10.9 Status of Non-Growing Plants Within Area of Ground Under Repair

**Q.** A bush, tree or other plant is rooted within an area of ground under repair, but there is a possibility that it may not be growing, e.g., because it is dead or dormant. The Definition of "Ground Under Repair" states in part "All ground and any grass, bush, tree, or other growing thing within the ground under repair is part of the ground under repair." Is the bush, tree or other plant considered ground under repair?

**A.** Yes. Provided the bush, tree or other plant is rooted within the ground under repair and thus fixed, it is part of the condition. It is often difficult to differentiate between plant life that is alive, dead or dormant.

### 25/11 Grass Cuttings

Grass cuttings are only ground under repair if they have been piled for removal — see Note 1 under Definition of "Ground Under Repair." If cuttings piled for removal interfere with a player's stance or swing, the player is entitled to relief under Rule 25-1b.

Grass cuttings are loose impediments (see Definition of "Loose Impediments"), whether or not they are piled for removal, and may be removed by the player — Rule 23-1.

### 25/12 Cracks in Earth

**Q.** Are cracks in the earth which occur in hot and dry conditions ground under repair? Do the Rules of Golf provide relief?

**A.** No. However, a player whose ball is in a large crack would be justified in requesting the Committee to declare the crack to be ground under repair, and the Committee would be justified in doing so.

### 25/13 Bunker Totally Under Repair

If an entire bunker is being renovated, it does not lose its status as a hazard. However, it is recommended that the Committee should, during the renovation period, define the bunker as ground under repair and classify it as through the green. If such a bunker has been defined as ground under repair but has not been classified as through the green, the player may, under Rule 25-1b(ii):

(a) drop the ball without penalty in the bunker as near as possible to the spot where the ball lay, but not nearer the hole, on ground which affords maximum available relief, i.e., ground which is most nearly normal, or

(b) drop the ball under penalty of one stroke behind the bunker, keeping the point where the ball lay between the hole and the spot on which the ball is dropped.

## 25/14 Explanation of "Hole Made by Greenkeeper" in Definition of "Ground Under Repair"

**Q.** What constitutes a "hole made by a greenkeeper"?

**A.** A "hole made by a greenkeeper" is usually ground temporarily dug up in connection with course maintenance, such as a hole made in removing turf or a tree stump, laying pipelines, etc.

## 25/15 Aeration Holes

**Q.** Is an aeration hole a hole made by a greenkeeper within the meaning of that term in the Definition of "Ground Under Repair"?

**A.** No.

## 25/16 Rut Made by Tractor

**Q.** Is a rut made by a tractor considered a hole made by a greenkeeper and thus ground under repair? If not, should the Committee declare such a rut to be ground under repair?

**A.** Such a rut is not a hole made by a greenkeeper. The Committee would be justified in declaring a deep rut to be ground under repair, but not a shallow indentation made by greenkeeping equipment.

**Competitor Announces Intention to Play Two Balls; Plays Original Ball Before Dropping Second Ball; Elects Not to Play Second Ball — See 3-3/7.5.**

**Ball in Rut; Competitor Drops One Ball in Accordance with Rules for Ground Under Repair and Unplayable Ball — See 3-3/11.**

## 25/17 Sunken Hole Plug

**Q.** Is an old hole plug which has sunk below the level of the surface of the putting green a hole made by a greenkeeper and therefore ground under repair?

**A.** No. Rule 16-1c applies.

**Hole on Putting Green Not in Use — See 16/7.**

## 25/18 Hole of Removed Stake Defining Water Hazard

**Q.** A stake defining the margin of a water hazard is removed. Is the hole in which the stake was previously located a "hole made by a greenkeeper" and thus ground under repair?

**A.** Yes. However, such a hole is in a water hazard (see Definition of "Water Hazard") and a player would not be entitled to relief from the hole if his ball was in the water hazard — see first paragraph of Rule 25-1b.

## [25/19 Reserved]

### 25/19.5 Footprint of Burrowing Animal, Reptile or Bird

**Q.** Is the footprint of a burrowing animal, a reptile or a bird a "hole, cast or runway" within the meaning of these terms in the Definition of "Abnormal Ground Conditions"?

**A.** No. A footprint is an irregularity of surface from which there is no relief without penalty.

### [25/20 Reserved]

### 25/21 Lifting Ball to Determine Whether It Lies in Burrowing Animal Hole

**Q.** May a player whose ball lies in a depression, other than in a water hazard, lift his ball to determine if it is in a hole made by a burrowing animal?

**A.** In equity (Rule 1-4), the player may lift the ball, without penalty, provided he announces his intention in advance to his opponent in match play or his marker or a fellow-competitor in stroke play, marks the position of the ball, and gives his opponent, marker or fellow-competitor an opportunity to observe the lifting. If the ball is in a burrowing animal hole, he is entitled to relief under Rule 25-1b. Otherwise, the ball must be replaced and the opponent, marker or fellow-competitor given an opportunity to observe the replacement. If the player fails to comply with this procedure, he shall incur a penalty of one stroke, but no additional penalty under Rule 20-1 shall be applied. A ball so lifted may not be cleaned unless it is found to be lying in a burrowing animal hole and the player elects to take relief under Rule 25.

**Ball Found in Burrowing Animal Hole After Five-Minute Search — See 27/7.**

### [25/22 Reserved]

### 25/23 Molehills

Molehills are casts made by a burrowing animal. Accordingly, a player having interference from a molehill, or the remains of a molehill, is entitled to relief under Rule 25-1b, provided, in the latter instance, the remains are still identifiable as a cast made by a burrowing animal.

### 25-1/1 Ball in Casual Water Difficult to Retrieve

**Q.** There is reasonable evidence that a player's ball came to rest in a large puddle of casual water. A ball is visible in the casual water, but the player cannot retrieve it or identify it as his ball without unreasonable effort. The player abandons the ball and proceeds under Rule 25-1c, which provides relief for a ball lost in casual water. Was the player justified in doing so?

**A.** Yes. A player is not obliged to use unreasonable effort to retrieve a ball in casual water, for identification purposes.

However, if it would not take unreasonable effort to retrieve a ball in casual water, the player must retrieve it. If it turns out to be the player's ball and he elects to take relief, he must proceed under Rule 25-1b(i); otherwise, he must proceed under Rule 25-1c(i).

### 25-1a/1 Ball Outside Ground Under Repair Area But Tree Within Area Interferes with Swing

**Q.** The margins of ground under repair do not extend vertically upward. If the ball lies outside ground under repair and a tree rooted within the ground under repair interferes with a player's swing, but there is no interference with his stance, is the player entitled to relief?

**A.** Yes. The Definition of "Ground Under Repair" states: "All ground and any grass, bush, tree or other growing thing within the ground under repair is part of the ground under repair." Therefore, the player may take relief under Rule 25-1 as the tree within the ground under repair interferes with the area of his intended swing.

**Ball in Tree in Ground Under Repair — See 25/10.5.**

**Status of Roots Outside Ground Under Repair Growing from Tree Inside Ground Under Repair — See 25/10.7.**

**Status of Non-Growing Plants Within Area of Ground Under Repair — See 25/10.9.**

### 25-1a/2 Casual Water on Putting Green Intervenes Between Ball Off Green and Hole

**Q.** A player's ball lies just off the putting green and casual water on the green intervenes between the ball and the hole. Is the player entitled to relief?

**A.** No. In addition, Rule 13-2 prohibits the player from removing casual water from his line of play.

**Casual Water on Putting Green; Whether Player Entitled to Relief for Intervention If Ball Is on Green and Nearest Point of Relief Is Off Green — See 25-1b/10.5.**

### [25-1b/1 Reserved]

### 25-1b/2 Diagrams Illustrating "Nearest Point of Relief"

The following diagrams illustrate the term "nearest point of relief" in Rule 25-1b(i) in the case of both a right-handed and left-handed player.

The "nearest point of relief" must be strictly interpreted. A player is not permitted to choose on which side of the ground under repair he will drop the ball, unless there are two equidistant nearest points of relief. Even if one side of the ground under repair is fairway and the other is bushes, if the nearest point of relief is in the bushes then the player, if taking relief, must drop the ball within one club-length of that point, even though he may have to drop the ball in a virtually unplayable lie.

B1 = position of ball in ground under repair, etc.

P1 = nearest point of relief

P1-A-A = shaded area within which ball to be dropped, radius of one club-length from P1, measured with any club

B2 = position of ball in ground under repair, etc.

▯▬ = notional stance required to play ball at P2 with club with which player would expect to play the stroke

P2 = nearest point of relief

P2-C-C = shaded area within which ball to be dropped, radius of one club-length from P2, measured with any club

B1 and B2 are the positions of the ball in ground under repair, etc.

P1 is the nearest point of relief for B1

P2 is the nearest point of relief for B2

Shaded area P1-A-A = dropping area for ball at B1

Shaded area P2-C-C = dropping area for ball at B2

▬▯ = player's notional stance to play ball at P1

The same procedure applies under Rule 24-2b dealing with immovable obstructions.

Player Does Not Follow Recommended Procedure in Determining Nearest Point of Relief — See 24-2b/2.

Player Determines Nearest Point of Relief But Physically Unable to Play Intended Stroke — See 24-2b/3.

Diagram Illustrating Player Unable to Determine Nearest Point of Relief — See 24-2b/3.7.

### 25-1b/3 Improving Line of Play When Taking Relief from Abnormal Ground Conditions

**Q.** In certain circumstances, in complying with Rule 25-1b, it is possible for a player incidentally to improve his line of play, e.g., avoid playing over a bunker or a tree. Is this permissible?

**A.** Yes. If a player's ball is in one of the conditions covered by Rule 25 and if, in taking relief in accordance with the procedure laid down in Rule 25-1b, his line of play is improved, this is his good fortune.

Player Entitled to Relief from Abnormal Ground Condition Lifts Ball; Player Then Replaces Ball and Plays It from Original Position — See 18-2a/12.

Player Entitled to Relief Without Penalty from Condition Lifts Ball; Chooses Not to Take Relief and Wishes to Proceed Under the Unplayable Ball Rule — See 18-2a/12.5.

### 25-1b/4 Casual Water Covering Teeing Ground

**Q.** After several groups have played a particular hole, a player arrives at the teeing ground of that hole which has become completely covered with casual water. What is the procedure?

**A.** In such a case, the matter should be brought to the attention of the Committee. Rule 25-1 is not applicable since the player's ball is not in play — see Definition of "Ball in Play."

In match play, the Committee may relocate the teeing ground.

In stroke play, if the conditions are such that removal of the casual water might be possible, the Committee should suspend play and attempt to remove the casual water. If the removal of the casual water is impossible, the Committee may (1) suspend play until the teeing ground is playable or cancel the round (Rule 33-2d) or (2) relocate the teeing ground if this could be done without giving any competitor an undue advantage or disadvantage.

Hole Surrounded by Casual Water — See 33-2d/2.

### 25-1b/5 Explanation of "Maximum Available Relief" from Casual Water in Bunker

**Q.** In a bunker completely covered by casual water, is the place providing "maximum available relief" the spot which will provide the most relief for both lie and stance or just lie?

**A.** The term applies to both lie and stance. The spot providing "maximum available relief" might be such that the ball will be in shallower water than the player's feet after he takes his stance, or vice versa.

### 25-1b/6  Ball Dropped from Casual Water in Bunker at Point of Maximum Relief Rolls Elsewhere

**Q.** A player whose ball lies in a bunker completely covered by casual water drops his ball under Rule 25-1b(ii) at a spot where there is ¼ inch of casual water. This spot is the nearest spot providing maximum available relief. The ball rolls into a spot where there is about ½ inch of casual water. What is the ruling?

**A.** In equity (Rule 1-4), and under the principle of Rule 20-2c(v), the player may re-drop and, if the ball so rolls again, place the ball where it first struck a part of the course when re-dropped.

### 25-1b/7  Ball to Be Dropped in Bunker Dropped Outside Bunker and Rolls into Bunker

**Q.** A player's ball lies in casual water in a bunker. The player elects to proceed under Rule 25-1b(ii)(a) and determines that the nearest point of relief in the bunker is close to the back of the bunker. The player drops his ball within one club-length of the nearest point of relief on a slope outside the bunker because he fears it will plug in the sand. The ball rolls down the slope and comes to rest in the bunker not nearer the hole than the nearest point of relief. Is the player subject to penalty?

**A.** Yes, unless he lifts the ball and proceeds correctly, as provided in Rule 20-6. Under Rule 25-1b(ii)(a), the player is required to drop the ball in the bunker. If the player, although proceeding under this Rule, drops the ball outside the bunker and plays it, he is in breach of Rule 25 and the penalty is loss of hole in match play or two strokes in stroke play.

### 25-1b/8  Player's Options When Bunker Completely Covered by Casual Water

**Q.** If a player's ball lies in a bunker completely covered by casual water, what are his options?

**A.** The player may play the ball as it lies or:

(1) drop the ball in the bunker without penalty at the nearest point, not nearer the hole, where the depth of the casual water is least — Rule 25-1b(ii)(a); or

(2) drop the ball behind the bunker under penalty of one stroke — Rule 25-1b(ii)(b); or

(3) deem the ball unplayable and proceed in accordance with Rule 28.

### 25-1b/9 Player Who Invokes First Option of Rule 25-1b(ii) Then Wishes to Invoke Second Option

**Q.** A player's ball is in a bunker completely covered by casual water. Under the first option of Rule 25-1b(ii), he drops the ball on ground in the bunker affording maximum available relief. He then decides he would have been better off to invoke the second option and drop behind the bunker. May he invoke the second option?

**A.** No. Rule 25-1b(ii) permits the player to proceed under one of two options. He is not entitled to invoke one option and then, if he does not like the result, invoke the other. Therefore, as Rule 25-1 no longer applies, the player must play the ball as it lies or proceed under the unplayable ball Rule, incurring the penalty stroke prescribed by that Rule.

**Player Who Lifts Ball Under First Option of Rule 24-2b(ii) Then Wishes to Proceed Under Second Option — See 24-2b/5.**

### 25-1b/10 Casual Water on Putting Green; Nearest Point of Relief Is Off Green

**Q.** A player whose ball is on a putting green is entitled to relief from casual water. However, the nearest position affording complete relief which is not nearer the hole or in a hazard is off the green in the rough. If the player opts to take relief, must he place the ball in the rough?

**A.** Yes. See Rule 25-1b(iii).

### 25-1b/10.5 Casual Water on Putting Green; Whether Player Entitled to Relief for Intervention If Ball Is on Green and Nearest Point of Relief Is Off Green

**Q.** In Illustration X, a player's ball lies at Point 1 in casual water on the putting green. In Illustration Y, a player's ball lies at Point 1 on the putting green with casual water intervening on his line of putt.

Under Rule 25-1b(iii), the player is not entitled to place the ball at Point 4, which is on the green, because Point 4 is farther from Point 1 than either Point 2 or Point 3, both of which are off the green. It would seem that Point 2 may be the correct point because there is no relief if a ball lies off the green and casual water on the green intervenes on the line of play. In taking relief, must the player place the ball at Point 2 or Point 3?

**A.** Since, in both illustrations, the ball lies on the putting green, the player is entitled to relief with respect to the lie of the ball and intervention on his line. Accordingly, in either case the player must place the ball at Point 3, the nearest point which affords complete relief with respect to both situations.

### 25-1b/11  Ball in Casual Water Within Ground Under Repair

**Q.** A ball lies in casual water within an area defined as ground under repair. May a player take relief from the casual water under Rule 25-1b, drop the ball in the ground under repair, and then either play the ball as it lies or take relief from the ground under repair under Rule 25-1b?

**A.** Yes.

### 25-1b/11.5  Ball in Casual Water Within Ground Under Repair; Whether Player Entitled to Take Relief from Both Conditions in Single Procedure

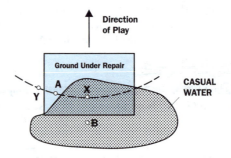

**Q.** The illustration above shows a player's ball which lies in casual water, at Point X, within an area of ground under repair. May the player, in a single procedure, drop the ball at Point Y, the nearest point of relief from both conditions?

**A.** No. The player has the option of taking relief from each condition in separate stages but not from both at the same time.

The player may take relief from the casual water at Point A and then may take relief from the ground under repair.

Alternatively, he may take relief from ground under repair at Point B and then may take relief from the casual water.

**Nearest Point of Relief from Cart Path Is in Casual Water; Nearest Point of Relief from Casual Water Is Back on Cart Path — See 1-4/8.**

**Player Takes Relief from Area of Casual Water and Ball Comes to Rest in a Position Where Another Area of Casual Water Interferes; Whether Re-Drop Required — See 20-2c/7.**

Rule 25   343

## 25-1b/12  Casual Water Mistaken for Water Hazard; Original Ball Played Under Water Hazard Rule

**Q.** A player whose ball is in casual water mistakes the casual water for a water hazard. He retrieves his original ball, drops it 10 yards behind the casual water in accordance with the water hazard Rule and plays it. His error is then discovered. What is the ruling?

**A.** The player did not follow the procedure prescribed in Rule 25-1b(i) for dropping a ball from casual water; he dropped the ball in a wrong place. In match play, he loses the hole — Rule 20-7b. In stroke play, he incurs a penalty of two strokes — Rules 25-1b(i) and 20-7c.

## 25-1b/13  Casual Water Mistaken for Water Hazard; Substituted Ball Played Under Water Hazard Rule

**Q.** A player whose ball is in casual water mistakes the casual water for a water hazard. The player does not retrieve his original ball, although he could have done so without unreasonable effort — see Decision 25-1/1. Rather, he drops another ball 10 yards behind the casual water in accordance with the water hazard Rule and plays it. His error is then discovered. What is the ruling?

**A.** Since the player could retrieve the ball without unreasonable effort, he was not permitted to substitute a ball in taking relief from the casual water. Additionally, as a result of proceeding under the water hazard Rule, he dropped the ball in a wrong place.

In match play, the player loses the hole (Rules 15-2, 25-1b(i) and 20-7b).

In stroke play, he incurs a total penalty of four strokes — two for wrongly substituting a ball (Rule 15-2) and two for playing from a wrong place (Rules 25-1b(i) and 20-7c).

**Player Proceeds Under an Inapplicable Rule; Committee's Decision — See 34-3/6.**

## [25-1b/14  Reserved]

## 25-1b/14.5  Ball Deemed Unplayable Dropped in Ground Under Repair from Which Play Prohibited; Ball Then Dropped Under Ground Under Repair Rule

**Q.** A player deemed his ball unplayable. In proceeding under Rule 28b or c, the player dropped his ball in an area of ground under repair from which play was prohibited by Local Rule. He then took the mandatory relief under Rule 25-1b. Is this procedure permitted?

**A.** Yes.

**Ball in Ground Under Repair Thought to Be Unfit for Play Lifted and Cleaned — See 5-3/6.**

**Whether Player May Drop Ball Into Area from Which Play Prohibited — See 20-7/3.**

**Obstruction in Ground Under Repair Interferes with Player's Swing** — See 24-2b/10.

**Ball Embedded in Ground Under Repair in Closely Mown Area** — See 25-2/4.

## 25-1b/15 Measuring Across Ground Under Repair in Obtaining Relief

**Q.** A player obtaining relief from a narrow strip of ground under repair through the green determines his nearest point of relief (Point A) which is not in a hazard or on a putting green. Point A is on the right-hand side of the ground under repair. Within one club-length of Point A is a point (Point B) on the left side of the ground under repair which meets the requirements of Rule 25-1b(i). May the player drop his ball at Point B?

**A.** Yes. There is nothing in Rule 25-1b prohibiting measuring the one club-length across ground under repair in obtaining relief.

**Ball Dropped from Ground Under Repair Area Rolls to Position Where Area Interferes with Stance; Whether Re-Drop Required** — See 20-2c/0.5.

## 25-1b/16 Ball Equidistant from Two Points Which Meet Requirements of Ground Under Repair Rule

**Q.** Through the green, the player's ball lies in ground under repair and he opts for relief under Rule 25-1b(i). There is no single nearest point of relief. Rather, there are two such points equidistant from the spot where the ball lies. May the player drop within one club-length of either point?

**A.** Yes.

**After Declaring Ball Unplayable and Lifting It, Player Discovers That Ball Was in Ground Under Repair** — See 28/13.

## 25-1b/17 Pine Needles Piled for Removal Interfere with Line of Play After Ball Dropped Away

**Q.** A player whose ball lies in pine needles piled for removal drops away under Rule 25-1b. The ball comes to rest in such a position that the pile of pine needles intervenes on his line of play. May the player remove the pine needles from his line of play?

**A.** Yes. Pine needles piled for removal are loose impediments or ground under repair. Initially, the player was entitled to remove the pine needles under Rule 23-1 (Loose Impediments) or drop away, as he did, under Rule 25-1b.

After the player dropped away a new situation existed and he was no longer entitled to invoke Rule 25-1b. However, he was not prohibited from removing the pine needles under Rule 23-1.

**Ball Played from Ground Under Repair Picked Up and Relief Taken Under Ground Under Repair Rule** — See 18-2a/8.

### 25-1b/18 Crawfish Mound Interferes with Stance or Swing

**Q.** When a crawfish digs a hole, it creates a sizable mound of mud. If such a mound interferes with a player's stance or swing, does he get relief under Rule 25-1b?

**A.** Yes, provided the player's ball does not lie in a water hazard — see first paragraph of Rule 25-1b. A crawfish is a burrowing animal.

**Touching Mound Made by Burrowing Animal with Backswing in Bunker — See 13-4/5.**

### 25-1b/19 Ball Lies on Mound Made by Burrowing Animal; Unreasonable to Play Stroke Due to Bush

**Q.** A player's ball lies under a bush and it is clearly unreasonable for the player to play a stroke at it. However, the ball lies on a mound made by a burrowing animal. Is the player entitled to relief without penalty under Rule 25-1b?

**A.** Under the Exception to Rule 25-1b a player may not obtain relief from an abnormal ground condition if it is clearly unreasonable for him to play a stroke due to interference by something other than such a condition. Therefore, in the circumstances described, the player is not entitled to relief.

**Stroke at Ball Not Reasonable Due to Interference by Immovable Obstruction and Casual Water — See 24-2b/19.**

### 25-1b/20 Stance Interfered with by Burrowing Animal Hole; Unreasonable to Play Stroke Because of Other Condition

**Q.** A player's ball is in an indentation at the base of a tree in such a position that it is clearly unreasonable for him to play a stroke. Despite this, the player claims relief without penalty under Rule 25-1 because his stance for a stroke at the ball in the indentation would be on a burrowing animal hole. Is the player entitled to relief without penalty under Rule 25-1b?

**A.** Under the Exception to Rule 25-1b a player may not obtain relief from an abnormal ground condition if it is clearly unreasonable for him to play a stroke due to interference by something other than such a condition. In the circumstances described above, the player's ball is unplayable as it lies in an indentation at the base of a tree. Therefore, the player is not entitled to relief under Rule 25-1 from the burrowing animal hole.

### 25-1b/21 Cast of Burrowing Animal Interferes with Stroke Towards Green; Tree Prevents Such Stroke

**Q.** A player's ball is immediately behind a tree. A cast behind the ball made by a burrowing animal would interfere with the player's backswing for a stroke towards the green, but not with a sideways stroke, which is the only reasonable stroke. If the player says he intends to play towards the green into the tree, may he take relief without penalty under Rule 25-1b?

**A.** Under the Exception to Rule 25-1b a player may not obtain relief from an abnormal ground condition if interference from such a condition would only occur through the player using an unnecessarily abnormal direction of play. Therefore, in the circumstances described above, the player is not entitled to relief.

### 25-1b/22 Cast of Burrowing Animal Interferes with Sideways Stroke; When Relief Granted

**Q.** A ball is behind a tree so that a sideways stroke is the only reasonable stroke for the player. However, a cast made by a burrowing animal interferes with the backswing for a sideways stroke. Is the player entitled to relief under Rule 25-1b?

**A.** Yes, and if relief gets the player out from behind the tree, he is entitled to play towards the green.

### 25-1b/23 Ball Enters Burrowing Animal Hole Out of Bounds and Comes to Rest in Bounds

**Q.** The entrance to a burrowing animal hole is out of bounds, but most of the burrow is in bounds under the course. A ball enters the hole from out of bounds and comes to rest in bounds under ground classified as through the green. What is the procedure?

**A.** Under Rule 25-1b, the player may drop the ball, without penalty, within one club-length of the point on the ground directly above its position in the burrow. In such cases, vertical distance is disregarded in applying the Rules.

### 25-1b/24 Ball Enters Burrowing Animal Hole in Bounds and Comes to Rest Out of Bounds

**Q.** A player's ball entered a rabbit hole, the mouth of which was in bounds but only about a foot from a boundary fence. The rabbit hole sloped steeply down below the fence, so that the ball came to rest beyond the boundary line. What is the ruling?

**A.** Whether or not a ball is out of bounds depends on where it lies in relation to the boundary of the course and this must be measured vertically upward or downward — see Definition of "Out of Bounds."

In the case cited, the ball was lying out of bounds and Rule 27-1 applied. Relief could not be obtained under Rule 25-1, i.e., from a hole made by a burrowing animal.

### 25-1b/25 Ball Enters Burrowing Animal Hole in Bunker and Is Found Underneath Putting Green

**Q.** A ball enters a burrowing animal hole in a greenside bunker and is found underneath the putting green. As the ball is not in the bunker or on the putting green, is relief taken in accordance with Rule 25-1b(i), i.e. through the green?

**A.** Yes. The player would drop the ball without penalty on a part of the course through the green within one club-length of the nearest point to its position in the burrowing animal hole that avoids interference from the condition and is not in a hazard, not on a putting green and not nearer the hole.

### 25-1b/26 Player Unaware Ball in Water Hazard Takes Relief from Interference by Burrowing Animal Hole

**Q.** A player, unaware that his ball is in a dry water hazard, lifts and drops the ball under Rule 25-1b(i) believing he is entitled to relief from a hole made by a burrowing animal. After dropping the ball in the hazard, he discovers his mistake. What is the ruling?

**A.** As the player's ball lay in a water hazard, he was not entitled to relief without penalty from a hole made by a burrowing animal — see first paragraph of Rule 25-1b. However, as his ball lay in a water hazard, he is not precluded from taking relief under Rule 26.

As the player had dropped the ball under an inapplicable Rule, he may correct his error under Rule 20-6 by:

1. lifting the ball and replacing it where it originally lay in the water hazard, in which case he incurs a penalty of one stroke under Rule 18-2a — see Decision 18-2a/12; or

2. proceeding under Rule 26-1. He incurs a penalty of one stroke under Rule 26-1, but no additional penalty is incurred. (Revised)

### 25-1c/1 Meaning of "Reasonable Evidence" in Rule 25-1c

**Q.** An area of casual water preceded by high rough is in a hollow not visible from the tee. A ball driven into this area is lost. The ball may be lost in the casual water or it may be lost in the high rough. Is there reasonable evidence that the ball is lost in the casual water?

**A.** No. In such circumstances, there is not reasonable evidence that the ball is lost in casual water. The player must proceed under Rule 27-1.

### 25-1c/1.5 Clarification of Point Where Ball "Last Crossed Outermost Limits" of Abnormal Ground Condition

**Q.** In the diagram above, a ball is lost in an area of casual water, having splashed at Point A. Point B represents the point where the ball crossed over the outermost limits of the casual water. For the purposes of proceeding under Rule 25-1c, where is the ball deemed to lie?

**A.** The ball is deemed to lie at Point B.

### 25-1c/2 Ball Dropped and Played Under Ground Under Repair Rule in Absence of Reasonable Evidence That Original Ball Lost in Ground Under Repair

**Q.** A player, after a search of less than one minute, considers that his ball is lost in ground under repair, although there is not reasonable evidence to that effect. He drops a ball under Rule 25-1c and plays it. His original ball is then found beyond the ground under repair. What is the ruling?

**A.** When the player dropped and played another ball under Rule 25-1c, it became the ball in play and the original ball was lost.

In the absence of reasonable evidence that the ball had been lost in ground under repair, the player was required to put another ball into play under Rule 27-1. In playing the ball dropped under Rule 25-1c, the player played from a wrong place.

In match play, he incurred a penalty of loss of hole (Rule 20-7b).

In stroke play, he incurred the stroke-and-distance penalty prescribed by Rule 27-1 and an additional penalty of two strokes for a breach of that Rule. If the breach was a serious one, he was subject to disqualification unless he corrected the error as provided in Rule 20-7c.

### 25-1c/2.5 Ball Dropped Under Rule 25-1c with Reasonable Evidence; Original Ball Then Found

**Q.** A player's ball is struck towards a large area of casual water. There is reasonable evidence that the player's ball is lost in the casual water and the player drops a ball under Rule 25-1c. Before he plays the dropped ball, his original ball is found within the five-minute search period. What is the ruling?

**A.** The player had reasonable evidence that his ball was lost in casual water when he put the substituted ball into play and, therefore, that ball was correctly substituted and he may not play the original ball.

If the original ball was found in the casual water and this discovery affects the reference point for proceeding under Rule 25-1c, resulting in the substituted ball having been dropped in a wrong place, the player must correct the error under Rule 20-6 and drop a ball under Rule 25-1c with respect to the correct reference point. Otherwise, Rule 20-6 does not apply, and the player must continue play with the dropped ball. In either case, the player incurs no penalty.

If the original ball was found outside the casual water, the player must continue play with the dropped ball without penalty.

The same answer would apply if there is reasonable evidence that the player's ball is lost in any other abnormal ground condition or an obstruction (Rule 24-3). (New)

**Ball Played Under Rule for Ball Lost in Ground Under Repair After Another Ball Played Under Stroke-and-Distance Procedure — See 15/8.**

**Ball Played from Ground Under Repair Abandoned and Relief Taken Under Ground Under Repair Rule — See 18-2a/8.5.**

**Ball Dropped Under Water Hazard Rule with Reasonable Evidence; Original Ball Then Found — See 26-1/3.5**

**Player Proceeds Under an Inapplicable Rule; Committee's Decision — See 34-3/6.**

## 25-1c/3  Ball Played in Ground Under Repair Area Lost in Same Area

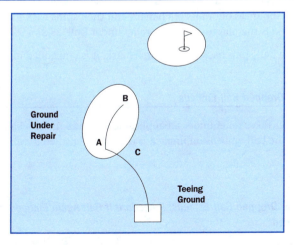

**Q.** In the illustration above, a player's tee shot comes to rest at Point A in a large area of ground under repair. He makes a stroke at his ball from within the ground under repair. He advances the ball to Point B, which is still in the ground under repair, and the ball never crossed the outermost limits of the ground under repair. The ball cannot be found. What is the ruling?

**A.** The player may drop a ball outside the ground under repair area, without penalty, as provided in Rule 25-1c and make his third stroke. In this case, the reference point is where the ball last crossed the outermost limits of the ground under repair with the player's tee shot (Point C).

Alternatively, the player may, under penalty of one stroke, drop a ball in the ground under repair as near as possible at the spot from which his original ball was last played (Point A) under Rule 27-1 and make his fourth stroke. Having dropped a ball under Rule 27-1, if the player then has interference from the ground under repair, he may take relief under Rule 25-1b without further penalty. (Revised)

#### Another Decision relating to Rule 25-1c:

**Whether Provisional Ball Becomes Ball in Play If Original Ball Lost in Ground Under Repair — See 27-2c/1.5.**

### 25-2/0.5 When Ball Embedded in Ground

For a ball to be considered embedded, it must be in its own pitch-mark with part of the ball below the level of the ground. However, the ball does not necessarily have to touch the soil to be considered embedded, e.g., grass or loose impediments may intervene between the ball and the soil.

### 25-2/1 Ball Bounces Out of Its Pitch-Mark and Spins Back into It

**Q.** A player's ball lands in soft ground in a closely mown area through the green, bounces out of its pitch-mark and then spins back into the pitch-mark. Is the player entitled to relief under Rule 25-2?

**A.** Yes. If a ball spins back into its pitch-mark, it is embedded in the pitch-mark.

### 25-2/2 Dropped Ball Embeds

**Q.** A player takes relief under an applicable Rule and drops a ball on a fairway. The ball embeds on impact. Is the player entitled to relief under Rule 25-2?

**A.** Yes.

### 25-2/2.5 Dropped Ball Embeds; Procedure If Ball Again Embeds When Re-Dropped

**Q.** According to Decision 25-2/2, if a ball dropped on a fairway embeds on impact, the player is entitled to relief under Rule 25-2. What is the proper procedure if a ball embeds each time it is dropped?

**A.** If a ball embeds when dropped and embeds again when re-dropped, the player may, in equity (Rule 1-4), place the ball as near as possible to the spot where it embedded when re-dropped, but not nearer the hole.

If the player drops the ball more than twice, the ball embeds each time and he then becomes aware that he was entitled to place the ball after the second drop, he may place the ball as near as possible to the spot where it embedded on the second drop.

### 25-2/3  Ball Returns to Pitch-Mark from Prior Stroke

**Q.** A player's ball embeds in its own pitch-mark in the ground in a closely mown area through the green. After taking relief under Rule 25-2, the player makes a stroke. The ball climbs a slope but rolls back down it and into the same pitch-mark. Is the player entitled to relief without penalty?

**A.** No. A player is only entitled to relief under Rule 25-2 when his ball is embedded in a pitch-mark created by the last stroke he made — but see Decision 25-2/2 with regard to a dropped ball that embeds.

### 25-2/4  Ball Embedded in Ground Under Repair in Closely Mown Area

**Q.** A player's ball is embedded in ground under repair in a closely mown area through the green. May the player drop the ball within the ground under repair under Rule 25-2 (Embedded Ball) and then elect whether to play the ball as it lies or take relief from the ground under repair under Rule 25-1b?

**A.** Yes.

**Ball in Casual Water Within Ground Under Repair; Whether Player Entitled to Take Relief from Both Conditions in Single Procedure — See 25-1b/11.5.**

### 25-2/5  Ball Embedded in Grass Bank or Face of Bunker

**Q.** Are grass banks or faces of bunkers considered to be "closely mown areas" under Rule 25-2 (Embedded Ball) and may relief be taken from them under that Rule?

**A.** No, not unless they are cut to fairway height or less.

**Ball Completely Embedded in Lip of Bunker — See 13/4.**

**Local Rule for Bunker Faces Consisting of Stacked Turf — See 33-8/39.**

### 25-2/6  Ball on Steep Bank Driven Straight into Ground

**Q.** A player's ball lies on a steep bank in the fairway. He plays a stroke and drives the ball straight into the bank, i.e., the ball is never airborne. Is the player entitled to relief without penalty under Rule 25-2?

**A.** No. Under Rule 25-2, relief is provided if a ball is embedded in its own pitch-mark. The word "pitch-mark" implies that the ball has become airborne.

### 25-2/7 Lifting Ball to Determine Whether It Is Embedded

**Q.** A player's ball lies on a fairway and he believes the ball may be embedded in its own pitch-mark. Is the player entitled to lift the ball to determine whether it is embedded?

**A.** In equity (Rule 1-4), the player may lift the ball, without penalty, provided he announces his intention in advance to his opponent in match play or his marker or a fellow-competitor in stroke play, marks the position of the ball, and gives his opponent, marker or fellow-competitor an opportunity to observe the lifting. If the ball is embedded in the ground, he is entitled to relief under Rule 25-2. Otherwise, the ball must be replaced and the opponent, marker or fellow-competitor given an opportunity to observe the replacement. If the player fails to comply with this procedure, he shall incur a penalty of one stroke, but no additional penalty under Rule 20-1 shall be applied. A ball so lifted may not be cleaned unless it is found to be embedded in the ground and the player elects to take relief under Rule 25-2.

### 25-2/8 Ball Embedded in Teeing Ground

**Q.** A player's tee shot strikes a tree and returns to the teeing ground, where the ball embeds in the ground. Is the player entitled to relief without penalty?

**A.** Yes. Although the Rules of Golf do not contemplate such a situation, in equity (Rule 1-4), the player is entitled to relief without penalty and must follow the procedure prescribed in Rule 25-2 for a ball that lies in a closely-mown area through the green.

The same principle would apply to other relief situations that do not contemplate relief being required within the teeing ground (e.g., Rule 24-1b). (New)

**Casual Water Covering Teeing Ground — See 25-1b/4.**

**Another Decision Relevant to Rule 25-2:**

**Pitch-Mark in Dropping Area Repaired Before Ball Dropped — See 13-2/10.**

### 25-3/1 Status of Half of Double Green Serving Hole Not Being Played

**Q.** One half of a U-shaped putting green serves as the 11th green and the other half serves as the 17th green. In play of the 17th hole, if a ball comes to rest on the part of the green serving the 11th hole, does Rule 25-3 (Wrong Putting Green) apply?

**A.** No, not unless the Committee divides the green by use of stakes or a line and declares one part to be the green of the 11th hole and the other part to be the green of the 17th hole. The Definition of "Putting Green" gives a Committee this right.

### 25-3/2 Player Makes Several Strokes on Wrong Putting Green

**Q.** In playing the 4th hole, a player plays his second shot onto the 7th green, believing it to be the 4th green. He marks the position of and lifts and cleans his ball. He then holes out in two putts on the 7th green before he is advised of his error. What is the ruling?

**A.** In equity (Rule 1-4), the player incurs no penalty under Rule 18-2a for lifting his ball in play without authority.

In match play, the player lost the hole when he made the first stroke on the wrong putting green — Rule 25-3.

In stroke play, Rule 25-3 does not contemplate a player making more than one stroke from the same wrong putting green. In equity (Rule 1-4), the player incurs a total penalty of two strokes under Rule 25-3. The two strokes made on the 7th green would count toward his score on the 4th hole.

When taking relief under Rule 25-3, the player would use the final location of the ball (in this case the hole on the 7th green) as the reference point for taking relief.

The same answer would apply to other areas on the course from which play is prohibited (e.g., ground under repair from which relief is mandatory or environmentally-sensitive areas).

#### Other Decisions Relating to Rule 25-3:

**Whether Player May Drop Ball Into Area from Which Play Prohibited — See 20-7/3.**

**Player Does Not Follow Recommended Procedure in Determining Nearest Point of Relief — See 24-2b/2.**

# Rule 26. Water Hazards (Including Lateral Water Hazards)

## Definitions
All defined terms are in *italics* and are listed alphabetically in the Definitions section — see pages 3-11.

### 26-1. Relief for Ball in Water Hazard
It is a question of fact whether a ball *lost* after having been struck toward a *water hazard* is lost inside or outside the *hazard*. In order to treat the ball as *lost* in the *hazard*, there must be reasonable evidence that the ball lodged in it. In the absence of such evidence, the ball must be treated as a *lost ball* and Rule 27 applies.

If a ball is in or is lost in a *water hazard* (whether the ball lies in water or not), the player may under penalty of one stroke:

a. Play a ball as nearly as possible at the spot from which the original ball was last played (see Rule 20-5); or

b. Drop a ball behind the *water hazard*, keeping the point at which the original ball last crossed the margin of the *water hazard* directly between the *hole* and the spot on which the ball is dropped, with no limit to how far behind the *water hazard* the ball may be dropped; or

c. As additional options available only if the ball last crossed the margin of a *lateral water hazard*, drop a ball outside the *water hazard* within two club-lengths of and not nearer the *hole* than (i) the point where the original ball last crossed the margin of the *water hazard* or (ii) a point on the opposite margin of the *water hazard* equidistant from the *hole*.

The ball may be lifted and cleaned when proceeding under this Rule.

(Prohibited actions when ball is in hazard — see Rule 13-4.)

(Ball moving in water in a water hazard — see Rule 14-6.)

### 26-2. Ball Played Within Water Hazard
#### a. Ball Comes to Rest in Same or Another Water Hazard
If a ball played from within a *water hazard* comes to rest in the same or another *water hazard* after the *stroke*, the player may:

(i) proceed under Rule 26-1a. If, after dropping in the *hazard*, the player elects not to play the dropped ball, he may:

(a) with reference to this *hazard*, proceed under Rule 26-1b, or if applicable Rule 26-1c, adding the additional penalty of one stroke prescribed by that Rule; or

(b) add an additional penalty of one stroke and play a ball as nearly as possible at the spot from which the last *stroke* from outside a *water hazard* was made (see Rule 20-5); or

(ii) proceed under Rule 26-1b, or if applicable Rule 26-1c; or

(iii) under penalty of one stroke, play a ball as nearly as possible at the spot from which the last *stroke* from outside a *water hazard* was made (see Rule 20-5).

**b. Ball Lost or Unplayable Outside Hazard or Out of Bounds**
If a ball played from within a *water hazard* is lost or declared unplayable outside the *hazard* or is *out of bounds*, the player may, after taking a penalty of one stroke under Rule 27-1 or 28a:

(i) play a ball as nearly as possible at the spot in the *hazard* from which the original ball was last played (see Rule 20-5); or

(ii) proceed under Rule 26-1b, or if applicable Rule 26-1c, adding the additional penalty of one stroke prescribed by the *Rule* and using as the reference point the point where the original ball last crossed the margin of the *hazard* before it came to rest in the *hazard*; or

(iii) add an additional penalty of one stroke and play a ball as nearly as possible at the spot from which the last *stroke* from outside the *hazard* was made (see Rule 20-5).

**Note 1:** When proceeding under Rule 26-2b, the player is not required to drop a ball under Rule 27-1 or 28a. If he does drop a ball, he is not required to play it. He may alternatively proceed under Rule 26-2b(ii) or (iii).

**Note 2:** If a ball played from within a *water hazard* is declared unplayable outside the *hazard*, nothing in Rule 26-2b precludes the player from proceeding under Rule 28b or c.

PENALTY FOR BREACH OF RULE:
Match play — Loss of hole; Stroke play — Two strokes.

## 26/1 When Ball Is in Water Hazard

**Q.** Is a ball in a water hazard when some part of the ball breaks the plane that extends vertically upward from the margin of the hazard even though the ball does not touch the ground or grass inside the hazard?

**A.** Yes, since the Definition of "Water Hazard" provides that "the margin of a water hazard extends vertically upwards."

### 26/2 Ball Within Natural Margin of Water Hazard But Outside Stakes Defining Margin

**Q.** Stakes defining the margin of a water hazard were improperly installed. As a result, an area which clearly was part of the water hazard was outside the stakes and, thus, technically was outside the hazard. A player's ball came to rest in water in this area. The player claimed that, in view of the alignment of the stakes, his ball was in casual water through the green. Was the claim valid?

**A.** No. The Committee erred in not properly defining the margin of the hazard as required by Rule 33-2a, but a player is not entitled to take advantage of such an error. Since it was clear that the place where the player's ball lay was within the natural boundaries of the water hazard, the claim should not be upheld.

### 26/3 Unmarked Water Hazard

**Q.** An unmarked ditch on the left of a hole is in bounds, but the left-hand margin is out of bounds. Accordingly, it is impossible to drop behind the water hazard under Rule 26-1b. A player's ball comes to rest in the ditch. Is the player restricted to playing the ball as it lies or proceeding under Rule 26-1a?

**A.** It is the responsibility of the Committee to define accurately the margins of water hazards and lateral water hazards — see Rule 33-2a. However, if the Committee has not done so, the ditch is, by definition, a lateral water hazard and the player should be permitted to proceed under Rule 26-1c(i).

### 26/3.5 Lateral Water Hazard Defined as Water Hazard

**Q.** A body of water which is both in front of and to the right of a putting green is so large that it is impossible to drop behind the water hazard as required by Rule 26-1b. May the Committee define the hazard or parts of the hazard as a water hazard even though it meets the Definition of a "Lateral Water Hazard"?

**A.** Yes — see Note 3 to the Definition of "Lateral Water Hazard." However, this should only be done when a Committee deems it necessary to preserve the integrity of the hole. In such cases the establishment of a Ball Drop or Dropping Zone as an additional option under the water hazard Rule (Rule 26-1) may be justified.

### 26/4 Man-Made Reservoir

**Q.** Is a man-made reservoir considered a water hazard?

**A.** Yes.

## 26/5 Unidentifiable Ball Played in Water Hazard and Lost

**Q.** A player's ball came to rest in a water hazard. He found a ball in the hazard but could not identify it. He played the ball into deep water within the hazard and the ball was lost. May the player assume that the ball he played in the hazard was not his ball, in which case the stroke played in the hazard would not count?

**A.** No. There was not reasonable evidence that the ball played was other than the player's ball. Lacking such evidence, he must count the stroke. The burden of proof is on the player.

## 26/6 Ball Assumed to Be in Water Hazard Found Outside Hazard After Another Ball Played Under Stroke-and-Distance Procedure

**Q.** A player assumes his original ball to be in a water hazard, although there was not reasonable evidence to that effect. Using the option in Rule 26-1a, he plays another ball at the spot from which the original ball was played. He then finds his original ball outside the hazard. What is the ruling?

**A.** The original ball is lost and the other ball is in play under penalty of stroke and distance — see Decision 27/17.

### Other Decisions relating to Rule 26:

Removal of Obstruction in Hazard Would Move Loose Impediment — See 1-4/5.

Player Who Told Opponent He Would Proceed Under Water Hazard Rule Changes Mind After Opponent Plays — See 9-2/13.

Flying Insect in Water Hazard — See 13-4/16.5.

Player Cleans Clubhead in Water Hazard When Ball Lies in Hazard — See 13-4/40.

Stone Broken Away from Retaining Wall in Water Hazard — See 24/6.

Overflow from Water Hazard — See 25/2.

Hole of Removed Stake Defining Water Hazard — See 25/18.

Player Unaware Ball in Water Hazard Takes Relief from Interference by Burrowing Animal Hole — See 25-1b/26.

Where to Place Lines or Stakes Defining Margin of Water Hazard — See 33-2a/4.

Pond Is Water Hazard from Back Tee and Lateral Water Hazard from Forward Tee — See 33-2a/6.

Deeming Body of Water as Both Water Hazard and Lateral Water Hazard — See 33-2a/7.

Treating Ocean and Beach as Through the Green — See 33-2a/8.

How to Mark Island Green — See 33-2a/10.

### 26-1/1 Meaning of "Reasonable Evidence" in Rule 26-1

The term "reasonable evidence" in Rule 26-1 is purposely and necessarily broad so as to permit sensible judgments to be reached on the basis of all the relevant circumstances of particular cases. As applied in this context, a player may not deem his ball lost in a water hazard simply because he thinks the ball may be in the hazard. The evidence must be preponderantly in favor of its being in the hazard. Otherwise, the ball must be considered lost outside the hazard and the player must proceed under Rule 27-1. Physical conditions in the area have a great deal to do with it. For example, if a water hazard is surrounded by a fairway on which a ball could hardly be lost, the existence of reasonable evidence that the ball is in the hazard would be more likely than if there was deep rough in the area. Observing a ball splash in a water hazard would not necessarily provide reasonable evidence as splashing balls sometimes skip out of hazards. It would depend on all the circumstances.

**Changing Relief Option When Re-Dropping Required — See 20-2c/5.**

### 26-1/1.5 Meaning of "Behind" in Rule 26-1

**Q.** With regard to the illustration above, a player makes a stroke from the tee and his ball comes to rest in the water hazard at Point A, having last crossed the margin of the hazard at Point B. The player wishes to proceed under Rule 26-1b, which requires that the player drop a ball behind the water hazard, keeping the point at which the original ball last crossed the margin of the water hazard directly between the hole and the spot on which the ball is dropped. May the player drop a ball on dotted line Y-Y?

**A.** Yes. The reference to "behind" in Rule 26-1b means that the ball must be dropped outside the hazard behind the point where the ball last crossed the margin of the water hazard. Therefore, the player may drop a ball on either dotted line X-X or dotted line Y-Y.

### 26-1/2 Player Proceeding Under Water Hazard Rule Drops Ball in Another Hazard

**Q.** A player's ball lies in a water hazard. In applying Rule 26-1b, the player drops a ball in a bunker or another water hazard. Is this permissible?

**A.** Yes.

**Ball Declared Unplayable Through the Green Dropped in Water Hazard; Player Elects Not to Play Ball and Wishes to Proceed Under the Water Hazard Rule — See 28/4.5.**

### 26-1/3 Ball Played Under Water Hazard Rule; Original Ball Then Found Outside Hazard

**Q.** A player believed his original ball came to rest in a water hazard. He searched for about a minute but did not find his ball. He therefore dropped another ball behind the hazard under Rule 26-1 and played it. He then found his original ball outside the hazard within five minutes of having begun to search for it. What is the ruling?

**A.** When the player dropped and played another ball behind the hazard, it became the ball in play and the original ball was lost.

If there was reasonable evidence that the original ball was in the water hazard, the player was entitled to invoke Rule 26-1. In the absence of reasonable evidence that the original ball was in the water hazard, the player was required to put another ball into play under Rule 27-1. In playing the ball dropped under Rule 26-1, the player played from a wrong place.

In match play, he incurred a penalty of loss of hole (Rule 20-7b).

In stroke play, he incurred the stroke-and-distance penalty prescribed by Rule 27-1 and an additional penalty of two strokes for a breach of that Rule. If the breach was a serious one, he was subject to disqualification unless he corrected the error as provided in Rule 20-7c.

### 26-1/3.5 Ball Dropped Under Water Hazard Rule with Reasonable Evidence; Original Ball Then Found

**Q.** A player's ball is struck towards a water hazard. There is reasonable evidence that the player's ball is in the water hazard and he drops a ball under Rule 26-1b. Before he plays the dropped ball, his original ball is found within the five-minute search period. What is the ruling?

**A.** The player had reasonable evidence that his ball was in the water hazard when he put the substituted ball into play and, therefore, that ball was correctly substituted and he may not play the original ball.

If the original ball was found in the water hazard and this discovery affects the reference point for proceeding under Rule 26-1b, resulting in the substituted ball having been dropped in a wrong place, the player must correct the error under Rule 20-6. The player must proceed in accordance with any of the applicable options under Rule 26-1 with respect to the correct reference point (see Decisions 20-6/2 and 26-1/16). Otherwise, Rule 20-6 does not apply and the player must continue play with the dropped ball. In either case, the player incurs a penalty of one stroke under Rule 26-1.

If the original ball was found outside the water hazard, the player must continue with the dropped ball under penalty of one stroke (Rule 26-1). (New)

**Substituting Ball When Re-Dropping — See 20-6/4.**

**Ball Dropped Under Rule 25-1c With Reasonable Evidence; Original Ball Then Found — See 25-1c/2.5.**

### *26-1/4 Ball Played Under Water Hazard Rule Without Reasonable Evidence Original Ball in Hazard; Original Ball Then Found in Hazard*

**Q.** A player's ball carried over a water hazard into some trees. It could not be determined whether the ball bounced back into the hazard or came to rest in the trees. Therefore, there was not reasonable evidence that the ball was in the hazard.

The player did not search for his original ball. He assumed that it was in the hazard, dropped a ball behind the hazard at a spot that conformed to Rule 26-1b and played that ball onto the green. As he was walking to the green, he found his original ball in the hazard. What is the ruling?

**A.** The first paragraph of Rule 26-1 states in part: "In order to treat the ball as lost in the hazard, there must be reasonable evidence that the ball lodged in it. In the absence of such evidence, the ball must be treated as a lost ball and Rule 27-1 applies." Therefore, the player was not entitled to assume that his original ball was in the hazard and the fact that it was subsequently found in the hazard is irrelevant. When the player dropped and played another ball behind the hazard, it became the ball in play and the original ball was lost. The player was required to proceed under Rule 27-1. In playing the ball dropped under Rule 26-1, he played from a wrong place.

In match play, he incurred a penalty of loss of hole (Rule 20-7b).

In stroke play, he incurred the stroke-and-distance penalty prescribed by Rule 27-1 and an additional penalty of two strokes for a breach of that Rule. If the breach was a serious one, he was subject to disqualification unless he corrected the error as provided in Rule 20-7c.

### 26-1/5  Ball Dropped and Played Under Water Hazard Rule; Original Ball Then Found in Hazard and Holed Out as Second Ball

**Q.** In stroke play, a competitor, unable to find his ball in a water hazard, drops another ball behind the hazard under Rule 26-1 and plays it. He then finds his original ball in the hazard. Not being sure of his rights, he holes out with both balls under Rule 3-3, opting to score with the original ball. What is the ruling?

**A.** When the competitor dropped and played the ball behind the hazard, that ball became the ball in play (see Definition of "Ball in Play"). The score with that ball was the competitor's score for the hole. The score with the original ball could not count because that ball was no longer the ball in play. However, the competitor incurs no penalty for holing out with the original ball.

### 26-1/6  Ball Played Back into Water Hazard from Putting Green Side of Hazard

**Q.** A player plays his second shot over a water hazard into a bunker behind the green. He skulls his third shot and the ball comes to rest in the water hazard. The ball is not playable. What are the player's options?

**A.** The player may, under penalty of one stroke:

(a) drop a ball behind the water hazard, keeping the point at which the original ball last crossed the hazard margin between the hole and the spot on which the ball is dropped — Rule 26-1b. This procedure would probably make it necessary for the player to return to the tee side of the hazard and play over the hazard again; or

(b) drop a ball in the bunker at the spot where his second shot came to rest — Rule 26-1a.

### 26-1/7  Ball Moved Out of Bounds by Flow of Water in Water Hazard

**Q.** The flow of water in a water hazard carries a ball out of bounds. May the player invoke Rule 26-1?

**A.** No. Since the ball lies out of bounds, the player must proceed under Rule 27-1. Water is not an outside agency — see Definition of "Outside Agency" — and thus the ball would not be replaced under Rule 18-1.

In a situation where it is likely that a ball will be carried out of bounds by the flow of water in a water hazard, it is suggested that a screen be installed to prevent such an occurrence.

### 26-1/8 Ball Moved into Bounds by Flow of Water in Lateral Water Hazard

**Q.** With regard to the illustration above, a player's ball lands in a river out of bounds at Point A and the flow of the water carries the ball into bounds to Point B. That part of the river which is in bounds is defined as a lateral water hazard. May the player invoke Rule 26-1?

**A.** Yes. The ball lies on the course in a lateral water hazard and it last crossed the margin of the hazard at Point C. Therefore, in taking relief in accordance with the Rule 26-1b or 26-1c, Point C is the reference point. As it is not possible to proceed under Rules 26-1b and 26-1c(i), it is likely that the player will proceed under Rule 26-1c(ii) by dropping a ball within two club-lengths of and not nearer the hole than Point D.

Alternatively, the player may proceed under Rule 26-1a or play the ball as it lies in the river.

### 26-1/9 Caddie Lifts Ball in Water Hazard Without Player's Authority

**Q.** A player's ball lying in a water hazard is lifted by the player's caddie without the player's authority. What is the ruling?

**A.** The player incurred a one-stroke penalty when his caddie lifted his ball — Rule 18-2a. The player may either replace the ball as required by Rule 18-2a or proceed under Rule 26-1 and incur an additional one-stroke penalty under that Rule.

### 26-1/10 Placing Ball on Bank of Water Hazard Instead of Dropping to Prevent Ball Rolling into Water

**Q.** A player's ball lies in a playable position on the bank of a water hazard. The player hits the ball out of bounds. If he proceeds under Rule 27-1 and drops a ball on the bank as nearly as possible at the spot from which the original ball was played, the ball will be likely to roll into deep water. May he place the ball in such circumstances, rather than drop it?

**A.** No. However, the player is not obliged to drop a ball within the hazard in accordance with Rule 27-1. He may take the penalty stroke provided in Rule 27-1 and then, under an additional penalty of one stroke, put a ball into play outside the hazard in accordance with either Rule 26-2b(ii) or 26-2b(iii).

**Ball Lost in Either Water Hazard or Casual Water Overflowing Hazard — See 1-4/7.**

**Players Inadvertently Exchange Balls Recovered from Water Hazard — See 15-1/4.**

**Ball Declared Unplayable in Water Hazard Is Dropped in Hazard and Played — See 20-7/2.**

**Casual Water Mistaken for Water Hazard; Original Ball Played Under Water Hazard Rule — See 25-1b/12.**

**Casual Water Mistaken for Water Hazard; Substituted Ball Played Under Water Hazard Rule — See 25-1b/13.**

### 26-1/11  Water Hazard Treated as Lateral Water Hazard

**Q.** In stroke play, a competitor played a stroke over a water hazard and the ball spun back into the hazard. The competitor, in error, treated the hazard as a lateral water hazard and dropped a ball under Rule 26-1c(i) within two club-lengths of where it crossed the hazard margin when it spun back into the hazard. He played the ball onto the green and then his procedure was questioned. What is the ruling?

**A.** The competitor incurred a penalty of one stroke under Rule 26-1. Furthermore, he was guilty of a serious breach of that Rule. He must, under an additional penalty of two strokes, rectify the error as provided in the second paragraph of Rule 20-7c or be disqualified.

### 26-1/12  Hazard Marked as Water Hazard Where Ball Last Crosses Margin and as Lateral Hazard Where Ball Comes to Rest

**Q.** A body of water is defined in part as a water hazard and in part as a lateral water hazard. A ball last crosses the hazard margin at a spot where it is marked as a water hazard but it comes to rest in that part of the hazard marked as a lateral water hazard. In addition to playing the ball as it lies, what are the player's options?

**A.** Since the ball last crossed the margin of the hazard where it is defined as a water hazard, the options in Rule 26-1c are not available. Thus, the player is limited to the options in Rules 26-1a and -1b.

### 26-1/13  Opposite Side of Lateral Water Hazard Defined as Water Hazard

**Q.** A player hit a ball into a lateral water hazard. The player wanted to drop within two club-lengths of a point on the opposite margin of the hazard equidistant from the hole, as permitted under Rule 26-1c. However, the opposite margin was marked as a water hazard. Was the player entitled to drop a ball within two club-lengths of the point in question on the opposite margin?

**A.** Yes. In such a case, relief is determined according to the status of the hazard at the point where the ball last crossed the hazard margin.

### 26-1/14 Clarification of "Opposite Margin" in Rule 26-1c(ii)

**Q.** Please clarify the words "opposite margin" in Rule 26-1c. With regard to the above illustration, "X1" indicates where a ball in the hazard last crossed the hazard margin. May the player drop a ball within two club-lengths of "Y1"? And, may a player whose ball last crossed the hazard margin at "X2" drop a ball within two club-lengths of "Y2," and so on?

**A.** With respect to "X1," "Y1" is "a point on the opposite margin of the water hazard equidistant from the hole." Accordingly, the player would be entitled to drop a ball within two club-lengths of "Y1."

The same applies in the cases of "X3" — "Y3" and "X4" — "Y4," but not in the case of "X2" — "Y2." A "point on the opposite margin" is a point across the hazard from "the point where the original ball last crossed the margin of the hazard." "Y2" is not across the hazard from "X2" because an imaginary straight line from "X2" to "Y2" crosses land outside the hazard.

### 26-1/15 Procedures for Relief from Lateral Water Hazard

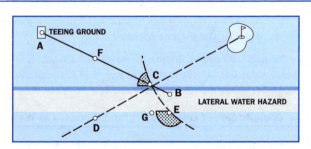

In the above illustration, a player has played a ball from the teeing ground (Point A) into the lateral water hazard at Point B. It last crossed the margin of the hazard at Point C. He may play the ball as it lies or, under penalty of one stroke:

(a) play another ball from the teeing ground — Rule 26-1a;

(b) drop a ball anywhere on the far side of the hazard on the dotted line from the hole through Point C, e.g., Point D — Rule 26-1b;

(c) drop a ball in the shaded area on the near side of the hazard which is all ground within two club-lengths of Point C, but not nearer the hole than Point C — Rule 26-1c(i); or

(d) drop a ball in the shaded area on the far side of the hazard which is all ground within two club-lengths of Point E, but not nearer the hole than Point E — Rule 26-1c(ii).

The player may not drop a ball on the so-called "line-of-flight" at Point F or anywhere else on the line the ball followed from A to B, except in the shaded area on the near side. Nor may he drop a ball within two club-lengths of Point G, the point on the far side of the hazard directly opposite Point C.

### 26-1/16 Point Where Ball Last Crossed Margin of Lateral Water Hazard Determined and Ball Dropped; Point Then Proves to Be Wrong Point

**Q.** In stroke play, A's ball goes into a lateral water hazard and is not found. A uses his best judgment in determining the point where the ball last crossed the hazard margin. B, A's marker and a fellow-competitor, agrees with that judgment and A drops a ball in accordance with Rule 26-1c, using the agreed point on the margin as the reference point. Before A plays his next stroke, C, another fellow-competitor, says that A's ball last crossed the hazard margin 20 yards beyond the point judged by A to be the point where the ball last crossed. A's ball is then found where C said it would be. What is the ruling?

**A.** When A dropped the ball under Rule 26-1, there was reasonable evidence that his original ball lay in the lateral water hazard. Therefore, Rule 26-1 was the applicable Rule and the player proceeded correctly in that he was permitted to put a ball into play under that Rule. However, as he dropped his ball in a wrong place, A must correct the error under Rule 20-6. He must proceed in accordance with any of the applicable options under Rule 26-1 with respect to the correct reference point (see Decision 20-6/2). A is precluded from playing the original ball from the hazard. (Revised)

**Substituting Ball When Re-Dropping — See 20-6/4**

### 26-1/17 Point Where Ball Last Crossed Margin of Lateral Water Hazard Determined and Ball Dropped and Played; Point Then Proves to Be Wrong Point

**Q.** In the circumstances described in Decision 26-1/16, what is the ruling if A, having dropped a ball in a wrong place, plays it before his error is discovered?

**A.** A must continue play with the ball played from a wrong place, without penalty. Applying a penalty under Rule 26-1 for playing from a wrong place (see Rule 20-7) is not appropriate. Otherwise, a competitor would risk incurring a penalty every time he makes an honest judgment as to the point where his ball last crosses a water hazard margin and that judgment subsequently proves incorrect.

### *26-1/18 Impossible to Drop Not Nearer Hole Than Point Where Ball Last Crossed Margin of Lateral Water Hazard*

**Q.** When a ball last crosses the margin of a lateral water hazard at the side of a putting green, it is sometimes impossible to drop a ball within two club-lengths of the point where the ball last crossed the hazard margin without dropping nearer the hole than that point. What is the procedure in such a case?

**A.** It is usually possible to drop a ball on the near side of a lateral water hazard and conform with Rule 26-1c(i) by dropping the ball close to the hazard margin. Where this is impossible, the player must proceed under one of the other options provided in Rule 26-1.

**Part of Lateral Water Hazard Where Impossible to Drop Not Nearer Hole; Procedure for Committee — See 33-2a/9.**

### *26-1/19 Permissible Dropping Area Under Lateral Water Hazard Rule So Narrow Player Has Difficulty Dropping Within It*

When a ball comes to rest in a lateral water hazard and relief is taken under Rule 26-1c, the ball must be dropped (1) outside the hazard and (2) not nearer the hole than the point where the ball last crossed the margin of the hazard (Point X). When the lateral water hazard is behind or to the side of the putting green, the permissible dropping area may be very narrow. If the ball, when dropped, first strikes a part of the course in the hazard or nearer the hole than Point X, the drop does not count for the purpose of determining when the ball must be placed under Rule 20-2c. The player must lift the ball and continue to drop it until the ball first strikes a part of the course within the permissible dropping area. Only if the ball has been dropped in the permissible dropping area twice and, each time, either rolls into the hazard or nearer the hole than Point X may it be placed as permitted by Rule 20-2c. If a ball is placed otherwise than as described, and is played, a breach of Rule 26-1c occurs.

Stakes and lines defining the margins of water hazards should be placed along the natural limits of the hazard. However, minor deviation to alleviate the dropping area problem would be appropriate. Alternatively, a Ball Drop (or Dropping Zone) should be established.

### 26-1/20 Allowing Drop Opposite Spot Where Ball Comes to Rest in Lateral Water Hazard

**Q.** A lateral water hazard is so situated that it is difficult to determine where a ball lying in the hazard last crossed the hazard margin. Would it be permissible to make a Local Rule to the effect that a player whose ball lies in this hazard may drop a ball, under penalty of one stroke, within two club-lengths of the point on the hazard margin opposite where the original ball came to rest in the hazard, instead of within two club-lengths of where the original ball last crossed the hazard margin, i.e., the Local Rule would modify Rule 26-1c?

**A.** No. Such modification of Rule 26-1c is not authorized. Moreover, the suggested Local Rule would be inoperable if the player's ball was lost in the hazard.

### 26-1/21 Example of Serious Breach of Lateral Water Hazard Rule

**Q.** In stroke play, A and B drive into a lateral water hazard. They determine where their original balls last crossed the hazard margin and elect to proceed under Rule 26-1c, taking a penalty of one stroke. A drops a ball slightly closer to the hole than the spot where his ball last crossed the hazard margin; B drops a ball 50 yards closer to the hole. A and B play their next strokes. What is the ruling?

**A.** A incurs an additional penalty of two strokes for a breach of Rule 26-1c and must play out the hole with the ball dropped in a wrong place and played — see Rule 20-7c.

B is guilty of a serious breach of Rule 26-1c. He incurs an additional penalty of two strokes and, before playing from the next teeing ground, he must drop another ball in accordance with Rule 26-1c and play out the hole; otherwise B is disqualified — see Rule 20-7c.

## 26-2/1 Explanation of Options Under Rules 26-2a and -2b

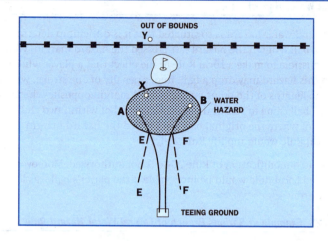

Regarding the above illustration, A and B play from the tee. A's ball comes to rest in the water hazard at Point A. B's ball comes to rest at Point B. Both A and B elect to play from the hazard. A fails to get out of the hazard. He plays to Point X, and his ball is not playable. B plays to Point Y, which is out of bounds.

Under penalty of one stroke, A may:

(a) drop a ball at Point A and play again from there, playing 4 (Rule 26-2a(i)); or

(b) drop a ball anywhere on dotted line E-E and play from there, playing 4 (Rule 26-2a(ii)); or

(c) play another ball from the tee, playing 4 (Rule 26-2a(iii)).

If A drops a ball at Point A and the ball comes to rest at a spot from which he judges he cannot play, he may, adding an additional penalty of one stroke, either drop a ball anywhere on the dotted line E-E or play another ball from the tee, playing 5.

B, after taking the penalty stroke prescribed in Rule 27-1, may drop a ball at Point B and play again from there, playing 4 (Rule 26-2b(i)).

Alternatively, B, after taking the penalty stroke prescribed in Rule 27-1, may drop a ball at Point B and elect not to play that ball or elect not to drop a ball at Point B. In either case, he shall then:

(a) under an additional penalty of one stroke, drop a ball anywhere on dotted line F-F and play from there, playing 5 (Rule 26-2b(ii)); or

(b) under an additional penalty of one stroke, play another ball from the tee, playing 5 (Rule 26-2b(iii)).

## 26-2/2 Ball Played from Within Hazard Comes to Rest in Same Hazard After Exiting Hazard

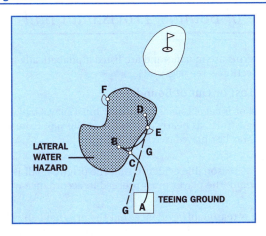

**Q.** In the above illustration, a player has played a ball from Point A (the teeing ground) into the lateral water hazard at Point B. The ball last crossed the margin of the hazard at Point C. The player elects to play the ball from the hazard and he succeeds in getting his ball out of the hazard, but it re-enters the hazard at point E. The ball comes to rest at Point D and it is not playable. What are the player's options?

**A.** The player may under penalty of one stroke:

(a) drop a ball at Point B and play again from there, playing 4 (Rule 26-2a(i)); or

(b) drop a ball anywhere on dotted line G-G and play from there, playing 4 (Rule 26-2a(ii)); or

(c) drop a ball within two club-lengths of and not nearer the hole than Point E, playing 4 (Rule 26-2a(ii)); or

(d) drop a ball within two club-lengths of and not nearer the hole than Point F, playing 4 (Rule 26-2a(ii)); or

(e) play another ball from Point A (the teeing ground), playing 4 (Rule 26-2a(iii)).

Point E is the reference point for proceeding under Rule 26-1b or 26-1c as it is the point where the original ball last crossed the margin of the water hazard.

If the player drops a ball at Point B and the ball comes to rest at a spot from which he judges he cannot play, he may, adding an additional penalty of one stroke, either drop a ball anywhere on the dotted line G-G, drop a ball within two club-lengths of and not nearer the hole than Points E or F, or play another ball from Point A (the teeing ground), playing 5.

**Stroke Played from Environmentally-Sensitive Area Defined as Water Hazard — See 33-8/43.**

# Rule 27. Ball Lost or Out of Bounds; Provisional Ball

**Definitions**
All defined terms are in *italics* and are listed alphabetically in the Definitions section — see pages 3-11.

### 27-1. Ball Lost or Out of Bounds

If a ball is *lost* or is *out of bounds*, the player must play a ball, under penalty of one stroke, as nearly as possible at the spot from which the original ball was last played (see Rule 20-5).

**Exceptions:**
1. If there is reasonable evidence that the original ball is *lost* in a *water hazard*, the player must proceed in accordance with Rule 26-1.
2. If there is reasonable evidence that the original ball is *lost* in an *obstruction* (Rule 24-3) or an *abnormal ground condition* (Rule 25-1c) the player may proceed under the applicable *Rule*.

PENALTY FOR BREACH OF RULE 27-1:
Match play — Loss of hole; Stroke play — Two strokes.

### 27-2. Provisional Ball

#### a. Procedure

If a ball may be *lost* outside a *water hazard* or may be *out of bounds*, to save time the player may play another ball provisionally in accordance with Rule 27-1. The player must inform his opponent in match play or his *marker* or a *fellow-competitor* in stroke play that he intends to play a *provisional ball*, and he must play it before he or his *partner* goes forward to search for the original ball.

If he fails to do so and plays another ball, that ball is not a *provisional ball* and becomes the *ball in play* under penalty of stroke and distance (Rule 27-1); the original ball is *lost*.

(Order of play from teeing ground — see Rule 10-3.)

**Note:** If a *provisional ball* played under Rule 27-2a might be *lost* outside a *water hazard* or *out of bounds,* the player may play another *provisional ball*. If another *provisional ball* is played, it bears the same relationship to the previous *provisional ball* as the first *provisional ball* bears to the original.

#### b. When Provisional Ball Becomes Ball in Play

The player may play a *provisional ball* until he reaches the place where the original ball is likely to be. If he makes a *stroke* with the *provisional ball* from the place where the original ball is likely to be or from a point nearer the *hole* than that place, the original ball is *lost* and the *provisional ball* becomes the *ball in play* under penalty of stroke and distance (Rule 27-1).

If the original ball is *lost* outside a *water hazard* or is *out of bounds*, the *provisional ball* becomes the *ball in play*, under penalty of stroke and distance (Rule 27-1).

If there is reasonable evidence that the original ball is *lost* in a *water hazard*, the player must proceed in accordance with Rule 26-1.

**Exception:** If there is reasonable evidence that the original ball is *lost* in an *obstruction* (Rule 24-3) or an *abnormal ground condition* (Rule 25-1c) the player may proceed under the applicable *Rule*.

### c. When Provisional Ball to Be Abandoned

If the original ball is neither *lost* nor *out of bounds*, the player must abandon the *provisional ball* and continue playing the original ball. If he makes any further *strokes* at the *provisional ball* he is playing a *wrong ball* and the provisions of Rule 15 apply.

**Note:** If a player plays a *provisional ball* under Rule 27-2a, the *strokes* made after this Rule has been invoked with a *provisional ball* abandoned under Rule 27-2c and *penalty strokes* incurred solely by playing that ball are disregarded.

## *27/1 Player Directs Caddie Not to Search for His Ball Until Others Can Assist*

**Q.** A hits a long drive into heavy rough. B hits a short drive into heavy rough. A's caddie starts walking towards the area where A's ball may be to search for A's ball. Everyone else, including A, walks towards the area where B's ball may be to look for B's ball. A directs his caddie also to look for B's ball and delay search for his (A's) ball until everyone else can assist. Is such procedure permitted?

**A.** Yes.

## *27/1.5 Time Permitted for Search for Lost Ball If Play Suspended During Search*

**Q.** A player has been searching for his ball for three minutes when play is suspended. How much time is he allowed for further search?

**A.** The player may continue searching for two more minutes. The suspension of play has no effect on the five-minute search period. Thus, even if the player searches for his ball during the suspension of play, he is still only permitted a total of five minutes to search for his ball.

## *27/2 Time Permitted for Search for Lost Ball After Wrong Ball Played*

**Q.** In stroke play, a competitor searches for his ball for three minutes, finds a ball, plays it and then discovers he has played a wrong ball. He returns to the area from which the wrong ball was played and resumes search for his ball. How much time is he allowed for further search — two minutes or five minutes?

**A.** Two minutes — see Definition of "Lost Ball."

### 27/3 Time Permitted for Search When Lost Ball Found and Then Lost Again

**Q.** A player finds his ball in high rough after a two-minute search, leaves the area to get a club and, when he returns, is unable to find the ball. Is he allowed three minutes or five minutes to find his ball?

**A.** Three minutes.

### 27/4 Time Permitted for Search for Original Ball and Provisional Ball

**Q.** Is a player allowed five minutes to search for his original ball and five more minutes to search for his provisional ball, or just a total of five minutes?

**A.** If the two balls are so close together that, in effect, both balls would be searched for simultaneously, a total of five minutes for search is allowed. Otherwise, the player is allowed to search five minutes for each ball.

### 27/5 Player Searching for Ball Mistakes His Ball for Opponent's

**Q.** In a match, A begins to search for his ball and after two minutes finds a ball which he believes to be his opponent's ball and resumes his search. The five-minute search period elapses and thereafter it is discovered that the ball which he found and believed to be his opponent's was in fact his ball. What is the ruling?

**A.** Once a ball has been found a player has an opportunity to identify it as his. In this case, the player had every opportunity to identify the ball as his within the five-minute search period and failed to do so. Therefore, the ball is, by definition, "lost."

### 27/5.5 Original Ball Found Within Five-Minute Search Period Not Identified Until After Period Has Elapsed

**Q.** A player plays a second shot, searches for his ball for just over four minutes and then starts to walk back down the fairway to play another ball under Rule 27-1. A ball is then found within the five-minute search period, but as the player is now a considerable distance away, he is unable to identify the ball as his before the search period has elapsed. What is the ruling?

**A.** As a ball was found within five minutes of beginning search, the player is allowed enough time to reach the area in order to identify it. If the player identifies the ball as his, it is not a "lost ball" even though the identification takes place after the five-minute search period has elapsed.

## 27/6 Player Unable to Find His Ball Because Another Player Played It

**Q.** A and B hit their tee shots into the same general area. A found a ball and played it. B went forward to look for his ball and could not find it. After a few minutes, B started back to the tee to put another ball into play. On the way, he found A's ball and knew then that A had played his (B's) ball in error. What is the ruling?

**A.** In match play, A lost the hole (Rule 15-3a).

In stroke play, A incurred a penalty of two strokes for playing a wrong ball and must then play his own ball (Rule 15-3b). A's ball was not lost even if A and B had been searching for more than five minutes because A had not "begun to search for it (his ball)"; the searching had been for B's ball — see Definition of "Lost Ball."

On the other hand, B began to search for his ball as soon as he went forward to look for it. If less than five minutes had elapsed before B found A's ball, B should have placed a ball on the spot from which A had wrongly played his (B's) ball and continued play, without penalty — see last paragraph of Rule 15-3. However, if five minutes had expired, B's original ball was lost and he was obliged to put another ball into play under penalty of stroke and distance (Rule 27-1).

## 27/7 Ball Found in Burrowing Animal Hole After Five-Minute Search

**Q.** A player's tee shot comes to rest in an area containing heavy rough and a large burrowing animal hole. After a search of five minutes, the players in the group determine that there is not reasonable evidence that the ball is lost in the burrowing animal hole. The player returns to the tee to put another ball into play under Rule 27-1. As the player is returning to the tee, the ball is found in the burrowing animal hole. May the player now proceed under Rule 25-1 on the basis that reasonable evidence did exist?

**A.** No. When five minutes elapsed and there was not reasonable evidence that the ball was lost in the burrowing animal hole, the ball was lost and Rule 27-1 was applicable.

**Ball Lost in Underground Drainpipe — See 24-3b/1.**

## 27/8 Ball Found After Search Exceeding Five Minutes Is Then Played

**Q.** A player searches for his ball for five minutes and does not find it. He continues to search, finds the ball and plays it. What is the ruling?

**A.** The ball was lost and therefore out of play when the five-minute period allowed for search expired — see Definitions of "Ball in Play" and "Lost Ball." When the player played a stroke with a ball out of play, he played a wrong ball — see Definition of "Wrong Ball" — and incurred a penalty of loss of hole in match play or two strokes in stroke play — Rule 15-3. In stroke play, he was disqualified if he did not correct the error by proceeding under Rule 27-1 before playing from the next tee — Rule 15-3b.

### 27/9 Player Searches for Lost Ball After Putting Another Ball into Play

**Q.** According to Rule 27, if a player hits his tee shot into the woods and tees up and plays another ball without announcing it as a provisional ball, the second ball becomes the ball in play and the original ball is lost. In such a case, is the player precluded from searching for his original ball?

**A.** No. But the player may not play the ball if he finds it and must not unduly delay play.

### 27/10 Player Unable to Distinguish His Ball from Another Ball

**Q.** A and B hit their tee shots into the same area. Both balls were found but, because A and B were playing identical balls and neither had put an identification mark on his ball, they could not determine which ball was A's and which was B's. What is the ruling?

**A.** Since neither player could identify a ball as his ball, both balls were lost — see Definition of "Lost Ball."

This incident underlines the advisability of the player putting an identification mark on his ball — see Rules 6-5 and 12-2.

### 27/11 Provisional Ball Not Distinguishable from Original Ball

A player entitled to play a provisional ball from the tee plays it into the same area as his original ball. The balls have identical markings and the player cannot distinguish between them. Following are various situations and the solutions, which are based on equity (Rule 1-4), when the above circumstances exist:

Situation 1: One ball is found in a water hazard and the other ball is not found.

Solution 1: The ball which was found must be presumed to be the provisional ball.

Situation 2: Both balls are found in a water hazard.

Solution 2: The player must return to the tee and play another ball; he would be playing 3.

Situation 3: One ball is found in a water hazard and one ball is found in the rough.

Solution 3: The player must return to the tee and play another ball; he would be playing 3.

Situation 4: One ball is found in bounds and the other ball is lost or found out of bounds.

Solution 4: The ball in bounds must be presumed to be the provisional ball.

Situation 5: Both balls are found in bounds and (1) both balls are playable, (2) one ball is playable and the other unplayable or (3) both balls are unplayable.

Solution 5: One could argue that both balls are lost. It would be inequitable to require the player to return to the tee, playing 5, when the player has found both balls but does not know which is the original and which the provisional. Accordingly, the player must select one of the balls, treat it as his provisional and abandon the other.

## 27/12 Identification of Ball Through Testimony of Spectator

**Q.** A's ball and B's ball came to rest close together. Neither A nor B could identify one of the balls as his ball because they were using balls with identical markings. A spectator who saw both shots land was able to state which ball belonged to A and which one belonged to B. May his testimony be accepted, or should both balls be deemed lost because they could not be identified by A and B?

**A.** If the Committee determined that, based on information given by the spectator, A and B were able to identify their balls, the balls should not be deemed lost. Otherwise, they would have to proceed under Rule 27-1.

## 27/13 Refusal to Identify Ball

**Q.** A player purposely refuses to identify a ball as his. What can the opponent or a fellow-competitor do in such a case?

**A.** An opponent or fellow-competitor has the right to be satisfied about the identification of a player's ball.

If a player has dishonestly not identified his ball, the opponent or fellow-competitor may refer the dispute to the Committee — Rule 34-3. In such a case, the Committee would be justified in imposing a penalty of disqualification under Rule 33-7.

**Identifying Ball by Brand and Number Only — See 12-2/1.**

### 27/14 Ball in Tree Identified But Not Retrieved

**Q.** A player's ball is lodged high in a tree. He identifies it with the aid of binoculars but is unable to retrieve it. Is the ball lost, in which case the player must invoke Rule 27-1?

**A.** No. Since the ball was identified, it was not lost — see Definition of "Lost Ball." The player may invoke the unplayable ball Rule (Rule 28).

### 27/15 Ball in Tree Visible But Not Identifiable

**Q.** A player is certain that his ball is lodged high in a tree. He can see a ball in the tree, but he cannot identify it as his ball. Is the player's ball lost, in which case he must proceed under Rule 27-1?

**A.** Yes.

### 27/16 Ball Declared Lost Is Found Before Another Ball Put into Play

**Q.** A player searched for his ball for two minutes, declared it lost and started back to play another ball at the spot from which the original ball was played. Before he put another ball into play, his original ball was found within the five-minute period allowed for search. What is the ruling?

**A.** A player cannot render a ball lost by a declaration — see Definition of "Lost Ball." The original ball remained in play — see Definition of "Ball in Play."

**Searching Ten Minutes for Lost Ball — See 6-7/2.**

### 27/17 Status of Original Ball if Another Ball Played Under Stroke-and-Distance Procedure

In general, if a player, after making a stroke, plays a ball under a stroke-and-distance procedure, the original ball is lost and the ball played under penalty of stroke and distance is the ball in play.

Such a position is supported by:

- (a) the Definition of "Ball in Play," which provides that a ball substituted for the ball in play becomes the ball in play, whether or not the substitution is permitted;

- (b) the Definition of "Lost Ball," which provides that a ball is lost if the player makes a stroke at a substituted ball, e.g., plays another ball under a stroke-and-distance procedure; and

- (c) Rule 27-2a, which provides: "The player must inform his opponent in match play or his marker or a fellow-competitor in stroke play that he intends to play a provisional ball, and he must play it before he or his partner goes forward to search for the original ball. If he fails to do so and plays another ball, that ball is not a provisional ball and becomes the ball in play under penalty of stroke and distance (Rule 27-1); the original ball is lost."

**Original Ball Found and Played After Another Ball Put into Play — See 15/5.**

## *27/18 Gate in Boundary Fence*

**Q.** A gate in a boundary fence swings onto the course. Sometimes the gate is open and sometimes it is closed. If the gate is open, may a player close it if it interferes with his swing?

**A.** A gate in a boundary fence, when closed, is part of the boundary fence, is not an obstruction (see Definition of "Obstructions") and may not be moved.

A gate in a boundary fence, if open, is not covered by the Rules. In equity (Rule 1-4), a player who finds a gate in a boundary fence open may leave it as he finds it or close it, but he must not move it to any other position.

**Removal of Boundary Stake Interfering with Swing — See 13-2/17.**

**Improving Position of Ball by Bending Boundary Fence — See 13-2/18.**

**Improving Area of Intended Swing by Moving Growing or Fixed Object Situated Out of Bounds — See 13-2/19.**

**Part of Fence Off Course Leans Across Boundary and Interferes with Swing — See 13-2/20.**

**Player Removes Boundary Post on Line of Play But Replaces It Before Playing — See 13-2/25.**

**Stroke Played with Ball Lying Out of Bounds — See 15/6.**

**Ball Lifted and Dropped Away from Boundary Stake Under Obstruction Rule — See 18-2a/3.**

## *27/19 When Ball Inside Boundary Fence Is Out of Bounds*

**Q.** In view of the Definition of "Out of Bounds," is it correct to say that, if the posts of a boundary fence are on the golf course side of the fence, the diameter of the posts is greater than the diameter of a golf ball and the fence is straight, a ball lying against the inside of the fence would be out of bounds?

**A.** Yes.

**Stile Attached to Boundary Fence — See 24/1.**

**Angled Supports or Guy Wires Supporting Boundary Fence — See 24/2.**

**Concrete Bases of Boundary Fence Posts — See 24/3.**

**Part of Boundary Fence Within Boundary Line — See 24/4.**

**Ball Moved Out of Bounds by Flow of Water in Water Hazard — See 26-1/7.**

**Ball Moved into Bounds by Flow of Water in Water Hazard — See 26-1/8.**

**Exposed Water Pipe Adjacent and Parallel to Boundary Fence — See 33-2a/1.**

### 27/20 Public Road Defined as Out of Bounds Divides Course; Status of Ball Crossing Road

**Q.** A public road defined as out of bounds divides a course. A ball crosses the road and comes to rest on the part of the course on the other side of the road. Is the ball out of bounds?

**A.** No. Since the ball lies on the course, it is in bounds unless a Local Rule provides otherwise. However, because it is unfair that a ball on the road is out of bounds and a ball beyond it is in bounds, it is suggested that the following Local Rule should be adopted:

"A ball which crosses a public road defined as out of bounds and comes to rest beyond that road is out of bounds, even though it may lie on another part of the course."

**Boundary Stakes Having No Significance in Play of Hole Being Played — See 24/5.**

**Tee Decreed to Be in Bounds for Tee Shot and Out of Bounds Thereafter — See 33-2a/13.**

**Internal Out of Bounds Applying to Stroke from Teeing Ground Only — See 33-2a/14.**

**Establishing Boundary Line Inside Fence on Property Line — See 33-2a/15.**

**Deeming Ball in Bounds Until Beyond Boundary Wall — See 33-2a/16.**

**Boundary Altered by Unauthorized Removal of Boundary Stake — See 33-2a/19.**

**Displaced Boundary Stake — See 33-2a/20.**

### 27-1/1 Original Ball Found Within Five-Minute Search Period After Another Ball Teed

**Q.** A player plays from the teeing ground, searches briefly for his ball and then goes back and tees another ball. Before he plays the teed ball, and within the five-minute search period, the original ball is found. May the player abandon the teed ball and play the original ball?

**A.** Yes. The teed ball was not in play since the player had not yet made a stroke at it (see Definition of "Ball in Play") and the original ball was not lost (see Definition of "Lost Ball").

### 27-1/2 Original Ball Found Within Five-Minute Search Period After Another Ball Dropped

**Q.** A player plays his second shot, searches for his ball briefly and then goes back and drops another ball under Rule 27-1. Before he plays the dropped ball, and within the five-minute search period, the original ball is found. Is the player required to continue with the dropped ball?

**A.** Yes. When the player put the substituted ball into play at the spot of the previous stroke with the intent to play a ball under Rule 27-1, he proceeded under an applicable Rule. Therefore, Rule 20-6 does not apply, and he must continue with the substituted ball. (Revised)

## 27-1/2.3 Original Ball Found Within Five-Minute Search Period After Another Ball Dropped; Original Ball Played

**Q.** In Decision 27-1/2, the player was required to proceed with the dropped ball. What would be the ruling if the player continues play with the original ball?

**A.** As the original ball is no longer the player's ball in play, it is a wrong ball, and the provisions of Rule 15-3 apply. (Revised)

**Original Ball Found and Played After Another Ball Put into Play — See 15/5.**

**Ball Believed to Be Original Found; Player Wishes to Ignore It and Continue Play with Provisional Ball — See 27-2c/2.**

## 27-1/2.5 Lost Ball Treated as Moved by Outside Agency in Absence of Reasonable Evidence to That Effect

**Q.** A player who is unable to find his ball treats it as moved by an outside agency, rather than lost, although there is no reasonable evidence to that effect. Accordingly, he drops a ball where he thinks his original ball came to rest (Rule 18-1) and plays it, rather than taking a stroke-and-distance penalty for relief for a lost ball (Rule 27-1). What is the ruling?

**A.** In the absence of reasonable evidence that the ball had been moved by an outside agency, the player was required to put another ball into play under Rule 27-1. In playing the ball dropped under Rule 18-1, the player played from a wrong place.

In match play, he incurred a penalty of loss of hole (Rule 20-7b).

In stroke play, he incurred the stroke-and-distance penalty prescribed by Rule 27-1 and an additional penalty of two strokes for a breach of that Rule. Because the breach was a serious one, he was subject to disqualification unless he corrected the error as provided in the second paragraph of Rule 20-7c.

**Original Ball Found and Played After Another Ball Put into Play — See 15/5.**

**Ball Believed to Be Lost in Bunker; Competitor Drops Another Ball in Bunker and Plays It; Original Ball Then Found Outside Bunker — See 20-7c/3.**

**Ball Lost in Tree in Ground Under Repair — See 25/10.**

## 27-1/3 Ball Dropped in Area Where Original Ball Lost; Ball Then Played

**Q.** A player, unable to find his ball, drops another ball in the area where his original ball was lost and plays that ball. What is the ruling?

**A.** In match play, the player loses the hole — Rule 20-7b.

In stroke play, the player incurs the stroke-and-distance penalty prescribed by Rule 27-1 and an additional penalty of two strokes for a breach of that Rule. If the breach was a serious one, he must rectify the error as provided in the second paragraph of Rule 20-7c; otherwise, he is disqualified.

**Other Decisions relating to Rule 27-1:**

**Ball Played from Outside Teeing Ground Goes Out of Bounds — See 11-4b/6.**

**Stroke Played with Ball Lying Out of Bounds — See 15/6.**

**Ball Thrown into Bounds by Outside Agency and Played; Caddie Aware of Action of Outside Agency — See 15/9.**

**Ball Thrown into Bounds by Outside Agency and Played; Neither Player Nor His Caddie Aware of Action of Outside Agency — See 15/10.**

**Ball Wrongly Thought to Be Out of Bounds Lifted; Competitor Proceeds Under Rule 27-1 — See 18-2a/11.**

**Ball Moved Accidentally by Backward Movement of Club After Stroke Misses; Ball Comes to Rest Out of Bounds — See 18-2a/22.**

**Ball Moves After Address and Comes to Rest Out of Bounds — See 18-2b/9.**

**Opponent's Caddie Lifts Player's Ball Which May or May Not Have Been Out of Bounds — See 18-3b/5.**

**Player's Ball Strikes Own Caddie and Comes to Rest Out of Bounds — See 19-2/2.**

**Player's Ball Strikes Own Caddie Standing Out of Bounds and Comes to Rest on Course — See 19-2/3.**

**Player's Ball Strikes Own Caddie Standing Out of Bounds and Comes to Rest Out of Bounds — See 19-2/4.**

**Ball Strikes Opponent Standing Out of Bounds and Comes to Rest Out of Bounds — See 19-3/1.**

**Dropped Ball Comes to Rest and Then Rolls Out of Bounds — See 20-2c/3.5.**

**Teed Ball Missed Then Hit Out of Bounds — See 20-5/1.**

**Player Proceeding Under Rule 20-5 Drops Ball on Different Part of Course — See 20-5/2**

**Ball Played from Spot Where Original Ball Deflected Out of Bounds by Maintenance Vehicle — See 20-7/1.**

**Ball Enters Burrowing Animal Hole Out of Bounds and Comes to Rest in Bounds — See 25-1b/23.**

**Ball Enters Burrowing Animal Hole in Bounds and Comes to Rest Out of Bounds — See 25-1b/24.**

**Ball Played in Ground Under Repair Area Lost in Same Area — See 25-1c/3.**

**Tee Shot Out of Bounds in Mixed Foursome in Which Different Tees Used by Men and Women — See 29/2.**

### 27-2/1  Provisional Ball Serving as Ball in Play If Original Ball Unplayable or in Water Hazard

**Q.** May a player announce that a second ball he is going to play is both (a) a provisional ball in case the original ball is lost outside a water hazard or out of bounds and (b) the ball in play in case the original ball is unplayable or in a water hazard?

**A.** No.

### 27-2/2  Member of Committee Finds Player's Original Ball; Player Prefers to Continue with Provisional Ball

**Q.** Is a member of the Committee or a forecaddie obliged to inform a player that his original ball has been found, even if it is clear that the player does not plan to search for it because he would prefer to continue play with the provisional ball he has played?

**A.** Yes.

#### Other Decisions relating to Rule 27-2:

Provisional Ball Used as Second Ball When Not Determinable Whether Original Ball Is Out of Bounds — See 3-3/1.

Condition Requiring Use of Ball on List of Conforming Golf Balls; Ball Not on List Played as Provisional Ball — See 5-1/3.

Order of Play for Provisional Ball Other Than from Teeing Ground — See 10/4

Wrong Ball Played in Belief It Is Provisional Ball — See 15/7.

Provisional Ball Moves After Being Addressed — See 15/7.

Original Ball Struck by Provisional Ball — See 18-5/2.

Provisional Ball Struck by Original Ball — See 19-5/5.

Who Plays Provisional Ball in Foursome — See 29-1/3.

Provisional Ball Played by Wrong Member of Side in Foursome — See 29-1/4.

### 27-2a/1  Announcement of Provisional Ball

**Q.** A player hits his ball into an area where it may be lost outside a water hazard or out of bounds. The player then drops another ball and plays it. The player intends the dropped ball to be a provisional ball, but he does not inform his opponent, marker or fellow-competitor that he is "playing a provisional ball." In such a situation, can a player's actions constitute announcement that he is playing a provisional ball?

**A.** No. Rule 27-2a specifically provides that the player must inform his opponent, marker or fellow-competitor that he intends to play a provisional ball.

The player's statement must specifically mention the words "provisional ball" or must make it clear that he is proceeding under Rule 27-2a. Therefore, a player who says nothing has put another ball into play.

The following are examples of statements that do not satisfy the requirement of announcing a provisional ball:

(a) "That might be lost. I am going to re-load."

(b) "That might be out of here."

(c) "I'd better hit another one."

(d) "I will never find that one. I'll play another."

### 27-2a/1.5 Meaning of "Goes Forward to Search"

**Q.** With respect to Rule 27-2a, when has a player gone forward to search for the original ball such that a provisional ball cannot be played?

**A.** The sole purpose of Rule 27-2 is to enable the player to save time. The only way he can effectively do so is to play the provisional ball before going forward for the purpose of searching for the original ball. However, this provision should not be so narrowly interpreted to preclude a player from playing a provisional ball even though he has proceeded from where he last played in the direction of the original ball, e.g., in retrieving a ball or a different club to play the provisional ball. The Committee must consider all of the relevant facts in determining if the player did in fact go forward to search for the original ball.

### 27-2a/2 Provisional Ball Played Solely in Belief Original Ball Might Be in Water Hazard

**Q.** A player's tee shot might be in a water hazard, but clearly it is not lost outside a water hazard or out of bounds. The player announces that, since his ball might be in the hazard, he is going to play a provisional ball and he does so. Rule 27-2a seems to prohibit a provisional ball in the circumstances. What is the ruling?

**A.** The player did not play a provisional ball which, according to the Definition of "Provisional Ball," is a ball played under Rule 27-2 for a ball which may be lost outside a water hazard or may be out of bounds. The second ball from the tee was in play since it was not a provisional ball.

### 27-2a/2.5 Player Plays Provisional Ball in Belief Original Might Be Lost Outside Water Hazard Then Discovers There Is No Possibility of Its Being Lost Outside Water Hazard

**Q.** A player's tee shot is struck towards an area of trees, bushes and tall grass. Believing his ball might be lost outside a water hazard, the player announces his intention to play a provisional ball and plays a ball from the tee. When he arrives at the area, he finds that the area in question is wetlands that has been defined as a lateral water hazard and that there is reasonable evidence that his ball is lost in it. What is the ruling?

**A.** As the player played the second ball from the tee in the belief that his original ball might be lost outside a water hazard, that ball was a provisional ball. The subsequent discovery that the area in question is in fact a lateral water hazard is irrelevant. Therefore, the player must abandon the provisional ball and proceed under Rule 26-1 — see Rule 27-2c.

### *27-2a/3  Play of Provisional Ball in Absence of Reasonable Possibility Original Ball Is Lost or Out of Bounds*

**Q.** In the absence of reasonable possibility that a ball is lost outside a water hazard or is out of bounds, may the player play a provisional ball?

**A.** No. If a player plays a ball under such circumstances, the ball is not a provisional ball but the ball in play — see Decision 27-2a/2.

### *27-2a/4  Three Balls Played from Same Spot; Only Second Ball Was Provisional Ball*

**Q.** A player, believing his tee shot might be lost or out of bounds, plays a provisional ball. His provisional ball is struck in the same direction as the original ball and, without any announcement, he plays another ball from the tee. This ball comes to rest on the fairway. What is the ruling?

**A.** If the original ball is not lost or out of bounds, the player must continue play with that ball without penalty.

If the original ball is lost or out of bounds, the player must continue play with the third ball played from the tee as, when this ball was played without any announcement, it rendered the provisional ball lost, regardless of the provisional ball's location. The player would lie 5 with the third ball played from the tee.

In both situations, the third ball bears a relationship only to the previous ball played, i.e. the provisional ball. (New)

### *27-2b/1  Continuation of Play with Provisional Ball Without Searching for Original Ball*

**Q.** At a par-3 hole, a player hits his tee shot into dense woods. He then hits a provisional ball which comes to rest near the hole. In view of the position of the provisional ball, the player does not wish to find his original ball. He does not search for it and walks directly towards his provisional ball to continue play with it. His opponent (or fellow-competitor) believes it would be beneficial to him if the original ball were found. May the opponent (or fellow-competitor) search for the player's ball?

**A.** Yes. In equity (Rule 1-4) he may search for five minutes provided that in the meantime the player does not play a stroke with the provisional ball, it being nearer the hole than the place where the original ball is likely to be. The player is entitled to play such a stroke. If he does, the original ball is then lost under Rule 27-2b and further search for it would serve no purpose. In match play, if the player so proceeds and his provisional ball is closer to the hole than his opponent's ball, his opponent may recall the stroke (Rule 10-1c). However, recalling the stroke would not change the status of the original ball, which was lost when the provisional ball was played out of turn. See also Decision 27-2c/2.

### 27-2b/2  When Provisional Ball Holed Becomes Ball in Play

**Q.** At a short hole, A's tee shot may be out of bounds or lost, so he plays a provisional ball, which he holes. A does not wish to look for his original ball. B, A's opponent or a fellow-competitor, goes to look for the original ball. When does the provisional ball become the ball in play?

**A.** In equity (Rule 1-4) the provisional ball becomes the ball in play as soon as A picks it out of the hole, provided his original ball has not already been found in bounds within five minutes of B starting to search for it.

### 27-2b/3  Original Ball Is Beyond Provisional Ball; Player Searches Briefly for Original Ball, Plays Provisional Ball and Then Finds Original Ball

**Q.** A player's provisional ball comes to rest short of where the original ball is likely to be. After a two-minute search for the original ball, the player goes back, plays a second stroke with the provisional ball and then his original ball is found within the five-minute time limit. What is the ruling?

**A.** The player must continue play with the original ball. Play of a provisional ball does not render the original ball lost until it has been played from the place where the original ball is likely to be or from a point nearer the hole than that place — Rule 27-2b.

### 27-2b/4  Provisional Ball Played from Beyond Where Original Ball Likely to Be But Not Beyond Where Original Ball Found

**Q.** A player, believing his tee shot might be lost or in a road defined as out of bounds, played a provisional ball. He searched for his original ball but did not find it. He went forward and played his provisional ball. Then he went further forward and found his original ball in bounds. The original ball must have bounced down the road and then come back into bounds, because it was found much farther from the tee than anticipated. Was the original ball still the ball in play?

**A.** No. The player played a stroke with the provisional ball from a point nearer the hole than the place where the original ball was likely to be. When he did so, the provisional ball became the ball in play and the original ball was lost — Rule 27-2b.

The place where the original ball in fact lay was irrelevant.

### 27-2b/5 Original Ball Played After Provisional Ball Played from Point Nearer Hole Than Original Ball Is Likely to Be

**Q.** A player, unable to find his original ball, goes forward and plays a second stroke with his provisional ball from a point nearer the hole than the place where the original ball is likely to be. His original ball is then found and he plays it. What is the ruling?

**A.** When the player played his second stroke with the provisional ball, the original ball was out of play and the provisional ball was in play — Rule 27-2b. In playing a stroke with a ball out of play (the original ball), the player played a wrong ball — see Definition of "Wrong Ball" — and was subject to penalty as prescribed in Rule 15.

### 27-2b/6 Player Abandons Original Ball and Walks Forward to Play Provisional Ball; Original Ball Then Found

**Q.** A player, having searched for a minute for his original ball, abandoned it and walked forward to continue play with his provisional ball. Before he played the provisional ball, some spectators found the original ball before the five-minute search period expired. What is the ruling?

**A.** The original ball remained the ball in play since it was found within five minutes after search for it had begun and the player had not played a stroke with the provisional ball from the place where the original ball was likely to be or from a point nearer the hole than that place — Rule 27-2b.

**Player Discovers Original Ball in Hole After Searching Five Minutes and Then Continuing Play with Provisional Ball — See 1-1/3.**

### 27-2b/6.5 Player Deems Provisional Ball Unplayable and Drops Ball; Original Ball Then Found

**Q.** A player hits his tee shot into heavy rough approximately 150 yards from the teeing ground and, since his ball may be lost outside a water hazard, he plays a provisional ball. After searching briefly for his original ball he goes forward to play his provisional ball which is in a bush approximately 200 yards from the teeing ground. He deems his provisional ball unplayable and drops it within two club-lengths of where it lay under Rule 28c. Before playing the provisional ball, the player's original ball is found by a spectator within five minutes of the player having begun to search for it. What is the ruling?

**A.** The original ball remained the ball in play since it was found within five minutes after search for it had begun and the player had not played a stroke with the provisional ball (see Rule 27-2b). The fact that the player lifted and dropped the provisional ball under Rule 28c is irrelevant.

**Player Declares First Ball from Tee Unplayable, Abandons Provisional Ball and Claims He Is Lying Three with Third Ball — See 28/2.**

### 27-2b/7 Provisional Ball Played in Erroneous Belief It Is Original Ball

**Q.** A player, believing his original ball may be out of bounds, plays a provisional ball which comes to rest in the same area. He finds a ball which he believes is his original ball, plays it and then discovers that the ball he played was his provisional ball. What is the ruling?

**A.** If a player reaches the place where his original ball is likely to be and plays another stroke with a provisional ball, the provisional ball is in play and the original ball is lost — Rule 27-2b.

### 27-2b/8 Provisional Ball Lifted in Erroneous Belief Original Ball Is in Bounds

**Q.** A player, believing his original ball might be out of bounds, played a provisional ball which came to rest short of where the original ball came to rest. He walked forward, saw his original ball and, believing the original ball to be in bounds, picked up the provisional ball. He then discovered that the original ball was out of bounds. What is the ruling?

**A.** Since the original ball was out of bounds, the provisional ball was in play — Rule 27-2b. When the player lifted the ball in play (provisional ball) without authority under the Rules, he incurred a penalty stroke and was required to replace it — Rule 18-2a.

### 27-2b/9 Provisional Ball Lifted Subsequently Becomes Ball in Play

**Q.** In stroke play, a competitor, believing his tee shot might be lost, plays a provisional ball. He finds a ball he believes is his original ball, plays a stroke at it, picks up his provisional ball and then discovers that the ball he played was not his original ball, but rather a wrong ball. He resumes search for his original ball but cannot find it. What is the ruling?

**A.** The competitor lifted a ball which was to become the ball in play, i.e., the provisional ball — see Rule 27-2b. Accordingly, the competitor incurred a stroke-and-distance penalty under Rule 27-1 as a result of losing his original ball, a two-stroke penalty under Rule 15-3b for playing a wrong ball and a one-stroke penalty under Rule 18-2a for picking up his provisional ball. He is required to replace and play out the provisional ball. The competitor would be playing his seventh stroke.

### 27-2b/10 Provisional Ball Lifted Subsequently Becomes Ball in Play; Competitor Then Plays from Wrong Place

**Q.** With regard to Decision 27-2b/9, what is the ruling if the competitor returns to the tee with the provisional ball and puts it into play again?

**A.** When the competitor played again from the tee rather than replacing and playing the provisional ball from where it was lifted, he incurred the general penalty of two strokes for a breach of Rule 18 (in accordance with Rule 20-7c), rather than a one-stroke penalty under Rule 18-2a. The competitor would be playing his eighth stroke from the tee.

When the competitor lifted the provisional ball he had no intention of playing again from the teeing ground, therefore, Rule 18-2a applies to the competitor's lifting of and failure to replace the provisional ball (i.e., the competitor cannot avoid the penalty under Rule 18-2a by proceeding under stroke and distance).

### 27-2c/1 Possibility That Original Ball Is in Water Hazard May Not Preclude Play of Provisional Ball

**Q.** Is it true that, if a player's original ball may have come to rest in a water hazard, the player is precluded from playing a provisional ball?

**A.** No. Even though the original ball may be in a water hazard, the player is entitled to play a provisional ball if the original ball might also be lost outside the water hazard or out of bounds. In such a case, if the original ball is found in the water hazard, the provisional ball must be abandoned — Rule 27-2c.

### 27-2c/1.5 Whether Provisional Ball Becomes Ball in Play If Original Ball Lost in Ground Under Repair

**Q.** A player hits his tee shot into an area of tall rough and, since the ball may be lost, he plays a provisional ball. During search for the original ball, the player discovers that the Committee has marked a large area of the rough as ground under repair. It is established that there is reasonable evidence that the original ball is lost in the ground under repair. Does the provisional ball automatically become the ball in play since the original ball was lost outside a water hazard?

**A.** No. The player may continue play with the provisional ball under Rule 27-2b or he may proceed under Rule 25-1c(i) as his ball was lost in ground under repair — see Exception to Rule 27-2b.

### 27-2c/2 Ball Believed to Be Original Found; Player Wishes to Ignore It and Continue Play with Provisional Ball

**Q.** At a par-3 hole, a player plays his tee shot into a heavy thicket. Since his ball may be lost, he hits a provisional ball that comes to rest near the hole. In the circumstances, it is advantageous to the player not to find his original ball. Accordingly, the player does not search for the original ball and walks directly toward his provisional ball. While the player is on his way to his provisional ball, a ball believed to be his original is found. The player is advised that his original ball may have been found. May the player ignore this ball and continue play with the provisional ball?

**A.** No. The player must inspect the ball that has been found and, if it is the player's original ball, he must continue play with it (or proceed under the unplayable ball Rule). The provisional ball must be abandoned — Rule 27-2c. See also Decision 27-2b/1.

**Original Ball Found Within Five-Minute Search Period After Another Ball Dropped; Dropped Ball Played — See 27-1/2.3.**

### 27-2c/3 Provisional Ball Played from Point Nearer Hole Than Original Ball Because Player Erroneously Thought Original Ball, Which Was Visible, Was Out of Bounds

**Q.** A player's ball came to rest 20 yards over a green and beyond a white stake which the player's caddie said was a boundary stake. The player played a provisional ball which came to rest short of the green, but closer to the hole than his original ball. The player played the provisional ball onto the green. At that point, he walked behind the green towards his original ball, which had been visible all along, and discovered that the white stake was not a boundary stake and that his original ball was in bounds. What is the ruling?

**A.** The player should have determined the status of his original ball before playing a second stroke with the provisional ball and, since the original ball was not out of bounds, he should have abandoned the provisional ball. When he failed to do so, the second stroke with the provisional ball was a stroke with a wrong ball — Rule 27-2c.

In match play, the player lost the hole (Rule 15-3a).

In stroke play, he incurred a two-stroke penalty (Rule 15-3b) and was required to hole out with the original ball.

## 27-2c/4 Original Ball and Provisional Ball Found Out of Bounds

**Q.** A player finds both his original ball and his provisional ball out of bounds. The balls were played from the tee. When the player returns to the tee and plays another ball, has he taken 3 strokes or 5?

**A.** The player will have taken 5 strokes when he plays the third ball from the tee. A stroke played with a provisional ball and any penalty related to it are not disregarded unless the provisional ball is abandoned as provided in Rule 27-2c.

# Rule 28. Ball Unplayable

**Definitions**

All defined terms are in *italics* and are listed alphabetically in the Definitions section — see pages 3-11.

The player may deem his ball unplayable at any place on the *course* except when the ball is in a *water hazard*. The player is the sole judge as to whether his ball is unplayable.

If the player deems his ball to be unplayable, he must, under penalty of one stroke:

a. Play a ball as nearly as possible at the spot from which the original ball was last played (see Rule 20-5); or

b. Drop a ball behind the point where the ball lay, keeping that point directly between the *hole* and the spot on which the ball is dropped, with no limit to how far behind that point the ball may be dropped; or

c. Drop a ball within two club-lengths of the spot where the ball lay, but not nearer the *hole*.

If the unplayable ball is in a *bunker*, the player may proceed under Clause a, b or c. If he elects to proceed under Clause b or c, a ball must be dropped in the *bunker*.

The ball may be lifted and cleaned when proceeding under this Rule.

PENALTY FOR BREACH OF RULE:

Match play — Loss of hole; Stroke play — Two strokes.

### 28/1 When Necessary to Find and Identify Ball Deemed Unplayable

**Q.** A player hits his tee shot into a deep canyon. The player immediately deems the ball unplayable and plays another ball from the tee under the stroke-and-distance option of Rule 28. May a player deem unplayable a ball which has not been found?

**A.** Yes. A player may proceed under the stroke-and-distance option (Rule 28a) without finding his ball.

However, since Rules 28b and c require reference to where the ball lay, the player must find and identify his ball in order to proceed under either of these options.

### 28/2 Player Deems First Ball from Tee Unplayable, Abandons Provisional Ball and Claims He Is Lying Three with Third Ball

**Q.** A player hit his tee shot deep into the woods on the right. The player then hit a provisional ball into the same woods. The player did not search for either ball.

The player deemed his first ball unplayable, said he was abandoning his provisional ball and hit a third ball from the tee. The player maintained that his third ball was in play and that he was lying 3. He based his argument on Rule 28, which states that the player is the sole judge as to whether his ball is unplayable, and on Decision 28/1, which says in effect that a player may proceed under the stroke-and-distance option of the unplayable ball Rule without finding his ball. The Committee ruled that the player's stroke with the third ball was his fifth stroke, but the wording of Decision 28/1 leaves a little doubt. Did the Committee rule correctly?

**A.** Yes. The player may not deem the first ball from the tee unplayable, disregard the provisional ball and put another ball into play under a stroke-and-distance penalty because, having played the provisional ball, he must find the original ball before he can declare it unplayable. Unless the original ball was found, the provisional ball would automatically become the ball in play.

This case differs from Decision 28/1. No provisional ball was played in that case.

**Player Deems Provisional Ball Unplayable and Drops Ball; Original Ball Then Found — See 27-2b/6.5.**

### 28/3 Ball Dropped Under Unplayable Ball Rule Comes to Rest in Original Position or Another Position at Which Ball Is Unplayable

**Q.** A player deemed his ball unplayable and, under Rule 28c, dropped his ball within two club-lengths of the spot where it lay. The ball came to rest in the original position or another position at which the ball was unplayable. What is the ruling?

**A.** The ball was in play when it was dropped — Rule 20-4. Thus, if the ball came to rest in the original position, the player must again invoke the unplayable ball Rule, incurring an additional penalty stroke, unless he decides to play the ball as it lies. The same applies if the ball came to rest in another position at which it was unplayable, assuming that the ball did not roll into a position covered by Rule 20-2c, in which case re-dropping without penalty would be required.

### 28/4 Ball Deemed Unplayable Through the Green Dropped in Hazard

**Q.** A player's ball lies through the green. The player deems the ball unplayable. In proceeding under Rule 28b or c, the player drops a ball in a hazard. Is this permissible?

**A.** Yes.

**Ball Deemed Unplayable in Water Hazard Is Dropped in Hazard and Played — See 20-7/2.**

**Ball Deemed Unplayable Dropped in Ground Under Repair from Which Play Prohibited; Ball Then Dropped Under Ground Under Repair Rule — See 25-1b/14.5.**

### 28/4.5 Ball Deemed Unplayable Through the Green Dropped in Water Hazard; Player Elects Not to Play Ball and Wishes to Proceed Under the Water Hazard Rule

**Q.** With regard to Decision 28/4, if the player drops a ball into a lateral water hazard and the ball rolls into a position where the player is unable to play the ball, how should he proceed?

**A.** The player's only option is to proceed under Rule 26-1a.

As the player deliberately dropped the ball directly into the water hazard "the point at which the original ball last crossed the margin of the water hazard" cannot be identified. Therefore, in the absence of this reference point, neither Rule 26-1b nor 26-1c can be applied.

**Player Proceeding Under Water Hazard Rule Drops Ball in Another Hazard — See 26-1/2.**

### 28/5 Regression Under Unplayable Ball Rule

**Q.** A player plays a stroke from Point A to Point B. Point B is in an area from which it is very difficult to extricate a ball. The player considers deeming the ball unplayable but this would result in a stroke-and-distance penalty (Rule 28a). Dropping behind under Rule 28b is impossible due to a boundary fence and dropping within two club-lengths under Rule 28c is not feasible because it would require a considerable number of such drops to escape the area. The player plays from Point B and moves the ball a few feet to Point C, where the ball is clearly unplayable. Under Rule 28a, may the player:

(a) deem the ball unplayable at Point C and drop a ball under penalty of one stroke at Point B, and then

(b) deem the ball unplayable at Point B and drop a ball, under an additional penalty of one stroke, at Point A?

**A.** No. Under Rule 28a, the player would be entitled to drop a ball only at the place from which he played his last stroke (Point B).

In the circumstances, the player's only alternative is to invoke Rule 28c a sufficient number of times (starting at Point C and dropping the ball sideways within two club-lengths each time) to get the ball into a playable position.

### 28/6 Player Plays Second Shot, Deems Ball Unplayable and Returns to Tee

**Q.** With regard to Decision 28/5, if Point A is the teeing ground and Point B is the spot from which the second shot was played, what is the penalty if the player, having deemed his ball unplayable at Point C, returns to the tee and plays out the hole from there?

**A.** The player was entitled to drop and play a ball at Point B under Rule 28a, but not Point A. When he played a ball from Point A, he played from a wrong place.

In match play, the player incurs a penalty of loss of hole for a breach of Rule 28 — see also Rule 20-7b.

In stroke play, a serious breach of Rule 28 is involved. Accordingly, the player is disqualified unless the serious breach is corrected as provided in Rule 20-7c.

Except in the special circumstances covered by Rule 26-2, the Rules do not allow a player to regress beyond the spot from which his last stroke was played, in this case Point B. Such action generally constitutes a serious breach, as in this case.

### 28/6.5 Player Deems Ball Unplayable a Second Time and Wishes to Proceed Under Stroke and Distance After Dropping a Ball Under Other Unplayable Option

**Q.** A player plays a stroke from Point A to Point B. The player deems his ball unplayable and proceeds under either Rule 28b or c. After dropping under penalty of one stroke, the ball comes to rest at Point C. The player deems his ball unplayable for a second time and wishes to proceed under Rule 28a, playing from Point A. Is this permissible?

**A.** Yes. The player may play from Point A because he did not make a stroke at the ball from either Point B or Point C. Point A was the spot from which the original ball was last played. The player would incur a total of two penalty strokes.

**Ball Dropped Under One Option of Unplayable Ball Rule Strikes Player; Player Wishes to Change Relief Option — See 20-2a/6.**

**Changing Relief Option When Re-Dropping Required — See 20-2c/5.**

**Changing Relief Option After Ball Dropped in Wrong Place — See 20-6/2.**

### 28/7 Player Misses Ball and Deems It Unplayable

**Q.** A player's tee shot comes to rest in tree roots. He makes a stroke, fails to move the ball and then deems the ball unplayable. May the player return to the tee, playing 4, under Rule 28a?

**A.** No. Rule 28a permits the player to play "a ball ... at the spot from which the original ball was last played." The original ball was last played from the tree roots, not the tee.

### 28/8 Ball Deemed Unplayable; Place from Which Previous Stroke Played Is Nearer Hole

**Q.** A player's ball strikes a rock and bounces farther away from the hole than the spot from which the stroke was played. The player deems the ball unplayable. May the player invoke the stroke-and-distance option of Rule 28 in the circumstances?

**A.** Yes.

### 28/9 Ball Lying on Grass-Covered Ground Within Bunker Deemed Unplayable

**Q.** A player's ball is lying on grass-covered ground within a bunker. The player deems the ball unplayable and elects to drop it under Rule 28b. Must he drop it in the bunker?

**A.** No. Grass-covered ground within a bunker is not part of the bunker. Accordingly, the player may drop the ball behind the bunker.

### 28/10 Ball Dropped Outside Bunker Under Option Requiring Drop in Bunker

**Q.** In stroke play, a competitor deems his ball unplayable in a bunker and, purporting to proceed under Rule 28b or c, drops a ball outside the bunker and plays it. What is the ruling?

**A.** In this case, Rules 28b and c require that a ball be dropped in and played from the bunker. Generally, if the ball is played from outside the bunker, the penalty should be disqualification for a serious breach of Rule 28, unless rectified under Rule 20-7c. However, if the position of the ball after it is dropped out of the bunker is not substantially different from what it would have been if the competitor had invoked the stroke-and-distance option under Rule 28a, he incurs the penalty stroke prescribed by Rule 28 and an additional penalty of two strokes for a breach of that Rule, rather than disqualification.

### 28/11 Ball Unplayable in Tree and Player Opts to Drop Within Two Club-Lengths

**Q.** A player's ball is eight feet off the ground, lodged in a tree. The player deems the ball unplayable. May the player proceed under option c of Rule 28 which permits him to drop a ball within two club-lengths of where his ball lay unplayable?

**A.** Yes. The player would be entitled to drop a ball within two club-lengths of the point on the ground immediately below the place where the ball lay in the tree. In some instances this may allow the player to drop a ball on a putting green.

**Ball Unplayable in Tree Dislodged by Shaking Tree or Throwing Club — See 18-2a/27.**

**Ball in Tree Identified But Not Retrieved Deemed Unplayable — See 27/14.**

## 28/12 Ball Unplayable at Base of Cliff and Player Wishes to Drop Within Two Club-Lengths of Point Above Ball

**Q.** Under Decision 28/11, if a ball in a tree is deemed unplayable, the player may, under Rule 28c, drop a ball within two club-lengths of the spot on the ground directly beneath where the ball lies.

Suppose a player deems unplayable a ball lying at the base of a cliff and wishes to proceed under Rule 28c. May the player drop a ball within two club-lengths of a point directly above where the ball lies in order to get himself onto the top of the cliff?

**A.** No.

In Decision 28/11, the player was permitted to ignore vertical distance in taking relief under Rule 28c only because his ball was off the ground. In this case, the ball at the base of the cliff is on the ground.

## 28/13 After Deeming Ball Unplayable and Lifting It, Player Discovers Ball Was in Ground Under Repair

**Q.** A player lifts his ball after deeming it unplayable and then discovers that the ball was lying in ground under repair. Does the declaration and the lifting of the ball commit the player to proceeding under Rule 28?

**A.** No. Provided the player has not put a ball into play under Rule 28, he is not precluded by that Rule from taking relief, without penalty, under the ground under repair Rule (Rule 25).

**Player Entitled to Relief Without Penalty from Condition Lifts Ball; Chooses Not to Take Relief and Wishes to Proceed Under the Unplayable Ball Rule — See 18-2a/12.5.**

## 28/14 Wrong Ball Deemed Unplayable Played Under Stroke-and-Distance Procedure; Original Ball Then Found

**Q.** A player finds a stray ball, which he mistakenly thinks is his, in a bad lie. He deems it unplayable and decides to adopt the procedure in Rule 28a. After going back, he plays the stray ball under penalty of stroke and distance at the spot from which his original ball was played. He then finds his original ball in a playable position. What is the ruling?

**A.** The original ball is lost and the stray ball played under penalty of stroke and distance is in play — see Decision 27/17.

The ruling would have been different if the player had decided to proceed under either Rule 28b or 28c — see Decision 28/15.

### 28/15 Wrong Ball Deemed Unplayable, Dropped Within Two Club-Lengths and Played Before Error Discovered

**Q.** A player finds a stray ball, which he mistakenly thinks is his, in a bad lie. He deems it unplayable and decides to adopt the procedure in Rule 28c. He drops the stray ball within two club-lengths of the spot where it lay and plays it. He then finds his original ball in a playable position. In Decision 28/14 the basic situation is exactly the same, but in that case the player elected to proceed under Rule 28a and it was ruled that the stray ball played under penalty of stroke and distance was in play. What is the ruling in this case?

**A.** The procedures in Rules 28b and 28c may not be applied except with reference to the position of the player's ball in play, which must first be found and identified (see Decision 28/1). In the present case, the stray ball dropped and played by the player was not his original ball; it was a substituted ball. Since the location of the original ball was not known at the time the substituted ball was dropped, he was required to proceed under Rule 27-1. As the substituted ball was not dropped at the spot required by Rule 27-1, he played from a wrong place (see Decision 15/14).

In match play, he incurred a penalty of loss of hole (Rule 20-7b).

In stroke play, he incurred a penalty of one stroke under Rule 27-1 and an additional penalty of two strokes under Rule 20-7c for playing from a wrong place. If the breach was a serious one, he was subject to disqualification unless he corrected the error as provided in Rule 20-7c.

**Stray Ball Dropped Under Unplayable Ball Rule But Not Played — See 15/13.**

#### Other Decisions relating to Rule 28:

**Ball Declared Unplayable in Bunker; Player Removes Loose Impediment from Bunker While Ball Lifted — See 13-4/35.7.**

**Caddie on Own Initiative Lifts Ball Considering It Unplayable — See 18-2a/15.**

**Ball Deemed Unplayable in Water Hazard; Another Ball Is Dropped in Hazard But Player Realizes Error Before Playing — See 20-7/2.5**

# OTHER FORMS OF PLAY

# *Rule 29.*
# *Threesomes and Foursomes*

**Definitions**
All defined terms are in *italics* and are listed alphabetically in the Definitions section — see pages 3-11.

### 29-1. General

In a *threesome* or a *foursome*, during any *stipulated round* the *partners* must play alternately from the *teeing grounds* and alternately during the play of each hole. Penalty *strokes* do not affect the order of play.

### 29-2. Match Play

If a player plays when his *partner* should have played, his *side* loses the hole.

### 29-3. Stroke Play

If the *partners* make a *stroke* or *strokes* in incorrect order, such *stroke* or *strokes* are canceled and the *side* incurs a penalty of two strokes. The *side* must correct the error by playing a ball in correct order as nearly as possible at the spot from which it first played in incorrect order (see Rule 20-5). If the *side* makes a *stroke* on the next *teeing ground* without first correcting the error or, in the case of the last hole of the round, leaves the *putting green* without declaring its intention to correct the error, the *side* is disqualified.

## 29/1 Changing Partners After Driving from First Tee

**Q.** A and B are to play C and D in a foursome match in which the conditions of the competition permit substitutions. D is absent at the time the match is to start. Accordingly, E is substituted for D. C plays the first stroke for side C-E. At that point, D arrives. May D be reinstated in the match since E has not played a stroke?

**A.** No. Once any player in a foursome match has played from the first tee, the composition of neither side may be changed.

## 29/2 Mixed Foursome in Which Different Tees Used by Men and Women; Tee Shot Out of Bounds

**Q.** In a mixed foursome in which the men play from the back tees and the women play from the forward tees, a man hits a tee shot out of bounds. Does his partner play the next stroke from the back tee or the forward tee?

**A.** The partner must play from the back tee.

### 29/3 Player in Foursome Match Practices Putts on Previous Green After Partner Has Driven from Next Tee

**Q.** A and B are partners in a foursome match. A was practicing putts on the 11th green after B drove off the 12th tee. Was A playing practice strokes during the play of a hole?

**A.** Yes. A and B lost the 12th hole for a breach of Rule 7-2.

**Player in Four-Ball Practices Putts on Previous Green After Partner Has Driven from Next Tee — See 30-3f/12.**

### 29/4 Dropping Ball in Foursome Competition

**Q.** Rule 20-2a provides that "the player himself" must drop a ball. Under the Definition of "Partner," it is stated that, in the case of threesomes and foursomes, the term "player" includes his partner where the context so admits. When a side in a foursome is required to drop a ball, may either member of the side drop it?

**A.** No. In view of the requirement of Rule 20-2a that the player himself must drop the ball, the member of the side whose turn it is to play next must drop the ball.

### 29/5 Hitting Sand in Bunker with Club After Failing to Extricate Ball; Foursome Match

**Q.** In a foursome match, A and B are partners. A plays a bunker shot, fails to get the ball out and takes a swing with his club into the sand. This action does not improve the position of the ball in the bunker.

Rule 13-4 provides that, when a ball lies in a hazard, the player "must not touch the ground in the hazard ... with a club." When A took the swing, it was B's turn to play the next stroke for side A-B. So, presumably, B was the "player" insofar as the Rules were concerned. Accordingly, it would appear A-B would incur no penalty under Rule 13-4 as a result of A's swing. Is this correct?

**A.** No. In a foursome, the word "player" includes his partner — see Definition of "Partner." A-B incur a penalty of loss of hole for a breach of Rule 13-4 — see Decision 13-4/35.

### 29/6 Signing of Score Card in Foursome Stroke Play

**Q.** Rule 31-4 dealing with scoring in four-ball stroke play states: "Only one of the partners need be responsible for complying with Rule 6-6b." What is the ruling in this regard in foursome stroke play?

**A.** Although Rule 29 is silent on the matter, in foursome stroke play only one of the partners need be responsible for complying with Rule 6-6b.

**Competitor Records Incorrect Handicap for Partner in Foursome Stroke Play Competition; Error Discovered After Competition Closed — See 6-2b/2.5.**

**Competitors in Foursome Competition Fail to Record Individual Handicaps on Score Card —**
See 6-2b/4.

## 29-1/1  Ball Played from Outside Teeing Ground in Foursome Match

**Q.** A and B are playing C and D in a foursome match. A plays from outside the teeing ground and Side A-B is required by C and D to replay the stroke. Should A or B replay it?

**A.** A must replay the stroke. The original stroke does not count.

## 29-1/2  Competitor Plays from Outside Teeing Ground in Foursome Stroke Play; Partner Replays Stroke

**Q.** In foursome stroke play A plays in correct order but from outside the teeing ground. B, his partner, then plays from within the teeing ground, whereas A should have done so. What is the ruling?

**A.** The side is penalized two strokes for playing from outside the teeing ground (Rule 11-4) and two strokes for playing in incorrect order (Rule 29-3). A must now play another ball from within the teeing ground. Otherwise, the side is disqualified.

## 29-1/3  Who Plays Provisional Ball in Foursome

**Q.** A and B are partners in a foursome. A drives and there is doubt whether the ball is out of bounds. They decide to play a provisional ball. Who plays it?

**A.** The provisional ball is played by B.

## 29-1/4  Provisional Ball Played by Wrong Member of Side in Foursome

**Q.** A and B were partners in a foursome competition. A drove from the tee and, since the ball might be lost, A-B elected to play a provisional ball. A played the provisional ball, whereas, under Rule 29, B should have played it. What is the ruling?

**A.** If the original ball was found in bounds and thus the provisional ball did not become the ball in play, there was no penalty.

If the original ball was lost and the provisional ball became the ball in play, A-B lost the hole in match play (Rule 29-2) or incurred a penalty of two strokes in stroke play (Rule 29-3). In stroke play, the provisional ball would have to be abandoned and B would have to play from the tee — Rule 29-3.

## 29-1/5  Order of Play If Player Accidentally Moves Ball After Address

**Q.** In a foursome match, a player accidentally moves the ball after addressing it and incurs a penalty of one stroke under Rule 18-2b. The ball is replaced. Does the player or his partner play the next stroke?

**A.** The player must play the next stroke. Penalty strokes do not affect the order of play (Rule 29-1).

### 29-1/6 Player Misses Ball Accidentally When Making Stroke

**Q.** In a foursome event, A and B are partners. A attempts to strike the ball and misses. Whose turn is it to play?

**A.** An accidental miss is a stroke — see Definition of "Stroke." It is B's turn to play.

### 29-1/7 Player Misses Ball Purposely So Partner Would Play Ball Over Water

**Q.** A and B, partners in a foursome competition, were faced with a difficult shot over a pond. A, a poor player, swung but purposely missed the ball. B, an expert player, then played the ball to the green. Is this permissible?

**A.** No. Since A had no intention of moving the ball, he did not play a stroke — see Definition of "Stroke" — and it remained his turn to play.

When B played instead of A, A and B incurred a penalty of loss of hole in match play or two strokes in stroke play — Rules 29-2 and -3. In stroke play, A must play a ball at the spot from which B played. If A did not do so before the side played from the next teeing ground, A and B were disqualified — Rule 29-3.

### 29-1/8 Order of Play in Foursome Stroke Play When Wrong Ball Played

**Q.** In foursome stroke play, A played a wrong ball. Who plays the next shot, A or his partner, B?

**A.** A must play the next stroke. In a foursome competition, penalty strokes do not affect the order of play — see Rule 29-1. The side A-B incurs a penalty of two strokes — Rule 15-3b.

### 29-1/9 Both Player and Partner Drive at Same Tee in Foursome Play

**Q.** A and B are partners in foursome play. At the 5th hole, forgetting that they were playing a foursome, A and then B drive. What is the ruling:

(a) if it was A's turn to drive?

(b) if it was B's turn to drive?

**A.** (a) If it was A's turn to drive, B's ball would be the side's ball in play and would be lying 3 — see Decision 27/17.

(b) If it was B's turn to drive, the side loses the hole in match play or incurs a penalty of two strokes in stroke play (Rules 29-2 and -3). In stroke play, the side must continue with B's ball which lies 3.

**Restriction on Which Partner in Foursome Competition May Play from 1st Tee — See 33-1/3.5.**

## 29-2/1 Wrong Partners Drive for Both Sides in Foursome Match

**Q.** A and B are playing C and D in a foursome match. A and C drive off at a hole at which B and D should have driven. The error is then discovered. What is the ruling?

**A.** The side which drove first loses the hole under Rule 29-2.

## 29-2/2 Side Drives for Three Holes in Wrong Order and Then Claim Is Made

**Q.** In a foursome match, A and B are playing C and D. A drives at the 9th hole and again, in error, at the 10th hole. B drives at the 11th and A drives at the 12th. The error is then discovered. C and D claim the 10th, 11th and 12th holes, and the matter is referred to the Committee. What is the ruling?

**A.** A and B lose the 12th hole under Rule 29-2.

C and D's claim of the 10th and 11th holes could have been considered only if C and D had been given wrong information by A and B and the claim had been based on facts previously unknown to C and D. A and B are deemed to have given wrong information to C and D — see first paragraph of Rule 9-2b(i). However, C and D must have seen A and B play out of order on all three holes. Therefore, the claim was not based on facts previously unknown to C and D.

# Rule 30. Three-Ball, Best-Ball and Four-Ball Match Play

**Definitions**
All defined terms are in *italics* and are listed alphabetically in the Definitions section — see pages 3-11.

### 30-1. Rules of Golf Apply
The Rules of Golf, so far as they are not at variance with the following specific Rules, apply to *three-ball*, *best-ball* and *four-ball matches*.

### 30-2. Three-Ball Match Play

#### a. Ball at Rest Moved by an Opponent
Except as otherwise provided in the *Rules*, if the player's ball is touched or *moved* by an opponent, his *caddie* or *equipment* other than during search, Rule 18-3b applies. That opponent incurs a penalty of one stroke in his match with the player, but not in his match with the other opponent.

#### b. Ball Deflected or Stopped by an Opponent Accidentally
If a player's ball is accidentally deflected or stopped by an opponent, his *caddie* or *equipment*, there is no penalty. In his match with that opponent the player may play the ball as it lies or, before another *stroke* is played by either *side*, he may cancel the *stroke* and play a ball without penalty as nearly as possible at the spot from which the original ball was last played (see Rule 20-5). In his match with the other opponent, the ball must be played as it lies.

**Exception:** Ball striking person attending *flagstick* — see Rule 17-3b.

(Ball purposely deflected or stopped by opponent — see Rule 1-2.)

### 30-3. Best-Ball and Four-Ball Match Play

#### a. Representation of Side
A *side* may be represented by one *partner* for all or any part of a match; all *partners* need not be present. An absent *partner* may join a match between holes, but not during play of a hole.

#### b. Maximum of 14 Clubs
The *side* is penalized for a breach of Rules 4-3a(iii) and 4-4 by any *partner*.

#### c. Order of Play
Balls belonging to the same *side* may be played in the order the *side* considers best.

#### d. Wrong Ball
If a player makes a stroke at a *wrong ball* that is not in a *hazard*, he is disqualified for that hole, but his *partner* incurs no penalty even if the *wrong ball* belongs to him. If the *wrong ball* belongs to another player, its owner must place a ball on the spot from which the *wrong ball* was first played.

#### e. Disqualification of Side
(i) A *side* is disqualified for a breach of any of the following by any *partner*:

- Rule 1-3 — Agreement to Waive Rules
- Rule 4-1 or -2 — Clubs
- Rule 5-1 or -2 — The Ball
- Rule 6-2a — Handicap (playing off higher handicap)
- Rule 6-4 — Caddie (having more than one caddie; failure to correct breach immediately)
- Rule 6-7 — Undue Delay; Slow Play (repeated offense)
- Rule 14-3 — Artificial Devices and Unusual Equipment

(ii) A *side is disqualified* for a breach of any of the following by all *partners*:

- Rule 6-3 — Time of Starting and Groups
- Rule 6-8 — Discontinuance of Play

(iii) In all other cases where a breach of a *Rule* would result in disqualification, the player is disqualified for that hole only.

**f. Effect of Other Penalties**

If a player's breach of a *Rule* assists his *partner's* play or adversely affects an opponent's play, the *partner* incurs the applicable penalty in addition to any penalty incurred by the player.

In all other cases where a player incurs a penalty for breach of a *Rule*, the penalty does not apply to his *partner*. Where the penalty is stated to be loss of hole, the effect is to disqualify the player for that hole.

**g. Another Form of Match Played Concurrently**

In a *best-ball* or *four-ball* match when another form of match is played concurrently, the above specific Rules apply.

## 30/1 Caddie Shared by Members of Opposite Sides in Four-Ball Match Moves Ball

**Q.** A caddie shared by A and C, who were on opposite sides in a four-ball match, moves A's ball. What is the ruling?

**A.** If the caddie was not acting upon directions of C, A is penalized one stroke — see Definition of "Caddie" and Rule 18-2a.

If the caddie was acting upon directions of C, C is penalized one stroke under Rule 18-3b.

## 30/2 Caddie Shared by Opponents' Side in Four-Ball Match Moves Player's Ball

**Q.** A and B are playing C and D in a four-ball match. A caddie shared by C and D accidentally moves A's ball. Who is penalized?

**A.** Rule 18-3b provides that, if a player's ball is moved by an opponent's caddie, that opponent incurs a penalty stroke. However, when opponents share a caddie, there is no fair way of assigning the penalty to one member of the side. Accordingly, in equity (Rule 1-4), both C and D incur a penalty stroke.

A must replace his ball — Rule 18-3b.

### 30/2.5 Player Touches Putting Green in Pointing Out Line for Putting for Partner and Incidentally Touches Own Line of Putt

**Q.** In a four-ball match, A and B are partners and their balls lie on the putting green. A touches the green in pointing out a line for putting for B. Incidentally, the spot which A touches is on his (A's) line of putt.

B is disqualified for the hole under Rule 8-2b. Is A disqualified for the hole under Rule 16-1a?

**A.** No.

**Player Who Has Holed Out Touches Partner's Line of Putt — See 1-2/3.5.**

### 30/3 Determination of Honor in Four-Ball Match in Which Points Awarded for Both Better-Ball and Aggregate Scores

**Q.** In a four-ball match, one point is awarded for the better-ball score at each hole and one point is awarded for the aggregate score at each hole. How is the honor determined?

**A.** The Rules of Golf do not cover such a match — see Definition of "Matches." It is recommended that the honor be determined by the better-ball score only.

### 30/4 Player Who Walks Off Green Under Mistaken Impression Partner Halved Hole Returns and Putts for Half

**Q.** A and B are playing C and D in a four-ball match. At one hole C and D hole out and their better-ball score is 4. A, who had marked the position of his ball and lifted it, has a putt for a 4 but he mistakenly thinks B has scored a 4. Accordingly, A walks off the green, leaving his ball-marker on the green. B immediately advises A that he (B) scored a 5. So A returns to the green, replaces his ball and holes out for a 4.

C and D claim the hole on the ground that A cannot come back and putt after walking off the green, thinking his partner had halved the hole. Are C and D correct?

**A.** No. Since A had not waived his turn to putt and there was no undue delay, A was entitled to proceed as he did. If, however, A had not left his ball-marker on the green, and therefore the position of his ball was no longer marked, he would have incurred a penalty stroke under Rule 20-1 and would no longer have had a putt for the half.

## 33-2a/10 How to Mark Island Green

**Q.** A putting green is situated on an island in a lake. The water between the tee and the green is defined as a water hazard. The water on each side is marked as a lateral water hazard. How should the water behind the island be marked?

**A.** The Committee would be justified in marking the water behind the island as a lateral water hazard.

Alternatively, the Committee might consider defining the entire lake as a water hazard, establishing a Ball Drop (or Dropping Zone) and adopting a Local Rule giving a player whose ball lies in the hazard the option of dropping a ball in the Ball Drop, under penalty of one stroke.

## 33-2a/10.5 Status of Tree Basins

**Q.** What is the status under the Rules of tree wells or tree basins?

**A.** There is no relief under the Rules from tree basins which are not made of artificial materials.

If a tree basin has an artificial wall, the wall is an obstruction unless the Committee deems it to be an integral part of the course under Rule 33-2a.

## 33-2a/11 Defining Body of Water Adjacent to Course

**Q.** A body of water (e.g., a river, lake or ocean) is adjacent to a hole and is off club property. The Definition of "Water Hazard" refers to a body of water "on the course." How may the Committee define the body of water?

**A.** The Committee may define the body of water as a water hazard (or lateral water hazard), even though it is off the club's property. The phrase "on the course" in the Definition of "Water Hazard" does not mean on property owned by the club; rather, it refers to any area not defined as out of bounds by the Committee.

When it is possible for a ball to finish on ground on the opposite side of a body of water, but it is impracticable for the Committee to define the opposite margin, the Committee may adopt a Local Rule stating that when marked on just one side, a water hazard is deemed to extend to infinity. Accordingly, all ground and water beyond the defined margin of the hazard is in the hazard. When it is not possible for a ball to finish on the opposite side of the body of water (e.g., as with a wide river, large lake or ocean), such a Local Rule is not necessary.

**A.** The pond should be defined as a water hazard with yellow stakes or a yellow line and there should be a Local Rule to the effect that the hazard is a lateral water hazard in play from the forward tee.

### 33-2a/7 Deeming Body of Water as Both Water Hazard and Lateral Water Hazard

A given part of a body of water must not be defined as both a water hazard and a lateral water hazard in play of a particular hole, except in the circumstances described in Decision 33-2a/6.

A given part of a body of water may be defined as a water hazard in play of one hole and a lateral water hazard in play of another hole.

A given part of a body of water may be defined as a water hazard and another part of the same body of water as a lateral water hazard.

### 33-2a/8 Treating Ocean and Beach as Through the Green

There is no authority in the Rules for a Committee to treat the ocean and adjoining beach and rocks as through the green. Such treatment results in a more severe penalty in many instances than is the case if the ocean, beach and rocks are properly defined as a water hazard or lateral water hazard.

**Permissible Dropping Area Under Lateral Water Hazard Rule So Narrow Player Has Difficulty Dropping Within It — See 26-1/19.**

### 33-2a/9 Part of Lateral Water Hazard Where Impossible to Drop Not Nearer Hole

If part of a lateral water hazard at the side of a putting green is so configured that it may be impossible to drop a ball within two club-lengths of the point where the ball last crossed the hazard margin without dropping nearer the hole than that point, the following is suggested:

(1) the part of the hazard where the situation exists should be distinctively marked;

(2) one or two Ball Drops (or Dropping Zones) should be established; and

(3) a Local Rule should state that, if a ball in the lateral water hazard last crossed the margin of the hazard in the marked area, the player may, under penalty of one stroke, drop a ball in the Ball Drop or, if two Ball Drops are established, in the nearer of the two Ball Drops.

Rule 33  435

area. B requests the Committee to declare the area ground under repair. Would the Committee be justified in declaring the area ground under repair in such circumstances?

**A.** Yes; this applies in either match or stroke play. However, it is preferable that all areas which warrant marking as ground under repair should be so marked before the start of a competition.

### 33-2a/3  Extensive Damage Due to Heavy Rain and Traffic

When heavy rains have resulted in many areas of unusual damage to the course (such as deep ruts caused by vehicles or footprints by spectators) and it is not feasible to define them with stakes or lines, a notice to players along the following lines is suggested:

"Ground under repair may include areas of unusual damage, including areas where spectators or other traffic have combined with wet conditions to affect materially the ground surface, but only when so declared by a Committee member."

Without such notice, Committee members have authority to declare unusual damage to be ground under repair, if so authorized. However, a notice has the advantage of advising all players that relief from unusual damage might be given.

**Old Hole Plug Sunk or Raised on Line of Putt** — See 16-1c/3.
**Fallen Tree Attached to Stump** — See 25/9.
**Cracks in Earth** — See 25/12.
**Rut Made by Tractor** — See 25/16.
**Marking Environmentally-Sensitive Areas** — See 33-8/41.

### 33-2a/4  Where to Place Lines or Stakes Defining Margin of Water Hazard

Lines and stakes defining the margins of a water hazard should be placed as nearly as possible along the natural limits of the hazard, i.e., where the ground breaks down to form the depression containing the water. See also Decision 26-1/19.

**Ball Within Natural Margin of Water Hazard But Outside Stakes Defining Margin** — See 26/2.

### [33-2a/5  Reserved]

### 33-2a/6  Pond Is Water Hazard from Back Tee and Lateral Water Hazard from Forward Tee

**Q.** A pond on a par-3 hole meets the Definition of a lateral water hazard in play from the forward tee but not from the back tee. How should the Committee handle this situation?

Rule 33    433

### 33-1/13 Competitor Disqualified from Handicap Event Claims Gross Prize

**Q.** In a stroke-play event, a competitor played off a higher handicap than that to which he was entitled. Although the event was primarily a handicap one, there was also a gross prize, and the competitor concerned had the lowest gross score.

The competitor was disqualified from the handicap competition under Rule 6-2b, but he claimed the gross prize. Should he receive the gross prize?

**A.** Yes.

### 33-1/14 Condition Regarding Footwear

**Q.** May a Committee, in the conditions of a competition, prohibit the use of shoes with metal or traditionally designed spikes?

**A.** Yes.

**Other Decisions relating to Rule 33-1:**

**Condition Requiring Use of Ball on List of Conforming Golf Balls; Penalty for Breach** — See 5-1/2.

**Permitting Players to Discontinue Play for Refreshment** — See 6-8a/2.5.

### 33-2a/1 Exposed Water Pipe Adjacent and Parallel to Boundary Fence Causes Problems; Suggested Procedure

**Q.** An exposed water pipe (obstruction) which is parallel to, and about six inches inside, a boundary fence is causing a problem. If a ball lies near the boundary fence, the prohibition against free relief from the fence is effectively negated because in most cases the player would be entitled to drop away from the fence by taking free relief from the water pipe under Rule 24-2b. Is there a solution to this dilemma?

**A.** It is suggested that the water pipe be declared an integral part of the course and thus not an obstruction — see Definition of "Obstructions" — in which case the player would have to play the ball as it lies or deem it unplayable.

**Stone Serving as Part of Drain in Bunker** — See 24/7.

### 33-2a/2 Declaring Area as Ground Under Repair During Competition Round

**Q.** A's ball is in a poor lie in a washed-out area which warrants being marked as ground under repair but is not so marked. He deems the ball unplayable and proceeds under Rule 28, incurring a one-stroke penalty.

Subsequently, in the same competition round, B's ball is in the same

33

## [33-1/9 Reserved]

### 33-1/9.5 Breach of Transportation Condition by Caddie

**Q.** The Committee has adopted the Transportation Condition in Appendix I as a condition of competition. During the stipulated round, a player's caddie accepts a ride on a golf cart without the authority of the Committee. Is the player penalized for the caddie's breach of the condition?

**A.** Yes. The player is responsible for any breach of a Rule during a stipulated round by his caddie and incurs the applicable penalty (Rule 6-1). (Revised)

## [33-1/10 Reserved]

## [33-1/11 Reserved]

### 33-1/11.5 Status of Team Captain or Coach

**Q.** May a Committee, in the conditions of a team competition, specify that, during the stipulated round, the team captain or coach is part of the match or part of the competitor's side, i.e., he is not an outside agency?

**A.** Yes. If such a condition is adopted, the player(s) or, in some circumstances, the team would be responsible for any breach of the Rules by the captain or coach.

**Team Captain Gives Advice While Playing** – See 8/2.

**Advice Given by Team Coach or Captain** – See 8-1/24.

### 33-1/12 Wrong Handicap Used Due to Committee Misinformation

**Q.** The players in a four-ball match were unsure as to the handicaps to which they were entitled under the conditions of the competition. They consulted a member of the Committee who wrongly advised them as to the condition regarding handicaps. This resulted in Player A receiving one less handicap stroke than he was entitled to receive. Player A's side lost the match, 4 and 3. The Committee representative's error was then discovered. What should the Committee do?

**A.** The Committee should resolve the matter in whatever manner it considers most equitable. The Committee could let the result stand or require a replay of the match.

All players except Player A received the correct number of handicap strokes and Player A received only one less stroke than he should have received. In view of this fact and the rather one-sided result, it is recommended that the fairest solution would be to let the result stand.

### 33-1/5 Competitor in Stroke-Play Event Plays with Two Players Engaged in Match

**Q.** A competitor in a stroke play competition had no other competitor with whom to play. So he joined two players engaged in a match and one of those players served as his marker. Is such procedure considered combining stroke play and match play, contrary to Rule 33-1?

**A.** No. The competitor was playing stroke play only and the other two players were playing match play only. The Committee should retrospectively appoint the player concerned as the competitor's marker — see Definition of "Marker."

### 33-1/6 One Player in Match Competes Concurrently in Stroke-Play Competition

**Q.** A and B played a match. A concurrently competed in a stroke play competition. What should the Committee do?

**A.** Under Rule 33-1, both the result of the match and the score returned by A in the stroke-play event were unacceptable.

If the match was to be played on any day in a prescribed period, A and B must replay the match within the prescribed period. If it was too late for A and B to replay the match within the period, A and B are disqualified, unless one concedes the match to the other — see Rule 2-4.

It would not be proper to allow A to replay the round in the stroke-play competition. A had already competed in that competition, and his score was unacceptable.

**Competing Simultaneously in Bogey or Stableford Competition and Stroke-Play Competition — See 32-1/1.**

### 33-1/7 Making Competitors Responsible for Adding Scores

**Q.** May the Committee make it a condition of a competition that competitors are responsible for the addition of scores?

**A.** No. Such a condition would modify Rule 33-5.

**Requirement That Alteration on Score Card Be Initialed — See 6-6a/6.**

**Requirement That Score Be Entered into Computer — See 6-6b/8.**

### 33-1/8 Use of Golf Carts in Competition

**Q.** May a player use a golf cart during a competition?

**A.** Yes, unless such equipment is prohibited in the conditions of the competition (Rule 33-1).

(d) cancel the third and fourth rounds and declare the leader after 36 holes to be the winner.

The third and fourth choices are undesirable. It is preferable not to reduce the number of rounds of a competition when the competition is in progress.

The Committee does not have the authority to reduce the number of holes of a stipulated round once play has commenced in that round.

### 33-1/3 Starting Players from 1st and 10th Tees

**Q.** May the Committee start play in a competition from both the 1st and the 10th tees?

**A.** Yes. See Definition of "Stipulated Round," which says that the holes are to be played in correct sequence unless otherwise authorized by the Committee.

### 33-1/3.5 Restriction on Which Partner in Foursome Competition May Play from 1st Tee

**Q.** Rule 29-1 states that in a foursome "The partners must play alternately from the teeing grounds and alternately during the play of each hole." However, it is a matter of personal choice which partner drives at the first tee.

May a Committee, in the conditions of a foursome competition, stipulate which partner must play from the first tee?

**A.** Yes.

### 33-1/4 Match Decided by Wrong Form of Play by Agreement of Players

**Q.** The four participants in a first-round match thought the competition was a foursome competition, whereas it was in fact a four-ball competition. They played the first hole on a foursome basis and then learned of their error. Rather than go back and begin again on a four-ball basis, they agreed (1) to continue playing a foursome and (2) that in the four-ball competition the side losing the foursome match would default to the winning side.

The matter came to the Committee's attention after the side receiving the default reached the semi-finals of the four-ball event. What should the Committee do?

**A.** The side should be disqualified under Rule 1-3 for agreeing to decide a match other than as prescribed in the conditions, and the Committee should decide how the competition should be concluded.

**Wrong Form of Play Used to Decide Which Side Concedes Match** – See 2-4/21.

**Wrong Form of Play Used in Match-Play Event** – See 6-1/1.

**Competition in Which Best Two of Four Scores Used to Determine Winner; Competitor Returns Score Card with Higher Handicap** — See 6-2b/5.

**Other Decisions relating to Rule 33:**

**Indicating Hole Numbers on Teeing Grounds** — See 11-5/2.

**Artificial Limbs** — See 14-3/15.

**Ball Assisting Fellow-Competitor on Putting Green; Procedure for Committee Member if Competitor Does Not Lift Ball** — See 22/7.

**Preventing Ball from Being Carried Out of Bounds by Flow of Water in Water Hazard** — See 26-1/7.

**Player's Ball Found by Committee Member; Player Prefers to Continue with Provisional Ball** — See 27-2/2.

### 33-1/1 Altering Conditions After Competition Starts

**Q.** A condition of a stroke-play competition provided that scores must be returned by 7:30 p.m. At 5 p.m., a member of the Committee extended the deadline to accommodate four late-arriving competitors. Is such action proper?

**A.** No. Once a competition has started, the conditions should be altered only in very exceptional circumstances. In this case, no such circumstances existed.

**Players Exclude Operation of Condition** — See 1-3/7.

### 33-1/2 Number of Holes of Stroke Play Competition Reduced During the Competition

**Q.** A 72-hole stroke-play competition is scheduled over four consecutive days. Eighteen holes are to be played each day. On the third day, all competitors finish the first nine holes but a number of competitors are still playing the second nine holes. At that point, the course becomes unplayable due to heavy rain and play is suspended. The rain continues and it is impossible to resume play that day. What are the Committee's options?

**A.** Under Rules 33-1 and 33-2d, the Committee has the following choices:

(a) resume play the next day and finish the third round, and then play the last 18 holes that day or on a subsequent day.

(b) cancel the third round, replay it on a subsequent day and then play the last 18 holes that day or on a subsequent day.

(c) reduce to three the number of rounds of the competition and finish the suspended third round on a subsequent day, or cancel the third round and replay it on a subsequent day, or

## [33/2 Reserved]

## 33/3 Match-Play Finalists Both Disqualified

If both finalists in a match-play competition are disqualified, the event must conclude without a winner.

## [33/4 Reserved]

## 33/5 Distance Markers

**Q.** May a Committee install markers on a hole to indicate distances to the green?

**A.** Yes.

## 33/6 Map of Putting Green Indicating Hole Position Displayed at Tee

**Q.** At the teeing ground of each hole, a Committee has displayed a map of the putting green. The position of the hole on the green is indicated on each map. Is this proper?

**A.** Yes. Displaying such maps is not contrary to the Rules.

## 33/7 Whether Player Disqualified in Match-Play Event Entitled to Prize Won Prior to Disqualification

**Q.** If a player in a match-play event is disqualified, should he be entitled to any prize he had previously won in the event?

**A.** Yes.

## 33/8 Application of Disqualification Penalty in Competition in Which Not All Scores Used to Determine Winner

**Q.** In a 72-hole stroke-play team competition with each team consisting of three players, a team's score for each round is the aggregate of the two best scores for the round. In the first of four rounds, a player is disqualified under Rule 6-3a. May he play in the subsequent rounds and have his score count?

**A.** Yes. The disqualification applies only to that round of the competition. This applies to all events in which not all scores are used to determine the winner (e.g., an individual competition in which the player counts his three best scores from four rounds).

However, if the player had been disqualified under Rule 33-7 or for a serious breach of Rule 1-2, it is up to the Committee to determine whether that disqualification should be for the round or the duration of the competition. (New)

## 33-6. Decision of Ties

The *Committee* must announce the manner, day and time for the decision of a halved match or of a tie, whether played on level terms or under handicap.

A halved match must not be decided by stroke play. A tie in stroke play must not be decided by a match.

## 33-7. Disqualification Penalty; Committee Discretion

A penalty of disqualification may in exceptional individual cases be waived, modified or imposed if the *Committee* considers such action warranted.

Any penalty less than disqualification must not be waived or modified.

If a *Committee* considers that a player is guilty of a serious breach of etiquette, it may impose a penalty of disqualification under this Rule.

## 33-8. Local Rules

**a. Policy**

The *Committee* may establish Local Rules for local abnormal conditions if they are consistent with the policy set forth in Appendix I.

**b. Waiving or Modifying a Rule**

A Rule of Golf must not be waived by a Local Rule. However, if a *Committee* considers that local abnormal conditions interfere with the proper playing of the game to the extent that it is necessary to make a Local Rule that modifies the Rules of Golf, the Local Rule must be authorized by the USGA.

### 33/1 Removal of Casual Water or Loose Impediments on Putting Green by Committee

**Q.** If casual water, leaves, sand or other loose impediments accumulate on a putting green during a round, would it be appropriate for the Committee to remove them?

**A.** Yes. The Committee may do what is necessary to eliminate the condition, e.g., use a squeegee or brush or blow the surface of the putting green. It is not necessary for the Committee to suspend play to take these actions.

In such cases, the Committee may, when necessary, enlist the help of players to eliminate the condition. However, a player would be in breach of Rule 13-2 if he were to mop up casual water on his line of play or line of putt without the Committee's permission.

**Casual Water Covering Teeing Ground** — See 25-1b/4.

**Dividing Double Green** — See 25-3/1.

do so. On any day of a stroke-play competition, the *Committee* should not normally permit practice on or to a *putting green* or from a *hazard* of the competition *course*.

**d. Course Unplayable**

If the *Committee* or its authorized representative considers that for any reason the *course* is not in a playable condition or that there are circumstances that render the proper playing of the game impossible, it may, in match play or stroke play, order a temporary suspension of play or, in stroke play, declare play null and void and cancel all scores for the round in question. When a round is canceled, all penalties incurred in that round are canceled.

(Procedure in discontinuing and resuming play — see Rule 6-8.)

### 33-3. Times of Starting and Groups

The *Committee* must establish the times of starting and, in stroke play, arrange the groups in which *competitors* must play.

When a match-play competition is played over an extended period, the *Committee* establishes the limit of time within which each round must be completed. When players are allowed to arrange the date of their match within these limits, the *Committee* should announce that the match must be played at a stated time on the last day of the period unless the players agree to a prior date.

### 33-4. Handicap Stroke Table

The *Committee* must publish a table indicating the order of holes at which handicap strokes are to be given or received.

### 33-5. Score Card

In stroke play, the *Committee* must provide each *competitor* with a score card containing the date and the *competitor's* name or, in *foursomes* or *four-ball* stroke play, the *competitors'* names.

In stroke play, the *Committee* is responsible for the addition of scores and the application of the handicap recorded on the score card.

In *four-ball* stroke play, the *Committee* is responsible for recording the better-ball score for each hole and in the process applying the handicaps recorded on the score card, and adding the better-ball scores.

In bogey, par and Stableford competitions, the *Committee* is responsible for applying the handicap recorded on the score card and determining the result of each hole and the overall result or points total.

**Note:** The *Committee* may request that each *competitor* record the date and his name on his score card.

426 Rule 33

## ADMINISTRATION

# Rule 33. The Committee

### Definitions

All defined terms are in *italics* and are listed alphabetically in the Definitions section — see pages 3-11.

### 33-1. Conditions; Waiving Rule

The *Committee* must establish the conditions under which a competition is to be played.

The *Committee* has no power to waive a Rule of Golf.

Certain specific Rules governing stroke play are so substantially different from those governing match play that combining the two forms of play is not practicable and is not permitted. The results of *matches* played and the scores returned in these circumstances must not be accepted.

In stroke play the *Committee* may limit a *referee*'s duties.

### 33-2. The Course

#### a. Defining Bounds and Margins

The *Committee* must define accurately:

(i) the course and *out of bounds*,
(ii) the margins of *water hazards* and *lateral water hazards*,
(iii) *ground under repair*, and
(iv) *obstructions* and integral parts of the course.

#### b. New Holes

New *holes* should be made on the day on which a stroke-play competition begins and at such other times as the *Committee* considers necessary, provided all *competitors* in a single round play with each *hole* cut in the same position.

**Exception:** When it is impossible for a damaged *hole* to be repaired so that it conforms with the Definition, the *Committee* may make a new *hole* in a nearby similar position.

**Note:** Where a single round is to be played on more than one day, the *Committee* may provide in the conditions of a competition that the *holes* and *teeing grounds* may be differently situated on each day of the competition, provided that, on any one day, all *competitors* play with each *hole* and each *teeing ground* in the same position.

#### c. Practice Ground

Where there is no practice ground available outside the area of a competition *course*, the *Committee* should establish the area on which players may practice on any day of a competition, if it is practicable to

Rule 33   425

## 32-2b/1 Breach of Rule by Both Partners at Same Hole in Four-Ball Stableford

**Q.** A and B are partners in a four-ball Stableford competition. During the play of a hole, A and B find they have exchanged balls at the previous hole. What is the ruling?

**A.** A and B are not disqualified from the competition but only for the hole at which they exchanged balls, for which they score no points.

marker inadvertently transposed the scores, recording a 5 (net 4) for A and a 4 (net 3) for B. The card was returned with these scores recorded. What is the ruling?

**A.** B's recorded score of 4 (net 3) was the lower recorded score. As this was lower than the score actually taken by B and was also lower than A's recorded score of 5 (net 4), the result of the hole was affected and the side is disqualified under Rule 32-2a for a breach of Rule 31-7a.

The same ruling would apply in a four-ball bogey or par competition on a handicap basis.

### 32-2a/3 Handicap Stableford Competition; Recording of Lower Gross Score Affects Result of Hole

**Q.** In a handicap Stableford competition against a fixed score of par, a competitor inadvertently returns his score card to the Committee with a score of 6 at the 9th hole when his score for the hole was actually 7. The 9th hole is a par 4 at which the competitor receives a handicap stroke. What is the ruling?

**A.** As the recording of the lower score affected the result of the hole, i.e., the competitor would be awarded 1 point for the hole when he should have received no points, the competitor is disqualified under Rule 32-2a for a breach of Rule 6-6d.

### 32-2a/4 Handicap Stableford Competition; Recording of Lower Gross Score Does Not Affect Result of Hole

**Q.** In a handicap Stableford competition against a fixed score of par, a competitor inadvertently returns his score card to the Committee with a score of 6 at the 11th hole when his score for the hole was actually 7. The 11th hole is a par 4 at which the competitor receives no handicap strokes. What is the ruling?

**A.** As the recording of the lower score did not affect the result of the hole, i.e., the competitor would be awarded no points for the hole despite recording a 6 instead of a 7, there is no penalty (Rule 32-2a).

### 32-2a/5 Handicap Bogey or Par Competition; Recording of Lower Gross Score Does Not Affect Result of Hole

**Q.** In a handicap bogey or par competition, a competitor inadvertently returns his score card to the Committee with a score of 3 at the 10th hole when his score for the hole was actually 4. The 10th hole is a par 4 at which the competitor receives a handicap stroke. What is the ruling?

**A.** As the recording of the lower score did not affect the result of the hole, i.e., the competitor would be awarded the hole despite recording a 3 instead of a 4, there is no penalty (Rule 32-2a).

## 32-1/1 Competing Simultaneously in Bogey or Stableford Competition and Stroke Play Competition

**Q.** Is it permissible for a player to compete simultaneously in a bogey or Stableford competition and a stroke-play competition?

**A.** Yes, since bogey and Stableford competitions are forms of stroke-play competition.

## 32-1/2 Omitting Holes in Bogey or Stableford Competition

**Q.** In a bogey or Stableford competition, may a player omit two holes of the round and return a score for 16 holes?

**A.** Yes. Under Rule 32-1a, any hole for which a competitor makes no return in a bogey competition is regarded as a loss. Under Rule 32-1b, if no score is returned on a hole in a Stableford competition, the competitor scores no points for that hole.

## 32-1/3 Determination of Honor in Handicap Stableford Competition

**Q.** In a handicap Stableford competition, if B has the honor at a hole and A and B have the same gross score at that hole but A receives a handicap stroke, who has the honor at the next hole?

**A.** A has the honor because of a better net score. (Revised)

## 32-2a/1 Four-Ball Stableford Competition on Handicap Basis; Side's Scores Transposed at a Hole But Not to Side's Advantage

**Q.** A and B were partners in a four-ball Stableford competition on a handicap basis. At a hole where A, but not B, received a handicap stroke, A scored a 4 (net 3) and B scored a 5. The marker inadvertently transposed the scores, recording a 5 (net 4) for A and a 4 for B. The card was returned with these scores recorded. What is the ruling?

**A.** There is no penalty. Although B's recorded score of 4 was lower than actually taken by him, since it was not lower than the recorded score of net 4 for A (which was higher than actually taken by A), there was no breach of Rule 31-7a. Nor was there a breach of Rule 32-2a, since the error did not affect the result of the hole.

The same ruling would apply in a four-ball bogey or par competition on a handicap basis.

## 32-2a/2 Four-Ball Stableford Competition on Handicap Basis; Side's Scores Transposed at a Hole to Side's Advantage

**Q.** A and B were partners in a four-ball Stableford competition on a handicap basis. At a hole, A scored 4 (net 3) and B scored 5 (net 4). The

**Note 1:** Maximum of 14 Clubs (Rule 4-4) — Penalties applied as follows: From total points scored for the round, deduction of two points for each hole at which any breach occurred; maximum deduction per round: four points.

**Note 2:** One Caddie at Any One Time (Rule 6-4) — Penalties applied as follows: From the points scored for the round, deduction of two points for each hole at which any breach occurred; maximum deduction per round: four points.

**Note 3:** Undue Delay; Slow Play (Rule 6-7) — *The competitor's* score is adjusted by deducting two points from the total points scored for the round.

### 32-2. Disqualification Penalties

**a. From the Competition**

A *competitor is disqualified* from the competition for a breach of any of the following:

- Rule 1-3 — Agreement to Waive Rules
- Rule 3-4 — Refusal to Comply with Rule
- Rule 4-1 or -2 — Clubs
- Rule 5-1 or -2 — The Ball
- Rule 6-2b — Handicap (playing off higher handicap; failure to record handicap)
- Rule 6-3 — Time of Starting and Groups
- Rule 6-4 — Caddie (having more than one caddie; failure to correct breach immediately)
- Rule 6-6b — Signing and Returning Score Card
- Rule 6-6d — Wrong Score for Hole, i.e., when the recorded score is lower than actually taken, except that no penalty is incurred when a breach of this Rule does not affect the result of the hole
- Rule 6-7 — Undue Delay; Slow Play (repeated offense)
- Rule 6-8 — Discontinuance of Play
- Rule 7-1 — Practice Before or Between Rounds
- Rule 14-3 — Artificial Devices and Unusual Equipment

**b. For a Hole**

In all other cases where a breach of a *Rule* would result in disqualification, the *competitor is disqualified* only for the hole at which the breach occurred.

# Rule 32. Bogey, Par and Stableford Competitions

**Definitions**
All defined terms are in *italics* and are listed alphabetically in the Definitions section — see pages 3-11.

## 32-1. Conditions

Bogey, par and Stableford competitions are forms of stroke play in which play is against a fixed score at each hole. The Rules for stroke play, so far as they are not at variance with the following specific Rules, apply.

### a. Bogey and Par Competitions

The scoring for bogey and par competitions is made as in match play. Any hole for which a *competitor* makes no return is regarded as a loss. The winner is the *competitor* who is most successful in the aggregate of holes.

The *marker* is responsible for marking only the gross number of strokes for each hole where the *competitor* makes a net score equal to or less than the fixed score.

**Note 1:** Maximum of 14 Clubs — Penalties as in match play — see Rule 4-4.

**Note 2:** One Caddie at Any One Time — Penalties as in match play — see Rule 6-4.

**Note 3:** Undue Delay; Slow Play (Rule 6-7) — The *competitor's* score is adjusted by deducting one hole from the overall result.

### b. Stableford Competitions

The scoring in Stableford competitions is made by points awarded in relation to a fixed score at each hole as follows:

| Hole Played in | Points |
|---|---|
| More than one over fixed score or no score returned | 0 |
| One over fixed score | 1 |
| Fixed score | 2 |
| One under fixed score | 3 |
| Two under fixed score | 4 |
| Three under fixed score | 5 |
| Four under fixed score | 6 |

The winner is the *competitor* who scores the highest number of points.

The *marker* is responsible for marking only the gross number of strokes at each hole where the *competitor's* net score earns one or more points.

count is lower than actually taken. The score recorded for A was not A-B's lower score for the 10th hole. Accordingly, no penalty is applicable.

**Side's Scores Transposed at a Hole in Handicap Competition But Not to Side's Advantage** — See 32-2a/1.

### 31-7a/2  Lower Gross Score Attributed to Wrong Partner

**Q.** A and B were partners in four-ball stroke play. At the 11th hole, A picked up and B holed out in 4 strokes. The marker inadvertently recorded a score of 4 for A. The card was returned. What is the ruling?

**A.** It was A's recorded score of 4 which was the side's gross score to count. As this was lower than the score actually taken by A, the side is disqualified under Rule 31-7a.

**Side's Scores Transposed at a Hole in Handicap Competition to Side's Advantage** — See 32-2a/2.

### 31-8/1  Competitor Lifts Loose Impediment in Bunker When His Ball and Partner's Ball Are in Bunker

**Q.** A and B are partners in a four-ball stroke play competition. A's ball and B's ball are in the same bunker. A lifts a loose impediment lying in the bunker. A is penalized two strokes for a breach of Rule 13-4. Does B incur a penalty?

**A.** If A's infringement assisted B's play, B also is penalized two strokes — Rule 31-8. Otherwise, B incurs no penalty.

### Other Decisions relating to Rule 31-8:

**Competitor Plays Away from Hole to Assist Partner** — See 30-3f/6.

**Competitor After Picking Up Drops Ball Where Partner's Ball Lies and Plays Practice Stroke** — See 30-3f/7.

### 31-5/1 Player Waives Turn to Play; Circumstances Under Which He May Complete Hole

**Q.** A and B are partners in four-ball stroke play. A's tee shot at a par-3 entirely over water comes to rest in the water hazard. As B's tee shot comes to rest on the putting green, A elects not to play a ball under Rule 26-1 and proceeds to the green. B four putts and scores 5 for the hole. May A return to the tee and put another ball into play under Rule 26-1?

**A.** Yes. However, he may be subject to penalty under Rule 6-7 for unduly delaying play.

### 31-5/2 Extent to Which Side May Play in Order it Considers Best

Rule 31-5, which is an exception to Rule 10-2 (Order of Play), permits a side to play in the order it considers best. Generally, a side will exercise its right under Rule 31-5 for strategic reasons. However, in doing so, the side must not unduly delay play (Rule 6-7).

The following are examples of a side (competitors A and B) playing in an order other than that set forth in Rule 10-2b and whether a penalty under Rule 6-7 would be appropriate:

(a) A's ball is on the putting green five feet from the hole and he plays before B, whose ball is on the putting green 20 feet from the hole — no penalty.

(b) A's ball is in an awkward lie in a hazard 30 yards from the hole and he plays before B, whose ball is in the fairway 50 yards from the hole — no penalty.

(c) A's ball is 220 yards from the hole on a par-5 hole and he plays his second stroke before B, whose ball is 240 yards from the hole plays — no penalty.

(d) In situation (c) above, A's ball comes to rest 30 yards from the green. The side then elects to have A play his third stroke before B plays his second stroke — B is penalized two strokes for a breach of Rule 6-7.

### 31-7a/1 Competitor Records Score for Hole Not Completed

**Q.** A and B are partners in four-ball stroke play. At the 10th hole, A picks up and B holes out in 5 strokes. The marker records a score of 6 for A and a score of 5 for B. The card is returned with these scores recorded. Is any penalty incurred because A-B returned a card containing a score for A at a hole which A did not complete?

**A.** No. Rule 31-7a provides that disqualification of a side under Rule 6-6d applies only when the recorded score of the partner whose score is to

**Flagstick Attended by Partner Without Express Authority of Competitor; Ball Strikes Flagstick or Partner** — See 17-3/4.

## 31-2/1 Absent Player Joins Partner After Fellow-Competitor Plays from Teeing Ground But Before Partner Plays

**Q.** In four-ball stroke play, A and B are playing with C and D. They have been given a starting time of 9:00 a.m. D arrives at 9:01 a.m. after A has played but before B and C have played. May D play the first hole?

**A.** D was late for his starting time and as such the answer depends on whether the Note to Rule 6-3a was in effect. If the Note was not in effect, D is disqualified for the first hole and may not play it — Rules 6-3a and 31-7c.

If the Note was in effect, D may play the first hole, adding the penalty of two strokes prescribed by the Note to his score for that hole. Rule 31-2 allows an absent player to join his partner before his partner has commenced play of a hole. As C had not yet played from the teeing ground, D may join him.

If D did not arrive until later in the round, he would be able to join his partner between holes without penalty, provided C had not yet played from the next tee, regardless of whether A and/or B had played.

### Decision relating to Rule 31-3:

**Breach of 14-Club Rule in Stroke Play Discovered at 8th Hole; Where Penalty Strokes Applied** — See 4-4a/10.

## 31-4/1 Gross Score of Partner with Better Net Score Omitted from Card

**Q.** In four-ball stroke play on handicap, partners A and B both holed out in 4 at the 8th hole; partner A did not receive a handicap stroke at the hole, but partner B did. The marker, who was a fellow-competitor, recorded a gross score of 4 for A, who did not receive a stroke, and no gross score for B. However, the marker also recorded a net 3 in the better-ball column.

On completion of the round, the card, in all other respects correct, was signed and returned to the Committee. Both the marker and the partners were interviewed, and it was established that in fact both partners had gross scores of 4 at the 8th hole. What is the ruling?

**A.** Under Rules 6-6b and 31-4, it was the responsibility of one of the partners to check the side's better-ball gross score for each hole before countersigning the card.

When checking the card, the partner concerned should have noticed that there was no gross score recorded for B at the 8th hole and should have corrected this mistake. As he did not do so, A's gross 4 was the side's score for the hole. It is the responsibility of the Committee — and not the competitor — to record the better-ball net score for each hole.

Rule 31 417

- Rule 1-3 — Agreement to Waive Rules
- Rule 3-4 — Refusal to Comply with a Rule
- Rule 4-1 or -2 — Clubs
- Rule 5-1 or -2 — The Ball
- Rule 6-2b — Handicap (playing off higher handicap; failure to record handicap)
- Rule 6-4 — Caddie (having more than one caddie; failure to correct breach immediately)
- Rule 6-6b — Signing and Returning Score Card
- Rule 6-6d — Wrong Score for Hole, i.e., when the recorded score of the *partner* whose score is to count is lower than actually taken. If the recorded score of the *partner* whose score is to count is higher than actually taken, it must stand as returned.
- Rule 6-7 — Undue Delay; Slow Play (repeated offense)
- Rule 7-1 — Practice Before or Between Rounds
- Rule 14-3 — Artificial Devices and Unusual Equipment
- Rule 31-4 — Gross Scores to Count Not Individually Identifiable

### b. Breach by Both Partners

A *side* is disqualified:

(i) for a breach by both of Rule 6-3 (Time of Starting and Groups) or Rule 6-8 (Discontinuance of Play), or

(ii) if, at the same hole, each *partner* is in breach of a *Rule* the penalty for which is disqualification from the competition or for a hole.

### c. For the Hole Only

In all other cases where a breach of a *Rule* would result in disqualification, the *competitor* is disqualified only for the hole at which the breach occurred.

### 31-8. Effect of Other Penalties

If a *competitor's* breach of a *Rule* assists his *partner's* play, the *partner* incurs the applicable penalty in addition to any penalty incurred by the *competitor*.

In all other cases where a *competitor* incurs a penalty for breach of a *Rule*, the penalty does not apply to his *partner*.

### Decisions relating to Rule 31:

Competitor Who Has Holed Out Touches Partner's Line of Putt — See 1-2/3.5.

# Rule 31.
# Four-Ball Stroke Play

**Definitions**
All defined terms are in *italics* and are listed alphabetically in the Definitions section — see pages 3-11.

## 31-1. General
In *four-ball* stroke play two *competitors* play as *partners*, each playing his own ball. The lower score of the *partners* is the score for the hole. If one *partner* fails to complete the play of a hole, there is no penalty.

The Rules of Golf, so far as they are not at variance with the following specific Rules, apply to *four-ball* stroke play.

## 31-2. Representation of Side
A *side* may be represented by either *partner* for all or any part of a *stipulated round*; both *partners* need not be present. An absent *competitor* may join his *partner* between holes, but not during play of a hole.

## 31-3. Maximum of 14 Clubs
The *side* is penalized for a breach of Rules 4-3a(iii) and 4-4 by either *partner*.

## 31-4. Scoring
The *marker* is required to record for each hole only the gross score of whichever *partner's* score is to count. The gross scores to count must be individually identifiable; otherwise the *side is disqualified*. Only one of the *partners* need be responsible for complying with Rule 6-6b. (Wrong score — see Rule 31-7a.)

## 31-5. Order of Play
Balls belonging to the same *side* may be played in the order the *side* considers best.

## 31-6. Wrong Ball
If a *competitor* makes a *stroke* at a *wrong ball* that is not in a *hazard*, he incurs a penalty of two *strokes* and must correct his mistake by playing the correct ball or by proceeding under the Rules. His *partner* incurs no penalty even if the *wrong ball* belongs to him.

If the *wrong ball* belongs to another *competitor*, its owner must place a ball on the spot from which the *wrong ball* was first played.

## 31-7. Disqualification Penalties
**a. Breach by One Partner**
A *side* is *disqualified from the competition* for a breach of any of the following by either *partner*:

**A.** A incurs a penalty stroke under Rule 18-2a and must replace his ball. Assuming the infringement did not assist B, B incurs no penalty — Rule 30-3f.

### 30-3f/10 Player's Ball Lifted Without Authority by Opponent in Four-Ball Match

**Q.** In a four-ball match, an opponent lifted a player's ball on the putting green after marking its position. He did this without the authority of the player. Is the opponent subject to penalty?

**A.** Yes. Rule 20-1 prohibits such action. Accordingly, the opponent incurs a penalty stroke under Rule 18-3b, but the penalty does not apply to his partner — see Rule 30-3f. The player must replace his ball.

### 30-3f/11 Request to Lift Ball That Might Assist Partner Not Honored

**Q.** A and B are playing C and D in a four-ball match. B's ball is near the hole in a position to serve as a backstop for A's ball. C requests B to lift his ball. B does not comply and A putts. What is the ruling?

**A.** B is disqualified for the hole for failing to comply with Rule 22-1. If A's ball strikes B's ball, A would also be disqualified from the hole since B's infringement assisted A – Rule 30-3f. If the balls do not collide, A is not penalized.

### 30-3f/12 Player in Four-Ball Practices Putts on Previous Green After Partner Has Driven from Next Tee

**Q.** A and B are partners in a four-ball competition. A was practicing putts on the 4th green after B drove from the 5th tee. Was A in breach of Rule 7-2?

**A.** Yes.

In match play, A is disqualified for the 5th hole. B incurred no penalty since A's breach did not assist him (Rule 30-3f).

In stroke play, A incurred a penalty of two strokes at the 5th hole. B incurred no penalty since A's breach did not assist him (Rule 31-8).

**Player in Foursome Match Practices Putts on Previous Green After Partner Has Driven from Next Tee — See 29/3.**

414 Rule 30

ball. The player then putts towards the hole, and the roll of his ball is helpful to his partner in determining how much his putt will break, etc. Is such procedure contrary to the Rules?

**A.** Such procedure is contrary to the spirit of the game. In match play, in equity (Rule 1-4), the player should be disqualified for the hole and, since his action assisted his partner's play, the partner should incur the same penalty — Rule 30-3f.

In stroke play, the player should incur a penalty of two strokes and, under Rule 31-8, the partner should incur the same penalty.

**Putting Out After Concession of Stroke; Act Assists Partner — See 2-4/6.**

**Advice Given on Request of Opponent in Four-Ball Match — See 8-1/25.**

**Player Plays Partner's Ball; Act Assists Partner — See 30-3d/1.**

### 30-3f/7 Player After Picking Up Drops Ball Where Partner's Ball Lies and Plays Practice Stroke

**Q.** In four-ball play, A and B are partners. A hits his tee shot out of bounds and decides not to complete play of the hole. B was undecided on club selection for his second shot, so A drops a ball near B's ball and hits a shot towards the green. What penalties were incurred?

**A.** Since the side, i.e., both A and B, had not completed the play of the hole, A was practicing during play of the hole and thus was in breach of Rule 7-2.

Since it must be assumed that the breach assisted B, he would also be penalized — Rules 30-3f and 31-8.

### 30-3f/8 Player Disqualified for Next Hole Plays Hole That Hole

**Q.** In a four-ball match, A practices chip shots to the 18th green between play of the 9th and 10th holes. Thus, A is disqualified for the 10th hole under Rule 7-2. If A plays the 10th hole, is B, A's partner, also subject to disqualification for the 10th hole if A's play of the hole assists B's, e.g., with regard to club selection?

**A.** Since A was disqualified for the 10th hole, the strokes played by him on that hole were practice strokes. Therefore, A was in breach of Rule 7-2 each time he played a stroke on the 10th and, if B was assisted by any such stroke, B incurred the applicable penalty.

**Absent Partner Joins Match During Play of Hole — See 30-3a/1.**

### 30-3f/9 Player's Ball Moved by Partner in Playing His Own Ball

**Q.** In four-ball match play, A and B are partners. In playing his own ball, B accidentally strikes A's ball with his club and causes it to move. What is the procedure?

### 30-3f/4 Wrong Information Given by Player Out of Contention in Four-Ball Match

**Q.** A and B are playing C and D in a four-ball match, and the situation is as follows:

- A's ball is on the green; he lies 3.
- B's ball is in a bunker; he lies 5 and it is his turn to play.
- C's ball is on the green; he lies 4.
- D has picked up.

After B addresses his ball in the bunker, the ball moves and B incurs a penalty stroke under Rule 18-2b. B does not inform anyone that he has incurred a penalty stroke. B then replaces his ball and plays onto the green.

A then holes out for a 5 and C does likewise.

B is disqualified for the hole under Rule 9-2 for failing to inform C or D, before C played his next stroke, that he (B) had incurred a penalty stroke. Is A also disqualified for the hole under Rule 30-3f on the ground that B's failure to inform C or D of his (B's) penalty stroke adversely affected C's play?

**A.** No. B was clearly out of contention, and the result of the hole was dependent upon A and C alone. Accordingly, B's failure to inform C or D about the penalty could not have adversely affected C's play.

### 30-3f/5 Player Attending Flagstick for Opponent Struck by Ball of Opponent's Partner Who Played Out of Turn

**Q.** A and B are playing C and D in a four-ball match. It is B's turn to play and C is attending the flagstick at B's request. A, whose ball is in a deep bunker in such position that he cannot see C, plays out of turn and his ball strikes C. What is the ruling?

**A.** B authorized C to attend the flagstick which is the equivalent of A having authorized attendance of the flagstick. See Definition of "Partner," which provides that in a four-ball match, where the context so admits, the word "player" includes his partner.

Accordingly, A is disqualified for the hole (Rule 17-3b), but the penalty does not apply to B (Rule 30-3f).

### 30-3f/6 Player Plays Away from Hole to Assist Partner

**Q.** In a four-ball competition, a player purposely putts away from the hole to a position slightly farther from the hole than the spot where his partner's ball lies and on the same line to the hole as his partner's

## 30-3f/1 Player Lifts Loose Impediment in Bunker When His Ball and Partner's Ball in Bunker

**Q.** A and B are partners in a four-ball match. A's ball and B's ball are in the same bunker. A lifts a loose impediment lying in the bunker. A is disqualified for the hole for a breach of Rule 13-4. Does B incur a penalty?

**A.** If A's infringement assisted B's play, B is also disqualified for the hole — Rule 30-3f. Otherwise, B incurs no penalty.

## 30-3f/2 Hitting Sand in Bunker with Club After Failing to Extricate Ball; Partner's Ball in Same Bunker

**Q.** In a four-ball match A and B were partners. A played a stroke in a bunker and failed to get the ball out of the bunker. He then swung his club into the sand in the bunker, but this action did not affect his new lie in the bunker:

(a) What is the ruling if B's ball lay in the same bunker when A swung his club into the sand?

(b) What is the ruling if B's ball lay elsewhere?

**A.** In either case, A is disqualified for the hole (Rule 13-4 and Decision 13-4/35). The penalty does not apply to B unless A's action assisted B's play or adversely affected an opponent's play (Rule 30-3f).

## 30-3f/3 Player's Ball Resting Against Flagstick Lifted Before Being Holed; Others in Match Pick Up Mistakenly Believing Player Won Hole

**Q.** In a four-ball match, A's ball rested against the flagstick but it was not holed in terms of the Definition of "Holed." Instead of proceeding under Rule 17-4, A picked up the ball without marking its position. The other three players, believing that A had won the hole, picked up. Before anyone played from the next tee, a spectator pointed out that A's ball had not been holed. The players immediately asked the Committee for a ruling. What would be the correct ruling?

**A.** A incurred a penalty stroke under Rule 20-1 when he lifted his ball without marking its position. Since A did not inform the opponents about the penalty before they picked up, A was disqualified for the hole for giving wrong information — Rule 9-2. Since A's infringement adversely affected the opponents, i.e., caused them to pick up, A's partner was also disqualified for the hole — Rule 30-3f. Thus, the opponents won the hole.

## 30-3d/3 Players on Opposite Sides Exchange Balls During Play of Hole and Their Partners Pick Up; Error Discovered at Next Hole

**Q.** A and B were playing C and D in a four-ball match. At the 2nd hole, by mistake A played C's ball and then C played A's. C holed out with A's ball, scoring 5. A holed out C's ball, scoring 4. B and D picked up. Thus, A and B "won" the hole. The error was discovered during play of the 3rd hole, and Side C-D lodged a claim. What is the ruling?

**A.** A and C were disqualified for the 2nd hole for playing wrong balls. They should have informed their opponents as soon as practicable, which in this case was as soon as they had the opportunity to discover that they had done so, i.e., when they reached the balls wrongly played to play them again. Because they failed to do so, they gave wrong information (Rule 9-2) and, under Rule 2-5, a belated claim that A (and C as well) was disqualified for the 2nd hole for a breach of Rule 30-3d should be upheld.

It could be argued that B and D's play of the 2nd hole was adversely affected (in that they picked up) and that accordingly Rule 30-3f applies. However, Rule 30-3d specifically provides that the "partner incurs no penalty." This applies even if play of the wrong ball would have assisted the partner — See Decision 30-3d/1 — and by implication it applies in the related case of an adverse effect on an opponent's play.

Furthermore, applying Rule 30-3f for the breaches of Rule 9-2 would not have been proper because those breaches were the direct result of the penalties incurred under Rule 30-3d.

Accordingly, if B picked up before D, Side C-D won the hole. If D picked up before B, Side A-B won the hole. If the order in which B and D picked up was not determinable, the Committee should have ruled that the 2nd hole was halved.

## 30-3d/3.5 Player Plays Partner's Ball; Error Discovered After Opponents Have Played Next Strokes

**Q.** A and B are playing C and D in a four-ball match. At the 2nd hole, after the tee shots A mistakenly plays B's ball. The error is discovered after C and D play their second strokes, and C and D claim the hole. What is the ruling?

**A.** A is disqualified for the hole because he played a wrong ball (Rule 30-3d). B incurs no penalty for A having played his ball (Decision 30-3d/1) and players B, C and D should continue play of the hole.

### 30-3c/2 Waiving Turn to Putt in Four-Ball Match

**Q.** In a four-ball match, A and B are playing C and D. All four balls are on the green in three strokes. The balls of A and C are about 10 feet from the hole; B's ball is two feet away and D's is three feet away. C picks up his ball. A leaves his ball on the green, but tells B and D to "battle it out." D putts first and holes; B then putts and misses. May A then putt for a half?

**A.** No. A and B abandoned A's right to complete the hole by allowing D to putt before A and B when it was A-B's turn to play. Under Rule 30-3c, A-B could have opted for B to putt before A. However, if B had done so and missed, it would then have been A's turn to play.

The answer is different if B's ball is three feet away, D's is two feet away and B putts and misses. In these circumstances, A may putt, provided he does so before D putts.

**Waiving Turn to Play in Four-Ball Stroke Play — See 31-5/1.**

### 30-3d/1 Player Plays Partner's Ball

**Q.** A and B are partners in a four-ball match. By mistake, A putts B's ball and A is disqualified for the hole under Rule 30-3d for playing a wrong ball. B replaces his ball as required by Rule 30-3d and holes his putt. The opponents then claim that B also is disqualified for the hole under Rule 30-3f because A's act of putting B's ball assisted B in determining how much his putt would break, etc. Is the claim valid?

**A.** No. Rule 30-3d specifically provides that B incurs no penalty. Rule 30-3f is not applicable.

### 30-3d/2 Player Wins Hole with Wrong Ball and Partner Picks Up; Error Discovered at Next Hole

**Q.** In a four-ball match, Side A-B holed out for a 4. C, a member of Side C-D, then holed a putt for a 3 and his partner, D, picked up what he thought was his ball. After playing from the next tee, it was discovered that C had putted out at the previous hole with D's ball. Side A-B claimed the hole. What is the ruling?

**A.** C gave wrong information to Side A-B when he did not inform Side A-B as soon as practicable that he had incurred a penalty for playing a wrong ball — see Rule 9-2. Accordingly, a belated claim by Side A-B was valid — Rule 2-5.

The Committee should have ruled that C was disqualified for the hole — Rule 9-2 or Rule 30-3d — and, since D did not complete the hole, Side A-B won the hole.

### 30-3a/1 Absent Partner Joins Match During Play of Hole

**Q.** Rule 30-3a states in part: "An absent partner may join a match between holes, but not during play of a hole." If A and B are to play C and D in a four-ball match and A is absent when the match begins, what is the ruling if A joins the match during play of a hole?

**A.** A incurs the general penalty prescribed in Rule 2-6 and thus is disqualified for the hole. If any of A's strokes assisted B's play, B is also disqualified for the hole — Rule 30-3f.

### 30-3a/2 Absent Partner Gives Advice Before Joining Match

**Q.** A and B are to play C and D in a four-ball match. A is absent when the match begins. A arrives just after B, C and D have teed off at the 3rd hole. According to Decision 30-3a/1, A is prohibited from joining the match until the 4th hole. Is it permissible for A to give B advice during the play of the 3rd hole?

**A.** Yes.

### 30-3a/3 Determination of Handicap Allowances in Four-Ball Match If One Player Unable to Compete

**Q.** In a four-ball handicap match, the player with the lowest handicap is unable to play. Should the absent player be disregarded in determining the handicap allowances?

**A.** No. Under Rule 30-3a, a side may be represented by one partner for all or any part of the match. In determining handicap allowances, the handicaps of the three players should be reduced by the handicap of the absent player.

If a wrong handicap is declared for the absent player, Rule 6-2a applies.

### 30-3c/1 Player Entitled to Putt Stands on Another Player's Line of Putt

**Q.** A and B are partners in a four-ball match. A's ball is closer to the hole than any other ball and it is B's turn to play. A-B decide that A will putt before B – Rule 30-3c. However, in doing so A would be standing on B's line of putt or the line of putt of an opponent. What is the ruling?

**A.** A would be entitled to putt first even if he would be standing on B's line. Rule 30-3c overrides Rule 16-1a which prohibits touching the line of putt.

A would also be entitled to putt first if he would be standing on an opponent's line of putt. However, it would be a sporting gesture for A-B to relinquish A's right to putt first in these circumstances.

(4) The balls of all four players lie on the putting green and A's ball is the farthest from the hole with B's ball on the same line. Side C-D concedes B's next stroke for the four-ball match only, but B goes ahead and putts before A. In the four-ball match, A is disqualified for the hole (see Decision 2-4/6).

(5) B moves A's ball without authority under the Rules. In the four-ball match, A incurs a penalty stroke (Rule 18-2a) but, in his singles match against C, he incurs no penalty. B incurs no penalty in any match.

(6) Other than during search, A moves D's ball. In the four-ball match, A incurs a penalty stroke (Rule 18-3b) but, in his singles match against C, he incurs no penalty.

(7) On the 3rd hole it is discovered that B started his round with 15 clubs. In the four-ball match, Side A-B has two holes deducted from the state of the match after the 3rd hole. B has two holes deducted from the state of his singles match against D. A incurs no penalty in his singles match against C.

(8) During the round, it is discovered that B started the round with a non-conforming club. In the four-ball match, Side A-B is disqualified (Rules 4-1 and 30-3e). B is disqualified in his singles match against D. A incurs no penalty in his singles match against C.

(9) On the 5th hole, B holes out in 3 to win the hole for Side A-B in the four-ball match. A has a putt left to win or halve the hole in his singles match against C and asks B for advice. There is no penalty to either player. A and B may exchange advice at any time until the four-ball match has been concluded, at which point A and B are no longer partners and become outside agencies with respect to each other. (New)

### 30-3/2 Effect of State of Match Penalties in Four-Ball Play

**Q.** In a four-ball match in which A and B are partners, A employs two caddies at the 3rd hole. Before play of the 3rd hole is completed, A discovers and corrects his breach of Rule 6-4. As the penalty for breach of Rule 6-4 requires an adjustment of the state of the match, how should the penalty be applied in four-ball match play?

**A.** At the conclusion of the 3rd hole, Side A-B must deduct one hole from the state of the match.

In four-ball match play, when a player breaches a Rule that requires an adjustment to the state of the match, the side is penalized. If a breach of a Rule that requires an adjustment to the state of the match in match play arises in four-ball stroke play, both partners incur the applicable stroke play penalty. (New)

## 30-2/1 Player Plays Out of Turn from Tee in Three-Ball Match; One Opponent Requests Replay and Other Does Not

Following are the rulings in a three-ball match if A, B and C are scheduled to play in that order from the tee, B inadvertently drives first and A and C disagree on whether B should be required to replay the stroke under Rule 10-1c:

(a) If A wants B to replay the stroke but C does not, B must complete the hole with two balls. He must replay the stroke in his match with A, and continue with his original ball in his match with C.

(b) If C wants B to replay the stroke but A does not, B must continue with his original ball in both matches. B did not play out of turn with respect to C. Accordingly, C has no right to require B to replay the stroke.

If A, B and C are scheduled to play in that order from the tee, C inadvertently drives first and A and B disagree on whether C should be required to replay, C must complete the hole with two balls. He must replay his stroke in his match with the opponent who requires him to replay and continue with his original ball in his match with the other opponent.

## 30-3/1 Examples of Rulings in Four-Ball Match with Concurrent Singles Matches

When players are involved in concurrent matches, whenever possible the Rules are applied only to the match affected. When it is not possible to separate the matches, the four-ball match takes precedence.

A and B are playing C and D in a four-ball match. There are also concurrent singles matches between A and C and between B and D. The following are examples of the application of the Rules in such a format:

(1) A concedes a stroke, hole or the match to C but stipulates that the concession is solely for their singles match. The concession is not valid in the four-ball match.

(2) A concedes a stroke, hole or the match to C and does not specify which match the concession is intended for. The concession applies to both the four-ball and the singles matches.

(3) A concedes a stroke, hole or the match to D. The concession applies only to the four-ball match as A has no authority to make concession in the B-D singles match.

## 30/5 In Four-Ball Match Player with Putt for Half Picks Up in Error at Suggestion of Opponent Based on Misunderstanding

**Q.** A and B are playing C and D in a four-ball match. A has holed out in 4, the better ball for his side. When C holes out, A remarks: "Nice 4, C. D, you may pick your ball up." C does not correct A by stating he had a 5 and allows his partner D to pick his ball up although D still has a putt for a half.

Upon leaving the putting green, it occurs to C that he has allowed D to pick up when D had an opportunity to halve the hole. In the circumstances, could A's remark be construed as a concession of D's putt?

**A.** No. A's suggestion that D might pick up D's ball was based on A's mistaken impression that C had scored a 4 and that therefore D's putt could have no bearing on the result.

C should have corrected A's mistaken impression before D picked up his ball. Since C failed to do so and D did not finish the hole, C's score of 5 for the hole was C-D's better-ball score. Thus, C and D lost the hole.

## 30/6 Player Plays Practice Putt After He and Partner Have Holed Out But Before Opponents Hole Out

**Q.** In a four-ball match, A plays a practice putt after he and his partner have holed out but before the opponents have holed out. Was A in breach of Rule 7-2?

**A.** No. Rule 7-2 prohibits practicing during play of a hole. A did not practice during play of the hole because he and his partner had completed it. However, A was guilty of a breach of etiquette.

**Another Decision relating to Rule 30:**

Flagstick Attended by Partner Without Express Authority of Player; Ball Strikes Flagstick or Partner — See 17-3/4.

## 30-1/1 Side Plays Out of Turn from Tee; Opponents Require One Member of Side to Replay But Not Other

**Q.** A and B are playing C and D in a four-ball match. At one hole A and B drive out of turn. C and D require that A abandon his ball and replay in correct order and that B continue with his original ball. A and B maintain that if A is required to drive again then B must also do so. What is the ruling?

**A.** Rule 10-1c states in part: "... the opponent may immediately require the player to cancel the stroke so made ..." In this context, "immediately" means before anyone else plays.

In some situations the Committee may decide to define such a body of water as out of bounds for safety reasons (e.g., to prevent players playing from an unstable bank or cliff) or to ensure that a hole plays as designed (e.g., not to give the players the ability to play from the beach).

### 33-2a/12 Internal Boundary Between Holes

**Q.** It is proposed to install boundary stakes between two holes as a safety measure. It would prevent players playing a "dog-leg" hole from driving onto the fairway of another hole in order to cut the "dog-leg." Is it permissible to establish such a boundary?

**A.** Yes. For the recommended status of such boundary stakes, see Decision 24/5.

### 33-2a/13 Tee Decreed to Be in Bounds for Tee Shot and Out of Bounds Thereafter

**Q.** A Committee has decreed that ground surrounding a certain teeing ground is in bounds for tee shots and out of bounds thereafter. Is this permissible?

**A.** No. In play of a particular hole, an area cannot be both in bounds and out of bounds.

### 33-2a/14 Internal Out of Bounds Applying to Stroke from Teeing Ground Only

A Committee may make a Local Rule under Rule 33-2a declaring part of an adjoining hole to be out of bounds when playing a particular hole, but it is not permissible for a Committee to make a Local Rule placing an area of the course out of bounds to a stroke played from the teeing ground only.

### 33-2a/15 Establishing Boundary Line Inside Fence on Property Line

**Q.** Along a fence on our property line, i.e., the fence is a boundary fence, there are flower beds. To save time and protect the flowers, it is proposed to move the boundary line inward several feet by establishing white stakes along the inside edge of the flower bed. Is this permitted by the Rules?

**A.** Yes.

**Stile Attached to Boundary Fence — See 24/1.**

**Concrete Bases of Boundary Fence Posts — See 24/3.**

### 33-2a/16  Deeming Ball in Bounds Until Beyond Boundary Wall

**Q.** Because a boundary wall is in disrepair and the inside face is irregular, the Committee has declared by Local Rule that a ball is not out of bounds until it is beyond the wall. Is this permissible or must the inside face of the wall serve as the boundary line?

**A.** Such procedure is permissible. There is nothing in the Rules stating that, in the case of a boundary wall, the inside face of the wall serves as the boundary line.

### [33-2a/17  Reserved]

### [33-2a/18  Reserved]

### 33-2a/19  Boundary Altered by Unauthorized Removal of Boundary Stake

In stroke play, a boundary line has been altered through unauthorized removal of a boundary stake, and therefore there is an area (Area X) which is in bounds if the removed stake is disregarded and out of bounds if the removed stake is replaced.

**Q1.** A's ball comes to rest in Area X. A is aware that the boundary has been altered. He asks the Committee for a ruling. What is the ruling?

**A1.** The Committee should replace the removed stake, i.e., restore the original boundary line and require A to proceed under Rule 27-1, unless the Committee knows that one or more preceding competitors had, in ignorance of the fact that a stake has been removed, played from Area X. In that case, the Committee should allow the altered boundary line to stand for the remainder of the competition, and A would play his ball as it lay.

**Q2.** What would be the ruling if the Committee determined that one or more competitors had, in ignorance of the fact that a stake was missing, played from Area X and one or more other competitors had treated Area X as out of bounds and proceeded under Rule 27-1?

**A2.** If the inconsistent treatment of Area X could significantly affect the result of the competition, the round should be canceled and replayed. Otherwise, the round should stand.

### 33-2a/20  Displaced Boundary Stake

**Q.** A boundary stake has fallen down, or has been removed without authority of the Committee. The stake is lying several feet from the hole in which it had been situated. It is obvious that the stake had been displaced.

A player's ball comes to rest in bounds near the hole in which the boundary stake had been situated. The ball is in such a position that, if the boundary stake were reinstalled, it would interfere with the player's swing.

Is the player required to replace the stake before playing his next stroke?

**A.** No. If a boundary fence or stake is leaning towards the course and as a result interferes with a player's swing, the player is not allowed to straighten the fence or the stake — see Decision 13-2/18. It follows that, if a boundary fence or stake is leaning away from the course, the player is not allowed to straighten it.

A displaced boundary stake is a movable obstruction. Therefore, the player may replace it but he is not required to do so.

**Another Decision relating to Rule 33-2a:**

Marking Environmentally-Sensitive Areas — See 33-8/41.

### 33-2b/1  Holes Relocated and/or Tee-Markers Moved During Stroke-Play Round

**Q.** During a round in a stroke-play competition, one or more holes were relocated and/or tee-markers moved. What is the proper procedure?

**A.** If this was authorized by the Committee, the round should be declared null and void. In stroke play, the Committee is prohibited from relocating a hole and from moving tee-markers except as provided in the Exception and Note to Rule 33-2b or in circumstances such as those in Decision 25-1b/4.

If this was done without the authority or sanction of the Committee, generally the round should be declared null and void. However, if the course has not been altered significantly and no competitor has been given an undue advantage or disadvantage, the Committee would be justified in letting the round stand.

### 33-2b/2  Relocating Hole After Ball Already Positioned Nearby on Putting Green

**Q.** A's ball comes to rest on the putting green four feet from the hole. B's ball then strikes the hole, severely damaging the hole before coming to rest off the putting green, 30 feet from the hole. The players attempt to repair the damage caused by the impact of the ball as permitted by Rule 16-1c, but they are unable to restore the hole to its proper dimensions and call for a ruling. What should the Committee do?

**A.** The Committee should attempt to repair the hole so that it conforms with the Definition of "Hole." If this is not possible, the players may complete the hole with the hole in its damaged state. It is not desirable to relocate the hole, as provided in the Exception to Rule 33-2b, before all players in the group have completed play of the hole. However, the Committee may relocate the hole in a nearby similar position if it is necessary to ensure the proper playing of the game.

If it was necessary to relocate the hole before A and B made their next strokes, as A's ball was on the putting green, in equity (Rule 1-4), the Committee should require A to relocate his ball to a position comparable to that which his stroke had given him originally. As B's ball was off the putting green, the Committee should require B to play his ball as it lies. The same principle would apply in match play.

**Damaged Hole; Procedure for Player — See 16-1a/6.**

### 33-2d/1 Guidelines on Whether to Cancel Round

**Q.** In stroke play, in what circumstances should a Committee cancel a round?

**A.** There is no hard-and-fast rule. The proper action depends on the circumstances in each case and must be left to the judgment of the Committee.

Generally, a round should be canceled only in a case where it would be grossly unfair not to cancel it. For example, if some competitors begin a round under extremely adverse weather conditions, conditions subsequently worsen and further play that day is impossible, it would be unfair to the competitors who started not to cancel the round.

**Number of Holes of Stroke-Play Competition Reduced During the Competition — See 33-1/2.**

### 33-2d/2 Hole Surrounded by Casual Water

If all the area around the hole contains casual water, in stroke play the course should be considered unplayable and the Committee should suspend play under Rule 33-2d. In match play, the Committee should relocate the hole.

**Casual Water Covering Teeing Ground — See 25-1b/4.**

### 33-2d/3 Competitor Refuses to Start or Picks Up Because of Weather Conditions; Round Subsequently Canceled

**Q.** In stroke play, A refuses to start at the time arranged by the Committee because of inclement weather, and B picks up during the round for the same reason. Subsequently, the course becomes unplayable and the Committee cancels the round and reschedules it for the next day. Are A and B entitled to play the next day?

**A.** Yes. When a round is canceled all penalties incurred in the round are canceled — see Rule 33-2d.

**Player Unable to Resume Suspended Match at Scheduled Time — See 6-8b/4.**

### 33-2d/4 Match Begun in Ignorance That Course Closed

**Q.** Two players began a match at 10 a.m. After the players had played two holes, a member of the Committee arrived and advised them that the course had been closed since 9 a.m., but no notice to this effect had been posted at the 1st tee. Should the match be replayed entirely or resumed at the 3rd hole?

**A.** The match should be replayed entirely. Play on the course while it was closed should be considered null and void.

**Replacement of Club Broken on Practice Ground While Play Suspended — See 4-3/11.**

**Ball Moved by Wind or Casual Water While Play Suspended — See 18-1/11.**

### 33-3/1 Status of Starting Time Fixed by Players

**Q.** It was a condition of a match-play competition that each match must be played on the day and at the time published unless the players agreed to a prior date and time. A and B agreed to play their match at a specified time on a prior date. However, B arrived late. Was B subject to disqualification under Rule 6-3a?

**A.** Yes. The starting time agreed by A and B had the same status as a starting time fixed by the Committee.

### 33-3/2 Player Not Present at Time of Starting; Course Closed at the Time

**Q.** A and B were scheduled to play a match at 9 a.m., at which time the course was closed due to weather conditions. A was present at the appointed time. B, assuming the course would be closed, was not present. B arrived at noon, at which time the course was still closed. A claimed the match because B was not present at 9 a.m. Was the claim valid?

**A.** No. As the course was closed, and it was impossible for A and B to start at the appointed time or within a reasonable time thereafter, a new starting time for the match should be arranged.

**Time of Starting; Player is Late but Group Unable to Play Due to Delay — See 6-3a/4.**

### 33-3/3 Competitors Determining Own Groupings and Starting Times

**Q.** May a Committee permit competitors in a stroke-play competition to determine their own groupings and starting times?

**A.** Yes. Rule 33-3 does not prohibit such an arrangement.

**Postponement of Final Match Due to Injury of Player — See 6-3a/1.**

**All Competitors Must Be Present at Time of Starting — See 6-3a/2.**

### 33-3/4 Groupings for Stroke-Play Play-Off

**Q.** Is there any Rule limiting the number of competitors in a group in a stroke play play-off? For example, if 11 competitors are in a play-off, should they be separated into a group of five and a group of six? Or should they be separated into two groups of four and one group of three?

**A.** There is no Rule. The matter is up to the Committee. However, it is suggested that normally there should be no more than five competitors in any group.

### 33-4/1 Alteration of Handicap Stroke Table

**Q.** As provided in the Definition of a "Stipulated Round," the Committee has authorized certain matches to begin at the 6th hole. The higher-handicapped player in such matches is disadvantaged because, under the Handicap Stroke Table, the first handicap stroke is allocated to the 5th hole and, thus, it is not used if a match is concluded in less than 18 holes. Would it be permissible to alter the Handicap Stroke Table for such matches?

**A.** Yes.

**Another Decision relating to Rule 33-4:**

Handicap Stroke Given at Incorrect Hole in Error — See 6-2a/2.

### 33-5/1 Score Cards in Sudden-Death Play-Off

**Q.** Must competitors involved in a sudden-death play-off in stroke play return score cards to the Committee?

**A.** Yes, but only if the Committee has issued a score card for each competitor in accordance with Rule 33-5. Otherwise, the competitors should not be penalized if they fail to return score cards.

### 33-5/2 Wrong Handicap Applied by Committee Results in Player Not Receiving Prize

**Q.** In a stroke-play competition, A returns a card showing the handicap to which he is entitled and the Committee applies the wrong handicap or miscalculates the correct net score. This results in another competitor receiving a prize to which A was entitled. The error is discovered after the competition has closed. What is the ruling?

**A.** The Committee should correct its error by retrieving the prize and awarding it to A. There is no time limit for correcting such an error. Rule 34-1b is not applicable since it deals with penalties and not with Committee errors.

## 33-5/3 Misapplication of Handicap Affects Match-Play Draw

**Q.** Misapplication of a player's handicap by the Committee on a score card for the qualifying round of a match-play event results in an incorrect draw. The error is discovered during the first round of match play. What should the Committee do?

**A.** The Committee should deal with the matter in the fairest way possible. The Committee should consider amending the draw and canceling the matches affected by the amendment if this is practicable.

**Other Decisions relating to Rule 33-5:**

**When Score Card Considered Returned — See 6-6c/1.**

**Total Score Recorded by Competitor Incorrect — See 6-6d/2.**

**Competitors Made Responsible for Adding Scores — See 33-1/7.**

## [33-6/1 Reserved]

## [33-6/2 Reserved]

## 33-6/3 Determining Winner and Positions in Stroke-Play Play-Off

If there is a stroke play play-off between two competitors and one of them is disqualified or concedes defeat, it is not necessary for the other to complete the play-off hole or holes to be declared the winner.

If there is a play-off involving more than two competitors and not all of them complete the play-off hole or holes, the order in which the competitors are disqualified or decide to withdraw shall determine their positions in the play-off.

## 33-6/4 Players Decide Method of Settling Tie When Committee Fails to Do So

**Q.** A and B, in a club match-play event in which the Committee had not prescribed how a halved match would be decided, finished their stipulated round all square. A suggested that the tie be decided by an 18-hole play-off. B reluctantly agreed. A won the play-off. B protested to the Committee. He argued that the match should have been settled by a sudden-death play-off, since that is the customary manner of deciding a tie in club events. What should the Committee do?

**A.** Since the Committee did not prescribe the method of settling the tie, it was appropriate for the players to determine the method. Since the players agreed to an 18-hole play-off, the match should stand as played.

**Groupings for Stroke Play Play-Off — See 33-3/4.**

### 33-7/1 Authority to Waive or Modify Disqualification Penalty

Only the Committee as a whole has authority to waive or modify a penalty of disqualification under Rule 33-7. A referee or an individual member of the Committee may not take such action.

### 33-7/2 Modifying Penalty for Not Holing Out in Stroke Play

**Q.** In stroke play, a competitor missed a short putt at the 16th hole, knocked his ball off the green, picked it up and teed off at the next hole without having holed out at the 16th.

After the competitor returned his score card, a fellow-competitor brought the matter to the attention of the Committee. The competitor admitted the error and expressed the view that his fellow-competitors were unsportsmanlike in not calling the error to his attention when the incident occurred.

In such circumstances, would the Committee be justified in modifying to two strokes the disqualification penalty provided in Rule 3-2?

**A.** No. Rule 33-7 should never be invoked in the case of disqualification for failing to hole out in stroke play. The competitor in such a case has not played the course.

Failure of the fellow-competitors to advise the competitor of his error is not a good reason for modifying the penalty. It is the responsibility of the competitor to know the Rules.

**Waiving or Modifying Penalty for Carrying Non-Conforming Club — See 4-1/1.**

**Modifying Penalty for Holing Short Putt with Club Whose Playing Characteristics Changed Other Than in Normal Course of Play — See 4-3/4.**

**Waiving or Modifying Penalty for Use of Non-Conforming Ball — See 5-1/1.**

**Circumstances Which Warrant Waiving of Disqualification Penalty Under Rule 6-3a — See 6-3a/1.5.**

**When Play Suspended by Committee, Modifying or Waiving Penalty for Resuming Play Other Than at Time Ordered by Committee — See 6-8b/6.**

**When Play Suspended by Committee and Immediate Discontinuance of Play Required; Waiving or Modifying Penalty for Failure to Discontinue Play Immediately — See 6-8b/7.**

### 33-7/3 Competitor's Failure to Countersign Card Blamed on Lack of Time Provided by Committee

**Q.** In a 36-hole stroke-play competition played in one day over two courses, a competitor returned his first-round score card to the Committee but he failed to countersign it. After the second round the Committee informed him that he was disqualified. The competitor blamed the Committee for the error. He said the

Committee, in attempting to get him to leave promptly for the course on which the second round was being played, caused him to return his first-round card hurriedly and that he had been given insufficient time to check and countersign the card. The competitor requested the Committee to waive the penalty under Rule 33-7. Would the Committee be justified in doing so?

**A.** No. If the competitor did not feel he was given sufficient time to check and sign his first-round card, he should have protested before he returned the card.

### 33-7/4  Modifying Penalty for Returning Wrong Score

**Q.** A marker inadvertently recorded a 4 for a competitor on a hole at which the competitor's score was actually 5. The competitor failed to check his score for each hole and therefore did not discover the error. The competitor returned his card to the Committee.

Later, the competitor discovered the error while observing the scoreboard. He immediately reported the error to the Committee. Would it be appropriate in such circumstances to invoke Rule 33-7 and waive or modify the disqualification penalty prescribed in Rule 6-6d?

**A.** No. A penalty of disqualification may be waived or modified only in exceptional circumstances. Under Rule 6-6d, the competitor is responsible for the correctness of the score recorded for each hole.

### 33-7/4.5  Competitor Unaware of Penalty Returns Wrong Score; Whether Waiving or Modifying Disqualification Penalty Justified

**Q.** A competitor returns his score card and the score for one hole is lower than actually taken due to failure to include a penalty of two strokes which he did not know he had incurred. The error is discovered before the competition has closed.

Would the Committee be justified, under Rule 33-7, in waiving or modifying the penalty of disqualification prescribed in Rule 6-6d?

**A.** No. It is the responsibility of the competitor to know the Rules.

**Players Agree Not to Tee Off in Prescribed Order to Save Time; Whether Waiving Penalty of Disqualification Justified** — See 1-3/1.

**Imposing Disqualification Penalty When Marker Attests Wrong Score Knowingly** — See 6-6a/5.

**Modifying Penalty for One Practice Stroke on Course Before Stroke Play Round** — See 7-1b/1.

**Waiving Penalty for Practice on Course** — See 7-1b/2.

**Waiving Penalty for Competitor Who Practices on Course After Qualifying Round and Is Subsequently in Play-Off on Same Day** — See 7-1b/3.

**Imposing Disqualification Penalty for Failing to Correct Opponent's Misunderstanding of State of Match** — See 9-2/12.

### 33-7/5 Play of Wrong Ball Not Rectified on Advice of Committee Member

**Q.** In stroke play, a competitor plays two strokes on the 14th hole and then plays a wrong ball for what he believed to be his third stroke. He plays a total of four strokes with the wrong ball, holing out with it. He then discovers the error. Before teeing off at the 15th, he asks a member of the Committee as to the procedure. The Committee member told the competitor to proceed and consult the Committee when the round was completed, instead of telling him to rectify the error as prescribed in Rule 15-3b.

Should the competitor be disqualified as prescribed in Rule 15-3b?

**A.** No. In the circumstances, the competitor should incur a penalty of two strokes for a breach of Rule 15-3b. The disqualification penalty that he also incurred under that Rule should be waived by the Committee under Rule 33-7, since the competitor's failure to correct his mistake was due to the error of the Committee member.

Generally, strokes played with a wrong ball do not count in the player's score. However, in this case such strokes must be counted. Otherwise, the competitor would not have a score for the hole. In equity (Rule 1-4), his score for the hole would be 8: the two strokes he played with his ball, the two penalty strokes for playing a wrong ball and the four strokes he played with the wrong ball.

**Referee Reverses Ruling After Player Subsequently Plays a Ball — See 34-2/6.**

**Committee Error and Scoring in Stroke Play — See 34-3/1.5.**

**Player Plays Based on Incorrect Ruling; Procedure for Player When Error is Discovered – See 34-3/3.**

**Player Placed at Serious Disadvantage Due to Incorrect Ruling — See 34-3/3.3.**

### 33-7/6 Competitor Repeatedly Replaces Ball Nearer Hole on Green

**Q.** On completion of a round in stroke play, a competitor's marker reports that the competitor, after lifting his ball on the putting green, repeatedly placed it nearer the hole than the spot from which it was lifted. The Committee, after gathering all available evidence, concludes that the marker's report is correct. What should the Committee do?

**A.** The competitor should be disqualified under Rule 33-7.

**Imposing Disqualification Penalty for Playing Two Holes Not Included in Stipulated Round — See 3/2.**

**Imposing Disqualification Penalty for Knowingly Giving Incorrect Information on Rules — See 9/1.**

**Imposing Disqualification Penalty for Altering Teeing Ground — See 11-2/2.**

**Imposing Disqualification Penalty for Refusing to Identify Ball — See 27/13.**

### 33-7/7 Competitor Seeks Help from Fellow-Competitor to Avoid Penalty

**Q.** A competitor's ball is lying through the green. He asks a fellow-competitor to remove a loose impediment lying near his ball because he believes that the removal of the loose impediment might cause his ball to move and knows that if the loose impediment is removed by an outside agency, the competitor incurs no penalty. The fellow-competitor removes the loose impediment. What is the ruling?

**A.** Irrespective of whether the ball moves as a result of removing the loose impediment, the action of the competitor is so contrary to the spirit of the game that the Committee should disqualify him under Rule 33-7.

The fellow-competitor incurs no penalty for removing the loose impediment unless the Committee is satisfied that he was aware of the competitor's intention to circumvent a Rule. In that instance, he should also be disqualified under Rule 33-7.

### 33-7/8 Meaning of "Serious Breach of Etiquette"

**Q.** In Rule 33-7, what is meant by a "serious breach of etiquette"?

**A.** A serious breach of etiquette is behavior by a player that shows a significant disregard for an aspect of the Etiquette Section, such as intentionally distracting another player or intentionally offending someone.

Although a Committee may disqualify a player under Rule 33-7 for a single act that it considers to be a serious breach of etiquette, in most cases it is recommended that such a penalty should be imposed only in the event of a further serious breach.

Ultimately, the application of a penalty for a serious breach of etiquette under Rule 33-7 is at the discretion of the Committee.

### 33-8/1 Local Rule for Temporary Putting Green Waives Requirement to Hole Out

**Q.** A course has been going through a period of renovation necessitating the use of temporary putting greens from time to time.

A Local Rule states that a player whose ball lies on a temporary green may either pick up his ball, counting two putts, or putt out.

Is such a Local Rule authorized?

**A.** No. Rule 1-1 provides: "The Game of Golf consists in playing a ball with a club from the teeing ground into the hole by a stroke or successive strokes in accordance with the Rules." Any Local Rule under which a player would not be required to play the ball into the hole waives this basic Rule and is not authorized.

### 33-8/2  Local Rule Allows Drop on Green Side of Water Hazard When Ball Fails to Clear Hazard

**Q.** The design of a hole is such that a player must hit the ball about 100 yards in order to carry a water hazard. A Local Rule has been adopted to assist players who cannot drive over the hazard by allowing them to drop a ball, under penalty of two strokes, in a Ball Drop (Dropping Zone) that is located across the hazard. Is such a Local Rule authorized?

**A.** No. Such a Local Rule substantially alters Rule 26-1b as it allows the player to drop a ball on a part of the course (i.e., on the green side of the water hazard) that the Rule would not have permitted him to reach. Furthermore, the penalty for taking relief under the water hazard Rule (Rule 26) is one stroke, and may not be increased to two strokes by a Committee through a Local Rule – see Rule 33-8b.

### 33-8/3  Local Rule Allowing Play of Second Ball in Match Play

**Q.** May a Committee make a Local Rule allowing play of a second ball in match play when a player is in doubt as to his rights?

**A.** No. Rule 3-3 specifically restricts the play of a second ball to stroke play.

### 33-8/4  Local Rule for Events in Which Motorized Golf Carts Permitted

**Q.** A competition involving stroke-play qualifying followed by match play is to be held. Motorized golf carts will be permitted. Play will be in couples. There are enough carts available to provide each couple with a cart. No caddies will be available. Should a Local Rule clarifying the status of the carts be made?

**A.** It is suggested that the following Local Rule be adopted:

"A motorized cart is part of the player's equipment:

(1) When one cart is shared by two players, the cart and everything in it are deemed to be the equipment of the player whose ball is involved except that, when the cart is being moved by one of the players, the cart and everything in it are deemed to be the equipment of that player.

(2) A player or players using a cart may appoint someone to drive the cart, in which case the driver is considered to be the caddie of the player or players.

(3) Use of a cart by anyone other than the player or players using it or the appointed driver is prohibited. Any player allowing unauthorized use of his cart is subject to penalty as follows:

Match play — At the conclusion of the hole at which the breach is discovered, the state of the match shall be adjusted by deducting one hole for each hole at which a breach occurred. Maximum deduction per round: two holes.

<u>Stroke play</u> — Two strokes for each hole at which any breach occurred; maximum penalty per round: four strokes. In the event of a breach between the play of two holes, the penalty applies to the next hole.

<u>In either form of play</u> — Use of any unauthorized automotive vehicle shall be discontinued immediately upon discovering that a breach has occurred. Otherwise, the player shall be disqualified."

If some caddies are available, it is suggested that they be assigned in an equitable way and that the above suggested Local Rule be adopted with item (2) amended to read as follows:

"A player or players using a cart may appoint someone to drive the cart if no caddie is available, in which case the driver is considered to be the caddie of the player or players."

**Status of Person in Shared Golf Cart — See 19/2.**

### 33-8/5 Local Rule Permitting Competitors to Discontinue Play by Agreement in Bad Weather

**Q.** May the Committee for a stroke-play event make a Local Rule permitting competitors to discontinue play by agreement among themselves in bad weather?

**A.** No. Such a Local Rule would modify Rule 6-8a.

### [33-8/6 Reserved]

### 33-8/7 Local Rule Requiring Player to Play Out of Turn on Putting Green

**Q.** A proposed Local Rule would require that, on the putting green, a player must play continuously until he has holed out. Would such a Local Rule be acceptable?

**A.** No. Such a Local Rule would modify Rules 10-1b and -2b, which require that the ball farther from the hole shall be played first.

### 33-8/8 Local Rule Providing Relief from Tree Roots

**Q.** May a Committee make a Local Rule providing relief without penalty if a player's stroke is interfered with by exposed tree roots?

**A.** No. A Local Rule is authorized only if an abnormal condition exists. The existence of exposed tree roots is not abnormal.

### 33-8/9  Local Rule Providing Relief from Damage to Bunkers Caused by Children

**Q.** Some holes are accessible to the general public, and children play in the bunkers leaving footprints, holes and sand castles.

May the Committee make a Local Rule allowing a player, without penalty, either to drop his ball outside a bunker damaged by children or to lift his ball from such damage, smooth out the sand and replace the ball?

**A.** No. This would be a modification of Rule 13-4.

### 33-8/10  Local Rule Prohibiting Removal of Flagstick

**Q.** May a Committee make a Local Rule for winter-time play prohibiting removal of the flagstick? The purpose would be to reduce traffic around the hole in the winter when the putting greens are very soft.

**A.** No. Such a Local Rule would modify the Rules of Golf.

### 33-8/11  Local Rule Waiving Penalty for Ball Striking Unattended Flagstick

**Q.** Is it permissible for a Committee to make a Local Rule for winter play waiving the penalty incurred under Rule 17-3c (Ball Striking Flagstick When Unattended) in order to reduce the damage caused to the area around the hole and to speed up play?

**A.** No.

### 33-8/12  Local Rule for Ball Deflected by Sprinkler Head

**Q.** May a Committee make a Local Rule allowing a player to replay a stroke, without penalty, if his ball has been deflected by a sprinkler head?

**A.** No. A sprinkler head is an outside agency (see Definition of "Outside Agency"). The deflection of a ball by it is a rub of the green and the ball must be played as it lies — see Rule 19-1.

### 33-8/13  Local Rule for Ball Deflected by Power Line

**Q.** An overhead power line is so situated that it interferes with the play of a hole. Would it be appropriate for the Committee to make a Local Rule allowing a player whose ball is deflected by this power line the option to replay the stroke, without penalty, if he wishes?

**A.** No. However, a Local Rule requiring a player to replay the stroke would be acceptable. The following text is suggested:

"If a ball strikes the power line during play of the ____ hole, the stroke is canceled and the player must play a ball as nearly as possible at the spot from which the original ball was played in accordance with Rule 20-5 (Making Next Stroke from Where Previous Stroke Made)."

In some cases the Committee may wish to include in the Local Rule the towers or poles supporting such lines when the towers or poles are positioned such that they interfere with the play of the hole. (Revised)

### 33-8/14 Local Rule Deeming Interior Boundary Fence to Be an Obstruction

**Q.** There is a practice range in the middle of the course. The range is surrounded by a fence which defines the range as out of bounds. Would a Local Rule be authorized under which this particular boundary fence, since it is within the course, is treated as an obstruction?

**A.** No, such a Local Rule is not authorized. An interior boundary fence is not an abnormal condition.

### 33-8/15 Local Rule Providing Relief from Interference by Immovable Water Hazard Stake for Ball Lying in Water Hazard

**Q.** If the stakes defining the margins of water hazards are immovable, may the Committee make a Local Rule providing relief without penalty if a player's ball lies in a water hazard and such a stake interferes with his swing or stance?

**A.** No. Such stakes are immovable obstructions (see Note 1 to Rule 24).

### 33-8/16 Local Rule Deeming All Stakes on Course to Be Immovable Obstructions

**Q.** It is proposed to adopt a Local Rule providing that all stakes on the course, i.e., stakes defining the margins of water hazards, ground under repair, etc., are deemed to be immovable obstructions. The Local Rule would not, of course, apply to boundary stakes since they are not on the course. Is such a Local Rule permissible?

**A.** Yes.

### 33-8/17 Local Rule Providing Line-of-Sight Relief from Irrigation-Control Boxes

**Q.** Irrigation-control boxes, which are about two feet wide and four feet high, have been installed near a number of fairways. Would it be appropriate for a Committee to adopt a Local Rule under which relief would be provided from such boxes when they intervene on the line of play, i.e., line-of-sight relief?

**A.** No. Providing line-of-sight relief from permanent immovable obstructions is not authorized, except in very unusual circumstances. It is not unusual for irrigation-control boxes to be located near fairways.

### 33-8/18 Local Rule Providing Line-of-Sight Relief from Protective Fence Near Line of Play

If a wire fence is erected to protect players on the tee of one hole from errant shots played at another hole, and it is relatively close to the line of play of the other hole, it would be permissible to make a Local Rule allowing a player whose ball is in such a position that the fence intervenes on his line of play to drop the ball, without penalty, not nearer the hole in a specified Ball Drop (or Dropping Zone).

### 33-8/19 Local Rule Permitting Relief on Specified Side of Paved Path

**Q.** A paved path is parallel to the left side of the 12th hole. If a ball is on the path and the nearest point of relief under Rule 24-2b is on the left side of the path, the player effectively gets no relief as there is a very sharp incline on the left of the path that goes down 30 feet. Would it be appropriate to make a Local Rule giving relief in all cases on the fairway side of this path?

**A.** No. Rule 33-8 states: "The Committee may establish Local Rules for local abnormal conditions." It is not abnormal for areas adjacent to paved paths to have dense underbrush, trees, sharp slopes, etc., thereby providing no practical relief.

Furthermore, it would not be appropriate to establish Ball Drops (or Dropping Zones) on the fairway side of the path to alleviate the problem.

### 33-8/20 Local Rule Providing Relief from Unsurfaced Road for Tee Shot Only

**Q.** A road which is not artificially-surfaced crosses a fairway 225 yards from the tee. May the Committee adopt a Local Rule granting relief of the type afforded by Rule 24-2b(i) or Rule 25-1b(i) for tee shots, but not subsequent shots, coming to rest on the road?

**A.** No. The Committee has authority to provide relief from interference by the road but does not have authority so to limit its application.

### 33-8/21 Local Rule for Damage Made by Insects

**Q.** Some types of insects, e.g., mole crickets, can create damage on a golf course that results in unreasonable playing conditions. May a Committee make a Local Rule treating this damage as ground under repair?

**A.** Yes. However, in some instances a Committee would be justified in denying relief from interference with the player's stance by such a condition — see Note under Rule 25-1a.

## 33-8/22 Local Rule Treating Ant Hills as Ground Under Repair

**Q.** An ant hill is a loose impediment and may be removed, but there is no other relief without penalty. Some ant hills are conical in shape and hard, and removal is not possible, but relief under Rule 25-1b is not available since an ant is not a burrowing animal. If such ant hills interfere with the proper playing of the game, would a Local Rule providing relief be authorized?

**A.** Yes. A Local Rule stating that such ant hills are to be treated as ground under repair would be justified.

Such a Local Rule is also justified on courses where fire-ants exist. A fire-ants' mound or hill is removable, but its removal will cause the fire-ants to swarm out of the ground. When this occurs, anyone in the vicinity is in danger of being bitten by the ants, and the bite of a fire-ant can cause serious illness.

If a Local Rule giving relief from fire-ants has not been adopted and a ball is so close to a fire-ants' mound that the player is in danger, the player is, in equity, entitled to relief as prescribed in Decision 1-4/10.

## 33-8/23 Local Rule Denying Relief from Ground Under Repair During Play of Particular Hole

**Q.** An area of ground under repair is situated on the fairway of the 2nd hole, which is parallel to the 1st hole. Is it permissible to make a Local Rule prohibiting relief from this ground under repair during the play of the 1st hole?

**A.** No.

## 33-8/24 Local Rule Permitting Relief from Edging Grooves Around Putting Green

**Q.** Edging grooves, which are about three inches deep and one-quarter to one-half inch wide, are cut at the perimeters of the putting greens to control the creeping of bermuda grass onto the greens. If a ball comes to rest on such a groove, it is impossible to putt the ball with any degree of accuracy. Would a Local Rule providing relief be authorized?

**A.** Yes. It would be proper to make a Local Rule giving relief if a ball lies on such a groove, but not solely because a groove might affect the player's stance. The Local Rule should read as follows:

"If a ball lies on an edging groove around a putting green, the player may, without penalty, lift the ball, clean it and place it out of the groove in the nearest position to where it lay, whether on or off the putting green, which is not nearer the hole."

**Local Rule for Mushrooms on Line of Putt — See 16-1a/15.**

### 33-8/25 Local Rule for Ground Under Repair Adjacent to Artificially-Surfaced Cart Path

**Q.** When ground under repair is adjacent to an artificially-surfaced cart path (an obstruction), sometimes a player, after obtaining relief from one condition, is interfered with by the other condition. Thus, another drop under another Rule results. This is cumbersome and could lead to complications. Would it be proper to eliminate the problem by means of a Local Rule under which ground under repair adjacent to an artificially-surfaced cart path would have the same status as the cart path?

**A.** Yes. If white lines are used to define ground under repair, a Local Rule is suggested as follows:

> "White-lined areas tying into artificially-surfaced roads or paths are declared to have the same status as the roads or paths, i.e., they are obstructions, not ground under repair. Relief, without penalty, is provided under Rule 24-2b(i)."

### 33-8/26 Local Rule Altering Ground Under Repair Relief Procedure

**Q.** It is planned to define an area containing young trees as ground under repair. Would it be permissible to make a Local Rule requiring that, if a player elects to take relief from this area, he must drop the ball behind the area, keeping the trees between himself and the hole?

**A.** No. However, if it is not feasible to proceed in conformity with the ground under repair Rule, establishment of special areas on which balls may be dropped is authorized.

### 33-8/27 Local Rule Providing Relief Without Penalty from Flooded Bunker

**Q.** May a Committee make a Local Rule allowing a player to drop out of any bunker filled with casual water, without penalty, notwithstanding Rule 25-1b(ii)?

**A.** No. Such a Local Rule is not acceptable as it waives a penalty imposed by a Rule of Golf, contrary to Rule 33-8b.

### 33-8/28 Local Rule Permitting Re-Dropping or Placing When Dropped Ball Embeds in Bunker

**Q.** Our bunkers frequently have casual water in them. The texture of the sand in the bunkers is such that a ball dropped under Rule 25-1b(ii)(a) embeds itself in the wet sand to the depth of the ball or deeper.

Would it be proper to make a Local Rule permitting a ball that embeds in a bunker after being dropped from casual water in the bunker to be re-dropped or placed?

**A.** No. It is not abnormal for a ball dropped in a bunker to embed itself in the sand.

### 33-8/29 Local Rule Requiring Player to Take Relief Under Penalty from Tree Nursery or Plantation

**Q.** May a Committee make a Local Rule requiring that a ball lying in a tree nursery or plantation be dropped outside it under penalty of one stroke?

**A.** No. If the Committee wishes to prohibit play in such an area, it may declare it to be ground under repair from which relief without penalty is mandatory. However, a Local Rule imposing a penalty of one stroke is not permitted.

### 33-8/30 Local Rule Permitting the Repair of Turf Plugs on the Putting Green That Are Not 4¼ Inches in Diameter

**Q.** Turf plugs which are not 4¼ inches in diameter or are not circular have been cut on some putting greens to repair damaged areas of turf. May a Committee adopt a Local Rule permitting the repair of these plugs?

**A.** Yes. If such areas exist it is recommended that a Local Rule permitting the repair of these plugs under Rule 16-1c be adopted. Otherwise, the repair of such turf plugs would be contrary to Rule 16-1c.

### 33-8/31 Local Rule Providing Relief from Accumulations of Leaves Through the Green

The Committee may make a temporary Local Rule declaring accumulations of leaves through the green at certain holes to be ground under repair (see Definition of "Ground Under Repair") and Rule 25-1 will apply.

The Local Rule should be restricted to the hole(s) at which trouble with leaves occurs and it should be withdrawn as soon as conditions permit. Particular attention is drawn to the opening paragraph of Rule 25-1c; unless there is reasonable evidence that a ball which cannot be found is lost in the leaves, it must be treated as lost elsewhere and Rule 27 applies.

For fallen leaves in a bunker — See Decision 13-4/33.

**[33-8/32 Reserved]**

### 33-8/32.5 Local Rule Treating Severe Damage by Non-Burrowing Animals as Ground Under Repair

**Q.** May a Committee make a Local Rule declaring areas severely damaged by non-burrowing animals to be ground under repair without marking them as such?

**A.** Yes. Furthermore, in some instances a Committee would be justified in denying relief from interference with the player's stance by such a condition — see Note under Rule 25-1a.

### 33-8/33 Local Rule Prohibiting Dropping on Apron When Ball on Wrong Putting Green

**Q.** Balls from the 13th tee frequently come to rest on the 15th green, and the point of nearest relief under Rule 25-3 is the closely mown apron of the green. Much damage is being caused to this apron. May the Committee make a Local Rule requiring that a ball be dropped not only clear of the putting surface but also clear of the apron of this green?

**A.** Yes. The following wording for a Local Rule is suggested:

"For the purpose of Rule 25-3, the putting green of the 15th hole includes the apron surrounding the green."

### 33-8/34 Local Rule Establishes Ball Drop or Dropping Zone; Procedure for Dropping

**Q.** The Committee has established a Ball Drop or Dropping Zone for relief from an immovable obstruction, ground under repair, a wrong putting green or a water hazard or for an unplayable ball (see Appendix I). If the player elects to take relief, what is the procedure for dropping and re-dropping?

**A.** (a) The player does not have to stand within the Ball Drop when dropping the ball.

  (b) The dropped ball must first strike a part of the course within the Ball Drop.

  (c) If the Ball Drop is defined by a line, the line is within the Ball Drop.

  (d) The dropped ball does not have to come to rest within the Ball Drop.

  (e) The dropped ball must be re-dropped if it rolls and comes to rest in a position covered by Rule 20-2c(i-vi).

  (f) The dropped ball may roll nearer the hole provided it comes to rest within two club-lengths of the spot where it first struck a part of the course within the Ball Drop and not into any of the positions covered by (e).

  (g) Subject to the provisions of (e) and (f), the dropped ball may roll and come to rest nearer the hole than:

  - its original position or estimated position (see Rule 20-2b);
  - the nearest point of relief or maximum available relief (Rule 24-2, 24-3, 25-1 or 25-3); or

- the point where the original ball last crossed the margin of the water hazard or lateral water hazard (Rule 26-1). (Revised)

## 33-8/35 Local Rule Treating Rough as a Lateral Water Hazard

**Q.** The areas immediately adjacent to the fairways consist of large embedded boulders, thick desert brush and prickly cactus. A player whose ball comes to rest in such areas has no opportunity to play a stroke. Would it be proper to make a Local Rule under which such areas would be treated as lateral water hazards?

**A.** No. There are many courses where the areas adjacent to the fairways are of such a nature that a ball therein is almost always lost or unplayable. Thus, such a situation is not abnormal.

## 33-8/36 Local Rule Giving Free Relief for Ball in Water Hazard

**Q.** A drainage ditch crosses a hole 190 yards from the tee. The Committee has marked that portion of the ditch within the limits of the fairway and a Local Rule allows a player relief, without penalty, if his tee shot lies in the ditch within the fairway limits.

Is this a proper Local Rule?

**A.** No. A drainage ditch is a water hazard — see Definition of "Water Hazard." Under Rule 26-1, the penalty for relief from a water hazard is one stroke. Rule 33-8b prohibits waiving this penalty by Local Rule.

## 33-8/37 Local Rule Allowing Drop in Water Hazard Behind Point Where Ball Lies Unplayable in Hazard

**Q.** A water hazard varies from 100 yards to 250 yards in width, and there is little or no water in it. In most cases a ball in the hazard can be played. However, it sometimes happens that a ball fails by a few yards to carry the hazard and ends up unplayable in water.

Under Rule 26-1, the player must either drop behind the hazard or at the spot from which his previous stroke was played. In either case, the relief point is up to 250 yards away. In such circumstances, may the Committee make a Local Rule permitting a player to drop a ball in the hazard under penalty of one stroke, as well as out of the hazard?

**A.** No.

**Local Rule Allowing Drop Opposite Spot Where Ball Comes to Rest in Lateral Water Hazard — See 26-1/20.**

**Local Rule When Pond Is Water Hazard from Back Tee and Lateral from Forward Tee — See 33-2a/6.**

**Local Rule for Part of Lateral Water Hazard Where Impossible to Drop Not Nearer Hole — See 33-2a/9.**

**Local Rule for Island Green — See 33-2a/10.**

### 33-8/38 Local Rule Deeming Out of Bounds Ball Which Crosses Boundary But Comes to Rest on Course

**Q.** Is it permissible to make a Local Rule that a ball is out of bounds if it crosses a boundary, even if it recrosses the boundary and comes to rest on the same part of the course? The purpose of the Local Rule would be to prevent players from cutting across a "dog-leg."

**A.** No. A ball is out of bounds only when all of it lies out of bounds — see Definition of "Out of Bounds."

The Local Rule suggested in Decision 27/20 deals with a different situation, i.e., one in which a ball crosses an out of bounds area and comes to rest on a different part of the course.

**Local Rule for Boundary Stakes Having No Significance in Play of Hole Being Played — See 24/5.**

**Local Rule for Public Road Dividing Course Which Is Defined as Out of Bounds — See 27/20.**

**Local Rule Deeming Ball in Bounds Until Beyond Boundary Wall — See 33-2a/16.**

### 33-8/39 Local Rule for Bunker Faces Consisting of Stacked Turf

**Q.** The face of a bunker that consists of stacked turf may be grass-covered or earthen. May a Committee make a Local Rule deeming that such faces are not "closely mown areas" (Rule 25-2)?

**A.** Yes.

**Ball Embedded in Grass Bank or Face of Bunker — See 25-2/5.**

### 33-8/40 Local Rule Clarifying Status of Material Similar to Sand

**Q.** A course has material other than sand (e.g., finely crushed shell or lava dust) filling its bunkers. May the Committee establish a Local Rule stating that such material is deemed to have the same status as sand or loose soil (i.e., loose impediments on the putting green but not elsewhere)?

**A.** Yes. (New)

### 33-8/41 Marking Environmentally-Sensitive Areas

If an appropriate authority prohibits entry into and/or play from an area for environmental reasons, it is the Committee's responsibility to decide whether an environmentally-sensitive area should be defined as ground under repair, a water hazard or out of bounds.

However, the Committee may not define the area as a water hazard or a lateral water hazard unless it is, by Definition, a water hazard. The Committee should attempt to preserve the character of the hole.

As examples:

(a) A small area of rare plants close to a putting green has been declared an environmentally-sensitive area. The Committee may define the area to be ground under repair or out of bounds, but it may not be defined as a water hazard or lateral water hazard. In view of the area's proximity to a putting green, it should not be defined as out of bounds because a stroke-and-distance penalty would be unduly harsh. It would be more appropriate to define the area as ground under repair.

(b) A large area of sand dunes along the side of a hole has been declared an environmentally-sensitive area. In contrast to (a) above, it should not be defined as ground under repair because the absence of a penalty would be unduly generous. It would be more appropriate to define the area as out of bounds.

(c) A large area of wetlands along the side of a hole has been declared an environmentally-sensitive area. As in (b) above, it could be defined as out of bounds, but it would be more appropriate to define it as a lateral water hazard.

An environmentally-sensitive area should be physically protected to deter players from entering the area (e.g., by a fence, warning signs and the like) and it should be marked in accordance with the recommendations in the Rules of Golf (i.e., by yellow, red or white stakes, depending on the status of the area). It is recommended that stakes with green tops be used to designate an environmentally-sensitive area.

### 33-8/42 Player Enters Environmentally-Sensitive Area to Retrieve Ball

**Q.** A player wrongfully enters an environmentally-sensitive area to retrieve his ball. What is the ruling?

**A.** There is no penalty under the Rules of Golf, but the player may have broken the law or be subject to other disciplinary action. A Local Rule which imposes a penalty for entering an environmentally-sensitive area is not authorized.

### 33-8/43 Stroke Played from Environmentally-Sensitive Area

**Q.** A player played a stroke at his ball in an environmentally-sensitive area from which play is prohibited or took his stance in such an area in playing a stroke. What is the ruling?

**A.** The answer depends on how the Committee has defined the environmentally-sensitive area.

*Ground Under Repair, Water Hazard* or *Lateral Water Hazard:* If the ball was in the environmentally-sensitive area, or if the player took his stance in the environmentally-sensitive area to play a stroke at his ball which was lying outside the environmentally-sensitive area, he loses the hole in match play or he incurs a penalty of two strokes in stroke play for a breach of the Local Rule. In stroke play, he must play out the hole with that ball unless a serious breach of the Local Rule has occurred — see Decision 33-8/44.

*Out of Bounds*: If the ball was in the environmentally-sensitive area, the player played a wrong ball — see Decision 15/6. Accordingly, in match play, the player loses the hole. In stroke play, he incurs a two-stroke penalty and is required to proceed under Rule 27-1, incurring the additional one-stroke penalty prescribed by that Rule.

If the player took his stance in the environmentally-sensitive area to play a ball which was in bounds, the ruling would be the same as that for *Ground Under Repair*, *Water Hazard* or *Lateral Water Hazard*.

In all cases, the player may have broken the law or be subject to other disciplinary action for having entered the environmentally-sensitive area.

**Player Makes Several Strokes on Wrong Putting Green — See 25-3/2.**

### 33-8/44 Significant Advantage Gained When Player Plays Stroke from Environmentally-Sensitive Area Defined as Water Hazard

**Q.** A player makes a stroke at his ball which is lying in an environmentally-sensitive area from which play is prohibited and which has been defined as a water hazard.

The point where his ball last crossed the margin of the water hazard is 150 yards behind the place where he made a stroke at his ball. What is the ruling?

**A.** In match play, the player loses the hole for a breach of the Local Rule.

In stroke play, playing from an environmentally-sensitive area does not, by itself, constitute a serious breach of the Local Rule. However, in this case the player gained a significant advantage by doing so and, consequently, was guilty of a serious breach of the Local Rule. Therefore, the player must correct his error and follow the procedure outlined in Rule 20-7c by playing a ball in accordance with Rule 26-1, incurring the penalty stroke prescribed by that Rule and an additional penalty of two strokes for a breach of the Local Rule; otherwise the player is disqualified. The stroke made with the original ball from within the environmentally-sensitive area and all subsequent strokes, including penalty strokes, with this ball do not count in the player's score.

# Rule 34. Disputes and Decisions

**Definitions**

All defined terms are in *italics* and are listed alphabetically in the Definitions section — see pages 3-11.

## 34-1. Claims and Penalties

### a. Match Play

If a claim is lodged with the *Committee* under Rule 2-5, a decision should be given as soon as possible so that the state of the match may, if necessary, be adjusted. If a claim is not made in accordance with Rule 2-5, it must not be considered by the *Committee*.

There is no time limit on applying the disqualification penalty for a breach of Rule 1-3.

### b. Stroke Play

In stroke play, a penalty must not be rescinded, modified or imposed after the competition has closed. A competition is closed when the result has been officially announced or, in stroke-play qualifying followed by match play, when the player has teed off in his first match.

**Exceptions:** A penalty of disqualification must be imposed after the competition has closed if a *competitor*:

(i) was in breach of Rule 1-3 (Agreement to Waive Rules); or

(ii) returned a score card on which he had recorded a handicap that, before the competition closed, he knew was higher than that to which he was entitled, and this affected the number of strokes received (Rule 6-2b); or

(iii) returned a score for any hole lower than actually taken (Rule 6-6d) for any reason other than failure to include a penalty that, before the competition closed, he did not know he had incurred; or

(iv) knew, before the competition closed, that he had been in breach of any other *Rule* for which the penalty is disqualification.

## 34-2. Referee's Decision

If a *referee* has been appointed by the *Committee*, his decision is final.

## 34-3. Committee's Decision

In the absence of a *referee*, any dispute or doubtful point on the *Rules* must be referred to the *Committee*, whose decision is final.

If the *Committee* cannot come to a decision, it may refer the dispute or doubtful point to the Rules of Golf Committee of the United States Golf Association, whose decision is final.

If the dispute or doubtful point has not been referred to the Rules of Golf Committee, the player or players may request that an agreed statement be referred through a duly authorized representative of the *Committee* to the Rules of Golf Committee for an opinion as to the correctness of the decision given. The reply will be sent to this authorized representative.

If play is conducted other than in accordance with the Rules of Golf, the Rules of Golf Committee will not give a decision on any question.

### 34-1a/1  Player Who Has Reached Third Round of Match Play Disqualified for Agreeing to Waive Rules in First-Round Match

**Q.** Rule 34-1a provides that there is no time limit on applying the disqualification penalty under Rule 1-3 for agreeing to waive a Rule. If A, who agreed with his opponent to waive a Rule in a first-round match, has advanced to the third round before the Committee becomes aware of the breach of Rule 1-3, what should the Committee do?

**A.** As A is disqualified, the Committee must rule in accordance with equity (Rule 1-4). For guidelines, see Decision 34-1b/8.

### 34-1b/1  Omission of Penalty Stroke When Score Returned

**Q.** In stroke play, a competitor returned an incorrect score for a hole due to failure to include a penalty stroke. After the competition closed the error was discovered. Does Rule 34-1b allow imposition of a disqualification penalty for a breach of Rule 6-6d?

**A.** As stated in Rule 34-1b, the Committee should impose a penalty of disqualification if the competitor knew, before the competition closed, that he had incurred the penalty but intentionally or unintentionally failed to add the penalty to his score, but not if the competitor did not know he had incurred the penalty.

**Omission of Penalty Strokes When Score Returned Is Due to Incorrect Ruling — See 34-3/1.**

### 34-1b/1.5  Competitor Correctly Advised by Fellow-Competitor That He Had Incurred a Penalty Disagrees with Fellow-Competitor and Fails to Include Penalty in His Score; Committee Advised of Incident After Competition Had Closed

**Q.** In stroke play, A, in ignorance of the Rules and with the concurrence of B, his marker, removed a stone from a water hazard when his ball lay in the hazard. Subsequently, A was advised by C, a fellow-competitor, that he (A) was in breach of Rule 13-4. A disagreed, failed to settle the doubtful point with the Committee at the end of the round and returned his score card without including a two-stroke penalty for a breach of Rule 13-4.

After the competition had closed, C advised the Committee of the incident. Should A be disqualified?

**A.** Yes. Rule 34-1b says in effect that a competitor shall be disqualified after the competition has closed if he had returned a score, failing to include a penalty which, before the competition closed, he knew he had incurred. As C pointed out to A that he had proceeded incorrectly and A took no action to check whether he had incurred a penalty before returning his card, the Committee should decide that A knew that he had incurred a penalty.

### 34-1b/2 Competitor's Failure to Sign Score Card Discovered After Competition Closed

**Q.** Shortly after a stroke-play competition had closed, it was discovered that the score card of the winner had not been signed by him. Should the Committee take any action?

**A.** The Committee must decide whether the competitor knew, before the competition closed, that he was in breach of the Rules by failing to sign his score card (Rule 6-6b). If he knew, he is disqualified. Otherwise, as provided in Rule 34-1b, no penalty may be imposed and the result of the competition must stand.

### 34-1b/3 Play of Wrong Ball in Stroke Play Not Rectified; Error Discovered After Competition Closed

**Q.** In stroke play, A played a wrong ball at the 5th hole but he did not realize it until he had holed out at that hole. Before teeing off at the 6th hole, A and B, who was A's marker, concluded that A had incurred a two-stroke penalty. Accordingly, B added two penalty strokes to A's score for the 5th hole and A and B teed off at the 6th hole without A having rectified his mistake as required under Rule 15-3b. A was not aware that he should have rectified the error.

Before returning his card, A advised the Committee of the incident. The Committee confirmed that the penalty was two strokes but did not ask A whether the error had been rectified.

A won the competition. Several days later the runner-up claimed that A should be disqualified under Rule 15-3b. What is the ruling?

**A.** The competition stands as played, with A the winner. Under Rule 34-1b, a penalty of disqualification may not be imposed after a competition is closed if the competitor did not know he had incurred the penalty.

### 34-1b/4 Competitor Changes Weight of Club During Round; Breach Discovered After Competition Closed

**Q.** It was reported a few days after conclusion of a stroke-play event that the winner had changed the weight of his putter twice during play. Should he be penalized?

**A.** The Committee must decide whether the competitor knew he was in breach of the Rules in changing the weight of his putter during the course of the round (Rule 4-2). If he knew, the Committee should disqualify him. Otherwise, as provided in Rule 34-1b, no penalty shall be imposed.

### 34-1b/5 Disqualification Penalty Wrongly Applied to Winner of Event; Error Discovered After Two Other Competitors Play Off for First Place

**Q.** In the final round of a stroke-play competition, the Committee disqualified A for recording on his score card a total score which was one stroke less than his actual score. A's hole-by-hole scores were correct. The Committee was in error. A would have won the event if he had not been disqualified.

As a result of A's disqualification, B and C play off for first place and B wins the play-off. Before the result of the competition is announced, the Committee discovers that A should not have been penalized.

Should the Committee rectify its error?

**A.** Yes. The penalty applied to A should be rescinded and A should be declared the winner — see Rule 34-1b.

### 34-1b/6 Winner's Score Not Posted Due to Committee Error

**Q.** In a stroke-play event, the winner's prize is awarded to B. The next day A advises the Committee that he had returned a lower score than B. A check reveals that A is correct and that, in error, the Committee had failed to post A's score. What should be done?

**A.** Rule 34-1b does not apply to Committee errors of this kind. The prize should be retrieved from B and given to A, the rightful winner.

Wrong Handicap Used Due to Error by Committee; Error Discovered Several Days Later — See 6-2b/3.

Wrong Handicap Applied by Committee Results in Player Not Receiving Prize — See 33-5/2.

### 34-1b/7 Wrong Score in Qualifying Round Discovered During Match Play

**Q.** On completion of the stroke-play qualifying round for a match-play competition, a player unintentionally failed to include in his score for a hole a penalty he knew he had incurred. After the player had advanced in the match-play phase, the error was discovered. What should be done?

**A.** The player should be disqualified. Under Rule 34-1b, the penalty for a breach of Rule 6-6d was applicable after the qualifying competition was closed.

**Wrong Handicap Used in Stroke Play by Mistake; Error Discovered After Competition Closed — See 6-2b/1.**

**Wrong Handicap Knowingly Used in Stroke Play; Error Discovered After Competition Closed — See 6-2b/2.**

**Competitor Records Incorrect Handicap for Partner in Foursome Stroke-Play Competition; Error Discovered After Competition Closed — See 6-2b/2.5.**

### 34-1b/8 Player Who Has Advanced in Match Play Is Disqualified for Wrong Score in Qualifying Round

**Q.** The Committee discovers that by mistake A, who has advanced to the fourth round of a match-play competition, returned a score lower than actually taken in the qualifying round. A was disqualified. What is the proper procedure with regard to the players beaten by A?

**A.** The Committee must determine further procedure in equity (Rule 1-4). The choices are:

(a) cancel the competition;

(b) consider the disqualification penalty applicable only from the time of its discovery, thus giving A's next opponent a default;

(c) reinstate the player last eliminated by A; or

(d) require all players eliminated by A to play off for his position.

### 34-2/1 Referee's Authority to Declare Ground Under Repair

**Q.** Does the referee of a match have authority to declare an area ground under repair during the match?

**A.** Yes.

### 34-2/2 Referee Authorizes Player to Infringe a Rule

**Q.** In error, a referee authorized a player to infringe a Rule of Golf. Is the player absolved from penalty in such a case?

**A.** Yes. Under Rule 34-2, a referee's decision is final, whether or not the decision is correct.

**Imposition of Penalty by Referee After Any Player in Match Has Played from Next Tee — See 2-5/12.**

### 34-2/3 Referee Warning Player About to Infringe Rule

**Q.** If the referee observes a player about to break a Rule, may he warn the player and thus prevent a breach?

**A.** Yes, but he is under no obligation to do so. If he volunteers information about the Rules, he should do so uniformly to all players.

### 34-2/4 Disagreement with Referee's Decision

**Q.** In match play, if a player disagrees with a referee's decision, may the player demand that the matter be considered by the Committee?

**A.** No. A referee's decision may be referred to the Committee only if the referee consents.

### 34-2/5 Referee Reverses Ruling Made at Last Hole of Match After Players Leave Putting Green

**Q.** In a match, A and B are all square playing the last hole. An incident occurs on the putting green and the referee rules incorrectly that A loses the last hole and the match, whereas he should have ruled that B lost the last hole and the match. A and B walk off the putting green without disputing the ruling. Subsequently, but before the result of the match is officially announced, the referee learns of his error, reverses his ruling and decides that B lost the last hole and the match. Did the referee act properly in reversing his ruling?

**A.** Yes. As the result of the match had not been officially announced and neither player had made any further strokes, the referee was correct in reversing his ruling (see also Decisions 2-5/14, 34-2/6, 34-3/3 and 34-3/3.3). (Revised)

**When Match Result "Officially Announced" — See 2-5/14.**

**Ball Thought to Be Unfit for Play; Committee Involvement When Opponent, Marker or Fellow-Competitor Not Readily Available — See 5-3/7.**

**Procedure for Referee in Determining Ball Farther from Hole — See 10-1b/1.**

**Flagstick Attended by Referee — See 17-1/3.**

### 34-2/6 Referee Reverses Ruling After Player Subsequently Plays a Ball

**Q.** In a match, an incident occurs on the putting green of the 17th hole and the referee rules incorrectly that A loses the hole. A and B walk off the putting green without disputing the ruling. After the players play from the next tee, the referee learns of his error, reverses the ruling and rules that B lost the 17th hole. Did the referee act properly in reversing the ruling?

**A.** No. If, after a referee has given a ruling, either player makes a stroke on the hole or, in circumstances where no more strokes are made on the hole, either player makes a stroke from the next teeing ground, the referee may not reverse his ruling. In the case of the last hole of the match, see Decision 34-2/5.

If the referee becomes aware of his error prior to a player making a stroke or, in circumstances where no more strokes are made on the hole, either player making a stroke from the next teeing ground, he should correct his error. Although Rule 34-2 states that the referee's decision is final, it is final only in the sense that the player has no right to appeal unless the referee consents. (Revised)

**Play of Wrong Ball Not Rectified on Advice of Committee Member – See 33-7/5**

**Committee Error and Scoring in Stroke Play – See 34-3/1.5**

**Player Plays Based on Incorrect Ruling; Procedure for Player When Error is Discovered – See 34-3/3**

**Player Placed at Serious Disadvantage Due to Incorrect Ruling – See 34-3/3.3**

## 34-3/1  Correction of Incorrect Ruling

**Q.** During the first round of a 36-hole stroke-play competition a competitor plays a wrong ball from a bunker at the 6th hole and the ball comes to rest on the green. The competitor holes out with it. He then realizes that he has played a wrong ball and corrects his mistake. The competitor reports the facts to the Committee before returning his card and is incorrectly advised that he has incurred no penalty since the wrong ball was played from a hazard.

During the second round the Committee realizes that it made a mistake and retrospectively adds to the competitor's first-round score two penalty strokes at the 6th hole, but does not disqualify the competitor under Rule 6-6d.

The competitor objects on the ground that the Committee reached a decision on the matter the previous day and that, as Rule 34-3 states that the Committee's decision is final, it cannot now impose a penalty.

Was the Committee's procedure correct?

**A.** Yes.

Under Rule 34-3, a Committee's decision is final in that the competitor has no right to appeal. However, Rule 34-3 does not prevent a Committee from correcting an incorrect ruling and imposing or rescinding a penalty provided that no penalty is imposed or rescinded after the competition is closed except in the circumstances set forth in Rule 34-1b.

## 34-3/1.5  Committee Error and Scoring in Stroke Play

A player is responsible for knowing the Rules (Rule 6-1), but there may be situations, immediately before and during a stipulated round, when an official representative of the Committee provides the player with incorrect information on the Rules. The player is entitled to act on such information in his subsequent play. Consequently, the Committee may be required to make a judgment as to both the duration of the player's entitlement and his proper score when, as a result of proceeding according to the incorrect information provided by the official, he is liable to a penalty under the Rules.

In these situations, the Committee should resolve the matter in whatever manner it considers most equitable, in light of all the facts and with the objective of ensuring that no player receives an undue advantage or disadvantage. In cases where the incorrect information significantly affects the results of the competition, the Committee may have no option but to cancel the round. The following principles, in equity (Rule 1-4), are applicable:

1. **General Guidance on the Rules**
   When a Committee member provides incorrect information in the nature of general guidance about the Rules, the player should not be exempt from penalty.

2. **Specific Ruling**
   When a Committee member makes a specific ruling that is contrary to the Rules in a specific situation, the player should be exempt from penalty. The Committee has the authority to extend this exemption for the duration of the round in circumstances where the player proceeds incorrectly on his own in exactly the same manner as advised by a Committee member earlier in the round. However, that exemption would cease if, in that round, the player becomes aware of the proper procedure or has his actions questioned.

3. **Guidance on Local Rules or Conditions of Competition**
   When a Committee member gives incorrect information on whether a Local Rule or condition of the competition is in effect, the player should be exempt from penalty for acting on that information. This exemption should be for the duration of the round unless corrected earlier, in which case, the exemption should cease at that point.

4. **Equipment Ruling**
   When a Committee member rules that a non-conforming club is conforming, the player should be exempt from penalty for carrying the club. This exemption should be for the duration of the competition unless corrected earlier, in which case, the exemption should cease at the completion of the round during which the correction was made. (New)

### 34-3/2 Committee Does Not Penalize Player in Breach of Pace of Play Condition Believing Player Had Already Lost Hole

**Q.** In a match between A and B without a referee, a pace of play condition was in effect. During play of the 10th hole, B was observed by a Committee member to breach the pace of play condition. The Committee member did not advise either player of the loss of hole penalty because he mistakenly believed that A had won the hole. During play of the 14th hole, another Committee member began to monitor the match's pace of play and informed B that he had previously breached the pace of play condition on the 10th hole. The Committee member also indicated that neither player was advised of the breach and the resulting loss of hole penalty because it was thought that A had already won the hole. The players indicated that A did not win the 10th hole and that the hole was halved. What is the ruling?

**A.** The result of the 10th hole stands as played. The Committee erred in failing to impose the loss of hole penalty for B's breach of the pace of play condition and may not do so after either player has played from the 11th tee. A was not given wrong information by B and could not therefore make a later claim when the Committee error came to his attention (Rule 2-5).

### 34-3/3 Player Plays Based on Incorrect Ruling; Procedure for Player When Error is Discovered

**Q.** A player obtains a ruling from a member of the Committee and proceeds on the basis of that ruling, which involves dropping a ball and playing from a wrong place. The Committee then learns of the incorrect ruling by the Committee member. Should the Committee require the player to disregard the stroke or strokes made after the incorrect ruling and proceed correctly?

**A.** In match play, an incorrect ruling may not be reversed or corrected after either side makes a stroke on the hole or, in the circumstances where no more strokes are made on the hole, either side makes a stroke from the next teeing ground. In the case of the last hole of the match, see Decision 34-2/5.

In stroke play, if a serious breach is not involved, the strokes made after the incorrect ruling must stand with no penalty. If a serious breach is involved and the player has not played from the next teeing ground or, in the case of the last hole of the round, has not left the putting green, the Committee must require the player to cancel the stroke made from the wrong place and any subsequent strokes and proceed correctly. The player incurs no penalty for playing from a wrong place. Otherwise, in the case of a serious breach, the strokes made after the incorrect ruling must stand with no penalty. (Revised)

### 34-3/3.3 Player Placed at Serious Disadvantage Due to Incorrect Ruling

If a member of the Committee makes a specific ruling that results in a player not only playing from a wrong place but being seriously disadvantaged, the Committee should, in equity (Rule 1-4), consider appropriate corrective action.

In match play, an incorrect ruling may not be reversed or corrected after an opponent makes a stroke. However if, after the incorrect ruling, an opponent does not make a stroke on the hole, the incorrect ruling may be reversed or corrected before either player makes a stroke from the next teeing ground. In the case of the last hole of the match, see Decision 34-2/5. Therefore, even if, for example, the player has conceded the opponent's next stroke and the opponent has lifted his ball, the Committee should direct the player to proceed correctly and the opponent to replace his ball, without penalty.

In stroke play, if the player has not played from the next teeing ground or, in the case of the last hole of the round, has not left the putting green, the Committee should direct the player to proceed correctly, disregarding the stroke made from the wrong place and any strokes subsequently made, including penalty strokes. The player should incur no penalty for playing from the wrong place. (New)

**Play of Wrong Ball Not Rectified Due to Incorrect Advice by Committee Member — See 33-7/5.**

**Referee Reverses Ruling After Player Subsequently Plays a Ball — See 34-2/6.**

### 34-3/3.5 Player Lifts Ball Without Authority Due to Misunderstanding Committee Member's Instructions

**Q.** A player's ball comes to rest against a movable obstruction and he seeks relief. A member of the Committee correctly advises him that he may remove the obstruction under Rule 24-1 and that he should mark the position of the ball in case it moves during the removal of the obstruction. The player marks the position of the ball and lifts it before the member of the Committee can stop him. The player was under the misapprehension that, having been requested to mark the position of the ball, he was entitled to lift it before the obstruction was removed. Should the player be penalized under Rule 18-2a in these circumstances?

**A.** No. Provided the Committee member is satisfied that the player misunderstood the instruction, the ball should be replaced without penalty.

## 34-3/4 Dispute as to Whether Competitor Played from Outside Teeing Ground

**Q.** In stroke play, B, A's fellow-competitor and marker, claimed at the completion of the round that A had played from outside the teeing ground at the 15th hole. A stated that he had played from within the teeing ground.

The Committee ruled that the claim was invalid because it was not made at the 15th tee and because A disputed the claim. Was the ruling correct?

**A.** It is a question of fact whether A played from outside the teeing ground. The matter should be resolved on the basis of the weight of evidence. The timing of a claim is not necessarily a factor.

In this case, it was B's word against A's and the weight of evidence did not favor either competitor. In such a case, the benefit of the doubt should be given to A, the player of the stroke.

## 34-3/5 True State of Match Not Determinable

**Q.** On completion of a match, A claims he is 1 up and B claims the match is all square. The matter is referred to the Committee. The Committee gathers all available evidence and is unable to determine the true state of the match. What should the Committee do?

**A.** It should resolve the matter in the fairest way. An equitable solution would be to order that the match be replayed.

## 34-3/6 Player Proceeds Under an Inapplicable Rule; Committee's Decision

When a player proceeds under a Rule that does not apply to his situation and then makes a stroke, the Committee must determine the Rule to apply in order to give a ruling based on the player's actions.

For examples of appropriate Committee decisions in such cases, see Decisions 20-7/2, 25-1b/13 and 25-1c/2 and the explanations below:

In Decision 20-7/2, the player deemed his ball unplayable in a water hazard, dropped it according to the procedure of option b or c of Rule 28 and played it from the water hazard. As Rule 26-1 was the only Rule that allowed the player to lift his ball for relief in that situation, the Committee determined that Rule 26 applied and ruled accordingly. As a result, the player was considered to have played from a wrong place (i.e., a place not permitted by Rule 26-1).

In Decision 25-1b/13, the player's ball lay in casual water that he mistook for a water hazard. He dropped and played a ball according to the procedure of option b under Rule 26-1. As Rule 25-1 was the only Rule that allowed the player to lift his ball for relief in that situation, the Committee determined that Rule 25 applied and ruled accordingly. As a result, the player was considered to have played from a wrong place (i.e., a place not permitted by Rule 25-1) and to have wrongly substituted a ball in breach of Rule 25-1 (see Rule 15-2).

In Decision 25-1c/2, a player did not know the location of his original ball but assumed, without reasonable evidence, that it was lost in ground under repair. He dropped and played another ball under Rule 25-1c. As the player did not know the location of his original ball, in these circumstances, Rule 27-1 was the only Rule that the player could have proceeded under. Therefore, the Committee determined that Rule 27-1 applied and ruled accordingly. As a result, the player was considered to have put a ball into play under penalty of stroke and distance and to have played from a wrong place (i.e., a place not permitted by Rule 27-1).

### 34-3/7 Player Proceeds on Basis of Ruling; Subsequent Facts Prove Ruling to Be Incorrect

**Q.** A player believes his ball in play may have moved after he addressed it and asks for a ruling from a member of the Committee. Based on the evidence available at the time, the member of the Committee determines that the ball did not move and instructs the player to play the ball as it lies without penalty. After the player plays, the member of the Committee becomes aware of evidence that indicates that the ball had in fact moved. What is the ruling?

**A.** As the ball moved after the player had addressed it, he was required to replace the ball with a penalty stroke under Rule 18-2b. When he failed to do so, he played from a wrong place. As he did so at the instruction of a member of the Committee, he does not incur the general penalty under Rule 18 for playing from a wrong place. However, he does incur the penalty stroke under Rule 18-2b as the ball had moved after address before the ruling from the member of the Committee. The player must continue with the ball played from the wrong place. (New)

### 34-3/8 Player Proceeds on Basis of Ruling; Player's Version of Facts Subsequently Found to Be Incorrect

**Q.** A player's ball in play moves, and the player asks for a ruling from a member of the Committee. When asked, the player informs the member of the Committee that he had not addressed the ball. As the player had done nothing else to cause the ball to move, the member of the Committee instructs the player to play the ball from its new location without penalty. After the player plays, the member of the

Committee becomes aware that the player had in fact addressed the ball. What is the ruling?

**A.** As the ball moved after the player had addressed it, he was required to replace the ball with a penalty stroke under Rule 18-2b. When he failed to do so, he played from a wrong place and loses the hole in match play or incurs a penalty of two strokes in stroke play under Rule 18.

The player must continue with the ball played from the wrong place except that, in stroke play, if a serious breach is involved and the player has not yet played from the next teeing ground or, in the case of the last hole of the round, before the player leaves the putting green, the member of the Committee must require the player to cancel the stroke made with the ball from the wrong place and any subsequent strokes and play from the original location of the ball.

The imposition of the general penalty in this situation is different from the ruling in Decision 34-3/7 in that, in this case, the player provided the incorrect information that led to the incorrect ruling. The player is responsible for providing the correct facts to the member of the Committee and is subject to penalty under the applicable Rule if his incorrect version of the facts led to his playing from a wrong place. (New)

# APPENDIX I

## CONTENTS

### Part A    Local Rules

1. Defining Bounds and Margins .................................................. 476
2. Water Hazards
    a. Lateral Water Hazards ..................................................... 476
    b. Provisional Ball ............................................................... 476
3. Areas of the Course Requiring Preservation;
   Enviromentally-Sensitive Areas .............................................. 476
4. Temporary Conditions — Mud, Extreme Wetness,
   Poor Conditions and Protection of the Course
    a. Lifting an Embedded Ball, Cleaning ................................. 477
    b. 'Preferred Lies' and 'Winter Rules' .................................. 477
5. Obstructions
    a. General .......................................................................... 477
    b. Stones in Bunkers .......................................................... 477
    c. Roads and Paths ............................................................ 477
    d. Immovable Obstructions Close to
       Putting Green ................................................................ 477
    e. Protection of Young Trees .............................................. 477
    f. Temporary Obstructions ................................................. 478
6. Dropping Zones (Ball Drops) .................................................. 478

### Part B    Specimen Local Rules

1. Areas of the Course Requiring Preservation;
   Enviromentally-Sensitive Areas
    a. Ground Under Repair; Play Prohibited ............................ 478
    b. Enviromentally-Sensitive Areas ...................................... 478
2. Protection of Young Trees ..................................................... 480
3. Temporary Conditions — Mud, Extreme Wetness,
   Poor Conditions and Protection of the Course
    a. Relief for Embedded Ball; Cleaning Ball .......................... 481
    b. 'Preferred Lies' and 'Winter Rules' .................................. 481
    c. Aeration Holes ............................................................... 482
4. Stones in Bunkers ................................................................. 482
5. Immovable Obstructions Close to
   Putting Green ........................................................................ 483
6. Temporary Obstructions
    a. Temporary Immovable Obstructions ............................... 484
    b. Temporary Power Lines and Cables ................................ 486

## Part C  Conditions of the Competition
1. Specifications of Equipment
    a. List of Conforming Driver Heads ............................................ 487
    b. List of Conforming Golf Balls .................................................. 487
    c. One Ball Condition ................................................................... 487
2. Time of Starting ................................................................................. 488
3. Caddie ................................................................................................. 488
4. Pace of Play ........................................................................................ 489
5. Suspension of Play Due to a Dangerous Situation ....................... 489
6. Practice
    a. General ........................................................................................ 490
    b. Practice Between Holes ........................................................... 490
7. Advice in Team Competitions ......................................................... 490
8. New Holes .......................................................................................... 490
9. Transportation .................................................................................. 490
10. Anti-Doping ....................................................................................... 491
11. How to Decide Ties .......................................................................... 491
12. Draw for Match Play ........................................................................ 492
    General Numerical Draw ................................................................. 492

# APPENDIX I
# LOCAL RULES; CONDITIONS OF THE COMPETITION

## Definitions
All defined terms are in *italics* and are listed alphabetically in the Definitions section — see pages 3–11.

## PART A

## *Local Rules*

As provided in Rule 33-8a, the *Committee* may make and publish Local Rules for local abnormal conditions if they are consistent with the policy established in this Appendix. In addition, detailed information regarding acceptable and prohibited Local Rules is provided in "Decisions on the Rules of Golf" under Rule 33-8 and in "How to Conduct a Competition."

If local abnormal conditions interfere with the proper playing of the game and the *Committee* considers it necessary to modify a Rule of Golf, authorization from the United States Golf Association must be obtained.

### 1. Defining Bounds and Margins
Specifying means used to define *out of bounds*, *water hazards*, *lateral water hazards*, *ground under repair*, *obstructions* and integral parts of the *course* (Rule 33-2a).

### 2. Water Hazards
#### a. Lateral Water Hazards
Clarifying the status of *water hazards* that may be *lateral water hazards* (Rule 26).

#### b. Provisional Ball
Permitting play of a *provisional ball* under Rule 26-1 for a ball that may be in a *water hazard* of such character that if the original ball is not found, there is reasonable evidence that it is *lost* in the *water hazard* and it would be impracticable to determine whether the ball is in the *hazard* or to do so would unduly delay play. The ball is played provisionally under any of the available options under Rule 26-1 or any applicable Local Rule. In such a case, if a *provisional ball* is played and the original ball is in a *water hazard*, the player may play the original ball as it lies or continue with the *provisional ball* in play, but he may not proceed under Rule 26-1 with regard to the original ball.

### 3. Areas of the Course Requiring Preservation; Environmentally-Sensitive Areas

Assisting preservation of the *course* by defining areas, including turf nurseries, young plantations and other parts of the course under cultivation, as "*ground under repair*" from which play is prohibited.

When the *Committee* is required to prohibit play from environmentally-sensitive areas that are on or adjoin the *course*, it should make a Local Rule clarifying the relief procedure.

## 4. Temporary Conditions — Mud, Extreme Wetness, Poor Conditions and Protection of Course

### a. Lifting an Embedded Ball, Cleaning
Temporary conditions that might interfere with proper playing of the game, including mud and extreme wetness, warranting relief for an embedded ball anywhere *through the green* or permitting lifting, cleaning and replacing a ball anywhere *through the green* or on a closely mown area *through the green*.

### b. "Preferred Lies" and "Winter Rules"
Adverse conditions, including the poor condition of the *course* or the existence of mud, are sometimes so general, particularly during winter months, that the *Committee* may decide to grant relief by temporary Local Rule either to protect the *course* or to promote fair and pleasant play. The Local Rule should be withdrawn as soon as the conditions warrant.

## 5. Obstructions

### a. General
Clarifying the status of objects that may be *obstructions* (Rule 24).

Declaring any construction to be an integral part of the *course* and, accordingly, not an *obstruction*, e.g., built-up sides of *teeing grounds*, *putting greens* and *bunkers* (Rules 24 and 33-2a).

### b. Stones in Bunkers
Allowing the removal of stones in *bunkers* by declaring them to be "movable *obstructions*" (Rule 24-1).

### c. Roads and Paths
(i) Declaring artificial surfaces and sides of roads and paths to be integral parts of the *course*, or

(ii) Providing relief of the type afforded under Rule 24-2b from roads and paths not having artificial surfaces and/or sides, if they could unfairly affect play.

### d. Immovable Obstructions Close to Putting Green
Providing relief from intervention by immovable *obstructions* on or within two club-lengths of the *putting green* when the ball lies within two club-lengths of the immovable *obstruction*.

### e. Protection of Young Trees
Providing relief for the protection of young trees.

### f. Temporary Obstructions

Providing relief from interference by temporary *obstructions* (e.g., grandstands, television cables and equipment, etc.).

### 6. Dropping Zones (Ball Drops)

Establishing special areas on which balls may or must be dropped when it is not feasible or practicable to proceed exactly in conformity with Rule 24-2b (Immovable Obstruction), Rule 24-3 (Ball Lost in Obstruction), Rule 25-1b or 25-1c (Abnormal Ground Conditions), Rule 25-3 (Wrong Putting Green), Rule 26-1 (Water Hazards and Lateral Water Hazards) or Rule 28 (Ball Unplayable).

---

**Part B**

# *Specimen Local Rules*

Within the policy established in Part A of this Appendix, the *Committee* may adopt a Specimen Local Rule by referring, on a score card or notice board, to the examples given below. However, Specimen Local Rules 3a, 3b, 3c, 6a and 6b should not be printed or referred to on a score card as they are all of limited duration.

## 1. Areas of the Course Requiring Preservation; Environmentally-Sensitive Areas

### a. Ground Under Repair; Play Prohibited

If the *Committee* wishes to protect any area of the *course*, it should declare it to be *ground under repair* and prohibit play from within that area. The following Local Rule is recommended:

> "The _____(defined by \_\_\_\_) is *ground under repair* from which play is prohibited. If a player's ball lies in the area, or if it interferes with the player's *stance* or the area of his intended swing, the player must take relief under Rule 25-1.
>
> PENALTY FOR BREACH OF LOCAL RULE:
> Match play — Loss of hole; <u>Stroke play</u> — Two strokes."

### b. Environmentally-Sensitive Areas

If an appropriate authority (i.e., a Government Agency or the like) prohibits entry into and/or play from an area on or adjoining the *course* for environmental reasons, the *Committee* should make a Local Rule clarifying the relief procedure.

The *Committee* has some discretion in terms of whether the area is defined as *ground under repair*, a *water hazard* or *out of bounds*. However, it may not simply define such an area to be a *water hazard* if it does not meet the Definition of a "*Water Hazard*" and it should attempt to preserve the character of the hole.

The following Local Rule is recommended:

"**I. Definition**
An environmentally-sensitive area is an area so declared by an appropriate authority, entry into and/or play from which is prohibited for environmental reasons. These areas may be defined as *ground under repair*, a *water hazard*, a *lateral water hazard* or *out of bounds* at the discretion of the *Committee* provided that, in the case of an environmentally-sensitive area that has been defined as a *water hazard* or a *lateral water hazard*, the area is, by Definition, a *water hazard*.

**Note**: The *Committee* may not declare an area to be environmentally-sensitive.

**II. Ball in Environmentally-Sensitive Area**
  **a. Ground Under Repair**
If a ball is in an environmentally-sensitive area defined as *ground under repair*, a ball must be dropped in accordance with Rule 25-1b.

If there is reasonable evidence that a ball is *lost* within an environmentally-sensitive area defined as *ground under repair*, the player may take relief without penalty as prescribed in Rule 25-1c.

  **b. Water Hazards and Lateral Water Hazards**
If a ball is in or there is reasonable evidence that it is *lost* in an environmentally-sensitive area defined as a *water hazard* or *lateral water hazard*, the player must, under penalty of one stroke, proceed under Rule 26-1.

**Note**: If a ball dropped in accordance with Rule 26 rolls into a position where the environmentally-sensitive area interferes with the player's *stance* or the area of his intended swing, the player must take relief as provided in Clause III of this Local Rule.

  **c. Out of Bounds**
If a ball is in an environmentally-sensitive area defined as *out of bounds*, the player must play a ball, under penalty of one stroke, as nearly as possible at the spot from which the original ball was last played (see Rule 20-5).

**III. Interference with Stance or Area of Intended Swing**
Interference by an environmentally-sensitive area occurs when the condition interferes with the player's *stance* or the area of his intended swing. If interference exists, the player must take relief as follows:

(a) Through the Green: If the ball lies *through the green*, the point on the *course* nearest to where the ball lies must be determined that (a) is not nearer the *hole*, (b) avoids interference by the condition and (c) is not in a *hazard* or on a *putting green*. The player must lift the ball and drop it without penalty within one club-length of the point so determined on a part of the *course* that fulfills (a), (b) and (c) above.

(b) In a Hazard: If the ball is in a *hazard*, the player must lift the ball and drop it either:

(i) Without penalty, in the *hazard*, as near as possible to the spot where the ball lay, but not nearer the *hole*, on a part of the *course* that provides complete relief from the condition; or

(ii) Under penalty of one stroke, outside the *hazard*, keeping the point where the ball lay directly between the *hole* and the spot on which the ball is dropped, with no limit to how far behind the *hazard* the ball may be dropped. Additionally, the player may proceed under Rule 26 or 28, if applicable.

(c) On the Putting Green: If the ball lies on the *putting green*, the player must lift the ball and place it without penalty in the nearest position to where it lay that affords complete relief from the condition, but not nearer the *hole* or in a *hazard*.

The ball may be cleaned when lifted under Clause III of this Local Rule.

**Exception**: A player may not take relief under Clause III of this Local Rule if (a) it is clearly unreasonable for him to play a *stroke* because of interference by anything other than a condition covered by this Local Rule or (b) interference by the condition would occur only through use of an unnecessarily abnormal *stance*, swing or direction of play.

PENALTY FOR BREACH OF LOCAL RULE:
Match play — Loss of hole; Stroke play — Two strokes.

**Note**: In the case of a serious breach of this Local Rule, the *Committee* may impose a penalty of disqualification."

## 2. Protection of Young Trees

When it is desired to prevent damage to young trees, the following Local Rule is recommended:

"Protection of young trees identified by _____ — If such a tree interferes with a player's *stance* or the area of his intended swing, the ball must be lifted, without penalty, and dropped in accordance with the procedure prescribed in Rule 24-2b (Immovable *Obstruction*). If the ball lies in a *water hazard*, the player must lift and drop the ball in accordance with Rule 24-2b(i) except that the *nearest point of relief* must be in the *water hazard* and the ball must be dropped in the *water hazard* or the player may proceed under Rule 26. The ball may be cleaned when lifted.

**Exception**: A player may not take relief under this Local Rule if (a) it is clearly unreasonable for him to make a *stroke* because of interference by anything other than the tree or (b) interference by the tree would occur only through use of an unnecessarily abnormal *stance*, swing or direction of play.

PENALTY FOR BREACH OF LOCAL RULE:
Match play — Loss of hole; Stroke play — Two strokes."

## 3. Temporary Conditions — Mud, Extreme Wetness, Poor Conditions and Protection of the Course

### a. Relief for Embedded Ball; Cleaning Ball

Rule 25-2 provides relief without penalty for a ball embedded in its own pitch-mark in any closely mown area *through the green*. On the *putting green*, a ball may be lifted and damage caused by the impact of a ball may be repaired (Rules 16-1b and c). When permission to take relief for an embedded ball anywhere *through the green* would be warranted, the following Local Rule is recommended:

"*Through the green*, a ball that is embedded in its own pitch-mark in the ground, other than sand, may be lifted without penalty, cleaned and dropped as near as possible to where it lay but not nearer the *hole*. The ball when dropped must first strike a part of the *course through the green*.

**Exception**: A player may not take relief under this Local Rule if it is clearly unreasonable for him to play a *stroke* because of interference by anything other than the condition covered by this Local Rule.

PENALTY FOR BREACH OF LOCAL RULE:
Match play — Loss of hole; Stroke play — Two strokes."

Alternatively, conditions may be such that permission to lift, clean and replace the ball will suffice. In these circumstances, the following Local Rule is recommended:

"(Specify area) a ball may be lifted, cleaned and replaced without penalty.

**Note**: The position of the ball must be marked before it is lifted under this Local Rule — see Rule 20-1.

PENALTY FOR BREACH OF LOCAL RULE:
Match play — Loss of hole; Stroke play — Two strokes."

### b. "Preferred Lies" and "Winter Rules"

Occasional local abnormal conditions that might interfere with fair play and are not widespread should be defined as *ground under repair* (Rule 25).

However, adverse conditions, such as heavy snows, spring thaws, prolonged rains or extreme heat can make fairways unsatisfactory and sometimes prevent use of heavy mowing equipment. When these conditions are so general throughout a *course* that the *Committee* believes "preferred lies" or "winter rules" would promote fair play or help protect the *course*, the following Local Rule is recommended:

"If a player's ball lies on a closely mown area *through the green* [or specify a more restricted area, e.g., at the 6th hole] the player may mark, lift and clean his ball without penalty. Before lifting, he must mark the position of the ball. The player must then place the ball on a spot within [specify area, e.g., six inches, one club-length, etc.] of and not nearer the *hole* than where it originally lay, that is not in a *hazard* or on a *putting green*.

A player may place his ball only once, and it is *in play* when it has been placed (Rule 20-4). If the ball fails to come to rest on the spot on which it was placed, Rule 20-3d applies. If the ball when placed comes to rest on the spot on which it is placed and it subsequently moves, there is no penalty and the ball must be played as it lies, unless the provisions of any other *Rule* apply.

If the player fails to mark the position of the ball before lifting it or moves the ball in any other manner, such as rolling it with a club, he incurs a penalty of one stroke.

*PENALTY FOR BREACH OF LOCAL RULE:
Match play — Loss of hole; Stroke play — Two strokes
*If a player incurs the general penalty for a breach of this Local Rule, no additional penalty under the Local Rule is applied."

### c. Aeration Holes

When a *course* has been aerated, a Local Rule permitting relief, without penalty, from an aeration hole may be warranted. The following Local Rule is recommended:

"*Through the green*, a ball that comes to rest in or on an aeration hole may be lifted without penalty, cleaned and dropped, as near as possible to the spot where it lay but not nearer the *hole*. The ball when dropped must first strike a part of the *course through the green*.

On the *putting green*, a ball that comes to rest in or on an aeration hole may be placed at the nearest spot not nearer the *hole* that avoids the situation.

PENALTY FOR BREACH OF LOCAL RULE:
Match play — Loss of hole; Stroke play — Two strokes."

### 4. Stones in Bunkers

Stones are, by definition, *loose impediments* and, when a player's ball is in a *hazard*, a stone lying in or touching the *hazard* may not be touched or moved (Rule 13-4). However, stones in *bunkers* may represent a danger to players (a player could be injured by a stone struck by the player's club in an attempt to play the ball) and they may interfere with the proper playing of the game.

When permission to lift a stone in a *bunker* is warranted, the following Local Rule is recommended:

"Stones in *bunkers* are movable *obstructions* (Rule 24-1 applies)."

## 5. Immovable Obstructions Close to Putting Green

Rule 24-2 provides relief without penalty from interference by an immovable *obstruction*, but also provides that, except on the *putting green*, intervention on the *line of play* is not, of itself, interference under this Rule.

However, on some courses, the aprons of the *putting greens* are so closely mown that players may wish to putt from just off the green. In these conditions, immovable *obstructions* on the apron may interfere with the proper playing of the game and the introduction of the following Local Rule providing additional relief without penalty from intervention by an immovable *obstruction* would be warranted:

"Relief from interference by an immovable *obstruction* may be taken under Rule 24-2. In addition, if a ball lies off the *putting green* but not in a *hazard* and an immovable *obstruction* on or within two club-lengths of the *putting green* and within two club-lengths of the ball intervenes on the *line of play* between the ball and the *hole*, the player may take relief as follows:

The ball must be lifted and dropped at the nearest point to where the ball lay that (a) is not nearer the *hole*, (b) avoids intervention and (c) is not in a *hazard* or on a *putting green*. The ball may be cleaned when lifted.

Relief under this Local Rule is also available if the player's ball lies on the *putting green* and an immovable *obstruction* within two club-lengths of the *putting green* intervenes on his *line of putt*. The player may take relief as follows:

The ball must be lifted and placed at the nearest point where the ball lay which (a) is not nearer the *hole*, (b) avoids intervention and (c) is not in a *hazard*. The ball may be cleaned when lifted.

PENALTY FOR BREACH OF LOCAL RULE:
Match play — Loss of hole; Stroke play — Two strokes."

## 6. Temporary Obstructions

When temporary *obstructions* are installed on or adjoining the *course*, the *Committee* should define the status of such *obstructions* as movable, immovable or temporary immovable *obstructions*.

### a. Temporary Immovable Obstructions

If the *Committee* defines these obstructions as temporary immovable *obstructions*, the following Local Rule is recommended:

> "**I. Definition**
>
> A temporary immovable *obstruction* is a non-permanent artificial object that is often erected in conjunction with a competition and is fixed or not readily movable.
>
> Examples of temporary immovable *obstructions* include, but are not limited to, tents, scoreboards, grandstands, television towers and lavatories.
>
> Supporting guy wires are part of the temporary immovable *obstruction* unless the *Committee* declares that they are to be treated as elevated power lines or cables.
>
> **II. Interference**
>
> Interference by a temporary immovable *obstruction* occurs when (a) the ball lies in front of and so close to the *obstruction* that the *obstruction* interferes with the player's *stance* or the area of his intended swing, or (b) the ball lies in, on, under or behind the *obstruction* so that any part of the *obstruction* intervenes directly between the player's ball and the *hole*; interference also exists if the ball lies within one club-length of a spot equidistant from the *hole* where such intervention would exist.
>
> **Note**: A ball is under a temporary immovable *obstruction* when it is below the outermost edges of the *obstruction*, even if these edges do not extend downward to the ground.
>
> **III. Relief**
>
> A player may obtain relief from interference by a temporary immovable *obstruction*, including a temporary immovable *obstruction* that is *out of bounds*, as follows:
>
> > (a) Through the Green: If the ball lies *through the green*, the point on the *course* nearest to where the ball lies must be determined that (a) is not nearer the *hole*, (b) avoids interference as defined in Clause II and (c) is not in a *hazard* or on a *putting green*. The player must lift the ball and drop it without penalty within one club-length of the point so determined on a part of the *course* that fulfills (a), (b) and (c) above.
> >
> > (b) In a Hazard: If the ball is in a *hazard*, the player must lift and drop the ball either:
> >
> > > (i) Without penalty, in accordance with Clause III(a) above, except that the nearest part of the *course* affording complete relief must be in the *hazard* and the ball must be dropped in the *hazard*, or, if complete relief is impossible,

on a part of the *course* within the *hazard* that affords maximum available relief; or

(ii) Under penalty of one stroke, outside the *hazard* as follows: the point on the *course* nearest to where the ball lies must be determined that (a) is not nearer the *hole*, (b) avoids interference as defined in Clause II and (c) is not in a *hazard*. The player must drop the ball within one club-length of the point so determined on a part of the *course* that fulfills (a), (b) and (c) above.

The ball may be cleaned when lifted under Clause III.

**Note 1**: If the ball lies in a *hazard*, nothing in this Local Rule precludes the player from proceeding under Rule 26 or Rule 28, if applicable.

**Note 2**: If a ball to be dropped under this Local Rule is not immediately recoverable, another ball may be substituted.

**Note 3**: A *Committee* may make a Local Rule (a) permitting or requiring a player to use a dropping zone or ball drop when taking relief from a temporary immovable *obstruction* or (b) permitting a player, as an additional relief option, to drop the ball on the opposite side of the *obstruction* from the point established under Clause III, but otherwise in accordance with Clause III.

**Exceptions**: If a player's ball lies in front of or behind the temporary immovable *obstruction* (not in, on or under the *obstruction*) he may not obtain relief under Clause III if:

1. It is clearly unreasonable for him to play a *stroke* or, in the case of intervention, to play a *stroke* such that the ball could finish on a direct line to the *hole*, because of interference by anything other than the temporary immovable *obstruction*;

2. Interference by the temporary immovable *obstruction* would occur only through use of an unnecessarily abnormal *stance*, swing or direction of play; or

3. In the case of intervention, it would be clearly unreasonable to expect the player to be able to strike the ball far enough toward the *hole* to reach the temporary immovable *obstruction*.

**Note**: A player not entitled to relief due to these exceptions may proceed under Rule 24-2, if applicable.

## IV. Ball Lost

If there is reasonable evidence that the ball is *lost* in, on or under a temporary immovable *obstruction*, a ball may be dropped under the provisions of Clause III or Clause V, if applicable. For the purpose of applying Clauses III and V, the ball is deemed to lie at the spot where it last crossed the outermost limits of the *obstruction* (Rule 24-3).

### V. Dropping Zones (Ball Drops)

If the player has interference from a temporary immovable *obstruction*, the *Committee* may permit or require the use of a dropping zone or ball drop. If the player uses a dropping zone in taking relief, he must drop the ball in the dropping zone nearest to where his ball originally lay or is deemed to lie under Clause IV (even though the nearest dropping zone may be nearer the *hole*).

**Note 1**: A *Committee* may make a Local Rule prohibiting the use of a dropping zone or ball drop that is nearer the *hole*.

**Note 2**: If the ball is dropped in a dropping zone, the ball must not be re-dropped if it comes to rest within two club-lengths of the spot where it first struck a part of the *course* even though it may come to rest nearer the *hole* or outside the boundaries of the dropping zone.

PENALTY FOR BREACH OF LOCAL RULE:
<u>Match play</u> — Loss of hole; <u>Stroke play</u> — Two strokes."

### b. Temporary Power Lines and Cables

When temporary power lines, cables or telephone lines are installed on the *course*, the following Local Rule is recommended:

"Temporary power lines, cables, telephone lines and mats covering or stanchions supporting them are *obstructions*:

1. If they are readily movable, Rule 24-1 applies.

2. If they are fixed or not readily movable, the player may, if the ball lies *through the green* or in a *bunker*, obtain relief as provided in Rule 24-2b. If the ball lies in a *water hazard*, the player may obtain relief under Rule 24-2b(i) except that the *nearest point of relief* must be in the *water hazard* and the ball must be dropped in the *water hazard* or the player may proceed under Rule 26.

3. If a ball strikes an elevated power line or cable, the *stroke* must be canceled and replayed, without penalty (see Rule 20-5). If the ball is not immediately recoverable, another ball may be *substituted*.

**Note**: Guy wires supporting a temporary immovable *obstruction* are part of the temporary immovable *obstruction* unless the *Committee*, by Local Rule, declares that they are to be treated as elevated power lines or cables.

**Exception**: A stroke that results in a ball striking an elevated junction section of cable rising from the ground must not be replayed.

4. Grass-covered cable trenches are *ground under repair*, even if not marked and Rule 25-1b applies."

## PART C

# *Conditions of the Competition*

Rule 33-1 provides, "The *Committee* must establish the conditions under which a competition is to be played." These conditions should include many matters such as method of entry, eligibility, number of rounds to be played, etc., that it is not appropriate to deal with in the Rules of Golf or this Appendix. Detailed information regarding these conditions is provided in "Decisions on the Rules of Golf" under Rule 33-1 and in "How to Conduct a Competition."

However, there are a number of matters that might be covered in the Conditions of the Competition to which the *Committee's* attention is specifically drawn. These are:

## 1. Specifications of Equipment

The following three conditions are recommended only for competitions involving expert players:

### a. List of Conforming Driver Heads

The USGA periodically issues a List of Conforming Driver Heads that lists driving clubheads that have been evaluated and found to conform to the Rules of Golf. If the *Committee* wishes to require players to carry a driver having a clubhead, identified by model and loft, that is on the List, the List should be posted and the following condition of competition used:

"The driver the player carries must have a clubhead, identified by model and loft, that is named on the current List of Conforming Driver Heads issued by the United States Golf Association.

PENALTY FOR BREACH OF CONDITION: Disqualification."

### b. List of Conforming Golf Balls

The USGA periodically issues a List of Conforming Golf Balls that lists balls that have been tested and found to conform. If the *Committee* wishes to require players to play a brand of golf ball on the List, the List should be posted and the following condition of competition used:

"The ball the player plays must be named on the current List of Conforming Golf Balls issued by the United States Golf Association.

PENALTY FOR BREACH OF CONDITION: Disqualification."

### c. One Ball Condition

If it is desired to prohibit changing brands and types of golf balls during a *stipulated round*, the following condition is recommended:

"Limitation on Balls Used During Round: (Note to Rule 5-1)

> **(i) One Ball Condition**
> During a *stipulated round*, the balls a player plays must be of the same brand and type as detailed by a single entry on the current List of Conforming Golf Balls.

**Note**: If a ball of a different brand and/or type is dropped or placed, it may be lifted, without penalty, and the player must then proceed by dropping or placing a proper ball (Rule 20-6).

PENALTY FOR BREACH OF CONDITION:
Match Play — At the conclusion of the hole at which the breach is discovered, the state of the match is adjusted by deducting one hole for each hole at which a breach occurred; maximum deduction per round — Two holes.
Stroke Play — Two strokes for each hole at which any breach occurred; maximum penalty per round — Four strokes.

> **(ii) Procedure When Breach Discovered**
> When a player discovers that he has played a ball in breach of this condition, he must abandon that ball before playing from the next *teeing ground* and complete the round using a proper ball; otherwise, the player is disqualified. If discovery is made during play of a hole and the player elects to *substitute* a proper ball before completing that hole, the player must place a proper ball on the spot where the ball used in breach of the condition lay."

### 2. Time of Starting (Note to Rule 6-3a)

If the *Committee* wishes to act in accordance with the Note, the following wording is recommended:

"If the player arrives at his starting point, ready to play, within five minutes after his starting time, in the absence of circumstances that warrant waiving the penalty of disqualification as provided in Rule 33-7, the penalty for failure to start on time is loss of the first hole to be played in match play or two strokes in stroke play. Penalty for lateness beyond five minutes is disqualification."

### 3. Caddie (Note to Rule 6-4)

Rule 6-4 permits a player to use a *caddie* provided he has only one *caddie* at any one time. However, when there may be circumstances where a *Committee* may wish to prohibit *caddies* or restrict a player in his choice of *caddie*, e.g., professional golfer, sibling, parent, another player in the competition, etc. In such cases, the following wording is recommended:

## Use of Caddie Prohibited
"A player is prohibited from using a *caddie* during the *stipulated round*."

## Restriction on Who May Serve as Caddie
"A player is prohibited from having _____ serve as his *caddie* during the *stipulated round*.

PENALTY FOR BREACH OF CONDITION:
Match play — At the conclusion of the hole at which the breach is discovered, the state of the match is adjusted by deducting one hole for each hole at which a breach occurred; maximum deduction per round — Two holes.
Stroke play — Two strokes for each hole at which any breach occurred; maximum penalty per round — Four strokes.
Match or stroke play — In the event of a breach between the play of two holes, the penalty applies to the next hole.
A player having a *caddie* in breach of this condition must immediately upon discovery that a breach has occurred ensure that he conforms with this condition for the remainder of the *stipulated round*. Otherwise, the player is disqualified."

## 4. Pace of Play (Note to Rule 6-7)
The *Committee* may establish pace of play guidelines to help prevent slow play, in accordance with Note 2 to Rule 6-7.

## 5. Suspension of Play Due to a Dangerous Situation (Note to Rule 6-8b)
As there have been many deaths and injuries from lightning on golf courses, all clubs and sponsors of golf competitions are urged to take precautions for the protection of persons against lightning. Attention is called to Rules 6-8 and 33-2d. If the *Committee* desires to adopt the condition in the Note under Rule 6-8b, the following wording is recommended:

"When play is suspended by the *Committee* for a dangerous situation, if the players in a match or group are between the play of two holes, they must not resume play until the *Committee* has ordered a resumption of play. If they are in the process of playing a hole, they must discontinue play immediately and not resume play until the *Committee* has ordered a resumption of play. If a player fails to discontinue play immediately, he is disqualified unless circumstances warrant waiving the penalty as provided in Rule 33-7.

The signal for suspending play due to a dangerous situation will be a prolonged note of the siren."

The following signals are generally used and it is recommended that all *Committees* do similarly:

- **Discontinue Play Immediately**: One prolonged note of siren.
- **Discontinue Play**: Three consecutive notes of siren, repeated.
- **Resume Play**: Two short notes of siren, repeated.

### 6. Practice
#### a. General
The *Committee* may make regulations governing practice in accordance with the Note to Rule 7-1, Exception (c) to Rule 7-2, Note 2 to Rule 7 and Rule 33-2c.

#### b. Practice Between Holes (Note 2 to Rule 7)
It is recommended that a condition of competition prohibiting practice putting or chipping on or near the *putting green* of the hole last played be introduced only in stroke-play competitions. The following wording is recommended:

"A player must not play any practice *stroke* on or near the *putting green* of the hole last played. If a practice *stroke* is played on or near the *putting green* of the hole last played, the player shall incur a penalty of two strokes at the next hole, except that in the case of the last hole of the round, he incurs the penalty at that hole."

### 7. Advice in Team Competitions (Note to Rule 8)
If the *Committee* wishes to act in accordance with the Note under Rule 8, the following wording is recommended:

"In accordance with the Note to Rule 8 of the Rules of Golf, each team may appoint one person (in addition to the persons from whom *advice* may be asked under that Rule) who may give *advice* to members of that team. This person (if it is desired to insert any restriction on who may be nominated insert such restriction here) must be identified to the *Committee* before giving *advice*."

### 8. New Holes (Note to Rule 33-2b)
The *Committee* may provide, in accordance with the Note to Rule 33-2b, that the *holes* and *teeing grounds* for a single round competition, being held on more than one day, may be differently situated on each day.

### 9. Transportation
If it is desired to require players to walk in a competition, the following condition is recommended:

"Players must walk at all times during a *stipulated round*.

PENALTY FOR BREACH OF CONDITION:
Match play — At the conclusion of the hole at which the breach is discovered, the state of the match is adjusted by deducting one hole for each hole at which a breach occurred. Maximum deduction per round: Two holes.

Appendix I 491

> Stroke play — Two strokes for each hole at which any breach occurred; maximum penalty per round: Four strokes.
> Match or stroke play — In the event of a breach between the play of two holes, the penalty applies to the next hole.
> Use of any unauthorized form of transportation must be discontinued immediately upon discovery that a breach has occurred. Otherwise, the player is disqualified."

## 10. Anti-Doping

The *Committee* may require in the Conditions of Competition, that players comply with an anti-doping policy.

## 11. How to Decide Ties

Rule 33-6 empowers the *Committee* to determine how and when a halved match or a stroke play tie is decided. The decision should be published in advance.

The USGA recommends:

### Match Play
A match that ends all square should be played off hole by hole until one *side* wins a hole. The play-off should start on the hole where the match began. In a handicap match, handicap strokes should be allowed as in the prescribed round.

### Stroke Play
(a) In the event of a tie in a scratch stroke-play competition, a play-off is recommended. The play-off may be over 18 holes or a smaller number of holes as specified by the *Committee*. If that is not feasible or there is still a tie, a hole-by-hole play-off is recommended.

(b) In the event of a tie in a handicap stroke-play competition, a play-off with handicaps is recommended. The play-off may be over 18 holes or a smaller number of holes as specified by the *Committee*. If the play-off is less than 18 holes the percentage of 18 holes to be played should be applied to the players' handicaps to determine their play-off handicaps. Handicap stroke fractions of one-half stroke or more should count as a full stroke and any lesser fraction should be disregarded.

(c) In either a scratch or handicap stroke-play competition, if a play-off of any type is not feasible, matching score cards is recommended. The method of matching cards should be announced in advance. An acceptable method of matching cards is to determine the winner on the basis of the best score for the last nine holes. If the tying players have the same score for the last nine, determine the winner on the basis of the last six holes, last three holes and finally the 18th hole. If this method is used in a handicap stroke-play competition, one-half, one-third, one-sixth, etc. of the handicaps should be deducted. Fractions should not be disregarded. If this method is used in a competition with a multiple tee start, it is recommended that the "last nine holes, last six holes, etc." is considered to be holes 10-18, 13-18, etc.

(d) If the conditions of the competition provide that ties are to be decided over the last nine, last six, last three and last hole, they should also provide what will happen if this procedure does not produce a winner.

## 12. Draw for Match Play

Although the draw for match play may be completely blind or certain players may be distributed through different quarters or eighths, the General Numerical Draw is recommended if matches are determined by a qualifying round.

### General Numerical Draw

For purposes of determining places in the draw, ties in qualifying rounds other than those for the last qualifying place are decided by the order in which scores are returned, with the first score to be returned receiving the lowest available number, etc. If it is impossible to determine the order in which scores are returned, ties are determined by a blind draw.

| UPPER HALF | LOWER HALF | UPPER HALF | LOWER HALF |
|---|---|---|---|
| 64 QUALIFIERS | | 32 QUALIFIERS | |
| 1 vs. 64 | 2 vs. 63 | 1 vs. 32 | 2 vs. 31 |
| 32 vs. 33 | 31 vs. 34 | 16 vs. 17 | 15 vs. 18 |
| 16 vs. 49 | 15 vs. 50 | 8 vs. 25 | 7 vs. 26 |
| 17 vs. 48 | 18 vs. 47 | 9 vs. 24 | 10 vs. 23 |
| 8 vs. 57 | 7 vs. 58 | 4 vs. 29 | 3 vs. 30 |
| 25 vs. 40 | 26 vs. 39 | 13 vs. 20 | 14 vs. 19 |
| 9 vs. 56 | 10 vs. 55 | 5 vs. 28 | 6 vs. 27 |
| 24 vs. 41 | 23 vs. 42 | 12 vs. 21 | 11 vs. 22 |
| 4 vs. 61 | 3 vs. 62 | 16 QUALIFIERS | |
| 29 vs. 36 | 30 vs. 35 | 1 vs. 16 | 2 vs. 15 |
| 13 vs. 52 | 14 vs. 51 | 8 vs. 9 | 7 vs. 10 |
| 20 vs. 45 | 19 vs. 46 | 4 vs. 13 | 3 vs. 14 |
| 5 vs. 60 | 6 vs. 59 | 5 vs. 12 | 6 vs. 11 |
| 28 vs. 37 | 27 vs. 38 | 8 QUALIFIERS | |
| 12 vs. 53 | 11 vs. 54 | 1 vs. 8 | 2 vs. 7 |
| 21 vs. 44 | 22 vs. 43 | 4 vs. 5 | 3 vs. 6 |

# APPENDICES II AND III

Any design in a club or ball which is not covered by Rules 4 and 5 and Appendices II and III, or which might significantly change the nature of the game, will be ruled on by the United States Golf Association.

The dimensions contained in Appendices II and III are referenced in imperial measurements. A metric conversion is also referenced for information, calculated using a conversion rate of 1 inch = 25.4 mm. In the event of any dispute over the conformity of a club or ball, the imperial measurement takes precedence.

# APPENDIX II
# DESIGN OF CLUBS

A player in doubt as to the conformity of a club should consult the United States Golf Association (USGA).

A manufacturer should submit to the USGA a sample of a club, which is to be manufactured, for a ruling as to whether the club conforms with the *Rules*. If a manufacturer fails to submit a sample or to await a ruling before manufacturing and/or marketing the club, the manufacturer assumes the risk of a ruling that the club does not conform with the *Rules*. Any sample submitted to the United States Golf Association becomes its property for reference purposes.

The following paragraphs prescribe general regulations for the design of clubs, together with specifications and interpretations. Further information relating to these regulations and their proper interpretation is provided in "A Guide to the Rules on Clubs and Balls."

Where a club, or part of a club, is required to have some specific property, this means that it must be designed and manufactured with the intention of having that property. The finished club or part must have that property within manufacturing tolerances appropriate to the material used.

## 1. Clubs

### a. General

A club is an implement designed to be used for striking the ball and generally comes in three forms: woods, irons and putters distinguished by shape and intended use. A putter is a club with a loft not exceeding ten degrees designed primarily for use on the *putting green*.

The club must not be substantially different from the traditional and customary form and make. The club must be composed of a shaft and a head. All parts of the club must be fixed so that the club is one unit, and it must have no external attachments except as otherwise permitted by the *Rules*.

### b. Adjustability

Woods and irons must not be designed to be adjustable except for weight. Putters may be designed to be adjustable for weight and some other forms of adjustability are also permitted. All methods of adjustment permitted by the *Rules* require that:

(i) the adjustment cannot be readily made;

(ii) all adjustable parts are firmly fixed and there is no reasonable likelihood of them working loose during a round; and

(iii) all configurations of adjustment conform with the *Rules*.

The disqualification penalty for purposely changing the playing characteristics of a club during a *stipulated round* (Rule 4-2a) applies to all clubs including a putter.

*Figure I*

### c. Length

The overall length of the club must be at least 18 inches (457.2 mm) and, except for putters, must not exceed 48 inches (1,219.2 mm). For woods and irons, the measurement of length is taken when the club is lying on a horizontal plane and the sole is set against a 60 degree plane as shown in Fig. I. The length is defined as the distance from the point of the intersection between the two planes to the top of the grip. For putters, the measurement of length is taken from the top of the grip along the axis of the shaft or a straight line extension of it to the sole of the club.

### d. Alignment

When the club is in its normal address position the shaft must be so aligned that:

(i) the projection of the straight part of the shaft on to the vertical plane through the toe and heel must diverge from the vertical by at least 10 degrees (see Fig. II);

*Figure II*

Figure III

(ii) the projection of the straight part of the shaft on to the vertical plane along the intended line of play must not diverge from the vertical by more than 20 degrees forward or 10 degrees backward (see Fig. III).

Figure IV

Except for putters, all of the heel portion of the club must lie within 0.625 inches (15.88 mm) of the plane containing the axis of the straight part of the shaft and the intended (horizontal) line of play (see Fig. IV).

## 2. Shaft

### a. Straightness

The shaft must be straight from the top of the grip to a point not more than 5 inches (127 mm) above the sole, measured from the point where the shaft ceases to be straight along the axis of the bent part of the shaft and the neck and/or socket (see Fig. V).

Figure V

### b. Bending and Twisting Properties

At any point along its length, the shaft must:

(i) bend in such a way that the deflection is the same regardless of how the shaft is rotated about its longitudinal axis; and

(ii) twist the same amount in both directions.

### c. Attachment to Clubhead

The shaft must be attached to the clubhead at the heel either directly or through a single plain neck and/or socket. The length from the top of the neck and/or socket to the sole of the club must not exceed 5 inches (127 mm), measured along the axis of, and following any bend in, the neck and/or socket (see Fig. VI).

*Figure VI*

**Exception for Putters:** The shaft or neck or socket of a putter may be fixed at any point in the head.

## 3. Grip (see Fig. VII)

The grip consists of material added to the shaft to enable the player to obtain a firm hold. The grip must be straight and plain in form, must extend to the end of the shaft and must not be molded for any part of the hands. If no material is added, that portion of the shaft designed to be held by the player must be considered the grip.

*Figure VII*

  (i) For clubs other than putters the grip must be circular in cross-section, except that a continuous, straight, slightly raised rib may be incorporated along the full length of the grip, and a slightly indented spiral is permitted on a wrapped grip or a replica of one.

  (ii) A putter grip may have a non-circular cross-section, provided the cross-section has no concavity, is symmetrical and remains generally similar throughout the length of the grip. (See Clause (v))

  (iii) The grip may be tapered but must not have any bulge or waist. Its cross-sectional dimensions measured in any direction must not exceed 1.75 inches (44.45 mm).

  (iv) For clubs other than putters the axis of the grip must coincide with the axis of the shaft.

(v) A putter may have two grips provided each is circular in cross-section, the axis of each coincides with the axis of the shaft, and they are separated by at least 1.5 inches (38.1 mm).

## 4. Clubhead

### a. Plain in Shape

The clubhead must be generally plain in shape. All parts must be rigid, structural in nature and functional. It is not practicable to define plain in shape precisely and comprehensively but features which are deemed to be in breach of this requirement and are therefore not permitted include:

(i) holes through the head,

(ii) transparent material added for other than decorative or structural purposes,

(iii) appendages to the main body of the head such as knobs, plates, rods or fins,

for the purpose of meeting dimensional specifications, for aiming or for any other purpose. Exceptions may be made for putters.

Any furrows in or runners on the sole must not extend into the face.

### b. Dimensions and Size

(i) Woods

When the club is in a 60 degree lie angle, the dimensions of the clubhead must be such that:

(a) the distance from the heel to the toe of the clubhead is greater than the distance from the face to the back;

(b) the distance from the heel to the toe of the clubhead is not greater than 5 inches (127 mm); and

(c) the distance from the sole to the crown of the clubhead is not greater than 2.8 inches (71.12 mm).

These dimensions are measured on horizontal lines between vertical projections of the outermost points of:

- the heel and the toe; and

- the face and the back (see Fig. VIII, dimension A); and on vertical lines between the horizontal projections of the outermost points of the sole and the crown (see Fig. VIII, dimension B). If the outermost point of the heel is not clearly defined, it is deemed to be 0.875 inches (22.23 mm) above the horizontal plane on which the club is lying (see Fig. VIII, dimension C).

### Figure VIII

The size of the clubhead must not exceed 28.06 cubic inches (460 cubic centimeters), plus a tolerance of 0.61 cubic inches (10 cubic centimeters).

(ii) Irons and Putters

When the clubhead is in its normal address position, the dimensions of the head must be such that the distance from the heel to the toe is greater than the distance from the face to the back. For traditionally shaped heads, these dimensions will be measured on horizontal lines between vertical projections of the outermost points of:

- the heel and toe; and
- the face and back.

For unusually shaped heads, the toe to heel dimension may be made at the face.

**Note**: For additional dimensional specifications regarding putters, please refer to "A Guide to the Rules on Clubs and Balls" on the USGA's Web site.

### c. Striking Faces

The clubhead must have only one striking face, except that a putter may have two such faces if their characteristics are the same, and they are opposite each other.

## 5. Club Face

### a. General

The material and construction of, or any treatment to, the face or clubhead must not have the effect at impact of a spring (test on file), or impart significantly more or less spin to the ball than a standard steel face, or have any other effect which would unduly influence the movement of the ball.

The face of the club must be hard and rigid (some exceptions may be made for putters) and, except for such markings listed below, must be smooth and must not have any degree of concavity.

### b. Impact Area Roughness and Material

Except for markings specified in the following paragraphs, the surface roughness within the area where impact is intended (the "impact area") must not exceed that of decorative sandblasting, or of fine milling (see Fig. IX).

The whole of the impact area must be of the same material. Exceptions may be made for wooden clubs.

*Figure IX*

### c. Impact Area Markings

Markings in the impact area must not have sharp edges or raised lips as determined by a finger test. Grooves or punch marks in the impact area must meet the following specifications:

(i) Grooves. A series of straight grooves with diverging sides and a symmetrical cross-section may be used (see Fig. X).

- The width and cross-section must be consistent across the face of the club and along the length of the grooves.

- Any rounding of groove edges shall be in the form of a radius which does not exceed 0.020 inches (0.508 mm).

- The width of the grooves must not exceed 0.035 inches (0.9 mm), using the 30 degree method of measurement on file with the United States Golf Association.

- The distance between edges of adjacent grooves must not be less than three times the width of a groove, and not less than 0.075 inches (1.905 mm).

- The depth of a groove must not exceed 0.020 inches (0.508 mm).

**Note: Exception — see US Decision 4-1/100.**

(ii) Punch Marks. Punch marks may be used.

- The area of any such mark must not exceed 0.0044 square inches (2.84 sq. mm).

- A mark must not be closer to an adjacent mark than 0.168 inches (4.27 mm) measured from center to center.

- The depth of a punch mark must not exceed 0.040 inches (1.02 mm).

- If punch marks are used in combination with grooves, a punch mark must not be closer to a groove than 0.168 inches (4.27 mm), measured from center to center

## Figure X

### d. Decorative Markings

The center of the impact area may be indicated by a design within the boundary of a square whose sides are 0.375 inches (9.53 mm) in length. Such a design must not unduly influence the movement of the ball. Decorative markings are permitted outside the impact area.

### e. Non-metallic Club Face Markings

The above specifications apply to clubs on which the impact area of the face is of metal or a material of similar hardness. They do not apply to clubs with faces made of other materials and whose loft angle is 24 degrees or less, but markings which could unduly influence the movement of the ball are prohibited. Clubs with this type of face and a loft angle exceeding 24 degrees may have grooves of maximum width 0.040 inches (1.02 mm) and maximum depth 1½ times the groove width, but must otherwise conform to the markings specifications above.

### f. Putter Face Markings

The specifications above with regard to roughness, material and markings in the impact area do not apply to putters.

# APPENDIX III  THE BALL

## 1. Weight
The weight of the ball must not be greater than 1.620 ounces avoirdupois (45.93 gm).

## 2. Size
The diameter of the ball must not be less than 1.680 inches (42.67 mm). This specification will be satisfied if, under its own weight, a ball falls through a 1.680 inches diameter ring gauge in fewer than 25 out of 100 randomly selected positions, the test being carried out at a temperature of 23 ± 1 °C.

## 3. Spherical Symmetry
The ball must not be designed, manufactured or intentionally modified to have properties which differ from those of a spherically symmetrical ball.

## 4. Initial Velocity
The initial velocity of the ball must not exceed the limit specified (test on file) when measured on apparatus approved by the United States Golf Association.

## 5. Overall Distance Standard
The combined carry and roll of the ball, when tested on apparatus approved by the United States Golf Association, must not exceed the distance specified under the conditions set forth in the Overall Distance Standard for golf balls on file with the United States Golf Association.

# MISCELLANEOUS DECISIONS

### Misc./1 Course Record

The term "course record" is not defined in the Rules of Golf. However, it is generally accepted that a record score should be recognized as the official "course record" only if made in an individual stroke play competition (excluding bogey, par or Stableford competitions) with the holes and tee-markers in their proper medal or championship positions.

It is recommended that a record score should not be recognized as the official "course record" if a Local Rule permitting preferred lies is in operation. (Revised)

### Misc./2 Whether Rakes Should Be Placed In or Outside Bunkers

**Q.** Should rakes be placed in or outside bunkers?

**A.** There is not a perfect answer for the position of rakes, but on balance it is felt there is less likelihood of an advantage or disadvantage to the player if rakes are placed outside of bunkers.

It may be argued that there is more likelihood of a ball being deflected into or kept out of a bunker if the rake is placed outside the bunker. It could also be argued that if the rake is in the bunker it is most unlikely that the ball will be deflected out of the bunker.

However, in practice, players who leave rakes in bunkers frequently leave them at the side which tends to stop a ball rolling into the flat part of the bunker, resulting in a much more difficult shot than would otherwise have been the case. This is most prevalent at a course where the bunkers are small. When the ball comes to rest on or against a rake in the bunker and the player must proceed under Rule 24-1, it may not be possible to replace the ball on the same spot or find a spot in the bunker which is not nearer the hole — see Decision 20-3d/2.

If rakes are left in the middle of the bunker the only way to position them is to throw them into the bunker and this causes damage to the surface. Also, if a rake is in the middle of a large bunker it is either not used or the player is obliged to rake a large area of the bunker resulting in unnecessary delay.

Therefore, after considering all these aspects, it is recommended that rakes should be left outside bunkers in areas where they are least likely to affect the movement of the ball.

Ultimately, it is a matter for the Committee to decide where it wishes rakes to be placed.

# DECISIONS APPLICABLE ONLY IN THE UNITED STATES OF AMERICA

## US/2-3/100  Player Who Wins First Nine Holes in Nassau Match Withdraws During Second Nine

**Q.** The "Nassau" System of scoring is used in a team match, i.e., in each match three points are awarded as follows: one point to the winner of the first nine holes, one point to the winner of the second nine and one point to the winner over 18 holes. In one match, a player who had defeated his opponent on the first nine holes withdrew due to illness during the second nine. Should the player retain the point he won on the first nine or, since he withdrew, should he lose all three points?

**A.** The player should be awarded one point; his opponent won the other two points by default.

## US/4-1/100  Club Face Markings

**Q.** May a player use a golf club with a groove spacing to groove width ratio of 2.3 to 1, if that club was manufactured before March 31, 1990, even though Appendix II 5c(i) requires that the groove spacing to groove width ratio must be no less than 3 to 1?

**A.** Yes. It is, however, the responsibility of the player to provide proof of the date on which the club was manufactured. If the player cannot provide such proof, the club must conform with the specifications described in Appendix II 5c(i).

## [US/5-1/100  Reserved]

## US/5-1/101  Status of Ball Not on List of Conforming Golf Balls

Brands of balls not appearing on the current List of Conforming Golf Balls fall into three categories:

1. Brands which have never been tested,

2. Brands which appeared on a previous List but which have not been re-submitted for inclusion on the current List, and

3. Brands which have been tested and found not to conform to the Rules and specifications set forth in Appendix III.

Balls in categories 1 and 2 are presumed to conform and the onus of proof is on the person alleging that the ball does not.

All balls of brands in category 3 are deemed to be non-conforming.

### US/5-1/102  Status of Ball to Be Removed from List of Conforming Golf Balls

**Q.** A brand of ball included on the current List of Conforming Golf Balls is tested further and found not to conform to the specifications set forth in Appendix III. The brand will therefore be deleted from the next List published. What is the status of the ball in the interim period?

**A.** Players are entitled to assume that all balls of a brand included on the current List of Conforming Golf Balls conform to the Rules and Appendix III. Accordingly, players may continue to use balls of the brand in question until the publication of the next List, unless by a condition of the competition the Committee has specifically excluded that brand. This applies whether or not it is a condition of the competition that only brands of golf balls on the List of Conforming Golf Balls may be used.

### US/17/100  Flagstick Dimensions

The USGA recommends that the flagstick be at least seven feet in height and that its diameter be not greater than three-quarters of an inch from a point three inches above the ground to the bottom of the hole.

### US/20-1/100  Placing Ball-Marker to Side

**Q.** If a player is requested to mark the position of his ball to the side of where it lies, must he place a ball marker behind the ball, measure a clubhead-length to the side of the marker and then move the marker to the side? Or may the player simply measure a clubhead-length from the side of the ball and eliminate one step?

**A.** The player may measure from the side of the ball.

### US/29/100  Penalty in "Pinehurst" Foursome Not Related to Ball Holed Out

**Q.** In a foursome competition played under the so-called "Pinehurst" format, A and B were partners. In accordance with the format, A hit a second shot with B's ball. B then hit a second shot with a ball he thought was A's, but which in fact was a wrong ball. Since B's shot with the wrong ball was a poor one, B picked up the wrong ball and he and A proceeded to play out the hole with B's ball. It was then discovered that the ball B picked up was not A's ball, but rather a wrong ball.

Do A and B incur any penalty because B played a wrong ball in view of the fact that the hole was completed with B's ball which was not related to the play of the wrong ball?

**A.** The Rules of Golf do not cover this form of play.

It is recommended that a penalty in this form of play should be incurred only if related to the ball ultimately holed out by the side. Thus, as the ball played by B from the tee was ultimately holed out, the side should not have incurred a penalty because B played a stroke with a wrong ball instead of A's ball.

## US/33-8/100 Local Rule for Lateral Water Hazard with Bunker Adjacent

**Q.** The 18th hole at the Pebble Beach Golf Links is bordered along the left side by Carmel Bay, and there is a sea wall which begins more than 100 yards short of the green and extends to the back of the green. There is a bunker approximately 12 feet wide between the sea wall and the fairway for much of this distance.

The bay is a lateral water hazard and the sea wall is the natural margin of the hazard. Accordingly, a player, when dropping a ball under Rule 26-1c(i), must drop in the bunker. The sand at this point is soft and a dropped ball usually plugs.

Would it be permissible to place the line defining the lateral water hazard along the right edge of the bunker, making the bunker part of the lateral water hazard, or alternatively, make a Local Rule to the effect that, when obtaining relief under the lateral water hazard Rule, the player may drop a ball to the right of the bunker?

**A.** In all cases, the hazard should be marked along its natural boundary, i.e., the sea wall — see Decision 33-2a/4.

If the Committee does not wish to require a player to drop a ball in the bunker when proceeding under the lateral water hazard Rule, the Committee may establish a series of Ball Drops along the right-hand side of the bunker and make a Local Rule stating that a player whose ball comes to rest in the lateral water hazard (having last crossed the hazard margin at a point where, when proceeding under Rule 26-1c(i), the player may drop a ball in the bunker) may drop a ball, under penalty of one stroke, on the nearest Ball Drop which is not nearer the hole.

## US/33-8/101 Local Rule for Breach of Sportsmanship Code

**Q.** A high school federation has a sportsmanship code for golfers who compete in high school matches.

May the federation make a Local Rule assessing a penalty for a breach of the code?

**A.** A Local Rule assessing a penalty for a breach of a sportsmanship code is not authorized. Penalties for a breach of a sportsmanship code should take a more generalized form, e.g., subjection to censure, suspension or revocation of the privilege of playing in events.

## US/34-3/100 Committee Intervention in Match Play

In the absence of a referee, a Committee has no authority to intervene in match play unless there is a reason to believe Rule 1-3 is being infringed or a breach of Rule 6-7 is involved. When there is no referee, the players must protect their own rights by invoking Rule 2-5 and by referring to the Committee any dispute they cannot resolve — see Rule 34-3.

## US/34-3/101 Committee Intervention in Match Play When Search for Lost Ball Exceeds Five Minutes

**Q.** Decision US/34-3/100 permits a Committee member to intervene in a match to which a referee has not been assigned in case of a breach of Rule 6-7 (Undue Delay).

Would it be in order for a Committee member to intervene in such a match if he has observed that a player has looked for his ball for five minutes and is continuing to search?

**A.** Yes. It would be appropriate for a Committee member to intervene and advise the player that the ball is lost under the Rules and, if he does not resume play immediately, a penalty for undue delay will result.

# PRINCIPAL CHANGES SINCE 2004-2005

## General

The United States Golf Association and The R&A have agreed to a two year revision cycle for the Decisions on the Rules of Golf. Therefore, no existing Decisions will be revised or withdrawn, and no new Decisions will be added to the book until the next edition is published in 2008.

Should extraordinary circumstances arise that would warrant amending the Decisions on the Rules of Golf in the interim, the USGA will notify its member clubs, all state and regional golf associations and appropriate media sources of any change.

## New Decisions

| | |
|---|---|
| 1-2/1.5 | Competitor Alters Line of Play of Fellow-Competitor |
| 1-2/3.8 | Player Jumps Close to Hole to Cause Ball to Drop; Ball Does Not Move |
| 1-2/7 | Player Purposely Deflects Partner's Ball in Motion on Putting Green |
| 4-4a/14 | Player Carries Pieces of Broken Club |
| 6-4/5.3 | Additional Persons Carry Items for Player |
| 6-8b/9 | Resumption of Play; When Players Must Be Present |
| 6-8d/3 | Player Who Drops Ball Immediately After Committee Has Ordered Resumption of Play Subsequently Lifts Ball Under Rule 6-8d(ii) |
| 8-2b/2 | Caddie Attending Flagstick Advises Player to Aim at his Foot |
| 9-2/3.5 | Player Refuses to Tell Opponent How Many Strokes He Has Taken |
| 10/4 | Order of Play for Provisional Ball Other Than from Teeing Ground |
| 13-2/8.7 | Player's Area of Intended Stance Affected by Another Player's Stroke |
| 13-2/12 | Player Presses Down Sand Behind Ball in Grounding Club |
| 13-4/35.8 | Player Deems Ball Unplayable in Bunker, Announces His Intention to Proceed Under Rule 28a Outside Bunker and Then Rakes Bunker on New Line of Play |

## Principal Changes

| | |
|---|---|
| 14-3/0.5 | Local Rule Permitting Use of Distance Measuring Device |
| 14-3/10.5 | Use of Stretching Devices |
| 16-1e/2 | Player Plays from Stance Astride Extension of Line of Putt Behind Ball |
| 16-2/4 | Ball Overhanging Lip of Hole Moves When Flagstick Removed |
| 16-2/5 | Ball Overhanging Lip of Hole Moves and Strikes Flagstick During Removal of Flagstick |
| 17/3.5 | Reflector on Flagstick |
| 18-2a/30.5 | Ball Moves After Removal of Loose Impediment Near Ball |
| 20-5/2 | Player Proceeding Under Rule 20-5 Drops Ball on Different Part of Course |
| 20-6/4 | Substituting Ball When Re-Dropping |
| 20-6/5 | Player Drops Ball Under Rules and Then Wishes to Replace Ball in Original Position |
| 20-7/2.5 | Ball Deemed Unplayable in Water Hazard; Another Ball Is Dropped in Hazard But Player Realizes Error Before Playing |
| 23/5.5 | Status of Insect-Like Creatures |
| 25-1c/2.5 | Ball Dropped Under Rule 25-1c with Reasonable Evidence; Original Ball Then Found |
| 25-2/8 | Ball Embedded in Teeing Ground |
| 26-1/3.5 | Ball Dropped Under Water Hazard Rule with Reasonable Evidence; Original Ball Then Found |
| 27-2a/4 | Three Balls Played from Same Spot; Only Second Ball Was Provisional Ball |
| 30-3/1 | Examples of Rulings in Four-Ball Match with Concurrent Singles Matches |
| 30-3/2 | Effect of State of Match Penalties in Four-Ball Play |
| 33/8 | Application of Disqualification Penalty in Competition in Which Not All Scores Used to Determine Winner |
| 33-8/40 | Local Rule Clarifying Status of Material Similar to Sand |
| 34-3/1.5 | Committee Error and Scoring in Stroke Play |
| 34-3/3.3 | Player Placed at Serious Disadvantage Due to Incorrect Ruling |

| | |
|---|---|
| 34-3/7 | **Player Proceeds on Basis of Ruling; Subsequent Facts Prove Ruling to be Incorrect** |
| 34-3/8 | **Player Proceeds on Basis of Ruling; Player's Version of Facts Subsequently Found to be Incorrect** |

## Revised Decisions

The following Decisions have been substantively revised:

| | |
|---|---|
| 1-1/1 | **Two Balls in Play Simultaneously at Different Holes.** Reference to Rule 2-3 changed to Rule 2-1. |
| 1-2/5.5 | **Player Purposely Stops or Deflects Ball; Where Next Stroke Must Be Played From.** Amended to address the situation where the player has deflected rather than stopped his ball in motion after a stroke. |
| 1-2/6 | **Player Removes Loose Impediment Affecting Lie of Opponent or Fellow-Competitor in Hazard.** Answer expanded to explain that the opponent or fellow-competitor is not required to replace the loose impediment. |
| 1-4/5 | **Removal of Obstruction in Hazard Would Move Loose Impediment.** Answer expanded to clarify the penalty if the player fails to replace the loose impediment |
| 1-4/12 | **Player Breaches Rules More Than Once Prior to Stroke; Whether Multiple Penalties Applied.** Expansion of example under Principle 4 and edits to chart of principles. |
| 2-1/1.5 | **Players Agree to Consider Hole Halved During Play of Hole.** Reference to Rule 2-3 changed to Rule 2-1. |
| 2-1/4 | **Two Holes Purposely Omitted in Match.** Reference to Rule 2-3 changed to Rule 2-1 (Formerly 2-3/3). |
| 3-3/0.5 | **Guidelines for Determining Which Ball Counts When Player Proceeds Under Rule 3-3.** Reference to Withdrawn Decision 3-3/5.5 removed. |
| 4-3/1 | **Meaning of Damage Sustained in "Normal Course of Play."** Meaning of "normal course of play" expanded to include a number of reasonable acts in addition to making a stroke, practice swing or practice stroke. |
| 4-3/7 | **Club Broken While Used as Cane.** Answer altered to allow replacement of the club due to change in meaning of damage in the "normal course of play." |
| 4-3/9 | **Club Broken Due to Habit of Hitting Head of Club on Ground.** Answer altered for consistency with interpretation of meaning of damage in the "normal course of play." |

# Principal Changes

| | | |
|---|---|---|
| 4-4a/13 | **Player Practices with Another Player's Club.** Answer revised to reflect that a breach did not occur because the stroke did not count in the player's score rather than that it could not count. | |
| 6-6a/7 | **Different Score Card Returned.** Clarified to include examples of why the original score card was not returned and to explain that the returned score card met the requirements of Rule 6-6. | |
| 6-6d/4 | **Competitor's Scores Recorded on Score Card with Fellow-Competitor's Name and Vice Versa.** Amended to recommend that the Committee rectify this administrative error by changing the names on the score cards. | |
| 6-8d/2 | **Lie in Bunker Altered Prior to Resumption of Play.** Reference to Rule 20-3b/5 removed due to revision to that Decision. | |
| 6-8d/4 | **Ball Visible from Tee Disappears While Play Suspended.** Answer clarified to explain that the player must proceed in accordance with Rule 6-8d(iii) — Formerly 18-1/2. | |
| 7-1b/5 | **Competitor's Caddie Practices on or Tests Putting Green Surfaces of the Course Before Stroke Play Round.** Reference to Rule 6-4 changed to Rule 6-1. | |
| 8-1/2 | **Exchanging Distance Information.** Revised to specify that the distance between any objects is a matter of public information and therefore not advice. | |
| 9-2/2 | **Incorrect Information Given by Caddie or Partner.** Clarified to be consistent with Rule 9-2 regarding its use of the term "wrong information." | |
| 9-2/3 | **Wrong Information on Strokes Taken Given Voluntarily.** Clarified to be consistent with Rule 9-2 regarding its use of the term "wrong information." | |
| 9-2/5 | **Incorrect Information Causes Opponent to Lift His Ball-Marker.** Clarified to be consistent with Rule 9-2 regarding its use of the term "wrong information." | |
| 9-2/7 | **Incorrect Information Given by Player Corrected Before Opponent Makes Next Stroke But After Opponent Has Conceded Player's Putt.** Clarified to be consistent with Rule 9-2 regarding its use of the term "wrong information." | |
| 9-2/14 | **Incorrect Information Causes Opponent Mistakenly to Think He Has Putt for Half; Opponent Holes Putt and Then Error Discovered.** Clarified to be consistent with Rule 9-2 regarding its use of the term "wrong information." | |

| | |
|---|---|
| 9-2/15 | **Wrong Information After Play of Hole; When Penalty Applicable.** Clarified to be consistent with Rule 9-2 regarding its use of the term "wrong information." |
| 12-1/5 | **Player Kicks Ball While Probing for It in Water Hazard.** Answer expanded to clarify that the movement of the ball was not directly attributable to the act of probing for the ball; therefore, a penalty was incurred under Rule 18-2a. |
| 13-2/26 | **Natural Object Interfering with Swing Moved to Determine Whether It Is Loose.** Answer revised to clarify that the player is in breach of Rule 13-2 if he moved a growing natural object other than for the purpose of determining whether it was loose or if he failed to replace such an object if it was not loose. |
| 13-2/29 | **Worsening and Then Restoring Line of Play.** Answer expanded to clarify that the player may not restore any areas covered by Rule 13-2 that he may have worsened prior to his stroke. |
| 13-4/25 | **Taking Firm Stance in Bunker Some Distance from Where Ball Lies in Bunker to Simulate Next Stroke.** Question modified to reflect that it is not relevant whether the player is holding a club. |
| 13-4/35.7 | **Player Deems Ball Unplayable in Bunker, Lifts Ball and Then Removes Loose Impediment from Bunker.** Answer revised to permit the player to remove the loose impediment without penalty if he has stated that he will proceed under Rule 28a and he does so. |
| 13-4/36 | **Smoothing Irregularities in Bunker After Stroke But Before Ball Extricated.** Reference to "test consistency of the sand during the first stroke" in the Answer deleted as the smoothing is specifically permitted by Exception 2 to Rule 13-4 |
| 14-2/4 | **Caddie Inadvertently Stands on Extension of Line of Play Behind Ball.** Revised to clarify that Rule 14-2b is applicable regardless of the part of the course on which the ball lies prior to the stroke. |
| 14-3/1 | **Distance Meter Attached to Golf Cart.** Reference to Decision 14-3/0.5 added to clarify that distance measuring equipment may be permitted by Local Rule. |
| 14-3/2 | **Pencil or Score Card Used to Assist in Gauging Distance.** Reference to Decision 14-3/0.5 added to clarify that distance measuring equipment may be permitted by Local Rule. |

| | |
|---|---|
| 14-3/3 | **Standard Spectacles and Field Glasses.** Reference to Decision 14-3/0.5 added to clarify that distance measuring equipment may be permitted by Local Rule. |
| 14-3/5.5 | **Electronic Device Providing Distances Between Various Points.** Reference to Decision 14-3/0.5 added to clarify that distance measuring equipment may be permitted by Local Rule. |
| 14-3/10 | **Use of Training or Swing Aid During Round.** Reference to Decision 4-4a/7 expanded for clarity. |
| 14-3/13.5 | **Golf Ball Artificially Warmed.** Amended to clarify that the use of a ball which was warmed prior to the stipulated round is not a breach of Rule 14-3. |
| 14-3/14 | **Electronic Instrument Used to Find Ball.** Answer expanded to clarify that the ball itself may be used only if it conforms with the Rules including any applicable conditions of competition. |
| 14-3/16 | **Use of Electronic Devices.** Reformatted and expanded to provide examples of uses of various electronic devices that would or would not be a breach of Rule 14-3. |
| 15/5 | **Original Ball Found and Played After Another Ball Put Into Play.** Amended in light of the revision to Decision 27-1/2. |
| 15/9 | **Ball Thrown into Bounds by Outside Agency and Played; Caddie Aware of Action of Outside Agency.** Reference to Rule 6-4 changed to Rule 6-1. |
| 15/13 | **Stray Ball Dropped Under Unplayable Ball Rule But Not Played.** Revised to clarify that the stray ball which is dropped is an improperly substituted ball; not a wrong ball. |
| 16-1a/11 | **Raised Tuft of Grass on Line of Putt Brushed to Determine Whether It Is Loose.** Answer revised to clarify that the player is in breach of Rule 16-1 if he moved a growing natural object other than for the purpose of determining whether it was loose or if he failed to replace such an object if it was not loose. |
| 16-1b/3 | **Ball Lifted from Putting Green; Ball Replaced While Another Ball in Motion Subsequently Deflects Ball.** Revised to clarify that A's ball was not on the putting green when B made his stroke from the putting green. |
| 16-1d/6 | **Caddie Roughens Surface of Putting Green But Player Does Not Benefit.** Reference to Rule 6-4 changed to Rule 6-1. |

# Principal Changes

**18-2a/12.5** **Player Entitled to Relief Without Penalty from Condition Lifts Ball; Chooses Not to Take Relief and Wishes to Proceed Under the Unplayable Ball Rule.** Answer expanded to explain that the player may proceed directly under Rule 28a without incurring a penalty under Rule 18-2a.

**18-2a/24** **Ball Moved by Flagstick When Measuring.** Revised to clarify that a ball moved by a dropped flagstick has not been moved in a manner directly attributable to the act of measuring.

**18-2b/10** **Ball Falls into Hole After Being Addressed.** Answer expanded to clarify that the player's ball has not been holed.

**19-2/1.5** **Ball Moves Prior to Address and Is Accidentally Stopped by Player's Club; Player Removes Club and Ball Rolls Away.** Amended to clarify the penalty incurred if the player fails to replace his ball on the spot at which it was stopped.

**20-3b/5** **Lie of Ball to Be Replaced Altered and Spot Where Ball Originally Lay Not Determinable.** Answer expanded to clarify the circumstances under which the player must proceed under Rule 20-3b and those under which he must proceed under Rule 20-3c.

**20-7c/4** **Competitor's Ball Played by Fellow-Competitor; Competitor Substitutes Another Ball at Wrong Place, Plays It and Then Abandons It and Plays Out Original Ball from Right Place.** Question modified to reflect that Rule 15-3 provides the proper procedure for Player A to follow when his ball is played by another player and is the applicable Rule under which he is penalized when he proceeds improperly.

**21/3** **Whether Ball Cleaned Through Act of Caddie Throwing It to Player.** Question revised to clarify that the player's ball did not lie on the putting green when it was lifted.

**23-1/7** **Loose Impediment Affecting Lie Moved When Ball Lifted.** Amended to clarify the penalty incurred if the player fails to replace the loose impediment.

**24-2b/20** **Interference by Line or Mark on Ground Consisting of Lime or Paint.** Answer expanded to clarify that a Local Rule may be adopted declaring such areas to be ground under repair.

**25-1b/26** **Player Unaware Ball in Water Hazard Takes Relief from Interference by Burrowing Animal Hole.** Answer expanded to clarify that the player has proceeded under an inapplicable Rule thus he is permitted to correct his error under Rule 20-6.

| | |
|---|---|
| 25-1c/3 | **Ball Played in Ground Under Repair Area Lost in Same Area.** Expanded to clarify that the ball did not cross the outermost limits of the area of ground under repair when it was played from within that area and that the player is entitled to relief without penalty under Rule 25-1b if, after having dropped a ball under Rule 27-1, he has interference from this condition. |
| 26-1/16 | **Point Where Ball Last Crossed Margin of Lateral Water Hazard Determined and Ball Dropped; Point Then Proves to Be Wrong Point.** Amended to clarify that the player may drop a ball in accordance with any of his options under Rule 26-1 when correcting his error. |
| 27-1/2 | **Original Ball Found Within Five-Minute Search Period After Another Ball Dropped.** Revised to specify that Rule 20-6 does not apply as the player has substituted a ball under an applicable Rule (Rule 27-1). |
| 27-1/2.3 | **Original Ball Found Within Five-Minute Search Period After Another Ball Dropped; Original Ball Played.** Revised to specify that the original ball, if played, is a wrong ball because the original ball is no longer the player's ball in play in view of the Revision to Decision 27-1/2. |
| 32-1/3 | **Determination of Honor in Handicap Stableford Competition.** Question clarified through the removal of unnecessary information. |
| 33-1/9.5 | **Breach of Transportation Condition by Caddie.** Reference to Rule 6-4 changed to Rule 6-1. |
| 33-8/13 | **Local Rule for Ball Deflected by Power Line.** Answer expanded to clarify that the Local Rule may include supporting poles which are located such that they interfere with play of the hole. |
| 33-8/34 | **Local Rule Establishes Ball Drop or Dropping Zone; Procedure for Dropping.** Part (e) of Answer amended to include Rule 20-2c(vi). |
| 34-2/5 | **Referee Reverses Ruling Made at Last Hole of Match After Players Leave Putting Green.** Clarification of circumstances under which ruling may be corrected. |
| 34-2/6 | **Referee Reverses Ruling After Player Subsequently Plays a Ball.** Clarification of circumstances under which ruling may be corrected. |
| 34-3/3 | **Player Plays Based on Incorrect Ruling; Procedure for Player When Error is Discovered.** Clarification of circumstances under which ruling may be corrected. |

## Withdrawn Decisions

| | |
|---|---|
| 3-3/5.5 | **Procedure If Both Original and Second Balls Dropped in Wrong Place and Played.** Withdrawn as the same information is contained in Decision 3-3/0.5. |
| 6-4/2 | **Who May Serve as Caddie.** Withdrawn as the information is contained in Appendix I; Part C. |
| 8-1/2.5 | **Players Exchange Distance Information to Determine Order of Play.** Withdrawn in light of revision to Decision 8-1/2. |
| 11-3/2 | **Lifting Ball in Play But Still Within Teeing Ground.** Withdrawn as the same information is contained in Decision 18-2a/1. |
| 16/6 | **Cutting Hole on Slope.** Withdrawn as not a Rules of Golf issue. |
| 26/7 | **Ball Apparently in Water Hazard Found Outside Hazard After Another Ball Played Under Stroke-and-Distance Procedure.** Withdrawn as the same information is contained in Decision 26/6. |
| 33/4 | **Direction Posts.** Withdrawn as not a Rules of Golf issue. |
| 33-1/9 | **Breach of Condition Prohibiting Golf Carts.** Withdrawn as the information is contained in Appendix I; Part C. |
| US/6-2a/100 | **Player in Match Uses Established Handicap but Handicap Too High Due to Player's Failure to Observe Provision of Handicap System.** Decision moved to USGA Handicap System Manual. |

## Re-Numbered Decisions

| | |
|---|---|
| 2-1/3 | **Hole Inadvertently Omitted in Match; Error Discovered After Match Concluded** (Formerly 2-3/2) |
| 2-1/4 | **Two Holes Purposely Omitted in Match** (Formerly 2-3/3) |
| 2-1/5 | **Three Holes Played Out of Sequence in Match** (Formerly 2-3/4) |
| 2-1/6 | **Replaying Match When Play Discontinued Instead of Resuming from Where Play Stopped** (Formerly 2-3/5) |
| 2-3/2 | **Result of Match When Player Dormie and Opponent Concedes** (Formerly 2-3/6) |
| 6-8d/4 | **Ball Visible from Tee Disappears While Play Suspended.** (Formerly 18-1/2) |

# THE USGA AND YOU

Contact us for:

**The Rules of Golf:**
For all of your Rules of Golf needs, including:

- Complete Rules of Golf and Decisions on the Rules of Golf on-line
- Frequently asked questions regarding the Rules
- Submitting your Rules questions to our staff
- Ordering Rules of Golf-related products

www.rulesofgolf.com

**USGA Publication Orders:**
A comprehensive selection of USGA books, pamphlets, software and videos. Publications include:

- The Rules of Golf — 2006-07 edition
- Decisions on the Rules of Golf — 2006-07 edition
- Golf Rules in Brief
- Golf Rules Illustrated
- USGA Handicap Publications
- USGA Green Section Publications

www.usgapubs.com • 1-800-336-4446

**USGA Catalog**
The ultimate source for clothing and memorabilia from our National Championships, including the U.S. Open and Women's Open, plus a full line of USGA Members clothing and accessories, golf gifts and books. Generous Member discounts apply.

www.usgacatalog.com • 1-800-755-0293

**USGA Members Program**
Find out more about becoming a Member of the USGA and learn how your contribution will help fund a wide range of programs committed to enhance your enjoyment of the game while ensuring its future.

www.usga.org • 1-800-223-0041